WILEY PLUS
www.wileyplus.com

This online teaching and learning environment integrates the entire digital textbook with the most effective instructor and student resources to fit every learning style.

With **WileyPLUS**:

Students achieve concept mastery in a rich, structured environment that's available 24/7

Instructors personalize and manage their course more effectively with assessment, assignments, grade tracking, and more

• manage time better

• study smarter

• save money

From multiple study paths, to self-assessment, to a wealth of interactive visual and audio resources, *WileyPLUS* gives you everything you need to personalize the teaching and learning experience.

»Find out how to MAKE IT YOURS»

www.wileyplus.com

5TH Edition

Human Geography in Action

MICHAEL KUBY
Arizona State University

JOHN HARNER
University of Colorado at Colorado Springs

PATRICIA GOBER
Arizona State University

Contributors

Dan Arreola
Arizona State University

Elizabeth Burns
Arizona State University (retired)

Kevin McHugh
Arizona State University

Ross Nelson
Thompson Rivers University

Breandán Ó'Uallacháin
Arizona State University

WILEY

John Wiley & Sons, Inc.

VICE PRESIDENT & EXECUTIVE PUBLISHER	Jay O'Callaghan
ACQUISITIONS EDITOR	Ryan Flahive
ASSISTANT EDITOR	Veronica Armour
SENIOR PRODUCTION EDITOR	Valerie A. Vargas
MARKETING MANAGER	Danielle Torio
CREATIVE DIRECTOR	Harry Nolan
SENIOR DESIGNER	Kevin Murphy
PRODUCTION MANAGEMENT SERVICES	Suzanne Ingrao Associates
SENIOR ILLUSTRATION EDITOR	Anna Melhorn
PHOTO ASSOCIATE	Sheena Goldstein
EDITORIAL ASSISTANT	Meredith Leo
MEDIA EDITOR	Lynn Pearlman
COVER DESIGN	Michael Boland

There are four photos being used for the Kuby Cover. The photo credits are as follows:
(Starting at top going clockwise)

Top Image, San Francisco: Satellite image courtesy of ©GeoEye www.geoeye.com. All rights reserved

Bottom Right Image, Denver 13th Street: Ken Schroeppel, DenverInfill.com
Bottom Center Image, Honolulu: Rob Reichenfeld/Getty Images, Inc.
Bottom Left Image, Portland Streetcar: Travel Portland

This book was set in 11/13 New Caledonia by Macmillan Publishing Services and printed and bound by Courier-Kendallville. The cover was printed by Courier-Kendallville.

To order books or for customer service please, call 1-800-CALL WILEY (225-5945).

ISBN-13 978-0-470-48479-1

Printed in the United States of America
10 9 8 7 6 5 4

To the next generation of geographers,

and to our children—Nora, Olivia, Cole, and Kelly.

I Hear and I Forget,

I See and I Remember,

I Do and I Understand.

Ancient Chinese Proverb

Contents

Preface for the Instructor

"DOING" HUMAN GEOGRAPHY

Higher education in North America is undergoing a metamorphosis. The traditional emphasis on instructor-centered teaching is being replaced by a focus on student-centered learning. Colleges and universities are searching for new models of communicating information whereby instructors are facilitators and students are active participants in the learning process. Students retain more with student-oriented approaches than with the traditional model of instructor as lecturer and student as listener. New models of learning necessitate new classroom materials.

Human Geography in Action is a response to the need for innovative alternatives to the standard human geography textbook. As its name implies, the purpose of *Human Geography in Action* is for students to learn geography by doing geography.

Human Geography in Action comprises 14 stimulating, hands-on chapters that challenge students to collect, manipulate, display, and interpret geographic information. Each freestanding activity provides hands-on experience with a basic concept in human geography, including scale, region, diffusion, spatial interaction, age-sex pyramids, economic specialization, development, agriculture, urban hierarchy, neighborhood characteristics, urban sprawl, segregation, nations and states, and environmental change. We have chosen activities that demonstrate the kinds of questions that geographers ask and the myriad ways they go about answering them. Our goal is to help students develop the geographic perspective and problem-solving skills that will prove valuable to them in the long run—in their other courses, in their careers, and for lifelong learning.

The idea of doing geography rather than reading about it makes *Human Geography in Action* an alternative to the strictly lecture-oriented course and its accompanying "reading-centered" textbook. Another key difference between the standard human geography text and *Human Geography in Action* is our focus on essential concepts rather than the never-ending cavalcade of facts in the typical introductory text—depth rather than breadth. Using the standard course syllabus in human geography as a framework for *Human Geography in Action*, we focus on the basics—5 to 10 of the most important ideas in each chapter—keeping the theoretical material useful but brief and keeping *Human Geography in Action* true to our goal of offering an active learning curriculum.

Human Geography in Action is a complete program for teaching and learning human geography. Yet it is perfectly understandable that some instructors—given their busy schedules, varying levels of resources, and individual preferences—might want to change their human geography curriculum incrementally by sprinkling their current courses and complementing their current texts with some or all of these activities. Not only is each chapter freestanding, but in many of the chapters, individual activities can be assigned independently. Thus, while *Human Geography in Action* is a cohesive instructional program, it has also been designed with flexibility in mind.

▶ HANDS-ON ACTIVITIES

Eleven of the 14 chapters in *Human Geography in Action* have computerized activities for your students to do. Nine of the chapters have activities that do not require a computer. Of course, this means that some chapters offer both computerized and non-computerized activities. This mix is fitting, because while technology has profoundly influenced what geographers do and how they do it, many aspects of geography today are practiced without the aid of computers.

For students who still think of geography as a dusty old pursuit, the computerized projects will be real eye-openers. Even computer whizzes will find them colorful, animated, and interactive. But the computerized activities are much more than high-tech "window dressing." They enable students to do analyses that they could not possibly do—or could only do very, very tediously—without computers. Chapter 1 (mapping the distribution of African-Americans in the United States) and Chapter 2 (defining the Middle East and American Southwest culture regions) demonstrate the power of geographic information systems (GIS) to change scales and map types and to layer information. Chapter 3 (tracking the AIDS epidemic) uses the computer to animate change over time. In Chapters 4 (modeling interstate migration flows) and 12 (analyzing segregation in Northern Ireland), students compute formulas and effortlessly link spreadsheets, maps, and graphs. In Chapter 5 (working with age-sex pyramids) and Chapter 9 (defining the market areas for baseball teams), students engage in "what-if" simulations. Chapter 8 (agriculture) makes extensive use of photographs for landscape recognition and introduces remote sensing for measuring land-use change. Chapter 10 (urban geography) includes a virtual field trip through Colorado Springs, and Chapter 11 (urban sprawl) animates a half-century of urban growth and uses GIS layering to explore the effects of different scenarios for future urban growth. Finally, in Chapter 14 students build a dynamic flowchart to analyze environmental problems within a systems-theory framework.

Many professional geographers gather and process information about the world without the use of computer technology, and *Human Geography in Action* introduces students to some of these methods as well. There is, for example, an extremely rich tradition of field observation and analysis in geography that we tap into in Chapter 10 on reading the urban landscape. Also valuable for geographers is the ability to adjudicate the perspectives of different stakeholders in the decision-making process and the ability to speak in public. These skills are honed in role-playing debates in Chapters 11 and 14. Students interpret newspaper, magazine, and Internet articles in Chapter 13 on the disintegration of Yugoslavia and the conflict in Iraq. They also collect data on regional imagery by using local postcards in Chapter 2, on imported foods by visiting local food stores in Chapter 8, and on the number of pizza restaurants in a town by using telephone directories in Chapter 9. Finally, students gain numeracy skills as they calculate regional multipliers in Chapter 6, development indices in Chapter 7, and impacts on global climate change in Chapter 14. Students are introduced to the concepts of outliers and extreme values in Chapter 4, rank-order in Chapter 7, and log-log graphs in Chapter 9. Students can do the non-computerized activities at home or in class using only the hard copy of the book.

Six of the projects can be customized to your city or state. Chapters 4 (migration) and 6 (economy) come with data for every U.S. state and Canadian province. Activity 2 of Chapter 2 (culture regions) asks students to identify culture traits for their own region. Local phone directories are data sources for Activity 1 of Chapter 9 (urban hierarchy). Chapter 10 (urban landscape) compares local census data to field observations. For the role-playing debate in Chapter 14, instructors can substitute an article about a local environmental issue for the ones we provide.

▶ FLEXIBLE TEXTBOOK AND SOFTWARE OPTIONS

Human Geography in Action and the associated computerized activities can be ordered and used in a variety of formats. There is, of course, the paperback book, which features perforated pages that students can tear out and hand in. There is also an online e-book with color photos and graphics available under the WileyPlus platform (see next section for details).

For the digital activities, instructors can choose among three main options. The first is for students to run the activities from the free online Student Companion Site. The second, though less preferred option, is to use CD-ROMs. Wiley can provide CDs if requested, but this technology is no longer actively maintained, and this option is recommended only if students or classrooms lack Internet service. Delivery of the CD can be arranged with each university's Wiley sales representative (who can be found at www.wiley.com/college/rep). For either of these first two options, students will explore the animations online and then answer the questions on the book's tear-out pages. The third option is for students to access the computerized animations via the WileyPlus platform. Students using WileyPlus submit their assignments electronically (see next section).

Some instructors may want to combine the paperback book with the WileyPlus interface. Some students prefer having a traditional book to read, and instructors may want students to bring the physical book with them for doing non-computerized activities during class. And yet it may be advantageous to combine those features with WileyPlus for its automated grading, expanded question sets, and other resources. In order for instructors to choose what's best for their class, we need to introduce you to WileyPlus.

▶ WILEYPLUS UPGRADE

WileyPlus is a course management and educational learning package from John Wiley & Sons. WileyPlus is the biggest change to *Human Geography in Action* since it was first published in 1998. For the past three years we have been developing the WileyPlus interface and testing it on our students at Arizona State University and University of Colorado at Colorado Springs. The *Human Geography in Action* WileyPlus interface seamlessly integrates an online version of the textbook with the interactive activities for which our book is known, plus automated grading of many questions, and grades that flow automatically into a grade book. It has been used successfully in both small and large classes, and is particularly well suited as a stand-alone platform for online classes.

For the student, WileyPlus offers a number of enhanced features—including an affordable price. The photos and graphics in the book are all in color, and there are a number of bonus features like map quizzes, flash cards, and area and demographic data for countries around the world. The links to related web pages are live and instantaneous. Most importantly, *all* of the activities are online, even those that do not feature a computerized animation. All of the questions are answered online and submitted electronically. When answering a question, students can click on links to refer to the Introduction or Case Study readings.

Whenever possible, we have converted the questions from the activities into true-false, multiple-choice, matching, text-entry, and numeric-entry questions that are graded automatically. Automated grading can save you hours of time each week, which can enable you to offer more hands-on activities to your students. Another way it benefits students is by providing instant feedback on their interpretation and analysis. The objective questions still require students to analyze and evaluate the animations and data sets. However, not all questions can be turned into good objective questions. In some cases, the answer depends on your state or province. In other cases, an open-ended written question promotes critical thinking. In such cases, we've kept them as open-ended written questions. Student scores for objective questions flow instantly into a grade book for each student in each class section. The written answers also flow into the grade book, where the instructor or TA can read them and assign a score.

When we first began converting *Human Geography in Action* to WileyPlus, we examined each existing question in the book and determined if we could—and should—convert it to an objectively graded question. But as we tested the questions on our students and gained experience with the technology, we came to realize that the WileyPlus technology offered more than just convenience. Therefore, in a second round of software development, we took advantage of Wiley Plus's capabilities by adding some entirely new sequences of questions to some of the activities. Since the instructor does not have to grade the objective questions, it liberates us to ask a sequence of pointed questions about the things we always hoped students would see in the animations. For instance, we now ask students an expanded series of questions about:

- Particular combinations of layers and what they say about the core/domain/sphere of the Middle East or the American Southwest in Chapter 2
- Cultural landscapes and regional imagery in Chapter 2
- S-curves of particular metro areas in Chapter 3
- The economic ratios of particular states and particular regions in Chapter 6
- The location of particular countries in the scatter plot of Chapter 7
- Theoretical definitions of nations, states, ethnonationalism, and irredentism in Chapter 13

All in all, we feel it has a nice mix of objective and open-ended questions. However—and here's another major attraction of WileyPlus—if you feel differently, you can change it!

WileyPlus is flexible. You can create your own questions to add to any assignment. For instance, you could create your own series of questions about migration to your state or employment shares in your province. You can delete questions you don't like and add ones you've always wanted to ask. You can replace an objective question with a written one, or vice versa. You can give students from one to five (or even unlimited) attempts at each question, give hints after a missed attempt, set due dates, assign point values, and give individual students extensions. You can set up the assignments so students lose some percentage of the possible points if they don't give the correct answer by the nth attempt. You can make announcements or post files for the class, and draw from the instructor resources for discussion questions or PowerPoint files of graphics, and organize and manage class rosters and grades. You can create rosters or allow students to pay and self-enroll online. The test banks and discussion questions from our earlier instructors manual are included among the resources for each chapter, and you can use these to create quizzes and tests for your students to take online. These can also be automatically graded and will flow into the grade book. Your investment of time to develop a good course using WileyPlus can be carried over to subsequent semesters and other instructors in your university.

WileyPlus does have some limitations, and it is important to acknowledge these to help you choose wisely. First, students are not able to digitally submit any maps and graphs that they manipulate in the WileyPlus environment. You could ask your students to print and hand in hard copies, or submit screen shots via email or digital drop box, but we have restructured the WileyPlus assignments so that students are not required to hand in maps and graphs. Second, there are some limitations to the length and types of new assignment questions you can create. As of Spring 2009, you cannot insert a link to a computerized animation into a new question you create, but students can access the animation in other ways. Third, WileyPlus does not yet have discussion boards or chat rooms for conducting online debates for role-playing activities in Chapters 11 and 14. The WileyPlus course, however, does include instructions for how we have organized online debates using another platform such as Blackboard®. We can personally vouch that the online instructions work well and the quality of the comments in online debates can be very good. In fact, some students who might be shy in a live debate may contribute more in an online debate.

Despite these minor limitations, WileyPlus revolutionizes the concept of a textbook, integrating technology with education for an efficient and enhanced learning environment. What's more, WileyPlus and *Human Geography in Action* are a perfect match, in that each can take advantage of the other's unique capabilities. Please contact your Wiley Representative if you would like a free "test-drive" of WileyPLUS.

▶ ORGANIZATION OF THE BOOK

Because of the interconnections among subfields of human geography, there is no single agreed-upon progression of building blocks for sequencing the chapters of a textbook. For the most part, our Table of Contents corresponds to a fairly typical model for a human geography syllabus and textbook, having evolved through the years by those who design and teach the course as a logical progression through a survey of the field. We begin with fundamentals such as mapping, scale, regions, and culture (Chapters 1 and 2). Next we cover two fundamental forms of movement that shape the human world: diffusion and migration (Chapters 3 and 4). After that we survey population, economic, and urban processes and spatial patterns (Chapters 5-12). Finally, we end with two subfields of geography that involve a substantial amount of synthesis: political and environmental geography (Chapters 13 and 14). This order of chapters, however, is by no means the only logical one. An alternative progression could begin with local-scale projects (Chapters 10 and 11), moving to regional/national-scale activities (Chapters 1, 2, 3, 4, 6, and 9) and finally to international topics (Chapters 2, 5, 7, 8, 12, 13, and 14). Others might prefer to examine world population trends (Chapter 5) in conjunction with development processes (Chapter 7) near the beginning of the course, before looking at diffusion, migration, and urban-economic geography.

▶ ORGANIZATION OF THE CHAPTERS

Each chapter and activity follows a consistent format and hierarchy. Each chapter has an Introduction that explains the theoretical concepts, then a Case Study that applies these concepts to some real-world situation or place, followed by the activities that analyze the case study. The Preface for the Student includes a sample of the actual features and pedagogy that the instructor and student can expect to find and follow in every chapter.

▶ LEARNING ENVIRONMENTS

The activities lend themselves to a wide variety of learning environments. Many of them are suited for either classroom activities or homework. They can be done individually or as small-group collaborative projects. Computer projects can be done in a lab or at home. We designed *Human Geography in Action* to be especially appropriate for small-group collaboration. In-class, small-group projects generate a great deal of excitement and discussion among students. For some of the projects, it works well to start in class and then have the students finish them at home, once they have gotten the hang of it. The amount of time needed to complete the projects varies according to the number of separate sections, the amount of reading and/or calculations, and the student's abilities. The range is from 1 to 4 hours per chapter. See the Instructor's Companion Site for time estimates by chapter and section as well as for ideas about what works best for each assignment. In addition, the WileyPlus platform is ideally suited for an online course.

▶ GRADING AND OUTCOME ASSESSMENT

The issue of grading is of obvious concern to instructors, especially those teaching large sections. Ideally, instructors want students to do a lot of writing, thinking, and calculating, but realistically they have limited time for grading. In the WileyPlus *Human Geography in Action* course, many but not all open-ended questions in the book's activities have been converted to objective questions that are graded automatically. WileyPlus instructors can customize the mix of objective and written questions in each assignment to meet their goals and constraints.

For instructors not using WileyPlus, there are numerous strategies you can adopt. We have had success in grading some activities on a pass-fail basis. Grading time is significantly reduced, but students still feel the need to do these chapters just as diligently as if they were graded because the material is covered in examinations. Also, we deduct for obviously halfhearted efforts. Another strategy for reducing grading workload is to use group grades for group work. Instructors also have the option to assign the readings for a chapter and discuss it in class without requiring students to do all the activities. Finally, the fifth edition includes three computerized activities that are self-correcting even outside of WileyPlus. These include activities on population pyramids (Chapter 5), agricultural landscapes (Chapter 8), and environmental systems (Chapter 14). By "self-correcting," we mean that the students are coached by the computer towards the correct answers, and cannot complete the assignments until they get it right.

▶ INSTRUCTOR'S COMPANION SITE

The Instructor's Companion Site (www.wiley.com/college/kuby) offers a range of resources for the instructor. It requires a password to gain access—contact your Wiley sales representative (who can be found at www.wiley.com/college/rep). The Instructor's Companion Site offers logistical advice, time estimates, a teaching outline, discussion questions, sample test questions, and an answer key for each chapter. Also included are e-mail links to the authors and useful people to contact at Wiley.

▶ CHANGES IN THE FIFTH EDITION

The most important change in the fifth edition of *Human Geography in Action* is the adaptation of the book to the WileyPlus platform for course management and enhanced learning. In addition to the interface change, we have improved many components from the fourth edition, including updated data and statistics, improved instructions for activities, reworded questions for increased clarity, updated Web resources and further readings, new and improved graphics, and some new key terms. A summary of the changes is included here:

Chapter 1
- Updated maps of population with B.A. degrees (Figures 1.4 and 1.5) to 2000 Census data.
- New discussion about racial change in America, including mention and photo (Figure 1.11) of Barack Obama elected as the first African-American president.
- Better explanation in Question 1.9 for changes seen in the regional scale population in Figure 1.11.
- Better instructions for using the interactive mapping graphic array with the State Choropleth maps, including changes to Questions 2.10 through 2.13 that ask about this map and compare it to the isoline map.
- Updated the Census mapping instructions.

Chapter 2
- Updates to geopolitical events in the Middle East Case Study Background, and clarifications for the American Southwest Background.
- New photo (Figure 2.3) illustrating regional symbolism.
- Improvements to graphics for the Mormon Culture Region and the physiographic regions of North America.
- Major additions relating to vernacular regions, cultural landscapes, and regional symbolism in Activities 2 and 3 in WileyPlus.

Chapter 3
- Updated graph with growth trend for hydrogen fueling stations (Figure 3.4).
- Improvement to map showing the early diffusion of AIDS (Figure 3.10).

- Updated world map of global HIV/AIDS rates (Figure 3.11) to 2007.
- Instructions added in Activity 1 to help students determine whether a new city crossing the high AIDS rate threshold lies within or outside of one of the top 15 metro regions.
- Question 2.2 reworded to ensure students use either New York or Miami as an illustration of hierarchical diffusion to answer this question.
- Greatly expanded questions in Activity 3 in WileyPlus about the S-curve diffusion model using graphs of cumulative AIDS rates for numerous cities.

Chapter 4

- Expanded discussion about international immigration, particularly the immigration history of Canada and the United States, and discussion about Mexican immigration to the U.S.
- New graph (Figure 4.2) showing historical immigration to the United States by world region from 1850 to 2000.
- New photo (Figure 4.3) of a person jumping the international border fence in Nogales (on the Arizona-Sonora border) to enter the United States illegally.
- Updated data on the graph of annual mobility rates (Figure 4.10).
- Modified the graph showing extreme values and outliers in a scatter diagram (Figure 4.14) to illustrate how the graph expands to better show the distribution of points when the extreme values are eliminated.
- Reword Question 4.7 to help student better understand residuals in the migration model.

Chapter 5

- Updated data in Table 5.1 for countries in various stages of the demographic transition, and Table 5.2 of ten most populous countries.
- New photo (Figure 5.7) of elderly population in Italy.
- Added discussion of upside-down pyramids and their societal implications.
- New photo (Figure 5.13) of India's high-tech sector.
- Questions and instructions changed in Activity 2 to help students better understand rates of population change and cohorts.

Chapter 6

- Revised regional multiplier diagram (Figure 6.7) to include purchases by basic industries from non-basic industries.
- New photo (Figure 6.12) reflecting the current recession and the Wall Street bailout.
- Updated Table 6.1 and descriptive text of the top 20 U.S. companies to reflect 2008 sales data.
- Case Study discussion updated to incorporate events related to the current economic crisis.
- Added outsourcing as a key term.
- Questions in Activity 1 greatly expanded in WileyPlus to help students better understand the NAICS categories, to think about some of the patterns they see on the maps of employment data, to interpret the employment ratios showing economic specialization and economic change over time.

Chapter 7

- Substantive changes to instructions for filling out the development spreadsheets. Changes help students understand what to do in case countries tie in their rankings, explain the meaning of several variables, tell how many decimal places to use for their values, and help to calculate the difference between economic versus human welfare rankings.

- Improved page layout of the first four maps showing global development variables.

- Added substitution of capital for labor as a key term and as a real-world strategy in the modernization school of thought in Table 7.1.

- Mentioned Nobel Prize for Grameen Bank founder.

- Expanded questions in WileyPlus Activity 3 to help students interpret the scatter diagram showing differences between economic and human welfare dimensions of development. Questions ask students about specific countries on the graph and interpretations of the patterns.

Chapter 8

- Case Study Background discussion has been greatly expanded to introduce two counter forces to the current model of globalized agriculture. The first addresses concerns from LDCs about agricultural subsidies that continue in the United States and Europe, including large subsidies in the 2008 U.S. Farm Bill, and the breakdown of the Doha trade negotiations. The second introduces environmental, ethical, and health and sustainability-related complaints about the global agricultural system that arise within the MDCs, and discusses alternatives that are becoming more popular within the United States—organic production, urban gardens, community supported agriculture, and farmers markets, to name a few.

- Updated and expanded discussion of NAFTA trade statistics.

- New photo (Figure 8.5) to illustrate high-yield, capital intensive agriculture.

- New photo (Figure 8.10) showing a farmer's market in an urban environment.

- Expanded questions in WileyPlus Activity 2 ask students about the environmental effects of long-distance transportation of food versus buying locally.

- Expanded questions in WileyPlus Activity 2 about North American food culture regions.

Chapter 9

- New photo (Figure 9.3) of a very small town illustrating a lower-order central place.

- New photo (Figure 9.5) of Broadway theaters in New York illustrating a higher-order central place.

- Added a new diagram (Figure 9.7) of overlapping and tangent circular market areas and how they lead to hexagonal market areas. Also improved the diagram showing the theoretical distribution of the hierarchy of central places (Figure 9.8) to include 3 levels of central places and 3 levels of market areas. Expanded text to explain these new figures.

- Improved the sample log-log scatter diagram showing line of best fit (Figure 9.17).

Chapter 10

- Census instructions updated.
- Questions and instructions in both Activity 1 and 2 reorganized and modified to better help students compare their census tract data to the metropolitan area overall, think about their neighborhood, and reflect upon the social environment they observe in their field study.
- Graphic of the urban land use models (Figure 10.1) improved.
- New map (Figure 10.5) illustrating urban realms added, using metropolitan Phoenix as an example.
- New graphic (Figure 10.6) added illustrating the factoral ecology concept—how the three models of concentric rings, sectors, and multiple nuclei reflect family status, economic status, and racial or ethnic status, and how these all form a composite that makes up the physical urban space.
- New photo (Figure 10.7) to better reflect the cultural heritage of the city.
- New diagram (Figure 10.14) added showing changes in the population density gradient away from the CBD across the twentieth century, with discussion added in the text.

Chapter 11

- New graphic (Figure 11.6) of competing shopping malls in two different political jurisdictions illustrates how municipal boundaries drive inefficient land use as neighboring cities try to grab their share of sales tax dollars.
- New graphic (Figure 11.7) added illustrating urban zoning.
- New graphic (Figure 11.8) showing the growth in population, car ownership, trips per day, average trip length, and vehicle miles traveled.
- Expanded discussion of the increase of single occupancy vehicle miles driven in the United States.
- New photo (Figure 11.12) showing an urban, mixed-use development.

Chapter 12

- Improved discussion of how to interpret the index of segregation values.
- New photo (Figure 12.1) illustrating Jewish ghettos in mid-20th Century Europe.
- Updated discussion of the political developments in Northern Ireland.
- New age-sex pyramids (Figure 12.7) for Northern Ireland Protestants and Catholics added.

Chapter 13

- Substantial text updates on the changing political situations in both the former Yugoslavia and Iraq.
- Map of pre- and post-breakup Yugoslavia (Figure 13.7) and map of historic Serbian boundaries (Figure 13.9) amended to now show Montenegro and Kosovo independence.
- Many questions added to WileyPlus activities that first reinforce students' understanding of Key Terms before case study questions are asked.

Chapter 14

- The case study on global warming has been supplemented with Pacala and Socolow's well-known diagram of carbon reduction "wedges" (Figure 14.17) and a table (Table 14.2) indicating the types of technologies capable of reducing 1 gigaton of carbon emissions over the next 50 years. This addition mirrors the evolution of the global warming debate from "whether or not it is human-caused?" to "what can we do about it?"

- Updated graph showing global change in temperature and atmospheric CO_2 levels (Figure 14.16).

Digital Activities

We suggest using a recent release web browser, such as Internet Explorer, Firefox, or Safari. Even the CD runs an engine called EduGen that works best with internet access. The Book Companion Site and CD also provide a link to free downloads of Shockwave, which is needed for Activity 1 of Chapter 5. Click on *Help* for system requirements and technical support.

PowerPoint Graphics

Instructors will find updated PowerPoint files on their Instructor's Companion Site. Instructors using the WileyPlus interface will find them under the *Prepare and Present* tab. PowerPoints can be downloaded to your computer from either web interface.

Preface for the Student

Human Geography in Action is not your standard human geography textbook. As its name implies, the purpose of *Human Geography in Action* is for you to learn geography as you do geography. Fourteen stimulating, hands-on activities challenge you to collect, manipulate, and interpret geographic information, with each activity demonstrating several basic concepts in human geography.

In some chapters, you will work with computers using the *Human Geography in Action* activities on the Internet. In others, you will discover geography in postcards, newspapers, libraries, and the Internet and in your own daily activities and neighborhood. You always will be working with maps, because human geography is the social science that describes and explains where human activities take place.

Compared with the traditional textbook, this book aims more for depth than breadth. Instead of an encyclopedic survey of the entire field of human geography, you will learn instead to view the world as a geographer. You will ask the spatial questions geographers ask, and you'll answer them using the methods professional geographers use. Our goal is to help you develop problem-solving skills that will prove valuable to you in the long run—in your other courses, in your career, and, we hope, in your lifelong interest in the world.

You will get as much out of this book as you put into it. In this course, you can't just sit back and passively take notes. To succeed, you will need to think logically about how theoretical concepts apply to real-world case studies. Read the instructions and questions carefully. Don't rush your answers, and express yourself clearly. After you've finished, reread your answers to make sure they actually say what you mean and that they answer the questions.

Because maps are a geographer's most basic tool, you will need to become comfortable with interpreting them. Practice your map-reading skills every chance you have. In some exercises, you will apply math in new ways. Study the formulas, and follow them one step at a time. Math is increasingly important in geography, as it is in other social sciences and in life.

Human Geography in Action has been designed with flexibility in mind. Don't be surprised if your instructor does not assign all 14 chapters or all activities within a chapter. You may complete some in class, in a lab, or as homework. Your instructor may also skip a project entirely but still assign you to read the introductory material.

Each chapter follows a standard format, illustrated on the following sample pages. The format introduces core ideas in human geography, which you will then apply to a particular case study using research methods employed by geographers solving real-world problems.

The Human Geography in Action software runs using your computer's Web browser software. You will find the interface very familiar and intuitive, but be aware that the performance of browser applications depends on your computer system configuration. Browser applications "ride" on the computer's operating system, printer drivers, and browser software. It is therefore very important that you carefully read and follow the computer requirements that can be found by clicking on *Help* on the Web site. Please do *not* attempt to use this product on a computer that does not meet the hardware and software specifications. You should run this program on a recent version of Mozilla Firefox, Internet Explorer, or Safari. If your usual computer doesn't satisfy the hardware or operating system requirements, we suggest that you find a computer on campus that does, and work there. So, just follow the instructions and get ready to enjoy some of the coolest educational software available anywhere!

We hope you enjoy and profit from this new approach to learning human geography.

CHAPTER 1

True Maps, False Impressions: Making, Manipulating, and Interpreting Maps

Each chapter is organized around a set of **core ideas** in human geography (second part of title) and a **case study** (first part of title).

▶ INTRODUCTION

Each chapter begins with an **Introduction** to the core ideas.

Human geography studies the distribution of humans and their activities on the surface of the earth and the processes that generate these distributions. People use geographic space and interact with the environment when they grow crops, build homes, drive cars, do jobs, raise children, practice religions, cast votes, and spend leisure time. Geographers help us understand the evolving character and organization of human life on the earth's surface.

Geographers subscribe first and foremost to the view that location matters. It is significant that 305 million persons live in the United States. More significant, however, is where these 305 million persons live. Are they urban or rural? Are they spreading out or becoming increasingly concentrated? What kinds of places are attracting people, and what kinds are losing them? These are geographic questions. Similarly, the world is capable of producing plenty of food to feed its current population of 6.8 billion. Relevant questions about world hunger are geographic ones. How are the supply of and demand for food distributed spatially? What environmental, economic, and political factors account for these distributions? How are demand and supply reconciled in the international marketplace for food?

Many of the topics that you will find in this workbook are common to other sciences. Geographers have no monopoly on the study of baseball franchises, migration, AIDS, the population explosion, civil war, and air pollution. Geographers bring to the table their unique spatial perspective and interest in human-environmental relations by asking ìwhere?î and ìwhy there?î questions about the same pressing human problems that engage other social and environmental scientists.

The ìwhereî question leads to five overarching themes in human geography that run through the various chapters of this book (Table 1.1). The first theme, **location**, refers not only to the exact coordinates of a point in space but also to where it is relative to other factors. **Place**, the second theme, involves the human and physical characteristics that uniquely define a place and impart meaning to its inhabitants. The third theme, **region**, defines areas that are bound together by common characteristics: Similar places and locations form common regions. In the fourth geographical theme, **movements** of information, goods, and people connect locations and regions to one another. The

Key terms in bold are defined at the end of the chapter and appear in the **Glossary** on the Internet Student Companion Site.

© 2010 John Wiley & Sons, Inc.

1

The **case study** begins after the concept-oriented Introduction.

The **goal** of each case study states what you will accomplish in the activity and what lifelong abilities you will acquire.

The **learning outcomes** are specific, measurable skills and knowledge that you gain from this activity. You can be tested on these outcomes.

Special materials are things you will need to complete the project that are not provided in the book. Be sure to have them handy.

The **background** section briefs you on the particular case study that you will analyze in the exercise to follow.

Case Study   **11**

▶ *CASE STUDY*

TRUE MAPS, FALSE IMPRESSIONS

GOAL

To interpret and critically evaluate maps, to understand how **scale** influences data representation on maps, and to recognize three types of map scale: representative fraction, verbal, and graphic. You will also learn how to represent data with different types of **thematic maps**óthe **dot map**, the **isoline map**, the **choropleth map**, and the **proportional symbol map**óand see that your choice of map type profoundly influences the resulting spatial pattern.

LEARNING OUTCOMES

After completing the chapter, you will be able to:

- Convert map scale to real-world distances.
- Recognize choropleth, proportional symbol, isoline, and dot maps.
- Recognize that changing the scale and type of a map changes its message.
- Understand the difference between changing scale and changing level of aggregation.
- Use GIS to change the class limits on a choropleth map.
- Describe the geographic distribution of African-Americans in the United States.

SPECIAL MATERIALS NEEDED

- Calculator
- Computer with high-speed Internet access and a recent release of a Web browser. If using the Student Companion Site with the printed book, click on *Tech Support* for system requirements and technical support. (If using the e-book in WileyPlus, click on *Help* for details about the system requirements.)

BACKGROUND

Africans were first brought to what is now the United States between 1619 and 1808 as slaves to work on tobacco, rice, sugar, and cotton plantations, mostly in the South. Although the practice of bringing slaves into the country was made illegal in 1808, some smuggling of slaves continued further into the nineteenth century. Importation was replaced by programs of slave breeding and trade within the South. Although most slaves were concentrated in the South, a small number of slaves escaped to the North and other parts of the country, where they were represented across many walks of life. A free black man living in Baltimore was commissioned by Thomas Jefferson to survey the District of Columbia. Black cowboys, based in Texas, were well known on cattle drives throughout the West.

Many people are surprised to learn that African-Americans represented a sizable share of the U.S. population during the seventeenth and eighteenth centuries. At the time of the first census in 1790, one of every five residents of the new country was African-American. Concentrations were highest in southern states: 54 percent of South Carolinaís population

was African-American, 40 percent of Virginiaís, 37 percent of Georgiaís, 34 percent of North Carolinaís, and 33 percent of Marylandís.

After emancipation in 1863, most African-Americans remained in the South, working as sharecroppers or tenants on white-owned cotton farms, barely getting by. Although the reasons to leave the South were compelling, including crushing poverty, antiblack terrorism, and a lack of civil rights, few actually left the region. Many black farmers were illiterate and therefore unaware of economic opportunities in other parts of the country. White landowners, desperate to preserve their favored way of life sustained by cheap black labor, promulgated an economic system that put sharecroppers in a position of permanent indebtedness, making departure illegal. In the late nineteenth century, Northern labor unions lobbied against the importation of African-Americans from the South, fearing it would depress their wages. They preferred European immigrants to meet the demand for new industrial workers in Americaís burgeoning manufacturing sector.

All of that changed after the end of World War I, beginning one of the most dramatic migration streams in U.S. history. At the turn of the twentieth century, 90 percent of the nationís African-American population lived in the South, mostly in the rural South. By 1970, barely 50 percent lived in the South (Figure 1.7), millions having sought a better life in northern cities. Reasons for leaving were many and complicated. The supply of cheap immigrant labor was cut off by World War I, and recruiters went south, bringing literally trainloads of African-American workers to the steel mills, automobile factories, and meatpacking plants of Pittsburgh, Detroit, Chicago, and other northern cities (Figure 1.8). Once these connections had been established, thousands of migrants followed and established themselves in predominantly black neighborhoods such as Harlem in northern Manhattan (Figure 1.9) and the South Side of Chicago. The Great Depression of the 1930s and the mechanization of cotton harvesting after 1945 further spurred the African-American exodus from the South. The mechanical cotton picker rendered sharecroppers obsolete by drastically reducing the need for their labor. Early models of the cotton picker reduced the costs of picking cotton from $40 to $5 per bale. Each machine did the work of 50 pickers. As the mainstay for southern African-American employment evaporated, many left the rural South in search of northern jobs. A second wave of black migration headed to California from 1940 to 1970, lured by both industrial and agricultural jobs.

The story does not end here, for migration flows between the South and North were reversed after 1970. Fewer African-Americans left the South, and many more moved from the North to the South. Race riots and deteriorating economic conditions in northern cities served as push factors, and the favorable economic opportunities and improved social conditions of the ìNew Southî attracted migrants from the North. Whereas the earlier migration streams connected the *rural* South to the *urban* North, todayís streams primarily link the *urban* North

© 2010 John Wiley & Sons, Inc.

Activity 3: Regional Imagery   **57**

Name: _____   Instructor: _____

Layers of Tradition: Culture Regions at Different Scales

▶ ACTIVITY 3: REGIONAL IMAGERY

In Activities 1 and 2 you tried to distinguish the key characteristics of a culture region based on maps and personal experience. Activity 3 uses another method to assess cultural characteristics of a region by looking at major themes that define the region on postcards. Themes on postcards project recognizable symbols or scenes that people from around the nation or world can identify as representing that region.

   A. Go to some local stores that sell postcards and identify the symbols, cultural characteristics, or features of the cultural landscape that best represent the region in which you live. Keep a tally of the number of times each theme appears. You should sample at least 20 to 30 postcards. The more you use, the easier your task will be.

3.1. Fill in the following table of the dominant themes that appear on the postcards and the number of times you saw cards in this group. The themes you define should be general categories that are represented by individual postcard images. Examples might be cowboys in the West, nature in the Rocky Mountains, city skylines in the East, or regional sports such as NASCAR in the South. Think about which themes struck you as repeatedly appearing and try to be thorough in creating the groups. The number of themes you should identify will vary for each region.

Theme (fill in as many as necessary)   Number of Appearances

   1.

   2.

   3.

   4.

   5.

   6.

   7.

   8.

   9.

  10.

© 2010 John Wiley & Sons, Inc.

The hands-on part of each chapter is divided into different **activities**. In some cases, your instructor may choose not to assign all activities.

Instructions that do not require a written answer are labeled with capital letters.

Questions that must be answered in writing (in the blank space provided) are labeled numerically. In this case, Question 3.1 is the first question of Activity 3. Students working in the WileyPLUS environment will have questions assigned by your instructor that will either require manually submitting written answers or digitally submitting answers, depending on what your instructor chooses.

Tear out your completed worksheets and hand them in, or submit digital answers in the WileyPLUS environment.

Definitions of key terms are short, concise summaries of each idea. These key terms are also found in the Glossary.

At the end of each chapter is a list of **further readings** for students who wish to learn more about the chapter's core ideas, methods, and case study. The readings are a mix of books, articles in scientific journals, popular articles, and data sources.

A list of **Web resources** will get you started on your online exploration.

At the very end of each chapter is a reminder list of **Items to hand in**. Listed are the written questions and any additional items, such as maps, graphs, spreadsheets, or typed essays.
Note: WileyPLUS users may have custom-assigned questions from your instructor that do not match the default list of Items to Hand in. Be sure you are clear on what your instructor requires.

---

368   Chapter 12. Do Orange and Green Clash? Residential Segregation in Northern Ireland

▶ DEFINITIONS OF KEY TERMS

Apartheid A system of forced segregation between races in South Africa in effect until 1993.

Enclave Residential clusters that result from voluntary segregation.

Ethnic Cleansing Forced residential segregation along ethnic lines.

Ghetto An urban area where, due to discrimination, ethnic segregation is largely involuntary.

Integration The residential mixing of subgroups within the larger population.

Plantation System An organized system of colonization used by the British government in the 1500s and 1600s to ìplantî British colonists on Irish land.

Residential Segregation The residential separation of subgroups within the larger population.

Segregation Index A numerical measure of the degree of separation of two or more distinct groups.

Social Distance A measure of the likelihood that dissimilar groups will interact in society. Influences the degree of assimilation for minority groups.

Spatial Convergence Increased integration over time.

Spatial Divergence Increased segregation over time.

Tenant Farmer A farmer who rents land to farm. Although tenant farmers often live in debt to the landowner, they are considered more fortunate than landless laborers, who neither own nor rent their own land.

▶ FURTHER READINGS

Alba, Richard, and Victor Nee. 1997. Rethinking Assimilation Theory for a New Era of Immigration. *International Migration Review* 31:826ñ874.

Allen, James Paul, and Eugene James Turner. 1988. *We the People: An Atlas of Americaís Ethnic Diversity*. New York: Macmillan.

Anderson, K. J. 1987. The Idea of Chinatown: The Power of Place and Institutional Practice in the Making of a Racial Category. *Annals of the Association of American Geographers* 77(4):580ñ598.

Boal, F. W. 1976. Ethnic Residential Segregation. In *Social Areas in Cities, vol. 1*, D. Herbert and R. Johnston (eds.). New York: Wiley.

Cherny, R. W. 1994. Patterns of Tolerance and Discrimination in San Francisco: The Civil War to World War I. *California History* 73:130ñ141.

Clark, William A. V. 1998. *The California Cauldron: Immigration and the Fortunes of Local Communities*. New York: Guilford.

▶ WEB RESOURCES

Conflict Archive on the Internet: *Northern Ireland*: cain.ulst.ac.uk/
Democratic Unionists Party: www.dup.org.uk/
Fianna F·il. *Fianna F·il: The Republican Party* : www.fiannafail.ie/
Irish Times. *Ireland.com*: www.ireland.com/
Loyalist and Orange Information Services: www.lois.itgo.com/main.html

▶ ITEMS TO HAND IN

Activity 1: • The three choropleth maps of percentage of Catholics
   • Questions 1.1–1.4, or answer all questions your instructor created in your WileyPlus assignments.
Activity 2: • The three completed spreadsheets
   • Questions 2.1–2.4, or answer all questions your instructor created in your WileyPlus assignments.

© 2010 John Wiley & Sons, Inc.

Acknowledgments

The list of people who helped with this book continues to grow with the release of this fifth edition.

At John Wiley & Sons, Executive Editor Ryan Flahive and Executive Publisher Jay O'Callaghan continued to provide strong support for this book and our integration of technology into the learning process. Veronica Armour handled all the organization and details marvelously, taking over from the great job that Courtney Nelson began. Bridget O'Lavin handled the technological issues with professionalism, especially the portage into the WileyPLUS environment. We are grateful to the WileyPlus programmers and developers at TES for their expertise and patience in adapting *Human Geography in Action* to WileyPlus. Other members of Wiley's superb production team include Valerie Vargas, (Production Editor), Suzanne Ingrao of Ingrao Associates (Production Services), Dorothy Sinclair (Production Services Manager), Meredith Leo (Editorial Assistant), Sheena Goldstein (photo research), and Anna Melhorn (graphics). We are also grateful for the support of Wiley's Higher Education Marketing Team, especially Danielle Torio, Jeff Rucker, and Melissa Kleckner.

A number of our colleagues and students helped us immeasurably with this fifth edition. We especially want to thank Mike Larkin of UC-Colorado Springs, who did the initial, pioneering work to convert the book's questions to the WileyPlus environment. At ASU, undergraduate student Hope Johnston produced a number of new maps, as did our standout staff cartographer, Barbara Trapido-Lurie. Former ASU PhD student Ken Madsen produced the PowerPoints that come with the book, and has contributed ideas, references, and data over the years. ASU teaching assistants Johnny Finn, Ann Fletchall, and Melinda Alexander provided valuable feedback on the WileyPlus adaptation. And of course, we especially want to thank our students at ASU and UCCS, especially those good sports who took our first online classes and helped us test the first version of WileyPlus.

Many people tested our product and provided crucial review comments. We thank Randy Alexson-Gabrys, University of Wisconsin; Christopher Badurek, SUNY Buffalo; Michaele Anne Buell, Northwest Arkansas Community College; Brian Crawford, West Liberty State College; Shannon Crum, University of Texas at San Antonio; Robert Czerniak, New Mexico State University; Satish Davgun, Bemidji State University; Mark Drayse, California State University, Fullerton; Jill Eastman, Southern Connecticut State University; Brian Forn, United States Military Academy; Bill Graves, University of North Carolina at Charlotte; Daniel Griffith, University of Miami; Charles Gunter, Eastern Tennessee State University; Ellen Hanson, Emporia State University; Jim Hipple, St. Mary's University; Craig Laing, University of Tennessee at Chattanooga; Olga Medvedkov, Wittenberg University; Peter Muller, University of Miami; Garth Myers, University of Kansas; Kenji Oshiro, Wright State University; Jeff Osleeb, Hunter College; Timothy Pitts, Edinboro University; Guo Quain, San Francisco State University; Thomas Schlitz, San Diego Miramar College; Derek Shanahan, Millersville University; Hunter Shobe, University of Oregon; Mandeep Singh, Hofstra University; Binita Sinha, Diablo Valley College; Bruce Smith, Bowling Green State University; Linda Wang, University of South Carolina, Aiken; Richard Wolfel, Southern Illinois University;

Benjamin Zhan, Texas State University. A number of our reviews were anonymous and we would also like to thank these reviewers for their comments.

We feel it is important to continue to recognize those who helped with previous editions of the book, since their contribution continues to benefit students:

1998 and 1999 NSF Workshop Participants
Jorge Brea, Ross Nelson, Katie Algeo, Nancy Hultquist, Michael Camille, Shannon O'Lear, Jeff Allender, Nancy Jonsson, Ed Chambless, Debra Paulson, Michelle Behr, Joan Kendall, Fiona Davidson, Julio Rivera, Sarah Brinegar, Sandra Nichols, Clint Davis, Carol Rosen, Henry Bullamore, Gordon Riedesel, Jim Davis, Paul Sabourin, Sam Couch, Paul Rollinson, Bonnie Hallman, Debra Sharkey, Cliff Craig, Lynnell Rubright, Dan Hammel, Dona Stewart, Anne-Marie d'Hautserre, Michael Solem, Neusa Hidalgo-Monroy, Sharon Thomas, Lillian Fleming, Tom Terich, James Jennings, Gerald Thomas, Heidi Glaesel, Craig Torbenson, Uchida Kazuhiro, Virginia Thompson, Janet Halpin, Katie Wilcoxen, Art Kieffer, Christine von Reichert, Miriam Helen Hill, Peter Cohen, Robert Kuhlken, Mike Wangler, and Lori LeMay.

Arizona State University
Kenneth Madsen, Kevin Romig, Kerstin Byorni, Alex Oberle, Breandán Ó'Uallacháin, Kevin McHugh, Elizabeth Burns, Dan Arreola, Anthony Brazel, Patricia Fall, Randy Cerveny, Malcolm Comeaux, Duncan Schaeffer, Dan Borough, Rodrigo Sierra, Robert Balling, Eric Matranga, Mike Pasqualetti, Linda Ellis, Jamie Goodwin-White, Denise Dorn, Kevin Blake, Jean Sol, Emily Skop, David Wasserman, Larry Joseph, and Chris Upchurch.

University of Colorado at Colorado Springs
Lori Haefner, Mike Duysen, Victor Grycenkov, Tom Huber, Carole Huber, Ruth Jackson, Matt Mayberry, Teri Hawley Valerie Brodar, Charlene(Kelly) Wooldridge, and Lisa Harner.

City of Colorado Springs/El Paso County
Phil Friesen, David Litzelman, Steve Vigil, Angela Bratton, and Carl Schueler.

Thompson Rivers University
Ross Nelson, who helps us develop and verify all Canadian aspects of the activities.

Universidad de Guadalajara
Hirineo Martínez Barragán, Armando Chávez Hernández, and María del Rocío Castillo Aja.

Reviewers and Data Providers
Michal Imort, Sharon Cobb, Art Kieffer, Jon Klipinen, James Lowry, Tom Maringer, Douglas Munski, Ross Nelson, Gordon Riedesel, Julio Rivera, Carol Rosen, Jamie Strickland, Sarah Bednarz, Jorge Brea, Phil Crossley, Stephen Cunha, Satish Davgun, Larry Dilsaver, Roger Downs, Leslie Duram, Thomas Graff, Lucy Jarosz, Sandra Kehoe-Forutan, David Ley, Miriam Lo, Tom Maringer, Richard Matthews, Daniel Montello, Curtis Roseman, John Rennie Short, Jean-Claude Thill, Michael

Wheeler, Bruce Newbold, James Lowry, William Wykoff, and the anonymous reviewers.

Software Developers for Prior Editions
Tom Kulesa, Lynn Pearlman, Lenox Softworx (Robert Kestyn), and Penn State's Deasy GeoGraphics Laboratory (David DiBiase).

John Wiley & Sons
Hillary Newman, Karen Ayoub, Denise Powell, Deepa Chungi, Tara Sanford, Chris Thillen, and Emily Autumn (GGS Book Services) and especially Nanette Kauffman, who put her faith in us and who had the vision for what *Human Geography in Action* could be.

About the Authors

MICHAEL KUBY received an A.B. from The University of Chicago in 1980 and a Ph.D. from Boston University in 1988, both in geography. He is a professor in the School of Geographical Sciences and Urban Planning at Arizona State University, where he has taught since 1988. Before writing *Human Geography in Action*, he developed an active-learning module on population and energy for the Commission on College Geography II. His research interests are in transportation, energy, and facility location. Kuby has served as Chair of the Transportation Specialty Group of the Association of American Geographers (AAG) and on editorial boards of the *Professional Geographer* and *Journal of Transport Geography* and as an Area Editor for *Networks and Spatial Economics*. His work with the World Bank on energy transport in China won a Citation Award in Applied Geography in 1993. His current research focuses on optimal location of alternative-fuel stations.

JOHN HARNER received a B.S. in geography from The Pennsylvania State University in 1986 and an M.A. and a Ph.D. in geography from Arizona State University in 1993 and 1996, respectively. He is an Associate Professor in the Department of Geography and Environmental Studies at the University of Colorado at Colorado Springs, where he has been since 1997. In 2005, Harner was visiting professor in geography at the Departamento de Geografía y Ordenación Territorial at the Universidad de Guadalajara, Mexico. His research areas include cultural and urban geography as well as topical expertise in GIS and regional interests in Mexico and the American Southwest. He has published in such journals as the *Annals of the AAG*, *Professional Geographer*, *Geographical Review*, and the *Journal of Cultural Geography*.

PATRICIA GOBER received a B.S. Ed in Geography from the University of Wisconsin-Whitewater in 1970 and M.A. and Ph.D. degrees in Geography from the Ohio State University in 1972 and 1975. She is currently a Professor at Arizona State University with a joint appointment in the School of Geographical Sciences and Urban Planning and the School of Sustainability. She is co-Director of the National Science Foundation's Decision Center for a Desert City which studies water management decisions in the face of growing climatic uncertainty in Greater Phoenix. Her current research centers on issues of water management and environmental change in metropolitan Phoenix, as well as population and urban geography. She is a past President of the Association of American Geographers, former member of the Population Reference Bureau's Board of Trustees and the Science Advisory Board of NOAA, and former Chair of the College Board's Advanced Placement Human Geography Committee. Her most recent book, *Metropolitan Phoenix: Place Making and Community Building in the Desert*, was published by the University of Pennsylvania Press in 2006. She holds an honorary doctorate of science from Carthage College in Kenosha, Wisconsin, is a fellow of the American Association for the Advancement of Science, and was awarded the Prince Sultan Abdulaziz International Price for Water in November 2008 and the ASU Alumni Association's Faculty Research Award in February 2009.

True Maps, False Impressions: Making, Manipulating, and Interpreting Maps

▶ INTRODUCTION

Human geography studies the distribution of humans and their activities on the surface of the earth and the processes that generate these distributions. People use geographic space and interact with the environment when they grow crops, build homes, drive cars, do jobs, raise children, practice religions, cast votes, and spend leisure time. Geographers help us understand the evolving character and organization of human life on the earth's surface.

Geographers subscribe first and foremost to the view that location matters. It is significant that 305 million persons live in the United States. More significant, however, is where these 305 million persons live. Are they urban or rural? Are they spreading out or becoming increasingly concentrated? What kinds of places are attracting people, and what kinds are losing them? These are geographic questions. Similarly, the world is capable of producing plenty of food to feed its current population of 6.8 billion. Relevant questions about world hunger are geographic ones. How are the supply of and demand for food distributed spatially? What environmental, economic, and political factors account for these distributions? How are demand and supply reconciled in the international marketplace for food?

Many of the topics that you will find in this workbook are common to other sciences. Geographers have no monopoly on the study of baseball franchises, migration, AIDS, the population explosion, civil war, and air pollution. Geographers bring to the table their unique spatial perspective and interest in human-environmental relations by asking "where?" and "why there?" questions about the same pressing human problems that engage other social and environmental scientists.

The "where" question leads to five overarching themes in human geography that run through the various chapters of this book (Table 1.1). The first theme, **location**, refers not only to the exact coordinates of a point in space but also to where it is relative to other factors. **Place**, the second theme, involves the human and physical characteristics that uniquely define a place and impart meaning to its inhabitants. The third theme, **region**, defines areas that are bound together by common characteristics: Similar places and locations form common regions. In the fourth geographical theme, **movements** of information, goods, and people connect locations and regions to one another. The

TABLE 1.1 Five Themes in Human Geography

Theme	Definition	Selected Examples in Chapters
Location	The absolute position of something on the surface of the earth and its relative proximity to other related things	Chapter 1: Where do African-Americans live, and why? Chapter 6: Where are different kinds of jobs concentrated, and why? Chapter 7: What is the spatial pattern of development, and why? Chapter 8: Where are different crops and livestock grown, and why? Chapter 9: Where are major league baseball teams located, and where should new ones be put, and why? Chapter 11: Where should new housing be built in the urban area, and why? Chapter 12: Are the locations of Catholics and Protestants in Northern Ireland growing more mixed or more segregated over time?
Place	The local human and physical characteristics that uniquely define a place and impart meaning to its inhabitants	Chapter 2: What symbolic imagery represents the characteristics of the place where you live? How are these themes presented to create a place identity? Chapter 10: What can you tell about a neighborhood by observing it, and how does it compare to census data? Chapter 13: Why are people of the former Yugoslavia and Kurdistan so attached to their places of birth?
Region	An area characterized by similarity or by cohesiveness that sets it apart from other areas	Chapter 2: What are the boundaries and cultural traits of the Middle East or American Southwest culture regions? Chapter 6: Which regions specialize in which industries, and why? Chapter 9: How and why would a new baseball team affect the market areas of existing teams? Chapter 10: What kinds of subregions exist within a city, and why? Chapter 11: How and why have urban regions expanded over time? Chapter 13: How did mismatches between political and ethnic regions lead to war in Yugoslavia and Iraq?
Movement	The flow of people, goods, money, ideas, or materials between locations near and far	Chapter 3: How and why has AIDS spread throughout the United States? Chapter 4: From where do people move to your state or province, and why? Chapter 8: What kinds of food are imported from other countries, and why? Chapter 11: How will different urban growth strategies affect traffic congestion? Chapter 13: When did Islam spread to Bosnia, and why? Chapter 14: How does the movement of water or beef, or barriers to the movement of mountain lions, lead to environmental problems?
Human-Environmental Interaction	The ways in which human society and the natural environment affect each other	Chapter 2: How have humans adapted to arid climates in the Middle East and the American Southwest? Chapter 5: How does population growth in India affect the environment? Chapter 8: Which crops grow best in which climates? Chapter 11: How does urban sprawl affect the environment? Chapter 14: What are the causes and effects of environmental problems, and what are the positions of the various stakeholders?

final theme is **human-environmental interactions**. Humans and their environment interact in both directions: environmental resources constrain and benefit human societies while human activities refashion and degrade their environments. Notice in Table 1.1 that some of the case studies in the book involve several themes (i.e., the themes are not mutually exclusive).

Geography's spatial perspective—and all five themes—lead to the heavy use of maps. In the broadest sense, **a map** is a two-dimensional graphical representation of the surface of the earth. No map can perfectly represent reality. People tend to think of maps as unalterable facts, as if produced by an all-seeing overhead camera. In practice, however, mapmakers (or cartographers, as they are known in the field) exercise considerable discretion in the spatial information they display and the way they display it. You must always keep in mind that any map you look at could have been made in countless different ways, sometimes drastically altering your perception of what you see.

Cartographers (mapmakers) make five critical decisions about map construction that greatly influence the message conveyed by the map. First, they choose a particular **map projection**, which is a systematic method of transferring the spherical surface of the earth to a flat map. There is an old saying that "all maps lie flat, and all flat maps lie." It is utterly impossible to represent the three-dimensional world on a flat, two-dimensional piece of paper or video screen without stretching or compressing it in some way. Every projection is therefore distorted in one way or another, and this distortion influences the impression in the viewer's mind about the size and proximity of different regions of the world (Figure 1.1).

For example, Figure 1.1A shows the Mercator projection of the world, a map used in early navigation because all compass bearings (directions) are correct. The British Empire, based on sea power, used the Mercator projection extensively, and spread it around the world. However, this projection grossly exaggerates area as you move away from the equator. For this reason, Mercator maps were a favorite of President Reagan during the Cold War because they made the Soviet Union appear much larger than it actually was, reinforcing the impression that the USSR was a dangerous threat and thereby justifying a tough anti-Soviet stance. For the same reason, Mercator projections are unpopular among equatorial countries, whose size appears diminished. A popular projection that attempts to preserve the area of map features and avoid high-latitude distortions is Mollweide, shown in Figure 1.1B. Many international agencies, such as the World Bank, have changed the map projections they use in an effort to more accurately depict relationships between countries, not biasing any one region. For example, Figure 1.1C shows the Van Der Grinten projection, which portrays both Russia and Canada at over 200 percent larger than they actually are. The National Geographic Society used this projection for over 50 years before changing to the Robinson projection (Figure 1.1D) in 1998. The Robinson projection better portrays the relationship between land and water areas in the world and does not distort countries at high latitudes nearly as much.

Although these four examples of map projections show distortions in shape and size that can occur, they all still adhere to certain conventions that can also mislead. For instance, they all split the world through the Pacific Ocean, making Japan appear far from Hawaii and the United States. This false impression may have contributed to the "surprise" Japanese attack on Pearl Harbor during World War II. Polar projections centered on the North Pole in Figure 1.1E clearly show how close the former Soviet Union and the United States were to each other over the Arctic Ocean, a relationship you cannot see in the first four projections. Looking at this

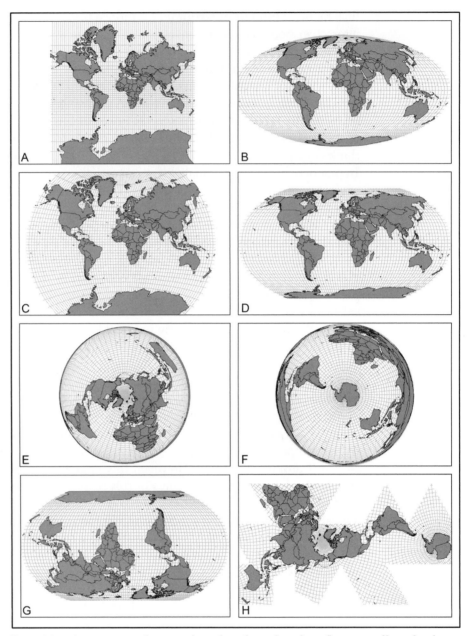

Figure 1.1 The projection chosen to draw the spherical earth on flat paper affects the shape of the map and our perception of the relationships between the map features.

projection, it becomes obvious that northern Canada and Alaska were good locations for warning stations designed to detect incoming Soviet nuclear missiles. A less common view of the polar projection focused on the South Pole and Antarctica (Figure 1.1F) makes Australia, New Zealand, Chile, and Argentina appear central to the world. In fact there is no compelling reason for adhering to the convention of showing north at the top on a map. Europe and North America typically occupy the privileged position on a map where our eyes tend to focus, reinforcing the perception of their dominant status in the world. The earth as seen from space could just as easily be depicted with south up (Figure 1.1G), a radical change that calls into question global geopolitical relations.

Finally, the Dymaxion Map™ (Figure 1.1H) reveals the landmasses situated in a worldwide ocean, without visible distortion of the relative shapes and sizes and without splitting any continents. This map, designed by the Buckminster Fuller Institute, is an attempt to show the global connections of all humanity rather than disassociated countries and places competing against each other.

The second critical decision cartographers routinely make is **simplification**. Simplification can take many forms, such as omission, straightening, exaggeration, and distortion, depending upon the map's ultimate use. Maps of Canada for educational purposes frequently omit small, uninhabited islands and straighten jagged coastlines in the Canadian Arctic, whereas maps for navigation try to show the same features with great accuracy as well as water depth and currents. Highly simplified subway maps emphasize information of potential use to a subway rider and ignore features of the human and natural environment that are unimportant to navigating the subway network (Figure 1.2). Stations five or six blocks apart in the central city appear on the map as far apart as suburban stations separated by several miles, because for most subway travelers, distance is unimportant. What matters is whether they are on the right line, how many stops until they need to get off, and whether they need to change trains. To make road lines readable on the map, they are drawn thicker than if they were drawn proportional to their width in the real world. Some buildings are considered important enough to include, but most are not. No two cartographers make these ultimately subjective decisions in the same way.

A third way to manipulate the way a map looks is by choosing a different map scale. **Map scale** refers to the degree to which a map "zooms in" on an area. Map scale can be defined as the ratio of map distance (distance between two points on a map) to earth distance (distance between those two points on the surface of the earth), measured in the same units. Every map has a scale, and the degree of generalization of information depends on that scale. A large-scale map depicts a small area (such as downtown Phoenix) with great detail. A small-scale map depicts a large area (such as the state of Arizona) but with less detail. You can remember this by considering the size of a particular feature on a map. For example, the larger your city or country appears on a map, the larger the map scale. Another way to remember it is by the fraction that defines the ratio of map distance to earth distance. On a large-scale map of downtown Phoenix, the scale might be 1/10,000, which is a larger number than 1/1,000,000 for a typical small-scale map of Arizona. A large fraction means large scale; a small fraction means small scale.

The case studies in this book explore human geography at a variety of scales. Activities at the global scale (i.e., small-scale maps) include Chapter 7 on international development levels, Activity 1 of Chapter 8 on global agriculture, and Activity 1 of Chapter 14 on global carbon dioxide emissions. At the national or regional scale are Chapter 2 on the Middle East and American Southwest culture regions, Chapter 3 on AIDS diffusion, Chapter 4 on migration to your state or province, Chapter 5 on India's population, Chapter 6 on economic specialization, Chapter 9 on baseball market areas, Chapter 12 on segregation in Northern Ireland, Chapter 13 on the wars in the former Yugoslavia and Iraq, and Chapter 14 on environmental case studies. Finally, the activities at the local scale (large-scale maps) include Activity 3 of Chapter 8 on local agricultural change in Latin America, Activity 1 of Chapter 9 on pizza restaurants in your state, Chapter 10 on your local urban landscape, and Chapter 11 on urban sprawl in Colorado Springs.

Defining the scale of analysis is important in geography. Many geographical research questions will have different answers when asked at different scales.

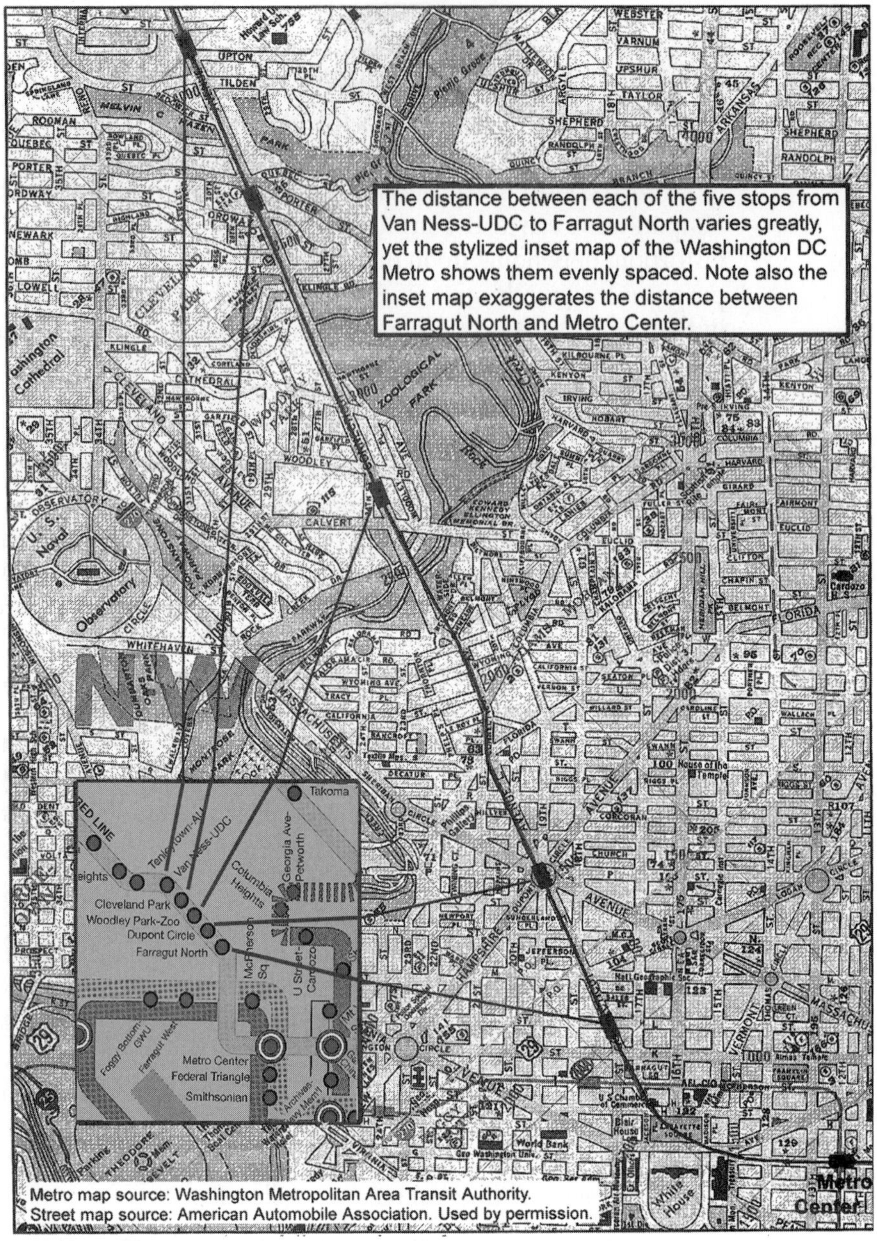
The distance between each of the five stops from Van Ness-UDC to Farragut North varies greatly, yet the stylized inset map of the Washington DC Metro shows them evenly spaced. Note also the inset map exaggerates the distance between Farragut North and Metro Center.
RED LINE
Takoma
Tenleytown-AU
Van Ness-UDC
Cleveland Park
Woodley Park-Zoo
Dupont Circle
Farragut North
Columbia Heights
Georgia Ave-Petworth
McPherson Sq
U Street-Cardozo
Foggy Bottom-GWU
Farragut West
Metro Center
Federal Triangle
Smithsonian
Metro Center
Metro map source: Washington Metropolitan Area Transit Authority.
Street map source: American Automobile Association. Used by permission.

Figure 1.2 The DC Metro inset map is highly selective in that it shows only the sequential relationship between subway stops. All underlying detail is suppressed so that even distance is distorted.

Take, for instance, airport location. America's airports are bursting at the seams. Departures have more than doubled since 1980, while only a single major new airport has been built. Most major airlines, with the notable exception of Southwest, operate a hub-and-spokes system, where flights converge at several times of day from all over the country, passengers debark and switch planes if necessary, and then an outgoing bank of flights take passengers to their final destinations. If the question is whether to locate a new hub airport at a central or peripheral location, the answer is very different at the national and local scales. At the national scale, most hubs for domestic airlines are located in the *central* region of the United States to minimize detours for passengers switching planes. Major hubs are at

Figure 1.3 Denver International Airport, built in 1995, is located 20 miles east of the city center.

Chicago (United, American), Atlanta (Delta), Dallas (Delta, American), Detroit (Northwest), Minneapolis (Northwest), Denver (United), Cincinnati (Delta), Salt Lake City (Delta), Charlotte (US Air), Philadelphia (US Air), and Phoenix (US Air). Cities on the periphery of the United States, such as Boston, Miami, San Diego, and Seattle, are not used as domestic hubs because they would create huge detours for passengers traveling between most U.S. airport pairs. At the local scale, on the other hand, it would be nearly impossible to locate a new airport in a central location, even though centrality would maximize the airport's accessibility to the entire metropolitan area. The cost of the land, the security risk, the number of residents and businesses it would displace, and the large populations that would be affected by noise and traffic would pose insurmountable problems for a new centrally located airport. The only major metropolitan airport built in the last two decades—Denver International Airport—is located on Denver's eastern periphery, out on the prairie (Figure 1.3). Airport location at the local scale thus depends on an entirely different range of issues from those at the national scale.

Related to map scale is the fourth cartographic issue of data **aggregation**. The level of data aggregation influences the spatial patterns we see. By level of aggregation, we are referring to the size of the geographic units under investigation (i.e., cities, counties, states, regions, countries, or groupings of countries, such as Central America, Western Europe, or Eastern Africa). A particular pattern that is revealed at one level of aggregation does not necessarily appear at another. For example, the spatial pattern of college graduates depends on whether you consider counties or states as your unit of analysis. If asked by a high-tech employer: "Where are the highest percentages of people with a college degree?" a good geographer would answer that it depends on the level of geographic resolution you have in mind. At the state level of aggregation, Massachusetts has the highest percentage of people with a bachelor's degree or higher at 33.2 percent, and West Virginia has the lowest at 14.8 percent (Figure 1.4). Maps at the county level, however, show that some urban counties and counties with universities in West Virginia have higher percentages of college graduates than do some rural counties in Massachusetts (Figure 1.5).

Finally, the fifth way to influence the way a map looks is through the type of map you choose. General-purpose maps with a variety of common features such as

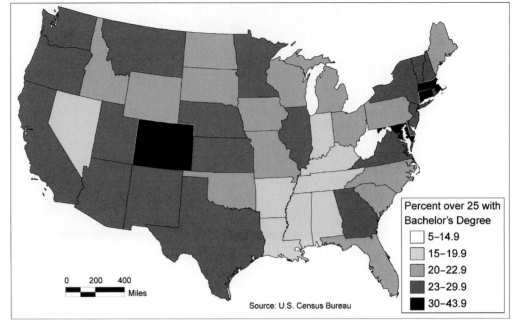

Figure 1.4 Percent of the population over 25 years old with a bachelor's degree, 2000.

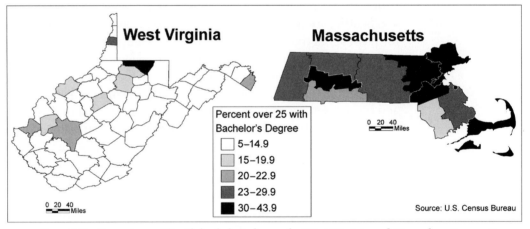

Figure 1.5 Percent over 25 with bachelor's degree for West Virginia and Massachusetts counties, 2000.

cities, boundaries, mountains, and roads are known as **reference maps**. Maps that highlight a particular feature or a single variable such as temperature, city size, or acreage in potatoes are called *thematic maps*. There are several types of **thematic maps** (Figure 1.6). **Isoline maps** show lines that connect points of equal value (*iso* means "equal" in Greek). A topographic map, for instance, shows lines of equal elevation above sea level. Crossing an isoline amounts to going up or down that surface (increasing or decreasing the value of the variable being mapped). **A choropleth map** shows the level of some variable within predefined regions, such as counties, states, or countries. It categorizes a variable into classes and depicts each class with different shading patterns or colors. **A proportional symbol map** uses a symbol such as a circle to show intensity or frequency; the size of the symbol varies with the frequency or size of the variable being mapped. Finally, **dot maps** use a

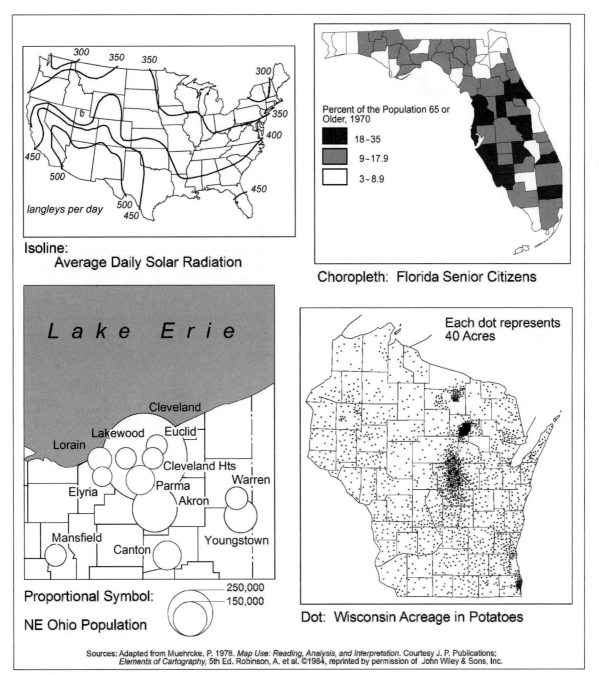

Isoline:
Average Daily Solar Radiation

Choropleth: Florida Senior Citizens

Percent of the Population 65 or Older, 1970
- 18–35
- 9–17.9
- 3–8.9

Proportional Symbol:
NE Ohio Population

Dot: Wisconsin Acreage in Potatoes

Each dot represents 40 Acres

Sources: Adapted from Muehrcke, P. 1978. *Map Use: Reading, Analysis, and Interpretation.* Courtesy J. P. Publications; *Elements of Cartography,* 5th Ed. Robinson, A. et al. ©1984, reprinted by permission of John Wiley & Sons, Inc.

Figure 1.6 Four types of thematic maps.

dot to represent the occurrence of some phenomenon in order to depict variation in density in a given area.

The project you will work on in this chapter asks you to use **spatial data**, which have a geographic or locational component. You can place them on the surface of the earth, and therefore you can map them. Geographers commonly use two types of geographic data: primary and secondary. **Primary data** are measured or obtained directly by researchers or their equipment without any intermediary. For instance, survey research involves asking people about their shopping behavior, travel patterns, or migration history. Traffic counts can be measured by video cameras, sensor plates or wires, or human observers. Geographers obtain **secondary data** from another source that has previously collected, processed, and catalogued the data. Agencies of international, national, state, and local governments collect and disseminate a veritable treasure trove of geographic information. Examples are agencies of the United Nations (www.un.org), the U.S. Census Bureau (www.census.gov), the National Oceanographic and Atmospheric Administration (www.nesdis.noaa.gov), state governments, and local planning agencies. Using secondary data can be efficient (imagine conducting your own census!) and can enable you to greatly extend the scope of your research by including a wide array of factors. In this book, most of the data you will use were obtained from secondary sources, but you will have a chance to collect primary data in Chapter 2 (postcards), Chapter 8 (foods available in your local supermarket), Chapter 9 (pizza restaurants in your state), and Chapter 10 (field observations of landscapes).

One of the most important recent trends in geography is the development of **geographic information systems (GIS)**. A GIS is, in short, a spatial database linked to a graphic display. Geographers and scientists in related fields use a GIS to store, access, analyze, and display geographic information in electronic form with user-friendly software. Addresses and locations can be given x,y earth coordinates (geocoded) within a GIS, enabling the user to pinpoint and interrelate a variety of phenomena in geographic space. The volume and variety of geographic data that can be linked using space as the reference grid literally have no limit. Different geographic information is stored in different layers that can be viewed in any combination, and their relations to each other can be analyzed.

A GIS has many useful applications in planning, environmental management, market research, and demographic analysis. You will use GIS in the following mapping exercise and observe its power to enrich geographic analysis.

► *CASE STUDY*

TRUE MAPS, FALSE IMPRESSIONS

GOAL

To interpret and critically evaluate maps, to understand how **scale** influences data representation on maps, and to recognize three types of map scale: representative fraction, verbal, and graphic. You will also learn how to represent data with different types of **thematic maps**—the **dot map**, the **isoline map**, the **choropleth map**, and the **proportional symbol map**—and see that your choice of map type profoundly influences the resulting spatial pattern.

LEARNING OUTCOMES

After completing the chapter, you will be able to:

- Convert map scale to real-world distances.
- Recognize choropleth, proportional symbol, isoline, and dot maps.
- Recognize that changing the scale and type of a map changes its message.
- Understand the difference between changing scale and changing level of aggregation.
- Use GIS to change the class limits on a choropleth map.
- Describe the geographic distribution of African-Americans in the United States.

SPECIAL MATERIALS NEEDED

- Calculator
- Computer with high-speed Internet access and a recent release of a Web browser. If using the Student Companion Site with the printed book, click on *Tech Support* for system requirements and technical support. (If using the e-book in WileyPlus, click on *Help* for details about the system requirements.)

BACKGROUND

Africans were first brought to what is now the United States between 1619 and 1808 as slaves to work on tobacco, rice, sugar, and cotton plantations, mostly in the South. Although the practice of bringing slaves into the country was made illegal in 1808, some smuggling of slaves continued further into the nineteenth century. Importation was replaced by programs of slave breeding and trade within the South. Although most slaves were concentrated in the South, a small number of slaves escaped to the North and other parts of the country, where they were represented across many walks of life. A free black man living in Baltimore was commissioned by Thomas Jefferson to survey the District of Columbia. Black cowboys, based in Texas, were well known on cattle drives throughout the West.

Many people are surprised to learn that African-Americans represented a sizable share of the U.S. population during the seventeenth and eighteenth centuries. At the time of the first census in 1790, one of every five residents of the new country was African-American. Concentrations were highest in southern states: 54 percent of South Carolina's population

was African-American, 40 percent of Virginia's, 37 percent of Georgia's, 34 percent of North Carolina's, and 33 percent of Maryland's.

After emancipation in 1863, most African-Americans remained in the South, working as sharecroppers or tenants on white-owned cotton farms, barely getting by. Although the reasons to leave the South were compelling, including crushing poverty, antiblack terrorism, and a lack of civil rights, few actually left the region. Many black farmers were illiterate and therefore unaware of economic opportunities in other parts of the country. White landowners, desperate to preserve their favored way of life sustained by cheap black labor, promulgated an economic system that put sharecroppers in a position of permanent indebtedness, making departure illegal. In the late nineteenth century, Northern labor unions lobbied against the importation of African-Americans from the South, fearing it would depress their wages. They preferred European immigrants to meet the demand for new industrial workers in America's burgeoning manufacturing sector.

All of that changed after the end of World War I, beginning one of the most dramatic migration streams in U.S. history. At the turn of the twentieth century, 90 percent of the nation's African-American population lived in the South, mostly in the rural South. By 1970, barely 50 percent lived in the South (Figure 1.7), millions having sought a better life in northern cities. Reasons for leaving were many and complicated. The supply of cheap immigrant labor was cut off by World War I, and recruiters went south, bringing literally trainloads of African-American workers to the steel mills, automobile factories, and meatpacking plants of Pittsburgh, Detroit, Chicago, and other northern cities (Figure 1.8). Once these connections had been established, thousands of migrants followed and established themselves in predominantly black neighborhoods such as Harlem in northern Manhattan (Figure 1.9) and the South Side of Chicago. The Great Depression of the 1930s and the mechanization of cotton harvesting after 1945 further spurred the African-American exodus from the South. The mechanical cotton picker rendered sharecroppers obsolete by drastically reducing the need for their labor. Early models of the cotton picker reduced the costs of picking cotton from $40 to $5 per bale. Each machine did the work of 50 pickers. As the mainstay for southern African-American employment evaporated, many left the rural South in search of northern jobs. A second wave of black migration headed to California from 1940 to 1970, lured by both industrial and agricultural jobs.

The story does not end here, for migration flows between the South and North were reversed after 1970. Fewer African-Americans left the South, and many more moved from the North to the South. Race riots and deteriorating economic conditions in northern cities served as push factors, and the favorable economic opportunities and improved social conditions of the "New South" attracted migrants from the North. Whereas the earlier migration streams connected the *rural* South to the *urban* North, today's streams primarily link the *urban* North

© 2010 John Wiley & Sons, Inc.

▶ *CASE STUDY (continued)*

Figure 1.7 Farmer and son in Daphne, Alabama.

Figure 1.8 Many of today's African-Americans, such as this construction worker at Newark Airport, continue to work in blue-collar industries.

Figure 1.9 African-American culture, featuring jazz and blues music, flourished in their neighborhoods in northern cities. Olympic great Jesse Owens and his wife danced at the opening of the Cotton Club in Harlem, September 25, 1936.

► *CASE STUDY (continued)*

with the *urban* South. California, after several decades as a magnet for black migrants, lost more than it gained in the late 1990s. Many blacks returned to the South, and others "spilled over" into nearby Arizona, Nevada, and Washington. College-educated African-Americans are migrating to the South at higher rates than are those with a high-school education or less (Figure 1.10).

In 2008, perhaps the ultimate race barrier was broken when Barack Obama was elected president of the United States (Fig. 1.11). Although of mixed race (his mother was white), he self-identifies as African-American, and his wife, Michelle, is descended from slaves in South Carolina. Obama's election was an emotional milestone for the many people who fought for equality during the long civil rights struggles, and also sent a powerful message to the entire world that past injustices are at last being resolved and that the United States truly is a land of opportunity. Young people of the post–Civil Rights era were some of Obama's most enthusiastic supporters, indicating that racial divisiveness is less prevalent in new generations than in past ones. Racism has not disappeared, but the election of an African-American president provides great hope that hatred and discrimination based purely on skin color might finally be eliminated.

This exercise, involving mapping the distribution of African-Americans, relies heavily on information about race from the U.S. Census. Census race data are used to enforce antidiscrimination laws on voting rights, equal job and housing opportunity, and access to credit, as well as in studies of migration, residential segregation, health, education, and poverty. Until recently, the U.S. Census Bureau had established five racial categories—American Indian or Alaskan Native, Asian or Pacific Islander, Black, White, and "Some Other Race"—and asked respondents to self-identify as one of the five groups. In 2000, for the first time, the census allowed Americans to select more

than one racial category, reflecting the growing rates of racial intermarriage and the increasing racial and ethnic diversity of the nation's population. In addition, the number of racial categories was increased to six, renamed as "American Indian

Figure 1.10 Recent data show a black "brain drain" from New York, Pennsylvania, and Ohio and a "brain gain" in Georgia, Maryland, Texas, and North Carolina, where the existence of a large black middle class in cities like Atlanta and Dallas exerts a strong attraction.

Figure 1.11 Barack Obama, with wife Michelle at his side, was sworn in as 44th President of the United States on January 20, 2009.

© 2010 John Wiley & Sons, Inc.

▶ **CASE STUDY (continued)**

or Alaskan Native," "Asian," "Black or African-American," "Native Hawaiian or Other Pacific Islander," "White," and "Some Other Race." Also, the census category "Hispanic or Latino" is independent of these racial categories; Hispanics can be of any race.

The United States is about to pass through a new demographic change that some refer to as the post-racial age—groups currently categorized as racial minorities will account for the majority of the population by 2042 (and by as soon as 2023 for Americans under the age of 18). The white population will be the minority when compared to all others. But more important is the increasing complexity of racial categorizations and identities. "Race" is in fact a social construct; there are no biological determinants that define one race as clearly distinguishable from another. Definitions have changed throughout history, so that at one time the Irish were not considered "white," and neither were Italians, Lebanese,

or Jews. Because more and more Americans are of mixed race or self-identify with one racial category with increasingly fuzzy barriers, race as a classification scheme may outlive its usefulness. Some claim that the very categories themselves serve a political purpose: to privilege the dominant white class above those of color. Racial politics continue to be an important part of the country, but whiteness is no longer a precondition for entry into the highest levels of public office or private-sector leadership. Racial strife and misunderstandings will certainly continue, but the demographic shifts that we are seeing will likely reduce the power of racial hierarchies in society so that all U.S. citizens are treated as individuals rather than members of a caste or identity group. While the 2000 census recognized greater racial diversity and intermixing, with 63 possible racial combinations, questions of what race means in our society and why we continue to collect data by race remain important social and political issues.

Name: _____   Instructor: _____

True Maps, False Impressions: Making, Manipulating, and Interpreting Maps

▶ ACTIVITY 1: SCALE

Map scale is the ratio of the distance on the map to the distance on the ground, where both are measured in the same units. Scale can be represented in three different ways:

Representative Fraction. The map distance to ground distance ratio is written as a simple fraction (e.g., 1/50,000) or ratio (1:50,000). In this example, it simply means that one unit (inches, centimeters, etc.) on the map represents 50,000 of the same units on the ground.

Verbal Scale. Words instead of numbers are used to express the scale. The verbal scale can thus be thought of as a "translation" of the representative fraction into words. For example, the scale of 1:100,000 can also be expressed as "one centimeter to one kilometer," or "one centimeter represents one kilometer." This is because there are 100 centimeters in 1 meter, and 1,000 meters in 1 kilometer.

$$100\,\frac{cm}{m} \times 1,000\,\frac{m}{km} = 100,000\,\frac{cm}{km}$$

Multiply 100 by 1,000 and cancel the *m*'s on top and bottom and you get 100,000 centimeters in a kilometer. Therefore, in a map with a scale of 1:100,000, one centimeter on the map represents 100,000 centimeters, or one kilometer, on the ground. Likewise, a verbal scale of "one inch to one mile" translates to a representative fraction of 1:63,360 because there are 63,360 inches in a mile:

$$12\,\frac{inches}{foot} \times 5,280\,\frac{feet}{mile} = 63,360\,\frac{inches}{mile}$$

Graphic Scale. This normally appears as a line or bar divided into conveniently numbered segments. You can think of this as a picture of the words in the verbal scale. In the example below, two centimeters represents one kilometer (use a ruler to test it out!).

© 2010 John Wiley & Sons, Inc.

Questions 1.1 to 1.3 assume a scale of 1:25,000. Note that this scale is different from those in either of the examples just given.

1.1. Suppose that City A is four centimeters away from City B on the map. How many *centimeters* apart are they on the surface of the earth?

1.2. How many *kilometers* apart are Cities A and B on the surface of the earth?

1.3. A bakery needs to supply bread to every store within a six-kilometer radius. How many centimeters will this radius be when drawn on the map? *Hint:* First convert 6 km to cm, and then multiply by the representative fraction: 1/25,000.

1.4. Which is the largest-scale map?
   a. 1/24,000   b. 1/62,500   c. 1/100,000   d. 1/250,000

1.5. Which of the following maps is larger scale?

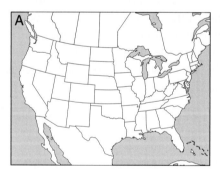 

1.6. Would your college campus appear larger on a map at a scale of 1:500 or 1:5,000?

Scale is more than just a way of zooming in or out for a closer look or a broader perspective. When you change scales, you can actually see a different spatial process at work. The process you will investigate in Questions 1.7 to 1.9 involves whether the northeastern U.S. population became more concentrated or more spread out during the twentieth century.

Figure 1.12 shows each county's percentage of the northeast regional population for 1900 (top) and 2000 (bottom) at a relatively small scale of 1:12,000,000. At this scale you can see the whole northeastern section of the United States, and each county is fairly small. We could call this a "regional-scale" map.

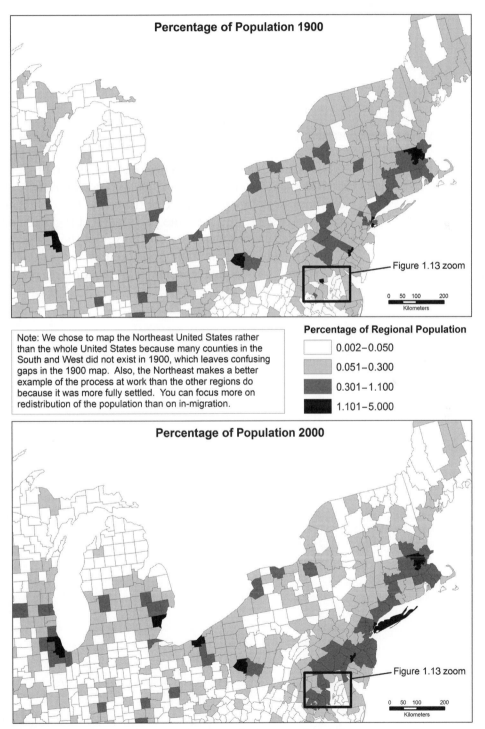

Percentage of Population 1900

Figure 1.13 zoom

0   50 100   200
Kilometers

Note: We chose to map the Northeast United States rather than the whole United States because many counties in the South and West did not exist in 1900, which leaves confusing gaps in the 1900 map. Also, the Northeast makes a better example of the process at work than the other regions do because it was more fully settled. You can focus more on redistribution of the population than on in-migration.

Percentage of Regional Population

0.002–0.050
0.051–0.300
0.301–1.100
1.101–5.000

Percentage of Population 2000

Figure 1.13 zoom

0   50 100   200
Kilometers

Figure 1.12   Regional-scale map of population by county in the northeastern United States, 1900 and 2000.

1.7. On the regional-scale maps (Figure 1.12), did the population become more spread out (people distributed more uniformly and evenly across counties) or more concentrated (more people living in a few places) from 1900 to 2000? Explain how you interpreted the map pattern to reach this conclusion.

Now look at Figure 1.13, which zooms in on the Baltimore-Washington region. This is a larger-scale map at 1:1,200,000. In fact, it is exactly 10 times larger. This is a more "local-scale" map. Notice that the level of aggregation has stayed the same as in Figure 1.12: It still shows the percentage of regional population by county. 1.8. On the local-scale maps (Figure 1.13), did the population of the Baltimore-Washington region become more spread out or more concentrated from 1900 to 2000? Explain how you interpreted the map pattern to reach this conclusion.

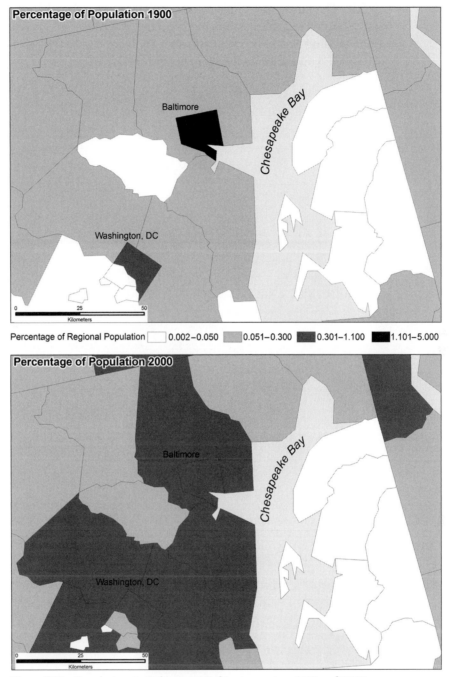

Percentage of Population 1900

Baltimore

Chesapeake Bay

Washington, DC

Percentage of Regional Population ☐ 0.002–0.050 ▨ 0.051–0.300 ▨ 0.301–1.100 ■ 1.101–5.000

Percentage of Population 2000

Baltimore

Chesapeake Bay

Washington, DC

Figure 1.13 Populations in Baltimore-Washington region, 1900 and 2000.

1.9. The patterns of change you see in the regional-scale maps (Figure 1.12) are the function of Americans moving from the countryside to cities due to mechanization of farming and industrial and service jobs in cities. What is behind the patterns of change you see at the local scale (Figure 1.13)?

Name: _____   Instructor: _____

True Maps, False Impressions: Making, Manipulating, and Interpreting Maps

▶ **ACTIVITY 2: THEMATIC MAPS**

This activity involves looking at the distribution of African-Americans in the United States (or Aboriginals in Canada) using different types of thematic maps. You will use some of the functions of a geographic information system (GIS) to look at the various maps and choose the most useful ones. A GIS is a software package that makes maps and allows the user to analyze spatial data. A GIS is a powerful tool used by utility companies, city planners, engineers, cartographers, environmental scientists, and many others. You will be using the mapping capabilities of a GIS to interactively change the maps on your computer screen.

A. To start your activity, click on the *Student Companion Site* at www.wiley.com/college/kuby. (For students using Wileyplus, log on to your class Web site, select the *Assignment* tab, locate and click on this assignment, and follow all instructions.)

B. Select this chapter from the drop-down list, and then click on *Computerized Chapter Activities*.

C. Click on *Activity 2: Thematic maps (USA)* or *(Canada)*, according to your instructor's directions.

D. Students who chose Canada should first read the short background article on the geography of the Aboriginal population in the window that appears. Following the background article, Canadian students will find the computer instructions and questions to answer and hand in for the Canadian case study. You can print these if you like. Proceed with the digital instructions for the Canadian version.

E. You will see the first of four types of thematic maps you will use to evaluate the distribution of African-Americans in the United States. In the right margin are the names for all of the maps. The map displayed is *County Choropleth*, which classifies each county into one of four classes and assigns a pattern as shown in the map **legend**. Notice that this map shows the *percentage* of African-Americans per county, not the actual number. Choropleth maps are usually used to show intensity, such as percentages, rather than magnitude, such as total numbers. You will later see maps that show magnitude, such as the total number of African-Americans.

If you wish, you can zoom in on portions of the map to get a better view of a smaller area (you would then be looking at a larger-scale map). Simply move the "slider" at the upper right toward the plus sign. To zoom back out, slide it toward the minus sign. The percentage enlargement is shown in the box below. Next to the percentage is a menu for choosing low, medium, or high resolution. You can move the map around on the screen if you click and hold the mouse button on the red square in

© 2010 John Wiley & Sons, Inc.

the small map in the upper right and move the square around. You also have a layer of boundaries of *States* and another of *City Names* that you can click on or off for reference.

2.1. According to the *County Choropleth*, where would you say most African-Americans live in the United States?

Based on the map, approximately what percentage of African-Americans would you guess live in the dominant region? No need to write an answer; just think about it. Would you say the overwhelming majority? Maybe two-thirds? Less than one-half?

In fact, only about one-half of all African-Americans live in the South. About the same number live outside the South in large urban areas of the Northeast, Midwest, and West.

F. Click on the *County Circle* icon in the right margin. Now do you believe the previous statement? This map is called a *graduated circle map*. A graduated circle is a type of proportional symbol whose size varies with the value for each county. This graduated circle map shows magnitude with each circle a different size, depending on the total number of African-Americans per county.

2.2. Based on this map, name four cities with the largest number of African-American residents. (Don't forget, you can zoom in and also turn on *City Names*.)

_____   _____

_____   _____

2.3. Now you see that the way in which data are presented on maps can greatly alter your perception of the distribution of the information being mapped. By using a different type of thematic map and by presenting the data in absolute rather than percentage terms, the latter map's message changes even though both maps are based on exactly the same data. What are the false impressions created by the *County Choropleth* and *County Circle* maps?

2.4. Zoom in on the New York City area. What graphic or visual problems do you see with the way the graduated circle map represents the African-American population of the counties adjacent to New York City?

G. Click on the icon entitled *County Dot*. Dot maps are another way to present the distribution of African-Americans. According to the legend, each dot represents 15,000 people. Any county with fewer than 15,000 African-Americans has no dots, those with 15,000 to 29,999 get one dot, those with 30,000 to 44,999 get two dots, and so on.

2.5. What is a drawback of using this kind of map to compare the number of African-Americans in different counties?

H. Change the threshold that sets the number of people per dot to 50,000 and then to 5,000 by clicking on the buttons with these resolutions. Toggle between the three dot resolutions to see the different impressions they portray.

2.6. Which map emphasizes urban areas while deemphasizing the rural South? Why?

I. The level of aggregation (i.e., the size of the spatial unit of analysis) is also important to the pattern depicted on the map. Click on the *County Choropleth* map again to get a fresh image of it in your mind, and then click on *State Choropleth*. This shows the same data but by state rather than by county. Note that as you move your mouse over each state, you see the state name and the percentage of African-Americans included in the state's total population.

2.7. What different impression of spatial pattern do you get from the state map as compared to the county map?

J. Experiment with the different *Color Scheme* options seen at the bottom of the window. Think about how the colors relate to the percentage of African-Americans.

2.8. Which color scheme, if any, does a poor job of portraying the percentage of African-Americans? Why?

K. Restore the original color scheme. Next you will interactively define your own class limits using the graphic array to the left of the map. This graph shows the distribution of data on the x-axis, in this case the percentage of African-Americans for each state, from low to high. The y-axis, which ranges from 0 to 50 states, shows the states ranked from highest to lowest percentage of African-Americans. As you move your mouse over the dots in the graph, the state name and percentage of African-Americans appear. Starting at the upper left, you can see that the lowest 13 states are between 0 and 2.2 percent, the next 13 states are between 2.2 and 6.8 percent, and so on. Cartographers use graphic arrays to help in setting class break points that divide the data into "natural classes" or groupings. Look for vertical groupings that indicate a group of states with similar percentages of African-Americans, and set your class limits in the empty horizontal gaps.

The vertical red bars show your class limits in this distribution. You can select a bar by clicking on the top triangle with your mouse. Holding the mouse button down on the triangle, move it left or right to set new class limits. The shading patterns between the bars match those of the map. The x-axis is labeled in percentages, and when you move the bars, the breakpoints in the boxes below change to reflect the new position. These boxes are also directly editable: click on a breakpoint box, type in a value, and hit return. You will use this interactive graphic array and/or the editable boxes to make your final map. Before then, experiment with some other options.

L. As you just discovered, changing break points between classes can alter the impression the map gives. Buttons at the lower left use standard cartographic rules for establishing break points, known as *Equal Frequency* and *Equal Interval*:

Equal Frequency	Divides the data distribution into classes with equal numbers of states (this is the default you first looked at). Click this button and look at the histogram (bar graph) below the map to see the number of states in each class.
Equal Interval	Divides the data distribution into classes (intervals) of equal size between the smallest and largest numbers. Click this button and look at the break points on the graphic array (the red vertical lines) to see that they are equally spaced. The boxes below the graphic array also list the break-point values, and they, too, will be evenly spaced between the minimum and maximum values.

The default map uses the equal frequency settings. Click back and forth between the *Equal Frequency* and *Equal Interval* buttons to see their effects on the maps.

M. Another way to customize a choropleth map is to change the *number* of classes. The initial map has only four classes. You can change the number of classes to 5 or 6 using the small window at the lower left. Set the map to 5 *classes* and click *Equal Interval* and then *Equal Frequency*. Finally, set 6 *classes* and click *Equal Interval* and *Equal Frequency*. From these six distinct maps (*Equal Frequency* with 4, 5, or 6 classes, and the same for *Equal Interval*), choose the map you consider to be the most misleading (i.e., it creates the most inaccurate impression of where African-Americans live). You may consult the actual data values for each state in Table 1.2 to compare actual values to perceived values from the map. You also may refer to the graphic array to look for natural groupings that you can separate with break points.

N. Using the window above the map, change the map title to the "Most Misleading Map." Click on the *Print* button in the lower-right corner. Hand in the map with this assignment.

TABLE 1.2   Number and Percentage of African-Americans by State, 2000 (ranked by %)

State	Total population	African-American	Percent African-American	State	Total population	African-American	Percent African-American
District of Columbia	572,059	343,312	60.0	California	33,871,648	2,263,882	6.7
Mississippi	2,844,658	1,033,809	36.3	Kansas	2,688,418	154,198	5.7
Louisiana	4,468,976	1,451,944	32.5	Wisconsin	5,363,675	304,460	5.7
South Carolina	4,012,012	1,185,216	29.5	Massachusetts	6,349,097	343,454	5.4
Georgia	8,186,453	2,349,542	28.7	Rhode Island	1,048,319	46,908	4.5
Maryland	5,296,486	1,477,411	27.9	Nebraska	1,711,263	68,541	4.0
Alabama	4,447,100	1,155,930	26.0	Colorado	4,301,261	165,063	3.8
North Carolina	8,049,313	1,737,545	21.6	Minnesota	4,919,479	171,731	3.5
Virginia	7,078,515	1,390,293	19.6	Alaska	626,932	21,787	3.5
Delaware	783,600	150,666	19.2	Washington	5,894,121	190,267	3.2
Tennessee	5,689,283	932,809	16.4	West Virginia	1,808,344	57,232	3.2
New York	18,976,457	3,014,385	15.9	Arizona	5,130,632	158,873	3.1
Arkansas	2,673,400	418,950	15.7	Iowa	2,926,324	61,853	2.1
Illinois	12,419,293	1,876,875	15.1	New Mexico	1,819,046	34,343	1.9
Florida	15,982,378	2,335,505	14.6	Hawaii	1,211,537	22,003	1.8
Michigan	9,938,444	1,412,742	14.2	Oregon	3,421,399	55,662	1.6
New Jersey	8,414,350	1,141,821	13.6	Utah	2,233,169	17,657	0.8
Texas	20,851,820	2,404,566	11.5	Wyoming	493,782	3,722	0.8
Ohio	11,353,140	1,301,307	11.5	New Hampshire	1,235,786	9,035	0.7
Missouri	5,595,211	629,391	11.2	South Dakota	754,844	4,685	0.6
Pennsylvania	12,281,054	1,224,612	10.0	North Dakota	642,200	3,916	0.6
Connecticut	3,405,565	309,843	9.1	Maine	1,274,923	6,760	0.5
Indiana	6,080,485	510,034	8.4	Vermont	608,827	3,063	0.5
Oklahoma	3,450,654	260,968	7.6	Idaho	1,293,153	5,456	0.4
Kentucky	4,041,769	295,994	7.3	Montana	902,195	2,692	0.3
Nevada	1,998,257	135,477	6.8				

Washington, D.C., has been omitted from the maps in the animated activity.

© 2010 John Wiley & Sons, Inc.

2.9. How many classes did your most misleading map have? (4, 5, or 6) _____ Which rule for establishing class break points did you choose? (Equal Frequency or Equal Interval) _____ In what way is the map you chose misleading?

O. It is clear that many African-Americans live in the South. So far, however, many of your maps have probably lumped all southern states into one "high-percentage" category. Suppose you want a map to differentiate *among* the southern states. Look at the data for each state in Table 1.2 and choose class categories that show differences in the percentage of African-Americans within the South. Set the map to 4 *classes*. Using either the graphic array or the editable boxes, set the break points to highlight the differences within the South. Study your map, and repeat the process if necessary. When finished, label the map "Differentiation among Southern States." Click on the *Print* button in the lower-right corner. Hand in this map with your exercise.

2.10. What happens to the West when you choose classes that differentiate among southern states? Would this map be useful for showing differences in the percentage of African-Americans in California and Oregon?

P. Finally, using the interactive graphics array and thinking about the various options you have already seen, set the number of classes and the break points to produce the "best" map. *Print* and hand in this map, clearly labeled "Best Map."

2.11. Describe the classification scheme you chose and explain why you thought it was best.

Q. Click on *State Isoline*. Isolines connect points of equal value—in this case, equal percentages of African-Americans. Therefore, as you cross an isoline, you are going into an area with either higher or lower percentages of African-Americans. By interpreting the spacing and configuration, you can "read" a third dimension portrayed on the map: an African-American "surface" with peaks of high percentage and valleys of low percentage (Figure 1.14).

The following six rules help you read an isoline map:

1. Evenly spaced isolines represent comparatively steady or constant slopes.
2. Closely spaced isolines represent steep slopes.
3. Widely spaced isolines represent slight slopes.
4. Isolines that form the "peaks" of your variable become closed circles.
5. Isolines either start and end at the edges of the map **or** form closed circles. There are no other possibilities.
6. Isolines **never split, intersect, or cross each other.**

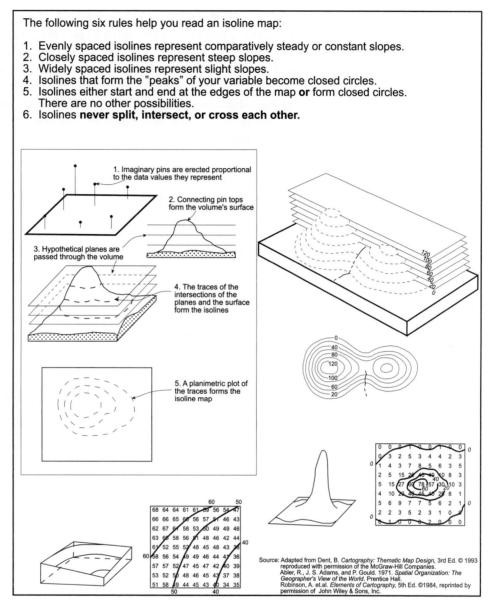

Source: Adapted from Dent, B. *Cartography: Thematic Map Design*, 3rd Ed. © 1993 reproduced with permission of the McGraw-Hill Companies.
Abler, R., J. S. Adams, and P. Gould. 1971. *Spatial Organization: The Geographer's View of the World*. Prentice Hall.
Robinson, A. et.al. *Elements of Cartography*, 5th Ed. ©1984, reprinted by permission of John Wiley & Sons, Inc.

Figure 1.14   Rules and visual aids for isoline maps.

© 2010 John Wiley & Sons, Inc.

The legend says the isoline interval is 3 percent. Therefore, the map has isolines at 3 percent, 6 percent, 9 percent, and on up to 33 percent. Try to picture the surface that the map represents. As you move from very low percentages in South Dakota toward the "peak" in Mississippi, each time you cross an isoline, you are going up by 3 percent. The surface peaks at higher than 33 percent in the ring centered over Mississippi and then starts back down as you head toward Florida, which is below 15 percent. Elsewhere in the map, you can really see the gradient decline sharply from New York to New England as the percentage of African-Americans drops rapidly. You can also see the West Virginia "gap."[1]

2.12. a. Is the change more rapid between South Carolina and Kentucky or between South Carolina and Alabama?

b. Is the change more rapid between New Mexico and Louisiana or between New Mexico and California?

c. Look at the range within which most of Oklahoma falls. Based on this, what impression does the map give for the average percentage of African-Americans in Oklahoma?

[1]The isoline maps are based on state data in Table 1.2. The surface is defined by 50 data points (excluding Washington, D.C.), not by thousands of county data points. Therefore, the map cannot be used for studying variations within states.

2.13. Look again at the *State Isoline* map to "read" the African-American "surface" with peaks of high percentage and valleys of low percentage. Compare these peaks and valleys with the *State Choropleth* map. Set the *State Choropleth* map to 4 classes with the Equal Frequency breakpoint setting (this should be the default) and toggle between this map and the *State Isoline* map.

Describe one difference between the State Isoline map and the State Choropleth map.

2.14. Think about TV shows and movies you have seen that prominently feature African-Americans. Based on the maps you have seen of the distribution of African-Americans, does Hollywood accurately represent where African-Americans live? What stereotypes are embodied in these media images?

Census 2000 asked Americans to list their race and Hispanic origin separately because *race* and *ethnicity* are two entirely different concepts. Of those who identified with a single race, 211.46 million (75.1 percent) considered themselves White, 34.66 million (12.3 percent) considered themselves to be Black or African-American, 2.48 million (0.9 percent) were American Indian or Alaskan Native, 10.24 million (3.6 percent) were Asian, and another 15.66 million (5.6 percent) belonged to other races. Reflecting increasing intermarriage and growing racial diversity, some 6.83 million (2.4 percent) regarded themselves as belonging to more than one racial group.

Separate from racial status is Hispanic or Latino origin. As of the 2000 Census, 35.31 million (12.5 percent) of the U.S. population identified as Hispanic. The vast majority of Hispanics considered themselves to be White (16.91 million) although some 710,000 individuals were both Black and Hispanic, many of them immigrants from Cuba and other parts of the Caribbean.

R. In the right margin, click on *Other Ethnic Groups*.

S. In the right margin, click on the *Choropleth* and *Circle* maps for these other groups (all maps based on county-level data).

2.15. Many atlases show ethnic population distribution via county choropleth maps rather than circle maps. In the following table, briefly summarize, in a few words, the overall impression you get from each map for each ethnic group. If the circle map gives the same impression, write "same."

T. When you have finished, close all browser windows.

Note: With the experience you now have in mapmaking and map reading, you might want to think about taking a GIS or cartography class next semester. You are also ready to make your own ethnic maps on the U.S. Census Bureau Web site. Keep in mind, however, that you can make only choropleth maps, which, as you know, will create a certain impression of the data. The Census Bureau site lets you make choropleth maps at either the state or national scale with either the state or county level of aggregation. You can select from varieties of ethnicities and other socioeconomic characteristics.

The following instructions were valid at the time this book went into production. Go to factfinder.census.gov. Under the *Decennial Census* heading, click on *get data*. Select a data set you want to use, then click *Thematic Maps*. You next select a *geographic type* and *geographic area* (these are your units of analysis and the location). Hit the *Next* button. Then pick a theme, which is the thematic variable you want mapped, and click *Show Results*. Once the map is displayed, you can change the zoom or elements visible on the map and then print it or download it to a file.

This exercise has demonstrated that maps can be manipulated in a variety of ways to produce different impressions of spatial data. We hope it has opened your eyes to the importance of careful use of symbols for representing data on maps. We also hope it has corrected any false impressions you may have had about the historical and contemporary geography of the African-American population of the United States.

	County Choropleth Map	County Circle Map
White		
Hispanic or Latino (of any race)		
Asian		
American Indian and Native Alaskan		

▶ DEFINITIONS OF KEY TERMS

Aggregation The level of detail for dividing a thematic map into geographic units, ranging from a coarse division (e.g., countries) to a fine division (e.g., zip codes).

Choropleth Map A thematic map in which ranked classes of some variable are depicted with shading patterns or colors for predefined zones.

Dot Map A thematic map in which a dot represents some frequency of the mapped variable.

Geographic Information Systems A computer hardware and software system that handles geographically referenced data. A GIS uses and produces maps and has the ability to perform many types of spatial analysis.

Human-Environmental Interaction The ways in which human society and the natural environment affect each other (the fifth theme of geography).

Human Geography The study of the distribution of humans and their activities on the surface of the earth and of the processes that generate these distributions.

Isoline Map A thematic map with lines that connect points of equal value.

Legend Explanatory list of symbols in a map. Usually appears in a box in a lower corner.

Location The absolute position of something on the surface of the earth and its relative proximity to other related things (the first theme of geography).

Map A two-dimensional graphical representation of the surface of the earth (or of events that occur on the earth).

Map Projection A systematic method of transferring a spherical surface to a flat map.

Map Scale The ratio of map distance to earth distance, measured in the same units.

Movement The flow of people, goods, money, ideas, or materials between locations near or far (the fourth theme of geography).

Place The local human and physical characteristics that uniquely define a place and give it meaning to its inhabitants (the second theme of geography).

Primary Data Information collected directly by the researchers or their equipment without any intermediary. This can include surveys, interviews, observations, or measurements obtained in the field.

Proportional Symbol Map A thematic map in which the size of a symbol varies in proportion to the frequency or intensity of the mapped variable.

Reference Map A general-purpose map that shows recognizable landmarks, roads, and political units.

Region An area characterized by similarity or by cohesiveness that sets it apart from other areas (the third theme of geography).

Secondary Data Information obtained indirectly from another source that was previously collected, processed, and made available to a larger audience.

Simplification Elimination of unimportant detail on maps and retention and possibly exaggeration and distortion of important information, depending on the purpose of the map.

Spatial Data Information that has a geographical or locational component.

Thematic Map A map that demonstrates a particular feature or a single variable. Four types of thematic maps are (1) **dot maps**, (2) **choropleth maps**, (3) **proportional symbol maps**, and (4) **isoline maps**.

▶ FURTHER READINGS

Allen, James R., and Eugene J. Turner. 1988. *We The People: An Atlas of America's Ethnic Diversity*. New York: Macmillan.

Asante, Molefi K., and Mark T. Mattson. 1991. *Historical and Cultural Atlas of African Americans*. New York: Macmillan.

Assiniwi, Bernard. 2000. *The Beothuk Saga: A Novel*. Translated by Wayne Grady. Toronto: M&S.

Dewar, Elaine. 2001. *Bones: Discovering the First Americans*. Toronto: Random House Canada.

Dwyer, Owen J. 1997. Geographical Research about African-Americans: A Survey of Journals, 1911–1995. *Professional Geographer* 49:441–451.

Fligstein, Neil. 1981. *Going North: Migration of Whites and Blacks from the South, 1900–1950*. New York: Academic Press.

Geography Education Standards Project. 1994. *Geography for Life*. Washington, DC: National Geographic Research and Exploration.

Hanson, Susan (ed.). 1997. *10 Geographic Ideas that Changed the World*. New Brunswick, NJ: Rutgers University Press.

Kent, Mary M. 2007. Immigration and America's Black Population. *Population Bulletin* 62(4):1–16.

Lee, Sharon M., and Barry Edmonston. 2005. New Marriages, New Families: U.S. Racial and Hispanic Intermarriage. *Population Bulletin* 60(2):1–36.

McHugh, Kevin E. 1987. Black Migration Reversal in the United States. *Geographical Review* 77:171–182.

McKittrick, Katherine, and Clyde Woods (eds.). 2007. *Black Geographies and the Politics of Place*. Cambridge, MA: South End Press.

Monmonier, Mark. 1991. *How to Lie with Maps*. Chicago: University of Chicago Press.

Monmonier, Mark. 1995. *Drawing the Line: Tales of Maps and Cartocontroversy*. New York: Henry Holt.

National Research Council. 1997. *Rediscovering Geography: The New Relevance for Science and Society*. Washington, DC: National Academy Press.

Schein, Richard (ed.). 2006. *Landscape and Race in America*. New York: Routledge.

Steedman, Marek D. 2008. How was Race Constructed in the New South? *DuBois Review: Social Science Research on Race* 5(1):49–68.

▶ WEB RESOURCES

Amistad Research Center: www.tulane.edu/~amistad

Assembly of First Nations: www.afn.ca

Association of Multiethnic Americans: www.amesite.org

Buckminster Fuller Institute: www.bfi.org/map.htm

Buckymap Puzzle: eris.bytecamp.net/~su/buckymap/index.htm

Dymaxion Projection Animation: www.westnet.com/~crywalt/unfold.html

FirstNations.com: firstnations.com

Frey, William H. 2004. *The New Great Migration: Black Americans' Return to the South, 1965–2000*: www.brookings.edu/urban/pubs/20040524_Frey.pdf

Geographer's Craft. *Map Projections*: www.colorado.edu/geography/gcraft/notes/mapproj/mapproj_f.html

Hsu, Hua. 2009. The End of White America? *The Atlantic*: www.theatlantic.com/doc/200901/end-of-whiteness

Indiana University. *Archives of African American Music and Culture*: www.indiana.edu/~aaamc

Kearl, Michael C. *Race and Ethnicity*: www.trinity.edu/~mkearl/race.html

Library of Congress. *The African-American Mosaic: A Library of Congress Resource Guide for the Study of Black History and Culture*: lcweb.loc.gov/exhibits/african/intro.html

Maps of the 2008 US Presidential Election Results: www-personal.umich.edu/~mejn/election/2008/?map

National Geographic Society. *Xpedition Hall (Xpedition I: Globe Projector)*: www.nationalgeographic.com/xpeditions/hall

National Geographic Society. *Map Machine*: maps.nationalgeographic.com/map-machine

Population Reference Bureau: www.prb.org

Social Explorer: www.socialexplorer.com/pub/home/home.aspx

Statistics Canada: www.statcan.gc.ca

U.S. Bureau of the Census: www.census.gov

U.S. Bureau of the Census: factfinder.census.gov

U.S. Department of the Interior: nationalatlas.gov

U.S. Geological Survey. *Geography*: geography.usgs.gov

USA Today. *Census 2000*: www.usatoday.com/news/nation/census/front.htm

▶ ITEMS TO HAND IN

Activity 1: • Questions 1.1–1.9, or answer all questions your instructor created in your WileyPlus assignments.

Activity 2: • Questions 2.1–2.15, including your most misleading map (2.9), the map that best differentiates among southern states (2.10), and your "best overall" map (2.11), or answer all questions your instructor created in your WileyPlus assignments.

© 2010 John Wiley & Sons, Inc.

CHAPTER 2

Layers of Tradition: Culture Regions at Different Scales

▶ INTRODUCTION

One of the most important aspects of humanity that differentiates people and shapes, the way we live, and the places we create is **culture**. *Culture* refers to a people's way of life, their behavior, and their shared understandings about themselves and the world. Culture serves as a guide for how we act and interpret the world around us. When studying how cultural characteristics of place come to be, geographers often focus on a **region**, or an area with common characteristics. Aspects of culture—the complexities of human lifestyles, including social arrangements, the use of land and resources, language, and spiritual and political beliefs—are some of the best features we can use to define regions in human geography.

Region is a concept that is used to identify and organize areas of the world. It is a form of classification as well as a basic building block of geographic analysis. A region is quite simply an area characterized by similarity or a cohesiveness that sets it apart from other regions. This similarity can take the form of a common characteristic such as geographic proximity (North America), a dominant crop (the Corn Belt), the prevailing livelihood (the Manufacturing Belt), a common history (Dixie), or a common set of trading partners (European Union). Some regions have clear-cut boundaries; others have indefinite boundaries.

All regions are mental constructs; nothing is absolute or sacred about them. One person's conception of "the South" will quite likely differ from the next person's, but that does not mean that the regional concept is not useful. Conceptualizing a region is a method for geographers to impose order on the messy complexities of the real world—to make sense out of geographic chaos. Just as organizing time into blocks called *eras* (e.g., Middle Ages, Great Depression) helps people understand history better, so does organizing space into regions help people understand geography better. The degree of detail in definitions of regions correlates to the familiarity people have with those regions, so that locals and outsiders often focus on different characteristics. Like maps, regions exist for particular purposes. Also like maps, regions vary in scale from local to global.

There are three types of regions: formal, functional, and perceptual (Figure 2.1). A **formal region** has a common human characteristic such as language, religion, or level of economic development or a common physical attribute such as climate, landform, or vegetation. The Dairy Belt shares a common agricultural specialization

34 © 2010 John Wiley & Sons, Inc.

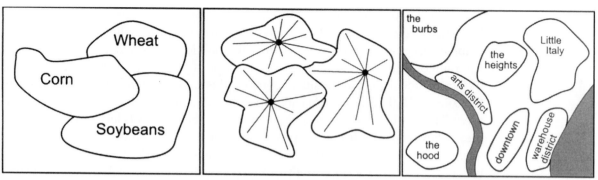

Formal regions based on dominant crop types.

Functional regions tied to a central node. These could be banks serving their branches, dairy farms providing milk to suppliers, etc.

Perceptual regions of a city.

Figure 2.1 Three types of regions.

in milk, cheese, and butter production. Dixie consists of states that seceded from the Union in the Civil War. Latin America is held together by a common location in the Western Hemisphere and by a common Spanish or Portuguese colonial heritage. A single criterion can be used to define a formal region as in the case of the Dairy Belt, or multiple criteria can be used. In addition to secession from the Union in the Civil War, Dixie may also be defined as the block of states where African-Americans represent more than 20 percent of the population or places where the typical breakfast menu includes a side order of grits.

Functional regions are held together by a common set of linkages or spatial interactions. These linkages are organized around one or several nodes. Criteria for defining functional regions take the form of transportation flows, information exchanges, and movements of people. A metropolitan area is a functional region bound together by movements of people to and from work, school, stores, cinemas, and doctors' offices; information flows from newspapers, television, radio, telephone calls, and facsimile messages; and movements of goods and services. Although city and suburban residents sometimes view themselves as separate, they are, in fact, inexorably intertwined by a complicated web of economic, social, and political interactions into one functional region. The region *from which* people travel to a movie theater is a functional region, as is the region *to which* goods are shipped from a seaport.

Sometimes the distinction between formal and functional region is fuzzy, as in the case of *megalopolis*, geographers' name for the coalescence of metropolitan areas into a continuous network of urban development. Megalopolis is a formal region in the sense that it represents a dense concentration of human activity and the dominance of urban over rural land uses. Megalopolis is also a functional region because it is linked by extensive movements of people, goods, and information. The fact that people living hundreds of miles apart in megalopolis are said to be "close neighbors" speaks to the importance of functional interactions over geographic proximity in defining closeness.

More elusive but equally important is the third type of region, the **perceptual region**. Perceptual regions are based on people's feelings or beliefs about areas and are subjective rather than objective in nature. Joel Garreau, an editor with *The Washington Post*, developed the "Nine Nations of North America," a regional geography of the United States based on how reporters perceived and described the places they visited. He classified North America into such regions as "MexAmerica," "The Bread Basket," and "The Foundry," regions that he believed captured geographic variation in culture better than the political units of states and provinces we commonly use. *Vernacular regions*, one type of perceptual region, are identified by local residents, not as outsiders perceive them. *Vernacular* refers to the traits of the common folk, such as vernacular speech, vernacular architecture, or vernacular dress. The way to discern vernacular regions is at the grassroots level: to ask people if they believe that they live in a region called "the South" or to ask them to outline on a map where "the South" starts and stops. Another way to define vernacular regions is to determine how local businesses use regional monikers such as Acadia, Delta, Dixie, Eastern, Northwestern, Midwestern, Pacific, and Western (Figure 2.2).

Perhaps the best way to think of a region is simply as a classification scheme using the characteristics that *best represent* the place to define it. Geographers use **culture traits**, which can be anything from religion, land use, or language to the type of eating utensils, grave markers, or headwear, to define a **culture region**. A key component of a culture region is that the inhabitants are aware to some degree of a common cultural heritage and differences from other territorial groups. This consciousness of belonging to a group united in a common territory is **regional identity**, which is what geographers look for when studying vernacular regions. Vernacular regions stem from human emotions and feelings about place. Regions have *meaning* to their inhabitants and form part of residents' cultural identity.

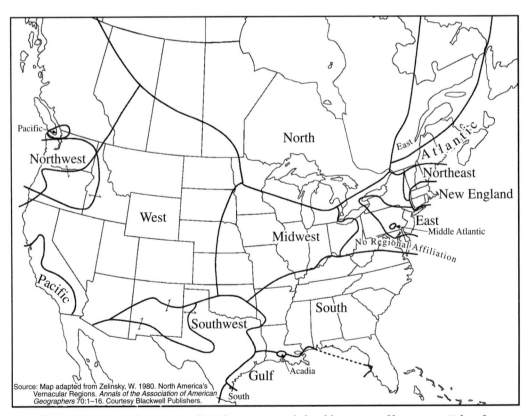

Source: Map adapted from Zelinsky, W. 1980. North America's Vernacular Regions. *Annals of the Association of American Geographers* 70:1–16. Courtesy Blackwell Publishers.

Figure 2.2 Vernacular regions of North America as defined by names of businesses. Taken from advertisements in phone books, the logic is that the frequency with which people use certain themes in commercial names is a function of group perceptions of regional identity.

A culture region, then, both shapes and is shaped by people's behaviors in their unique geographic setting, or *milieu*. In more traditional societies, there was much interaction between the physical characteristics of regions and the cultural lifestyles that developed over time, something early French geographers called the *genres de vie*, or "ways of life"—an integration of environmental, spiritual, and cultural practices in a region. People incorporate this organic construction of space through the long coevolution of lifestyles and landscapes into their regional identity and attachment to place. In today's postindustrial, globalized world, culture regions still exist, but perhaps with less influence from the physical geography of place. Many expressions of regional uniqueness today are reactions against the homogenized, consumer-oriented "placeless" characteristic of the global economy. Culture, and culture regions, are continually constructed by people as they shape their world and express their identity.

One way to study which characteristics best define a region would be to actually go there and engage in fieldwork involving detailed observation. Each culture region develops a distinctive **cultural landscape** as people modify their environment to their specific needs, technologies, and lifestyles. Terraced rice paddies, for instance, represent a distinctive feature of the cultural landscape in the humid, hilly terrain of Southeast Asia. Humid, hilly terrain in the southeastern United States looks very different, however, because the U.S. culture formed at a different time and with a different mix of population, capital, diets, technology, and trade relations.

The value system of a culture affects the way people perceive and use the natural environment and, thus, the way the cultural landscape looks. Native Americans of the northeastern United States, for instance, modified their environment with paths and villages and fields of corn and other crops. Although often agriculturalists, they were still very dependent on hunting and gathering and therefore perceived the forest and its wildlife as the most valuable resource. Whether left intact or, more commonly, modified by fire, the pre-European eastern forests were in fact a cultural landscape used to sustain many people. The farm-oriented European successors on the landscape, however, perceived the soil as more valuable and an individually owned resource, and they cut down many forests and leveled terrain to till the land and plant crops. Later, with the advent of industrialization, energy came to be seen as a prized resource. Streams were dammed for waterpower, and coal mines were excavated. The wilderness was something to be overcome, and the natural environment had value only in being able to provide raw materials and energy for human consumption. Today, society has begun to question the unbridled use of the environment for human consumption. Contemporary values now respect pristine wilderness as an end in itself, as a place that lifts and sustains the human spirit. As a result, some dams are being removed, mines are being reclaimed, and much of New England has been reforested.

Culture is evident everywhere throughout the landscape, not only in adaptations to the natural landscape but also in such things as names of places, types of architecture, and designs of cities. People express cultural beliefs through **symbols**, such as monuments, flags, slogans, or religious icons, as well as through symbolic meaning that is associated with artifacts such as landscaping, house types, and commercial signs (Figure 2.3). Symbols express people's identities, whether that identity be soccer mom, union worker, feminist, hippie, or gang member. Symbols can promote ideology, such as the western image of the cowboy as an expression of individualism. Geographers who study the cultural landscape have come to recognize that the concept of **regional identity** as we have discussed it so far can be problematic. There

Figure 2.3 This giant lobster used as a commercial sign is an expression of regional identity in Bar Harbor, Maine. A second shop towards the end of the street also uses the lobster imagery.

is often no central, unifying cultural "belief," no single "identity" in any given place, but a multiplicity of belief systems and group allegiances. Much of the landscape we see and live in reflects the cultural beliefs of those with power, such as the classical Greek architecture of our government buildings that celebrates a European heritage and democratic ideals, skyscrapers that serve as corporate advertising, monuments to founding fathers and war heroes, and churches and other symbols of Christianity. These symbols can be used to construct a regional identity, but they are usually symbols from the majority and often do not represent minorities or disenfranchised groups. For example, the South still faces controversies about the Confederate Stars-and-Bars flag in public spaces and on official seals. To many southerners, the Stars-and-Bars is a symbol of southern pride and membership in Dixie, but to others it represents slavery, racism, and oppression. Rarely do we see expressions of disenfranchised groups—gay couples walking hand in hand, Rastafarian communal living, migrant worker union halls, Black Muslim organizations—used as expressions of the broader regional identity.

Setting aside for a minute the complexities of multiple subcultures in any given place, culture regions are still a valuable tool to understand a place and its people. A problem remains, however, with drawing precise boundaries around them. How can you determine where a culture region starts and where it ends? The answer is that you can't with any degree of precision. For this reason, it is best to think not in terms of one fixed boundary between culture regions but of gradations between them. Geographer Donald Meinig first conceptualized these gradations when studying the Mormon culture region in the western United States. Based on Meinig's work, we can define three terms that express the decreasing influence of a culture with increasing distance from the center of the culture region. The first is the **core**, the centralized zone of concentration, or the "most pure" area that possesses all of the culture traits used to define the region (Figure 2.4). This represents the heart

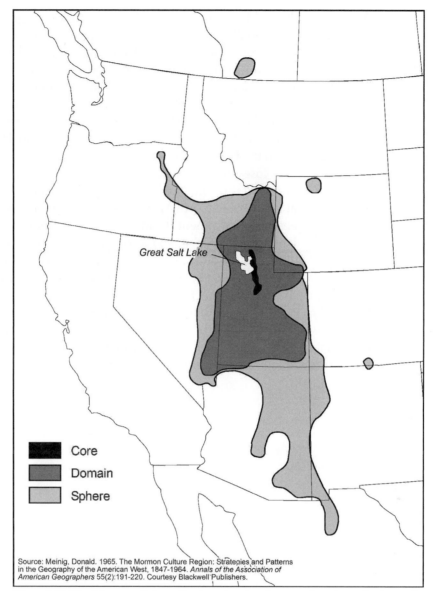

Great Salt Lake

Core

Domain

Sphere

Source: Meinig, Donald. 1965. The Mormon Culture Region: Strategies and Patterns in the Geography of the American West, 1847-1964. *Annals of the Association of American Geographers* 55(2):191-220. Courtesy Blackwell Publishers.

Figure 2.4 The Mormon Culture Region, showing the core, domain, and sphere of a culture region.

and soul of a culture region, its vital center and focus of circulation. The second is the **domain**, the area in which the particular culture is dominant but less intense. Finally, the **sphere** is the zone of outer influence where people with the culture traits in question can even be a minority within another culture region.

You'll want to keep two things in mind when thinking about cores, domains, and spheres. First, one culture's core can lie within another culture's sphere. For instance, the core of Tibetan Buddhist culture, the Tibetan plateau, is also part of the Chinese cultural sphere because China conquered Tibet in the eighteenth century and has occupied it since 1950. Second, the transitions between core, domain, and sphere can be gradual or abrupt. Barriers to movement have historically created abrupt transitions. Political barriers such as the Berlin Wall and the Great Wall of China sharply separated the capitalist West from the communist East and Chinese Confucians from Mongolian invaders. Physical barriers including the

Alps sharply divided Roman civilization from Northern European "barbarians." On the other hand, in Southeast Asia, a very gradual transition occurs over a thousand miles between the curry-based flavors of Indian cuisine to the soy-based flavors of Chinese cuisine, with Thai cuisine halfway between featuring major influences of both. Thai cuisine is an example of **syncretism**, when new cultural traits emerge as a cultural hybrid of two distinct parent traits. Syncretism occurs in many aspects of culture, such as the fusion of African religion with Catholicism in Brazil and the change in food such as the Mexican taco or Chinese chow mein into the variety we are familiar with in the United States and Canada. Another example is Japanese-style capitalism, which fuses the free-market ideas of the capitalist West with the group-oriented social relations of the Confucian East. The result is a form of capitalism much different from that in North America, where corporations offer lifelong jobs to their employees and government decides which industries should be phased out.

Activity 1 of this chapter asks you to construct a cultural region, either the Middle East or the American Southwest, depending on your instructor's choice. Ask yourself: "What's it like there? What do you think is the essence of the region? What are its signature traits? Which cities, states, or countries does it include?" Deciding the criteria for regional definition will help you to better understand the region. In Activity 2, you will look for the linguistic, culinary, landscape, or other cultural traits that mark your local culture region. In Activity 3, postcards will serve as clues to the regional identity of your own culture region.

▶ **CASE STUDY**

LAYERS OF TRADITION

GOAL

To introduce the concept of a **culture region** by evaluating **culture traits** and **cultural landscapes** of the Middle East and/or the American Southwest (check with your instructor). You will define your own core of the region, identify the traits of your own culture region, and explore how symbolism is used to represent **regional identity**.

LEARNING OUTCOMES

After completing the chapter, you will be able to:

- Evaluate map layers using a geographic information system (GIS).
- Define the core of a culture region on the basis of its main cultural traits.
- Define the domain of a culture region based on the degree of agreement between culture trait boundaries.
- Discuss the history and geography of the Middle East and/or American Southwest.
- Identify the cultural traits that make your subregion distinctive versus those that are shared with the entire North American culture region.
- Recognize symbolism as it is used to promote regional identity.
- Recognize that regional imagery often promotes one group's identity while excluding that of others.

SPECIAL MATERIALS NEEDED

- Computer with high-speed Internet access and a recent release of a Web browser. If using the Student Companion Site with the printed book, click on *Tech Support* for system requirements and technical support. (If using the e-book in WileyPlus, click on *Help* for details about the system requirements.)

BACKGROUND

Despite the arid climates they share, the Middle East and the American Southwest are marked by distinctive culture traits and cultural landscapes. Both regions consist of a relatively uniform core, surrounded by an increasingly mixed **domain** and **sphere**. Residents of both regions perceive that they belong to their region, and use *vernacular* terms to refer to it. Although these regions are at different scales, geographers analyze them in a similar fashion.

Unless you have lived or traveled in these regions, your knowledge of them could be sketchy. You probably have a mental picture of each region, and you can probably name at least one city that definitely belongs to each one. On the other hand, you could have a number of misconceptions about each region, and you probably don't have an exact idea where each region ends and the neighboring region begins. The regional background section that follows will help you to put the maps in Activity 1 into historical and geographical context.

What most North Americans know about the "Middle East" consists of snippets and images from TV, newspapers, and movies. We don't hear much about it unless there is a crisis going on. For the first half of the twentieth century, the Middle East was perceived as a vast, stark, beautiful, waterless emptiness as featured in the movie epic *Lawrence of Arabia*. American perceptions were dominated by sun-baked men in white robes and headdresses, riding camels and living in tents. Female stereotypes were performing as belly dancers or shrouded in veils (Figure 2.5). The movie *Raiders of the Lost Ark* imprinted similar images onto a new generation of North Americans. Both movies, interestingly, set the Middle East not as a region in its own right but as a stage for European conflict.

In the second half of the twentieth century, romantic mental images of the region were replaced by images of war and conflict. First, in 1948 the Jewish state of Israel was inserted into a Muslim-dominated region. A string of wars in 1948, 1956, 1967, 1973, and 1982 followed. Peace came haltingly and only partially to the region: a land-for-peace deal with Egypt in 1979, partial autonomy for Palestinians in the Gaza Strip and parts of the West Bank in the late 1990s, and Israeli withdrawal from occupied southern Lebanon in 2000. As of 2009, peace talks between Israelis and Palestinians had broken down amid ongoing violent clashes between Israel and the Hamas organization in Gaza, and between Israel and the Hezbollah group in Lebanon, and continued construction of Israeli settlements in the West Bank. Meanwhile, other conflicts added new images to the American mental map of the Middle East. An Arab embargo of oil exports to western supporters of Israel in 1974 quadrupled oil prices. Another oil price hike in 1979 coincided with the overthrow of the American-backed Shah of Iran by Muslim fundamentalists and the taking of hostages at the U.S. Embassy in Tehran. Then the apparent unity of the Middle East appeared to crack. A long war ensued between Iran and Iraq in the 1980s. In 1990, Iraq invaded Kuwait and threatened

Figure 2.5 Iranian women wearing their *chadors*, or veils, outside a mosque during Friday prayers in Tehran. The veils symbolize the sheltered status of women in many Middle Eastern countries.

© 2010 John Wiley & Sons, Inc.

Saudi Arabia. The western powers led by the United States intervened during the Gulf War, ostensibly to protect their allies and uphold international law, and not coincidentally to ensure the continued flow of oil to the West.

The twenty-first century dawned with more troubled relations between much of the Middle East and the Western world. On September 11, 2001, radical fundamentalist Muslim terrorists hijacked commercial airliners and crashed them into the World Trade Center towers in New York City and the Pentagon in Arlington, Virginia—two of the most prominent symbols of U.S. military and economic power. Some experts see this as a clash of civilizations, with Middle Easterners feeling that their independence and traditions are threatened by the globalization of Western influence and culture (see Chapter 8). Others say the attacks were motivated by anger specifically against U.S. foreign policy in the region, which is widely seen as hypocritical and biased against Muslims. Anti-American resentment at the time focused on U.S. military bases in Muslim holy lands in Saudi Arabia, including in Mecca; favoring of Israelis over Palestinians; economic sanctions against Iraqi civilians; and U.S. support for repressive and corrupt regimes in oil-rich countries. It is safe to say that most Middle Easterners share some of these political complaints but were horrified by the September 11 attacks carried out by the al-Qaeda terrorist group, led by Osama bin Laden (Figure 2.6).

Following September 11, an international coalition led by the United States invaded Afghanistan to wipe out the al-Qaeda network and the fundamentalist Taliban regime that had allowed the terrorists to train there. In 2002, the United States renewed pressure on Iraqi President Saddam Hussein to reveal and eliminate any weapons of mass destruction, as per previous United Nations (UN) resolutions (see Chapter 13). When Iraq did not comply, the United States, the United Kingdom, and several other countries—without UN backing—invaded Iraq in March 2003 and deposed Saddam Hussein's totalitarian regime. Critics of American policy decried the lack of evidence linking Iraq with al-Qaeda and pushed for a diplomatic solution. Other critics pointed out that in the 1980s the United States had provided military and economic support to both Saddam Hussein in Iraq and fundamentalist Muslim guerillas in Afghanistan to help each fight enemies considered more dangerous to the United States at that time. Even though Iraqi citizens turned out in large numbers for democratic elections of a transitional government, the U.S. military occupation and the transitional Iraqi government continued to face fierce resistance by insurgents. By May 2009, when this book was finished, the United States was still involved in costly economic and political reconstructions of Afghanistan and Iraq.

Both sides in the so-called "war on terrorism" possess, and even promote, cultural stereotypes. Al-Qaeda paints the Western system as a unified threat led by the United States. Westerners often see the Middle East as a hostile, war-torn area of radical fundamentalists and suicide bombers. At a more detailed scale, both pictures distort the great diversity in both the West and the Middle East. Al-Qaeda's attempts to promote a pan-Muslim Middle Eastern identity try to paint over regional diversity, but these attempts are challenged by

Figure 2.6 Osama bin Laden.

basic geographic realities. Just as not all Americans are white, English-speaking Christians, not all Middle Easterners are Arab (Turks and Persians are just two other groups), not all are Muslim (Jews and Coptic Christians are numerous), not all practice the same form of Islam (Sunni and Shia are the two main sects), and many countries have moderate, pro-Western governments (such as Turkey).

Westerners are not the only ones who trade in cultural stereotypes: al-Qaeda also ignores the region's rich history and cultural identities. This history goes back to the dawn of civilization, when agriculture, domestication of animals, and the very first cities originated some 10,000 years ago. The setting was the "Fertile Crescent," a quarter-moon-shaped zone of the rain-catching hilly flanks of the Zagros and Taurus Mountains, plus the smaller mountains of Lebanon and Palestine, where barley and emmer wheat grew wild (Figure 2.7). Although not necessarily the first culture hearth where farming, herding, and permanent towns were "invented," archaeological evidence points to the Fertile Crescent—ideally situated at the crossroads of three continents and near several perennial rivers—as the major source region for the diffusion of agriculture worldwide.

Later, great empires ruled these lands and produced lasting works of art, architecture, science, philosophy, and, of course, religion. One of the first known maps is on a stone tablet from Babylon dated around 2500 B.C. In addition to the pyramids, Egypt developed the great library at Alexandria, which became the intellectual center of the Western world in the second century A.D. Middle Eastern scholars not only kept the knowledge of the ancient Greeks and Romans alive during the European

▶ **CASE STUDY** *(continued)*

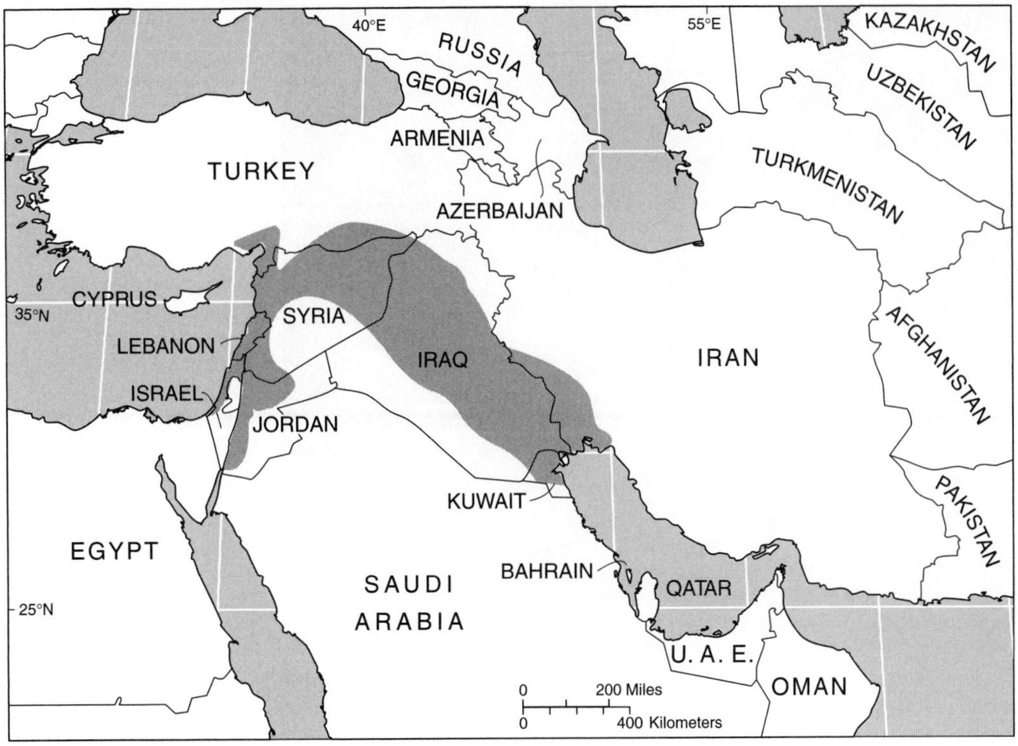

Figure 2.7 The Fertile Crescent, an early culture hearth and likely source for the diffusion of agriculture.

Dark Ages but also significantly advanced mathematics, which is why our numbers are referred to as *Arabic numerals.*

The Middle East "holy land" produced the Jewish and Christian faiths. Later, when Islam arose in the early seventh century A.D., it swept through the region in an extraordinarily short period of time. Within a century, Islam had spread to current-day Spain and Morocco in the west, to Pakistan in the east, south into Africa, and north to the Black Sea. Developed and spread by the Prophet Mohammed and codified in the holy book of the Koran, the practice of Islam is largely defined by the "Five Pillars." The Five Pillars are (1) recognizing Allah (God) and Mohammed as his messenger; (2) praying five times a day toward Mecca, Mohammed's birthplace; (3) giving alms to the poor and protecting the weak; (4) abstaining from food, drink, tobacco, and sex during daylight hours during the entire month of Ramadan; and (5) making a pilgrimage to Mecca at least once during a lifetime. Mohammed recognized the validity of the other monotheistic "peoples of the book," namely Jews and Christians, which helps explain how isolated Jewish and Christian communities survived in the Middle East over the next 1,400 years. (*Note*: the *Country Facts* spreadsheet contains data on the leading religions for every country in the world.)

A unique combination of adaptations evolved in the Middle East that enabled human society to survive the arid conditions. Geographers refer to this culture complex as the **ecological trilogy** because it involved sophisticated interactions among three kinds of communities: village, tribe, and city. Each part of the trilogy represented a unique cultural landscape that

adapted to the environment but also modified the environment. First, there were the sedentary villages that produced agricultural products (Figures 2.8 and 2.9). Villagers settled in river valleys, coastal areas, oases, and foothills, where sporadic rain and the availability of irrigation water made farming possible. The second element of the equation was the nomadic tribe, which added several essential factors. Tribes provided the protein in the Middle Eastern diet by nomadic herding of sheep, goats, and camels, which were used for meat, milk, and yogurt (Figure 2.10). Two primary variations are horizontal nomadism, in which herds are moved from one known pasture to the next, moving frequently so as not to deplete the pastures, and vertical nomadism, in which herds are moved to the highlands in summer and lowlands in winter. Nomads also provided long-distance transportation and military protection to the trilogy. Cities formed the third element of the trilogy. Traditional Middle Eastern cities were centered on the mosque for religious and political leadership and the bazaar for trading, craftmaking, and services (Figure 2.11).

Contrary to popular perceptions, significant parts of the Middle East are not desert. The true desert, which is characterized by a year-round deficit of moisture in the soil, is bordered by semidesert climate zones known as *steppe* that can sustain short grasses and scattered shrubs. The coasts of North Africa, Israel, and Turkey enjoy a Mediterranean climate similar to that of Italy and Southern California with dry summers and cool, moist winters. The mountains of the Fertile Crescent and Morocco's Atlas Mountains get significant amounts of snow.

▶ *CASE STUDY (continued)*

Figure 2.8   Mud bricks, like those shown here, have been used for thousands of years in the Middle East.

Figure 2.9   A small village with walled fields in the Al Bawn depression near Raydah, North Yemen.

Figure 2.10   Bedouin shepherd in the hills near Bethlehem in the occupied West Bank of Israel.

The ecological trilogy is an important cultural feature of the Middle East, but the region also has a common colonial heritage. Like much of the developing world, the Middle East was colonized by European powers, including Russia, in the eighteenth and nineteenth centuries, with only the Ottoman Empire (Turkey), Morocco, and Iran remaining independent. The country boundaries we see today were largely drawn by the European colonizers as they divided and redivided the region with no regard for the local people and land. In retrospect, the Arab-Israeli wars, the Iran-Iraq war, the Gulf War, and the

▶ **CASE STUDY** *(continued)*

Figure 2.11 The minarets of a mosque tower above the stalls of a market in Istanbul, Turkey.

Figure 2.12 Saguaro and cholla cactus dot the slopes surrounding the thirteenth- to fifteenth-century cliff dwellings at Tonto National Monument, Arizona. The Salado (Salt) people, famous for beautiful polychrome pottery, farmed crops and supplemented their diets by hunting and gathering.

Iraq invasion were all fought over European-imposed boundaries! In the colonies, traditional regional ties were replaced with exports of raw materials to the colonial power. The technological benefits of industrialization were rarely transferred back, other than through sales of Western goods. Except for a few landowners in several oil-rich countries, most Middle Eastern people now face the same problems as those in other less-developed countries (see Chapter 7). It is within this historical context that today's conflicts must be seen.

Although the history and cultural landscape of the American Southwest are markedly different from those of the Middle East, both regions are dominated by vast tracts of arid land. The Sonoran, Chihuahuan, Great Basin, and Mojave deserts converge in the Southwest and extend from southeastern California to southern New Mexico and west Texas. Many of the plants that grow in these deserts, such as creosote bush, saguaro cactus (Figure 2.12), joshua trees, and yuccas, are typical symbols of the Southwest. Semiarid grasslands also cover much of the region, especially in mid-altitude areas such as southeastern Arizona, the fringes of the Great Plains in eastern New Mexico, and much of the canyon country around the "Four Corners" (where Arizona, New Mexico, Colorado, and Utah meet). Yet the entire Southwest is not arid. Coastal Southern California, which may or may not be included in the Southwest, actually has a Mediterranean climate with hot, dry summers and cool, moist winters. The region is also punctuated by mountain ranges that receive abundant precipitation and are the source for such notable southwestern rivers as the Rio Grande, Colorado, Salt,

Gila, San Juan, and Pecos. These rivers and the many dams and reservoirs that were constructed to store their water for year-round use were crucial to the early settlement of the region. At the beginning of the twenty-first century, water supply looms as an important issue facing the Southwest.

The topography of the American Southwest could be even more diverse than its climate. The boundaries of the American Southwest can encompass hundreds of thousands of square miles and extend into numerous physiographic or "landform" regions (Figure 2.13). Four of these regions lie within most people's perception of the Southwest: the Basin and Range, Colorado Plateau, the Rocky Mountains, and Great Plains. The Basin and Range cover a considerable area of the western United States from eastern Washington through Nevada, then extend across much of southern and central Arizona and New Mexico and then extends into the "Big Bend" of west Texas. Large flat areas (basins) are interspersed with rather narrow, often steep but short mountain chains (ranges). Sometimes referred to as *sky islands* within a *desert sea*, the ranges frequently reach an elevation high enough to support different types of forest ecosystems such as those in the Rocky Mountains or Sierra Nevada. The second region, the Colorado Plateau, is an expanse of plateaus, mesas, and canyons that includes much of the area around the "Four Corners" (Figure 2.14). The Grand Canyon is cut down into the Colorado Plateau. The southern and southwestern edge of the Colorado Plateau literally drops off into the lower-elevation Basin and Range; a several-hundred-mile-long escarpment (i.e., cliff) called the *Mogollon Rim* marks its edge in Arizona. Third, the Rocky Mountains extend into the American Southwest as far south as Santa Fe, New Mexico. Finally, the Great Plains extend all the way into eastern New Mexico and west Texas. Note that many other physiographic regions may be considered part of

© 2010 John Wiley & Sons, Inc.

▶ *CASE STUDY (continued)*

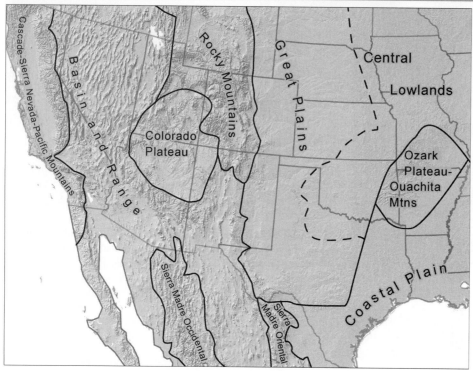

Figure 2.13 Physiographic regions of the Southwest.

Figure 2.14 Rainbow Bridge, the longest natural bridge in the world, towers above Lake Powell in southeastern Utah. Tourists to the Four Corners area can also visit Bryce, Zion, Arches, Grand Canyon, and Mesa Verde National Parks, plus Monument Valley and the Painted Desert.

the Southwest as well, such as the Pacific Coast Mountains, Mexico's rugged Sierra Madre Occidental, or the Gulf Coastal Plain of Texas.

Although the landforms and vegetation define the boundaries of the American Southwest in one way, many geographers, historians, and others also define the region by its cultural characteristics. The population of the Southwest is a distinctive blend of Native Americans, Hispanics, and Anglo-Americans (Figure 2.15). Native Americans, both historically and in contemporary times, have exerted a powerful influence on the Southwest. Prehistoric civilizations such as the Anasazi, Sinagua, and Mogollon constructed cliff dwellings and road networks while others including the Hohokam established irrigation canals that subsequent groups of Native Americans and European settlers used. These early groups flourished, and although they no longer exist, contemporary agricultural tribes including the Pima, Tohono O'odham, Hopi, and Pueblo Indians are their likely descendents. Numerous other Native American tribes exist in large numbers across the American Southwest. More than 200,000 Navajo live on the largest reservation in the United States in northeast Arizona, northwest New Mexico, and southeast Utah. The Apache, Utes, and Comanche, like the Navajo, were nomadic tribes that subsisted from hunting and gathering instead of agriculture. Separate Apache tribes currently exist in reservations across New Mexico and Arizona. The Utes have two substantial reservations in southwest Colorado. The Comanche, although originally inhabitants of the American Southwest, were forcibly relocated to reservation lands in Oklahoma. By raiding Spanish and Anglo settlements and forcefully defending their territory from European encroachment, the Utes, Comanche, and especially Apache were pivotal in limiting the spread of settlement in the Southwest.

The Hispanic element of the Southwest is evocative in the minds of many Americans. Symbols such as chile peppers

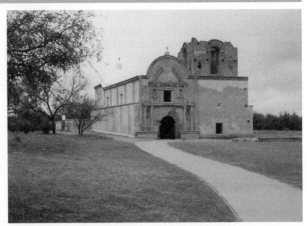

Figure 2.15 A mural on a wall in Douglas in southeastern Arizona honors the "Three Peoples" that settled in this region and contributed cultural traits to its distinctive culture.

Figure 2.16 One of the most important traits introduced by the Spanish to the Southwest was Catholicism. The Spanish built spectacular missions such as San Cayetano de Tumacácori, south of Tucson, Arizona, dating to 1691. Father Kino, the founder of the mission, established 27 others throughout the Southwest, all designed to convert the indigenous people into Christians and into tax-paying colonial subjects. Indians were enticed to the missions by food, clothing, supplies, and education.

(a crop Spaniards adopted from Native Americans), tortillas, adobe homes, and luminarias (traditional Christmas lights made of candles set in paper bags) are common characterizations of this region. The term *American Southwest* should be used carefully because most of the region was under Spanish control until 1821 and governed by Mexico until 1848 (Figure 2.16). The Southwest's Hispanic population, like that of the remainder of the United States, is not homogeneous and includes two diverse, although related, groups: Hispanos and Mexican-Americans. Hispanos were the first of the Hispanic groups to settle in the Southwest, with the earliest villages appearing in the early 1600s in what is now central New Mexico. Early Hispanos were Spaniards with little Native American ancestry, although racial mixing later occurred over the subsequent centuries. Traditions and customs maintained by Hispanos were more similar to Spanish culture and not directly linked to Mexico. The center of Hispano influence in the Southwest is the upper Rio Grande Valley of New Mexico extending roughly from Santa Fe into south-central Colorado. Other groups of settlers with Spanish ancestry settled in south Texas (Tejanos) and along the coast of southern California (Californios); yet the influence of these groups on the local area was not as lasting as that of the Hispanos on New Mexico, probably because settlement of California and Texas occurred much later than in New Mexico, and Spanish settlers were quickly outnumbered by Anglos.

After the initial Hispano settlement, Mexicans began arriving in the Southwest. Distinct from Hispanos, many Mexicans were of mixed Spanish and indigenous descent with cultural characteristics that exhibited both Spanish and Aztec or other Mexican Indian roots. Many Mexicans fled political unrest and economic stagnation in Mexico and arrived in the Southwest from the late 1800s into the early 1900s to work in mining and agriculture.

Anglo and European settlers in the Southwest also began arriving in the mid- to late 1800s and accounted for rapid population growth in the twentieth century. Early Anglo groups such as Mormons and settlers from Texas came and established extensive farms and ranches across the American Southwest. Others emigrated directly from Europe and formed ethnic enclaves, mostly in mining communities such as Bisbee, Arizona, and Silver City, New Mexico. After World War II, the Anglo population of the region increased rapidly due to postwar economic development, the widespread use of air conditioning, and construction of the interstate highway system. The population of the Southwest has mushroomed over the past 50 years with areas such as metropolitan Phoenix expanding from less than 200,000 in 1950 to 3.1 million by 2000.

The economy of the Southwest is now quite diversified. Economic activities commonly associated with the region such as ranching, irrigated farming, and mining are dwarfed by a burgeoning service sector related to retail trade and tourism. Industrial development in this region has always been somewhat limited, yet the number of high-tech firms (such as Motorola, Intel, and Sumitomo) has surged. In addition to the strong economy, migrants are lured by the sunny skies, mild winters, and perceptions that the Sun Belt has a "laid-back" lifestyle. The Mexican-American population of the Sun Belt has been steadily increasing through immigration from Mexico and higher rates of fertility among existing Mexican-American residents.

This history and geography of the Middle East and the American Southwest gives you some background for defining the regions' boundaries. Where does the Middle East begin and end? What makes the American Southwest different from the regions to the north, south, east, or west? Can the Middle East be defined based on physical characteristics including deserts or oil, or cultural characteristics such as Arabic language,

▶ *CASE STUDY (continued)*

Islam, goat milk, and camels? Is the American Southwest best defined by sunshine, Hispanics, cactus, or coyotes? These are some of the points you need to consider in Activity 1 of this chapter. You will use GIS (Chapter 1) to overlay different data layers to define your conception of the region.

The concept of a culture region with defining traits can be applied at different scales. In Activity 2, you will look within the North American culture region and downsize to the smaller subregion in which you live. Certainly, growing up in the American Midwest is not the same experience as growing up in the Northeast, the South, the Rockies, or Québec. We will ask you to identify some of the traits in the popular culture, the traditional culture, and the landscape that distinguish your culture region from others.

Finally, the Middle East and American Southwest are not the only regions in which media images dominate people's perceptions. In Activity 3, we ask you to look at tourist postcards of the culture region where you live. Postcards are created to "sell" your region to outsiders. They feature an ideal or symbolic landscape that may not much resemble where you live. Who benefits from projecting these images of your region to the outside world, and who is left out? You may never have thought about it before, but the cultural identity of your region is up for grabs in your local souvenir shop and gas station.

Name: _____   Instructor: _____

Layers of Tradition: Culture Regions at Different Scales

▶ ACTIVITY 1: MAPPING CULTURE REGIONS

In this exercise, you will use a GIS to look at a series of maps that portray different definitions of the Middle East and/or the American Southwest (check with your instructor). By discriminating between the maps and by overlaying them in combinations, you will define your own composite culture region.

A. To start your activity, click on the *Student Companion Site* at www.wiley. com/college/kuby. (For students using WileyPlus, log on to your class Web site, select the *Assignment* tab, locate and click on this assignment, and follow all instructions.)

B. Select this chapter from the drop-down list, and then click on *Computerized Chapter Activities*.

C. Click on *Activity 1: Mapping Culture Regions (American Southwest)* or *(Middle East)*, according to your instructor's directions.

D. A blank map of the general vicinity of the region will appear on your screen. Think about what the region means to you. What makes Middle Eastern culture different from European, African, Russian, Chinese, or South Asian culture? What makes southwestern culture different from that of the South or Pacific Northwest? What is different about its culture, landscape, and people? Now, click and hold your mouse button on the map to trace a boundary (go slowly!) around what you consider to be the culture region. Click on *Reset Drawing* to erase and start over. Don't worry about whether your region is "correct"; it won't be graded. The purpose is simply to think about your preconceptions before you look at some regional data. When you have drawn your regional boundary, click on *Save My Initial View*.

E. Computer mapping packages and geographic information systems are able to store many different layers. We have several different maps, each representing a separate definition of the region. The names of the map layers are visible in the right margin. The bottom layer titled *My Initial View* is what you just drew. Click any layer and the first map will appear overlaid on the base map. This map layer text is now also highlighted, indicating it is turned on. To turn the layer off, simply click on it again. Click on *Cities* or *Place Names* to identify cities and either states or countries.

© 2010 John Wiley & Sons, Inc.

1.1. Turn on each layer one at a time and look closely at each map. Write the name of each layer and the map title in the spaces that follow.

Name		Title
1	_____	_____
2	_____	_____
3	_____	_____
4	_____	_____
5	_____	_____
6	_____	_____
7	_____	_____
8	_____	_____
9	_____	_____
10	_____	_____
11	_____	_____
12	_____	_____
13	_____	_____
14	_____	_____
15	_____	_____
16	_____	_____
17	_____	_____
18	_____	_____

1.2. Think about what the region means to you and consider whether each map corresponds to your image of the region. In your opinion, which three maps best define the Middle East or American Southwest?

1._____ 2._____ 3._____

1.3. Justify the inclusion of *each* of your three layers. Why, in other words, do you believe each of these three variables represents the way of life of the culture region?

F. Turn on your three chosen layers at the same time. Regions that overlap are progressively shaded. The darkest shading therefore will be where all three definitions overlap. (Note that the red outline around each data layer appears only when you first turn on a layer.)

Think of the area of maximum overlap as the core of the Middle East or American Southwest. Print this view of your three-layer map by clicking on the *Print* button.

1.4. How closely do the boundaries of your three variables agree? What does this say about the presence of a domain (the zone of transition between culture regions) for the American Southwest or the Middle East?

1.5. What other variable that was not on our list could be used to define the Middle East or American Southwest as a culture region?

1.6. With your three layers still showing, click on *My Initial View*. How does your initial perception of the region differ from your composite view? What have you learned about the culture region?

G. When you have finished, close all browser windows.

Name: _____ Instructor: _____

Layers of Tradition: Culture Regions at Different Scales

▶ **ACTIVITY 2: CULTURE TRAITS OF YOUR CULTURE SUBREGION**

Most people would agree that life in Kansas is different from life in Alabama, California, Montana, New York, Alaska, Québec, or Nova Scotia. Had Dorothy awakened in Philadelphia instead of Oz, however, she might still have said, "Toto, I've a feeling we're not in Kansas anymore." Of course, we recognize that all of these North American places culturally have more in common with each other than with Ecuador, Kenya, Malaysia, or Japan.

In Activity 2, we ask you to think about the region where you live and what sets it apart from neighboring regions. There may be many right answers to the following questions, but that doesn't mean there are no wrong answers. Try to keep your focus at the regional geographic scale. Your answers should apply to the whole region, not just your town or neighborhood, and not to the United States or Canada as a whole.

2.1. Find the location of your college in Figure 2.2. Write its *vernacular region* here:

- Common vernacular name _____

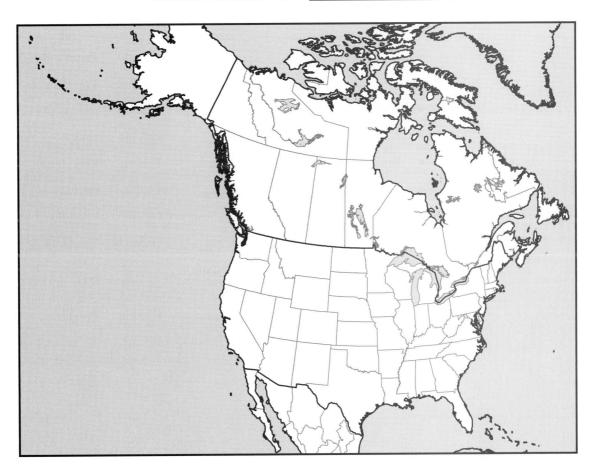

© 2010 John Wiley & Sons, Inc.

2.2. Now, on the map on the preceding page, draw your best approximation of the boundaries of your culture region. This exercise will not be graded by your instructor. Its purpose is for you to have the whole of this region in mind when answering the next set of questions.

2.3. To start you thinking about the cultural geography of your region, identify:

- Common or unique characteristics of the natural landscape
  _____

- Unofficial capital city _____

- Famous tourist site for visitors who want to experience the essence of your region _____

- Movie or TV show set in and symbolic of your region
  _____

- Novel about your region _____

2.4. For each of the following culture traits, identify a notable example associated with your region. For each trait, make your best guess about whether it is unique (found exclusively in your region), prevalent (not unique to your region but more prevalent or widespread in your region than elsewhere), or the same (as most of the United States and Canada).

- Food _____ Unique___ Prevalent___ Same ___
- Clothing _____ Unique___ Prevalent___ Same ___
- Crop _____ Unique___ Prevalent___ Same ___
- Livestock _____ Unique___ Prevalent___ Same ___
- Music _____ Unique___ Prevalent___ Same ___
- Sport or game _____ Unique___ Prevalent___ Same ___
- Architectural style _____ Unique___ Prevalent___ Same ___
- Building material _____ Unique___ Prevalent___ Same ___
- Mode of transportation _____ Unique___ Prevalent___ Same ___
- Religion _____ Unique___ Prevalent___ Same ___
- Local expression _____ Unique___ Prevalent___ Same ___
- Accent (spell phonetically an example of the pronunciation)

  _____ Unique___ Prevalent___ Same ___

2.5. Which of the cultural traits in your list in Question 2.4 was the least distinctive to your region? Why do you think that your region has lost its distinctiveness in this aspect of culture?

2.6. Does your region have any prominent cultural traits that originated outside of Canada and the United States? If so, describe one of these traits. What is it, where did it come from, and when do you think it was brought to your area?

2.7. Is the "nonnative" cultural trait in Question 2.6 an example of syncretism, and if so, how has it been modified and fused with a North American cultural element?

2.8. To the extent that regional culture traits are disappearing in the United States and Canada as the global economy becomes more pronounced, list two positive and two negative aspects of this "cultural homogenization."

Name: _____ Instructor: _____

Layers of Tradition: Culture Regions at Different Scales

▶ ## ACTIVITY 3: REGIONAL IMAGERY

In Activities 1 and 2 you tried to distinguish the key characteristics of a culture region based on maps and personal experience. Activity 3 uses another method to assess cultural characteristics of a region by looking at major themes that define the region on postcards. Themes on postcards project recognizable symbols or scenes that people from around the nation or world can identify as representing that region.

A. Go to some local stores that sell postcards and identify the symbols, cultural characteristics, or features of the cultural landscape that best represent the region in which you live. Keep a tally of the number of times each theme appears. You should sample at least 20 to 30 postcards. The more you use, the easier your task will be.

3.1. Fill in the following table of the dominant themes that appear on the postcards and the number of times you saw cards in this group. The themes you define should be general categories that are represented by individual postcard images. Examples might be cowboys in the West, nature in the Rocky Mountains, city skylines in the East, or regional sports such as NASCAR in the South. Think about which themes struck you as repeatedly appearing and try to be thorough in creating the groups. The number of themes you should identify will vary for each region.

Theme (fill in as many as necessary)   Number of Appearances

1.

2.

3.

4.

5.

6.

7.

8.

9.

10.

© 2010 John Wiley & Sons, Inc.

B. Buy five postcards that you believe are most representative of the themes you identified (these should cost you very little). You will hand in these five postcards with the assignment, and your instructor will return them to you.

3.2. What were the dominant themes in the postcards that you selected?

Card 1:

Card 2:

Card 3:

Card 4:

Card 5:

3.3. What is surprising to find or not find in this list of dominant themes?

3.4. Postcards are representations of a region designed for a specific purpose. What is the intent of these postcards? What message are they conveying about the region?

3.5. You read in the introduction to this chapter that culture regions have different subcultures, each with its own identity. Did you see examples of any "minority" cultures represented in your postcard themes, and if so, were those portrayals realistic? What groups, if any, were not represented?

3.6. Whose regional identity do you think these cards represent? In other words, whose belief system determines what imagery appears for your region?

▶ DEFINITIONS OF KEY TERMS

Core The zone of greatest concentration or homogeneity of the culture traits that characterize a region.

Cultural Landscape Modifications to the environment by humans, including the built environment and agricultural systems, that reflect aspects of their culture.

Culture The shared understandings that guide behavior and values and condition a group's perception of the world. Culture is learned from one generation to the next and evolves over time.

Culture Region A region defined by similar culture traits and cultural landscape features.

Culture Trait A defining characteristic of the culture that is shared by most, if not all, members.

Domain The area outside of the core of a culture region in which the culture is still dominant but less intense.

Ecological Trilogy The traditional symbiotic relationship among villages, cities, and nomadic tribes in the Middle East, in which villages grow irrigated crops, cities provide the central mosque and bazaar, and tribes herd livestock and provide transportation and protection.

Formal Region An area of near uniformity (homogeneity) in one or several characteristics.

Functional Region A region created by the interactions between a central node and surrounding locations.

Perceptual Region An area defined by subjective perceptions that reflect the feelings and images about key place characteristics. When these perceptions come from the local, ordinary folk, a perceptual region can be called a vernacular region.

Region An area characterized by similarity or by cohesiveness that sets it apart from other areas.

Regional Identity An awareness of being a part of a group of people living in a culture region.

Sphere The zone of outer influence for a culture region.

Symbol A material object that represents some greater meaning or refers to something else.

Syncretism The fusion of two distinctive cultural traits into a unique new hybrid trait.

▶ FURTHER READINGS

Alderman, Derek H. 2000. A Street Fit for a King: Naming Places and Commemoration in the American South. *Professional Geographer* 52(4):672–684.

Alderman, Derek H., and Daniel B. Good. 1997. Exploring the Virtual South: The Idea of a Distinctive Region on "The Web." *Southeastern Geographer* 37(1):20–45.

Allen, Rodney F., and Laurie E. S. Molina. 1992. People and Places on Picture Postcards: A High-Interest Source for Geographic Education. *Journal of Geography* 91(3):106–112.

Amery, Hussein A., and Aaron T. Wolf (eds.). 2000. *Water in the Middle East: A Geography of Peace*. Austin: University of Texas Press.

Barber, Benjamin. 1992. Jihad vs. McWorld. *The Atlantic* (March):53–55, 58–63.

Byrkit, James W. 1992. Land, Sky, and People: The Southwest Defined. *Journal of the Southwest* 34(3):257–387.

Childs, Craig. 2007. *House of Rain: Tracking a Vanished Civilization Across the American Southwest*. New York: Little Brown & Co.

Cosgrove, Denis. 1989. Geography Is Everywhere: Culture and Symbolism in Human Landscapes, pp. 118–135 in *Horizons in Human Geography*, Derek Gregory and Rex Walford (eds.). Totawa, NJ: Barnes & Noble Books.

Foote, Kenneth E., Peter J. Hugill, Kent Mathewson, and Jonathon M. Smith, eds. 1994. *Re-Reading Cultural Geography*. Austin: University of Texas Press.

Freeman-Grenville, G. S. P. 1993. *Historical Atlas of the Middle East*. New York: Simon & Schuster.

Garreau, Joel. 1981. *The Nine Nations of North America*. New York: Avon Books.

Gilbert, Martin. 1993. *The Dent Atlas of the Arab-Israeli Conflict*, 6th ed. London: J. M. Dent.

Haverluk, Terrence W. 1997. The Changing Geography of U.S. Hispanics, 1850–1990. *Journal of Geography* 96(3):139–145.

Haverluk, Terrence W. 2003. Chile Peppers and Identity Construction in Pueblo, Colorado. *Journal of the Study of Food and Society* 6(1):45–59.

Hecht, M. 1975. The Decline of the Grass Lawn Tradition in Tucson. *Landscape* 19(3):3–10.

Held, Colbert C. 1994. *Middle East Patterns: Places, Peoples, and Politics*. Boulder, CO: Westview Press.

Jordan, Terry G. 1992. The Concept and Method, pp. 8–24 in *Regional Studies: The Interplay of Land and People*, Glen E. Lich (ed). College Station: Texas A&M Press.

Kemp, Geoffrey. 1997. *Strategic Geography and the Changing Middle East*. Washington, DC: Brookings Institution.

Larkin, Robert P., and John Harner. 2002. Low Slung and Far Flung: The Urban Southwest. *Journal of the West* 41(2): 41–49.

Larkin, Robert P., Carole J. Huber, and Thomas P. Huber. 1998. Defining the Southwest: The Use of Geographic Information Systems for Regional Description. *Journal of the Southwest* 40(2):243–260.

Meinig, Donald W. 1965. The Mormon Culture Region: Strategies and Patterns in the Geography of the American West, 1847–1964. *Annals of the Association of American Geographers* 55(2):191–220.

Meinig, Donald W. 1971. *Southwest: Three Peoples in Geographical Change, 1600–1970.* New York: Oxford University Press.

Melamid, Alexander. 1991. *Oil and the Economic Geography of the Middle East and North Africa.* Princeton, NJ: Darwin Press.

Nabhan, Gary Paul. 2008. *Renewing America's Food Traditions: Savoring and Saving the Continent's Most Endangered Foods.* White River Junction, VT: Chelsea Green Publishing.

Rossum, Sonja, and Stephen Lavin, 2000. Where Are the Great Plains? A Cartographic Analysis. *Professional Geographer* 52(3):543–552.

Roudi-Fahimi, Farzaneh, and Mary M. Kent. 2007. Challenges and Opportunities—The Population of the Middle East and North Africa. *Population Bulletin* 62(2): 1–20.

Shortridge, Barbara G., and James R. Shortridge (eds). 1998. *Taste of American Place: A Reader on Regional and Ethnic Foods.* Lanham, MD: Rowman and Littlefield.

Shortridge, James R. 1985. The Vernacular Middle West. *Annals of the Association of American Geographers* 75(1):48–57.

Spencer, William (ed.). 2000. *Global Studies: The Middle East,* 8th ed. Guilford, CT: Dushkin.

Zakaria, Fareed. 2001. Why Do They Hate Us? *Newsweek* (Oct. 15, 2001):22–40.

Zelinsky, Wilbur. 1980. North America's Vernacular Regions. *Annals of the Association of American Geographers* 70:1–16.

Zelinsky, Wilbur. 1992. On the Superabundance of Signs in Our Landscape: Selections from a Slide Lecture. *Landscape* 31(3):30–38.

▶ WEB RESOURCES

Anasazi Heritage Center: www.blm.gov/co/st/en/fo/ahc.html

Al Jazeera News: english.aljazeera.net

Burek, Josh. Clash of Civilizations: A Reading Guide. *Christian Science Monitor*: www.christiansciencemonitor.com/specials/sept11/flash_civClash.html

Clements Center for Southwest Studies: www.smu.edu/swcenter

Electronic Cultural Atlas Initiative: ecai.org

Ford, Peter. 2001. Why Do They Hate Us? *Christian Science Monitor* (Sept. 27, 2001):1. www.christiansciencemonitor.com/2001/0927/p1s1-wogi.html

Harvard University, Center for Middle Eastern Studies: cmes.hmdc.harvard.edu/

Indian Pueblos Cultural Center: www.indianpueblo.org

Israel Ministry of Foreign Affairs: www.mfa.gov.il

Lebanon Atlas: www.lebanonatlas.com

Munson, Henry. 2004. Lifting the Veil: Understanding the Roots of Islamic Militancy. *Harvard International Review* 25(4): 20–23: www.harvardir.org/index.php?page=article&id=1184

National Hispanic Cultural Center: www.hcfoundation.org

North American Center for Transborder Studies, Arizona State University. Various culture region maps: nacts.asu.edu/knowledge_Center/North_American_Migration

University of Arizona, Center for Middle Eastern Studies: www.cmes.arizona.edu

World News Network. *Iraq Daily News*: www.iraqdaily.com

▶ ITEMS TO HAND IN

Activity 1: • Questions 1.1–1.6, including your overlay map for Question 1.4, or answer all questions your instructor created in your Wiley plus assignments.

Activity 2: • Questions 2.1–2.8, or answer all questions your instructor created in your Wiley plus assignments.

Activity 3: • Questions 3.1–3.6, including the five postcards of dominant regional themes or answer all questions your instructor created in your Wiley plus assignments.

Tracking the AIDS Epidemic in the United States: Diffusion through Space and Time

▶ INTRODUCTION

Places can affect other places through a process called **spatial diffusion**. It is the spread of some phenomenon over space and through time from a limited number of origins. Phenomena take the form of ideas, innovations, products, new technology, culture traits, and contagious diseases. At first glance, comparing the spread of agriculture at the dawn of civilization to the spread of dress styles, popular music, or a new strain of flu virus may seem like comparing apples and oranges. Upon more careful analysis, however, geographers have discovered that all phenomena that diffuse, no matter how dissimilar, share some general spatial patterns and processes.

There are two types of diffusion: relocation diffusion and expansion diffusion. **Relocation diffusion** occurs when the items being diffused leave the original areas behind as they move to new areas. People move to a new area and take their language, religion, and other cultural items with them, as in the case of African-Americans who moved from the rural South to the urban North during the mid-twentieth century and brought blues music to Chicago and of contemporary Mexicans who migrated to America and brought Mexican cuisine with them. Although cultural traits are carried with the people who move, the number of adopters stays the same—at least initially.

Expansion diffusion is the process whereby the item spreads geographically by passing *from* one person *to* another while remaining with the first person. In this case, the number of people adopting the item expands. The phenomenon being diffused often intensifies in the origin region as new areas are affected by the phenomenon. An example of this type is the diffusion of a new strain of hybrid rice in India or the diffusion of AIDS in the United States, the topic of this chapter.

Relocation diffusion is often followed by expansion diffusion, depending partly on how much the new residents interact with the preexisting population. After African-American migrants brought the blues north, and Mexican migrants brought tortillas and salsa north, these cultural traits spread beyond the black and Mexican populations to other Americans. In addition to food, migrants bring countless other cultural traits with them, such as religion, technology, and even sports. Europeans brought Christianity with them to the New World (relocation diffusion), where it

© 2010 John Wiley & Sons, Inc.

spread to native peoples (expansion diffusion). Likewise, settlers carried guns with them to the American and Canadian West (relocation). Native American peoples witnessed the effectiveness of firearms firsthand and quickly acquired guns for themselves (expansion). The British are credited with inventing several of the world's most famous sports, including soccer, golf, and cricket. While soccer and golf spread throughout the world, cricket gained popularity mainly in the United Kingdom itself and the former British colonies that make up the British Commonwealth (Figure 3.1). The British have played cricket since at least the sixteenth century, with the first recorded rules in the Code of 1744. British colonists and soldiers played cricket wherever they went, and while it spread to the local populations, its complexity and leisurely pace may have prevented it from spreading to areas that were never settled by the British.

The adoption of phenomena generally follows an S-shaped curve (Figure 3.2). Take the case of cellular phone purchases as an example. Initially, only a small number of purchases were made because very few people knew about the product, and few distributors offered it for sale. Later, the number of adopters grew exponentially as the early buyers spread the word through a large, susceptible population (people who could afford but had not yet purchased a cellular phone). During this middle phase, the majority of people who will eventually adopt do so. Ultimately, the rate of adoption will taper off as the remaining number of susceptible people shrinks and the novelty and excitement of cellular phones wears off. The number of cell phone subscribers in the United States is still growing rapidly (Figure 3.3), but will eventually have to taper off as it approaches the total U.S. population of just over 300 million. The level of adoption never quite reaches 100 percent. Even in the most modern and wealthiest societies, there will always be people who choose to live without telephones and electricity. In addition, many products and diseases taper off at levels much lower than 100 percent, for example, snowboards, colored contact lenses, hip-hugger jeans, and the flu. If the saturation level is low, say at 10 percent of the population, the innovators might constitute the first 1 percent, the majority adopters from 2 to 9 percent, and the laggards the last 1 percent.

Figure 3.1 Cricket is especially popular in India, Pakistan, Australia, and the British West Indies. This group of formerly British islands in the Caribbean Sea had one of the best squads of the late twentieth century. International matches can take five days to play.

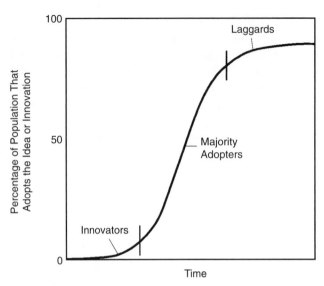

Figure 3.2 Typical S-shaped curve for the adoption of some idea or innovation.

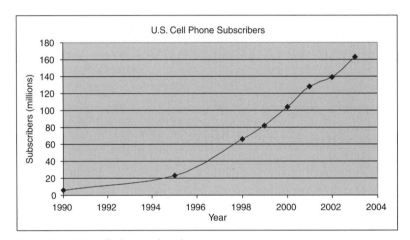

Figure 3.3 U.S. cell phone subscribers.
Source: U.S. Census Bureau, *Statistical Abstract of the United States: 2004–2005*, p. 278.

The S-curve also applies to innovations introduced by businesses and governments (Figure 3.4). A technology with the potential to transform the twenty-first century, but still in its infancy, is the hydrogen-powered vehicle. Hydrogen vehicles, which emit only water vapor from the tailpipe, can reduce urban smog, slow global warming, and lessen our dependence on imported oil. But which will be commercialized first: hydrogen vehicles or refueling stations? To break this chicken-and-egg dilemma, government agencies in partnership with automobile and energy companies are seeding an initial refueling infrastructure so that consumers and businesses will be able to use hydrogen vehicles as they become commercially available. As Figure 3.4 shows, there are now over 200 stations worldwide, with most growth occurring in Europe and North America. What you see in Figure 3.4 is the very beginning of an S-curve that might someday—if technology keeps improving and costs keep coming down—level off at over a million stations worldwide. In comparison, the first gasoline station was built in 1907, and the United States alone now has

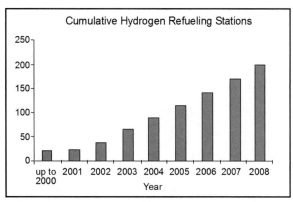

Figure 3.4 Hydrogen, which has been used as a fuel in the space program for many years, is the most common and lightest element in the universe but is not found in its pure form in nature. Currently, it is most cheaply made from natural gas (CH_4) using a process called steam reforming, but the vision for the hydrogen economy is to generate electricity from renewable sources such as solar or wind power, and then use this electricity to generate hydrogen from water (H_2O) using a process called electrolysis. The hydrogen can then be shipped and stored for use when and where it is needed. Hydrogen vehicles will use either an internal combustion engine to burn hydrogen or a fuel cell to generate electricity for a quiet but powerful electric motor. Most hydrogen stations today deliver compressed, pressurized hydrogen to the vehicle's fuel tank.

Adapted from Nicholas Huleatt-James, *2008 Hydrogen Infrastructure Survey*. www.fuelcelltoday.com. With permission of Fuel Cell Today ©2008.

an estimated 175,000 stations. In the United States, hydrogen fueling stations are diffusing most rapidly in California, which has a history of forward-looking measures to combat its severe air pollution.

How is it that some people adopt an innovation, purchase a hot new product, or catch a disease earlier than others? *Where* you live has something to do with *when* the diffusing phenomenon reaches you. The diffusion process has two spatial regularities. The first is a **contagious effect**, which says that places near the origin are usually affected first (Figure 3.5a). The farther you are from the point or points of origin, the later you will be affected. Think of a pebble tossed in a pond. The ripple spreading through the water is akin to the contagious effect in diffusion. This process is strongly influenced by distance because you are more likely to come in contact with nearby persons than with more remote persons. Contagious diffusion tends to characterize things that spread via direct contact or communication with, or observation of, another individual. Illnesses and slang spread rapidly among schoolmates, while farmers often rely on neighbors for proof that new equipment or seeds are better than the old. The spread of Islam from its birthplace in Mecca in what is now Saudi Arabia is a good example of contagious diffusion at work (Figure 3.6).

Diffusion processes do not, however, always follow the rule of distance. Sometimes distance is less important to the spread of an idea or disease than contact with major cities or influential people. **Hierarchical effects** occur when phenomena spread first to major cities, then to intermediate-size places, and later to small towns and rural areas (Figure 3.5b). New clothing and music fads, for example, spread quickly among major world cities such as New York, Los Angeles, London, Paris, and Tokyo. Only later do they filter down the **urban hierarchy**, in other words, down from large cities to smaller places (see Chapter 9 for a complete

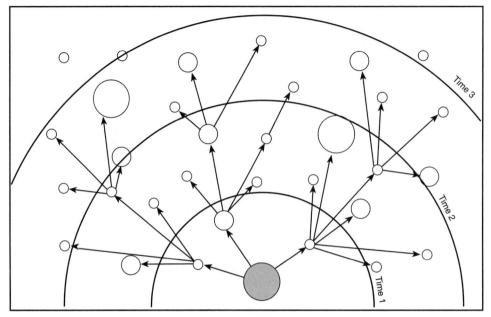

Figure 3.5a Typical contagious diffusion spreading like a wave.

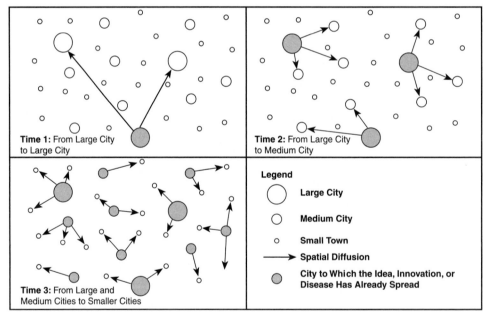

Figure 3.5b Typical sequence of hierarchical diffusion.

discussion of urban hierarchies). This occurs for several reasons. First, larger places have a greater potential for interaction. Far more travel and contact occur between large cities than between smaller cities, due in part to their complex air, road, and communication links. With more carriers of ideas coming to a place, large cities have more interactions with other people and places and, therefore, are first to find out about new styles and trends (you will see the effects of size on the number of interactions in Chapter 4). Second, the people in larger cities tend to be more diverse, wealthier, and more accustomed to change; cities attract more risk-taking

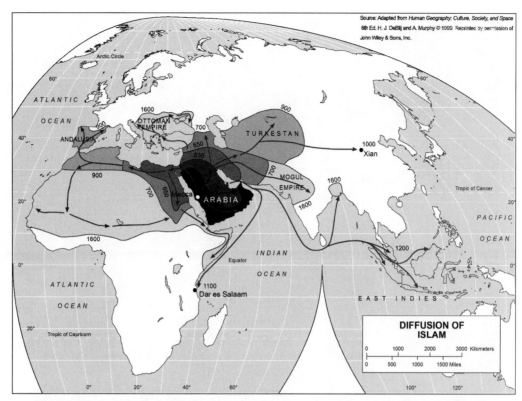

Source: Adapted from *Human Geography: Culture, Society, and Space* 6th Ed. H. J. DeBlij and A. Murphy © 1999. Reprinted by permission of John Wiley & Sons, Inc.

Figure 3.6 The spread of Islam from its origin in Mecca shows the process of contagious diffusion.

persons. Third, the same can be said for the industries in larger cities: They also tend to be more diverse and more able and willing to adopt new technologies and practices.

A classic example of hierarchical diffusion is the spread of radio broadcasting in the "Roaring 20s." From an initial set of cities (Pittsburgh, Detroit, Los Angeles, Seattle, and Oklahoma City) in 1920, radio diffused to a total of 126 small, medium, and large cities by 1924. In this case, the limiting factor was the need for a large enough audience within a limited broadcasting range to make it worthwhile to invest in transmission equipment and a tower. Half a century later, the musical genre of "punk rock" diffused hierarchically from its breeding grounds in New York and London to the next set of cities such as Cleveland and Los Angeles in the United States, and Belfast and Manchester in the United Kingdom. The hierarchical diffusion of punk rock in the 1970s relied on a different mechanism than the diffusion of radio did in the 1920s. Trendsetting musicians including Iggy Pop, Lou Reed, David Bowie, The New York Dolls, The Ramones, The Clash, and The Sex Pistols were attracted to cosmopolitan cities such as New York and London (Figure 3.7). They traveled frequently between New York and London, cross-fertilizing new music, and they found a market for their avant-garde music in these cosmopolitan cities.

It can be difficult to disentangle contagious and hierarchical diffusion because both are usually at work in any real situation. One indicator of which diffusion process is dominant is the extent to which the innovation skips over large areas in jumping from city to city (hierarchical) versus the extent to which it spreads from place to place like a wave (contagious). Also, to qualify as hierarchical diffusion, larger cities should have a disproportionately higher number of cases than do

Figure 3.7 The Ramones perform at the Bottom Line in New York City in May of 1976.

smaller cities; that is, they should have a higher adoption rate *per person*. If a city of 1,000,000 people had only 10 times as many cases as a city of 100,000 people, there would be no evidence of hierarchical diffusion.

Above and beyond the contagious and hierarchical effects, the spatial pattern of diffusion is influenced by **barriers to diffusion**. These barriers can be physical in nature, such as rivers, oceans, lakes, and mountain ranges; or they can be cultural. Language barriers thwart the easy flow of ideas and fads from the United States and English-speaking Canada to French Canadians in Québec. Similarly, a political boundary can impede or slow down the dissemination of disease. Economic factors play a role if people in a certain place cannot afford to purchase a new commodity.

Cultural and social factors can also *facilitate* diffusion. Geographically varying acceptance of gay lifestyles and differing intravenous drug-use rates influence the diffusion of the AIDS epidemic in the United States. On a global scale, Thailand, with an exploitative but legal prostitution industry (so-called sex tourism), has a high AIDS rate, whereas China, with more conservative attitudes toward sex and less contact with the West, has a lower rate.

The purely spatial model of diffusion has been criticized by some geographers. These critics talk about **biased innovations** that diffuse according to social context rather than spatial context. Biased innovations are less accessible to people of a certain gender, class, ethnicity, or age, or less appropriate for them. Many people simply cannot afford expensive innovations and are denied loans to purchase them, even if the products would help them to be more productive (e.g., computers, chemical fertilizers for farming, anti-HIV drug "cocktail"). Others lack the necessary education, which in turn can be gender based or class based. In some countries, girls lag 20 to 30 percent behind boys in school enrollment, and poor children in some countries are taken out of school and put to work. In some countries, women are denied access to normal channels of information, and the elderly have low literacy rates. The concept of biased innovations can be extended to diseases that strike different groups of people unequally.

This chapter asks you to look for evidence of contagious and hierarchical effects in the spread of AIDS in the United States. What were the early origins of the epidemic? What paths did it follow? Do there appear to be any barriers to diffusion of the epidemic? Understanding the geographic spread of this disease will help to plan for its effects and to predict (and hopefully dampen) the course of future epidemics.

▶ *CASE STUDY*

TRACKING THE AIDS EPIDEMIC IN THE UNITED STATES

GOAL

To see how ideas, behavior, products, technology, and disease spread through time and across space as illustrated by the spread of AIDS in the United States.

LEARNING OUTCOMES

After completing the chapter, you will be able to:

- Define and give examples of hierarchical diffusion.
- Define and give examples of contagious diffusion.
- Interpret a scatter diagram.
- Interpret animated maps that change over time.
- Calculate cumulative totals and make a cumulative graph.
- Describe the diffusion of AIDS in the United States.

SPECIAL MATERIALS NEEDED

- Computer with high-speed Internet access and a recent release of a Web browser. If using the Student Companion Site with the printed book, click on *Tech Support* for system requirements and technical support. (If using the e-book in WileyPlus, click on *Help* for details about the system requirements.)

BACKGROUND

You may never have considered geography and the medical sciences to be related, but in fact they have an old partnership. In particular, the subfield of *epidemiology* is the study of how disease spreads. Geographers have long considered the spread or diffusion of phenomena across space.

AIDS remains a major health concern around the world. It is estimated that 30 to 40 million people have died from the disease, including over 2 million in 2007. Another 33 million are currently infected with HIV/AIDS, of whom 2 million are children. In fact, nearly 1 percent of all adults ages 15 to 49 in the world are living with HIV, including 0.6 percent of Americans and 0.4 percent of Canadians. About 2.7 million people contract HIV each year, or about 7,400 per day. Globally, half of all people infected with HIV are women. About 95 percent of new infections occur in less-developed countries. More than 16 million children have been orphaned by AIDS worldwide. Another 4 million people will likely die of AIDS in the next two years.

Acquired immunodeficiency syndrome (AIDS) is caused by the human immunodeficiency virus (HIV). HIV is a retrovirus that attacks T4 lymphocytes, white blood cells that are an integral part of the body's immune system. People with AIDS usually die of opportunistic diseases such as pneumonia, tuberculosis, and certain forms of cancer. Opportunistic diseases use the opportunity of a depleted immune system to take hold. Until the recent introduction of potent and expensive new drugs called *protease inhibitors*, AIDS was usually fatal within 10 years. In much of the developing world, however, these drugs are too expensive or unavailable.

HIV is transmitted via bodily fluids. Because of a very long incubation period (time between infection and appearance of distinctive symptoms), the HIV virus spreads undetected for many years, resulting in seeding for a worldwide AIDS pandemic. In the United States, homosexual males and intravenous drug users are among those most commonly infected. Infants born to women infected with HIV and people who received blood transfusions before blood was screened for HIV also have disproportionately high infection rates.

The origins of HIV have been traced to Africa, but how this disease originated remains unknown. Two strains of HIV have been co-circulating in Africa, HIV-1 originating in East-Central Africa and HIV-2 in West Africa. Virologists did not identify HIV-1 and HIV-2 until 1982 and 1985, respectively. Simian immunodeficiency viruses (SIVs) found in wild monkey populations in Africa bear similarities to HIV, particularly HIV-2. The occurrence of HIV-2 is also highly correlated with the habitat of the sooty mangabey, the monkey with the closely related SIV. The source of HIV-1 has been more difficult to identify, but many point to a related SIV in chimpanzees as the most probable source. The earliest documented HIV-1 infection is a man in Kinshasa, Congo, in 1959. Researchers measuring the rate of genetic change of HIV believe that current strains evolved from SIVs in about 1931. We do not know how these SIVs passed from monkeys to humans (a process called *zoonosis*), but cross-transmission of blood from animal populations, perhaps by people butchering monkeys for meat, is most likely. A more controversial interpretation has been that polio vaccines administered in the 1950s were made with kidneys from infected chimpanzees and led to the zoonosis from SIV to HIV. Although several researchers still believe this to be a possibility, subsequent testing of the original vaccine found no trace of the virus. The relatively late date of the vaccinations also makes this interpretation less likely.

No matter how the disease spread to humans, it might have remained an isolated event in rural African villages had not rural-to-urban migration and trade routes spread the virus throughout sub-Saharan Africa from its origins in East Africa (HIV-1) and West Africa (HIV-2). AIDS in Africa largely has spread through and relocation diffusion processes. Heterosexual transmission, the dominant mode in Africa, has led to alarming rates of HIV infection—as high as 39 percent of the adult population of Botswana, and 5 million people in South Africa alone.

Several factors have contributed to the African AIDS. First, as a result of postcolonial development patterns (see Chapter 7), many African men looking for jobs have choice but to leave their wives and children behind to live in male-only hostels in mines, plantations, and cities. Prostitution typically thrives in these kinds of situations, and many men inadvertently spread AIDS to their wives or girlfriends on their few trips back home every year. Second, abject poverty, famine, war, and other perils often threaten a much more imminent demise than the delayed risk of contracting AIDS. Many African prostitutes complain of no other means of feeding their starving children. Third, ignorance and misinformation about AIDS and AIDS prevention is

▶ **CASE STUDY** *(continued)*

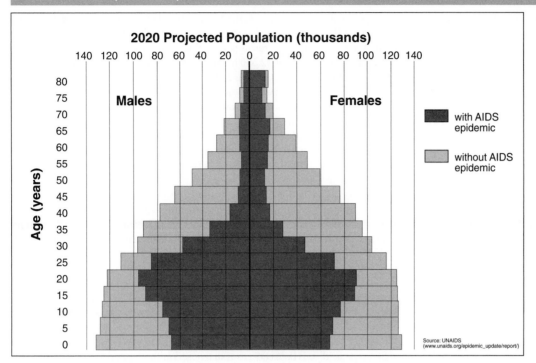

Figure 3.8 Projected population for Botswana in 2020 with and without the AIDS epidemic. Each horizontal bar shows the population (labeled on the vertical bars) for five-year age groups (labeled on the left axis). Notice that by 2020, the 30- to 55-year-old age brackets—composed of today's 15- to 35-year-old young adults—will be decimated, creating a society devoid of middle-aged expertise and leadership and a generation without parents.

rampant, and traditional cultural taboos often enforce a code of silence surrounding the entire issue.

AIDS is having a devastating effect upon the development of many sub-Saharan countries, shortening life expectancies by 30 to 50 percent to as low as 30 years (Figure 3.8). Unlike diseases that tend to target infants and the elderly, AIDS kills sexually active adults in the prime of their lives. This increases the ratio of dependent population (children and elderly) to the labor force while requiring more workers and resources for the health care industry. This double whammy adversely diverts a country's labor force, savings, and resources away from other pressing needs such as agriculture, industry, education, transportation, and services. In Zimbabwe, a country of about 13 million people in southern Africa, more than 780,000 children have been orphaned by the AIDS epidemic. Many are forced to stop their educations and go into migratory labor or prostitution to feed themselves and their younger siblings. Annual basic care and treatment for a person with AIDS can cost as much as two to three times per capita gross domestic product (GDP) in the poorest countries. There will likely be 68 million deaths because of AIDS in the 45 most affected countries between 2000 and 2020, more than five times the death toll of AIDS in the previous two decades in those countries.

Young women are the hardest hit in Africa. In sub-Saharan Africa, 76 percent of young people living with HIV are female. They are four times more apt than men to contract AIDS

during heterosexual sex, they progress to full-blown AIDS faster, and they die sooner. Because of unequal economic and social power relations between the genders, women often cannot control when and with whom they have sex, let alone insist that their partner wear a condom (Figure 3.9).

For the first time, the rate of new infections in sub-Saharan Africa stabilized in 2000. Some countries, such as Uganda and Senegal, have been successful at slowing the diffusion of

Figure 3.9 A Tanzanian woman stricken with AIDS with her son and a nurse.

▶ *CASE STUDY (continued)*

AIDS. Successful anti-AIDS policies include three mutually reinforcing initiatives: (1) limiting the transmission of AIDS by advocating the use of condoms, (2) reducing the transmission of AIDS to newborn children from infected mothers by administering inexpensive ($4) antiviral drugs to the mother just before birth, and (3) most important, empowering women and girls by better education. Educated and economically independent girls and young women are less likely to be coerced into relationships with older men—major carriers of HIV.

From its origins in Africa, HIV spread throughout most of the world via the global network of travel and migration (Figures 3.10 and 3.11; see HIV data for different countries in the *Area and Demographic Data* on the Web site). In the Western Hemisphere, Haiti was one of the first countries with high rates of AIDS. The disease has now spread to all Latin American and Caribbean nations, the United States, and Canada. It is believed that the first case in the United States entered via Haiti. In 1981, the sexual contacts of 40 homosexual men with AIDS were carefully traced. HIV infection from the sexual contacts among this sample of 40 homosexual men produced a geographic trail defining early epicenters of AIDS (Los Angeles, New York City, San Francisco, Miami—all of which have large gay communities).

The number of *new* AIDS cases in the United States peaked in 1993 and then began to decline due to increasing prevention programs. Activists have raised public awareness of AIDS and demanded that governments and pharmaceutical companies devote resources to this issue (Figure 3.12). AIDS deaths (about 12,500 in 2005) have declined, but new HIV infections (over 56,000 in 2006) have remained relatively stable since the early 2000s. Studies in San Francisco have shown, however, that new HIV infections are again increasing as many in the homosexual community again engage in risky sexual behavior. Infection rates for gay men in New York were found to be more than 12 percent, and some 80 percent were unaware they were infected. The most widely cited cause of increases in risky behavior and new HIV infections is the widespread belief that, due to the availability of new drugs, AIDS has changed from being a death sentence to a treatable disease. This has led to a growing complacency about AIDS, a trend that worries many health officials. The number of new AIDS cases diagnosed has remained fairly stable at around 41,000 from 2000 to 2005.

Although the homosexual community and intravenous drug users continue to have the highest HIV/AIDS rates in the United States, AIDS is not restricted to these subpopulations. As seen in Africa and Asia, heterosexual activity can also be a prevalent source for the diffusion of AIDS—34 percent of all HIV/AIDS cases diagnosed in the United States in 2003 were transmitted through heterosexual contact.

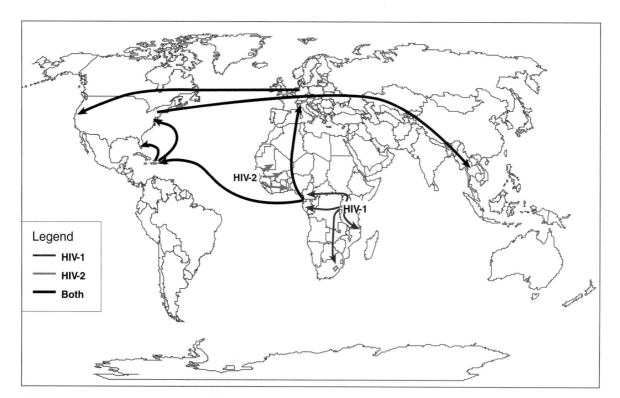

Figure 3.10 Probable early diffusion of AIDS.

Source: Adapted from Shannon, Gary W., Gerald F. Pyle, and Rashid L. Bashshur. 1993. *The Geography of AIDS: Origins and Course of an Epidemic*. New York: Guilford Press.

© 2010 John Wiley & Sons, Inc.

► *CASE STUDY (continued)*

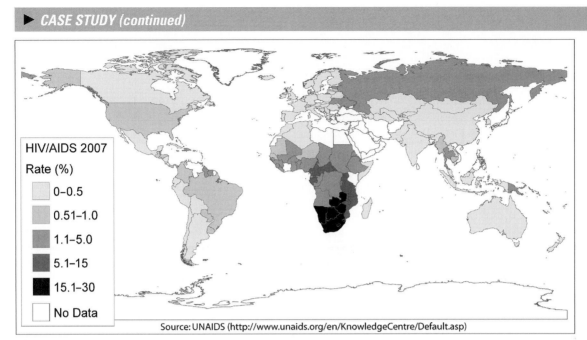

Source: UNAIDS (http://www.unaids.org/en/KnowledgeCentre/Default.asp)

Figure 3.11 World HIV/AIDS rate for adults, 2007.

Figure 3.12 AIDS awareness activists in the United States demand that more resources be allocated to the study of this disease.

Name: _____   Instructor: _____

Tracking the AIDS Epidemic in the United States

► **ACTIVITY 1: MAPPING THE DIFFUSION OF AIDS**

A. To start your activity, click on the *Student Companion site* at www.wiley.com/college/kuby. (For students using WileyPlus, log on to your class Web site, select the *Assignment* tab, locate and click on this assignment, and follow all instructions.)

B. Select this chapter from the drop-down list and then click on *Computerized Chapter Activities*.

C. Click on *Activity 1: Mapping the Diffusion of AIDS*.

On the map of the United States, you can visualize the diffusion of the AIDS epidemic across the country by changing the year with the slider bar below the map. You will be mapping the rate of AIDS cases per 100,000 population reported from 1986 to 2003, an 18-year span. Each metropolitan area appears on the map when it exceeds the threshold of 100 cases per 100,000 people. All metro areas are highlighted with a black diamond in the first year they appear and then convert to a blue square for subsequent years. Metro area names can be identified by "mousing over" the black diamonds in the year they appear. Notice that for the first year, 1986, only the metro areas of New York and San Francisco appear. They were the only two metro areas with more than 100 AIDS cases per 100,000 people in that year.

At any time, you can click on the *Population* icon to turn on a graduated circle map of metropolitan area populations, in green. You may also click on *AIDS Rate/100,000 People* to see graduated circles in red that change from year to year as the AIDS rate of each metro area changes.

You need to consider many geographical factors as you study the maps and graphs of the spread of AIDS in the United States. First, the most vulnerable populations (homosexuals and intravenous drug users) are not equally distributed throughout the United States but tend to be more prevalent in certain kinds of locations. Second, as you saw in Chapter 2, regional cultures differ across the United States. Third, cultural differences can be related to the size of a place. Fourth, you must consider the amount and types of movement of people between the initial source regions and secondary places, keeping in mind that once AIDS has spread to a new place, the new place becomes a potential source region. Unfortunately, the data tell us only where AIDS appears, not which places infected which other places.

D. With the entire U.S. map visible, slide the bar back and forth to see the diffusion through U.S. metro areas across the 18-year time span.

E. Click on *Top 15 Metro Regions*. The boundaries of the 15 most populous metropolitan regions in the United States in 1990 (see box) are highlighted in red. See whether there is a relationship between when a metro area passes the 100-cases-per-100,000-people level and whether it is in one of the largest metropolitan regions of the urban hierarchy. Please note: it is sometimes hard to tell whether certain cities fall within a Top

© 2010 John Wiley & Sons, Inc.

15 metro region because they lie very near the CMSA boundary. If you are not sure if the black diamond is in a metro region, try going to the following year when the large black diamond will change to a smaller blue square—the smaller symbol will make it easier to determine which side of the boundary the city is on.

As each metro area appears, determine whether it is within one of the 15 largest metropolitan regions.

Metropolitan areas are functional regions defined and ranked by the U.S. Census Bureau. They are composed of a central "downtown" or "nucleus" county plus all surrounding nonagricultural counties that are connected to the nucleus via intercounty commuting patterns. Cities such as Atlanta that have only one central nucleus are defined as a standard metropolitan statistical area (MSA). Sometimes metropolitan areas overlap with each other and merge together. The Census Bureau recognizes these cases by defining *consolidated metropolitan statistical areas* (CMSAs) that are made up of smaller component metro areas called *primary metropolitan statistical areas* (PMSAs). For instance, the New York CMSA in 1990 was made up of 15 PMSAs stretching from the Monmouth–Ocean, NJ, PMSA to the New Haven, CT, PMSA (see Chapter 10 for more information about census-defined metropolitan areas).

The Top 15 layer shows MSA or CMSA boundaries (which we call *metropolitan regions*), and the dots that appear on the map represent the central cities of MSAs or PMSAs (which we call *metro areas*). Boundaries for 1990 are shown because they are most representative of conditions during the crucial early stages of diffusion.

1.1. How many metro areas of each population level are *added* to your map in *each* year? (The first two rows are already completed to guide you.)

Year	Number of *New* Metro Areas Appearing on Map *within* the Top 15	Number of *New* Metro Areas Appearing on Map *not within* the Top 15	Total Number of *New* Metro Areas Appearing on Map (add the two columns to the left)
1986	2	0	2
1987	1	0	1
1988			
1989			
1990			
1991			
1992			
1993			
1994			
1995			
1996			
1997			
1998			
1999			
2000			
2001			
2002			
2003			

1.2. In the table on the previous page, does the sequence of small and large metro areas over time provide evidence for hierarchical effects in the diffusion of AIDS? Explain.

1.3. Miami, Florida, had a 1986 population of 1,769,500. Seattle, Washington, had a 1986 population of 1,751,100. Seattle crossed the 100-per-100,000 threshold in 1991; Miami did so in 1988. Why did Miami have such a high early rate of AIDS? (*Hint*: Refer to Figure 3.10.)

1.4. San Francisco, California, had a 1986 population of 1,588,000. San Jose, California, had a 1986 population of 1,401,600. Both are part of the Bay Area CMSA (ranked #5). San Jose crossed the 100-per-100,000 threshold in 1993, and San Francisco did so in 1986. Why did San Francisco have such a high early rate of AIDS?

1.5. Go back to the national map and move the time slider slowly back and forth between 1985 and 2003. Do you see any particular barriers blocking AIDS diffusion or pathways promoting it?

1.6. In Question 1.1, you should have found several metro areas not within the Top 15 that appeared on the map between 1986 and 1990. Go back to the national map and identify them and write their names here.

1.7. At first glance, it might seem that these smaller metro areas with early high rates of AIDS do not fit the hierarchical diffusion pattern of big cities first and small cities later. What is it about the locations of the metro areas in Question 1.6 that might explain their earlier-than-expected AIDS outbreaks? (Going back to look at Figure 3.5 might help you.)

F. When you have finished the activity, proceed to *Activity 2* to continue. Otherwise, close all browser windows.

Name: _____   Instructor: _____

Tracking the AIDS Epidemic in the United States

► ACTIVITY 2: AIDS RATES AND DISTANCE FROM INITIAL CENTERS

AIDS diffusion prior to 1986 is not well documented, but we know that concentrations of reported AIDS cases in the early 1980s were in New York, San Francisco, and Miami, as well as Los Angeles, Houston, and Denver. Here we examine the relationship between the AIDS rate and distance from three regional source cities: New York, Miami, and San Francisco. Select the metro area that is closest to your college or that is assigned by your instructor and answer questions about the relationships you see.

A. To start your activity, click on the *Student Companion Site* at www.wiley.com/college/kuby. (For students using WileyPlus, log on to your class Web site, select the *Assignment* tab, locate and click on this assignment, and follow all instructions.)

B. Select this chapter from the drop-down list and then click on *Computerized Chapter Activities*.

C. Click on *Activity 2: AIDS Rate and the Distance from Initial Centers.*

D. Click on the metro area you wish to examine: *New York, San Francisco,* or *Miami.*

► DISTANCE FROM THE INITIAL CENTERS

You can now see a scatter diagram that plots the AIDS rate in 1986 against distance from New York City (or Miami or San Francisco, depending on your choice) for 46 nearby metropolitan areas. A *scatter diagram* depicts the relationship between two variables. One variable (distance) is measured on the x-axis (horizontal), and another (AIDS rate) is measured on the y-axis (vertical). The placement of the dots tells you the x and y values for the place in question (see Figure 3.13). As you move the cursor around, red crosshairs that move along the x- and y-axes show you the x and y values of the tip of the cursor arrow. Try "mousing over" any of the dots to see a temporary window with the name of the metro area the dot represents, the population, and the distance from the source city (x) and AIDS rate (y) for that metro area. The scatter diagram is a "scatter" of these dots, which show groupings or trends in the relationship between the two variables. Note that the source city (New York), at distance $= 0$, is on the y-axis.

A best-fitting, smoothed blue curve through this scatterplot shows the general trend in the relationship between the AIDS rate and distance. A horizontal red line shows the 100-AIDS-cases-per-100,000-population threshold above which metro areas appeared on the map in Activity 1.

E. Slowly move the slider to the right to see the graph interactively change over an 18-year time period. Pay attention to how the graph changes, particularly the line of best fit.

© 2010 John Wiley & Sons, Inc.

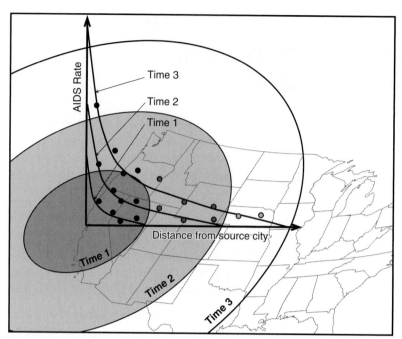

Figure 3.13 The graph shows the typical downward-sloping scatterplot of AIDS rates versus distance from a source node (in this case, San Francisco) and the associated line of best fit. The graph is superimposed over a diagram of contagious diffusion spreading like a wave (which is overlaid on a map of the United States). As time increases, more cities become adopters (or cross the threshold of AIDS rates) at farther distances.

2.1. Look at changes in the *height* of the curve. What has happened to the rate of AIDS for most of these metro areas over the 18-year interval?

2.2. Using either New York or Miami (not San Francisco), move the slider all the way to the right-hand side so that the graph stops at 2003.

(a) What is the relationship between the rate of AIDS and distance from your initial source metro area in 2003?

(b) Does the graph provide evidence of spatially contagious diffusion?

(c) How much scatter is there around your best-fitting curve?

2.3. Metro areas that fall farthest from the best-fitting curve are termed *outliers* because they deviate from the general trend. Click on the outliers in the graph to see their names and populations. What factors might explain why some metro areas have a much higher AIDS rate than expected given their distance from New York (or Miami or San Francisco) while others are far below the trend? You could go back and look at the population layer on the diffusion map in Activity 1 to help answer this question.

F. When you have finished the activity, proceed to *Activity 3* to continue. Otherwise, close all browser windows.

Name: ———————————————— Instructor: ————————————————

Tracking the AIDS Epidemic in the United States

▶ **ACTIVITY 3: *S*-CURVES**

In most diffusion processes, the number of cases follows an S-shaped curve (Figure 3.2). Growth is usually slow at first because only a few people and places adopt the new idea or catch the new disease. Growth then accelerates as the idea or disease spreads rapidly. Finally, growth slows down again as the susceptible population approaches the saturation point. In Activity 3 you will make one S-curve by hand and look at others on your computer screen to see how well AIDS diffusion fits the model.

A. Return to Question 1.1 in Activity 1 and copy the last column into the middle column of the table below.

Year	Number of New Metro Areas Added Each Year	Cumulative Number of Metro Areas
1986	2	2
1987	1	3
1988		
1989		
1990		
1991		
1992		
1993		
1994		
1995		
1996		
1997		
1998		
1999		
2000		
2001		
2002		
2003		

B. In the last column, calculate the cumulative number of metro areas that have passed the 100-cases-per-100,000-persons threshold for each year. The cumulative number is the running total of the added metro areas each year. The first two entries are already filled in to get you on the right track.

C. On the following graph paper, plot the cumulative number of metro areas surpassing the AIDS threshold for each year. The *y*-axis of the graph goes to 100. Note that 98 metro areas with a population over 500,000 people were included in this study.

© 2010 John Wiley & Sons, Inc.

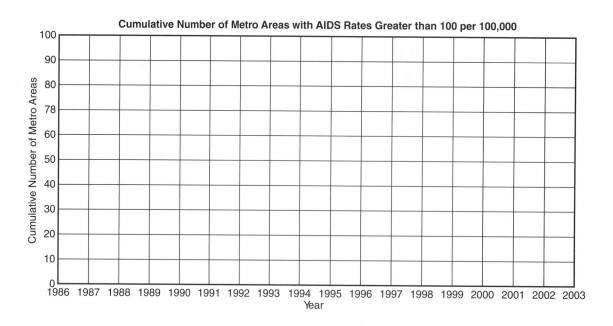

Cumulative Number of Metro Areas with AIDS Rates Greater than 100 per 100,000

3.1. Figure 3.2 (page 64) shows transition points on the diffusion S-curve that define three stages: innovators, majority adopters, and laggards (late adopters). Based on the shape of your graph in Step C, what year marks the end of the innovator stage and beginning of the majority adopter stage?

3.2. Based on the shape of your graph in Step C, in which year (if any) did the majority adopter stage end and the laggard stage begin? Why did you pick this year (or why did you not pick any)?

D. To start your activity, click on the *Student Companion Site* at www.wiley.com/college/kuby. (For students using WileyPlus, log on to your class Web site, select the *Assignment* tab, locate and click on this assignment, and follow all instructions.)

E. Select this chapter from the drop-down list and then click on *Computerized Chapter Activities.*

F. Click on *Activity 3: S-Curves.*

G. A map of the United States will be visible, showing all metropolitan areas with populations over 500,000. "Mouse over" any metro area to see its name and click on any metro area to see its S-curve. The variable on the y-axis is different than in the graph you just made by hand. The graph on the screen shows the actual AIDS rate in the metro area. As such, it is possible for the AIDS rate to go down as AIDS patients die. If the rate is seen to be increasing, it means that new cases are increasing even faster than AIDS patients are dying.

H. Click on your metro area or the one closest to where you live.

The Centers for Disease Control, which collects the data graphed here, updated the definition of AIDS several times as more was learned about the disease. The greatest change began with the 1993 data, when the 23 clinical conditions in the previous definition were extended to include HIV-infected persons with CD4+ T-lymphocyte counts of less than 200 cells/μL or a CD4+ percentage of less than 14 (a measure of a compromised immune system), and persons diagnosed with pulmonary tuberculosis, recurrent pneumonia, and invasive cervical cancer (three opportunistic diseases seen among AIDS patients). Other changes were implemented in 1987 and 1994. State reporting requirements have also varied across this time period, and the CDC estimates that reporting of AIDS cases in the United States is now more than 85 percent complete.

3.3. Based on the shape of your metro area's graph, in which year did the transition from innovator to majority adopter occur?

3.4. Has the AIDS rate for your metro area leveled off (entered into laggard stage) or even declined? If so, when?

I. Click *Print.*

J. When you have finished, close all browser windows.

▶ DEFINITIONS OF KEY TERMS

Barriers to Diffusion Physical, political, cultural, or economic impediments to diffusion.

Biased Innovations Innovations (or diseases) that are less (or more) accessible to people of a certain gender, class, age, or ethnicity. The biased innovation diffusion theory emphasizes social context in addition to spatial context.

Contagious Effects Diffusion of a disease, cultural trait, idea, or innovation that spreads outward from a node or epicenter in wavelike fashion. Spatially contagious diffusion emphasizes the frictional force of distance in explaining the spread of things in time and space.

Expansion Diffusion A process in which the items being diffused remain and often intensify in the origin area as new areas are being affected (i.e., the items diffuse from person to person).

Hierarchical Effects Diffusion of a disease, cultural trait, idea, or innovation from larger to smaller places, leaping over nearby but small places in the early stages. Hierarchical diffusion emphasizes the size distribution of urban places (i.e., the urban hierarchy) in explaining the spread of things over time and space.

Relocation Diffusion A process in which items being diffused leave the originating areas as they move to new areas (i.e., the items diffuse with people migrating).

Spatial Diffusion The spread of some phenomenon over space and through time from a limited number of origins.

Urban Hierarchy A system of cities consisting of various levels with few cities at the top level and increasingly more settlements on each lower level. The position of a city within the hierarchy is determined by the types of central place functions it provides.

▶ FURTHER READINGS

Cliff, A. D., and M. R. Smallman-Raynor. 1992. The AIDS Pandemic: Global Geographical Patterns and Local Spatial Processes. *Geographical Journal* 158(2):182–197.

Cohen, Jon. 1999. AIDS Virus Traced to Chimp Subspecies. *Science* 283:772–773.

Comer, Jonathan C., and Thomas A. Wikle. 2008. Worldwide Diffusion of the Cellular Telephone, 1995–2005. *Professional Geographer* 60(2):252–269.

Crimp, D. (ed.). 1988. *AIDS: Cultural Analysis, Cultural Criticism*. Cambridge, MA: MIT Press.

Gladwell, Malcolm. 1997. The Coolhunt. *The New Yorker* (March 17):76–88.

Gould, Peter. 1969. *Spatial Diffusion*. Resource Paper No. 4, Commission on College Geography. Washington, DC: Association of American Geographers.

Gould, Peter. 1993. *The Slow Plague: A Geography of the AIDS Pandemic*. Cambridge, MA: Blackwell.

Hagerstrand, Torsten. 1967. *Innovation Diffusion as a Spatial Process*. Chicago: University of Chicago Press.

Hillis, David M. 2000. How to Resolve the Debate on the Origin of AIDS. *Science* 289:1877–1878.

Karon, J. M., P. L. Fleming, R. W. Steketee, and K. M. DeCock. 2001. HIV in the United States at the Turn of the Century: An Epidemic in Transition. *American Journal of Public Health* 91:1060–1068.

Koch, Tom. 2005. *Cartographies of Disease: Maps, Mapping, and Medicine*. Redlands, CA: ESRI Press.

Lamptey, Peter R., Jami L. Johnson, and Marya Khan. 2006. The Global Challenge of HIV and AIDS. *Population Bulletin* 61(1):1–24.

Lamptey, Peter, Merywen Wigley, Danra Carr, and Yvette Collymore. 2001. Facing the HIV/AIDS Pandemic. *Population Bulletin* 57(3):3–39.

McGeary, Johanna. 2001. Death Stalks a Continent. *Time* (Feb. 12):36–54. See also photo essay by James Nachtwey-Magnum, Crimes Against Humanity, pp. 26–35 in the same issue.

Morrill, Richard, Gary L. Gaile, and Grant Ian Thrall. 1988. *Spatial Diffusion*. Newbury Park, CA: Sage.

Nina, Siu-Ngam Lam, Ming Fan, and Kam-biu Liu. 1996. Spatial-Temporal Spread of the AIDS Epidemic, 1982–1990: A Correlogram Analysis of Four Regions of the United States. *Geographical Analysis* 28:93–107.

Oppong, Joseph R. 1998. A Vulnerability Interpretation of the Geography of HIV/AIDS in Ghana, 1986–1995. *Professional Geographer* 50:437–448.

Patton, C. 1990. *Inventing AIDS*. London: Routledge.

Pyle, Gerald F., and William A. Gross. 1997. The Diffusion of HIV/AIDS and HIV Infection in an Archetypal Textile County. *Applied Geographic Studies* 1:63–81.

Shannon, Gary W., Gerald F. Pyle, and Rashid L. Bashshur. 1991. *The Geography of AIDS: Origins and Course of an Epidemic*. New York: Guilford.

The Economist. 2000. A Turning Point for AIDS? (July 15):77–79.

Yapa, Lakshman. 1996. Innovation Diffusion and Paradigms of Development, pp. 230–272 in *Concepts in Human Geography*, Carville Earle, Kent Mathewson, and Martin S. Kenzer (eds.). London: Rowman & Littlefield.

Zhu, Tuofu, Bette K. Korber, Andre J. Nahmias, Edward Hooper, Paul M. Sharp, and David D. Ho. 1998. An African HIV-1 Sequence from 1959 and Implications for the Origin of the Epidemic. *Nature* 391:594–597.

▶ WEB RESOURCES

AIDS Map: www.aidsmap.com
The AIDS Memorial Quilt: www.aidsquilt.org
Body Health Resources Corporation. *The Body*: www.thebody.com/index.shtml (Very informative for those with AIDS)
Center for AIDS Prevention Studies: www.caps.ucsf.edu
Centers for Disease Control. *National Prevention Information Network*: www.cdcnpin.org/scripts/index.asp
Centers for Disease Control and Prevention. *Discussion of HIV/AIDS Prevention*: www.cdc.gov/hiv/pubs/mmwr.htm
Eberstadt, Nicholas. 2002. The Future of AIDS. *Foreign Affairs* (Nov./Dec.): www.foreignaffairs.org/20021101faessay9990/nicholas-eberstadt/the-future-of-aids.html
Fuel Cell Today. Surveys: www.fuelcelltoday.com
MAP Secretariat, U.S. Census Bureau. Monitoring the AIDS Pandemic (MAP): www.mapnetwork.org
National Center for Health Statistics. *Faststats A to Z: AIDS/HIV*: www.cdc.gov/nchs/fastats/aids-hiv.htm
Population Reference Bureau. *HIV/AIDS Focus Area*: www.prb.org
United Nations. *AIDS Epidemic Update 2004*: www.unaids.org/wad2004/report_pdf.html
United Nations. UNAIDS. *Joint United Nations Programme on HIV/AIDS*: www.unaids.org
United Nations. UNAIDS 2008 Report on the Global AIDS Epidemic: www.unaids.org/en/KnowledgeCentre/HIVData/GlobalReport/2008/2008_Global_report.asp
World Bank. *HIV/AIDS*: www1.worldbank.org/hiv_aids
World Health Organization: www.who.int/health-topics/hiv.htm (especially the fact sheet on Women and HIV/AIDS)

▶ ITEMS TO HAND IN

Activity 1: • Answers to Questions 1.1–1.7, or answer all questions your instructor created in your WileyPlus assignments.
Activity 2: • Answers to Questions 2.1–2.3, or answer all questions your instructor created in your WileyPlus assignments.
Activity 3: • Answers to Questions 3.1–3.4, or answer all questions your instructor created in your WileyPlus assignments.

CHAPTER 4

Newton's First Law of Migration: The Gravity Model

▶ INTRODUCTION

Places are connected with one another at the local, regional, and global scales through systems of **spatial interactions**. These interactions involve movements of ideas, information, money, products, and people. **Migration**, the movement of people, is defined as a permanent change in residence to outside of one's community of origin. Conceptually, someone who moves to a new home within his or her community but does not have to change his or her place of work, shop in new stores, find new doctors, and establish new friendships is considered a local mover but not a migrant. Officially, migration is defined as crossing an administrative boundary, such as between counties or states. Tourists, temporary residents, and seasonal workers may play important roles in some places, but they are not considered migrants if they don't intend to stay at least one year. There is, of course, some gray area regarding how far one has to move and how long one has to stay to be considered a migrant, but that is just one of the factors that makes the study of migration so fascinating.

Migration can occur at many spatial scales, including rural-to-urban movements from hinterlands to cities (Figure 4.1), urban-to-urban moves between regions, and global migration between countries. The size, composition, and spatial organization of migration flows tell us a great deal about the places involved. In that people tend to move from less-desirable places toward more-desirable places, the system of migration flows provides clues about how places stack up relative to one another. Place desirability can result from economic factors such as job availability, high wages, and affordable housing and from noneconomic considerations such as a favorable climate, clean air, low crime rates, nearness to friends and relatives, and the absence of war and environmental disaster.

Geographers sometimes differentiate between migration as a within-country move and **immigration** as a move across international borders. Whereas internal movements rise and fall with the ebb and flow of regional and national economies, international movements have steadily grown due to population pressure in some less-developed countries (see Chapter 7), economic globalization (see Chapter 8), and growing income differences between rich and poor countries, civil wars, and natural disasters. Both the United States and Canada are nations built on immigration. Apart from Native Americans (who most believe also migrated to North America

Figure 4.1 Rural-to-urban migrants at a train station in China.

from Asia several millennia ago), both countries were founded and populated by immigrants. Early colonial immigrants were European settlers and African slaves. Beginning in the 1850s, immigration increased rapidly (Figure 4.2). Immigration in the second half of the 1800s came mainly from northern and western Europe for three reasons. First, Great Britain, France, Sweden, and the Netherlands were countries with the original colonial outposts on the continent, so migration streams with those places were well developed. Second, Northwest Europe industrialized earlier than the rest of the world, and as a result, not only did their populations grow rapidly but mechanization in agriculture created excess labor (see Chapter 5). While many migrated from rural areas to cities in their home countries, many others emigrated to America for land and opportunity. Third, Northern Europeans were racially and culturally similar to nineteenth-century Americans and so were more accepted than people of different religions, race, ethnicities, and lifestyles.

From the early twentieth-century until the Great Depression of the 1930s, immigration rates remained high but the source areas shifted more toward eastern and southern Europe, because by then these places were transitioning to an industrial economy and population pressure was growing. The influx of Catholics and Orthodox Christians from southern Europe, often with darker skin complexion, led to immigration laws in 1921 and 1924 that for the first time restricted the numbers of immigrants from European countries. English and Dutch immigrants could continue to enter the United States easily, whereas Italians and Greeks were more restricted. In fact, racial and ethnic discrimination had been institutionalized in U.S. immigration law since 1882 when the United States banned immigration from China. As Figure 4.2 shows, there was hardly any immigration from Asia, Africa, and Latin America from 1850 to 1940, but in 1965, the United States finally eliminated country quotas and began to apply hemispheric quotas more fairly. Since then, immigration from Latin America has exploded, with immigration from Asia and, to a lesser extent Africa, also growing rapidly.

In 2009, an estimated 200 million people lived outside their countries of birth. International movements have profound impacts for sending and receiving countries. For sending countries, immigration tends to relieve pressure from unemployment and generate substantial **remittances**—money immigrants send home to support their families. In 2008, immigrants around the world transferred an estimated $337 billion to their home countries. Returning migrants are often agents of modernization for their home communities. For most receiving countries, immigration provides

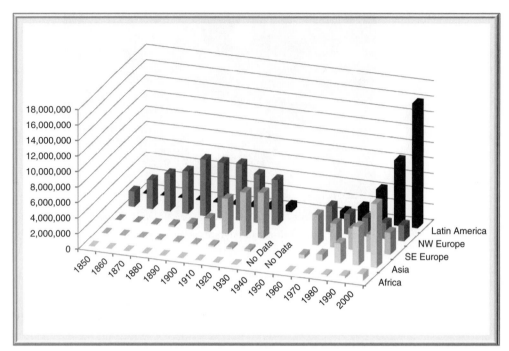

Figure 4.2 This graph shows the region of birth for the foreign-born population in the United States since 1850. The trend clearly shows that immigrants (who are recorded as foreign born in the U.S. Census) came early from northwestern Europe, but by the early 20th century, this shifted to southeastern Europe. In recent decades Latin America and Asia have grown to be major immigrant origin regions.
Source: U.S. Census Bureau

a flexible labor force to support aging populations and increases cultural diversity; but it strains social, educational, and health services in some places.

Globally, some of the largest immigration flows are from Latin America (particularly Mexico) to the United States, and from Africa and the Middle East to Western Europe. Other sizeable immigration flows are from Southeast Asia and the Philippines to oil-producing countries on the Arabian Peninsula, and from countries across southern Africa into their wealthier neighbor, the Republic of South Africa. Much of this immigration is undertaken illegally, meaning that the migrants often do not have official permission to enter the destination country and seek employment. Countries regulate this movement with different policies, from sponsored guest worker programs that have long been in effect in Germany, to increasing attempts to stop illegal immigration, as in the United States. It is estimated that 450,000 Mexicans enter the United States each year (Figure 4.3). Many more are stopped and sent back, plus many others attempt entry from countries other than Mexico. In response, the United States is constructing a steel wall along much of the U.S.-Mexican border. The wall has raised concerns among environmentalists, who worry that it will hinder flows of wildlife, and among many others who see it as an insult from the United States to a friendly neighboring country.

The increase in undocumented Mexican migration to the United States in recent years is in large part a response to a global economic system that has strongly integrated flow of capital and goods between the two countries (see Chapter 8), but continues to inhibit the flow of labor. Rural population growth and mechanization of agriculture have forced large numbers of farmers from the Mexican countryside to seek jobs elsewhere, but employment in Mexican cities has not grown rapidly enough to absorb

Figure 4.3 A Mexican immigrant jumping the fence into the United States in Nogales, Arizona. This photo was taken some 100 feet from the new U.S. Immigration border station being constructed in the early 1990s. Since then, a large steel wall has been put up to replace the chain link fence.

the displaced people. The result is immigration out of desperation. Immigrants seek some way to support themselves and their families by illegally crossing into the United States, where many employers are more than willing to hire them for wages that are considered relatively low in the United States but would be high in Mexico. Life for undocumented migrants can be very difficult—there is usually a large fee to pay for guides to cross the border, then constant fear of arrest and deportation, loneliness from the separation from loved ones, culture shock from immersion in a foreign place with a foreign language, and an often hostile reception from some American citizens who resent these newcomers and their different ways in their communities.

Refugees are a special class of immigrant. They are people who were persecuted in their homelands or have a well-founded fear of persecution there on account of race, religion, nationality, membership in a particular social group, or political opinion. The United States and Canada accept refugees from war-torn parts of the world, in part because of their early histories as places of refuge from political and economic persecution in Europe. The Displaced Persons Act of 1948 brought 400,000 Eastern Europeans to the United States, and between 1953 and 1956 another 200,000 refugees arrived from "Iron Curtain" countries. After Fidel Castro took power in Cuba in 1959, more than 400,000 Cubans fled to the United States, many of them settling in south Florida. This "first wave" of Cuban refugees was followed by a "second wave" of 125,000 during the Mariel boatlift of 1980, and a "third wave" who came in response to a 1994 decision by Castro to allow people to leave Cuba on their own crafts. Vietnamese and other Southeast Asian refugees arrived after the war in Vietnam ended in 1975, and more recently, the United States has resettled substantial numbers of refugees from regions of turmoil, including Bosnia, Iraq, Iran, Somalia, Sudan, and Ethiopia. Major refugee flows to Canada originate in Pakistan, Colombia, China, and Sri Lanka.

Migration patterns are the result of millions of individual and household decisions about where to live. For those who move, a combination of push and pull factors triggers the decision to move. **Push factors** can include exorbitant housing costs, growing gridlock, rising crime rates, skyrocketing tax rates, a poor climate, and the

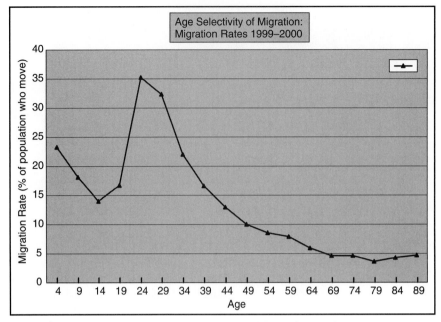

Figure 4.4   Migration rates are highest for young adults in their early 20s.

lack of a satisfying, well-paying job. **Pull factors** can include the promise of a higher-paying job, a pleasant physical setting, the availability of affordable housing, a desirable climate, or the lure of nearby family members. Sometimes a push for some people is a pull for others. Take, for example, closeness to family. Many believe that living near family members provides a valuable and comforting social support system; others see it as claustrophobic, stifling their independence. Similarly, a climate that is too hot and a push for some can be just right and a pull for others. High school taxes can be perceived as desirable for a young family with children but as onerous for a childless single person or an elderly couple. How we perceive various place characteristics and how much weight we attach to them is very much a personal matter.

The effects of migration on places of origin and destination are influenced by a process called **migration selectivity**. Certain individuals are more likely to migrate based on their personal characteristics, including age, education, and other sociodemographic characteristics. Age is the most important factor in influencing whether someone is a migrant or not (Figure 4.4). People are most prone to move during their early adult years between the ages of 18 and 30. The average individual makes approximately one-half of his or her 12 lifetime moves by age 25. During these young adult ages, people leave their parents' home to attend school, join the military, or take a job, leave college to find employment or change jobs, marry, and begin families. All these life-course events are usually associated with changes in residence. Movement rates are also high among young children, who typically have parents in their 20s.

A second migration selectivity factor is education. People with higher levels of education are more likely to make long-distance moves. Getting a college education often means moving to a new city and then returning or moving again upon graduation. In addition, education exposes us to new ideas and people from other places. It also qualifies us for, and provides information about, a wide variety of jobs in many different geographical areas. The selectivity of migration alters the population characteristics of origin and destination places. As a general rule, places

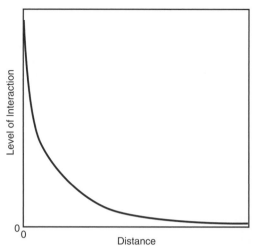

Figure 4.5 Distance decay curve showing decreasing interaction as distance increases.

experiencing net out-migration lose a disproportionate share of their young, well-educated residents while areas of net in-migration gain such individuals. There is a double whammy for places experiencing out-migration. They lose not only population numbers but also their youngest and best-educated residents. Especially troublesome is that this process can snowball, making origins less attractive to future migrants and less capable of retaining their current residents.

People do not move randomly across the landscape. The tendency for migration, or any other form of spatial interaction, to decrease with distance is called **distance decay** (Figure 4.5). Distance exerts more drag or friction on some kinds of moves than upon others and at some times more than others. Before the advent of modern transportation, it was very difficult to overcome distance. Think of the impediment of distance for the mountain men who explored the frontier and the wagon trains bringing settlers to the American West. Only the hardiest and most adventuresome people moved long distances. Today, it is much easier to travel, and the friction of distance has declined significantly. Airline fares are only weakly related to the distance traveled. Similarly, there is little difference in whether an e-mail message is sent 5 meters, 5 blocks, 5 kilometers, or 5,000 kilometers. Despite the declining cost of overcoming space, distance continues to exert an influence on migration because people are far more familiar with nearby than faraway places. Of the 40 million annual changes in residence in the United States, almost 60 percent occur near to home within the county of residence; only about 20 percent involve a move across state lines. People are unlikely to move to faraway places they know little or nothing about.

Distance, however, is not the only factor affecting migration. Migrants tend to move in well-defined channels from specific origins to specific destinations called **migration streams**. Migration streams result from information flows between origins and destinations. Letters, telephone calls, and return visits from earlier migrants communicate opportunity at the potential destination. These pioneer migrants assist newcomers in finding a place to live, getting a new job, and adjusting to a new community. Information about places also comes from newspapers, television, magazines, business contacts, and personal travel. Most people, however, know surprisingly little about the range of potential places to live. Their migration decisions are based on a narrow set of options dictated by first- or secondhand information about what it is like to live there.

Wherever a migration stream develops, a **migration counterstream** of people moving in the opposite direction occurs. Not everyone who migrates—for example, college students—intends to remain permanently at the place of destination. Others are unhappy with the circumstances of their move, their personal situation changes, or they are military or corporate personnel who are reassigned. Divorce might create a return migration. An elderly couple who moved from the North to a Sunbelt retirement community while in their 60s could return home when they are in their 80s in fragile health and in need of family support. Also important to understanding migration counterstreams is the presence of information linking the two places. Once, for whatever reason, the channels of communication are opened and interpersonal relationships are built, movement will occur in both directions, although not necessarily at the same rate.

Migration streams involving faraway places get started in a variety of ways. Large streams connecting New York and New Jersey with Florida arose after World War II with the migration of retirees and snowballed as contact between the two areas grew. Historically strong ties between California and midwestern states began as labor force migration. The stream between Oklahoma and California originated with Depression-era Dust Bowl migrants. The experience of Dust Bowl migrants, eloquently portrayed in Steinbeck's *The Grapes of Wrath*, changed conventional wisdom about migrants from hardy pioneers in search of opportunity to disadvantaged families trying to survive (Figure 4.6).

The most geographically focused migration streams in the United States today are among newcomers to the country who are strongly attracted to immigrant communities or enclaves (see Chapter 12 for a fuller discussion of enclaves). Immigrant communities offer familiar language, food, music, and religious institutions. They also help newcomers to locate all-important housing and jobs. Many immigrants find work in businesses owned by their compatriots, or they establish their own small businesses, providing goods and services to immigrant niche markets.

The internal migration streams of Cuban- and Mexican-born immigrants demonstrate the different conditions under which they migrated to the United States (Figure 4.7). Mexicans are immigrants who, for the most part, moved voluntarily to the United States, largely for economic reasons. Cubans are refugees who were forced

Figure 4.6   A "Dust Bowl" migrant family from Oklahoma recently arrived in California to join the harvest, November 1936.

10 Largest Domestic Migration Streams of Persons Born in Cuba

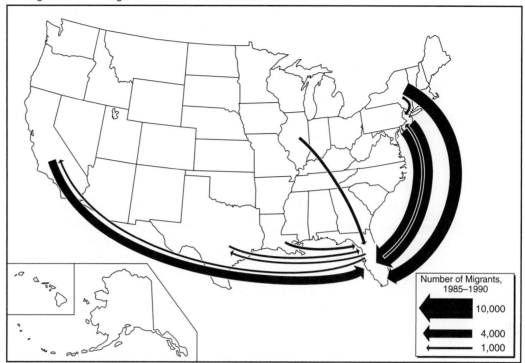

10 Largest Domestic Migration Streams of Persons Born in Mexico

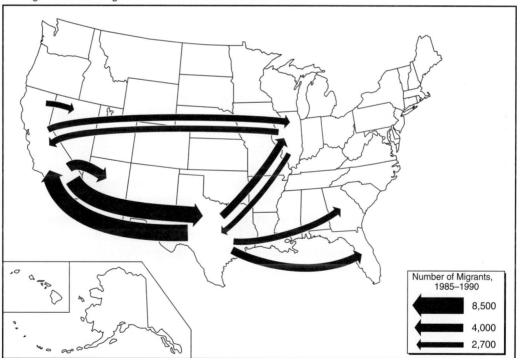

Figure 4.7 Examples of migration streams for two ethnic groups.

Source: 1990 Census of Population, Public Use Microdata Sample (PUMS), 5 Percent Sample. U.S. Census Bureau, Washington, DC.

© 2010 John Wiley & Sons, Inc.

by political crisis to flee their homeland. Even today, 20 or 30 years after their move to the United States, some Cubans continue to see themselves more as exiles hoping to return to Cuba than as immigrants seeking a permanent home and future in the United States. South Florida has emerged as the surrogate homeland for Cuban émigrés. Much political activity is organized around political change and post-communist Cuba, and high value is placed on preserving *cubanidad* or "Cubanness." Cuban migration streams are strongly directed toward Florida; the counterstreams are extremely weak. These uneven flows are redistributing the Cuban population in favor of Florida. The Mexican migration system is quite different. Six of the 10 largest interstate flows interconnect the three largest concentrations of Mexican-born population in California, Texas, and Illinois. Unlike the Cuban flows, the Mexican flows are self-compensating. Streams and counterstreams are about equal in size; thus, very little population redistribution occurs as a result of Mexican internal migration.

Having introduced these key migration concepts, we now shift our focus to the task of predicting migration flows. Being able to predict flows is important in making accurate population projections and in monitoring the health of regional economies and their quality of life. Migration flows are a major determinant of whether a region grows and by how much. Although many population projections simply extrapolate past trends into the future, more detailed systems take account of the geography of migration. A state's economic situation may not change greatly, but if the economy or attractiveness of its major migration partner changes dramatically, the balance between in-migration and out-migration will be affected. Accurate predictions of migration and population growth allow state and regional governments to plan for new schools, roads, public facilities, and programs required to accommodate newcomers. Accurate predictions help places losing population to plan for a shrinking tax base and school-age population.

Geographers use a mathematical formula known as the **gravity model** because it resembles Isaac Newton's formula for the gravitational attraction between any two celestial masses, which you might have learned in physics class. Newton's law has been adapted to social science research for the purpose of estimating the spatial interaction or movement between any two places. Spatial interaction can take the form of trade, transportation, communication, commuting, shopping, or, in the case of this chapter, migration.

The following example will help you to understand the idea behind the gravity model. Figure 4.8 shows the populations of several states and their distance from California. Would you expect California to attract more migrants from North Carolina or from South Carolina? Their distances are about equal, but North Carolina has twice as many inhabitants. All other things being equal, you'd probably expect about two times as many migrants from North Carolina because there are two times more *potential* movers. Next, would you expect more migration to California from Arizona or from Maryland? Their populations are both around 5.3 million, but Maryland is five times farther away. Surely more people will move from Arizona; but probably not five times more, because each additional mile matters less and less. As shown in Figure 4.5, distance decay tends to be nonlinear: steep at first but gradually flattening out. The first 100 miles reduces migration substantially, the second 100 miles less so, and the twentieth 100 miles (i.e., the difference between 1,900 miles and 2,000 miles) hardly matters to people at all.

In the gravity model formula, as in the California example in Figure 4.8, population size and distance are used to explain the interaction flow, I_{ij}, between origin

© 2010 John Wiley & Sons, Inc.

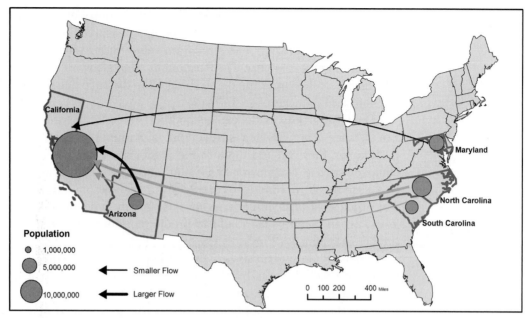

Figure 4.8 Although North Carolina and South Carolina are the same distance from California, we expect more migrants from North Carolina because it is larger. Although Arizona and Maryland have about the same population, we expect more migrants from Arizona because it is closer to California.

i and destination j. Unlike our example, however, the gravity model allows both size and distance to vary simultaneously:

$$I_{ij} = k\frac{P_i P_j}{d_{ij}^{\beta}}$$

where:

I_{ij} = predicted interaction between origin i and destination j

k = a scaling constant

P_i = a measure of size, usually population, for origin i

P_j = a measure of size, usually population, for destination j

d_{ij} = distance between origin i and destination j

β = an exponent that adjusts for the rate of distance decay unique to the type of *interaction* being measured

Let's look at the formula piece by piece. The mass or size variables in the numerator of the fraction will have a positive relationship with spatial interaction. This means that as the population of the state increases, both for origins and destinations, the interaction between them increases. Distance, being in the denominator, will be negatively or inversely related to interaction, meaning interaction decreases as distance increases. Dividing by distance creates a distance decay curve with the shape shown earlier in Figure 4.5.

The other two factors in the formula are constants that are calculated statistically to produce the most realistic estimates (we give them to you in this chapter).

The k factor scales the *relative* levels of interaction between places, so its value depends on the type of interaction being measured: a large value of k could exist for phone calls per year, a medium value for air travelers per year, and a low value for migrants per year. The β exponent affects how steeply interaction declines with distance: the larger the β, the steeper the distance decay effect. For simplicity, we won't use β in this case study.

The basic gravity model can be modified to model all types of spatial interaction. For instance, if geographers suspect that high unemployment rates are a significant push factor, they can add them to the model and test them statistically. A moving company such as Mayflower or a trailer and truck rental company such as U-Haul could use the gravity model to predict future migration patterns in order to choose new office locations. Similarly, airlines use gravity-type models to predict passenger flows, urban planners use them to predict commuting, and retailers use them to predict shopping.

When we designed this activity, we hoped that you would learn not only how the gravity model works but also how to think critically about models. Thinking critically about models means neither blindly accepting their outputs nor completely rejecting the model for not being perfectly true to reality. *Thinking critically* means assessing the strengths and weaknesses of a model, judging where it fits well and where it doesn't, and understanding what has been included in the model and what has been omitted. Certainly, people are different from the atoms and planets studied by physicists. Human actions are not mechanistically controlled by the size of their origins and destinations or the distances between them. In addition, the basic gravity model does not include migration selectivity factors such as age or education level, nor does it incorporate channelized migration streams and counterstreams. Nevertheless, human behavior is fairly predictable when the actions of millions of people are aggregated, and certain general tendencies emerge that are well represented by the gravity model.

After you have used the model to predict migration flows to your state or province in Activity 1, you will learn how to assess the effectiveness of the gravity model using graphs and maps. This will give you an idea of where the model fits well and where it doesn't. Moreover, you can determine which factors in addition to population size and distance could be influencing migration patterns. The failures of the model will reveal to you as much about migration as its successes do, and possibly more. You will learn that your state or province is more interconnected with some states than with others, which in turn can tell you about its economy, history, and culture.

▶ **CASE STUDY**

NEWTON'S FIRST LAW OF MIGRATION

GOAL

To model spatial interaction, in this case migration, using the **gravity model**. You will use the gravity model to predict the number of migrants to your state or province from all other U.S. states or Canadian provinces. The accuracy of the model will be assessed, and **residuals** will be mapped to show where actual migration differs from what the gravity model predicts.

LEARNING OUTCOMES

After completing the chapter, you will be able to:

- Apply principles of spatial interaction to patterns of movement.
- Identify the major source areas for migration to your state.
- Use functions of a spreadsheet.
- Produce and interpret a scatter diagram.
- Discriminate between positive and negative residuals.
- Identify outliers on a scatter diagram.
- Think critically about models in human geography.

SPECIAL MATERIALS NEEDED

- Computer with high-speed Internet access and a recent release of a Web browser. If using the Student Companion Site with the printed book, click on *Tech Support* for system requirements and technical support. (If using the e-book in WileyPlus, click on *Help* for details about the system requirements.)

BACKGROUND

Seeking a new life in a new place has always been a fundamental part of the American dream. High levels of mobility have been linked to settlement of the frontier, an innate restlessness, the drive for change, and an inherent dynamism in American culture. *Geographic mobility*, defined as a move from one

Figure 4.9 This scene of a family packing their belongings in a moving van is a familiar one in the highly mobile United States.

residence to another, is higher in the United States than in Western European countries, where many people have lived in the same area for many generations (Figure 4.9).

Higher-than-average levels of mobility found in the United States, Canada, Australia, and New Zealand suggest that something about the history and culture of these countries encourages movement. One explanation is that they are all high-immigration countries. Immigration from abroad brings people with weak ties to the new place. One of the strongest predictors of whether people move in the future is whether they have moved in the past. Migration begets further migration in the sense that once ties to home are broken, they are easier to break again. A second explanation is that the United States, Canada, Australia, and New Zealand share cultures that value personal freedom above loyalty to any particular group or place. A geographic move is, at its essence, an exercise of such freedom. Finally, in all four countries, land and housing costs are relatively cheap, and liberal government controls on housing codes, land use, and real estate markets make it easy for people to buy and sell homes, and thus to move.

Despite the popular conception that mobility is on the rise and Americans are continually on the move, mobility rates in the United States actually are at a post–World War II low (Figure 4.10). During most of the 1950s and 1960s, 20 percent of the population changed its residence every year. By the beginning of the 1980s, this figure was down to 16 percent. The most recent census figure was 11.9 percent in 2007–2008. The decline in mobility is attributed, in part, to the aging of the population. Older people are far less likely to move than younger ones, and an older population will have lower mobility rates than a younger one has. Even among people in their 20s, however, mobility rates are lower today than they were 50 years ago. One reason is that we have become a nation of homeowners, and people who own their own homes are far less likely to move than renters are. Also, rising labor-force participation among women and the growing number of dual-career households retard mobility because couples must consider the work and family responsibilities of both spouses in deciding to move.

An exception to the overall decline in U.S. mobility was during the mid-1980s, when an upward spike in mobility followed a sharp recession in which unemployment rates were high, inflation skyrocketed, and the housing market slumped. These conditions seriously curtailed the desire and ability to move. When the recession ended and interest rates fell, pent-up demand for movement briefly returned mobility rates to levels of the 1950s and 1960s. Since that unusual period, however, mobility rates have continued to decline. The most recent sharp drop in the 2007–2008 mobility rate reflects the most severe economic downturn since the Great Depression. Mobility rates track economic prosperity, so that in difficult times, people tend to stay put. Even though people may be experiencing economic hardships, at least the place and circumstances they are familiar with often seem better than increased uncertainties associated with migration to a new location.

© 2010 John Wiley & Sons, Inc.

▶ *CASE STUDY (continued)*

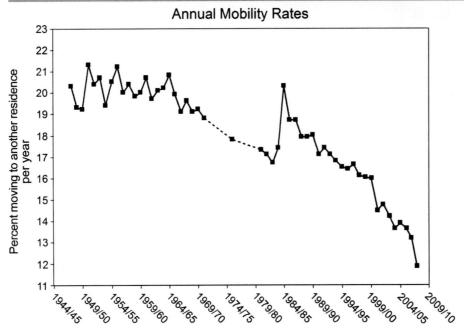

Figure 4.10 Annual mobility rate equals the number of people who moved to a new residence between March of one year and March of the next, divided by the population age 1 or older. Note the lower rates in the last few decades since the peak years of the 1950s and 1960s.
Source: U.S. Census Bureau.

The likelihood of moving varies markedly across major regions of the United States. The Northeast has the lowest moving rate—11.7 percent—well below the national rate of 15.9 percent. It is followed by the Midwest at 15.1 percent, the South at 17.1 percent, and the West at 18.5 percent. The South and West have higher mobility in part because they have been destinations for recent migrants from the Northeast and Midwest, and as noted earlier, once someone moves, he or she is more likely to move again. The West, in addition, has a long tradition of transience and impermanence dating from frontier days.

The largest interstate migration streams between 1995 and 2000 demonstrate the significance of population mass in generating large flows, the principle of migration streams and counterstreams, the importance of pull factors to high-amenity states, and the emergence of California as a major source for migrants to other western states (Figure 4.11). That California, the country's most populous state, and New York, the third-largest state, accounted for 10 of the 15 largest migration streams speaks to the importance of population—the numerator in the gravity model—as a generator of large flows. Population alone, however, does not explain the entire map of migration streams, because movement evolves from the economic, social, and political relationships between particular origins and destinations. New York and Florida, for example, share a common bond that began with post–World War II retirement migration and solidified with later labor-force flows. Large streams often create large counterstreams, as is the case between California and Texas and between Florida and Georgia.

The dominant Frostbelt-to-Sunbelt patterns of the 1970s and 1980s gave way to a more complicated system of migration in the 1990s. Although Florida continued to attract large numbers of people from New York and New Jersey, and North Carolina emerged as an important migration destination, the big story of the decade was the emergence of California as a major source area for domestic migrants. Until the early 1990s, California had attracted migrants from the East and Midwest and exchanged migrants with other western states. California, for example, was always Arizona's major migration partner, but the two states simply sent people back and forth, with little overall effect on either state's population. All that changed after California's deep and persistent recession of the early 1990s. Weak job growth, in conjunction with expensive home prices and the influx of immigrants from abroad, stimulated a large exodus of domestic migrants seen in the extensive flows leaving California for Oregon, Washington, Nevada, Arizona, and Colorado. These latter states grew rapidly, not only from the force of their own economic growth and their discovery as interesting and pleasant places to live, but from California's declining attractiveness to domestic migrants.

Americans vote with their feet and tell us how they feel about places through their net migration patterns. **Net migration rate** is the difference between in-migration and out-migration during a given period, expressed as a percentage of the total population. Positive net migration indicates that more migrants entered the state than left it during that period. A negative net migration means that more migrants left than entered the state. Net migration is usually presented as a rate

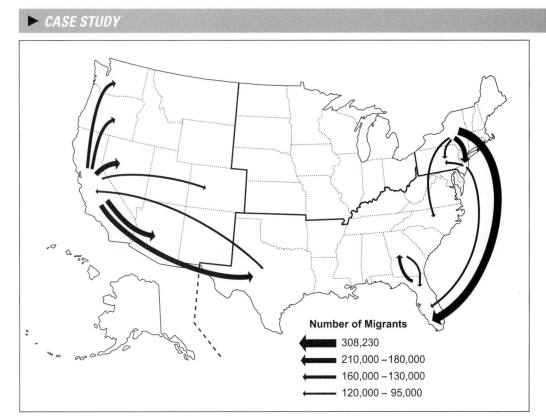

Figure 4.11 Fifteen largest interstate migration streams, 1995–2000.
Source: Raw data matrix from the Internal Revenue Service and U.S. Bureau of the Census.

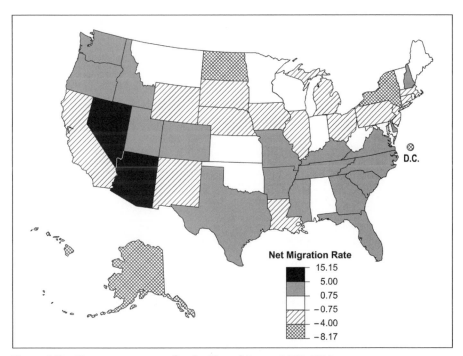

Figure 4.12 Net migration rates for the United States, 1995–2000.

© 2010 John Wiley & Sons, Inc.

▶ *CASE STUDY*

or percentage of the population to give an idea of the amount of migration change relative to the total population base. In New York State, for example, between 1995 and 2000 there were 726,000 in-migrants and 1,600,000 out-migrants. When divided by New York's 1995 population base of 17.8 million, these totals translate into a net migration rate of −4.9 percent. For every 100 people who lived in New York State in 1995, the state lost almost five people due to domestic migration. (*Note*: Net migration rates for every country can be found in the *Area and Demographic Data* on the Web site.)

Although Nevada and Arizona led the nation in net migration with rates of 15 and 7 percent respectively, the largest regional concentration of positive migration rates occurred in the Southeast, where Florida, Georgia, and North Carolina were among the top destination states (Figure 4.12). Positive net migration also occurred in Nevada, Arizona, Colorado, Oregon, and Idaho, where Californians and others were attracted by affordable housing, healthy job growth, and high-amenity lifestyles. The same forces created positive net migration to the upper New England states of Maine, Vermont, and New Hampshire. Alaska, Hawaii, and New York State registered the highest negative net migration rates. The urban

Northeast fared poorly in general, as did some parts of the Midwest, particularly Illinois. Great Plains states had difficulty retaining population, as did Louisiana in the South and New Mexico in the Southwest. Overall, the map of regional desirability reveals the strong preference among domestic migrants for high-amenity regions with warm climates, picturesque seashores, striking mountain views, and outdoor lifestyle.

Today's migration patterns reflect the location of states relative to one another (nearby states tend to exchange migrants), historical patterns of movement (i.e., longtime linkages between Florida and New York and between California and Texas), the changing geography of economic opportunity in the nation, and the public's perceptions about the attractiveness of places, including intangibles such as an agreeable climate, being near family and friends, and an ocean view. You are asked in this exercise to examine recent migration flows between your state (or Canadian province) and all others in the nation in 2002–2003 and to hypothesize about why your state or province is more connected to some than to others. Use your basic knowledge of migration trends in the nation and your knowledge of the circumstances of your particular state or province.

Name: _____ Instructor: _____

Newton's First Law of Migration: The Gravity Model

▶ ACTIVITY 1: PREDICTING MIGRATION WITH THE GRAVITY MODEL

Use the simplified format of the following gravity model to estimate migration flows to your state or province in 2003. The destination population term, P_j, has been left out because you will be looking at a single destination j—your state or province—that is the same for all origins. The distance exponent also has been left out for simplicity.

$$M_{ij} = k\frac{P_i}{d_{ij}}$$

where:

M_{ij} = gravity model prediction of migration between origin i and destination j

P_i = population of origin state i

d_{ij} = distance from origin i to destination j

k = a constant that adjusts the gravity model estimates so that the total numbers of actual and estimated migrants are approximately equal

You will obtain the data you need and perform calculations using a spreadsheet. If you've never used a spreadsheet, you will learn a valuable skill here. Just follow the step-by-step instructions.

A. To start your activity, click on the *Student Companion Site* at www.wiley .com/college/kuby. (For students using WileyPlus, log on to your class Web site, select the *Assignment* tab, locate and click on this assignment, and follow all instructions.)

B. Select this chapter from the drop-down list and then click on *Computerized Chapter Activities*

C. Click on *Activity 1: Predicting Migration with the Gravity Model.*

D. Choose your country, USA or Canada.

E. Choose the destination state or province to which you wish to measure migration. As you move the mouse over the names, the location on the map is highlighted. Click on your state or province.

You now will be looking at a spreadsheet with all the information you need. You can scroll down the spreadsheet to look at all the values by using the scroll bar. The columns are as follows:

© 2010 John Wiley & Sons, Inc.

Column A	*State*	State or province abbreviations.
Column B	P_i	Population of each state or province in 2002.
Column C	d_{ij}	Distance in miles from the geographic center of that state to the geographic center of the state you selected. Notice that your state has a value of 0 because it is zero miles away from itself.
Column D	P_i/d_{ij}	State or province population divided by the distance to your state or province.
Column E	*Predicted migration*	The number of migrants, M_{ij}, predicted by the gravity model.
Column F	*Actual migration*	The actual number of migrants from that state or province to your state or province from 2002 to 2003. The U.S. data come from the Internal Revenue Service (IRS), which tracks where claimants filed their returns in 2002 as opposed to where they filed in 2003. Any claimant crossing a state line between those years is considered an interstate migrant. Canadian data are estimated in the same way and are obtained from Statistics Canada for 2002 to 2003. Notice that your own state or province has a value of 0 because we are not concerned here with movements within a state or province.
Column G	*Residual %*	Actual migration minus the predicted migration, divided by the actual migration, and multiplied by 100. These residuals show the percentage error in your predictions.

Note: At the top of the screen, you are provided with the k coefficient that has already been calculated for your particular state or province.[1]

The spreadsheet software will compute values much like a calculator if you give it a formula to use. In a spreadsheet, the letter of the column and the number of the row identify a cell. For instance, the population (Column B) of California (row 6) is in cell B6. Multiplying or dividing a number by cell B6 is the same as multiplying or dividing by the population of California.

F. Your first step is to divide the population of the first origin state (or province) by the distance between that origin and your state. Click on cell D2, the first empty cell, where you will calculate P_i/d_{ij}. Because the population of the first origin is in B2 and its distance from your state is in C2, you can calculate P_i/d_{ij} by entering the following formula:

$$= B2/C2$$

The "=" is a code that tells the spreadsheet you are entering a formula, not a number. The formula simply says divide cell B2 by cell C2 and store the answer in D2. You can type this formula directly in cell D2 using the

---

[1] For you math mavens, we estimated k by doing a least-squares linear regression of M_{ij} on P_i/d_{ij} with the constant term forced to zero (that is, using the functional from $Y = kX$, where $Y = M_{ij}$ and $X = P_i/d_{ij}$).

keyboard or create it using the formula buttons at the top right. Click the "=" button, then type B2, then click on the "÷" button, and then type C2. Whichever way you enter the formula into the cell, if you did so correctly, the *Copy* button in the upper left is highlighted. You have now calculated your first value. The answer will appear in the cell itself. If you make a mistake, you will get an error message telling you the formula you have entered is incorrect and asking you to try again. Click *Try again* and edit the formula. If at any time you wish to return to the original blank spreadsheet, go to the browser's *View* menu and select *Refresh*.

G. Now comes one of the best features of spreadsheets—you can transfer this formula to the entire Column D. First, click on *Copy* in the upper left. This copies the formula from cell D2 into a buffer, which the computer remembers. Second, click on the Column D header to highlight the entire column. Third, click on the word *Paste* in the upper left. The computer has now copied the formula from cell D2 into each of the cells below it and has modified each formula to divide by the B and C column cells immediately to the left, rather than always dividing cell B2 by C2. You have just saved yourself much time compared with typing this formula 50 times.

Notice that the value for your state or province—infinity—is not a valid result. This is so because you tried to divide by zero (the distance), and zero can go into anything an infinite number of times. This is okay; you will not need a value from your own state, so ignore it.

H. Finish calculating the predicted migration to your state by multiplying the P_i/d_{ij} value in Column D by the coefficient k, which we have calculated and provided to you for each state and province. Because the *Human Geography in Action* software checks to make sure that you complete the spreadsheet correctly, k must be entered into the formula *exactly* as it appears at the top of the spreadsheet. The easiest and safest way to do this is to use the k button in the upper right to enter the value. **Whatever you do, don't type the letter k.** Click on cell E2 and type "=D2*" and then click on the k button (* means multiply in computer language). Your formula should look something like:

$$= D2 * 2.6183 \text{ (for Alberta)}$$
$$= D2 * 0.1974 \text{ (for Alabama)}$$

Follow the *Copy* and *Paste* commands from the previous step to copy this formula into all the cells for Column E. Column E is the predicted migration to your state or province based on the gravity model. Think about what these numbers mean. Based on the population of each state or province and its distance from your state or province, you have *predicted* the number of migrants in 2003.

I. Your final step in completing the spreadsheet is to calculate residuals in Column G. You will learn more about residuals and how to use them in Activity 3, but you must calculate them now while the spreadsheet is still active.

© 2010 John Wiley & Sons, Inc.

A **residual** is the difference between the actual migration and the predicted migration. Residuals indicate how well the gravity model predicted the actual migrant flow. To calculate the residuals, simply subtract your predicted migration, Column E, from the actual migration, Column F. then, to put the resideuals in percentage terms, divide the result by the actual migration (Column F) and multiply by 100. In cell G2, enter this formula exactly as shown here, and press *Enter:*

$$= 100 \circ (F2–E2) / F2$$

Again, use the *Copy* and *Paste* commands you learned in the previous steps to copy the formula from cell G2 to all cells in column G. If this step is done correctly, you will receive a message on the screen that says you have completed the spreadsheet. Click *OK.*

The numbers in Column G are interpreted as percentage errors. For instance, a–2.6 means that the actual migration was 2.6 percent less that the predicted migration, as a percentage of the actual migration. Putting the residuals into percentage terms allows you to compare, on an equal footing, how well the gravity model predicts migration from states of different sizes.

J. Click the *Print* button.

K. Click on *Activity 2: Scatter Diagram.* Do not close the spreadsheet window; you will need to return to it later.

Name: _____ Instructor: _____

Newton's First Law of Migration: The Gravity Model

► ACTIVITY 2: SCATTER DIAGRAM

You now see a **scatter diagram** next to the U.S. or Canada map. A scatter diagram depicts the relationship between two variables. One variable is measured on the x-axis (horizontal), and another is measured on the y-axis (vertical). Each dot represents a different origin state or province. Each dot is placed at the intersection of that state or province's x value and y value. The diagram, therefore, is a "scatter" of these dots, which show groupings or trends in the relationship between the two variables.

In this scatter diagram, the x-axis measures actual migration, and the y-axis measures predicted migration (Figure 4.13). Perfectly predicted migration values fall exactly along the 45° line (i.e., the predicted value was exactly equal to the actual value). In the case of those dots that deviate from the 45° line, the gravity model was less successful in estimating migrant flows to your state or province. All points above the line had predicted values that are larger than the actual migration flows. Points above the line are therefore *over*predicted and have negative residuals. All points below the line had predicted values that are smaller than the actual migration flows. Points below the line are therefore *under*predicted and have positive residuals.

A. Beware of states or provinces that have x and y values far greater than any other state. To fit such **extreme values** in the upper-right corner of the graph, a large number of other points usually end up getting "squished" into the bottom-left corner (see Figure 4.14). Eliminating the very large values can give you a more spread-out scatter so that you can see each dot better. To eliminate an extreme value, click on that dot in the graph to highlight it. The state or province will also be highlighted in red on the map (your state or province is shown in gray). Click *Hide*

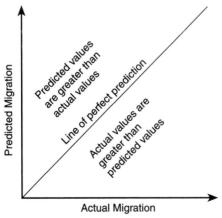

Figure 4.13 Over- and underpredicted areas of a scatter diagram.

© 2010 John Wiley & Sons, Inc.

Selected Area(s). Repeat as necessary. You can click *Show All Areas* to restore all dots to the graph. Be sure to discuss in your write-up whether you have eliminated an extreme value.

B. When you have finished customizing your graph, click the *Print* button.

C. Return to the computer and identify up to five poorly predicted states (**outliers**) on your graph. The outliers are dots that are farthest from the line of perfect prediction, in percentage terms. As the actual migration value gets larger on the graph, however, it takes a bigger deviation from the 45° line to qualify as an outlier. Thus, in Figure 4.14, dots falling in the darker shading are the most serious outliers, and dots in the white area are not considered outliers at all. Move your mouse over an outlying dot to highlight it in red on the map and display its name, its actual migration to your state or province, and the migration predicted by the gravity model. By hand, label the outliers on your printed map (use two-letter abbreviations if needed).

D. When you have finished, close the *Activity 2: Scatter Diagram* window and return to the *Activity 1: Spreadsheet* window, where you should click on *Activity 3: Residual Map*.

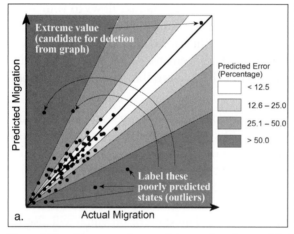
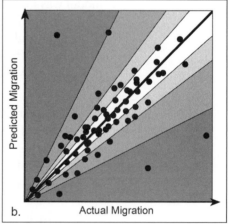

Figure 4.14a   Extreme values to delete and outliers to label.
Figure 4.14b   When you remove extreme values from your scatter diagram, the points that were previously clustered in the lower left corner expand out to the full dimensions of the graph so that you can better see their distribution.

Name: _____ Instructor: _____

Newton's First Law of Migration: The Gravity Model

► ACTIVITY 3: RESIDUAL MAP

You now see a choropleth map showing the accuracy of the gravity model across space. The difference between the actual value and the predicted value is called a residual. We have defined our residuals in percentage terms so that the residual of a big state or province such as California can be compared with that of a small state or province such as Vermont. The data displayed on the map are from the spreadsheet's Residual column, which was calculated as: $100 \times$ (Actual Migration − Predicted Migration)/Actual Migration. Each state or province is shaded according to its residual. Move the mouse over the map to see each state's name and residual.

A. The map's default break-point settings split the residual values into six equal intervals. These default break points are not particularly good ones because the map does not lend itself to easy interpretation. Interactively define your own class break points using the graphic array to the left of the map. This graph shows the range of data on the x-axis, in this case the percentage error between your predicted value and the actual migration value for each state or province. The gray vertical line shows the zero value where your predicted migration values equal the actual migration values. The y-axis, which ranges from 0 to 50 states or 0 to 13 provinces, ranks the origin states or provinces from highest to lowest residual. You can move your mouse over the dots to see which states or provinces they represent.

The vertical red bars show the break points between classes. You can select a bar by clicking on the top triangle with your mouse. Holding down the mouse button on the triangle, move it left or right to set new class limits. The shading patterns between the bars match those of the map. When you move the bars, the break points in the boxes below change to reflect the new position. These boxes are also directly editable: click in a break-point box, edit a value, and press *Enter*. You will use this interactive graphic array and/or the editable boxes to make your final map.

B. You can follow a number of possible strategies in defining the break points. First, you can define a break point at 0 (gray vertical line on the graph) that divides the states or provinces into those with positive residuals and those with negative residuals. You could then define two other break points to separate the small positive residuals from the large, and the small negative residuals from the large. You can choose to have only one or two extreme outliers in the large positive and large nega-tive classes, or you can have many. A second strategy, related to the first, defines six classes with small, medium, and large residuals on both the positive and negative side. A third strategy is to define a class that groups residuals that are close to zero (i.e., that are closely predicted by

© 2010 John Wiley & Sons, Inc.

the model) regardless of whether they are positive or negative. Fourth, you could use the graphic array to set class break points that divide the data into "natural classes" or groupings. Vertical groupings in the array indicate a group of states or provinces with similar residuals. Setting your break points in the empty horizontal gaps would avoid putting two states or provinces with very similar percentage residuals into different categories (i.e., you could avoid "splitting hairs"). You can also experiment with the *Equal Frequency* and *Equal Interval* buttons.

Set the break points to make what you consider to be the most informative choropleth map of the residuals. However you choose your limits, justify your choices in the write-up in Activity 4.

C. You can change the number of classes using the menu in the lower left. By setting the number of classes to four and moving Break Point 1 to the lower limit, and Break Point 3 to the upper limit and positioning Break Point 2 at 0, it is possible to create a two-color map with one shade for all positive residuals and another for all negative residuals.

D. At the bottom of the screen, pick a *Color Scheme* that best portrays the residual classes. You should try to use shades that indicate residual sign (+ or −) and size.

E. Click on the *Print* button. Study your map and make any changes necessary. Sometimes colors look good on the screen but print poorly. Make sure the categories are easily distinguished on the final map you print. Don't use any two patterns that look very similar. Hand in the map with this assignment.

F. When you have finished, close all browser windows.

Name: _____ Instructor: _____

Newton's First Law of Migration: The Gravity Model

▶ ACTIVITY 4: EVALUATION

Type (double-spaced) the answers to the following questions:

4.1. Report any extreme values eliminated from the scatter plot in Activity 2, and justify your choice of color scheme and class break points for the choropleth map of residuals in Activity 3.

4.2. Assess the gravity model's ability to predict migrant flows during the study period. How close were the predicted values to the actual flows?

4.3. The gravity model assumes that distance is a barrier to migration. Specifically, how does distance act as a deterrent to migration?

4.4. Justify the use of population as the numerator in the gravity model function. Can you suggest a variable that might be preferable to population as a measure of the "sending" power of a state or province?

4.5. We have said that points that fall along the 45° line on the graph are predicted accurately by the gravity model. What does it mean if a point is below the line? Above the line? Which one is overpredicted, and which one is underpredicted? (*Hint*: Look at the Residual column and compare those values with the location of the points on the graph.)

4.6. Can you detect any spatial patterns (groups of states or provinces) on the map of residuals that are overpredicted or that are underpredicted? What explanations can you suggest for these patterns?

4.7. Based on your answer to Question 4.6, think about any factors that could explain the spatial pattern of positive and negative residuals. Does this pattern suggest any variables that would be good to add to the gravity model that could account for factors other than population and distance?

▶ DEFINITIONS OF KEY TERMS

Distance Decay The declining intensity of an activity with increasing distance from its point of origin.

Extreme Value A point on a scatter diagram that is roughly in line with the main trend but is separated from the main group of points because of its extremely high or low value. Contrast with *outlier*.

Gravity Model A model to predict spatial interaction, where size (population) is directly related to interaction and distance is inversely related to interaction.

Immigration A move across international borders.

Migration A permanent change in residence to outside one's community of origin.

Migration Counterstream Migration that runs opposite to a migration stream.

Migration Selectivity The tendency for certain types of people to migrate. Age, education, and other socio-demographic characteristics are migration selectivity factors.

Migration Stream A well-defined migration channel from a specific origin to a particular destination.

Net Migration Rate The percentage gain or loss of population due to migration. It is calculated as in-migrants minus out-migrants divided by the total population, all times 100. Positive numbers indicate net gain; negative numbers indicate net loss.

Outlier Point on a scatter diagram that lies far off the trend line. Outliers on the graph correspond to cases that are poorly predicted by the model. Outliers are not to be confused with extreme values, which may lie far from any other point but which are still close to the best-fitting line (see Figure 4.14).

Pull Factors Reasons to move to a particular place.

Push Factors Reasons to move from a particular place.

Refugee A person who is outside his or her country due to a well-founded fear of persecution and who is unable or unwilling to return.

Remittances Money sent by immigrants from host country to home country.

Residuals The difference between an actual observed value of some variable and its predicted value using the gravity model.

Scatter Diagram A scatter of dots showing the relationship between two variables. Each dot on the graph represents the x and y coordinates of a different observation or case.

Spatial Interaction Movements of ideas, information, money, products, and people between places.

▶ FURTHER READINGS

Castles, Stephen, and Mark J. Miller. 1998. *The Age of Migration: International Population Movement in the Modern World*. New York: Guilford Press.

Chant, Sylvia M. (ed.). 1992. *Gender and Migration in Developing Countries*. New York: Belhaven Press.

Ellis, Mark, and Richard Wright. 1999. The Balkanization Metaphor in the Analysis of U.S. Immigration. *Annals of the Association of American Geographers* 88:686–698.

Fielding, Tony. 1992. Migration and Culture, pp. 201–212 in *Processes and Patterns Volume I: Research and Prospects*, Tony Champion and Tony Fielding (eds.). London: Bellhaven Press.

Frey, William H. 1995. Immigration, Domestic Migration, and Demographic Balkanization in America: New Evidence for the 1990s. *Population and Development Review* 22:741–763.

Gober, Patricia. 1993. Americans on the Move. *Population Bulletin* 48:1–40.

Long, Larry. 1988. *Migration and Residential Mobility in the United States*. New York: Russell Sage Foundation.

Manson, Gary A., and Richard Groop. 2000. U.S. Intercounty Migration in the 1990s: People and Income Move Down the Urban Hierarchy. *Professional Geographer* 52(3):493–504.

Martin, Philip, and Elizabeth Midgely. 2006. Immigration: Shaping and Reshaping America (2 ed.) *Population Bulletin* 61(4):1–28.

Martin, Philip, and Jonas Widgren. 2002. International Migration: Facing the Challenge. *Population Bulletin* 57(1):1–40.

Martin, Philip, and Gottfried Zürcher. 2008. Managing Migration: The Global Challenge. *Population Bulletin* 63(1):1–20.

McHugh, Kevin E. 2000. Inside, Outside, Upside Down, Backward, Forward, Round and Round; A Case for Ethnographic Studies in Migration. *Progress in Human Geography* 24:71–89.

McHugh, Kevin E., Ines M. Miyaris, and Emily H. Skop. 1997. The Magnetism of Miami: Segmented Paths in Cuban Migration. *Geographical Review* 87:504–519.

Pandit, Kavita, and Suzanne Davies Withers. 1999. *Migration and Regional Restructuring in the United States*. New York: Rowman & Littlefield.

Shumway, J. Matthew, and Samuel M. Octerstrom. 2001. Spatial Patterns of Migration and Income Change in the Mountain West: The Dominance of Service-Based, Amenity-Rich Counties. *Professional Geographer* 53(4): 492–502.

Skeldon, R. 1995. The Challenge Facing Migration Research: A Case for Greater Awareness. *Progress in Human Geography* 19:91–96.

Tocalis, Thomas R. 1978. Changing Theoretical Foundations of the Gravity Concept of Human Interaction, pp. 66–124 in *The Nature of Change in Geographical Ideas*, Brian J. L. Berry (ed.). DeKalb, IL: Northern Illinois University Press.

White, Paul, and Peter Jackson. 1995. (Re)Theorizing Population Geography. *International Journal of Population Geography* 1:111–123.

White, Stephen E. 1994. Ogallala Oases: Water Use, Population Redistribution, and Policy Implications in the High Plains of Western Kansas, 1980–1990. *Annals of the Association of American Geographers* 84:29–45.

Woltman, Kelly, and K. Bruce Newbold. 2009. Of Flights and Flotillas: Assimilation and Race in the Cuban Diaspora. *Professional Geographer* 61(1):70–86.

▶ WEB RESOURCES

International Organization for Migration: www.iom.int

Martin, Philip. *Migration News*: migration.ucdavis.edu/mn

Migration Research Unit at the University College, London: www.geog.ucl.ac.uk/mru

Miner & Silverstein, LLP. *Predictive Gravity Modeling*: www.msac.com/pptm/page2.html

North American Center for Transborder Studies, Arizona State University. *The North American Migration Project*: nacts .asu.edu/Knowledge_Center/North_American_Migration

Statistics Canada. *Population and Demography*: www.statcan.gc.ca/start-debut-eng.html

United Nations Population Division: www.un.org/esa/population

U.S. Census Bureau. *Geographic Mobility/Migration*: www.census.gov/population/www/socdemo/migrate.html

University of California, Davis. *Migration News*: Migration.UCdavis.edu/mn

University of Pennsylvania. *Mexican Migration Project*: www.pop.upenn.edu/mexmig

▶ ITEMS TO HAND IN

Activity 1: • The completed spreadsheet table or answer all questions your instructor created in your WileyPlus assignments.

Activity 2: • The scatter diagram, including the labels of poorly predicted states or answer all questions your instructor created in your WileyPlus assignments.

Activity 3: • The residual map or answer all questions your instructor created in your WileyPlus assignments.

Activity 4: • Typed answers to Questions 4.1–4.7, or answer all questions your instructor created in your WileyPlus assignments.

CHAPTER 5

One Billion and Counting: The Hidden Momentum of Population Growth in India

▶ INTRODUCTION

At the end of 2008, about 6.75 billion people lived on planet Earth. After reaching the 1 billion mark somewhere around 1830, the world's population reached 2 billion around 1930 (100 years) and then, in each of the following years, added another billion: 1959 (29 years), 1974 (15 years), 1987 (13 years), and 1999 (12 years). Every second there are about 4.2 births and 1.8 deaths, and thus an additional 2.4 people on the planet. Most of the world's population lives in the less-developed countries of Asia, Africa, and Latin America. From 1950 to today, the combined populations of Asia, Africa, and Latin America have soared from 71 percent of the world's total to 83 percent, and they are expected to comprise 87 percent by 2050 (Figure 5.1). In this chapter you will learn why the world's population is growing so fast, why this growth is concentrated in less-developed countries, and what are some of the factors that go into population forecasting.

The size, composition, and growth of populations affect the economic and environmental well-being of nations. Rapid population growth in regions such as Asia, sub-Saharan Africa, and the Middle East requires huge commitments of national resources for food, housing, education, and health care and exacerbates problems of poor air and water quality, soil erosion, deforestation, and desertification. Not all countries today are growing too fast, however. Many European countries are experiencing negative growth or population decline. These countries devote considerable economic resources to support large elderly populations. About 17 percent of Western Europe's population currently is over 65 years of age and is increasing steadily over time.

First, here are a few basics about the dynamics of population growth. Population change in any country results from four demographic forces: (1) births, (2) deaths, (3) immigration (people moving to a country), and (4) emigration (people leaving a country):

$$P_2 = P_1 + B - D + I - O$$

where: P_1 = population in time 1
P_2 = population in time 2

© 2010 John Wiley & Sons, Inc.

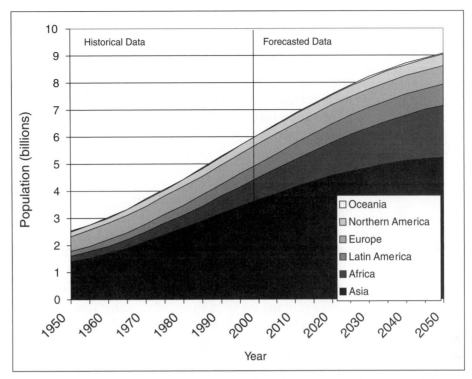

Figure 5.1 As you look at these historical data and the forecast to 2050, keep in mind that population forecasting is an inexact science. This graph shows the medium variant of the United Nations forecast, with a population of 9.1 billion in 2050. This medium variant is sandwiched between a high estimate of 10.6 billion and a low estimate of 7.67 billion. In the high variant, population would still be growing at almost 100 million per year in 2050; in the low variant, population would have peaked in 2040 and be starting a gradual decline.

Source: Population Division of the Department of Economic and Social Affairs of the United Nations Secretariat, World Population Prospects: The 2004 Revision and World Urbanization Prospects: The 2003 Revision, http://esa.un.org/unpp, 08 July 2005; 6:21:51 p.m.

$$B = \text{births}$$
$$D = \text{deaths}$$
$$I = \text{in-migrants}$$
$$O = \text{out-migrants}$$

The formula shows that births (B) and in-migration (I) add to the base population (P_1), while deaths (D) and out-migration (O) subtract from it. For many countries in the world (the United States is a notable exception), in-migration and out-migration do not contribute significantly to the overall balance sheet of population change, and we ignore them in discussions of current and future population change.

The **crude birth rate (CBR)**, the number of births per 1,000 persons, is a measure of the birth performance of a population. Similarly, the **crude death rate (CDR)**, the number of deaths per 1,000 persons, is an indicator of death experience of a population. Both measures are called crude because they fail to account for the different age structures of populations. This explains why Germany has a crude death rate of 10 while Mexico has a crude death rate of 5. You would be incorrect in concluding that life expectancy, medical care, and the overall quality of life are higher in Mexico. Germany's inflated crude death rate is a statistical artifact of its substantial elderly population. Some 19 percent of the German population is over 65 years of age, when the odds of dying are high. In Mexico a mere 6 percent of the population is older than 65 years. Relatively few Mexicans are in age classes where the likelihood of dying is high; thus, its crude death rate is low.

The **crude rate of natural increase** is the difference between the crude birth rate and the crude death rate. Take Burkina Faso in western Africa as an example. Burkina Faso's crude birth rate of 45 and the crude death rate of 15 yield a crude rate of natural increase of 30. Keep in mind that these are rates per 1,000, so an increase of 30 per 1,000 translates into a growth rate of 3.0 per 100, or 3.0 percent. The U.S. crude birth rate of 14 and death rate of 8 result in a crude rate of natural increase of 6 per 1,000, or 0.6 percent. Russia's rates are the reverse of those in the United States. The Russian crude birth rate of 12 and crude death rate of 15 produce a crude rate of natural increase of −3 per 1,000, or −0.3 percent (with rounding). If this rate were sustained, each year Russia's population would be 0.3 percent smaller.

As these examples indicate, birth, death, and growth rates across the world's countries vary markedly (Figure 5.2). (*Note*: These and other variables for every country can be found in the *Area and Demographic Data* on the *Human Geography in Action* Web site.) Geographers and demographers use the **demographic transition model** as a framework for understanding the dramatic variations in birth, death, and growth rates worldwide. Based on the demographic history of European countries, the demographic transition model offers a generalized perspective of the way birth, death, and growth rates change through time.

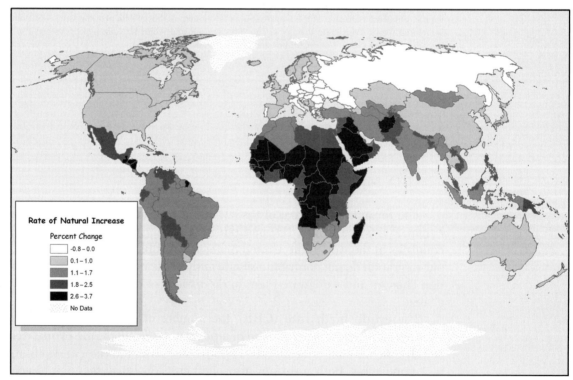

Figure 5.2 Annual rate of natural increase, 2004.

Source: Population Reference Bureau, *World Population Data Sheet 2004* (www.prb.org).

© 2010 John Wiley & Sons, Inc.

The demographic transition model says that preindustrial populations begin with high crude birth and death rates, somewhere between 40 and 50 per 1,000 (Figure 5.3). These conditions hold in primitive societies where people die young from poor diets, inadequate housing, rampant contagious disease, and the absence of modern medicine. To keep from becoming extinct, societies have many children and high birth rates. High birth rates and high death rates maintain an **equilibrium**, a state in which the forces making for change are in balance. This balance is reflected in extremely low rates of population growth.

Conditions of high birth and death rates and low growth prevailed for most of the time that humans occupied the earth. Populations eked by with infinitesimal growth rates of 0.56 per 1,000 from A.D. 1 to the time of the Industrial Revolution (Figure 5.4). High birth rates, high death rates, and low population growth characterize countries in the first stage of the demographic transition.

Modernization disrupts the balance between birth and death rates in the second stage of the demographic transition, which is characterized by declining death rates, continued high birth rates, and rapid rates of population growth. Death rates fall as food is transported from surplus to deficit regions, as housing improves, as knowledge about public health reduces contagious diseases, and as antibiotics, immunizations, and other innovations in science and medicine significantly prolong life. Birth rates, however, are slow to respond to the changing death situation because large family norms are deeply rooted in a society's cultural traditions. In addition, in agrarian areas, children are economic assets to the family, fetching water, gathering

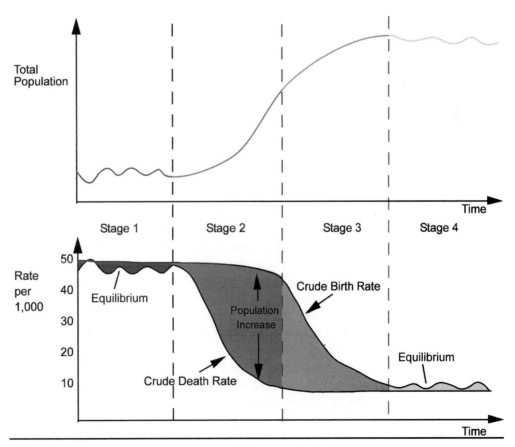

Figure 5.3 The demographic transition model.

© 2010 John Wiley & Sons, Inc.

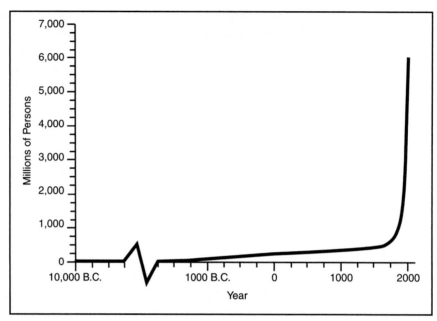

Figure 5.4 World population growth showing the rapid increase since the 1700s, which corresponds with the beginnings of the Industrial Revolution. Population growth before that time was very little. The zigzag you see shows a break in the data from 9250 B.C. until 1750 B.C. in order to extend the scale back to 10,000 B.C.

firewood, working the fields, tending the animals, looking after smaller children, and caring for aged parents. Because the world's population is still more than half (51 percent) rural, it is not surprising that many less-developed countries today are still in the second stage (Table 5.1).

In the third stage of the demographic transition, birth rates begin to fall in response to lower death rates, urbanization, and other changes associated with modernization. Fertility falls in modern societies as women derive status from activities other than childbearing and motherhood and as the cost of raising children mushrooms. Children in modern societies become economically active at much later ages than those in agrarian societies do, and they marry later. Families learn that it is no longer necessary to have six children if they want three of them to survive to adulthood. In addition, as literacy increases and contraceptive technology improves, people are better able to achieve their desired family size.

Ultimately, birth rates decline, and the demographic transition is complete. In the fourth stage, population returns to equilibrium, this time under conditions of low birth rates and low death rates. All more-developed countries are in the fourth stage of the demographic transition. In addition, China, with a crude birth rate of 12, crude death rate of 7, and growth rate of 0.5 percent, is moving rapidly toward stage 4.

Table 5.1 shows some of the range in birth, death, and natural increase rates. There are no countries in the world today still in stage 1 of the demographic transition, or even in early stage 2: crude death rates everywhere are below 32 per 1,000. The early twenty-first century finds countries in stage 2 that still have very high CBRs, countries in stage 3 with declining CBRs and low CDRs, and the more demographically stable countries in stage 4. Note the positive correlation between stage of the demographic transition and the percent urban, and the negative association between transition stage and the percentage of the workforce in agriculture.

TABLE 5.1 Key Population Indicators for Select Countries

Country	Demographic Transition Stage	Crude Birth Rate (per 1,000)	Crude Death Rate (per 1,000)	Rate of Natural Increase (percent)	Percent Urban	Percent of Workforce in Agriculture
Afghanistan		47	21	2.6	20	80
Nigeria	2	43	18	2.5	47	70
Palestinian Territory		37	4	3.3	72	15
Brazil		20	6	1.3	83	6
Mexico		20	5	1.6	76	15
Philippines	3	26	5	2.1	63	35
South Africa		23	15	0.8	59	9
Sri Lanka		19	7	1.2	15	34
Australia		14	7	0.7	87	4
Canada		11	7	0.3	81	2
Cuba	4	10	7	0.3	76	20
Germany		8	10	−0.2	73	2
Italy		9	10	0.0	68	4
United States		14	8	0.6	79	1
Bulgaria	Severe Population	10	15	−0.5	71	9
Ukraine	Decline	10	16	−0.6	68	19

Sources: Population Reference Bureau, *World Population Data Sheet 2008*, http://www.prb.org;
Central Intelligence Agency, *World Factbook 2008*, http://www.odci.gov/cia/publications/factbook
Natural increase does not always equal CBR-CDR/10 due to rounding.

Although the demographic transition is a compelling and extremely useful framework for viewing contemporary demographic change, it is not universally applicable. Some countries, such as Bulgaria and Ukraine (Table 5.1), do not fit in any stages of the demographic transition model. With high CDR and low CBR, they are losing about half of 1 percent of their population annually. Demographers do *not* consider their strongly negative population growth as a next stage beyond stage 4, because Russia and Ukraine are *not* more advanced economically and socially than Europe, North America, or Japan. Rather, the high death rates and low birth rates in Russia and Ukraine are viewed as a temporary anomaly resulting from the poverty, unemployment, and instability associated with their rocky transition from Soviet-style communism toward democracy and capitalism.

We must also be careful in using the demographic transition model to predict the future of less-developed countries currently in the second or third stages. Their economies and populations are so profoundly different from those of European countries when they went through the second or third stages of the demographic transition that we cannot be sure the demographic transition will be resolved in the same way. During the nineteenth century, most European countries experienced a massive exodus of population to the United States, Canada, Australia, New Zealand, and Latin America. Few such "migration escape hatches" exist now for rapidly growing less-developed countries.

In addition, populations in less-developed countries are much larger, densities are higher, and rates of growth are much faster. The death rates of less-developed countries fell much faster during stage 2 of their demographic transitions than they did for the more-developed countries (Figure 5.5). For instance, the death

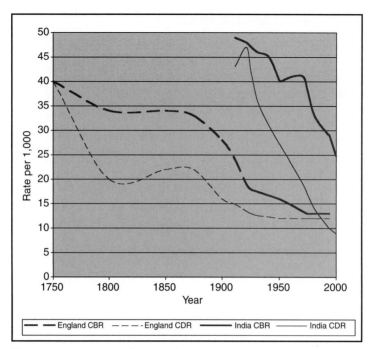

Figure 5.5 Contrasting demographic transitions of a more- and less-developed region: England and India. For both regions, the crude death rate (CDR) declined prior to the crude birth rate (CBR), but England started the demographic transistion much earlier and the changes occurred over a much longer time span. India is still undergoing the transition, so its CBR remains higher than the CDR.

rate of England declined gradually over a century or more with invention and diffusion of scientific improvements in agriculture, medicine, and modern sanitation. Comparable declines in less-developed countries such as India occur more quickly as countries acquire mortality-reducing technologies from more-developed countries. The steeper drop in death rates translates into growth rates that are higher than any experienced in the history of more-developed countries.

Also complicating completion of the demographic transition today is the nature of age structures in less-developed countries. There is momentum for continued population growth built into the extremely young age structures currently found in less-developed countries. Put simply, this means that future population growth cannot be avoided, even if countries are able to achieve small family sizes immediately. Take China as an example, Strict family-planning policies in China have reduced the average number of children to 1.6, lower than the 2.1 children per family average in North America. Still, the population of China continues to grow at a rate of 0.5 percent annually due to the large number of people in reproducing age groups.

The age structure of a population often is depicted in a **population pyramid**, a two-sided bar chart showing the distribution of population in various age categories, or **cohorts** as demographers call them (Figure 5.6). The horizontal axis shows the percentage of the population in a particular age group. The vertical axis shows ages, typically represented in 5-year intervals. Males are represented on the left side of the pyramid and females on the right. The term *pyramid* comes from times past, when there were more young than old people in national populations. Thus, the younger bars near the bottom were longer than the older ones near the top,

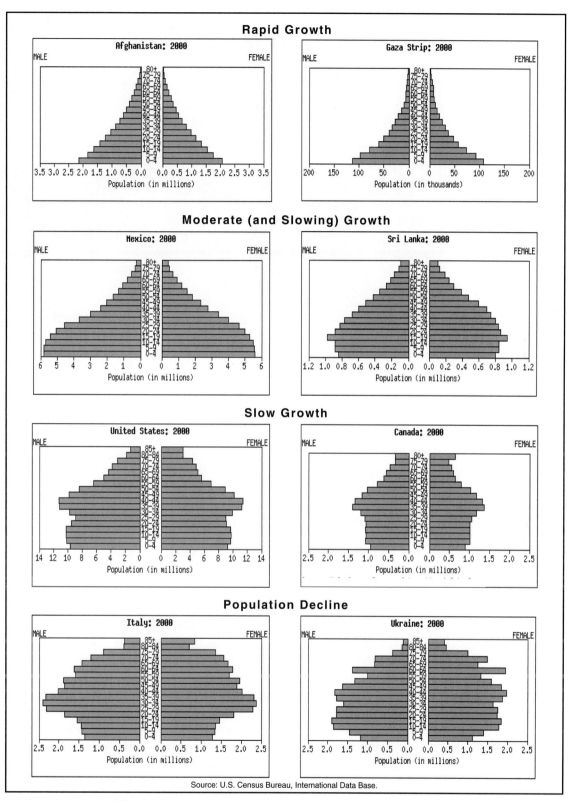

Source: U.S. Census Bureau, International Data Base.

Figure 5.6 Examples of different countries' population pyramids.

Figure 5.7 Elderly populations in a few countries, such as Italy, are now 20 percent of the total population and rising fast. How will these societies meet their growing needs for food, housing, transportation, and medical care?

creating a pyramid-shaped diagram. Today, however, the population pyramids for many countries are no longer shaped like pyramids.

The shape of a population pyramid is determined by the history of fertility (birth) and mortality (death) circumstances of a population. Countries with high birth and low death rates characteristic of stages 2 and 3 of the demographic transition model have age-sex structures with steeply sloping concave sides, large bases, and tiny tops (e.g., Afghanistan and Gaza Strip in Figure 5.6). In stage 4 of the demographic transition model, under conditions of low birth and death rates, age-sex structures do not look like pyramids at all. They resemble beehives with relatively straight sides sloping inward at the top (e.g., United States and Canada in Figure 5.6). Women usually outnumber men, especially in older age categories, because of the longer life expectancies for females than males. The typical life expectancy of women in North America is 81 years compared to 76 years for men. In Western Europe, 18 percent of the population is 65 and over, compared with just 3 percent in Africa and 7 percent in Asia. Already, wealthier countries with aging populations, such as Italy, are developing upside-down or tornado-like pyramids (Figure 5.6) and are starting to face the relatively new societal problem of a shrinking labor force having to provide for the needs of a burgeoning elderly population (Figure 5.7)

Of particular interest in an age-sex structure is the relationship between the generation that is currently bearing children, the so-called reproducing generation between the ages of 20 and 40, and their children at the base of the structure. In less-developed countries with triangular age-sex structures, the reproducing generation gives birth to a generation of children that is much larger than itself, often by a factor of 2 or even 3. This is symptomatic of high fertility and rapid growth.

Now contrast this situation with a beehive-shaped structure characteristic of more-developed countries. The reproducing generation is giving birth to a new generation that is about the same size as itself. These roughly equal-sized cohorts indicate that fertility is at or near the level needed for each generation merely to replace itself. The fact that older people eventually die leads to a tapering off at the top of the beehive.

The shapes of age-sex structures are strongly affected by **age-specific birth rates**. An age-specific birth rate is a precise indicator of the number of births occurring in each age cohort. More specifically, it is the number of births to women in a certain age cohort, say 25 to 29 years of age, divided by the number of women in that age cohort. Age-specific birth rates can be computed for all age categories in which women bear children, typically between 15 and 49 years. An age-specific birth rate tells us the likelihood that a woman of a certain age will bear a child in any given year.

If we add the current age-specific birth rates for all years from 15 to 49, we have a measure called the *total fertility rate*. Another way to think about the total fertility rate is that it is the number of children that an average woman would bear as she passes through her reproductive years. The **total fertility rate (TFR)**, often called the *average family size*, is a cross-sectional look at current fertility conditions. TFR ranges from a high of 7.1 children per woman in Niger and Guinea Bissau to a low of 1.1 in Taiwan. The TFR for the entire human race is 2.6 children per woman, which masks the differences between the more-developed countries (1.6) and the less-developed world (2.8, or 3.2 excluding China). China is a special case, with a one-child policy designed to dramatically slow (and eventually reverse) growth in its massive population of 1.3 billion people. The policy uses a variety of financial, medical, educational, and housing penalties and incentives; laws setting a minimum marriage age; and "birth planning" programs to convince people to have only one child. Originally designed in 1979 to cap the population at 1.2 billion by 2000, it has succeeded in lowering TFR only to 1.6, because of exceptions granted to farmers and ethnic minorities. Nevertheless, without the highly controversial one-child policy, China would have hundreds of millions more people today.

When the total fertility rate is about 2.0, the average woman and her spouse or partner are having just enough children to replace themselves. The population is said to be near replacement fertility. In developed societies such as North America or Europe, a total fertility rate of slightly more than 2.0 is needed to achieve **replacement fertility** because a small number of females will die before they reach an age at which they will reproduce. In high-mortality countries, a larger surplus of births is needed to account for the fact that many females born today will not live to an age when they will bear children. In such countries, a total fertility rate of 2.5 or 2.6 translates into replacement fertility.

The growth trajectory of a country is not determined by fertility conditions alone. The difference between the crude birth rate and the crude death rate determines the level of growth. When the number of births is equal to the number of deaths, the CBR minus the CDR equals 0, and the country is said to be at **zero population growth (ZPG)**. ZPG refers to the *current* relationship between births and deaths.

One of the more perplexing concepts for students to understand is how a population can have a total fertility rate at or below the replacement level and continue to expand through natural increase. Yet this is exactly what is happening in China, France, Thailand, Ireland, South Korea, and some other countries, including Canada, with a TFR of 1.6 children per woman and a natural increase rate of 0.3 percent per year. **Demographic momentum** (or hidden momentum) is what population geographers call this tendency for a population to continue to grow long after replacement fertility has been achieved. This phenomenon originates with young, triangular age structures similar to those found in less-developed countries today. When the base of the age-sex structure is wide, many people are at or will soon be in age groups that will bear children, that is, typically between ages 20 and 40. Very few people are at the top of the pyramid in age groups where the likelihood of death is high. Thus, even if the population were to achieve replacement fertility today, the sheer number of people in or near the base results in large numbers of births. The small number of old people at the top results in a small number of deaths. Remember that growth is the numerical difference between births and deaths, not between births and parents. ZPG is almost impossible to achieve in pyramids with large bases. It takes many years for the large base to work itself upward into older age groups where deaths typically occur. In Activity 2 of this chapter, you will see several scenarios that illustrate the hidden momentum of population growth.

Students interested in the population structure of Canada can view animations of population pyramids through time for the entire country or its provinces at www .statcan.gc.ca/kits-trousses/animat/edu06a_0000-eng.htm. This site demonstrates demographic momentum, as well as examples for rapid, moderate, slow, and declining growth.

The hidden momentum issue is the subject of this chapter. You will be asked to simulate demographic conditions in India based on how long it takes India to lower its total fertility rate from 3.2 in 2000 to approximately 2.4, the level that would lead to a stable population in the long run. Understanding this process will enable you to interpret the geographic distribution of current and future population growth.

► *CASE STUDY*

ONE BILLION AND COUNTING

GOAL

To learn how to interpret **population pyramids** and to apply that knowledge to understand population projections. You will simulate the effects of future fertility rate assumptions on the shape of pyramids and interactively examine the **hidden momentum** of population growth (i.e., why a long lag occurs between declining fertility and the end of population growth).

LEARNING OUTCOMES

After completing the chapter, you will be able to:

- Relate the shape of population pyramids to a country's birth, death, and growth rates.
- Differentiate population pyramids of countries with rapid, slow, and negative population growth.
- Understand the hidden momentum built into current population pyramids.
- Recognize the hypothetical nature of population projections.

SPECIAL MATERIALS NEEDED

- Computer with high-speed Internet access and a recent release of a Web browser. If using the student Companion Site with the printed book, click on *Tech Support* for system requirements and technical support. (If using the e-book in WileyPlus, click on *Help* for details about the system requirements.)

BACKGROUND

Sometime in 2000, India joined China in the One-Billion Club of demographic giants (Table 5.2). Because of its higher

TABLE 5.2   Ten Most Populous Countries, 2008

Rank	Country	Population in 2008 (millions)
1	China	1,325
2	India	1,149
3	United States	305
4	Indonesia	240
5	Brazil	195
6	Pakistan	173
7	Nigeria	148
8	Bangladesh	147
9	Russia	142
10	Japan	128

Source: 2008 World Population Data Sheet of the Population Reference Bureau.

fertility, India is expected to surpass China within 30 years as the world's largest population. To understand India's current and future population prospects, it is important to know about its demographic history, the status of Indian women, efforts at family planning, connections with the rest of the world through international migration, and the environmental and societal effects of rapid population growth.

As with other developing nations, India's population growth before World War II was slow, owing to high death rates and low life expectancies (Figure 5.8). Epidemics of plague and cholera and famines kept the death rate high and population growth low. Fertility was high to compensate for the loss

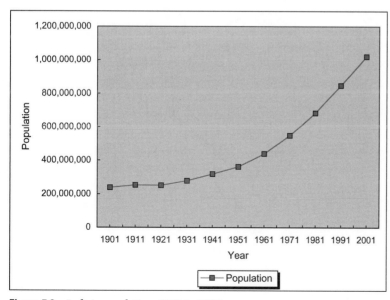

Figure 5.8   India's population, 1901 to 2000.
Source: www.censusindia.net.

© 2010 John Wiley & Sons, Inc.

► **CASE STUDY** *(continued)*

of children and to ensure that families would have enough sons to work the land and to take care of them in old age. India was in Stage 1 of the **demographic transition** with high fertility, high mortality, and slow population growth.

The beginnings of modernization after World War II improved health and diet. Life expectancy, which was only 32 years at the time of Indian independence in 1947, rose to 58 years in the 1980s and to 65 years today. The **infant mortality rate**, the number of babies who die before their first birthday (per 1,000 live births), fell from between 200 and 225 in 1947 to 90 during the 1980s and to 57 today. Initiated during the 1970s, the national government's program to provide free immunization to all children reduced the risk of contagious diseases such as tuberculosis, diphtheria, pertussis, tetanus, polio, and measles and was a major factor in reducing childhood death. Still, India's childhood immunization program misses a considerable percentage of children, especially in rural areas. Studies also show that children of illiterate mothers are less likely to be immunized than children of literate mothers, and girls are less likely to be immunized than boys.

As the demographic transition model predicts, the decline in birth rates in India lagged the decline of death rates (Figure 5.5). Norms of high fertility were, and still are, deeply ingrained in traditional Indian culture. Although India is the home of three of the world's 15 largest cities (Mumbai, Calcutta, and Delhi), 72 percent of the population lives in the rural countryside where incomes depend on agriculture, illiteracy is high, and the status of women is low (Figure 5.9). Despite rapid economic

growth, there are still not enough jobs for the recent flood of young people entering the workforce, and a rigid class structure inhibits upward mobility. India is home to 40 percent of the world's poor, and among these lower classes, illiteracy, hopelessness, and dependence on traditional value systems keep birth rates high. India today falls squarely in the third stage of the demographic transition with high but falling birth rates, low death rates, and rapid population growth.

Although fertility in India is high by world standards, it has fallen rapidly since the early 1970s. The **total fertility rate**—the average number of children a woman would have under current age-specific fertility rates—provides the best indication of fertility change over time. From a six-child average in the 1960s, the TFR fell to 3.1 by 2005, the base year for the simulation in Activity 2 (Figure 5.9), and to 2.8 by 2008 (Figure 5.10). This decline is substantial and significant in the context of the country's rural roots and traditional culture, but fertility remains above the replacement standard of two children per woman that prevails in societies that have completed the demographic transition. Pivotal factors in fertility decline have been an increase in the average age at marriage for women, from 16 in 1961 to about 22 today, and higher rates of contraceptive use, from 13 percent in 1970 to 56 percent today.

One of the biggest barriers to further fertility decline is the low status of Indian women. Evidence from the rest of the world shows the strong link between women's status and fertility. Literate, working women define their worth beyond the number of children they produce for the family. In most Indian

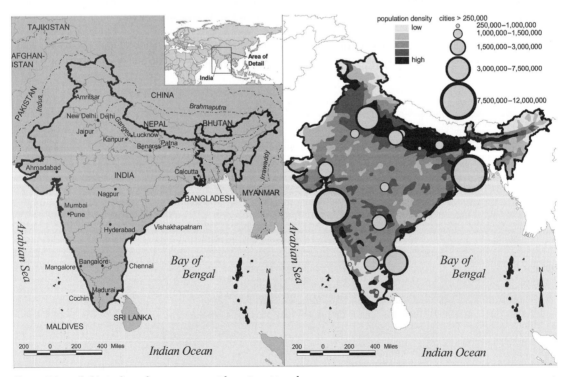

Figure 5.9a (left): India reference map, with major cities shown.
Figure 5.9b (right): India population density and major city population.

© **2010 John Wiley & Sons, Inc.**

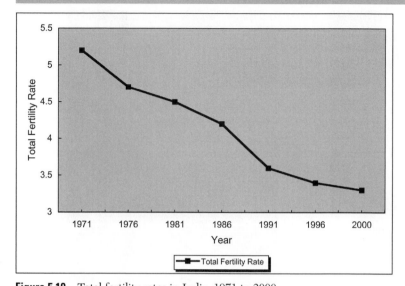

Figure 5.10 Total fertility rates in India, 1971 to 2000.

Source: Vital Rates for India 1971–1996, based on the Sample of Registration System (SRS). New Delhi: Registrar General of India, 1998.

families, males continue to make decisions about finances, work, social relationships, and selection of spouses. Marriage customs rely on arranged marriages, patrilineal inheritance systems, and wives who move in with their husband's family and then have little contact with their family of birth.

Related to the status and position of women in Indian society, a strong cultural preference for sons over daughters continues. This preference promotes neglect of female children, especially in poor families. Neglect can be extreme as in the case of outright infanticide among girl babies or more subtle as in failing to inoculate girls against childhood diseases or not sending them to school. Neglect of females leads to a deficit of women in the Indian population. Most populations contain more women than men because of higher across-the-board mortality among males. Because of the extremely low status of women, India's population has 5 percent more males than females.

Faced with high fertility and unprecedented population growth, India initiated a family-planning program during the 1950s. The program evolved from one focused on increasing the availability of family planning methods to a more all-encompassing view of family planning as integrated with efforts to improve overall health, reduce poverty, protect women's rights, and maintain the environment. Early efforts at family planning stressed methods over motivation and failed because Indian couples were not ready to accept family planning or were concerned about the risks of contraceptive use. In one ill-fated example, 800,000 to 900,000 Indian women were fitted with intrauterine devices (IUDs) in the mid-1960s. Real and perceived IUD-related health risks caused IUD use to plunge, and the method has never again gained widespread popular acceptance.

Frustrated by slow progress toward fertility reduction, many government officials rejected family planning as a means to slow population growth in the mid-1970s. At the 1974 World Population Conference in Bucharest, the Indian delegation articulated the now-familiar slogan that "development is the best contraceptive." In their minds, contraceptives are only a means to an end—a vehicle to help people achieve the family size they desire, however large that size may be. Without development and all that it includes—education, rising income, upward mobility, and urbanization—the view was that family planning would be unable to reduce fertility. This view has been moderated subsequently with growing evidence from India and elsewhere that family-planning programs can reduce fertility even without the obvious benefits of development. For instance, in neighboring Bangladesh, a small, mostly rural, country the size of Wisconsin with almost half as many people as the United States, TFR has fallen to 2.7 children per woman as a result of a strong government program of community-based family planning.

In the late 1970s, the Indian government established sterilization clinics around the country and offered financial and material incentives (e.g., money, bags of rice, radios) to those agreeing to the procedure (Figure 5.11). The national government gave local officials sterilization "targets" to achieve, and rumors of forced sterilizations soon swept India. As a result, the Indian people voted President Indira Gandhi out of office, and subsequent democratically elected governments have been careful not to cross the line to the kinds of punitive methods of fertility control practiced in nondemocratic China.

Today's program in India offers a wide range of contraceptives, including permanent sterilization and more reversible methods, such as oral contraceptives and IUDs, that appeal to a wide range of couples; administration is decentralized so programs can be sensitive to local area differences in language, religion, literacy, and economic development; and family planning is linked to women's reproductive health rather than viewed merely as a means of population control.

India has a vast **diaspora** across the world, with people who maintain close contact with families at home and are agents

© 2010 John Wiley & Sons, Inc.

▶ *CASE STUDY (continued)*

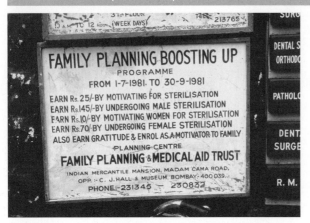

Figure 5.11 A sign outside a medical facility in Mumbai in 1978 entices passersby with money in payment for voluntary sterilization.

Figure 5.12 Women of Indian descent shopping at an Indian market in Durban, South Africa. Mohandas "Mahatma" Gandhi practiced law in South Africa from 1893 to 1914, where he was mistreated by whites for defending Asian immigrants. He developed the strategy of passive resistance there, which he used to lead India to independence from Britain in 1947.

of economic and social change. While India was a colony of Great Britain, many Indians emigrated to countries of the Commonwealth to provide plantation labor and to help build railroads. Large communities grew up in Guyana, Trinidad, Kenya, South Africa, and other British colonies and protectorates (Figure 5.12). More recently, Indians have moved to more-developed countries in search of high-wage jobs. This so-called brain drain draws off some of India's most ambitious and best educated people, but because emigrants send more than $3 billion to family at home, migration is a major source of income for the nation. There is considerable debate about whether remittances to family from Indians living abroad are spent on unproductive consumer goods (houses, cars, clothing, etc.) or used for education and to start businesses—investments that reap long-run returns for the Indian economy.

Major destinations for highly educated Indian migrants today are the United States, Great Britain, Canada, and Australia. Until 1990, the Persian Gulf also had drawn many Indian migrants, but they were forced to return home during the Persian Gulf crisis between Iraq and Kuwait. Slowing economies and the reluctance of Middle East governments to allow workers to bring their families or settle eventually reduced this historically and economically significant migration stream.

The social and environmental implications of rapid population growth in India are serious. The challenge of feeding more than 1 billion people puts extreme pressure on environmental resources. Supplies of fresh water are stretched to the limit, and soil exhaustion and erosion become major problems when farmland is overworked. In an effort to develop remaining arable land, farmers expand into marginal areas by cultivating low-lying, hurricane-prone islands in the Ganges delta, building terraces on steep mountainsides prone to landslides, and overgrazing arid lands. Thus far, increased use of fertilizers, pesticides, irrigation, and hybrid seeds (see discussion of the

Green Revolution in Chapter 8) has enabled India to become more or less self-sufficient in food supply, but 20 percent of the population is undernourished, and many poor people cannot afford the food that is available.

India's growth is outstripping the country's ability to provide social services and education to its entire population. Tens of millions have left rural India for the major cities, which cannot accommodate the huge influx of migrants. Millions of people are estimated to live in makeshift housing in squatter settlements around Mumbai, Calcutta, and Delhi without adequate sanitation and water supply, electricity, schools, and medical care. All three cities are predicted to grow by more than 33 percent from 2000 to 2015, with Mumbai surpassing 26 million people and possibly becoming the world's largest city.

It is hardly all doom and gloom, however. In addition to being the world's largest democracy, India has the largest middle class in the world. Its universities are first rate, its railway system is extensive, and it is industrializing rapidly. From 1990 to 2005, India's economy grew at an average rate of 6 percent per year—faster than any country in the world except China. Knowledge-based industries, particularly software engineering, are leading India's economic expansion and attracting foreign investment (Figure 5.13). Yet the rapid population growth puts the brakes on the rate of development by siphoning off capital

Figure 5.13 India is training ground for one of the world's largest technology work forces. Bangalore, home to the Indian Institute of Technology in South-Central India, is one of India's main high-tech centers.

surpluses that could have been invested in industrial infrastructure and technology but instead must be used for food, clothing, housing, health care, and education for the large cohort of children (Figure 5.14).

You will be asked in this exercise to put this background information to work in interpreting the shape of India's age-sex pyramid and in explaining the consequences of different future population scenarios. Due to the process of **demographic momentum** discussed earlier in this chapter, India is locked into future population growth by virtue of the high fertility in its recent past.

Figure 5.14 Children in Bangalore, India.

Name: _____ Instructor: _____

One Billion and Counting: The Hidden Momentum of Population Growth

▶ ACTIVITY 1: MATCHING DEMOGRAPHIC DESCRIPTIONS WITH POPULATION PYRAMIDS

A. To start your activity, click on the *Student Companion Site* at www.wiley.com/college/kuby. (For students using WileyPlus, log on to your class Web site, select the *Assignment* tab, locate and click on this assignment, and follow all instuctions.)

B. Select this chapter from the drop-down list and then click on *Computerized Chapter Activities*.

C. Click on *Activity 1: Matching Demographic Descriptions with Population Pyramids*.

1.1. Match the verbal description of a country's demographic composition (at the top of the screen) with the correct population pyramid. Click on the pyramid to check your answer. To go to the next description, click on the *Next Description* arrow in the right margin. Write the correct answer and the country name here:

Description 1: "A country with rapid population growth" matches population pyramid _____ Country name _____.

Description 2: "A country that shows the demographic effects of World War II" matches population pyramid _____ Country name _____.

Description 3: "A country at close to ZPG (zero population growth)" matches population pyramid _____ Country name _____.

Description 4: "A country that has undergone a recent shift from high to low fertility" matches population pyramid _____ Country name _____.

Description 5: "A country with many temporary immigrant workers" matches population pyramid _____ Country name _____.

Description 6: "A country with a declining population" matches population pyramid _____ Country name _____.

D. When you have finished, close all browser windows.

Name: _____   Instructor: _____

One Billion and Counting: The Hidden Momentum of Population Growth

► ACTIVITY 2: DEMOGRAPHIC MOMENTUM

Activity 2 of this chapter will use the population pyramid for India. To demonstrate the hidden momentum of population, you will run several scenarios of population change. Underlying these scenarios are two assumptions that relate to (1) the final total fertility rate (TFR) and (2) the number of years until that rate is achieved. You will experiment with changing the final TFR and the length of time it takes to get there. Once these assumptions are set, you will scroll through the years and watch India's population pyramid and total population change. This simulation will enable you to see when, if ever, population growth stabilizes, and at what level.

India begins with a TFR of 3.1 and a population of 1.1 billion in 2005 (based on U.S. Census Bureau and Census India estimates). By changing the final TFR either upward or downward, you can determine in the long run the number of children Indian women will bear. By changing the number of years to achieve that rate, you determine how long it will take for India to move to the new TFR position. Although the graphs start in 2000, your TFR assumptions will be put into effect starting in 2005.

In addition to these two assumptions, the computer incorporates (1) age-specific mortality rates, (2) age-specific fertility rates, and (3) the sex ratio of newborn children. The simulation resembles a conveyor belt that moves each cohort ahead in 5-year increments. Every five years, deaths are "trimmed off" the bar graph according to the age-specific, gender-specific death rates that generally increase with age. As the conveyor belt moves women through their childbearing years, children are added to the bottom of the pyramid according to the TFR you have specified and the age-specific birth rates of women 10 through 49. These births are added at a sex ratio of 51.2 percent male and 48.8 percent female, the biological average. Fortunately, the computer will automatically perform all calculations rapidly, and you can visualize the changes over time based on your assumptions.

It is important to recognize that any population simulation or projection is hypothetical in nature. One must exercise caution in dealing with simulations. One of the dangers of projecting future population change is assuming that various demographic parameters will stay the same in the future. Fifty years ago, few demographers would have imagined European countries with fertility rates barely above 1.0 or that a disease called AIDS would kill tens of millions of people in Africa. Fifty years from now, future demographers might say that no one foresaw the dramatic increase in life expectancy that resulted from artificial organs, a cure for cancer, or the mapping of the human genome—changes that would render most of today's population projections too low. In our case, although we allow total fertility to change, we assume that age-specific death rates, life expectancy, and the ages at which women give birth will all remain the same. Although we acknowledge the hypothetical nature of future projections by asking you to perform multiple "what-if" simulations, keep in mind that other parameters besides TFR will also change.

A. To start your activity, click on the *Student Companion Site* at www.wiley .com/college/kuby. (For students using WileyPlus, log on to your class Web site, select the *Assignment* tab, locate and click on this assignment, and follow all instuctions.)

B. Select this chapter from the drop-down list and then click on *Computerized Chapter Activities*.

C. Click on *Activity 2: Demographic Momentum*.

D. On the left side of the screen you will see the 2000 population pyramid of India. Try moving the mouse over the bars of the pyramid to see the exact population in both absolute and percentage terms. This will be especially useful for certain scenarios in which there will not be room to display an entire bar because the cohort in question surpasses the maximum of 15 percent that can be displayed.

On the upper right is a graph of India's population growth since 1900, and on the lower right is a demographic transition graph. These will change as you run different simulations. Try moving the mouse over the dots on the graphs.

Below the pyramid, in the bottom two gray boxes, you will see the variables you can adjust in these simulations. *Final Total Fertility Rate* is set to 3.1, the 2005 level; the allowable range is 0–10. *Years to Achieve Final TFR* is set to 0; it refers to years beyond 2005, the base year. For the following scenarios, you will adjust these variables and see what effect they have.

Scenario 1: Base Case, No Change in Total Fertility Rate

E. Assume no changes in India's fertility rate. Leave the *Final Total Fertility Rate* at 3.1, the 2005 value for India. Leave *Years to Achieve Final TFR* at 0, meaning this level is reached immediately. Click *Animate* and watch as the pyramid and graph evolve. To review the animation and freeze it at any year, use the up and down arrows on the screen to change the *Currently Shown Year*.

2.1. What would India's population be in 2050? _____.

2.2. The Population Reference Bureau reports the world's mid-2005 population as 6,396 million (or 6.396 billion). If India were to maintain its current fertility rate, how would its 2100 population compare to the current global population, in percentage terms?

India's population in 2100 would be roughly _____ percent of the 2005 global total.

2.3. India's 2005 population was 1,103 million. Approximately when would that population double, assuming the current fertility rate? _____.

2.4. Describe the shape of the population pyramid in 2100. _____
_____.

2.5. The gap between the crude birth rate (CBR) and the crude death rate (CDR) equals the rate of population change. Would this gap ever close if the TFR remains at 3.1? _____.

© 2010 John Wiley & Sons, Inc.

2.6. What would the annual rate of change of population be in 2100, in percentage terms? Calculate it as (CBR – CDR)/10, which gives you the rate of change in percentage terms. You can find out the exact CBR and CDR by mousing over the CBR and CDR dots in the graph._____.

Scenario 2: Instant Replacement Level

F. Next, assume that *overnight*, as of 2005, Indian women average 2.4 children. Use the up and down arrows to set the *Final Total Fertility Rate* to 2.4 and the *Years to Achieve Final TFR* to 0 (since we are assuming this level is reached immediately).

2.7. When would India's total population stop growing and more or less stabilize? _____.

2.8. What would be the approximate population when it stops growing? _____.

2.9. What would happen to the birth and death rates at the time when the population stops growing? _____.

G. Change the *Currently Shown Year* to 2020. Compare the size of the newly born 0- to 19-year-old generation (i.e., the children) with the size of the 20- to 39-year-old generation (i.e., their parents). (As you add up the cohorts, you can round each one to the nearest million before adding them up.)

2.10. Would the children's generation "replace" the parents' generation in terms of *approximately* equal numbers of people (+/– 25 million)? _____.

H. The comparison in Question 2.10 between parents and children does not, in the short term, control whether the population grows or not. For that you must compare births to deaths. Move the year shown back and forth between 2005 and 2025. Compare the size of the oldest four cohorts in 2005 (all of whom die between 2005 and 2025) to the youngest four cohorts in 2025 (all of whom were born between 2005 and 2025).

2.11. Would there be more births or elderly deaths between 2005 and 2025? _____.

2.12. By the year 2100, which of the four types of pyramids in Figure 5.6 would India's population pyramid most resemble? _____.

2.13. Assuming that achieving replacement-level fertility is desirable, is the assumption of 0 years to reach replacement fertility realistic, optimistic, or pessimistic? _____. Why? _____ _____.

Scenario 3: Forty Years until Replacement Fertility

I. Assume that a replacement-level TFR of 2.4 is India's ultimate goal but be more realistic about when that goal can be achieved. Leave the *Final Total Fertility Rate* at 2.4. Set the *Years to Achieve Final TFR* to 40, giving India until 2045 to achieve the replacement fertility rate.

© 2010 John Wiley & Sons, Inc.

2.14. How much larger would India's peak population be than in the previous scenario with no delay in achieving replacement fertility?

_____.

2.15. How many people will there be when the population peaks?

_____.

Scenario 4: Seventy-Five Years of Delay until Replacement Fertility

J. Now assume India will not achieve replacement fertility for 75 years. Leave the *Final Total Fertility Rate* at 2.4 but set the *Years to Achieve Final TFR* to 75.

2.16. Does India's total population completely stop growing before 2100?

_____.

2.17. What is the approximate population in 2100? _____.

Scenario 5: High Fertility

K. According to the *2005 Population Data Sheet* the country in which women have the largest number of children is Niger, with a TFR of 7.5. Assume that India reaches the same TFR as Niger by 2015. Set the *Final Total Fertility Rate* to 7.5 and the *Years to Achieve Final TFR* to 10.

2.18. What would India's total population be in the year 2100?

_____.

2.19. Under this high-fertility assumption, in which 5-year period would India's population surpass the world's current entire population of 6.396 billion?

_____.

2.20. What would happen to the base of the pyramid over the first 25 years?

_____.

Scenario 6: Low Fertility

L. In order to control population growth in China—a country with more than 1.3 billion people—the government enforced strict economic and social incentives for families to have only one child. Because not everybody complied with the policy, the 2000 TFR in China was 1.7 (rather than the sought-after TFR of 1.0). Assume the Indian government applied the same measures and this TFR was reached by 2015. Set the *Final Total Fertility Rate* to 1.7 and the *Years to Achieve Final TFR* to 10.

2.21. In what year would death rates surpass birth rates?

_____.

2.22. What would happen to the total population at that time? _____.

2.23. At what total population would it peak? _____.

2.24. What would be the difference in population between the peak year and the final year, 2100? _____.

2.25. What would be the annual rate of change of population in 2080, in percentage terms? Calculate it as (CBR − CDR)/10. _____.

Scenario 7: One-Child Policy

M. Assume a one-child policy was adopted and there was perfect compliance instantly. Set the *Final Total Fertility Rate* to 1.0 and the *Years to Achieve Final TFR* to 0.

2.26. When would the population completely stop growing? _____.

2.27. At what total population would it peak? _____.

2.28. What would be the difference in population between the peak year and the final year, 2100? _____.

2.29. How would you describe the shape of the age-sex distribution in 2100? _____.

2.30. Why would the crude death rate get so high near the end of the twenty-first century? _____.

N. When you have finished the activity, close all browser windows.

Name: _____   Instructor: _____

One Billion and Counting: The Hidden Momentum of Population Growth

▶ ACTIVITY 3: INTERPRETING POPULATION CHANGE

3.1. Using the understanding you have gained by projecting India's population pyramids into this hypothetical future, give a carefully worded explanation of how it is possible for a population to continue growing for several generations after women begin averaging only two children each. It may be particularly helpful to review your answers for Scenario 2 in Activity 2.

▶ DEFINITIONS OF KEY TERMS

Age-Specific Birth Rate The number of births to women in a certain age cohort divided by the number of women in that cohort.

Cohort All individuals in a certain age range.

Crude Birth Rate (CBR) Annual number of live births per 1,000 population.

Crude Death Rate (CDR) Annual number of deaths per 1,000 population.

Crude Rate of Natural Increase The difference between the crude birth rate and the crude death rate.

Demographic Momentum Continued population growth long after replacement-level fertility rates have been reached.

Demographic Transition Model A model of population change from an equilibrium with high birth and death rates through a high-growth transition period in which death rates decline sooner than birth rates, to a new equilibrium with low birth and death rates.

Diaspora Scattered settlements of a particular national group living abroad.

Equilibrium A state in which forces of change are in balance.

Hidden Momentum Same as demographic momentum.

Infant Mortality Rate Number of deaths of children under 1 year of age per 1,000 live births in a year.

Population Pyramid A graph showing the number of males and females in discrete age cohorts (age categories).

Replacement Fertility The fertility rate at which each female in a population produces on average one female baby who survives to the time when she herself can reproduce.

Total Fertility Rate The average number of children a woman would have during her reproductive years assuming the current fertility rates of women across all ages.

Zero Population Growth (ZPG) A state in which the crude birth rate minus the crude death rate equals zero. The number of deaths exactly offsets the number of births.

▶ FURTHER READINGS

Bloom, David E., and David Canning. 2006. Booms, Busts, and Echoes. *Finance & Development* 43(3).

Cohen, Joel E. 2005. Human Population Grows up. *Scientific American* (August): 48–55.

Gavin, Michelle. 2007. Africa's Restless Youth. *Current History* (May):220–226.

Gelbard, Alene, Carl Haub, and Marym Kent. 1999. World Population Beyond Six Billion. *Population Bulletin* 54:1–40.

Haub, Carl, and O.P. Sharma. 2006. India's Population Reality: Reconciling Change and Tradition. *Population Bulletin* 61(3):1–20.

Hopper, Gordon R. 1999. Changing Food Production and Quality of Diet in India, 1947–98. *Population and Development Review* 25:443–477.

India on Fire. 2007. *The Economist* (Feb. 3):77–80.

Kent, Mary M., and Carl Haub. 2005. Global Demographic Divide. *Population Bulletin* 60(4):1–24.

Lee, Ronald, and Andrew Mason. 2006. What is the Demographic Dividend? *Finance & Development* 43(3).

Levine, Ruth. 2006. Educating Girls, Unlocking Development. *Current History* (March):127–131.

Malthus, Thomas R. 1952. An Essay on Population. *Everyman's Library, Vol. 1.* New York: Dutton.

McFalls Jr., Joseph A. 2007. Population: A Lively Introduction (5th ed.). *Population Bulletin* 62(1): 1–31.

McMichael, Anthony J. 2008. Population, Human Resources, Health, and the Environment. *Environment* 50(1):46.

Meadows, Dana H., Dennis L. Meadows, and Jorgen Randers. 2004. *Limits to Growth: The 30-year Update.* White River Jct., VT: Chelsea Green.

O'Neill, Brian, and Deborah Bulk. 2001. World Population Futures. *Population Bulletin* 56(3):1–40.

Pinstrup-Andersen, Per and Fuzhi Cheng. 2007. Still Hungry: One Eighth of the World's People Do Not Have Enough to Eat. *Scientific American* (September):96–103.

Population Reference Bureau. 2008. World Population Highlights: Key Findings From PRB's 2008 World Population Data Sheet. *Population Bulletin* 63(3):1–12.

Riley, Nancy E. 2004. China's Population: New Trends and Challenges. *Population Bulletin* 59(2):1–36.

Singer, Max. 1999. The Population Surprise. *Atlantic Monthly* (Aug.):22–25.

United Nations. 1998. *Long-Range World Population Projections: Two Centuries of Population Growth, 1950–2150.* New York: United Nations.

Walker, Martin. 2006. India's Path to Greatness. *The Wilson Quarterly* 30(3):22–30.

Wilson, Chris. 2006. The Century Ahead. *Daedalus* 135(1):5–8.

Zakaria, Fareed. 2006. India Rising. *Newsweek* (March 6, 2006):32–42.

▶ WEB RESOURCES

Brinkhoff, Thomas. *City Population:* www.citypopulation.de
Census India. *Census of India*: www.censusindia.net
GeoHive: www.geohive.com/default1.aspx
International Monetary Fund. 2006. Picture This: Global Demographic Trends. *Finance & Development* 43(3): www.imf.org/external/pubs/ft/fandd/2006/09/picture.htm
Musee de L'homme. *6 Billion Human Beings*: www-popexpo.ined.fr/english.html
National Geographic. *Millennium@NationalGeographic.com*: magma.nationalgeographic.com/2000/population/main.html
Population Council: www.popcouncil.org
Population Reference Bureau. *World Population Data Sheet*: www.prb.org
Statistics Canada. *Population Pyramids*: www.statcan.ca/english/kits/animate/pyone.htm
UN Department of Economic and Social Affairs, Population Division. *India Becomes a Billionaire*: www.un.org/esa/population/pubsarchive/india/india.htm
UN Population Fund: www.unfpa.org
United Nations Statistics Division. Demographic, Social and Housing Statistics: unstats.un.org/unsd/demographic/default.htm
U.S. Census Bureau. *International Data Base (IDB)*: www.census.gov/ipc/www/idbnew.html
World Gazeteer: www.world-gazetteer.com

▶ ITEMS TO HAND IN

Activity 1: • Question 1.1, or answer all questions your instructor created in your WileyPlus assignments.
Activity 2: • Questions 2.1–2.30, or answer all questions your instructor created in your WileyPlus assignments.
Activity 3: • Question 3.1, or answer all questions your instructor created in your WileyPlus assignments.

CHAPTER 6

Help Wanted: The Changing Geography of Jobs

▶ INTRODUCTION

Places are highly differentiated in terms of what they produce, how they produce it, and how much they earn. Consider the differences among a subsistence rice-farming region in Bangladesh, the highly industrial Tokyo–Osaka region in Japan, and the service-based economy of greater New York (a major provider of services for finance, insurance, publishing, fashion, communication, and tourism). Economic geographers try to understand how and why production and service activities are distributed across the surface of the earth.

Let's start with a simple classification system for economic activity. **Primary activities**, which extract raw materials directly from the earth, include agriculture, forestry, fishing, trapping, and mining. Humans use some raw materials in their natural form, such as bananas, eggs, and coal. Many others, such as wheat, cattle, and unrefined oil, are not used in raw form. Copper ore, which can be less than 1 percent copper and 99 percent other materials, requires extensive processing before people can use it. **Secondary activities** are manufacturing operations that transform raw materials into more usable forms. They add value by making wheat into flour, copper ore into wire, and silicon into computer chips and by assembling sophisticated components into computers, airplanes, and cars.

The third sector of the economy, **tertiary activities**, takes the goods that are produced and manufactured by the primary and secondary sectors and either sells them to consumers or uses them to perform **services** for consumers. Services, quite simply, are tasks that you pay others to do for you. The tertiary sector thus includes wholesale and retail trade, restaurants, finance, transportation and communications, medicine, law, education, tourism, and entertainment. The service sector involves many occupations that do not require a high level of education or training (which are referred to as low-skill jobs), such as fast-food workers, janitors, cashiers, and bus drivers. The most dynamic part of today's service sector, however, includes highly skilled, information-based services called **quaternary activities** concerned with research and development (R&D), management and administration, and processing and disseminating information. The distinction between tertiary and quaternary activities is somewhat fuzzy. Technically, quaternary activities are a subset of the tertiary sector in that they are services that people do for other people using equipment (e.g., computers, telephones, copiers) manufactured by the secondary sector. In practice, however, the quaternary or "knowledge sector" is fundamentally different from other services. Your local bank clerk is a tertiary worker, whereas an investment banker brokering a merger between two large companies is a quaternary worker.

Now that we have defined *what* is produced in an economy, let's move to *where*. As a general principle, in market economies such as ours, in which firms are free to choose locations, economic activities locate where they can maximize profits. Profit equals revenues minus costs. For this introductory chapter, we focus on locations that minimize the cost side of the profit equation, although a firm's revenues can also vary depending on its location because demand and prices are spatially uneven.

The **cost-minimizing** location for any economic activity depends on what it is producing. Different economic activities have different cost structures: Some pay a lot for raw materials or transportation costs, whereas others pay a lot for land, unskilled labor, skilled labor, capital, or information. Cost structures vary not only among the primary, secondary, tertiary, and quaternary sectors but also within them. The cost structure of aluminum production, in which energy costs are very high, differs from that of computer programming, in which the costs of skilled labor and information are high. Some costs (for example, labor) vary tremendously from one location to another, whereas others (such as water) vary less. Cost structures even vary across the different stages of production within a single company, so that a company will locate some operations in one location and other operations elsewhere. In this chapter, we take a divide-and-conquer approach to discussing separately the locational strategies for minimizing each kind of cost.

One cost-minimizing locational orientation is toward locations with low wages. If unskilled labor accounts for the dominant part of a firm's manufacturing costs, as in textiles, furniture, shoes, or toys, the optimal location is in regions with cheap labor. This explains why the labor-intensive textile industry, once based mainly in New England, moved first to the nonunionized southern states and then overseas to the Caribbean islands and East Asia, for example, where workers earn only a few dollars per day. Many industries that require low-skilled assembly work have moved across the U.S. border to Mexico (Figure 6.1). In many cases, parts are manufactured

Figure 6.1 Women sew designer clothing at a maquiladora in the town of Matamoros in the state of Tamaulipas, Mexico.

in the United States, shipped to a **maquiladora** in Mexico for assembly, and then shipped back to the United States for sale to U.S. consumers. Low wages in Mexico more than make up for the extra transport costs. Labor quality must also be factored into the labor cost equation in terms of speed of work, reliability, absenteeism, work ethic, communications barriers, fringe benefits, length of work week, and so on. The presence of labor unions also can affect work rules and the cost of labor.

Transportation costs quite obviously depend on where the company is located. Firms for which transportation costs account for a large share of total costs tend to locate their factories where the total transportation cost of (1) assembling their physical inputs plus (2) distributing their products is as low as possible. Transport cost minimization can lead to three distinctly different locational orientations. If a firm's raw materials are quite heavy relative to the weight of the final product, and if those raw materials are found in only a few locations, transport costs are minimized by locating near the raw material sites (Figure 6.2a). Paper manufacturing is a classic **raw-material-oriented industry.** Approximately 3 tons of wood are used to make 1 ton of paper. In addition, boxes of paper are easier to handle than logs and therefore cheaper to ship per ton. It makes more economic sense to process logs into paper near the logging site and then ship the paper goods to markets than it does to ship heavy and unwieldy logs all the way to the market location. A second example of raw material orientation is the ore-producing industry, such as copper or iron ore. It is very common to build a concentrating plant right at the mine site to remove mine waste from iron and copper ore before shipping it to a smelter. A third and more complex example is steel manufacturing, which has not one but two main raw materials: coal and iron ore. In the 1800s, the "recipe" for making 1 ton of steel was 5 to 10 tons of coal plus 2 to 3 tons of iron. Steel manufacturing was pulled strongly toward the location of suitable metallurgical-quality coal near places such as Pittsburgh. However, changes in steel-making technology and changes in the locations of raw materials and final destinations have altered optimal locations. Today, some steel factories use natural gas furnaces. The natural gas source locations do not exert as strong a pull as the coal mines did because natural gas is a more efficient fuel that can be moved cheaply by pipeline. The new steel plants can also use scrap steel from junkyards as a source of iron. As a result, the optimal locations are now pulled away from the fuel sources and toward cities, which are major sources of scrap steel *and* markets for final products in the construction industry. Thus, a new wave of "mini" steel mills has sprung up in cities across the country.

The second type of transport-cost-minimizing location is near major markets for the products. If the transport costs of the final product exceed those of the raw materials, an industry is said to be **market oriented** and will profit by locating near its customers (Figure 6.2b). This can be the case if some of the raw materials are **ubiquitous;** that is, they can be found almost anywhere and therefore do not need to be transported to the factory. This is the case with soft drinks, which are made with approximately 1 part sugary syrup and 9 parts water. Why would a manufacturer add the water to the syrup near the sugar plantations in Florida or Cuba and ship the full cans over thousands of miles when it could much more cheaply ship the syrup to each city and add the water there? Glassmaking is market oriented not only because its main raw material—sand—is ubiquitous but also because the final product is so fragile. It is much cheaper to ship a ton of sand than a ton of glass. Beer, bread, and mattresses are other examples of market-oriented industries. Budweiser® and Miller®, for instance, have breweries not only in St. Louis and Milwaukee but also in numerous other cities.

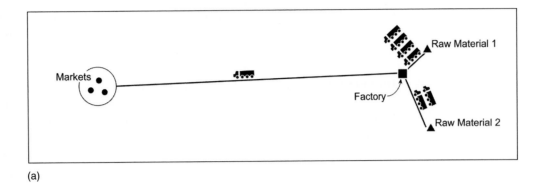

(a)

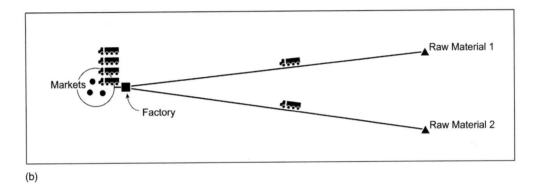

(b)

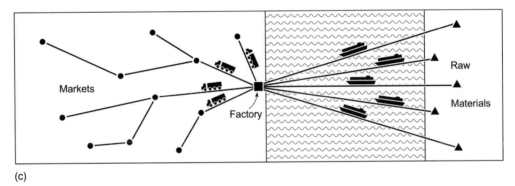

(c)

Figure 6.2 (a) Raw material orientation; (b) Market orientation; (c) Break-of-bulk orientation.

Sometimes a location between the raw materials and the market can minimize transport costs. This third type of transport cost minimization is at **break-of-bulk** points. These are places where a large shipment of raw materials is divided into smaller lots, often at ports where goods must be unloaded from one mode of transportation and reloaded onto another (Figure 6.2c). The loading and unloading costs are part of the transportation costs, and an additional loading/unloading stage at the factory can be avoided by locating the factory right at the break-of-bulk point itself. This is especially true when the port acts as a funnel location for the raw materials collected from, or final products bound to, many destinations in the port's "functional region." (See Chapter 2 for discussion of functional regions.) For instance, the ports of Philadelphia and northern New Jersey are funnel points for imported oil,

© 2010 John Wiley & Sons, Inc.

and they have evolved into major petrochemical refining sites. The oil arrives from various countries by tanker, and before it is transferred to pipelines and rail for the entire Northeast, it is refined into gasoline and other products.

Other types of companies are attracted to locate near other firms by **agglomeration economies**, which are cost savings (i.e., "economies") obtained by clustering (i.e., "agglomeration"). By locating within an agglomeration, firms can minimize their **transaction costs**, which are the additional costs of purchasing or selling a good or service beyond its actual price and transportation costs. Transaction costs include the costs of identifying buyers and sellers, finding and attracting skilled workers and investors, working out technological specifications and delivery schedules with parts suppliers and customers, learning new technologies and acquiring other information, and dealing with delays and shortages. Transaction costs are sometimes referred to as the *hidden costs* of doing business because they are very difficult to measure. Even though these costs don't appear as a separate item in a company's financial statement, they are very real costs that can make or break a company. These costs are highest in complex and rapidly changing industries.

The transaction cost savings accrued from locating within an agglomeration are considered **externalities**, that is, effects that are external to any one firm but internal to the cluster as a whole. We can distinguish between two kinds of agglomeration, depending on whether the externalities extend mainly to firms within a single industry (known as *localization effects*) or to all firms in the area (*urbanization effects*).

Examples of **localization economies** are carpets in Dalton, Georgia; glass in West Virginia; chemicals in Texas; lace in Brussels, Belgium; pharmaceuticals in Philadelphia; entertainment in Hollywood; finance in New York City; fashion in Milan; and aircraft in Seattle. This type of agglomeration can occur in an area as small as a few city blocks (Figure 6.3) or as large as a metropolitan area. Several mechanisms act to reinforce an initial industrial cluster and create a snowballing effect that attracts more activity to the cluster. First, agglomerations allow specialized support networks of suppliers and services to emerge, but not until a critical mass of demand for their products and services is reached. Specialized suppliers need sufficient demand in order to justify their investment in the specialized equipment and labor. For instance, Houston's petrochemical agglomeration is large enough to support firms that specialize in cleaning up oil spills and disposing of or recycling toxic waste. Hollywood benefits from the presence of special-effects companies, casting agents, film editors, film processors, sound engineers, and a host of other specialists. The transaction costs of producing a film away from this support network can be crushing.

A second type of localization economy is the presence of skilled labor. Agglomerations attract specialized workers, who migrate to agglomerations despite the high cost of living and traffic congestion. The draw of Hollywood for talented actors, comedians, and musicians is world famous. Similarly, the pharmaceutical industry of Philadelphia benefits from the largest output of medical students in the United States. The critical mass of skilled workers then attracts more companies needing top workers, which in turn attract more skilled workers, and so on in a self-reinforcing cycle that minimizes transaction costs for employers and workers.

The third mechanism for localization is **technological spillovers**—technological, scientific, and business information that passes among people and companies. The essence of technological spillovers is captured by the phrase "being in the loop." If your firm is "out of the loop," it could suffer critical delays in bringing new products to market or make massive investments in a technology that ends up being eclipsed by something else (e.g., Betamax video recorders). Technological spillovers occur not

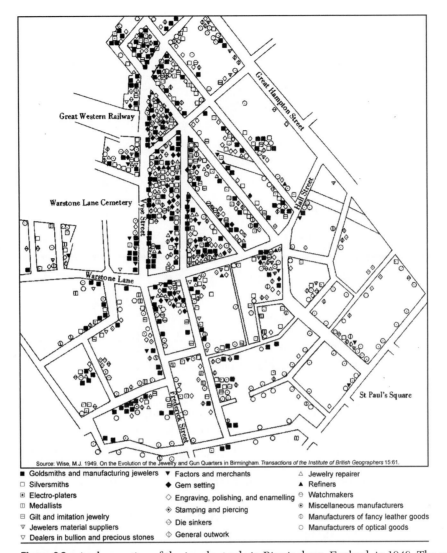

Source: Wise, M.J. 1949. On the Evolution of the Jewelry and Gun Quarters in Birmingham. *Transactions of the Institute of British Geographers* 15:61.

- ■ Goldsmiths and manufacturing jewelers
- ▽ Silversmiths
- ⊡ Electro-platers
- ⊞ Medallists
- ⊟ Gilt and imitation jewelry
- ▽ Jewelers material suppliers
- ▽ Dealers in bullion and precious stones
- ▼ Factors and merchants
- ◆ Gem setting
- ◇ Engraving, polishing, and enamelling
- ◈ Stamping and piercing
- ◇ Die sinkers
- ◇ General outwork
- △ Jewelry repairer
- ▲ Refiners
- ⊖ Watchmakers
- ⊙ Miscellaneous manufacturers
- ⊕ Manufacturers of fancy leather goods
- ○ Manufacturers of optical goods

Figure 6.3 Agglomeration of the jewelry trade in Birmingham, England, in 1948. The many specialty trades, manufacturers, and suppliers create localization economies by their geographical proximity.

only at business meetings and scientific conferences but also at backyard barbecues and kids' soccer games. Although technological spillovers are, by definition, free, we can think of them as the avoidance of very expensive costs of reproducing the same cutting-edge information at in-house research labs. One of the best examples of technological spillovers is the early history of the semiconductor industry in and around Santa Clara–San Jose, California, popularly known as *Silicon Valley* (Figure 6.4). The first semiconductor firm was started in 1955 by William Shockley, one of the inventors of the transistor. In 1957, eight of Shockley's scientists left to start their own firms. By 1965, there were 10 more spin-offs and 50 more by 1980—all located near Santa Clara–San Jose. The pace of technological innovation in this rapidly emerging industry made it imperative that producers keep abreast of the latest developments in the field. Innovation in semiconductors soon spawned a host of other related industries in the same area, including computers, digital networks, and software. As a result, at the zenith of the "dot-com" boom in 1999, Silicon Valley by itself attracted almost 40 percent of the national total of high-tech venture capital.

© 2010 John Wiley & Sons, Inc.

Figure 6.4 Location of semiconductor design houses, 1991.

Silicon Valley is a preeminent example of all three mechanisms driving localization economies: specialized networks of suppliers and support businesses, a specialized labor market, and technological spillover. Companies such as Oracle, Cisco, Apple, Yahoo!, Advanced Micro Devices, Hewlett-Packard, Intel, Xilinx, and countless others agglomerate there (Figure 6.5). All around the world, regions have tried to duplicate the synergy found in Silicon Valley, with self-proclaimed "silicon wannabes" such as Silicon Desert (Phoenix), Silicon Forest (Portland), Silicon Mountain (Colorado Springs), and Silicon Mesa (Albuquerque), not to mention Silicon Fen in the United Kingdom, Silicon Glen in Scotland, Silicon Bog in Ireland, Silicon Wadi in Israel, and Silicon Plateau in India. A few, such as Route 128 around Boston, which attracted 12 percent of high-tech venture capital in 1999, have reached a critical mass of companies, suppliers, investors, and workers to lower transaction costs.

Figure 6.5 Intel headquarters in Santa Clara, California.

Often overlooked are the additional transportation costs created by localization economies. An industry with but a few locations worldwide must ship the product from those few locations to the rest of the world. It is not coincidental, therefore, that many of the most highly agglomerated industries produce goods with an extremely high value-to-weight ratio. Computer chips, films, and pharmaceuticals are so valuable they are often shipped by air.

A second type of agglomeration economy is based on **urbanization economies**, in which cost-saving externalities derive from an increase in the size of the place and accrue to most firms in most industries. This is partly because larger cities provide large markets, but it is also because larger cities provide many goods and services—nearby airports, water and fire services, emergency health care, and job training—that a firm located in a smaller city or rural area might otherwise have to provide in-house. Most large cities offer a wide array of **producer services** (also known as *business services*), which include engineering firms, advertising agencies, printing shops, accounting firms, corporate law firms, temporary employment agencies, freelance editors, corporate trainers, office equipment repair, payroll-processing companies, freight forwarders, and the like. Economic clustering of secondary, tertiary, and quaternary companies in metropolitan areas including Toronto, New York, Chicago, and Los Angeles is partly the result of urbanization economies that minimize the transaction costs among myriad urban businesses.

Primary activities also attempt to minimize production, transportation, and transaction costs. Because primary activities consume large amounts of land to produce generally low-value products, most cannot afford to locate in expensive urban locations. They are influenced by environmental conditions such as rainfall, soil quality, and length of growing season. Some, however, can afford to locate near urban locations if they use small amounts of land and produce high-value products such as milk, mushrooms, strawberries, and grapes (see Chapter 8 for more on agriculture). Mining operations are particularly constrained by natural conditions and the availability of natural resources. Even with mining, factors such as distance to market, costs of labor, availability of capital, and technological know-how come into play. Sand and gravel, for instance, which the construction industry uses, are often mined in or near urban areas to minimize the transportation costs.

Initial cost advantages based on raw materials, markets, break of bulk, or labor often account for the early location of a particular industry. In other cases, there is no explanation other than a region's good luck in being home to a particularly brilliant entrepreneur—Detroit, for example, was home to Henry Ford. Early locations often act as the initial seed around which an agglomeration grows. Cheap hydroelectricity was the reason for the power-hungry aluminum-smelting industry to locate in the Pacific Northwest, which then gave Seattle an advantage in making aluminum airplanes. At this point, however, the know-how of the local labor force and the critical mass of aircraft industry suppliers keep Boeing production facilities rooted in the Seattle area, even though Boeing has moved its headquarters to Chicago.

Firms seek a balance to minimize their total costs. Thus, the labor savings of locating in distant low-wage countries must be weighed against higher transportation and transaction costs. One way companies get around this trade-off is through a **spatial division of labor**. Different stages of production can be spatially separated, with each located to minimize its own particular cost structure. Headquarters, management, and research and development functions are often located in "world cities" such as New York, Los Angeles, Toronto, Atlanta, London, Paris, Frankfurt, Tokyo, and Singapore that are well served by global transport and communications networks, capital markets, and highly educated labor pools. More routine manufacturing or information-processing tasks are frequently relocated to "branch plants" and "back offices" in areas with lower labor costs. For instance, semiconductor *fabrication* is far less agglomerated in Silicon Valley (Figure 6.6) than semiconductor *design* (Figure 6.4). Intel's headquarters and main research labs are in Silicon Valley, but branch plants are found across the Southwest. Similarly, banks and insurance companies are mainly headquartered in New York, London, and Tokyo, but their back-office credit-card-processing operations are located in places such as Phoenix, Omaha, and Ireland. The spatial division of labor occurs at the local scale as well. More command-and-control tasks requiring face-to-face interactions with other professionals are located in downtowns of large cities, whereas more routine functions are moved to suburban areas with lower rents.

Industries have distinctive life-cycle patterns with characteristic geographies. Infant industries are typically led by start-up companies located where the new technology was invented. As the industry reaches maturity, competition increases, and the product becomes a mass-produced standardized commodity, as semiconductors have become. The industry then consolidates from many small firms to fewer successful large firms. As the core region becomes more expensive and markets for the product become widespread, the production tasks that have now become routine are decentralized. Finally, the industry reaches the decline stage when the market becomes saturated or the technology is eclipsed by something new. Firms look to trim costs to stay competitive, and some reconcentration of production can occur as less efficient plants are "rationalized," that is, closed. Workers must retrain, migrate, or seek unemployment compensation, and the plant closures can create a ripple effect on the local economy.

States and provinces compete fiercely to attract new employers. Low unemployment, good jobs, and a strong tax base are on every region's wish list. Regions are interested in attracting new **basic industries**, which are those that sell outside

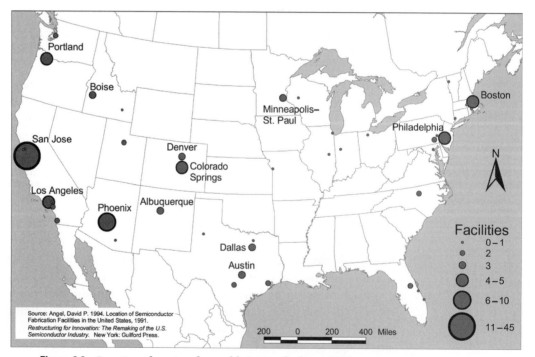

Figure 6.6 Location of semiconductor fabrication facilities, 1991.

© 2010 John Wiley & Sons, Inc.

the local region and thus bring new money into the region. In contrast, **nonbasic industries** produce mainly for the local market, supplying the needs of the region's inhabitants and businesses. According to the **economic base model**, exports from basic industries are the engine of regional development (Figure 6.7). They bring in money from outside to employ workers in the basic industries; further, each job created in the basic sector creates more jobs in the nonbasic sector. This relationship is called the **regional multiplier**. The multiplier is the total number of jobs created in the basic *and* nonbasic sectors for each new basic job in a region.

Two mechanisms multiply the impact of each new basic job. The first focuses on basic workers and where they spend their wages. For instance, a new software company sells its products to a national or international market and, with those revenues, pays workers in the local region. These workers, in turn, purchase food, housing, fuel, and other products and pay for services by doctors, teachers, and hairdressers, who in turn spend their wages to employ waitresses, mechanics, and so on. The second mechanism relates to where the new basic industry acquires the inputs it uses to produce goods or services. A new firm can purchase parts, packing boxes, and stationery from other local firms and can employ the services of local accounting firms, law offices, or truck repair stations. Alternatively, its inputs can come from faraway regions, for example, iron ore from Venezuela or electronic components from Texas. The size of the regional multiplier will depend on how much consumers and firms buy locally versus externally.

The regional multiplier effect cuts both ways. Job losses are multiplied in the same way as job gains. When a large factory closes (Figure 6.8), it is often followed

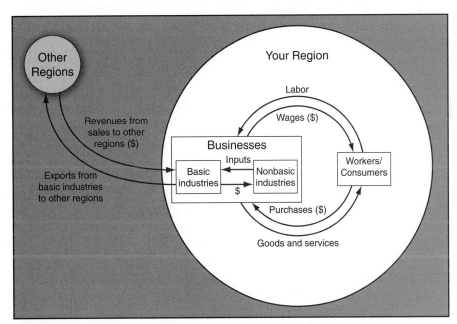

Figure 6.7 The underlying mechanism of the economic base model is shown in this simplified diagram. The economy of a region can be thought of as a cycle. Money, in the form of wages, flows from businesses to people in exchange for their labor. Money flows back from people to businesses as purchases of goods and services. When goods and services are sold by the region's basic industries to other regions, money flows in. Some of this money flows to additional local workers who are hired, and some flows back to nonbasic industries from which the basic industries purchase goods and services they need as inputs to their business. In addition, the new basic and non basic workers purchase local goods and services. The local, nonbasic firms then hire more workers for this additional demand, creating a multiplier effect.

Figure 6.8 Flint, Michigan, the birthplace of General Motors and a "company town," was economically devastated by the closure of the GM factory there in the mid-1980s. Tens of thousands of workers lost their jobs at GM, and countless businesses in the nonbasic sector closed shortly thereafter. The effects on the people of Flint were chronicled in the documentary film *Roger & Me*.

by bankruptcies of local nonbasic businesses (service stations, boutiques, restaurants, and grocery stores), not to mention suppliers of raw materials, components, and producer services.

Basic and nonbasic industries can come from any sector of the economy. In the primary sector, milk production and gravel mining are usually nonbasic industries that serve the local area, whereas citrus farming and gold mining are basic. In the secondary sector, manufactured goods that are sold nationally or globally such as airplanes and computer chips are basic, whereas goods that are sold locally such as bread and glass are nonbasic. In the tertiary sector, tourism, investment banking, and national television networks are basic, whereas auto repair, branch banking, and local TV stations are nonbasic. These examples illustrate two important points about the basic-nonbasic distinction. First, you can't lump an entire industry into basic or nonbasic. Second, basic or nonbasic depends on the scale of the region. A product sold to a four-state region is basic at the city and state scales but nonbasic at the national scale.

Activity 1 of this chapter asks you to look at a profile of economic activities for your state or province. You will compare it to the national profile to see how the economy of your state or province is different. You will also compare it to the profile for your state or province three decades earlier to see how the economy has changed over time. Then Activity 2 asks you to apply economic base theory to some hypothetical regions.

► *CASE STUDY*

HELP WANTED

GOAL

To introduce the different types of economic activities and to explain why certain industries locate where they do. You will better understand the economic profile of your state and country and changes over time. You will also be introduced to regional development, the relationships between what is produced by the economic activity (primary, secondary, tertiary, and quaternary), and where output is sold or consumed (basic and nonbasic activity).

LEARNING OUTCOMES

After completing the chapter, you will be able to:

- Differentiate among primary, secondary, tertiary, and quaternary activity.
- Explain how and why certain kinds of economic activities minimize certain kinds of costs.
- Identify and explain employment patterns on maps.
- Define the economic specializations of your state or province in relation to the nation, and understand why those specializations exist.
- Describe how your state's or province's economic profile has changed over time.
- Differentiate between basic and nonbasic activity.
- Calculate a regional multiplier from the ratio of total to basic activity.

SPECIAL MATERIALS NEEDED

- Calculator
- Computer with high-speed Internet access and a recent release of a Web browser. If using the Student Companion Site with the printed book, click on *Tech Support* for system requirements and technical support. (If using the e-book in WileyPlus, click on *Help* for details about the system requirements.)

BACKGROUND

What are your plans after college or graduate school? Do you have an ideal job in mind? Equally important, where would you like to live? If you stay in your current state or province after college, how will your job opportunities be different from those in other regions? How are your job options different from those of your parents and grandparents? The changing economic geography of jobs is something that every college graduate must consider. Average income varies greatly by state as a function of the types of industries located there and the cost of living (Figure 6.9).

As you complete your college degree, you will enter a labor market in which competition is fierce. The percentage of workers with college degrees has increased from 7 percent in 1952 to 26 percent in 2000. Furthermore, women have flooded the workforce, from just 10 percent of women in 1940 to 60 percent in 2000. *Downsizing* is everywhere as firms and government

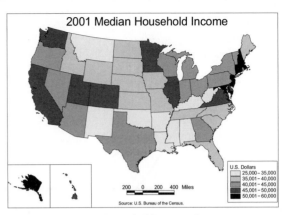

Figure 6.9 Median household income by state, 2001.

agencies try to do more with fewer workers. Increasingly, employers subcontract tasks that once were performed in-house, creating more temporary or contingent workers. Moreover, today's workers operate in a global labor market in which they compete with workers in less-developed countries who sometimes earn pennies per hour. They also compete with robots that never eat and sleep and make almost no mistakes.

Despite these unsettling aspects of today's labor market, workers in the United States, Canada, Japan, Australia, and Western Europe at the turn of the millennium live in the most affluent societies in the history of mankind (see Chapter 7 for a more international perspective on economic development). Over time, the basis of the economy has changed from primary activities, to industrial activities, and finally to postindustrial and information-based functions. This evolution has generated higher levels of productivity and higher levels of wealth per worker. Under preindustrial conditions, almost the entire society was needed to produce the basic necessities of life: food (primary production), shelter, and heat. As a society produces more efficiently, increasing numbers of workers are freed to work in manufacturing (secondary activity) and ultimately in services (tertiary and quaternary activities) (Figure 6.10).

In highly developed and technologically sophisticated countries such as the United States and Canada, primary activities represent only a tiny proportion of the total workforce. This is a drastic change from the 1700s and 1800s, when such activities dominated the economy, as they still do in many less-developed countries. Mechanization has enabled a tiny portion—3.7 million of 123 million employed persons in the United States—to produce enough food, fish, timber, and minerals for the entire country, thus freeing the other 97 percent of workers to perform other functions.

The **industrial economy** achieved great wealth through three processes: (1) mechanization, (2) economies of scale, and (3) specialization—all of which increased the productivity of labor. **Labor productivity** is a measure of output per worker per hour. The more each worker produces per hour, the more wages and/or profits increase. Mechanization, or substitution

© 2010 John Wiley & Sons, Inc.

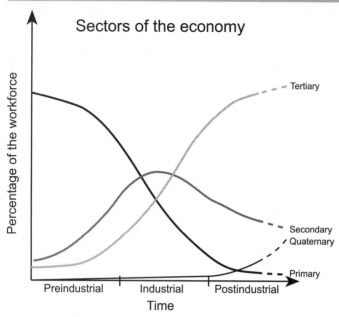

Figure 6.10 The percentage of the workforce engaged in primary, secondary, tertiary, or quaternary activities changes dramatically as an economy matures. Initially, the primary activities dominate as farming, mining, and fishing compose the majority of jobs. Later, secondary activities take over when an industrial economy develops. In the postindustrial era, tertiary service activities are most prevalent, and eventually quaternary activities also grow rapidly.

of capital for labor, is one way to increase labor productivity. **Capital goods,** defined as those used to produce other goods, include machines, tools, computers, buildings, and vehicles. Most goods and services can be produced with varying proportions of capital and labor. Toothpicks, for instance, can be made by hundreds of workers whittling with knives, or by a handful of workers operating saws, lathes, sanders, and conveyor belts. If the machine is to do the work of many workers, it needs a source of power other than humans and animals, which is why energy became so important to the industrial economy. In particular, electricity is a key to unleashing productivity because it allows myriad small devices to be powered.

The second key to increasing productivity of the industrial economy is through **economies of scale**, defined as cost savings that result from producing a larger amount of output. Economies of scale result partly from larger machines. In coal mining, larger and more efficient equipment increased the average output per worker from 0.7 ton per worker-hour in 1950 to 7 tons per worker-hour in 2000. In Wyoming, which recently eclipsed West Virginia as the leading coal-producing state, some mines average an astonishing 50 tons per worker-hour with the help of gargantuan surface-mining equipment (Figure 6.11).

Economies of scale also result from spreading overhead, management, accounting, marketing, and so forth over a larger volume of production. Thus, McDonald's, with more than 30,000 restaurants in 120 countries, can produce hamburgers at extremely low prices. Huge businesses such as Wal-Mart, with more than 7,000 stores and 2 million employees, can undersell the competition not only by spreading advertising and other management costs over a larger number of stores

but also by extracting discounts from suppliers, who are willing to sell to Wal-Mart at low prices in order to achieve their own economies of scale.

Economies of scale also can be achieved through horizontal and vertical integration. *Horizontal integration* refers to buying other companies at the same stage of the production process, which allows production of a wider range of products and more pricing power in the marketplace. When German automaker Daimler Motors, producer of Mercedes-Benz, acquired Chrysler and its diverse line of vehicles, the goal was to offer a wider range of products and achieve cost savings by integrating German and American car-making know-how. *Vertical integration* involves expanding into upstream and downstream businesses, that is, companies at earlier or later stages in the production and distribution process. During the early twentieth century, Ford Motor Company purchased everything from coal mines and lumber companies to steel mills and tire factories to bring the entire car production process under its control.

A third method for increasing productivity involves the process of specialization. As firms get larger, they can hire particular people for narrowly defined jobs: welder, accountant, seamstress, computer network specialist. **Division of labor** enables specialized workers to do individual tasks better than a generalist and to save time by not switching among tasks. And as workers specialize, so does the capital equipment they use and the training they receive.

Today's **postindustrial economy** (also known as the *New Economy or the Information Economy*) applies the same principles of mechanization, economies of scale, and specialization to services, education, leisure activities, and the

© **2010 John Wiley & Sons, Inc.**

► **CASE STUDY** *(continued)*

Figure 6.11 At the largest and most productive strip mines, workers average more than 50 tons produced per person per hour.

processing and exchange of information by telecommunications and computers. Information is now the most valuable resource in increasing productivity, even more than energy. The Information Economy employs only 8 percent of U.S. workers, according to the U.S. Council of Economic Advisors, but it accounted for one-third of the economic growth in the 1990s. Of course, the post-industrial economy does not completely replace the industrial economy, but rather supplements it and permeates it. Table 6.1 identifies the top 20 U.S. corporations on the Fortune 500 list of the largest U.S. companies in terms of sales. The changes in the list illustrate the grafting of the New Economy onto the Old, as well as the result of corporate mergers (horizontal and vertical). Gone are heavy-industry stalwarts such as U.S. Steel, Western Electric, and Ling-Temco-Vought, replaced by high-technology companies.

Computer and software giant IBM has been joined (and passed!) in the Top 20 by computer/printer manufacturer Hewlett-Packard, followed by computer maker Dell (#34), software giant Microsoft (#44), chip maker Intel (#60), and network/communications companies Motorola (#65) and Cisco (#71).

Of course, all of the other companies on the list are infused with advanced technology, either in their actual products (e.g., drugs, phones, electrical equipment, medical supplies), their manufacturing processes (oil, autos), their management of information (insurance, finance, health care providers), or their supply-chain management (autos, retail). Traditional energy and industrial companies—ExxonMobil, Chevron, GM, ConocoPhillips, General Electric, and Ford—still comprise six of the top seven, showing that oil, cars, and electricity of the Old Economy remain important, although they are produced with fewer employees due to automation and outsourcing.

Service corporations are now among the largest corporations in America. The number of financial service companies on the list has risen from one in 1969 (Prudential Life Insurance) to seven in 2004 (Citigroup, Bank of America, Berkshire-Hathaway, JPMorgan Chase, AIG Insurance, and Goldman Sachs, plus General Electric, which *Fortune* magazine lists as a "diversified financial" corporation because of its insurance, lending, credit card, and investment operations). Health care also figures more prominently, up from 0 to 2 (McKesson and Cardinal Health), with three others in the top 30 (CVS Caremark, United Health Group, and Amerisource Bergen). Large retail companies continue to do well, although major players have changed from Sears, A&P, Safeway, and J.C. Penney to Wal-Mart (and in the top 30: Home Depot, Kroger, and Costco). Wal-Mart—which took over the top spot in 2002—has more employees than the next 11 companies on the list combined. Ranked by number of employees, Wal-Mart would be followed by United Parcel Service (#46 by sales, with 425,000 employees) and McDonalds (#106 by sales, with 390,000 employees). The dramatic difference in how some companies rank in terms of sales and employees reveals the growing divide between the vast numbers of low-wage service workers and the expanding class of highly educated and highly compensated information workers in the New Economy. This wage and productivity gap is evident in the stark contrast between the two largest companies in Table 6.1: ExxonMobil took in nearly the same revenues as WalMart but with 19 times fewer employees.

Another huge change in the economy is increasing globalization (see also Chapter 8). Firms globalize to achieve economies of scale and greater specialization through larger markets, as well as cheap labor and resources. In 1950, large corporations operated mainly in their home countries. By 1975, most had become multinational corporations by setting up foreign subsidiaries in other countries. By 2000, multinational corporations had evolved into transnational corporations, which implies integration of global operations into a seamless supply chain linked by global transportation and communications

© 2010 John Wiley & Sons, Inc.

▶ **CASE STUDY** *(continued)*

TABLE 6.1   Top 20 U.S. Companies in Terms of Sales, 1969 and 2008

	1969				2008			
Rank	Top Companies	Head-quarters	Revenues (billion)	Employees	Top Companies	Head-quarters	Revenues (billion)	Employees
1	General Motors	Detroit, MI	$24.3	793,924	Wal-Mart Stores	Bentonville, AR	$378.8	2,055,000
2	AT&T (telephone)	New York, NY	$15.7	735,856	Exxon Mobil (oil refining)	Irving, TX	$372.8	107,100
3	Standard Oil, NJ (became Exxon)	New York, NY	$14.9	145,000	Chevron-Texaco (oil refining)	San Ramon, CA	$210.8	65,035
4	Ford Motor	Dearborn, MI	$14.8	436,414	General Motors	Detroit, MI	$182.4	266,000
5	Sears (retail)	Chicago, IL	$8.9	355,000	Conoco-Phillips (oil refining)	Houston, TX	$178.6	32,600
6	General Electric (machinery)	Fairfield, CT	$8.4	400,000	General Electric (machinery, finance, TV)	Fairfield, CT	$176.7	327,000
7	IBM (computers)	Armonk, NY	$7.2	258,662	Ford Motor	Dearborn, MI	$172.5	246,000
8	Chrysler (autos)	Highland Park, MI	$7.1	234,941	Citigroup (finance)	New York, NY	$159.2	380,500
9	Mobil (oil)	New York, NY	$6.6	76,000	Bank of America	Charlotte, NC	$119.2	209,718
10	Texaco (oil)	New York, NY	$5.9	72,572	AT&T (telecom)	San Antonio, TX	$118.9	309,050
11	A&P (groceries)	New York, NY	$5.7	135,000	Berkshire-Hathaway (insurance and finance)	Omaha, NE	$118.2	232,781
12	International Telephone & Telegraph	New York, NY	$5.5	353,000	JP Morgan Chase (bank)	New York, NY	$116.4	180,667
13	Gulf Oil	Pittsburgh, PA	$5.0	60,000	American International Group (AIG) (insurance)	New York, NY	$110.1	116,000
14	Western Electric (manufacture)	New York, NY	$4.9	203,608	Hewlett-Packard (computers)	Palo Alto, CA	$104.3	172,000
15	U.S. Steel	New York, NY	$4.8	204,723	International Business Machines (IBM) (computers)	Armonk, NY	$98.8	386,558

(continued)

© **2010 John Wiley & Sons, Inc.**

▶ **CASE STUDY** *(continued)*

TABLE 6.1 (*continued*)

	1969				2008			
Rank	Top Companies	Head-quarters	Revenues (billion)	Employees	Top Companies	Head-quarters	Revenues (billion)	Employees
16	Safeway Stores	Oakland, CA	$4.1	72,128	Valero Energy	San Antonio, TX	$96.8	21,651
17	Standard Oil of California (Chevron)	San Francisco, CA	$3.8	91,400	Verizon Communica-tions (telecom)	New York, NY	$93.8	234,971
18	J.C. Penney (retail)	New York, NY	$3.8	105,000	McKesson (health care)	San Francisco, CA	$93.6	31,800
19	Ling-Temco-Vought (man-ufacture)	Dallas, TX	$3.8	120,582	Cardinal Health	Dublin, OH	$88.4	43,500
20	Prudential Life Insurance	Newark, NJ	$3.7	56,356	Goldman Sachs Group	New York, NY	$88.0	30,522

Source: Fortune 500, © 1970, 2008, Time Inc. All rights reserved

networks. Transnational corporations locate different corporate functions in different places around the world where the factors of production (land, raw materials, skilled and unskilled labor, capital) and agglomeration economies minimize costs.

Globalization of manufacturing and the spatial division of labor would not have been possible without technological advances in transportation and communications, including cheap overseas container shipping, air travel by engineers and management, and instant communications with subsidiaries by telephone, fax, e-mail, and air couriers.

The New Economy, with its emphasis on innovation, has spawned an increasing number of local agglomerations of particular industries (see Introduction). These local agglomerations have been associated with a shift in industrial organization away from vertically integrated mass-production processes and toward a more flexible production process. Flexibility includes more flexible use of equipment (programmable machinery), more flexible organizational strategies (alliances, **outsourcing** of parts production and corporate tasks to subcontractors, vertical disintegration), a more flexible range of products for a more diverse market of consumers, more flexibility in bringing innovative products to market faster, more flexible relations with employees (less job security, hiring temporary workers, telecommuting, family leaves, flex time), and more flexible mobility of capital around the world. Some companies find they can maximize their versatility regarding what to make and how to make it by locating within an agglomeration of suppliers, competitors, customers, and skilled labor. The motion picture industry, for example, is highly agglomerated in the Los Angeles area. In the Golden Age of Hollywood before 1950,

seven large studios performed almost all the steps of making a movie using in-house employees and equipment. Today producers outsource many of these steps to a flexible cluster of firms that are brought together to create a single movie and disbanded when the movie is complete. Studios organize financing and distribution but subcontract for editing, sound, lighting, special effects, film processing, marketing, and so on. Co-location in Los Angeles facilitates the complicated interactions that occur in this highly flexible production environment.

The economy has always had ups and downs, changes in technology, and regions that have surged ahead while others were left behind. As we write this in March 2009, no one is at all certain how long or deep the current global financial crisis that began in September 2008 will be, and what regions, industries, companies, and professions will emerge from it weakened or strengthened. One thing the crisis has shown us, however, is how tightly linked the regions of the world and the sectors of the economy are in the world today. A crisis that began in the mortgage and real estate industries of the United States (Figure 6.12) quickly spread to banks, insurance companies, auto companies, and other sectors across the world. The Fortune Top 20 List (Table 6.1) will likely look very different in the coming years, as some of the companies on the 2008 list were teetering on the edge of bankruptcy in spring 2009 and receiving bailout funds because the federal government saw them as being "too big to let fail." In the new globalized Information Economy changes happen much faster, often as a result of decisions and events far away.

As you consider the economic profile of jobs in your state or province in Activity 1 and experiment with regional multipliers

© **2010 John Wiley & Sons, Inc.**

▶ *CASE STUDY (continued)*

Figure 6.12 The collapse of the U.S. financial industry in 2008 left many white-collar professionals out of work. This financial engineer resorted to street networking on Park Avenue in Manhattan to find employment.

in Activity 2, think about how these concepts affect your livelihood and that of your family and friends. Do you know people who work in each of the three sectors? Whose jobs bring money into your state or province? If you know any small-business owners (or employees) in the tertiary sector, how might they be affected if a basic industry opens or shuts nearby?

Name: _____   Instructor: _____

Help Wanted: The Changing Geography of Jobs

► ACTIVITY 1: REGIONAL ECONOMIC SPECIALIZATION

Before we can investigate how economic activities vary over space and time, we need to define the different kinds of activities. With the passage of the North American Free Trade Agreement (NAFTA), a new classification system was developed jointly by the United States, Canada, and Mexico to provide comparability in statistics about business activity across North America. The North American Industry Classification System (NAICS) will reshape the way we view our changing economy. The NAICS system replaces the Standard Industrial Classification (SIC) codes that had been used for decades. NAICS is an improvement over SIC not only because it is uniform across major North American trading partners but also because it more closely reflects today's deregulated Information Economy. For instance, the new Information category (NAICS group 51) combines data processing and broadcasting with activities such as telecommunications (formerly classified as a public utility) and publishing and sound recording (formerly classified as manufacturing).

1.1. What do you think are the *top* 5 economic categories in terms of employment in your state or province? Rank your choices from 1 to 5. This question will not be graded, so *do it solely based on your preconceptions.* Do not look up these figures; just make an educated guess.

Economic Category	Rank (1 to 5 only, where 1 = the highest)
Agriculture, Forestry, Fishing, and Hunting (NAICS 11)	_____
Mining and Oil/Gas Extraction (NAICS 21)	_____
Construction (NAICS 23)	_____
Manufacturing (NAICS 31–33)	_____
Public Utilities, Wholesale, Transportation, and Warehousing (NAICS 22, 41, 48, 49) (the category *utilities* includes electric power generation and distribution, natural gas, and water and sewer systems; *wholesaling* refers to the intermediaries (distributors) between manufacturing and retailing; *transportation* includes road, rail, water, air, and pipeline modes for passengers and freight; *warehousing* is inventory management and storage)	_____
Retail Trade (NAICS 42)	_____
(includes stores, gas stations, vending machines, and mail-order catalogs)	
Information (NAICS 51)	_____
(includes publishing, motion pictures, sound recording, TV and radio broadcasting, telecommunications, information services, and data processing)	
Finance, Insurance, and Real Estate (NAICS 52–53)	_____
Producer Services (NAICS 54–56)	_____
(includes legal, architectural, accounting, engineering, management consulting, employment agencies, advertising, copying, janitorial, credit, collection, travel agents, telemarketing, waste management and remediation, etc.)	
Educational Services (NAICS 61)	_____
(includes schools, vocational training, colleges, and testing; in the U.S. data, this category is private education only; in the Canadian data, this category includes public and private education)	
Health Care and Social Assistance (NAICS 62)	_____
(includes doctors, dentists, mental health, diagnostics, ambulance, hospitals, nursing homes, day care, shelters, child/youth/family services, etc.)	
Entertainment, Lodging, and Food Services (NAICS 71–72)	
(includes performing arts, spectator sports, amusement parks, museums, historical sites, skiing, golf, gambling, hotels, RV parks, camps, bars, restaurants, etc.)	
Public Administration (NAICS 91)	_____

1.2. Table 6.2 shows the percentage of total employment for the major economic categories for each state and for the United States as a whole in 2000. Table 6.3 does the same for Canada in 2001, using Canadian provinces. Fill in the percentages in columns A and B of the following table. Leave column C blank for now.

Economic Category	A Your State or Province	B U.S. or Canada	C = A/B Ratio
Agriculture, Forestry, Fishing, and Hunting	_____	_____	_____
Mining and Oil/Gas Extraction	_____	_____	_____
Construction	_____	_____	_____
Manufacturing	_____	_____	_____
Public Utilities, Wholesale, Transportation, and Warehousing	_____	_____	_____
Retail Trade	_____	_____	_____
Information	_____	_____	_____
Finance, Insurance, and Real Estate	_____	_____	_____
Producer Services	_____	_____	_____
Educational Services	_____	_____	_____
Health Care and Social Assistance	_____	_____	_____
Entertainment, Lodging, and Food Services	_____	_____	_____
Public Administration	_____	_____	_____

Notes about the data.

The U.S. employment data were estimated from two separate sources. The 2000 data were based on the Census Bureau's County Business Patterns NAICS data. The County Business Patterns (CBP) database, however, is for private, nonfarm firms, excluding sole proprietors and government employees. Therefore, agriculture and public administration employment data were estimated from the Department of Commerce's Regional Economic Information System (REIS) database, which includes farmers, sole proprietors, and government employees but in 2000 had a very simplistic breakdown of economic activities based on neither SIC nor NAICS categories. The 1969 CBP database has not yet been converted to NAICS categories, so these categories were reconstructed from REIS and CBP data. For these reasons and because the "Other Services" category was excluded, the employment totals for each state, province, and country may not add up to 100 percent.

U.S. employment statistics are classified according to each establishment's final product, not by the job of the employee (e.g., assembly-line workers, truck drivers, and computer specialists for a manufacturing firm are all classified as manufacturing employees). The overall numbers, therefore, may not reflect the true occupational breakdown.

Canadian data are derived from Statistics Canada's table, "Total Labour Force 15 Years and Over by Industry." The data were based on 20 percent (2001) and 33 percent (1971) samples of the population. Canadian data for 1971 are not grouped by NAICS categories, so these had to be reconstructed from more detailed industrial categories. Canadian data for 1971 do not include the province of Nunavut, which was part of the Northwest Territories at the time.

The category of educational services includes public and private education in the Canadian data, but only private education in the U.S. data.

These data were estimated for the purpose of this book only and should not be used for research or policy purposes.

© 2010 John Wiley & Sons, Inc.

TABLE 6.2   U.S. State and National Employment Percentages by Industry, 2000

USA, 2000	AL	AK	AZ	AR	CA	CO	CT	DE	DC	FL	GA	HI	ID
Primary													
11 Agriculture, forestry, fishing and hunting#	3.48	4.72	2.38	5.62	3.75	2.83	1.50	0.87	0.00	3.03	2.53	2.91	7.67
21 Mining and oil and gas extraction	0.36	2.60	0.44	0.26	0.13	0.54	0.04	0.08	0.00	0.08	0.16	0.03	0.42
Secondary													
23 Construction	5.25	4.94	7.33	4.06	4.90	6.90	3.74	5.00	1.05	5.08	4.84	3.95	6.96
31-33 Manufacturing	16.35	3.78	8.80	19.66	11.37	7.25	13.04	9.44	0.39	5.69	12.40	2.48	11.87
Tertiary													
22,41,48,49 Pub util, wholesl, transp, warehse	7.16	9.04	7.29	8.11	8.29	7.16	6.84	6.56	1.95	7.47	8.53	7.47	7.16
44-45 Retail trade	11.25	11.17	11.17	11.28	9.67	10.98	10.70	11.66	2.88	12.35	11.12	10.60	12.37
51 Information	1.94	2.02	2.08	1.87	3.42	4.03	2.90	1.89	3.76	2.37	3.34	1.40	1.96
52-53 Finance, insurance, and real estate	4.74	3.25	6.71	3.75	5.83	6.34	8.49	11.19	3.91	6.10	5.33	5.46	3.89
54-56 Producer services	10.86	7.88	15.75	9.39	16.31	15.34	13.74	15.64	17.02	19.39	15.08	9.59	10.92
61 Educational services	0.98	0.89	1.07	0.92	1.70	1.23	3.06	1.30	6.02	1.30	1.53	2.21	1.18
62 Health care and social assistance	9.89	10.46	8.76	11.02	8.57	8.32	11.97	9.70	8.81	10.13	8.19	8.44	9.38
71-72 Arts, ent, recr, lodging, & food svcs	7.05	8.10	10.39	7.00	8.81	10.56	7.68	7.59	7.15	10.14	7.94	15.88	9.09
91 Public administration#	15.97	23.33	12.87	13.72	12.91	12.91	11.31	12.84	32.52	12.16	14.14	21.61	14.55

	IL	IN	IA	KS	KY	LA	ME	MD	MA	MI	MN	MS	MO
Primary													
11 Agriculture, forestry, fishing and hunting#	2.27	3.06	7.03	5.65	6.07	2.93	4.00	1.73	1.27	2.28	3.93	5.06	4.50
21 Mining and oil and gas extraction	0.14	0.17	0.13	0.47	1.08	2.06	0.01	0.07	0.03	0.14	0.25	0.32	0.18
Secondary													
23 Construction	4.15	4.92	4.29	4.92	4.59	6.72	4.48	6.18	3.50	4.29	4.29	4.45	4.97
31-33 Manufacturing	13.33	20.74	16.12	13.62	15.81	8.07	13.29	6.16	11.23	17.23	13.56	17.96	12.14
Tertiary													
22,41,48,49 Pub util, wholesl, transp, warehse	9.23	7.63	7.46	7.50	8.12	7.78	6.07	6.35	6.82	6.65	8.23	6.12	8.71
44-45 Retail trade	9.96	11.48	12.12	10.88	11.90	11.62	12.88	11.05	9.97	11.45	10.92	11.54	11.09
51 Information	2.23	1.55	2.62	3.04	1.61	1.50	1.93	2.76	3.68	1.96	2.05	1.59	2.88
52-53 Finance, insurance, and real estate	6.71	4.71	6.11	4.82	4.48	4.88	4.98	6.01	7.39	4.69	6.16	3.51	5.83
54-56 Producer services	16.05	9.46	8.18	10.52	8.81	9.57	9.06	16.18	14.69	14.51	13.92	7.10	11.38
61 Educational services	1.89	1.52	2.09	1.17	1.36	1.62	2.12	2.10	4.66	1.18	1.73	1.20	2.04
62 Health care and social assistance	9.88	10.36	11.79	10.99	11.11	11.60	14.49	10.09	12.66	10.28	11.64	10.07	11.30
71-72 Arts, ent, recr, lodging, & food svcs	7.48	8.48	8.23	7.85	8.17	9.52	8.21	7.64	7.94	7.99	8.32	9.86	8.57
91 Public administration#	12.06	11.70	13.02	15.58	14.71	16.91	13.51	16.66	11.07	12.05	11.64	17.87	13.28

	MT	NE	NV	NH	NJ	NM	NY	NC	ND	OH	OK	OR	PA
Primary													
11 Agriculture, forestry, fishing and hunting#	7.56	6.93	1.50	1.86	1.23	3.64	1.28	3.03	9.58	2.37	5.96	5.16	2.17
21 Mining and oil and gas extraction	1.14	0.12	0.98	0.06	0.06	1.78	0.04	0.08	1.19	0.19	1.66	0.14	0.28
Secondary													
23 Construction	4.89	4.73	7.99	4.16	3.95	5.92	3.60	5.45	4.45	4.25	4.14	4.92	4.34
31-33 Manufacturing	5.50	11.90	3.70	14.74	9.30	5.14	7.99	17.72	7.35	16.97	11.07	12.47	13.60
Tertiary													
22,41,48,49 Pub util, wholesl, transp, warehse	7.37	7.87	6.38	6.85	11.12	5.71	7.82	7.11	8.82	7.40	7.00	8.22	7.52
44-45 Retail trade	13.66	12.04	10.47	14.66	10.56	12.28	9.55	10.90	12.81	11.06	11.05	11.90	11.39
51 Information	2.07	2.98	1.86	2.18	3.13	1.82	3.57	1.86	2.05	2.00	2.27	2.06	2.30
52-53 Finance, insurance, and real estate	4.94	6.88	4.99	4.69	6.35	4.40	8.45	4.52	5.30	5.40	4.77	5.45	5.92
54-56 Producer services	7.55	10.71	11.06	11.72	17.15	10.86	13.90	11.11	6.72	12.58	10.82	11.64	12.56
61 Educational services	1.29	1.71	0.39	3.53	1.85	1.29	3.34	1.54	1.42	1.61	1.12	1.98	3.34
62 Health care and social assistance	12.64	11.02	6.42	10.95	10.08	10.12	13.38	9.53	14.41	11.12	11.09	9.53	12.67
71-72 Arts, ent, recr, lodging, & food svcs	12.08	7.83	29.83	9.06	7.05	10.92	7.04	7.70	9.00	8.19	8.24	9.18	7.52
91 Public administration#	15.25	13.67	10.19	10.80	12.66	19.48	14.06	15.02	15.99	11.97	15.84	12.71	11.16

	RI	SC	SD	TN	TX	UT	VT	VA	WA	WV	WI	WY	USA
Primary													
11 Agriculture, forestry, fishing and hunting#	1.35	2.51	8.64	3.95	3.54	2.30	4.04	2.45	4.06	3.37	4.00	5.54	3.15
21 Mining and oil and gas extraction	0.04	0.09	0.32	0.15	1.09	0.67	0.24	0.28	0.11	2.60	0.10	6.82	0.33
Secondary													
23 Construction	3.89	5.88	4.33	4.68	5.33	5.71	4.67	5.36	5.59	4.14	4.38	6.27	4.80
31-33 Manufacturing	13.94	16.86	12.36	16.93	9.92	10.94	14.77	9.71	11.20	10.44	20.29	4.07	12.04
Tertiary													
22,41,48,49 Pub util, wholesl, transp, warehse	6.14	5.84	6.68	8.33	8.41	8.14	5.94	5.57	7.57	6.30	7.52	6.10	7.72
44-45 Retail trade	10.77	11.28	13.11	11.09	10.48	11.06	12.53	10.74	11.14	12.92	11.43	11.88	10.85
51 Information	2.11	1.54	1.88	1.86	2.52	2.43	2.22	3.43	3.16	1.86	1.84	1.56	2.59
52-53 Finance, insurance, and real estate	5.87	4.11	7.05	4.85	5.45	5.18	3.93	5.10	5.28	4.04	5.51	4.15	5.78
54-56 Producer services	11.16	11.82	5.51	12.69	15.32	15.18	7.43	15.70	11.24	7.21	9.40	5.63	13.76
61 Educational services	3.78	1.08	1.87	1.54	1.16	2.17	4.02	1.39	1.39	1.32	1.56	0.55	1.85
62 Health care and social assistance	13.98	8.67	13.60	10.15	9.46	7.45	11.76	8.19	10.01	14.35	10.79	10.66	10.31
71-72 Arts, ent, recr, lodging, & food svcs	8.59	8.92	9.77	7.84	8.18	8.29	11.63	7.74	8.76	8.56	8.16	11.59	8.50
91 Public administration#	13.11	16.64	13.64	11.96	13.97	14.55	12.96	18.22	15.35	17.10	11.73	19.22	13.58

Source: U.S. Department of Commerce, Bureau of the Census. County Business Patterns 2000: http://www.census.gov/epcd/cbp/view/cbpview.html
Source: U.S. Department of Commerce, Bureau of Economic Analysis. Regional Economic Information System 2000 (CD ROM). Washington, DC: U.S. Government Printing Office
The raw numbers underlying these percentages are based mainly on 2000 Regional Economic Information System data.
All percentages in the table are based on denominators combining County Business Patterns and REIS data.
Numbers do not add to 100% due to rounding and omission of the All Other Services category.

© 2010 John Wiley & Sons, Inc.

TABLE 6.3 Canada National Employment Percentages by Industry, 2001

	NFLD	PEI	NS	NB	QUE	ONT	MAN	SASK	ALTA	BC	YUK	NWT	NUN	CANADA
Primary														
11 Agriculture, forestry, fishing and hunting	6.68	12.96	5.18	5.59	2.79	2.06	6.48	14.43	5.03	3.90	1.61	1.47	1.16	3.64
21 Mining and oil and gas extraction	2.12	0.29	0.76	0.89	0.45	0.35	0.73	2.87	5.11	0.70	2.43	6.95	2.33	1.09
Secondary														
23 Construction	6.47	7.23	6.05	6.39	4.62	5.54	4.97	5.40	7.73	5.89	7.93	7.49	6.66	5.64
31–33 Manufacturing	10.33	10.63	9.99	12.56	17.58	16.43	11.78	5.83	8.02	9.65	2.18	1.30	1.72	13.96
Tertiary														
22,41,48,49 Public utilities, wholesale, transportation, & warehousing	7.12	6.28	8.047	7.973	9.867	10.08	9.413	8.794	9.808	8.765	4.557	5.165	3.728	9.58
44–45 Retail trade	12.65	10.69	12.35	11.22	11.38	11.21	10.49	10.66	10.88	11.56	10.98	8.94	12.26	11.27
51 Information	2.03	1.76	2.40	1.97	2.63	2.87	2.09	2.17	2.33	3.09	3.93	2.59	2.14	2.68
52–53 Finance, insurance, and real estate	3.05	2.78	4.66	4.05	5.13	6.70	4.98	5.02	5.01	6.06	3.23	3.26	3.68	5.75
54–56 Producer services	6.18	6.23	8.94	8.28	9.38	11.58	7.26	5.93	10.98	10.88	7.56	7.59	4.10	10.29
61 Educational services	7.19	5.94	7.16	6.60	6.61	6.19	7.38	7.26	6.48	6.93	6.68	7.64	13.42	6.55
62 Health care and social assistance	12.32	10.26	11.09	11.05	10.21	8.87	12.41	11.04	8.92	9.93	8.97	9.79	9.74	9.70
71–72 Arts, entertainment, recreation, lodging, & food services	7.58	9.82	9.06	8.23	7.88	8.38	8.55	8.78	9.19	10.59	12.17	7.42	7.08	8.67
91 Public administration	8.77	9.67	8.55	7.81	6.29	5.16	6.97	6.21	4.60	5.60	21.14	21.10	23.95	5.81

Source: Statistics Canada, *Census of Canada*, "Total Labour Force 15 Years and Over by Industry—1997 North American Industry Classification System—20% Sample Data."

163

1.3. Now rank the actual top five economic categories for your state or province.

1_____ 2_____ 3_____

4_____ 5_____

1.4. a. What, if any, economic categories were actually larger than you thought they would be in Question 1.1?

b. What economic categories were actually smaller than you thought they would be in Question 1.1?

1.5. Compare the share of employment in your state or province with that of the entire United States or Canada in Question 1.2. In which two economic categories does your state or province greatly exceed the national average in *ratio* terms? Divide Column A by Column B and write the result in Column C (you need to do this only for categories in which your state or province exceeded the national percentage). This ratio tells you *how many times larger* your state's or province's employment percentage is than the national percentage (see the following box on interpreting ratios). For the two economic categories with the highest ratios, discuss *why* you think your state or province specializes in those activities. Factors to think about include raw materials availability, labor cost, education levels, the demand of large urban markets, agglomeration economies, political factors, and economic growth or decline.

Interpreting Ratios

Suppose your state's employment percentage in a certain category is 3 percent, compared with the national percentage of 2 percent. Then 3 divided by 2 equals a ratio of 1.50, or 50 percent higher than the national average. This is a more significant difference than if your state percentage was 12 percent versus a national share of 10 percent: 12 divided by 10 equals 1.20, or only 20 percent higher. What about ratios greater than 2? A state percentage of 5 percent compared with a national percentage of 2 percent gives a ratio of 2.50, or two and a half times larger (150 percent larger).

1.6. Look at the choropleth maps of employment in each of the 13 economic categories (Figure 6.13). Which other states or provinces have high employment in each of the two economic specializations that yours does (identified in Question 1.5)?

1.7. Some of the maps in Figures 6.13a–6.13m show a strong regional concentration of particular industries, with the high-percentage states clustered together, whereas maps of other categories do not show this. Which economic categories are strongly regionalized, and in which parts of the United States and Canada? Why do you think these economic categories might be concentrated in those particular regions?

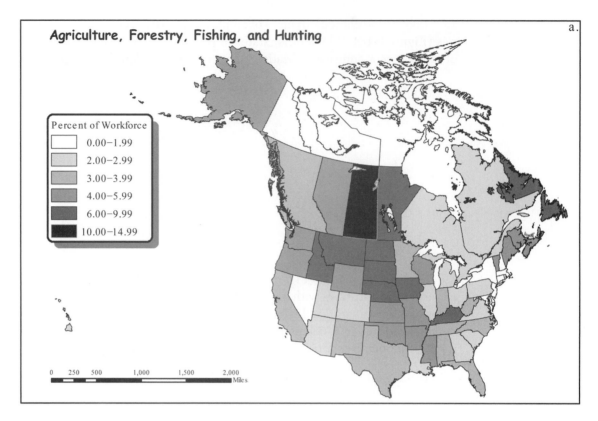

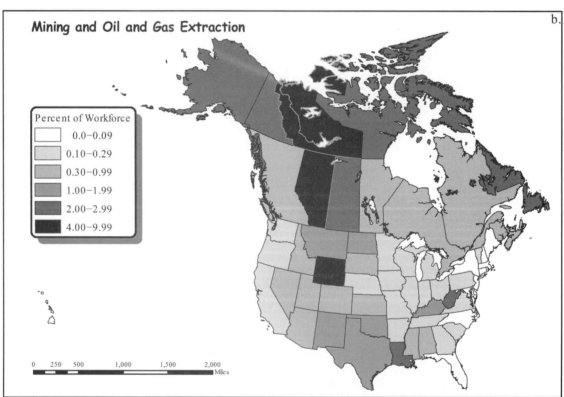

Figures 6.13a and 6.13b   Percentage employed by economic sector, 2000 (USA) and 2001 (Canada). (Figure continues on following pages.)

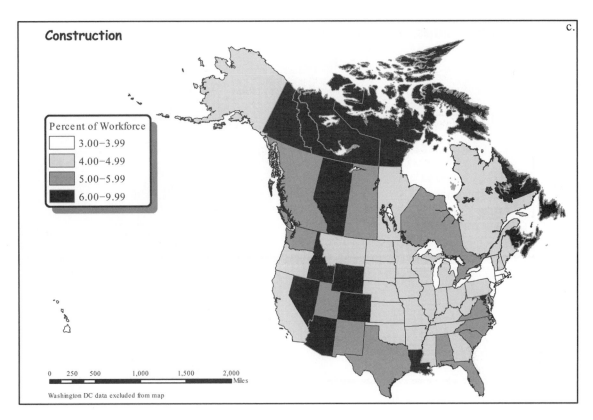

Construction

Percent of Workforce
- 3.00–3.99
- 4.00–4.99
- 5.00–5.99
- 6.00–9.99

0 250 500 1,000 1,500 2,000 Miles

Washington DC data excluded from map

c.

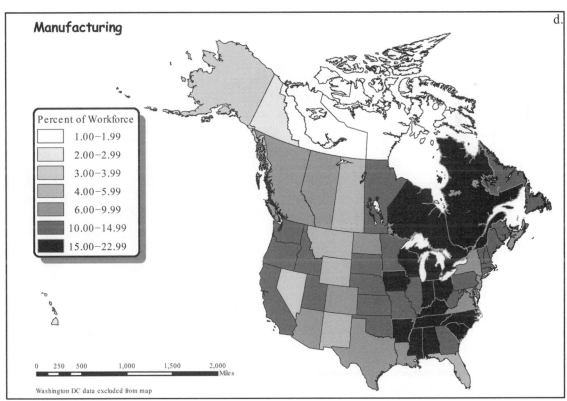

Manufacturing

Percent of Workforce
- 1.00–1.99
- 2.00–2.99
- 3.00–3.99
- 4.00–5.99
- 6.00–9.99
- 10.00–14.99
- 15.00–22.99

0 250 500 1,000 1,500 2,000 Miles

Washington DC data excluded from map

d.

Figures 6.13c and 6.13d Percentage employed by economic sector, 2000 (continued).

© 2010 John Wiley & Sons, Inc.

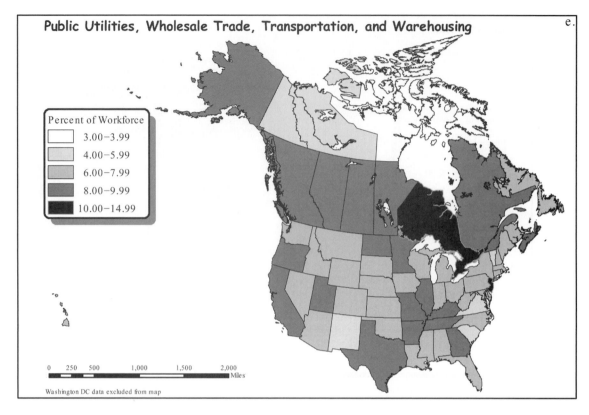

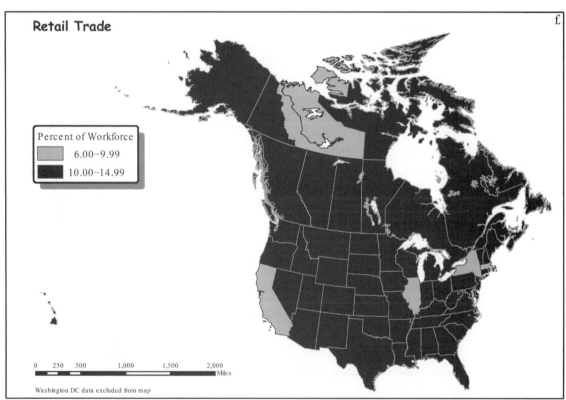

Figures 6.13e and 6.13f Percentage employed by economic sector, 2000 (continued).

© 2010 John Wiley & Sons, Inc.

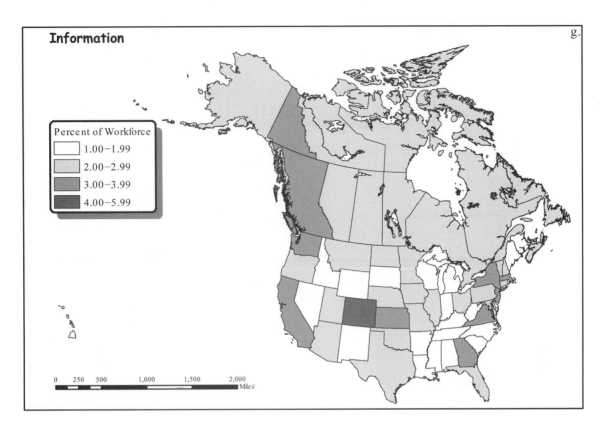

Information

g.

Percent of Workforce
- 1.00–1.99
- 2.00–2.99
- 3.00–3.99
- 4.00–5.99

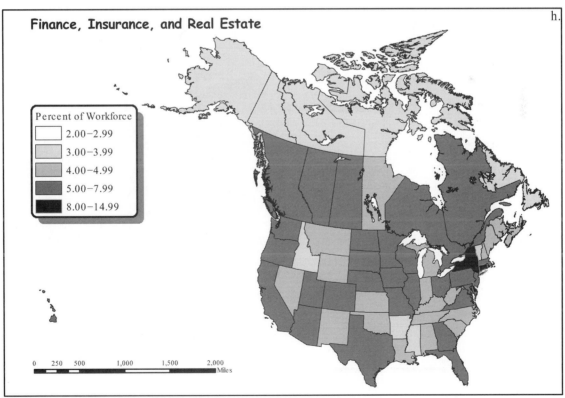

Finance, Insurance, and Real Estate

h.

Percent of Workforce
- 2.00–2.99
- 3.00–3.99
- 4.00–4.99
- 5.00–7.99
- 8.00–14.99

Figures 6.13g and 6.13h   Percentage employed by economic sector, 2000 (continued).

© 2010 John Wiley & Sons, Inc.

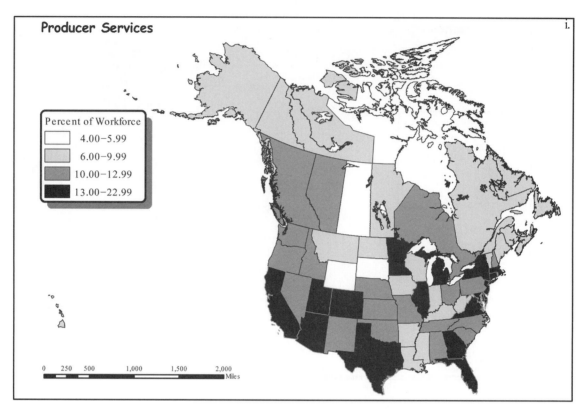

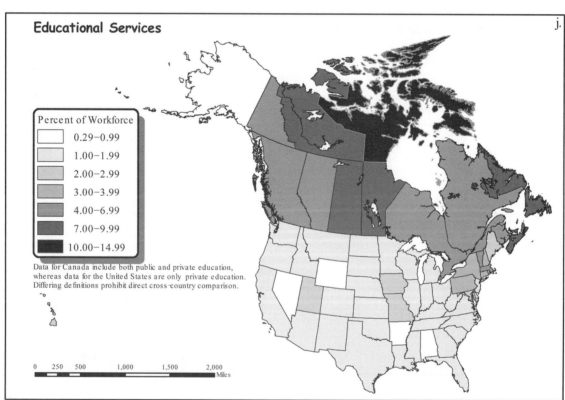

Figures 6.13i and 6.13j   Percentage employed by economic sector, 2000 (continued).

© 2010 John Wiley & Sons, Inc.

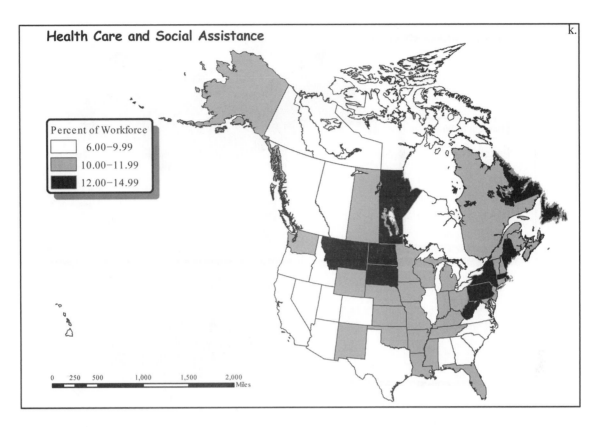

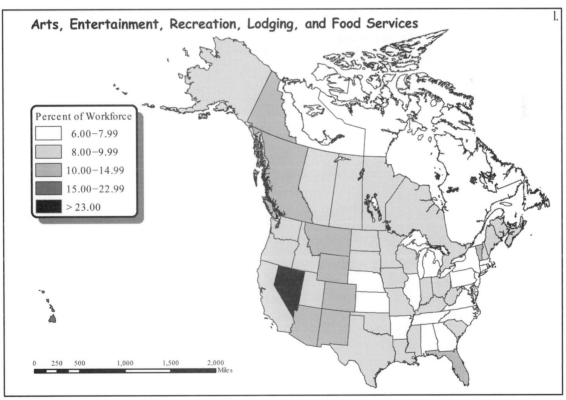

Figures 6.13k and 6.13l　Percentage employed by economic sector, 2000 (continued).

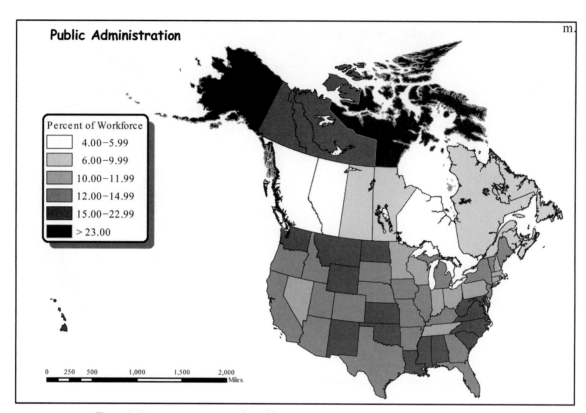

Figure 6.13m Percentage employed by economic sector, 2000 (continued).

Sources: U.S. Department of Commerce Bureau of the Census. *County Business Patterns 2000*: http://www
.census.gov/epcd/cbp/view/cbpview.html. U.S. Department of Commerce, Bureau of Economic Analysis,
Regional Economic Information System, 2000. Statistics Canada, Census of Canada, "Total Labour Force 15
Years and Over by Industry—1997 North American Industry Classification System—20% Sample Data."

1.8. Certain economic categories thrive in the states or provinces with the largest metropolitan areas, shown here in size order for your convenience (both lists are cut off at the 2.35 million mark):

Rank	United States	Canada
1	New York, NY	Toronto
2	Los Angeles, CA	Montreal
3	Chicago, IL	
4	Washington, DC–Baltimore, MD	
5	San Francisco, CA	
6	Philadelphia, PA	
7	Boston, MA	
8	Detroit, MI	
9	Dallas, TX	
10	Houston, TX	
11	Atlanta, GA	
12	Miami, FL	
13	Seattle, WA	
14	Phoenix, AZ	
15	Cleveland, OH	
16	Minneapolis, MN	
17	San Diego, CA	
18	St. Louis, MO	
19	Denver, CO	
20	Pittsburgh, PA	

Compare each map with the map above. Which economic categories thrive in states and provinces with the largest cities and don't do as well in states without big cities? Why do these activities concentrate in major cities?

1.9. Which economic categories are spread fairly evenly across the nation, with little difference between the highest and lowest states, and why?

1.10. Now look at the percentage of employment in the major economic categories several decades ago (Table 6.4: 1969 for the United States; Table 6.5: 1971 for Canada). Fill in the percentages in Column A of the following table for your state or province and then copy the 2001 (Canada) or 2000 (U.S.) values for your state or province from Question 1.2 (Column A) into Column B. Calculate Column C for all economic categories by dividing Column B by Column A. A ratio such as 2.5 (larger than 1.0) means that the percentage *grew* 2.5 times larger. A ratio such as 0.5 (smaller than 1.0) means that the later year's percentage *shrank* to be only half as large as the earlier percentage.

Economic Category	A Your State in 1969 (or Province in 1971)	B Your State in 2000 (or Province in 2001)	C = B/A Ratio of Change
Agriculture, Forestry, Fishing, and Hunting	_____	_____	_____
Mining and Oil/Gas Extraction	_____	_____	_____
Construction	_____	_____	_____
Manufacturing	_____	_____	_____
Public Utilities, Wholesale, Transportation, and Warehousing	_____	_____	_____
Retail Trade	_____	_____	_____
Information	_____	_____	_____
Finance, Insurance, and Real Estate	_____	_____	_____
Producer Services	_____	_____	_____
Educational Services	_____	_____	_____
Health Care and Social Assistance	_____	_____	_____
Entertainment, Lodging, and Food Services	_____	_____	_____
Public Administration	_____	_____	_____

TABLE 6.4 U.S. State and National Employment Percentages by Industry, 1969

	AL	AK	AZ	AR	CA	CO	CT	DE	DC	FL	GA	HI	ID
Primary													
11 Agriculture, forestry, fishing and hunting	7.68	3.55	4.67	13.68	1.85	5.27	1.35	3.49	0.34	4.60	4.95	3.80	14.67
21 Mining and oil and gas extraction	0.60	2.57	2.87	0.83	0.41	1.70	0.08	0.04	0.03	0.29	0.35	0.02	1.25
Secondary													
23 Construction	4.78	5.61	5.98	5.28	4.13	5.22	5.04	5.84	3.04	7.04	4.94	6.12	4.79
31–33 Manufacturing*	23.15	4.66	12.99	21.16	20.14	11.19	33.03	27.41	1.72	11.22	22.55	5.63	12.93
Tertiary													
22,41,48,49 Pub util, wholesl, transp, warehse*	7.13	7.35	6.60	6.62	8.18	8.52	6.31	6.31	5.96	8.70	8.66	8.36	7.40
44–45 Retail trade*	10.62	7.10	12.37	11.52	11.26	11.81	11.65	12.44	7.03	13.19	11.00	8.81	12.21
51 Information*	1.62	1.93	2.21	1.81	2.82	2.39	2.07	1.44	3.97	2.21	1.88	1.69	2.09
52–53 Finance, insurance, and real estate	4.19	3.41	7.08	5.17	7.76	8.43	6.94	5.92	6.54	7.79	5.82	9.10	5.70
54–56 Producer services*	6.90	5.99	7.25	4.06	10.36	8.41	7.14	12.05	14.18	9.63	7.47	7.55	6.26
61 Educational services*	0.93	0.77	1.05	0.73	1.19	1.49	2.21	0.99	5.39	1.31	1.14	1.70	0.13
62 Health care and social assistance*	3.93	3.59	5.54	4.91	5.22	6.64	5.11	4.18	4.80	0.45	2.60	3.85	5.00
71–72 Arts, ent, recr, lodging, & food svcs*	3.30	4.39	8.12	4.74	6.11	7.00	4.19	4.68	5.63	9.48	4.60	10.21	6.59
91 Public administration	19.88	49.42	20.72	14.88	20.15	22.88	12.74	17.52	42.81	18.33	20.47	33.80	18.87

	IL	IN	IA	KS	KY	LA	ME	MD	MA	MI	MN	MS	MO
Primary													
11 Agriculture, forestry, fishing and hunting	3.17	5.38	14.22	11.05	11.27	5.75	5.68	2.28	1.00	3.15	8.45	12.33	7.78
21 Mining and oil and gas extraction	0.53	0.40	0.34	1.85	2.19	3.92	0.08	0.16	0.06	0.39	0.91	0.88	0.47
Secondary													
23 Construction	4.51	4.94	4.94	4.84	5.69	6.60	5.14	5.99	4.77	4.46	5.01	4.76	4.59
31–33 Manufacturing*	26.55	31.86	17.10	13.90	18.72	12.39	25.99	16.51	24.85	32.39	19.15	18.46	20.64
Tertiary													
22,41,48,49 Pub util, wholesl, transp, warehse*	10.01	7.13	7.25	7.74	6.92	10.42	6.56	7.49	7.97	7.28	9.16	5.50	10.11
44–45 Retail trade*	11.93	11.80	13.12	12.57	11.32	11.80	12.00	12.95	12.57	11.76	12.23	10.50	11.95
51 Information*	2.56	2.26	2.44	2.42	1.79	1.81	2.02	2.06	2.38	1.90	2.10	3.53	2.27
52–53 Finance, insurance, and real estate	6.52	5.34	6.36	6.07	4.74	4.81	4.55	6.29	6.69	5.61	6.70	3.92	7.08
54–56 Producer services*	8.48	4.33	4.47	4.15	4.60	8.58	3.25	10.89	9.15	6.93	7.28	5.02	7.17
61 Educational services*	1.39	1.14	1.52	0.99	1.24	1.39	1.57	1.77	3.47	0.79	1.24	0.71	1.63
62 Health care and social assistance*	4.33	3.75	6.40	6.52	5.18	4.55	6.31	4.77	6.28	4.94	6.39	3.12	5.06
71–72 Arts, ent, recr, lodging, & food svcs*	5.06	4.96	5.50	5.55	4.79	5.28	4.38	4.79	5.05	4.89	5.50	4.02	4.87
91 Public administration	13.90	13.16	14.12	20.21	18.10	19.75	18.95	24.34	14.47	13.71	15.09	20.58	15.04

	MT	NE	NV	NH	NJ	NM	NY	NC	ND	OH	OK	OR	PA
Primary													
11 Agriculture, forestry, fishing and hunting	13.25	13.03	2.07	2.56	1.06	6.11	1.24	8.68	22.03	2.66	9.04	6.51	2.09
21 Mining and oil and gas extraction	2.37	0.41	1.79	0.13	0.15	4.83	0.13	0.17	0.84	0.51	4.58	0.20	0.83
Secondary													
23 Construction	4.89	5.20	5.52	6.09	4.77	5.44	3.83	5.25	4.34	5.13	5.05	4.78	4.82
31–33 Manufacturing*	8.10	12.15	3.04	28.85	29.05	5.06	21.18	29.57	3.01	31.26	11.67	19.97	29.87
Tertiary													
22,41,48,49 Pub util, wholesl, transp, warehse*	7.82	7.84	6.16	5.32	9.59	6.90	10.43	6.78	7.41	7.91	8.02	9.19	8.49
44–45 Retail trade*	12.46	13.35	11.04	12.51	11.75	12.02	10.76	10.08	12.57	11.90	11.53	11.78	11.69
51 Information*	2.78	2.76	2.59	1.91	2.26	2.77	3.22	1.46	2.43	2.23	1.84	2.16	2.24
52–53 Finance, insurance, and real estate	6.47	6.19	5.79	5.14	5.76	5.57	9.93	4.64	4.91	5.71	5.78	7.36	5.48
54–56 Producer services*	4.24	5.87	7.15	3.53	9.19	13.08	12.58	4.48	2.44	6.76	5.80	6.39	6.74
61 Educational services*	0.84	1.45	0.22	2.81	1.19	1.13	1.89	1.42	1.02	1.00	0.75	1.12	1.93
62 Health care and social assistance*	8.48	6.73	2.59	5.16	4.25	4.99	4.70	2.98	11.44	4.61	5.99	5.95	4.93
71–72 Arts, ent, recr, lodging, & food svcs*	6.73	6.53	31.03	6.50	4.44	6.35	5.29	3.48	5.58	5.23	5.10	6.30	4.87
91 Public administration	20.14	17.67	19.49	14.79	15.02	28.11	15.20	16.83	22.93	12.75	22.40	16.49	13.21

	RI	SC	SD	TN	TX	UT	VT	VA	WA	WV	WI	WY	USA
Primary													
11 Agriculture, forestry, fishing and hunting	1.07	6.75	21.26	8.08	6.50	5.37	7.04	5.20	5.52	4.92	8.08	9.94	4.92
21 Mining and oil and gas extraction	0.05	0.16	0.97	0.40	2.75	2.95	0.58	0.71	0.13	7.45	0.19	8.27	0.81
Secondary													
23 Construction	4.36	5.35	4.09	5.03	6.05	4.26	6.48	5.47	4.76	5.27	4.61	5.67	4.91
31–33 Manufacturing*	28.93	29.36	5.21	26.00	14.96	11.88	21.15	17.16	18.07	20.18	26.53	4.36	21.53
Tertiary													
22,41,48,49 Pub util, wholesl, transp, warehse*	6.64	5.09	6.60	7.82	9.45	8.83	5.69	6.56	8.17	8.62	7.08	7.95	8.32
44–45 Retail trade*	11.13	9.26	12.80	10.34	12.32	12.08	11.57	10.81	10.97	11.87	12.78	11.95	11.58
51 Information*	1.71	1.41	1.96	2.11	1.96	2.29	2.62	1.69	2.15	2.31	2.04	2.62	2.40
52–53 Finance, insurance, and real estate	5.05	3.71	5.99	5.92	6.30	6.28	5.21	5.49	7.37	4.30	5.06	4.83	6.50
54–56 Producer services*	5.36	5.36	2.43	6.76	7.96	5.67	3.27	6.55	7.47	3.79	4.87	4.17	5.89
61 Educational services*	2.14	0.96	1.65	1.55	1.15	1.65	4.77	1.48	0.91	0.78	1.19	0.35	1.46
62 Health care and social assistance*	5.92	2.55	9.25	3.81	4.62	5.49	7.03	4.41	5.68	5.32	6.03	4.06	4.84
71–72 Arts, ent, recr, lodging, & food svcs*	4.57	3.73	6.08	3.92	5.26	5.49	4.26	4.26	5.40	4.48	5.73	8.92	4.79
91 Public administration	21.19	20.99	20.67	15.14	18.03	25.69	14.51	28.19	22.69	16.40	14.04	23.22	17.41

Source: U.S. Department of Commerce, Bureau of Economic Analysis. *Regional Economic Information System 1969* (CD ROM). Washington, DC: U.S. Government Printing Office.

Source: U.S. Department of Commerce, Bureau of the Census. *County Business Patterns 1969*. Washington, DC: U.S. Government Printing Office.

* These numbers adjusted with 1969 County Business Patterns data to provide additional detail comparable to 1997 NAICS categories.

Numbers do not add to 100% due to rounding and omission of All Other Services category.

176

TABLE 6.5 Canadian Provincial and National Employment Percentages by Industry, 1971

	NFLD	PEI	NS	NB	QUE	ONT	MAN	SASK	ALTA	BC	YUK	NWT	CANADA
Primary													
11 Agriculture, forestry, fishing, and hunting	7.62	20.50	5.88	7.65	4.88	4.44	12.35	29.25	13.83	6.44	1.47	5.03	7.23
21 Mining and oil and gas extraction	3.59	0.11	2.29	1.53	1.28	1.29	2.00	2.12	4.13	1.74	16.29	12.38	1.73
Secondary													
23 Construction	11.28	7.14	8.01	7.38	6.03	6.53	5.73	5.15	8.15	7.54	7.69	4.72	6.70
31–33 Manufacturing	12.50	10.30	14.80	17.01	24.80	25.27	13.85	5.24	9.19	16.58	1.68	3.36	20.62
Tertiary													
22,41,48,49 Public utilities, wholesale, transportation, and warehousing	17.04	11.75	12.58	14.64	12.27	11.33	15.18	11.60	12.62	14.74	17.97	12.85	12.46
44–45 Retail trade	11.35	9.97	11.55	11.81	9.49	10.82	10.92	9.91	10.68	11.59	8.67	7.92	10.57
51 Information	2.14	1.67	2.32	2.09	2.16	2.32	2.58	2.06	2.42	2.75	3.50	2.78	2.32
52–53 Finance, insurance, and real estate	1.96	2.18	3.41	3.10	4.68	5.12	4.18	3.12	4.17	5.12	2.80	1.15	4.62
54–56 Producer services	1.39	1.04	1.67	1.53	2.60	2.93	1.86	1.29	2.65	3.04	1.40	1.05	2.60
61 Educational services	7.42	6.99	7.31	7.03	7.54	6.64	6.35	6.80	7.50	6.04	5.59	7.97	6.91
62 Health care and social assistance	6.41	6.58	6.64	6.49	6.54	6.19	6.88	6.54	6.61	6.22	4.27	5.72	6.39
71–72 Arts, entertainment, recreation, lodging, and food services	4.04	4.87	4.27	3.91	4.81	4.67	4.99	4.37	4.94	6.46	10.49	4.77	4.88
91 Public administration	8.57	12.01	14.34	10.51	7.06	7.85	8.73	7.59	8.42	6.73	14.48	26.01	7.96

Source: Statistics Canada, *Census of Canada*, "Persons 15 Years and Over in the Experienced Labour Force, by Detailed Industry Canada, Provinces and Territories," 1971 Census (33% Sample Data).

Note: These categories were derived to match the 1997 NAICS categories.

177

1.11. Which *two* economic categories experienced the greatest growth over this time period (in ratio terms) and why? What types of industries and which particular companies contributed to the rapid growth of this category in your state or province?

1.12. Which two categories experienced the greatest decline over the time period (in ratio terms) and why? What types of particular industries or particular companies in this category contributed to this decline in your state?

Name: _____ Instructor: _____

Help Wanted: The Changing Geography of Jobs

▶ ACTIVITY 2: REGIONAL MULTIPLIERS

In Activity 1 of this chapter, you saw the ways in which your state or province mirrors the economic structure of the nation and the ways in which it differs. In particular, in Question 1.5, you identified the economic categories in which the employment of your state or province exceeds the national average for that category. These are regional specializations of your state or province. Their share of employment exceeds the national average because your state or province is exporting these goods or services to other states or provinces and countries. In other words, they are the economic base or basic industries for your state or province.

The basic industries of a state or province are the driving forces of its economic growth. When the basic industries grow, they create additional jobs in other nonbasic industries, as explained in the Introduction section of this chapter. One way to determine how many additional nonbasic jobs will be created by job growth in a basic economic category is to calculate a regional multiplier.

We can define a regional multiplier as

$$k = E_t/E_b$$

where:

k = regional multiplier
E_t = total regional employment
E_b = regional employment in basic jobs

This is equivalent to the relationship

$$E_t = kE_b$$

which shows that total regional employment is an outcome of basic employment times k, the regional multiplier.

2.1. Region A has a total labor force of 1,000. Of these jobs, 400 are in the basic sector, and 600 are nonbasic. What is the size of the regional multiplier?

2.2. General Motors plans to build a new parts factory in Region A employing 200 new people in basic jobs. Using the regional multiplier calculated in Question 2.1, how many total new jobs will be created in Region A?

2.3. Region B has a total workforce of 800, of which 400 are basic jobs. Region C has 500 total workers, 300 in the basic sector. Calculate each region's multiplier; then calculate the total number of new jobs in each region if a new plant located there with 100 new basic jobs. Which region will get more new jobs?

2.4. Lockheed announced on June 27, 1995, that it would close a defense contract plant in Tucson, Arizona, laying off 385 workers. If all of these jobs were basic and the Tucson region has a regional multiplier of 2.3, how many total jobs did Tucson lose?

▶ DEFINITIONS OF KEY TERMS

Agglomeration Economies Cost savings resulting from location near other firms.

Basic Industry An industry producing goods or services for sale to other regions.

Break of Bulk The stage of transportation when a bulk shipment is broken into smaller lots and/or different modes of transportation.

Capital Goods Goods used to produce other goods.

Cost Minimization An industrial location strategy that seeks to minimize what the firm pays to produce and distribute its products or services.

Division of Labor The specialization of workers in particular tasks and different stages of the production process.

Economic Base Model A demand-driven model in which exports to other regions drive regional development.

Economies of Scale Lower production costs as a result of larger volume of production.

Externalities Effects that extend beyond any single company. External economies of scale, for instance, are cost savings due to a larger volume of production in the region as a whole rather than a large volume within any one company.

Industrial Economy The dominant mode of production and consumption of the late nineteenth and early twentieth centuries, emphasizing large domestic corporations engaged in food processing, heavy equipment manufacturing, and energy products.

Labor Productivity Amount produced per worker per hour.

Localization Economies Savings resulting from local specialization in a particular industry.

Maquiladora An export assembly plant in Mexico that relies on cheap labor to assemble imported components that are then re-exported as finished goods.

Market Oriented The tendency for an industry to locate near population centers in order to save on transport costs, which usually occurs when the final product is more expensive to transport than the raw materials.

Nonbasic Industry An industry producing goods or services for sale within the local region.

Outsourcing An arrangement in which a service or a manufacturing process that was previously produced in-house is subcontracted to an outside company.

Postindustrial Economy The emerging mode of production and consumption of the late twentieth and early twenty-first centuries, featuring huge transnational corporations and localized agglomerations that produce and/or utilize information technology and telecommunications, with greater employment in tertiary and quaternary services.

Primary Activity An economic activity that directly extracts or harvests resources from the earth.

Producer Services Services provided by businesses to other businesses. Also known as *business services*.

Quaternary Activity Highly skilled, information-based services.

Raw Material Oriented The tendency for an industry to locate near the source of raw materials in order to save on transport costs, which usually occurs when raw materials lose weight in the production process.

Regional Multiplier A numerical relationship showing the number of total jobs created for each new basic job in a region.

Secondary Activity An economic activity that transforms raw materials into usable products, adding value in the process.

Services Tasks done for consumers or businesses for a fee.

Spatial Division of Labor The specialization of different regions in different stages of the production process.

Technological Spillovers Leakage of technological know-how to other people and firms usually located in close proximity.

Tertiary Activity An economic activity that links the primary and secondary sectors to the consumers and other businesses either by selling goods directly or by performing services utilizing those goods.

Transaction Costs The unseen costs of doing business; the costs required for gathering information about, negotiating, and enforcing contracts in the exchange of a product or service.

Ubiquitous Available nearly everywhere.

Urbanization Economies Savings resulting from locating in or near urban areas that have a large and diverse labor pool, large markets, developed infrastructure, and availability of a wide variety of goods and services.

▶ FURTHER READINGS

Amin, A. (ed.). 1994. *Post-Fordism: A Reader*. Malden, MA: Blackwell.

Angel, David. 1994. *Restructuring for Innovation: The Remaking of the U.S. Semiconductor Industry*. New York: Guilford Press.

Anselin, Luc, A. Varga, and Z. Acs. 2000. Geographical Spillovers and University Research: A Spatial Econometric Perspective. *Growth and Change* 31:501-515.

Barff, Richard. 1995. Multinational Corporations and the New International Division of Labor, pp. 50–62 in *Geographies of Global Change*, R.J. Johnston, P.J. Taylor, and M.J. Watts (eds.). Oxford: Blackwell.

Bhatta, S.D., and J. Lobo. 2000. Human Capital and Per Capita Product: A Comparison of U.S. States. *Papers in Regional Science* 79:393–411.

Blumenfeld, H. 1955. The Economic Base of the Metropolis. *Journal of the American Institute of Planners* 21:114–132.

Boettcher, Jennifer. 1996. NAFTA Promotes a New Code System for Industry—The Death of SIC and Birth of NAICS. *Database* 19(2):42–45.

Brunn, Stanley D. (ed.). 2006. *Wal-Mart World: The Worlds Biggest Corporation in the Global Economy*. New York: Routledge.

Castells, Manuel. 2000. *End of Millennium, The Information Age: Economy, Society and Culture Vol. III* (2nd ed.). Cambridge, MA: Blackwell.

Dicken, Peter. 2007. *Global Shift: Mapping the Changing Contours of the World Economy* (5th ed.). New York: Guilford Press.

Florida, Richard. 2008. How the crash will Reshape America. *Atlantic Monthly* 303(2): 44–56.

Florida, Richard. 2008. *Who's Your City? How the Creative Economy is Making Where to Live the Most Important Decision of Your Life*. New York: Basic Books.

Glaeser, E.J., and Kohlhase, J.E. 2004. Cities, Regions, and the Decline of Transport Costs. *Papers of the Regional Science Association* 83:197–228.

Gross, Daniel. 2008. Southern Comfort: What Detroit Got Wrong. *Newsweek* (Dec. 22): 24–27.

Howells, J.R.L. 2002. Tacit Knowledge, Innovation and Economic Geography. *Urban Studies* 39:871–884.

Isserman, Andrew. 1977. The Location Quotient Approach to Estimating Regional Economic Impacts. *Journal of the American Institute of Planners* 43:33–41.

Krikelas A.C. 1992. Why Regions Grow: A Review of Research on the Economic Base Model. *Economic Review.* Federal Reserve Bank of Atlanta, (July/August): 16–29.

Moore, Michael. 1989. *Roger & Me* [videorecording]. Dog Eat Dog Films; written, produced, and directed by Michael Moore. Burbank, CA: Warner Home Video.

Ò hUallacháin, B. 2005. Spatial Convergence and Spillovers in American Invention. *Annals of the Association of American Geographers* 95:866–886.

Polèse, Mario, and Richard Shearmur. 2004. Culture, Language, and the Location of High-Order Service Functions: The Case of Montreal and Toronto. *Economic Geography* 80(4):329–350.

Rauch, Jonathan. 2001. The New Old Economy: Oil, Computers, and the Reinvention of the Earth. *Atlantic Monthly* (Jan.):35–49.

Scott, Allen J. 2006. *Geography and Economy.* New York: Oxford University Press.

Ullman, E.L., and Dacey, M.F. 1960. The Minimum Requirements Approach to the Urban Economic Base. *Regional Science Association Papers* 6:175–194.

▶ WEB RESOURCES

American Federation of Labor-Congress of Industrial Organizations (AFL-CIO): www.aflcio.org

Bureau of Economic Analysis, *Regional Economic Accounts:* www.bea.doc.gov/bea/regional/reis

BusinessWeek: www.businessweek.com

Center for Spatially Integrated Social Science: www.csiss.org

Clark University. *Economic Geography:* www.clark.edu/ECONGEOGRAPHY

Economy.com. *The Dismal Scientist:* www.economy.com

The Economist: www.economist.com.

Engardio, Pete. 2006. The Future of Outsourcing: How It's Transforming Whole Industries and Changing the Way We Work. *BusinessWeek* (Jan. 30): www.businessweek.com/magazine/content/06_05/b3969401.htm

Executive Office of the President, Council of *Economic Advisers. Economic Report of the President:* www.access.gpo.gov/eop

Fortune, Inc.: www.fortune.com

Glaeser, E.J. 2005. *Smart Growth: Education, Skilled Workers, and the Future of Cold-Weather Cities:* www.hks.harvard.edu/taubmancenter/pdfs/skilledcities.pdf

Glaeser, E.L. 2005. *Urban Colossus: Why is New York America's Largest City?:* www.economics.harvard.edu/pub/hier/2005/HIER2073.pdf

Google Finance: www.google.com/finance

North American Industry Classification System Association: www.naics.com

Public Citizen. *Global Trade Watch:* www.citizen.org/trade/nafta/index.cfm

Rodrigue, Jean-Paul, Claude Comtois, and Brain Slack. 2009. *The Geography of Transport System* (2 ed.). Companion Website: people.hofstra.edu/geotrans

Statistics Canada: www.statcan.ca/start.html
The Motley Fool: www.fool.com
U.S. Census Bureau. *County Business Patterns*: www.census.gov/epcd/cbp/view/cbpview.html
U.S. Department of Labor: www.dol.gov
University of Virginia, Geospatial and Statistical Data Center. *County Business Patterns*: fisher.lib.virginia.edu/cbp
The Wall Street Journal: online.wsj.com/public/us

▶ ITEMS TO HAND IN

Activity 1: • Answers to regional economy questions 1.1–1.12, or answer all questions your instructor created in your WileyPlus assignments.
Activity 2: • Answers to regional multiplier questions 2.1–2.4, or answer all questions your instructor created in your WileyPlus assignments.

CHAPTER 7

Rags and Riches: The Dimensions of Development

▶ INTRODUCTION

Huge differences in human welfare and standards of living now separate the countries of the world. For instance, Italy has 1 physician for every 238 people; Chad has 1 for every 25,000. The United States has 1.27 persons per motor vehicle; Afghanistan has 167 persons per vehicle. In Norway, 100 percent of the rural population has access to clean drinking water in their homes or nearby; only 30 to 40 percent have it in Somalia and Papua New Guinea. Indeed, many indicators of development show that the gap between the rich and the poor is increasing over time. In 1900, the ratio between the average income of the typical rich country and typical poor country was 4 to 1. In 2000 that ratio was 16 to 1!

More careful analysis of national differences in well-being requires that we define more precisely what we mean by rich and poor. Generally, countries are seen as falling along a continuum of **development**. Development, which implies modernization and progress, was once defined in strictly economic terms, but human progress cannot be measured in monetary terms alone. The usual indicators of development (see the *Area and Demographic Data* online) include variables such as **gross domestic product (GDP)** per capita (Figure 7.1), percent of the workforce in nonagricultural activities (Figure 7.2), infant mortality rate (deaths of children less than 1 year of age) (Figure 7.3), and female literacy rate (Figure 7.4). To geographers and others, *development* has come to mean the extent to which a society is making effective use of its resources, both human and natural. This definition recognizes that different regions have different resources with which to work and, indeed, different societies may aspire to different goals.

Although the income gap between the very richest and very poorest countries has widened, the middle has become more muddled. In much of the twentieth century, the distinction between more-developed countries (MDCs) and less-developed countries (LDCs) was relatively clear. The MDCs consisted of the northern tier of countries (United States, Canada, Europe, the Soviet Union, and Japan) plus Australia and New Zealand. All other countries and regions were classified as LDCs. Although this classification system always had snags (Israel and South Africa, for example, are more-developed than other countries in their regions), it was a useful starting point in discussions of world patterns of development.

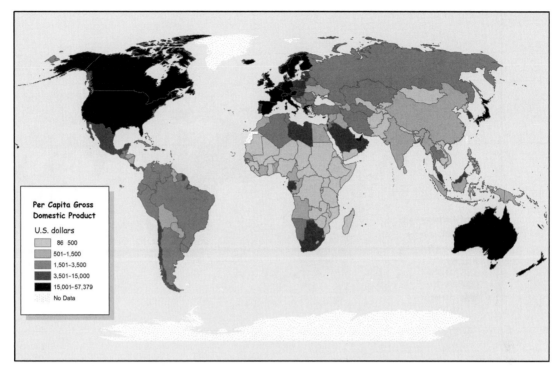

Figure 7.1 Per capita gross domestic product, 2003.

Source: United Nations (http://unstats.un.org/unsd)

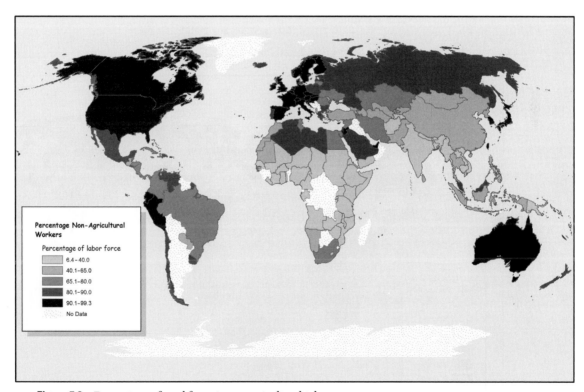

Figure 7.2 Percentage of workforce in nonagricultural jobs.

Source: U.S. Central Intelligence Agency World Factbook 2005 (http://www.odci.gov/cia/publications/factbook)

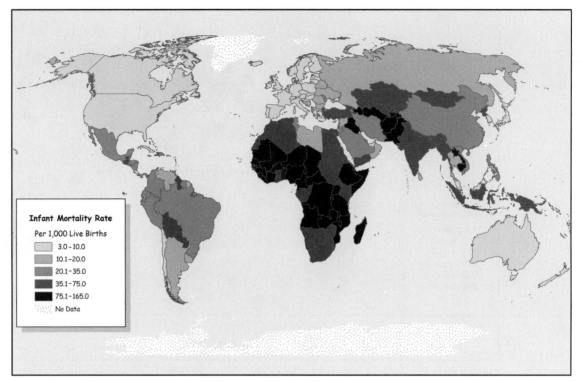

Figure 7.3 Infant mortality rate, 2005.
Source: United Nations (http://unstats.un.org/unsd)

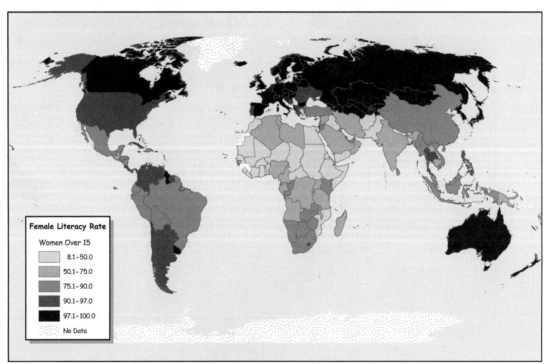

Figure 7.4 Female literacy rate, women over 15 years of age, 2004.
Source: United Nations (http://unstats.un.org/unsd)

Economic collapse of the former Soviet Union and its allies; dynamic growth among the newly industrializing East Asian countries such as Taiwan, South Korea, and Singapore; and rapid income growth among the oil-rich countries of the Middle East have blurred the distinction between more-developed and less-developed. South Korea, traditionally a less-developed country, today has a per capita income of more than $24,750 per year, an overall life expectancy of 79 years, and an infant mortality rate of 4 infant deaths per 1,000 live births, a profile more similar to the southern European countries of Spain, Portugal, and Greece than to LDCs such as Indonesia or Peru. Russia, traditionally a more-developed country with the capability of putting a space station into permanent orbit, now has a per capita income of $14,400, an overall life expectancy of 67, and an infant mortality rate of 9, a profile more like Mexico or Brazil than Europe or North America. Saudi Arabia, with a per capita income of $23,000, is creating as much wealth per person as are many European countries but has not made similar progress in women's rights or education; almost one-third of all women there are unable to read and write. Meanwhile, Chile, Argentina, and Mexico are following in the footsteps of the East Asian dynamos, and China quadrupled the size of its economy from 1980 to 2000. Clearly, many of the old stereotypes no longer apply.

During the last half of the twentieth century, the way social scientists think about development evolved, and so did the real-world strategies to combat poverty (Table 7.1). Development of poor countries first became a major international issue after World War II as they began to declare their independence from their colonial rulers, starting with India and Pakistan in 1947. The **modernization** school of thought dominated the postwar era. The predominant idea was that the former colonies should follow the path taken by Western Europe and North America during the Industrial Revolution. According to economists, the MDCs progressed through **structural change** in the makeup of their economies. The MDCs passed through a series of stages from a traditional, **subsistence economy** dominated by agriculture to a modern, commercial economy dominated first by industry and later by the service sector. The modernization of the MDCs was made possible by building (1) the physical infrastructure of transport, energy, and water systems and (2) the social institutions needed for capitalism, such as currency, private property, taxes, banks, insurance, and a legal system. The keys to creating wealth were seen as mass production, specialization, and **substitution of capital for labor** (Figures 7.5 and 7.6). The World Bank, the International Monetary Fund, the U.S. Agency for International Development (USAID), and other agencies were created to facilitate investment and **technology transfer** from rich to poor countries. Many of the first development projects were huge, Western-style power plants, factories, roads, and port facilities. These projects were expected to jump-start an industrial economy, the benefits of which would eventually trickle down to the masses.

After several decades of modernization policies in which few LDCs progressed linearly from stage to stage as had been expected, a new school of thought began to take root (Table 7.1). The **dependency** school of the 1970s argued that the *dynamic* between the developed and developing worlds kept the latter poor and economically "dependent." Central to this thinking is the **core-periphery** model, a spatial framework for how economies develop over time and space. The model says that the preindustrial order is characterized by small inequalities in wealth and development with regions that function in relative isolation from each other (Figure 7.7a). The beginnings of industrialization bring the concentration of investment into a single strong center, or core. Growth in the modern, dynamic core is distinguished

TABLE 7.1   A Brief History of Ideas and Strategies in Development

School of Thought	Time Period	Main Ideas	Real-World Strategies
Modernization	1940s–1960s	• Progressive stages of economic growth • Economic structural change • Trickle-down economics	• Investment • Substitution of capital for labor • Technology transfer • Large-scale industrialization projects
Dependency	1970s	• Human welfare • Core-periphery model • Circular and cumulative causation • Neocolonialism • Bottom-up economics	• Small-scale and rural enterprises • Import substitution • Nationalization
Neoliberal Counterrevolution	1980s	• Free-market economics • Transition economies	• Privatization • Foreign direct investment • Reduced role of the state • Free trade • Currency devaluation
Sustainable Development	1990s	• Global environmental change • Environmental economics • Women and development • Children and development	• Partnership with developed countries • Market mechanisms for environmental regulation • Resource conservation • Renewable resources • Loans to women and very poor (microcredit) • Women's and children's rights • Appropriate technology

Figure 7.5   In less-developed countries, where labor is cheap and capital expensive, goods are produced in some of the most labor-intensive ways imaginable. Here, unskilled workers (mostly women, children, and the elderly) in Trivandrum, India, are manufacturing gravel by chipping away at rocks with hammers. In more-developed countries, one worker operating a large piece of heavy machinery could conceivably do the work of a thousand workers with hammers—and maybe more.

Figure 7.6 The expense of getting around aboard the Train à Grand Vitesse (TGV, or high-speed train) can be justified only in a very high-income country such as France. These trains represent a massive substitution of capital and energy for labor compared with walking. The office buildings in the background represent the service economy.

by secondary, tertiary, and quaternary activity, and it occurs at the expense of a more traditional periphery dominated by primary economic activities (see Chapter 6 for definitions of primary, secondary, tertiary, and quaternary activities). The periphery supplies raw materials at cheap prices to the urban-industrial core, and the core supplies expensive manufactured goods back to the periphery (Figure 7.7b). Regional inequalities in development are greatest in this stage. Later, the simple core-periphery structure is transformed into a multinuclear structure with strong subcenters emerging in the periphery (Figure 7.7c). Ultimately, according to the model, a mature and functionally interconnected national economy should arise in which the periphery has been absorbed into nearby metropolitan economies (Figure 7.7d). Regional inequalities in wealth are again small at this stage of development.

The growth and then decline of inequalities between rich and poor regions are driven by processes of concentration and deconcentration. The forces of concentration are called **polarization effects**. Polarization effects reinforce growth in the core at the expense of the periphery. One way this works is through **circular and cumulative causation** in which forces set into motion a sequence of other forces that create a self-sustaining "snowballing" effect. There are four pathways to this: capital, labor, innovation, and services. First, capital investment is attracted to the core, retarding growth in the periphery. Second, young, educated workers migrate to the core, leaving an older, less dynamic labor force behind. Third, more innovation in the core leads to the creation of new or enlarged industries, which in turn breed more innovation, and so on. Fourth, faster growth in the core is multiplied into a more service-rich support environment, thus making it more attractive for future economic activity.

Forces of deconcentration are called **spread effects**. Eventually, growth in the core stimulates demand for goods and services from the periphery, and regional subcenters emerge to lead the peripheral areas. High density, congestion, high labor costs, and environmental decay in the core and the diffusion of technology to the periphery also encourage the outward dispersion of growth.

The core-periphery model has been used to explain both national and international differences in economic development. At the national scale, stage 1

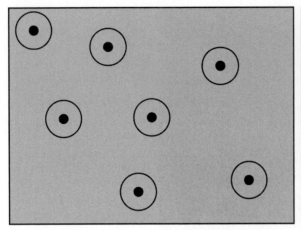

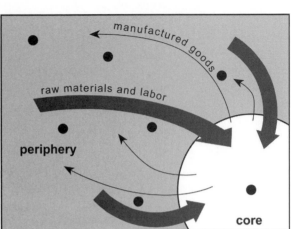

a. Stage One: The preindustrial structure of independent local centers with small market areas and little interaction.

b. Stage Two: Early industrialization brings concentration of investment, wealth, and power into a single, strong core. The periphery provides raw materials and labor to the core, and the core provides manufactured goods to the periphery. The net result is a draining of wealth from the periphery to the core.

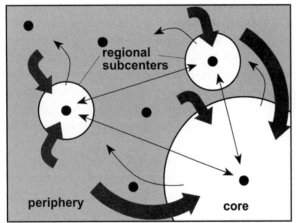

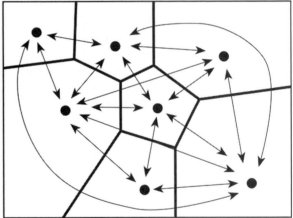

c. Stage Three: As industry develops, the core remains the dominant center, but regional subcenters begin to emerge. The core and regional subcenters exchange manufactured goods and services while continuing to receive raw materials and labor from the periphery.

d. Stage Four: Ultimately a mature and functionally interconnected space economy emerges in which the periphery has been absorbed into nearby metropolitan economies.

Figure 7.7 The core-periphery model shows changing spatial inequalities that occur during the process of industrialization. Many countries remain in stage 2 or 3, seemingly stalled in the global periphery and lacking a strong internal economy.

corresponded to the American colonial period of relatively isolated port towns from Virginia to Massachusetts. In stage 2, the East Coast ports evolved into industrial cities, and all areas west of the Appalachians and much of the South were an agricultural periphery. In stage 3, peripheral cities such as Chicago, Dallas, and Atlanta developed into regional subcenters, but surrounding areas still lagged far behind. Finally, by stage 4, most of the United States and Canada had achieved high levels of economic development. Many LDCs are still in stage 2 or 3, with capital/port cities (for example, Bangkok, Thailand, and Lagos, Nigeria) that are often far more advanced than their interior regions.

The same process can be seen internationally. More-developed core regions are in North America and Western Europe, and less-developed peripheries are in Asia, Africa, and Latin America. At this scale, polarization forces continue to concentrate growth and development in the core, and inequalities between rich and poor countries grow. We can also see some trickle-down effects, however, as labor-intensive industries such as footwear, clothing, toys, and electronic assembly disperse outward from the high-wage core to the low-wage periphery.

The dependency school of thought invokes the existence of core-periphery relationships at the global scale to explain the persistent lack of development in the periphery. Most of today's LDCs were colonized during the nineteenth century to supply cheap and/or exotic raw materials to European factories in the core and to serve as peripheral markets for the output of these factories. Education lagged, little industrial base was developed, and export-oriented transport systems were constructed with the sole purpose of funneling the products of forests, farms, and mines to coastal ports (Figure 7.8). Taxes frequently were imposed to force subsistence farmers to produce crops that could be sold for cash, which could then be used to pay the colonial tax. When most Third World countries became independent, their economies depended heavily on the former colonial rulers to purchase the raw materials they produced, they lacked economic and political leadership, and their transport networks were woefully inadequate for independent economic development. Their initial dependence on colonial mother countries set into motion a type of economic development that continues to render them economically dependent, a process called **neocolonialism**. Production and trade are now controlled by multinational corporations rather than by colonial governments, but former colonies

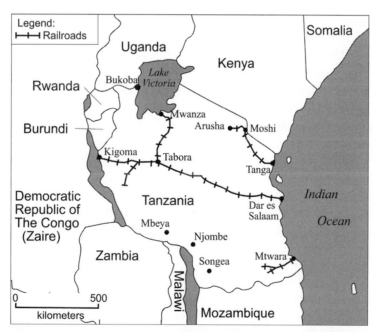

Figure 7.8 Railroads in Tanzania, 1965. Patterns show that the transportation system left by the British colonial government was designed to funnel raw materials to the ports for export rather than to foster a strong local economy by connecting the Tanzanian urban centers together.

© 2010 John Wiley & Sons, Inc.

remain locked into an overdependence on exporting unprocessed raw materials at cheap prices to rich countries. Countries that rely on single-commodity primary material exports include São Tomé and Príncipe (93 percent from cocoa, or cacao), Iran (85 percent from oil), Chad (76 percent from cotton), Zambia (50 percent from copper), and Martinique (40 percent from bananas).

To rectify this dependency, one popular development policy during the 1970s was **import substitution**. Countries were encouraged to produce internally what they previously had relied on from the mother country, especially basic, low-tech consumer goods. Often, high import tariffs were imposed on foreign goods to protect infant home-grown industries, a policy called protectionism. Another widespread practice in the postcolonial period was nationalization of foreign-owned assets, such as the Mexican oil industry. Some LDCs adopted socialist economic philosophies, in light of what they saw as a historic pattern of exploitation by the West.

Apart from the purely economic development strategies of the dependency school, a central concern was also to improve human welfare by providing the basic physical and social needs of citizens. The goal was to improve the overall quality of life for the masses. Unlike the top-down, structural-change model of the postwar era, the approach to development of the 1970s argued for a bottom-up strategy. More resources were directed toward traditionally poor sectors of society, such as day laborers and agricultural peasants, to meet their education, health, food, water, and shelter needs. Emphasis on human welfare concerns represented a deliberate effort to redistribute capital more evenly, in order to generate a strong middle class that would have the buying power to purchase the nationally produced goods that import substitution encouraged. Many governments in the developing world, dissatisfied with persistent poverty, took an active role in trying to raise standards of living. The choice to focus on human welfare needs rather than strictly economic development directly affects the **human welfare indicators** used to measure development, as you will see in this chapter's activities.

The next stage in development thinking was the **neoliberal counterrevolution** (Table 7.1), which dovetailed with the free-market approaches of the 1980s and the end of the Cold War. These policies were championed by Ronald Reagan in the United States and Margaret Thatcher in the United Kingdom. They advocated that protectionism and state-owned industries perpetuated dependency rather than cured it. Protected state-owned industries were not forced by the market to be competitive in price and quality. International agencies like the World Bank and International Monetary Fund (IMF) imposed economic reforms such as selling of government-owned industries to the private sector and free trade as conditions for getting economic assistance. Instead of protectionism to keep out foreign competition, the neoliberal approach advocates that countries allow their own currencies to devalue relative to other currencies in order to make their exports more attractive. With the 1980s and 1990s came the creation of the General Agreement on Tariffs and Trade (GATT), the World Trade Organization (WTO), and the North American Free Trade Agreement (NAFTA). Developing countries competed to attract foreign direct investment: China, for example, attracted investment from Boeing, and Vietnam from Nike. Neoliberal reforms are not only economic phenomena but also social ones. Social welfare programs from health care to education have been opened up to market competition by cost-cutting governments.

The People's Republic of China has undergone a dramatic makeover under neoliberalism. The change began in 1976 after the death of Mao Zedong, who led the

Communist Revolution in 1949 and later organized hundreds of millions of Chinese peasants into agricultural communes and state-owned factories with little contact with the outside world. The ideological Mao was succeeded by the pragmatic Deng Xiaoping, who declared that "to get rich is glorious" and "it doesn't matter if the cat is black or white, as long as it catches mice." Deng initiated a series of step-by-step and place-by-place reforms. Individual farmers were granted long-term allotments of land and permitted to sell their surplus produce to anyone for any price they could get. China established four special economic zones in coastal cities near Taiwan and Hong Kong where foreign investors could co-own factories with Chinese companies, using cheap local labor and foreign technology and management. Gradually, economic reforms were widened to other places and deepened to other sectors. Competition was permitted in a variety of industries, and subsidized prices were scaled back. State-owned factories were given smaller subsidies and more freedom to make decisions; the factories also were forced to compete based on price, quality, and timeliness. Banks have more freedom in making and turning down loans instead of just giving money to projects approved by the government. Many young people now leave the security of the "Iron Rice Bowl" of government employment to "jump into the sea" and work for foreign companies or as entrepreneurs. The result of two decades of reform is officially known as "Socialism with Chinese Characteristics" and unofficially as "Market Leninism." The effect of China's neoliberal reforms has been nothing short of spectacular: China's GDP per capita has reached $5,400, and its total GDP now ranks second in the world after the United States and ahead of Japan and Germany.

Countries converting from socialist to capitalist economies are known as **transition economies**. Regardless of whether the transition is step-by-step as in China or overnight "shock therapy" as in Russia, the transition is guaranteed to be both painful and exciting and to create winners and losers. With the improving business conditions and the lure of the world's largest consumer market, China in 1995 attracted 38 percent of the foreign investment for the entire developing world, yet the transition has also created huge disparities of wealth between the rich coastal provinces and the poor interior. Air pollution and traffic congestion plague most cities, political reforms have failed to match the economic reforms, drugs and crime are increasing, and many Chinese complain of the loss of the old Confucian and Communist value systems.

The latest thinking among development specialists focuses on the idea of **sustainable development**—that progress should not come at the expense of future generations by warming the climate, reducing biodiversity, depleting forests, increasing pollution, and reducing the resource base (Table 7.1). Most LDCs would like to protect their environments, but not at the cost of reducing their standard of living. Sustainability proponents argue that development and environmental protection are not necessarily conflicting goals: efficient energy and water use, renewable resources, pollution reduction, and protection of forests and wetlands actually make long-term economic sense. The sustainable development movement aims to help the LDCs skip the inefficient dependency on fossil fuels that the MDCs experienced and vault right to efficient, renewable technologies. Popular sustainable policies include ecotourism, partnerships with developed countries to introduce clean technologies, and Western pharmaceutical companies paying royalties on drugs developed from rain-forest species. New kinds of statistical indicators include air and water quality, percentage of land in nature preserves, deforestation rate, energy efficiency, and number of threatened species.

Coincident with sustainable development, the idea of **appropriate technology** has regained favor. Instead of the large-scale technology suited to the capital-rich, labor-scarce industrial world, what are needed are technologies appropriate to the capital-poor, labor-abundant, predominantly agricultural developing world—production by the masses rather than mass production. These ideas have been debated and practiced since the 1970s, when E. F. Schumacher, the economist who coined the phrase *appropriate technology*, said that the LDCs needed small-scale industries for "Two Million Villages." Appropriate technology goes hand in hand with the renewed emphasis that sustainable development places on ecologically and culturally sensitive development strategies. Appropriate technology is not a return to the primitive technology of the past but involves tools that are inexpensive and simple enough to be widely adopted and maintained by peasants, do not degrade the environment or human dignity, and are in keeping with the local culture. Examples of appropriate technology include looms for weaving, efficient cooking stoves, simple clay-pot water filters, electric irrigation pumps, composting systems, bicycle rickshaws, easy-to-read paper strips for testing for diseases and pregnancy, and technology for extracting usable fibers from pineapple leaves (Figures 7.9 and 7.10). Technologies that have been criticized as inappropriate are oil-fired power plants, automated factories, infant formula replacement for breast milk, combine harvesters, and chain saws.

The concept of sustainability has been broadened to include sustainability in a social sense. During the 1990s the focus on the roles of women and children in development increased (Figure 7.11). For example, the widespread use of child labor in the oriental carpet industry in Asia is not considered sustainable because these children have had their educations cut short. As they get older, their fingers are not as nimble as they once were; but without an education, they could be unable to get a decent job. Gender issues also have moved to the forefront of the development debate. Gender differences exist throughout the world, but they tend to be more pronounced in LDCs. Inequalities exist not only in political and social freedoms but also in the allocation of resources such as education, health care, food, and bank credit. The pattern of inequality begins at an early age, with female infanticide in countries such as India and China that favor male children and the practice of having boys stay in school longer and visit doctors more frequently

Figure 7.9 Women all over the developing world can be seen carrying heavy loads on their heads, as these women in New Delhi, India, are doing.

Figure 7.10 A bicycle rickshaw is a classic appropriate technology. This man, also in New Delhi, can do the work of 10 people carrying loads on their heads as in Figure 7.9. The capital investment is affordable with a small loan, repairs are cheap and simple, and the health benefits are many.

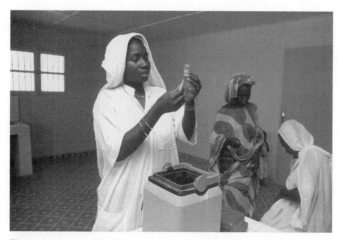

Figure 7.11 Health clinics are a successful strategy for delivering basic health care to children, women, the elderly, and the infirm in rural areas. Here a health care worker prepares a tetanus syringe in a clinic in Mauritania.

than girls. In South Asia, female literacy rates are 20–30 percentage points below male rates, which translates into fewer employment opportunities for females outside the home. Overall, in MDCs there are about 8 women for every 10 men in the labor force, but there are only 4 women for every 10 men in the Middle East and North Africa labor markets. African women perform about 90 percent of the work of processing food crops, providing household water and fuelwood, hoeing, and weeding. Women who do get jobs usually must continue to bear the brunt of household chores (Figure 7.12).

The Grameen (or "Village") Bank in Bangladesh is a successful and widely imitated program to integrate women into the development process. The bank was founded in 1976 by a professor of rural economics at the University of Chittagong, who has been awarded the Nobel Peace Prize for his work. The Grameen Bank offers "microcredit" loans averaging $160 (but as low as $1) to people with no collateral (e.g., assets that banks seize if debtors fail to repay their loans). The bank has 2.3 million borrowers, of which 94 percent are women. An astonishing 95 percent repay their loans. More than 223 similar banks have been opened in 58 countries.

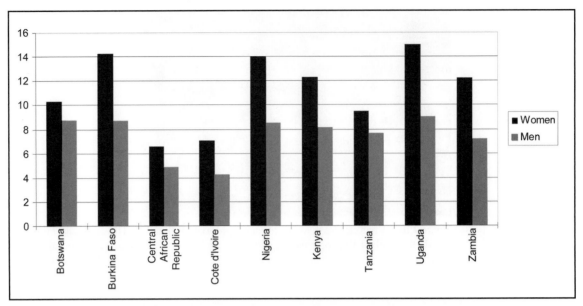

Figure 7.12 Daily productive hours (home and work) for men and women in selected African countries.

Source: *Gender, Growth, and Poverty Reduction: Special Program of Assistance for Africa: 1998 Status Report on Poverty in Sub-Saharan Africa* (English Edition). Washington, DC: World Bank. Copyright 1999 by World Bank. Reproduced with permission of World Bank in the format textbook via Copyright Clearance Center.

The sustainability paradigm holds that until women have equal access to resources and assets, have equal say in household and governmental decisions, and their unpaid household work is valued as highly as men's paid labor, society will not be making full productive use of its human resources.

In Mexico, the social sustainability advocates have raised gender issues regarding the free-trade policies of the neoliberal school. To promote industrialization, Mexico established export assembly plants called maquiladoras that rely on cheap labor to assemble imported components that are then reexported as finished goods. Initially restricted to the border region with the United States, today these plants are located throughout Mexico. The labor used in such plants is overwhelmingly female. Corporate rationale is that women are more dexterous and better suited to perform detailed work in such fields as garment production and electrical component assembly. Critics believe the emphasis on hiring women exists because employers know they can pay women lower wages and believe that they are more "moldable" to rigid work schedules and policies and less likely to join militant unions than men are. These assembly plants provide desperately needed jobs, but often the wages are well below what is needed to support a family. Also, women in Mexico are usually still required to perform the traditional roles of cooking, housework, and child care in addition to their newly found jobs in manufacturing. The result places great stress on traditional gender roles for both men and women in a society known for *machismo* (male emphasis on masculine traits). Compounding these changes is the reduction in social services such as day care and health care provided by the state as the Mexican government evolves from a protectionist institution to a neoliberal one.

In the latter half of the twentieth century, many LDCs accumulated crippling amounts of debt on money they borrowed from banks and governments in the MDCs to finance development. The total debt owed by LDCs has increased 25 times from around US$100 billion in 1970 to more than US$2500 billion in 2000.

Since 1984, the interest payments on loans plus the scheduled repayments of the principal have exceeded new loans, resulting in a net transfer of money *from the LDCs to the MDCs*. Many LDCs owe more than their entire GDP, and their annual interest payments alone can exceed one-quarter of their total earnings of foreign currency from exports. Advocates in both LDCs and MDCs consider the debt situation unsustainable and are calling for banks and other lenders to forgive interest payments.

Because neoliberal development policies tear down global protection barriers, advocates of sustainable development (and many others) question the growing global inequalities. Protesters have rallied against the World Trade Organization, the World Bank, and the International Monetary Fund (Figure 7.13) all over the world against policies that seem to benefit corporations at the expense of citizens and MDCs at the expense of LDCs. Central to the complaints about neoliberal globalization (see Chapter 8) are the undemocratic policies of these international trade organizations. Countries that enter into neoliberal trade agreements often find national or local interests at odds with "fair" trade practices that interfere with corporate profit making. For instance, Californians voted to ban a carcinogenic gasoline additive, causing a Canadian corporation that manufactures the product to sue the United States for violating the free-trade accords. Mexican fishermen complain that U.S. dolphin-safe restrictions on tuna nets inhibit their ability to sell tuna in the United States. The European Union sued the United States for allowing corporations to avoid taxes by locating headquarters "offshore" on Caribbean islands (thereby gaining an unfair competitive advantage). A U.S. company that wanted to open a toxic dump next to an impoverished neighborhood in northern Mexico was even awarded $16 million compensation after local citizens stopped the landfill! Should a country agree to international trade agreements, it could be forced to overrule local rules

Figure 7.13 Protests erupted against the World Trade Organization, the World Bank, and the International Monetary Fund.

© 2010 John Wiley & Sons, Inc.

put in place by the democratic process. In a further affront to democratic decision making, NAFTA-related lawsuits are heard by a closed-door tribunal without input from or responsibility to citizens. Protesters see this as favoring the right of global corporations to make money over the right of local citizens to decide what's good for their own country or community. Who should have the final say about local environmental, labor, or financial rules?

Sustainability and globalization are not always at odds, however, because the global economy can bring better-paying, badly needed jobs to an LDC. Better jobs reduce child labor and increase literacy when parents make enough money to send their children to school, not work. Jobs attributed to the global economy may also be the only source of employment for women, thereby increasing their economic independence and social status.

As development theory has evolved, many of the problems, solutions, policies, and institutions from older schools of thought remain important. Development is a highly complex phenomenon with no easy explanations. In the activities in this chapter, you will explore that complexity by producing different measures and rankings of development.

▶ *CASE STUDY*

RAGS AND RICHES

GOAL

To introduce the different ways of defining and measuring the multifaceted phenomenon of **development**. You will recognize that certain countries perform better on human welfare than on economic dimensions.

LEARNING OUTCOMES

After completing the exercise, you will be able to:

- Define development in economic and human welfare terms.
- Identify countries where economic and human welfare measures yield different rankings of development.
- Interpret the reasons for these different rankings.
- Consult UN documents and Web sites to identify other development indicators.

SPECIAL MATERIALS NEEDED

- Calculator
- Computer with high-speed Internet access and a recent release of a Web browser. If using the Student Companion Site with the printed book, click on *Tech Support* for system requirements and technical support. (If using the e-book in WileyPlus, click on *Help* for details about the system requirements.)

BACKGROUND

We are all aware that some countries are better off than others. Because no measures of development are universally accepted, development can mean different things to different people,

depending upon how much weight they place on particular dimensions of progress and well-being. Just as individuals can be rich in money but poor in health, family ties, or sense of community, so also can countries rank high in economic terms but low in human welfare terms.

Economic indicators of development measure a country's development by assessing its economic base, comparing such variables as **gross domestic product (GDP)** per capita with percentage of the labor force engaged in agricultural activities. **Human welfare indicators** define development by how well a country is able to provide necessary resources for its citizens and measure development with variables such as life expectancy, female literacy, and infant mortality rates.

Countries that score high on the economic dimension do not always score well on human welfare indicators. Some countries experience rapid economic growth with little improvement in human welfare. Similarly, other countries experience relatively high levels of human welfare without high economic development by purposely allocating resources to meet the basic needs of their citizens. In this exercise, rather than collapsing these differences into a single composite ranking, you will examine development as a multidimensional phenomenon.

You will also be asked to develop your own measures and to justify them. Remember that there are no universally agreed upon indicators of development. What you put in determines what you get out.

The 20 countries (Figure 7.14) examined in these activities allow you to see different stages of development as measured by human welfare and economic variables. They have been selected to provide a broad coverage of political systems, continents, cultures, and, more generally, development strategies (Table 7.2).

© 2010 John Wiley & Sons, Inc.

▶ *CASE STUDY (continued)*

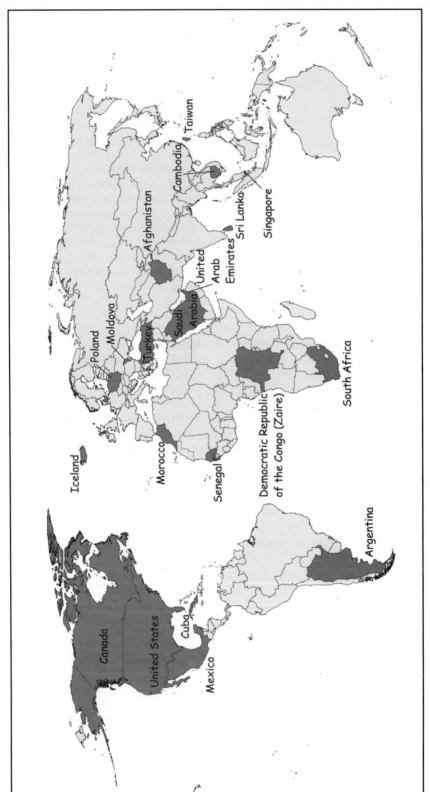

Figure 7.14 Countries selected for this exercise.

► **CASE STUDY** *(continued)*

TABLE 7.2   Description of the Selected 20 Countries

Name	2008 Population	Government	Description
Afghanistan	32.7 million	Transitional	Extremely poor, landlocked, arid, and mountainous country. Highly dependent on farming and livestock raising. After end of Soviet occupation in 1989, Islamic law imposed by Taliban, which U.S. military action overthrew in 2002 for supporting the al-Qaeda terrorist network, resulting in a new interim government and constitution. Is currently occupied by U.S. and Allied troops. New president elected in 2004, but the government's sustainability without Allied occupation is unclear. Afghanis are overwhelmingly Muslim (99%).
Argentina	39.7 million	Democracy	Temperate climate varying physically from rich plains to the high Andes Mountains. Was a very prosperous country last century; still maintains high levels of education and middle-class values. Although better off than other Latin American countries, has an inequitable distribution of wealth. Economy characterized by years of mismanagement and a current major financial crisis associated with neoliberal reforms.
Cambodia (formerly Kampuchea)	14.7 million	Democracy, transition economy	Tropical and rainy with a monsoon season. Much rice farming along the Mekong River, and gemstone mining elsewhere. Suffered mass genocide during the Khmer Rouge reign in the mid- to late 1970s. Destroyed by decades of war; later occupied by Vietnam; elections in 1998 brought new political stability. Economic growth hindered by undeveloped infrastructure.
Canada	33.3 million	Confederation, parliamentary democracy	Large land area with a climate varying from arctic to temperate. An affluent, high-tech, postindustrial society with great natural resources and a skilled labor force. However, there is potential for its dissolution along French/English linguistic lines.
Cuba	11.2 million	Communist state	Tropical island with a centrally planned economy. Suffered from the withdrawal of foreign aid upon Soviet Union collapse. Aggressively seeks new foreign investors and tourism while the United States maintains a trade embargo on Cuba. Relies on agricultural products but has a strong medical tradition. Is racially mixed, with 51% mulatto, 37% white, and 11% black.
Democratic Republic of Congo (formerly Zaire)	66.5 million	Dictatorship	Tropical, humid, or wet-dry. An ethnically diverse country composed of numerous indigenous groups. Has a vast potential for natural resource wealth but a history of rebellion and corruption that has resulted in little foreign investment. Long-running civil war and foreign occupation plagued the country from 1997 to 2002. Exports of minerals and tropical plantation agriculture.

▶ *CASE STUDY (continued)*

TABLE 7.2   Description of the Selected 20 Countries *(continued)*

Name	2008 Population	Government	Description
Iceland	0.3 million	Constitutional republic	Despite its northerly location, has a largely temperate climate and quite homogeneous population, with important historical, cultural, and linguistic ties with the remainder of Scandinavia. Has a Scandinavian-type capitalist economy characterized by an extensive welfare system, low unemployment, and an even income distribution. Economy heavily dependent on fishing but is beginning to diversify with manufacturing and tourism. Planning to become the first country in the world to get 100% of its energy from renewable sources.
Mexico	107.7 million	Federal republic	Great diversity of climate and physical features from tropical rain forest to desert and high mountains. Possesses a great wealth of natural resources, including oil. Changed economy to open-market policies after decades of government protectionism and management resulting in severe recession in 1994 that caused hardships for the transition. Like most of Latin America, has an inequitable distribution of wealth, is 89% Catholic, and has a sizable Amerindian population (30%).
Moldova	4.1 million	Republic, transition economy	A former Soviet Republic and a landlocked country with a steppe climate. Culturally and linguistically similar to Romania. Has an agriculturally based economy with the need to import almost all of its electricity and fossil fuels. Poorest country in Europe; elected a communist president in 2001.
Morocco	31.2 million	Constitutional monarchy	Mediterranean climate, more arid in the interior. Predominantly Muslim country suffering from foreign debt and unemployment causing many of its citizens to work temporarily in Europe, but has key resources—fishing, phosphates, and tourism—to develop.
Poland	38.1 million	Democracy, transition economy	Temperate climate with cold winters and industrial pollution. Historically a conflict zone on the plains between Europe and Russia. Conversion to democracy replacing the communist state in 1990. Underwent an economic shock when converted to capitalism. Large strides made toward privatization, but much of the economy still government controlled. Is 95% Catholic. Joined the European Union in 2004.
Saudi Arabia	28.1 million	Monarchy	Harsh, dry desert with great extremes of temperature. Mostly uninhabited sandy desert. Has a well-to-do, oil-based economy with strong government controls over economic activity but a highly inequitable distribution of wealth. Almost all export earnings and 75% of revenues from the petroleum sector. Has the world s largest petroleum reserves and exports the most. Is 90% Arab and 100% Muslim. Government has seen increasing threats from domestic terrorism.

(continued)

► **CASE STUDY** (continued)

TABLE 7.2 **Description of the Selected 20 Countries** (continued)

Name	2008 Population	Government	Description
Senegal	12.7 million	Republic	Tropical, wet-dry climate with multiethnic population of numerous indigenous groups, many of whom are Muslim. Recently made modest economic gains including a steady growth of its GDP and an increase in information technology, but still suffers from serious unemployment and drug abuse in the urban centers.
Singapore	4.8 million	Democracy	A tropical hot and humid island country at the tip of the Malay Peninsula whose location is a focal point for Southeast Asian sea routes that led to excellent international trading links. A prosperous country with an open and entrepreneurial economy whose people are 77% Chinese, 14% Malay, and 8% Indian.
South Africa	48.3 million	Democracy	Mostly semiarid to subtropical on the east coast with a high plateau immediately inland from most of the coasts. Rich in mineral resources. Population of 75% black, 14% white, 8% colored (mixed), and 3% Indian. Officially discriminated against blacks who lacked basic rights of citizenship under the system of apartheid, which ended in 1994. Still racially divided with most whites living on a par with the affluent West but most blacks living in poverty and Third World status. Many hardships created by change to an export-based economy.
Sri Lanka	20.3 million	Democracy	A tropical island at the tip of India with monsoonal rains and ethnicity of 74% Sinhalese, 18% Tamil, and 7% Moor. Has been in near civil war between the Sinhalese and Tamils since the mid-1980s, but with cease-fire signed in 2002. Some terrorism as the groups struggle for power. Economy relies on apparel industry exports and agriculture. Still in transition from state-run economy to export orientation. Religiously, 70% Buddhists and 15% Hindu.
Taiwan	23.0 million	Democracy	An island with tropical monsoon climate. Formerly a province of China that split from it in 1949 and whose status remains con-tested. Has a sparse natural resource base but a vibrant economy. Known as one of the Asian Tigers. A newly industrialized country (NIC) with rapid industrialization over the past half century.
Turkey	74.8 million	Parliamentary democracy	Mountains and high plateaus with hot summers. Straddles Europe and Asia and controls the strategic straits between the Black Sea and the Mediterranean Sea. Internal tensions between the tradition of Western government and more fundamentalist Muslims. Kurdish minority (20% of the population) want political autonomy. Economy hurt by fiscal deficits and inflation but economic and judicial reforms and a thriving private sector likely to increase prosperity Has long exported workers to Europe; currently seeking membership in the European Union.

▶ *CASE STUDY (continued)*

TABLE 7.2   Description of the Selected 20 Countries *(continued)*

Name	2008 Population	Government	Description
United Arab Emirates	4.5 million	Federation	A flat, desert nation that is largely Muslim with a mixed population of Arabs, Iranians, and South Asians. Has one of the world's highest per capita incomes, the result of its oil and natural gas production and its low population. Imports labor from Asia to work in oil and other sectors.
United States	304.5 million	Federal republic	Diverse physical environments with population of 80% white, 12.9% African-American, and 15.1% Hispanic. Most powerful, diverse, and technologically advanced economy in the world. Market-oriented and open. Predominantly Christian (79%), with many minority groups with diverse religious beliefs.

Source: Central Intelligence Agency, *The World Factbook* 2008: www.cia.gov/cia/publications/factbook/, and Population Reference Bureau, *2008 World Population Data Sheet*.

Name: _____ Instructor: _____

Rags and Riches: The Dimensions of Development

▶ ACTIVITY 1: ECONOMIC MODEL OF DEVELOPMENT

In this section, you will use two indicators to assess a country's level of economic development. These indicators are GDP per capita and percentage of the labor force engaged in nonagricultural labor:

- GDP per capita, the most typical indicator of economic development, measures the total dollar value of all goods and services produced by a country divided by its population.

- Percentage of the population involved in nonagricultural activities is another commonly used indicator of development. Because a subsistence economy is extremely labor intensive, a country with an economy based primarily on subsistence agriculture has few resources to invest in industry and services. As a country develops its technological capabilities, a smaller and smaller percentage of the labor force is needed to produce enough food for the entire population, and a larger and larger percentage of workers are diverted into manufacturing, trade, and services.

You will find values for each of these indicators listed by country in *Columns B* and *D* of Table 7.3 and will calculate a composite economic development ranking for each country based on these two indicators. This index will appear in *Column F*.

A. *Column B* lists GDP per capita for each country; *Column D* lists the percentage of the labor force in nonagricultural activities for each country. Columns C and E are for ranking the countries from best to worst according to the data in Column B and D, respectively. Column C is already filled out to show you how to do it. Your task in this question is to fill in the correct values for Columns E and F.

B. Let's start with Column E, which ranks the countries by values given for *Column D*. Generally, as a country develops, its percentage of workers engaged in nonagricultural activities increases. Therefore, the country with the highest value in *Column D* should be ranked 20 (highest), and the country with the lowest value in *Column D* should be ranked 1 (lowest). In the event of a tie, both countries should receive the same highest ranking. For example, if two countries share the highest value for GDP per capita, both would be ranked 20. The country in third place would receive a ranking of 18. Remember to skip a ranking number after assigning two identical rankings for a tie (See Column C for an example). Fill in Column E using whole numbers (no decimal points.)

C. *Column F* is a composite economic development ranking for each country based on rankings for GDP per capita and the percentage of the labor force involved in nonagricultural activities. To complete *Column F*, calculate the average of values in *Columns C* and *E*. Example: A country

© 2010 John Wiley & Sons, Inc.

TABLE 7.3 Composite Ranking

	A	B	C	D	E	F	G	H	I	J	K	L
	Country	GDP Per Capita* ($US)	GDP Per Capita* Ranking	Non-Agricultural Employment (%)	Non-Agricultural Employment Ranking	Economic Development Ranking	Infant Mortality Rate per 1,000	Infant Mortality Rate Ranking	Female Literacy Rate	Female Literacy Rate Ranking	Human Welfare Ranking	Human Welfare Ranking–Economic Ranking
United States	36,200	20	98				6.69		97			
Singapore	26,500	19	100				3.6		90			
Canada	24,800	18	97				4.95		97			
Iceland	24,800	18	95				3.53		100			
United Arab Emirates	22,800	16	93				16.12		80			
Taiwan	17,400	15	92				6.8		79			
Argentina	12,900	14	88				17.2		96			
Saudi Arabia	10,500	13	88				49.59		70			
Mexico	9,100	12	80				24.52		87			
Poland	8,500	11	73				9.17		98			
South Africa	8,500	11	70				61.78		85			
Turkey	6,800	9	60				45.77		77			
Morocco	3,500	8	50				46.49		31			
Sri Lanka	3,250	7	62				15.65		87			
Moldova	2,500	6	60				42.16		94			
Cuba	1,700	5	76				7.27		95			
Senegal	1,600	4	30				55.41		29			
Cambodia	1,300	3	20				64		22			
Dem. Rep. of the Congo (Zaire)	1,100	2	35				98.05		68			
Afghanistan	800	1	20				144.76		21			

Note that these figures are the most recent available; some may supersede those found in the *Area and Demographic Data* online
*Based on purchasing power parity.
Source: Central Intelligence Agency. 2002. *CIA Factbook:* www.cia.gov/cia/publications/factbook/index.html

206

with a GDP ranking of 4 (*Column C*) and a nonagricultural ranking of 3 (*Column E*) would have an economic development ranking (*Column F*) of 3.5. To confirm that you are calculating the values correctly, calculate the composite ranking for the United States; the answer should be 19.5.

Fill in Column F using one decimal place, even when none in needed (e.g., enter 10.0 instead of 10).

Name: _____ Instructor: _____

Rags and Riches: The Dimensions of Development

▶ ACTIVITY 2: HUMAN WELFARE MODEL OF DEVELOPMENT

In this question you will do a calculation similar to that in Activity 1 but for a composite human welfare development ranking for each country, based on two indicators. You will rank the countries separately for each of the two human welfare indicators in Columns H and J. Then you compute an average human welfare ranking for each country and enter it in Column K. Finally, in Column L, you will subtract the economic ranking from the human welfare ranking to get a measure of how "balanced" development is in each country. That's the big picture—now let's take it step by step.

The two human welfare indicators we have chosen are infant mortality and female literacy:

- The infant mortality rate is the annual number of deaths of infants 1 year of age or younger per 1,000 live births. It is frequently used as a measure of human welfare because it measures a society's ability to provide for its most vulnerable members. MDCs tend to have lower infant mortality rates than do LDCs because the populations of MDCs have better medical care, housing, nutrition, sanitation, and education.

- The female literacy rate—the percentage of women who can read and write—is also a common indicator of human well-being because literate labor forces can adopt new technologies and interact with the world market. The female literacy rate also reflects the status of women in society and whether the society is taking care of the needs of *all* of its citizens.

  A. *Column G* shows infant mortality rates for all 20 countries. In *Column H*, rank these countries by their infant mortality rates. As a country develops, its infant mortality rate generally decreases. As a result, the country with the *lowest* infant mortality rate will be ranked 20, and the country with the *highest* infant mortality rate will be ranked 1. Don't forget the tie-breaker rules from Activity 1. If two countries are tied, give both the higher ranking and then skip the lower of the two rankings (see Column C). Use whole numbers only in Column H (no decimals).

  B. *Column I* displays female literacy rates for all 20 countries. In *Column J*, rank countries according to their female literacy rates. The MDCs generally have higher female literacy rates. Therefore, the country with the highest female literacy rate would be ranked 20, and the country with the lowest female literacy rate would be ranked 1. Use whole numbers only in Column J (no decimals).

  C. *Column K* is a human welfare development ranking for each country based on its rankings for infant mortality and female literacy rates. To complete *Column K*, calculate the average of values in *Columns H* and *J*.

Enter the average ranks with one decimal place always, even if it is not needed (e.g., enter 10.0 instead of 10).

D. In *Column L*, subtract the economic development ranking (*Column F*) from the human welfare development ranking (Column *K*). That is, L = $K - F$. This calculation allows you to see how a country ranks differently, depending on whether development is measured economically or with a human welfare model. A country with a negative value in *Column L* has a better ranking for economic development than for human welfare development, and a country with a positive value in *Column L* has a better ranking for human welfare development than for economic development. If L is zero or close to zero, it means the country had similar rankings on the economic and human welfare indicators and is somewhat "balanced" in its development levels. Thus, we might say that a country's value in Column L represents where it falls on the economic (negative numbers) to human welfare (positive numbers) spectrum. (*Note*: we are not attaching negative or positive judgments to these negative and positive numbers.)

Name: _____   Instructor: _____

Rags and Riches: The Dimensions of Development

▶ ACTIVITY 3: COMPARING ECONOMIC DEVELOPMENT AND HUMAN WELFARE DEVELOPMENT MODELS

A. Transfer the values from *Column K* of Table 7.3 to *Column C* of Table 7.4 (on page 216). Notice that *Column B* in Table 7.4 has been copied from *Column F* on Table 7.3. The countries in Table 7.4 are in the same order as in Table 7.3.

B. Using the graph on page 212, create a scatter diagram of economic and human welfare development rankings for all 20 countries. Notice that both axes are scaled from 0 to 20. Locate the economic and human welfare ranks for the first country, the United States, in *Columns B* and *C* of Table 7.4. On the x-axis (horizontal) of the grid, locate the economic rank for the United States. On the *y*-axis (vertical) of the grid, locate the U.S. human welfare rank. Plot a point at the intersection of these rankings with a small abbreviation for the country name beside the point. Thus, you should have a point for the United States at the point (19.5, 17.5) on your scatter diagram. Complete this process for each country and label each point.

C. Notice that points fall into one of three sectors on the scatter diagram. Countries in Sector I have much higher human welfare scores than economic scores. Countries in Sector II have similar economic and human welfare development scores even though they may be low in both dimensions on the lower left or high in both dimensions on the upper right. Countries in Sector III have high economic scores compared to their human welfare measures of development. Also notice the relative position of each country away from the graph's diagonal. This position should reflect values in *Column L* of Table 7.3. Draw in a 45° diagonal line from (0, 0) to (20, 20). Countries with similar economic and human welfare rankings are arranged near or on the 45° line (Sector II). Countries with different rankings are represented by points situated well off the 45° line. Countries with large positive numbers in *Column L* are located far above the diagonal line (Sector I); countries with large negative numbers are located far below the line (Sector III).

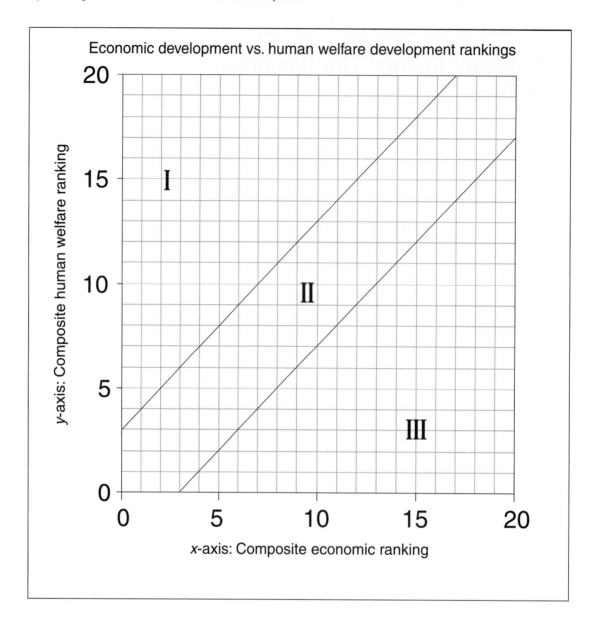

Economic development vs. human welfare development rankings

y-axis: Composite human welfare ranking

x-axis: Composite economic ranking

3.1. Why do Cuba, Poland, Sri Lanka, and Moldova rank higher on the human welfare than on the economic dimension? (*Hint*: Look at Table 7.2.)

3.2. Why do Saudi Arabia and the United Arab Emirates rank higher on the economic than on the human welfare dimension?

3.3. What are the long-term ramifications of investing heavily in economic production at the expense of human welfare investment?

3.4. What are the long-term ramifications of investing heavily in human welfare at the expense of economic production?

Name: _____   Instructor: _____

Rags and Riches: The Dimensions of Development

▶ ACTIVITY 4: ALTERNATIVE INDICATORS OF DEVELOPMENT

The first three activities have examined two models of development, each based on different indicators of development. What other indicators can you think of that might measure a country's success in realizing its full development potential? Look on the Internet to find international development indicators. From the Web Resources list at the end of the chapter, good data can be found at the Central Intelligence Agency, United Nations, U.S. Agency for International Development, U.S. Census Bureau, World Bank, and World Health Organization sites. Search the Web for other databases. Alternatively, go to your library and consult the United Nations' *Human Development Report; Demographic Yearbook; Compendium of Social Statistics and Indicators; World Population Profiles*; and the *Statistical Yearbook*, as well as the World Bank's *World Development Report*. Regional UN reports such as the *Statistical Yearbook for Latin America and the Caribbean* or *Asia and the Pacific* also are useful tools. Do not use any variables from the *Area and Demographic Data* online. We want you to develop your Internet and library skills.

A. Choose four development indicators not used in Activities 1 through 3. Use any sources you wish other than our *Area and Demographic Data*, but be sure to note the sources from which you acquire data. Indicators can be either economic or human welfare in nature. Attempt to measure a different aspect of development with each indicator. Many options are available. Although there are no absolutely correct indicators, there are many incorrect or flawed indicators that you should avoid. These include so-called mass variables that measure the grand total of something in a country, such as total GDP or total number of doctors. Mass variables tend to be large for large countries and small for small countries. *All of your variables should therefore be in the form of a rate, a percentage, or a per capita variable.* Also avoid variables that are determined largely by factors other than development. Inflation rate, oil production, and population density are variables that could easily be very low or very high regardless of a country's level of development. Be able to justify the indicator's importance to development. Choose four new indicators and record the data for each of the 20 countries on Table 7.4 in *Columns D, F, H, and J*.

   If you use multiple sources for a single variable, be sure units of measurement are the same. Beware of metric versus imperial units, rates per 100 versus rates per 1,000, or such things as electricity or energy units that differ. Try to find data for the same year. If you are unable to find data for a variable for one or two countries, leave them blank. If more than two countries are missing, use other sources or choose a new variable.

B. In *Columns E, G, I, and K*, respectively, rank values from *Columns D, F, H, and J*, respectively. Ranks will be from 1 to 20, and each country

© **2010 John Wiley & Sons, Inc.**

TABLE 7.4 Alternate Indicators

A	B	C	D	E	F	G	H	I	J	K
Country	Economic Development *Ranking*	Human Welfare *Ranking*	First Indicator Value	First Indicator *Ranking*	Second Indicator Value	Second Indicator *Ranking*	Third Indicator Value	Third Indicator *Ranking*	Fourth Indicator Value	Fourth Indicator *Ranking*
United States	19.5									
Singapore	19.5									
Canada	18.0									
Iceland	17.5									
United Arab Emirates	16.0									
Taiwan	15.0									
Argentina	14.0									
Saudi Arabia	13.5									
Mexico	12.0									
Poland	10.5									
South Africa	10.0									
Turkey	8.0									
Morocco	6.5									
Sri Lanka	7.5									
Moldova	6.5									
Cuba	8.0									
Senegal	3.5									
Dem. Rep. of the Congo (Zaire)	3.0									
Cambodia	2.5									
Afghanistan	1.0									

216

should have a different, whole number ranking (except in the case of ties). The country with the value indicating the highest level of development (relative to that variable) will be ranked 20. The country with the value indicating the lowest level of development (relative to that variable) will be ranked 1. Think carefully about whether a high value of your variable indicates a high level of development. Remember, for example, that *low* infant mortality rates and *high* literacy rates both indicate high development.

4.1. List each of your four variables, how it is measured (if necessary), and where you obtained the data. Give a justification for the choice of each variable as an indicator of development.

Variable 1 (*Column D*):

Source:

Justification:

Variable 2 (*Column F*):

Source:

Justification:

Variable 3 (*Column H*):

Source:

Justification:

Variable 4 (*Column J*):

Source:

Justification:

4.2. How did the rankings for your variables differ from those provided earlier in the exercise? Which countries scored higher? Which scored lower? Why?

▶ DEFINITIONS OF KEY TERMS

Appropriate Technology Small-scale technology that rural peasants can afford and use.

Circular and Cumulative Causation Self-sustaining economic growth that builds on itself as capital, skilled labor, innovation, and services attract and create more of the same.

Core Periphery A model of the economic development process over time and space that focuses on the evolving relationships between a rich, productive, innovative core region and a poor, dependent periphery.

Dependency School A school of thought that explains low development levels as being a result of the LDCs' economic dependency on the MDCs. See *core periphery* and *neocolonialism*. It also stressed that development be measured in terms of human welfare indicators rather than economic indicators.

Development The extent to which a society is making effective use of resources, both human and natural.

Economic Indicators Development indicators based on a country's economic production (how much it produces, e.g., GDP), what kinds of things it produces (ranging from raw materials to manufactured goods and services), and how it produces (ranging from labor-intensive, subsistence production to capital-intensive, specialized production).

Gross Domestic Product (GDP) The total dollar value of all final goods and services sold in monetary transactions in a country in a given year, excluding overseas transactions.

Gross National Product (GNP) The total dollar value of all final goods and services sold in monetary transactions in a country in a given year, including international transactions.

Human Welfare Indicators Development indicators based on a country's success in meeting the basic needs of its citizens.

Import Substitution A development strategy whereby an LDC tries to develop its own industries instead of importing manufactured goods from the MDCs.

Modernization The change from traditional ways of life to more up-to-date ways involving more use of specialization, technology, and capital. Also, the name given to the dominant school of thought from the 1940s to the 1960s.

Neocolonialism When a previously colonized country has become politically independent but remains economically dependent on exporting the same commodities (raw materials and foodstuffs) as it did during its colonization.

Neoliberal Counterrevolution The 1980s school of development emphasizing free-market approaches and participation in global trade.

Polarization Effects Concentrating tendencies, which reinforce growth in the core at the expense of the periphery.

Spread Effects Forces of deconcentration from the core to the periphery.

Structural Change Change in the structure of an economy, from one dominated by agriculture to one dominated by industry and services.

Subsistence Economy Food and craft production primarily to meet consumption needs at the household or community level.

Substitution of Capital for Labor Replacement of workers by machines, vehicles, and other capital goods operated by a smaller number of workers and usually powered by inanimate energy sources. Capital goods are produced goods used to produce others goods (see Chapter 6).

Sustainable Development Development providing for the needs of the present generation without diminishing the options of future generations. Also the name given to the emerging school of thought in the 1990s.

Technology Transfer The diffusion or transfer of technology, usually from a more-developed country to a less-developed country.

Transition Economies Countries in the process of converting from a centrally planned to a capitalist economy.

▶ FURTHER READINGS

Brown, Lawrence A. 1991. *Place, Migration and Development in the Third World*. New York: Routledge.

Cohen, Jessica, and William Easterling. 2009. *What Works in Development? Thinking Big and Thinking Small*. Washington DC: Brookings Institution Press.

Daly, Herman. 1991. *Steady State Economics. Washington*, DC: Island Press.

Easterly, William. 2007. The Ideology of Development. *Foreign Policy* 161:31–35.

Fennel, David A. 1999. *Ecotourism: An Introduction*. London: Routledge.

Fik, T. J. 1997. *The Geography of Economic Development: Regional Changes, Global Challenges*. New York: McGraw-Hill.

Kovasevic, Natasa. 2007. Child Slavery. *Harvard International Review* 29(2):36–42.

Potter, Robert B., J. A. Binns, J. A. Elliott, and D. Smith. 1999. *Geographies of Development*. London: Longman.

Sachs, Jeffrey. 2005. *The End of Poverty*. New York: Penguin.

Sachs, Jeffrey. 1999. Helping the World's Poorest. *The Economist* (Aug. 14):17–20.

Schumacher, Ernst F. 1973. *Small Is Beautiful: Economics as if People Mattered*. New York: Harper & Row.

Silva, Julia A., and Robin M. Leichenko. 2004. Regional Income Equality and International Trade. *Economic Geography* 80(3):261–286.

Straussfogel, Debra. 1997. Redefining Development as Humane and Sustainable. *Annals of the Association of American Geographers* 87:280–305.

Thomas, Alan. 1994. *Third World Atlas*, 2nd ed. Washington, DC: Taylor & Francis.

Zakaria, Fareed. 2008. *The Post-American World.* New York: W.W. Norton.

► WEB RESOURCES

Central Intelligence Agency: www.cia.gov/cia/library/publications/the-world-factbook/index.html

Engineers Without Borders: www.ewb-usa.org

Gap Minder: www.gapminder.org

One World: US.oneworld.net

Grameen Banking for the Poor: www.grameen-info.org

International Monetary Fund. *Finance & Development* Quarterly Magazine: www.imf.org/external/pubs/ft/fandd/fda.htm

International Monetary Fund. Country Information: www.imf.org/external/country/index.htm

Program for Appropriate Technology in Health: www.path.org/index.htm

United Nations Conference on Trade and Development. 2007. The Least Developed Countries Report, 2007. New York: United Nations: www.unctad.org/en/docs/ldc2007_en.pdf.

United Nations Educational, Scientific, and Cultural Organization. Photo Bank: portal.unesco.org/ci/photos

United Nations Statistics Division: unstats.un.org/unsd

U.S. Agency for International Development: www.usaid.gov/about_usaid

U.S. Census Bureau, International Programs Center: www.census.gov/ipc/www

World Bank. *Data and Statistics*: www.worldbank.org/data

World Bank: www.worldbank.org

World Health Organization. *World Health Report*: www.who.int/whr/en/index.html

World Resources Institute. *Earth Trends*: earth trends.wri.org

► ITEMS TO HAND IN

Activities 1 and 2: • The completed spreadsheets, or answer all questions your instructor created in your WileyPlus assignments.

Activity 3: • Scatter diagram with points recorded for each of 20 countries
  • Questions 3.1–3.4, or answer all questions your instructor created in your WileyPlus assignments.

Activity 4: • The completed spreadsheet with alternative development indicators
  • Questions 4.1 and 4.2, or answer all questions your instructor created in your WileyPlus assignments.

CHAPTER 8

Food for Thought: The Globalization of Agriculture

▶ INTRODUCTION

Unlike most of the chapters in this book, which focus on a single big idea in human geography, this chapter deals with two of them. This chapter looks at agriculture and the traditional geographic idea of how and what people farm in different places. It also looks at the contemporary idea of **globalization**—the increasing tendency for distant places and people to link together in a global market by fast, cheap transportation and communication (Figure 8.1). These old and new ideas will come together to explain how the forces of globalization are changing local agricultural systems in Latin America.

Students need to know more about agriculture for three reasons. First, much of the land surface of the planet is devoted to agriculture. Even some of earth's water bodies are being farmed. Second, although only 2 percent of Americans are farmers, half of all families in less-developed countries (LDCs) earn their living by

Figure 8.1   A Coca-Cola advertisement in Vietnam demonstrates the contemporary idea of globalization.

farming. Third, agriculture is a major contributor to environmental change in the form of pesticide and fertilizer runoff, soil erosion, freshwater depletion, damming of rivers for irrigation purposes, and deforestation (Figure 8.2).

It is important to recognize that **agriculture**, defined as intentional planting of crops and raising of domesticated animals (**livestock**), is not synonymous with food production (Figure 8.3). Some crops and livestock are raised for nonfood purposes: corn for ethanol, rubber for tires, and minks for fur coats. Likewise, many food (and nonfood) products are produced from plants and animals through methods other than agriculture. They can be artificially synthesized—as are NutraSweet® (a sweetener), Tang® (a breakfast drink), and Simplesse® (a fat-free oil)—or collected from nature via **hunting and gathering** of wild plants and animals. Hunting and gathering usually brings to mind a primitive, preagricultural society that is rapidly disappearing from the earth; but if you think about it, most fishing and forestry are in fact modern-day forms of hunting wild fish and gathering wild trees. Sometimes agriculture overlaps hunting and gathering (not shown in Figure 8.3), blurring the distinction between the two, as when people prune or weed around wild plants from which they gather food, or when people throw food scraps to attract wild animals. The true distinction between agriculture and hunting and gathering is not the technological level, but whether humans raise the plants and animals or they grow wild. Therefore, forestry and fishing, while usually a modern-day form of hunting and gathering, *can also be* forms of agriculture if the trees are planted (plantation forestry) and the fish raised in enclosures (aquaculture). Finally, Figure 8.3 also

Figure 8.2 Irrigated fields in Oregon. Damming of rivers and pumping water from deep aquifers for irrigation purposes are major contributons to environmental change.

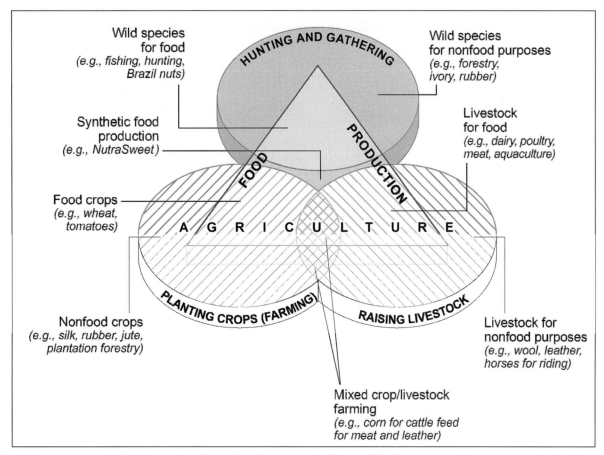

Figure 8.3 The relationship between agriculture and food production.

makes it clear that growing crops and raising livestock can overlap in **mixed farming** systems that grow crops for the purpose of feeding livestock.

Over the course of human history, three periods of technological change have led to the agricultural system we see today. In the **first agricultural revolution** during the Neolithic era some 8 to 14 thousand years ago, humans first planted and harvested edible plants and domesticated wild animals. The Fertile Crescent (see Chapter 2) was one important area of agricultural origins, but archaeological evidence points also to other and perhaps earlier source regions in China, Southeast Asia, the Indus Valley (present-day Pakistan), the Ethiopian highlands, West Africa, the Andes Mountains of South America, and Mexico/Central America (Figure 8.4). From these source regions, agriculture diffused (see Chapter 3) to other peoples around the world.

Numerous innovations have been made over the millennia to the basic idea of burying a seed in the ground and harvesting the results. Traditional innovations that we now take for granted include irrigation to deliver water to fields, plowing to loosen and turn the soil, fencing to keep animals out of fields, building terraces to provide level fields on hillsides, fertilizing with plant and animal waste, and weeding. Also important were various cultural and political practices, such as land tenure (private in some regions, communal in others), and division of labor (between humans and animals, men and women, adults and children, and among different occupations).

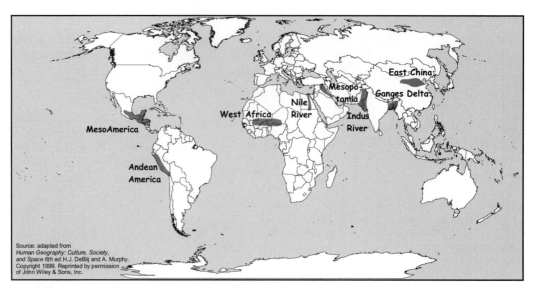

Source: adapted from
*Human Geography: Culture, Society,
and Space 6th ed.* H.J. DeBlij and A. Murphy.
Copyright 1999. Reprinted by permission
of John Wiley & Sons, Inc.

Figure 8.4 Probable culture hearths and origins of agriculture.

A **second agricultural revolution** began in western Europe in the 1600s. The second phase of agrotechnological change, which intensified agriculture in the sense of promoting higher yields per acre and per farmer, helped feed the growing urban populations in European cities. The second revolution actually began before the invention of machines with ideas such as crop rotation for sustaining soil fertility, increased use of fertilizers, and improved collars for draft animals to pull heavier plows. Then, in the nineteenth and early twentieth centuries, the Industrial Revolution introduced tractors for plowing soil, reapers for cutting crops, threshers for separating grain from stalks, and motors for pumping water to do the work of people and animals, not to mention better transport, storage, and barbed wire fencing. Industrially produced chemicals for fertilizers, herbicides (weed killers), and pesticides (insect killers) were also introduced in the twentieth century.

A dramatic **third agricultural revolution** began in the 1960s and continues to this day. The **Green Revolution**, as it is now known, introduced and diffused hybrid strains of staple grains by cross-pollinating different native strains of grain. These hybrids, known by names such as miracle rice and miracle wheat, mature in a shorter time period than conventional seeds, which means that farmers can grow an extra crop each year. Hybrid crops also respond better to chemical fertilizers and produce more grains per plant in closer proximity to other plants. Yields in both more-developed countries (MDCs) and LDCs increased by 50 to 100 percent in the space of a few years, which allowed global food production to keep pace with the exponential growth of population in the twentieth century. Unfortunately, the benefits of the Green Revolution have not spread to farmers everywhere; poor farmers lack the savings to invest in seeds, fertilizers, and pesticides. Critics also decry the Green Revolution's reliance on artificial fertilizers made from fossil fuels, the less flavorful grains, and the focus on corn, wheat, and rice, none of which are important crops in Africa.

The science of genetic engineering has breathed new life into the Green Revolution. Instead of crossing two varieties of plant or animal and hoping that a desirable combination of characteristics will emerge in some individuals of the next generation, genetic engineers leave little to chance. They identify the particular genes on the DNA molecules that produce the desirable characteristic and splice the gene directly into the chromosomes of the other plant or animal. Genetically engineered products are already on the market, mainly corn and soybeans that perform very well with particular weed-killing herbicides. The "Holy Grail" of bio-engineering is to identify the gene that allows legume crops to take nitrogen out of the air instead of through their roots and splice it into crops such as rice and wheat; these new plant varieties will eliminate the major need for chemical fertilizers. As is often the case, however, technological change carries risks, and some environmentalists and consumers are concerned about the effect of these "unnatural" crops on human health and on other species, such as monarch butterflies that pollinate corn. European consumers in particular have rejected genetically engineered crops, forcing U.S. farmers to carefully separate genetically engineered from traditional crops. Concerns also focus on the potential threat to natural species from aggressive bioengineered crops. Such was the outcry when genetically modified corn was discovered in Oaxaca, Mexico, the culture hearth of domesticated corn and home to dozens of diverse corn plants.

Geographers look at the spatial variation in *what* crops or livestock are produced and *how* they are produced. The natural environment plays an important role in determining what can be grown where (see the agricultural regions map layer in Activity 1). Rice needs more water than corn and wheat do. Wine-quality grapes need cool, wet winters and hot, dry summers. Citrus crops can be ruined by a winter freeze, whereas dairy cattle can thrive in cold and hilly areas. Tea and cacao (cocoa) are tropical crops, and, as we all know, Folgers® coffee is "mountain grown®." The physical environment alone does not, however, determine what is grown. If bananas, a plant native to the tropics, can be grown in Iceland in geothermally heated greenhouses (they can and they are!), then surely we must realize that climate is only one factor that determines where crops are grown. In fact, much of the farmland in the world is suitable for a variety of crops, and new varieties of grapes and rice are proving successful outside their traditional climate zones.

Culture is a second factor determining what is grown where. No meal is complete without rice in East and South Asia or corn tortillas in Mexico, whereas in Europe, the United States, and Canada, restaurants automatically serve bread made of wheat with every meal. Although it is true that traditional diets evolved based on available local ingredients, migration of cultural groups spread certain crops and livestock to other regions. Islamic and Jewish rules against eating pork, for instance, are not due to any difficulty of raising pigs in arid regions.

A third factor is economic. Rational farmers produce the crop that makes the greatest profit in any particular location. A German landowner, Johann Heinrich von Thünen, wrote a still classic work of economic geography in 1826 detailing how agriculture was organized into a series of concentric rings around each town. In von Thünen's model, climate and soils are assumed not to vary among sites. Location relative to the market determines what crops are grown. The farther a farm is from the market, the more transportation costs eat into the farmer's profits. Therefore, the agricultural land closest to the market will be the most valuable, all else being equal, and distant land will be least valuable. Different crops will be grown at different distances from the major metropolitan markets depending on factors such as **yield** (tons per acre per year), market price, production cost, and unit transport cost per ton. Generally speaking, crops with the highest annual transportation costs for an acre's worth of annual production, such as vegetables, eggs, and milk, tend to be produced in the ring immediately surrounding the market. Crops with low annual transportation costs, such as forestry (one crop every 20 to 50 years) or wheat (only the actual grains, not the stalks, are transported), can afford to be located far from markets. Other crops fall somewhere between. Thus, crops are not necessarily grown in their ideal bioclimate. Although wheat is better suited to the Ohio River valley, it is mainly grown in the Great Plains because other crops can make a greater profit in the Ohio Valley and few crops besides wheat can make a profit in the Plains.

The focus in Activity 1 is on *how* crops are grown in different parts of the world. As you will see, the same crop can be grown in remarkably different ways. The first distinction in agricultural methods is between labor-intensive and capital-intensive agriculture. **Capital** refers to goods that are used in the production of other goods, such as machinery, tools, facilities, vehicles, and transport networks. **Labor-intensive agriculture** employs large numbers of people and relatively little capital to produce a given amount of output. Some capital, such as hoes and plows and baskets and wells, is employed but not much, and most work is done by hand. **Capital-intensive agriculture** allows a single farmer to produce as much as 100 labor-intensive farmers can by substituting capital for labor (Figure 8.5). By using tractors for plowing, seed drills for planting, airplanes for spreading fertilizers, "combines" for reaping (cutting the plants) and threshing (separating the grains from the stalks), silos for storage, and railroads for transport, nearly every step of the agricultural process can be automated. Whether a region uses capital-intensive or labor-intensive methods depends largely on the price of capital and labor. As countries develop (see Chapter 7), wages increase, people have fewer children, people save more money, and bank loans become easier to obtain. As a result, labor becomes more scarce and capital more abundant. Farmers gradually automate their production process and become more capital intensive.

The second distinction, between intensive and extensive agriculture, refers to the intensity of land use. **Intensive agriculture** yields a large amount of output

Figure 8.5 The immense scale of capital-intensive agriculture is captured in this image from Montana. One combine can harvest many square miles of wheat, a feat that would have required hundreds of field workers prior to mechanization.

per acre through concentrated application of labor and/or capital, usually to small land holdings. In contrast, **extensive agriculture** yields a much smaller output per acre as farmers or ranchers spread their labor and capital over large areas of land. Intensity of land use depends on several factors, including the price of land (higher price, more intensive use) and the population density (more people per square mile, more intensive use). The intensive-extensive spectrum is largely independent of the capital-intensive–labor-intensive spectrum. Thus, intensive land use can be capital intensive as in greenhouses and hydroponics or labor intensive as in rice paddies with hundreds of workers per acre. Similarly, extensive land use can be capital intensive for a U.S. wheat farmer with a 500-acre farm and gigantic farm equipment or labor intensive for a nomadic goat herder ranging over many square miles.

A third distinction is between commercial and subsistence agriculture; and it, like the others, involves shades of gray. In pure **subsistence agriculture**, farmers and ranchers produce animals or crops to feed their families. Families and villages are nearly self-sufficient and do not depend on trade with other regions. In pure **commercial agriculture**, farmers and ranchers sell all of their output for money and buy their families' food at stores. Most subsistence farmers today sell some of their excess output on the market and link to other regions for specialized products. Similarly, many commercial farmers consume small amounts of output themselves. Generally speaking, regions shift from subsistence to commercial agriculture as a result of increasing wealth, trade, and specialization within the entire economy (i.e., as a result of development; see Chapter 7). However, political factors also play a role. Colonialism forced local people to convert from subsistence farming to commercial farming in order to pay colonial taxes in cash. Similarly, Chinese communism forced farmers into self-sufficient village communes in the 1950s to 1970s until a new regime let farmers sell their output for a profit in the 1980s. Today nearly pure subsistence farming is practiced only in some parts of Latin America, Africa, and Southeast Asia. However, farmers in nearly all LDCs subsist at least partly on their own production.

A fourth distinction is between sedentary and nomadic forms of agriculture. **Sedentary** refers to farmers and ranchers who live and work in a single location, whereas *nomadic* refers to production that shifts from place to place. **Nomadism** is usually associated with livestock herders who move from place to place in search of fresh pasture. As noted in Chapter 2 (the Middle East), nomadism is not random wandering but a systematic movement pattern among proven locations. Nomadic herding can be horizontal, from one water source to another, or vertical, from lowlands in the winter to highlands in the summer (also known as *transhumance*). In tropical rain forests, a nomadic form of farming known as **shifting cultivation** has also evolved. Farmers work the land for several years before moving on to another area. This form of farming is also known as slash-and-burn because the farmers cut the undergrowth and smaller trees and burn them. The burning clears the field of debris, and the resulting ash provides a short-term source of fertilizer to the relatively infertile rain-forest soils. Shifting cultivation can be a sustainable form of agriculture but only if the farmers stay for only a few years, do not return for several decades, and leave enough large trees standing to keep the torrential rains from eroding the soil. Thus nomadism is an adaption to life in difficult environments where sedentary agriculture would quickly exhaust water and soil resources.

A fifth broad categorization of agricultural systems is between irrigated and non-irrigated lands. **Irrigation** simply refers to artificial watering of farmland; it has many forms, including wells, tunnels, diversion channels, spraying, drip systems, and dams of all sizes. Irrigation is necessary in arid lands and areas with uncertain or seasonal precipitation.

Beyond these five universal dimensions, many other forms of agriculture relate to land ownership. Within commercial forms of agriculture, many organizational types exist: family farms, tenant farmers, sharecroppers, plantations, state-owned farms, garden plots, and agribusiness. Family farms are the traditional North American farm. In many parts of the world, however, most farmers rent their land and struggle to produce enough to pay the rent and still have enough to feed themselves and set some aside for next season's seed. A variation on tenant farming is *sharecropping*, by which farmers pay rent in the form of a percentage of the crop, which allows the farmers to share the risk with landowners. Located in LDCs, **plantations** are mainly historical leftovers from colonialism. They produce tropical crops such as bananas, cotton, rubber, coffee, cocoa, and peanuts by labor-intensive methods for export to MDCs. Individuals or corporations from MDCs still own many plantations, but local landowners or even local governments have taken over some plantations and continue to exploit local labor.

Socialist countries have experimented with many forms of farming on state-owned land. Workers can be collectivized into cooperatives or communes, rent from the state, be employed on state-run farms, or some other variation. In some such countries, workers are given small garden plots for their own use, which they farm very intensively. Yields from these backyard, quasi-private plots, which are also found in Latin America, can be several times higher than those achieved on the state farms because the worker gets to keep the proceeds. *Land reform* is a general term encompassing policies designed to give more of the population access to land that they can manage and steward themselves.

Finally, **agribusiness**, an industrialized, corporate form of agriculture, is organized into integrated networks of agricultural inputs and outputs beginning with seed, fertilizer, and pesticide production all the way through to processing and distributing food consumables. A small number of large corporations rather than a large number of independent farmers control agribusiness.

Similar to multinational industrial companies, telecommunications companies, and financial institutions, agribusinesses are increasingly extending their sources, sales, and power over a global network. The globalization of agriculture brings benefits to consumers in the MDCs of North America, Europe, Japan, and Australia (see Activity 2), but it also creates many negative local effects in peripheral LDCs (Activity 3) and often environmental and health concerns in the MDCs themselves. As the chief beneficiaries of globalized agriculture, we should be aware of these effects.

▶ *CASE STUDY*

FOOD FOR THOUGHT

GOAL

To understand how and why agricultural practices and agricultural landscapes vary around the world, to investigate where your food comes from, and to use remote sensing to evaluate land use and land cover change in Latin American agriculture.

LEARNING OUTCOMES

After completing the chapter, you will be able to:

- Differentiate among agricultural landscapes.
- Understand how and why the same crops and livestock are produced in different ways in different regions of the world.
- Collect primary data in your local supermarket.
- Describe global food chains.
- Recognize different land uses in satellite images.
- Use remote sensing to study land use change.

SPECIAL MATERIALS NEEDED

- Computer with high-speed Internet access and a recent release of a Web browser. If using the Student Companion Site with the printed book, click on *Tech Support* for system requirements and technical support. (If using the e-book in WileyPlus, click on *Help* for details about the system requirements.)

BACKGROUND

We now live in a global economy. Rapid transport and instantaneous communications technologies shrink space and stretch time, something geographers call **time-space convergence**. The **friction of distance** (i.e., the time, cost, or effort of movement) is continually being reduced, bringing distant places closer together. **Globalization** is a popular term used to describe the economic integration of different countries and regions around the world. The goods we use, including the food we eat, are now produced all around the globe. Globalization has affected local landscapes and economies even in what were previously very isolated places. This is perhaps most true for agriculture because so much of the world's land area is used for crops and livestock.

Globalization affects different people and places in various ways. In North America, the benefits have been great for some industries and farmers; they now export to larger markets around the world. Consumers benefit from the import of foods from all over the world. Imports produced more cheaply elsewhere (including food), however, have put many people in agriculture or related industries out of business. Globalization leads to a more unequal distribution of wealth and land. The number of small farmers in North America has declined for decades as more efficient **agribusinesses** underprice them and take advantage of the larger markets that globalization brings. Globalization of agriculture leads to a growing monopolization of the world food production in the hands of a

few multinational corporations. In 1996, the world's 10 largest agrochemical corporations captured 82 percent of global sales of fertilizers and pesticides, and the 10 largest seed corporations sold 40 percent of the seeds. Globalization also diffuses new agricultural innovations rapidly around the world.

Globalization thrives under **free trade**. Markets must be accessible to the supplier that can produce the best product for the lowest price. Absent restrictive trade barriers, regions around the world now produce those products in which they have a **comparative advantage**, and trade with other regions for what they need. Comparative advantage depends on the relative efficiency with which a region can produce a product compared with other products and other regions. Comparative advantage can lead to beneficial trade even when one region can produce all products for a lower cost. Why trade for something that could be produced more cheaply at home? Well, think about a lawyer who also happens to be a very fast typist and a sparkling receptionist. It still makes financial sense for the lawyer to hire someone to type documents and answer the phones, which would allow the lawyer to spend more time billing clients at a lawyer's high hourly rate. Likewise, regions can afford a higher standard of living by specializing in products in which they have a comparative advantage and using the profits to import other products.

One of the most daring experiments in free trade has been the North American Free Trade Agreement (NAFTA), which is the gradual removal of trade and investment restrictions among Canada, the United States, and Mexico. Between its inception in January 1994 and 2007, trade among the NAFTA countries more than tripled, from $297 billion to $930 billion. The three countries don't just trade with each other—they make things together, moving parts and assemblies up and down supply chains, back and forth across borders, until the final products are ready for market in any of the countries. The relationship—or better yet, partnership—between the United States and Canada is especially strong and generates millions of jobs in each country. Canada is the leading export market for 36 of the 50 U.S. states, and the United States exports more to Canada than to the 27 countries of the European Community combined. Mexico was the second largest trading partner of the United States until passed by China in 2005, but on a per capita basis, the United States exports about 25 times more to each Mexican citizen than to each person in China.

Although much of the growth has occurred in industry, NAFTA also has greatly affected agriculture. Mexico holds a comparative advantage in many agricultural products, such as tomatoes and vegetables, and has greatly increased the export of these crops to the United States (Figure 8.6). Traditional peasant lifestyles based on the production of maize (corn), beans, squash, and other staple crops for the local market and subsistence are becoming less common (Figure 8.7). Now many agricultural regions in Mexico produce goods for corporations that export crops to the United States, Canada, and Europe.

▶ **CASE STUDY** *(continued)*

Farms and entire regions that traditionally produced a mixture of crops are increasingly changing to **monoculture**—production of one crop year after year—with factories located nearby to process and package the product for export. Monoculture increases a region's vulnerability to the vicissitudes of bad weather, pests, and global price swings.

Planting a variety of crops is actually a type of community insurance against unforeseen disasters. In Central America, entire regions that relied predominantly on banana plantations as their economic base were devastated when fungi wiped out the entire banana crop. Monoculture creates a heavier reliance on pesticides as the biodiversity of the natural predators of the pests disappears. Furthermore, in traditional Mexican agriculture, intermixed planting of maize, beans, and squash also provided environmental benefits. Beans helped refertilize the soil with nitrogen, maize provided physical support for smaller vines, and squash planted between the rows as groundcover reduced soil erosion and evaporation.

Figure 8.6 U.S. Customs agent on the border of Nogales, Sonora, Mexico.

Figure 8.7 A traditional Mexican peasant house and small field of maize.

From a strictly economic perspective, the phasing out of peasant near-subsistence economies based on maize production in Mexico makes perfect sense. Traditional lifestyles were inefficient and labor intensive compared with monoculture. Mexico could never compete against the highly mechanized corn production in the United States, but Mexico's changing agricultural economy has had negative cultural and societal impacts on some people and regions. Maize production takes on religious significance to many Native Americans in Mexico. For them to change their lifestyles and take industrial jobs challenges their fundamental identities. Just as important, Mexico's pre-NAFTA land tenure system was communal in peasant villages called *ejidos*. In the mid-twentieth century, the Mexican government rewarded peasants in ejidos with land distribution and subsidized prices in return for votes. It also fostered allegiance with strong messages of nationalism. To implement NAFTA, Mexico had to amend its constitution to allow private sale of farmland on ejidos and stop many subsidies for peasant agriculture. These changes, plus the new emphasis on multinational corporations running the agricultural economy (which was previously seen as a threat to Mexican nationalism; see Chapter 7 on theories of development), have caused great upheaval and debate in rural Mexico. One expression of concern with globalization was the Zapatista uprising by indigenous people in southern Mexico that began on the very day NAFTA went into effect in 1994. To Native Americans in the state of Chiapas, globalization threatens lifestyles and strengthens a political system that does not represent their interests.

Elsewhere in Latin America, local economies and landscapes also are changing in response to globalization. One land use change is the conversion of forest to cattle production to satisfy the growing demand for beef in the more-developed world. In the Amazon Basin, much of the tropical rain forest cut down each year is eventually converted into ranches (Figure 8.8). Often the rain forest is first opened for oil and mineral exploration. Settlers fleeing poverty and crowding in urban areas soon follow using newly constructed roads for access to previously undeveloped areas (Figure 8.9). Homesteaders clear-cut the rain forest in hopes of establishing farms, most of which are productive only for a few years. Later, however, the land is abandoned because of encroaching weeds and depleted nutrients in soils not suitable for sedentary agriculture. Eventually, deforested areas are converted to ranching using grasses that thrive in tropical ecosystems, and the agricultural frontier moves on to repeat the process.

We have stressed the way globally driven free trade influences local landscapes, but the **global-local continuum** is not a one-way street. Local people, places, and regions have the power now to affect the global economy. Once-local innovations such as livestock feedlots and organic farming are spreading globally, as are once-local pests and crop diseases. The discovery of mad cow disease and the outbreak of hoof-and-mouth disease in Britain sent shock waves through the global beef distribution system, and a flood or labor strike in the Andes can drive up coffee prices in Toronto. The global-local continuum also refers to the fact that actions by millions of

Figure 8.8 Homesteaders clear the forest in the Amazon Basin for farming and ranching.

Figure 8.9 Roads for mineral extraction open the rain forest to migrants.

small producers can add up to produce significant global change, as in the piecemeal destruction of the Amazon rain forest. Also, each local place adapts differently to the forces of globalization. Some local farmers lose their land to agribusinesses, but others band together to form cooperatives and find new markets for their specialty products over the Internet.

You can see from the discussion in this chapter that globalization has caused profound changes throughout the world with many winners but also many losers. Among those who benefit from the global agricultural system are consumers who now have access to increased supplies of inexpensive products throughout all seasons and from around the world, large multinational corporations that control trade networks and key inputs (such as seeds and chemical fertilizers), and technologically advanced producers that can exploit economies of scale to serve the global market. However, proponents of globalization have recently met challenges to unfettered and ever-expanding agribusiness from a variety of fronts. One main force of opposition came from the LDCs when they stopped the expansion of agricultural trade accords at a series of meetings from 2003 to 2007. In what are referred to as the Doha trade negotiations, LDCs objected to what they see as unfair practices by the United States and the European Union. In spite of the push by the powerful world leaders for open markets to sell agricultural commodities, both the United States and the European Union continue to subsidize their own agricultural industries. For instance, the 2008 Farm Bill passed in the United States cost U.S. taxpayers $307 billion, much of it for subsidies to agribusiness. About 75 percent of the subsidies are for a few commodities (mostly wheat, corn, and oilseeds) that are sold in the global market. The effect is that agricultural products from the United States are cheaper in the LDCs than locally produced goods, and products grown in the LDCs cannot compete on the global market. This puts farmers in the developing world out of business and enriches large corporate agricultural entities in the United States and Europe. These hardships are particularly difficult for developing countries where agriculture typically accounts for a much higher share of economic output, exports, and employment than in developed countries. The agricultural sector is critical to many developing countries' overall economic growth. Brazil, India, and other developing countries are now demanding that, in exchange for removing trade barriers and agricultural subsidies in their own countries, the United States and the European Union must do the same.

A second source of resistance to the increasing globalization of agriculture comes from people concerned about environmental and community health. Their arguments are many: that the system of global production and trade is based on cheap oil for the transportation of products around the world and for the production of petrochemical fertilizers and is therefore unsustainable; that the environmental effects of fertilizers, pesticides, and herbicides are severely damaging our ecosystems; that the mass production of animals in corporate feedlots and factory farms is unethical and inhumane; that emphasis on monoculture and mass processing endangers food security by facilitating disease vectors and contamination of the food supply; that the current system produces inexpensive but highly processed products that are low in nutritional content and contribute to obesity, diabetes, and other diseases; and that the corporatization of agriculture puts small family farmers out of business and therefore weakens local cultures and local economies. Health and environmental activists in the United States are enraged that federal subsidies in the Farm Bill promote the production of the raw ingredients for food sweeteners, junk food, and livestock feed, using a system reliant on petrochemical inputs. Nearly 70 percent of farm subsidies

▶ *CASE STUDY (continued)*

go to the top 10 percent of the country's biggest growers while small farmers growing fruits and vegetables serving local communities receive nothing (and are actually put at an economic disadvantage). In response, a series of movements has grown rapidly in recent years promoting local agriculture and local food traditions, organic farming, urban and community gardens, and grass-fed/free-range livestock ranching. Outlets for these alternative production methods include farmers' markets (Figure 8.10), various forms of direct marketing such as community-supported agriculture (where consumers invest in farm shares and receive a weekly delivery), and restaurants with chefs who prefer local, fresh produce. Whether these social movements will affect the powerful global agribusiness system is uncertain, but alternatives to the global production model increasingly are available and much in demand.

Geographers analyze **land use** and **land cover** change with **remote sensing**, a process by which we acquire images of Earth from orbiting satellites. With the 1972 launch of the first Landsat satellite by the United States, images from space have been used to measure land cover change, monitor environmental health, explore for geologic resources, make maps, and predict crop production.

Satellite remote-sensing images are not photographs (although photos are taken from manned spacecraft such as the space shuttle). If a satellite took a photo, how would we get the film back to Earth to develop it, and how would we "reload" the satellite with more film? Satellites instead look at one small part of Earth and record a brightness value, which usually is just reflected sunlight (although some sensors actually emit a radar-like beam or signal that is recorded when

it bounces back). This value can range from a low number (zero) if that part of Earth is very dark and no reflected light is recorded, to a high number if that area is very bright and much light is reflected. After the satellite sensor records its brightness value, it moves on to the next small part of the earth and repeats the process. This all happens incredibly fast because the satellite is whizzing by overhead at a very fast speed. Each brightness value is called a *pixel*, which represents an average reflectance value for all features in that area of Earth. The size of the pixel varies by satellite. Some are as detailed as 1 square meter. Others, like weather satellites, use pixel resolutions of 5 kilometers.

Rather than record a brightness value for *all* reflected light, however, most sensors break the light (which is really just energy) into different colors with a prism. They can then record a brightness value for blue light, green light, red light, and many other parts of the electromagnetic spectrum such as infrared or ultraviolet that our eyes (which are also "remote sensors") cannot see. We call each of these "colors" a *band* because the spectral bandwidth refers to the energy wavelength that defines each color.

Satellite images are digital images, nothing more than a bunch of numbers in a matrix. The photos that we produce from these images are like paint-by-number images. Which spectral bands are painted with which colors determines how the image appears. If we use a band that corresponds to blue light and color it blue and do the same for green and red, we will produce an image that appears in "natural" color as it would look from the satellite through a telescope. More frequently, satellites use bands that gather brightness values in the infrared part of the

Figure 8.10 Farmer's markets are an increasingly attractive alternative for urban dwellers to purchase fresh produce, connect with the people who grow their food, support a local agricultural economy, and reduce the environmental impact of the food they eat.

© 2010 John Wiley & Sons, Inc.

▶ **CASE STUDY** *(continued)*

electromagnetic spectrum because they tend to cut through atmospheric haze much better and produce clearer images. For the same reason, early satellites' sensors excluded blue light because it scatters easily and adds haze. The near-infrared bands are also better at monitoring the health of vegetation, which reflects infrared light very brightly. The drawback with the infrared band is that it must be "painted" on the image with a color humans can see when in fact it is invisible to us, with the net result that the image won't look "natural." The most widely used band/color combination is called a "false-color infrared" in which the blue on an image is actually green light, the green is actually red light, and the red is actually near-infrared light. The result is an image in which healthy vegetation is bright red, bare fields range from white or gray to a bluish green, and urban areas look white or cyan (greenish blue).

Because all features have a unique reflectance pattern across the electromagnetic spectrum (called their *spectral signature*), we can classify the numbers that make up a digital image to find out where different features are located. Forests have a different spectral signature than grasses, and both are different from roads, water, and rooftops. The smaller the pixel size and the more spectral bands used, the more accurate

classifications can be. We can also easily detect changes from images acquired at one date to those at a later date.

In Activity 1, you will focus on seven agricultural products to look at the various ways the same product can be produced around the world. This will enable you to understand how landscapes are modified in different places by agricultural activities. You will then link these to a map of the world to see *where* these different modes of production occur.

In Activity 2, you will go to a local grocery store and gather evidence of the global agricultural economy by finding products produced outside the United States and Canada. This will reinforce your understanding that time-space convergence has brought faraway places to your door.

Finally, in Activity 3 you will look at an early satellite image (from the 1970s or 1980s) and a later satellite image (from the late 1990s or 2000) for three areas in Latin America. By overlaying these images, you can highlight all pixels that have changed. You will be able to calculate the area of change between these scenes using geographic information systems (GIS) operations and see how globalization of agriculture has affected these remote Latin American locations.

Name: _____   Instructor: _____

Food for Thought: The Globalization of Agriculture

▶ ## ACTIVITY 1: AGRICULTURAL LANDSCAPES AND PRODUCTION METHODS

If you have driven around North America, you are probably accustomed to seeing cows or wheat or vegetables produced in a particular way, and you could form the mistaken impression that it is the only way to produce them. In fact, we think you'll be much surprised at the many different ways that the same product is grown or raised in different places. In this activity, you will match strikingly different photographs of agricultural landscapes for the same crops to some of the key geographical terms you learned in this chapter. Then, once you have categorized the landscapes, you will match the photos to different regions of the world with the help of thematic map layers for various physical and human factors. If you get a wrong answer, don't worry; the animation will steer you in the right direction!

A. To start your activity, click on the Student Companion Site at www.wiley .com/college/kuby. (For students using WileyPlus, log on to your class Web site, select the *Assignment* tab, locate and click on this assignment, and follow all instructions.)

B. Select this chapter from the drop-down list and then click on *Computerized Chapter Activities*.

C. Click on *Activity 1: Agricultural Landscapes and Production Methods*.

D. In the right margin you will see your choices of livestock and agriculture. Click on *Cattle* to begin.

E. You will see several photographs of different methods of raising cattle from around the world, each with a different label. Above that you will see text that describes one of the methods using the key terms from the Introduction. Match the written description to the correct photo by clicking on the photo. If your answer is wrong, the computer will give you feedback on why it is wrong; read it and click *Try Again*. If your answer is correct, read the description of this landscape and production method and then click *Continue*.

F. When you have successfully matched all of the cattle-raising landscape descriptions to the proper photo, the screen will automatically change to a world map.

On the map you will see highlighted several regions that specialize in cattle, with a star showing the location where the photo was taken. The regions are darker in the center and lighter-colored around the edges to indicate a "core region" (see Chapter 2) where this type of agriculture is commonplace and a "fringe region" where it is also found but is not necessarily dominant. (*Note:* In some cases, the photo was taken in the fringe.) It is important to recognize that these regions are not the only areas on Earth where these crops are grown with these methods. The colors

© 2010 John Wiley & Sons, Inc.

simply delimit a region around where each photo was taken; they do not show all similar places around the world. For instance, cattle are grazed on the open range not only in the region shown but also in Australia and Argentina.

G. Your task is to match the photos to the regions and report several characteristics about the regions. Several thematic maps can be layered on the world maps. Click on *Population* to see a dot map of population density. Click on *Mountains* to see the mountainous areas of the world. Click on *Climate* to see the climate regions of the world. Click on *Precipitation* to see a map of rainfall plus the rain-equivalent amount of snowfall. Click on *Agriculture* to see a division of the world into broadly homogeneous agricultural regions. Click on *Development* to see the World Bank's grouping of countries into low-, lower-middle-, upper-middle-, and high- income countries. Click on *Subsistence* to see regions of primarily subsistence livelihoods (keeping in mind that many other areas practice a mix of subsistence and commercial agriculture). These are some of the leading factors under which traditional and modern agricultural systems have evolved. You can use these overlay maps as clues to figuring out where each photo was taken, and you will have to record certain data from these maps for each location. Click on *Photo Location* to return to the map of the crop in question.

H. If you wish, you can click *Enlarge Maps* to bring up a larger window. Close the larger map window with the "X" in the upper right window to return to the main map page.

I. Click on the star where you think this photograph was taken. If you get a wrong answer, use the computer's feedback and the thematic map overlays to guide you to a better answer. (We can't stop you from using trial and error, but we simply point out that random guessing won't help you prepare for the inevitable exam!) When you choose correctly, answer the following questions for that location (note that the animation automatically advances to the next photo after you correctly select each location). You can always click the back arrow to return to a previous photo.

▶ CATTLE

A capital-intensive, commercial, intensive land-use system in which cattle are raised in feedlots with automatic feeding, watering, and ventilation systems.

Location: _____

Population: _____

An extensive commercial system in which cattle are raised on the open range using natural grasslands as pasture.

Location: _____

Population: _____

An extensive subsistence system in arid regions in which cattle are herded nomadically among different locations of water and natural pastures.

Location: _____

Population: _____

An extensive commercial system in humid tropical regions in which settlers clear patches of rain forest, plant grass, and graze cattle.

Location: _____

Population: _____

J. After you have located all photos for cattle, the program automatically moves on to the next agricultural product. Complete the same steps and answer the questions for the other products. You can return to any product by clicking on its name in the right margin (*Cattle, Wheat, Rice, Bananas, Vegetables, Seafood, Hogs*). When asked to record a value from thematic map layers, check the map legend. Record your answers as before.

► WHEAT

A capital-intensive, commercial, extensive production system for growing and harvesting wheat.

Location: _____

Precipitation per year: _____

A capital-intensive, commercial, extensive system for irrigating wheat fields.

Location: _____

Precipitation per year: _____

A labor-intensive subsistence/commercial system for growing and harvesting wheat.

Location: _____

Precipitation per year: _____

A labor-intensive subsistence system for irrigating wheat fields.

Location: _____

Precipitation per year: _____

► RICE

A labor-intensive, subsistence/commercial, intensive land-use system in which rice is cultivated in rice paddy fields on flat land.

Location: _____

Development level: _____

A labor-intensive, subsistence/commercial, intensive land-use system in which rice is cultivated in terraced hillside rice paddies.

Location: _____

Development level: _____

A capital-intensive, commercial, extensive land-use system for cultivating and harvesting rice.

Location: _____

Development level: _____

A somewhat capital-intensive, commercial, highly intensive land-use system for cultivating and harvesting rice.

Location: _____

Development level: _____

A labor-intensive, extensive, subsistence system in humid tropical regions in which settlers slash and burn patches of rain forest and plant rice.

Location: _____

Development level: _____

▶ BANANAS

A labor-intensive, commercial, intensive land-use system in which bananas are grown in corporate plantations.

Location: _____

Climate: _____

A subsistence system in which banana trees are grown in villages as supplemental food sources.

Location: _____

Climate: _____

A capital-intensive commercial system in which bananas are grown in geothermally heated greenhouses.

Location: _____

Climate: _____

▶ VEGETABLES

A commercial, intensive land-use system in which seasonal vegetables are grown on "truck farms" for nearby cities.

Location: _____

Agriculture: _____

A capital-intensive, commercial, intensive land-use system in which vegetables are cultivated hydroponically in soilless containers in greenhouses.

Location: _____

Agriculture: _____

A large-scale, labor-intensive, commercial, intensive land-use system for cultivating and harvesting vegetables using migrant workers.

Location: _____

Agriculture: _____

A labor-intensive, subsistence/commercial, intensive land-use system for vegetables in small, backyard, urban plots.

Location: _____

Agriculture: _____

A labor-intensive, subsistence, intensive land-use system for growing vegetables in desert oases.

Location: _____

Agriculture: _____

► SEAFOOD

A capital-intensive commercial system in which fish are caught in a trawl net, processed, and frozen aboard a "factory ship."

Location: _____

Development level: _____

A capital-intensive commercial aquaculture system in which fish are raised in tanks.

Location: _____

Development level: _____

A commercial system in which a moderate amount of capital and labor are used to catch lobsters in traps using medium-sized boats.

Location: _____

Development level: _____

A labor-intensive subsistence/commercial system in which fish are caught in small canoes.

Location: _____

Development level: _____

► HOGS

A capital-intensive, large-scale, commercial, intensive land-use, agribusiness system in which hogs are raised in feedlots with mechanized feeding, watering, and ventilation systems.

Location: _____

Subsistence: _____

An extensive subsistence system of hunting wild boars.

Location: _____

Subsistence: _____

A subsistence production system in which village food waste is fed to domesticated "free-range" hogs.

Location: _____

Subsistence: _____

A medium-scale, commercial, mixed production system in which family farmers grow corn and use some of it to feed hogs.

Location: _____

Subsistence: _____

1.2. By now you may have noticed several common themes across the different agricultural products. List three examples of agricultural production systems that share some of the same characteristics. Fill in the blanks for the product and the location:

a. Labor-intensive agricultural systems:
_____ production in _____
_____ production in _____
_____ production in _____

b. Capital-intensive agricultural systems:
_____ production in _____
_____ production in _____
_____ production in _____

c. Intensive agricultural systems:
_____ production in_____
_____ production in _____
_____ production in _____

d. Extensive agricultural systems:
_____ production in _____
_____ production in _____
_____ production in _____

e. Commercial agricultural systems:
_____ production in _____
_____ production in _____
_____ production in _____

f. Subsistence agricultural systems:
_____ production in _____
_____ production in _____
_____ production in _____

g. Irrigated agricultural systems:
_____ production in _____
_____ production in _____
_____ production in _____

K. When you have finished, close all browser windows.

Name: _____ Instructor: _____

Food for Thought: The Globalization of Agriculture

► ACTIVITY 2: GLOBAL SOURCES FOR YOUR LOCAL SUPERMARKET

Hundreds of years ago, the vast majority of people ate the food they grew, gathered, or caught by themselves or bartered for it with others in the community. In many places, especially in LDCs, this is still true today, but our food increasingly comes from faraway places. Don't take our word for it, however—go see for yourself.

In Activity 2, we ask you to do a little field research while shopping at your local supermarket, and while we're at it, we just might get you to try a new taste! Your assignment is to browse the aisles and look for products that were imported from a country other than the United States or Canada.

Some foods are imported because the environmental conditions to grow them do not exist in the United States and especially Canada. Others, however, are imported for economic or cultural reasons. Furthermore, in the past, only nonperishable, packaged food products were imported because perishable products could not survive lengthy journeys. Today, however, inexpensive and fast long-distance transportation delivers perishable foods to your supermarket while they are still relatively fresh. For this reason, we ask you to find both perishable and packaged imports, some of which have domestic competitors (produced in the United States or Canada) and some of which don't.

Important: Questions 2.1 and 2.2 involve a task to be done at your local supermarket, such as browsing the aisles recording data (2.1) and making a purchase (2.2). *Make sure that you have dealt with these questions before you leave the market.* Questions 2.3 and 2.4 can be answered at home.

2.1. In the following table, list four perishable food products and four packaged food products that were imported from countries other than the United States and Canada. Perishable products include fruit, vegetables, baked goods, meats, and dairy products. Packaged goods are boxed, bagged, canned, bottled, and contained in any other long-term packaging. Record brand names if any are given, as well as the name of the importer, if it is different. Also give the name of a similar domestic product if it is available and the comparable unit prices (per ounce, liter, pound, or kilogram).

Product	Imported Product			Domestic Equivalent	
	Country of Origin	Brand Name (if any)	Unit price per___	Brand Name (if any)	Unit price per___
Perishable Product (4) 1. 2. 3. 4.					
Nonperishable Product (4) 1. 2. 3. 4.					

2.2. Purchase one perishable imported item and one nonperishable imported item and tape their labels in the space below to verify your selection.

2.3. For the imported products that have domestic competitors, speculate why people would buy the imported version over the domestic version. Use any clues that you can find (price, label, advertising, season, or quality).

2.4. For the imported products that do not have domestic competitors, speculate as to why they do not.

Name: _____ Instructor: _____

Food for Thought: The Globalization of Agriculture

► **ACTIVITY 3: REMOTE SENSING AND AGRICULTURAL LAND USE CHANGE**

Activity 3 involves using satellite images to determine land use change in three areas of Latin America (Figure 8.11). You will look at earlier and later satellite images for each area, and you'll measure changes between the two years that occurred during the globalization of agriculture.

A. To start your activity, click on the *Student Companion Site* at www.wiley .com/college/kuby. (For students using WileyPlus, log on to your class Web site, select the *Assignment* tab, locate and click on this assignment, and follow all instructions.)

B. Select this chapter from the drop-down list and then click on Computerized Chapter Activities.

C. Click on *Activity 3: Remote Sensing and Agricultural Land-Use Change*.

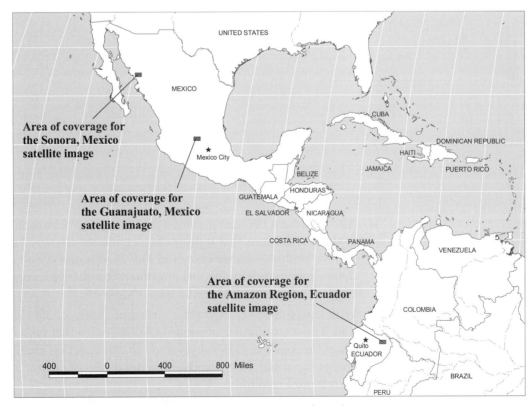

Figure 8.11 Case study areas in Latin America for land use change activity.

© **2010 John Wiley & Sons, Inc.**

The first scene is an area in Sonora, Mexico, where desert has been converted into irrigated agriculture. Irrigating the desert was begun at the end of the nineteenth century by U.S. investors. After the Mexican government completed large dams in the 1940s and 1950s, irrigated agriculture rapidly filled the desert areas on the lower deltas of rivers that flow out of the mountains. This process continued throughout the late twentieth century. Now canals bring water to fields throughout coastal areas. Agribusiness is a huge industry here, with crops such as wheat, cotton, and vegetables grown for the Mexican and global markets.

D. You initially will see a satellite image from April 12, 1973. Below the image is an interpretation of the land cover you see.

E. Click on *2000 Scene* and the screen changes to an image of the same place from April 6, 2000. Toggle back and forth between the two dates and look for areas that change. Note that when the later scene appears, you have the option to view this date in "natural color," which could help you to interpret the image (natural color is not available in the early scene because what we see as blue light was not collected by the sensor).

F. Click on *Split Screen* to view the images side by side.

G. Return to *Full Scene* and click *Photos on the Ground* to see photographs and interpretive text of that area.

3.1. What were the major land uses in 2000?

H. After you have become familiar with what you are looking at, select any of the four buttons that represent categories of change. Look closely at all four land-use change classes in *Full Screen* mode. Select the 1973 or 2000 scene to redraw the image without the change category on and then toggle the land-use Change Classes on and off.

I. With any land-use change class turned on, click on the *Calculate Area* tool. The total number of square kilometers for that type of change is listed for you. The GIS simply finds all pixels in that change class and counts them and then calculates the total area of change based on the known pixel resolution.

3.2. Which of the four types of change affected the most land? _____
How many square kilometers were affected? _____

3.3. For the answer to Question 3.2, describe the spatial pattern (if any) of where the change took place.

3.4. Fill in the following table, describing how this change affected people and their environment in both Mexico and the United States and Canada. Identify the positive and negative effects (the winners and losers) in both regions.

	Positive Effects	Negative Effects
In Mexico		
In the United States and Canada		

3.5. Rank the remaining three classes of change in decreasing order of area changed and briefly explain what is occurring in each class.

a. Second-most-important change:

b. Third-most-important change:

c. Fourth-most-important change:

J. Click on *Guanajuato, Mexico,* in the lower right margin. The second scene is in central Mexico in the states of Guanajuato and Querétaro. This area of central Mexico is called the *Bajío,* a rich agricultural area worked by Native Americans for centuries. Traditional peasant agriculture consisted of small plots where people grew a mixture of crops for market and subsistence. The staple crops traditionally have been corn (maize), beans, squash, and chilies. Today much of this is changing as Mexico produces export crops such as broccoli, cauliflower, lettuce, and strawberries for the U.S. market. Production is now more mechanized, with fewer traditional mixed-crop fields and more monoculture. Just as farmers in the United States do, small farmers in Mexico are selling out to agribusiness corporations that have better access to capital, technology, and global markets and can take advantage of economies of scale.

You will initially see a scene from March 28, 1976. Repeat the steps you did for the Sonora image so that you become familiar with this area. Note that the second image date is March 20, 2000.

3.6. What were the major land uses in 2000?

3.7. Which of the four types of change affected the most land?_____

How many square kilometers were affected? _____

3.8. For the answer to Question 3.7, describe the spatial pattern (if any) of where the change took place (note the presence of mountains to the north, south, and east of the photo, where it would be very difficult to farm).

3.9. Fill in the following table describing how this change has affected people and their environment in both Mexico and the United States and Canada. Identify the positive and negative effects (the winners and losers) in both regions.

	Positive Effects	Negative Effects
In Mexico		
In the United States and Canada		

© 2010 John Wiley & Sons, Inc.

3.10. Rank the remaining three classes of change in decreasing order of area changed and briefly explain what is occurring in each class:

a. Second-most-important change:

b. Third-most-important change:

c. Fourth-most-important change:

K. Click on *Amazon Region, Ecuador,* in the lower right margin. The third and final scene is from the Amazon rain forest in eastern Ecuador, where much deforestation has occurred since the 1970s. Initial development was for oil, but settlers followed using the roads built by the oil companies. The types of satellite images used in these scenes did not allow us to distinguish among different post-deforestation land uses, but studies of the region have shown that about 70 percent of the deforested area is ranch land for grazing cattle. Of the other 30 percent, some is for crops such as oil palm. Most of the farms are not sustainable because of the infertile rain-forest soils and will be converted to ranch land later unless the landowners have the money to invest in heavy applications of fertilizer.

The initial scene is of the Amazon rain forest in eastern Ecuador in 1986. You should look at the later scene from 1996, photos on the ground and experiment with split and full screen just as you did with the previous two images.

L. For this area, we have given you three buttons that show deforested areas (for 1977, 1986, and 1996), and two buttons that show change in the deforested areas, from 1977 to 1996 and from 1986 to 1996. Also included are two other GIS layers showing *Roads* and *Oil Wells* that you can turn on and off for reference.

3.11. What were the major land uses in 1996?

3.12. What was the total deforested area in 1977? _____

3.13. How many square kilometers of rain forest were cleared between 1977 and 1996? _____

3.14. How many square kilometers of rain forest were cleared between 1986 and 1996? _____

M. Turn on the Change Class for deforestation between 1977 and 1996. Click on the *Oil Wells* and *Roads* links to turn these layers on and off.

3.15. Describe the spatial pattern (if any) of where the change took place. In particular, does most of the land appear to have been cleared for oil-well construction or for other land uses? Are there many areas cleared that are far away from roads and rivers, and if not, why not?

3.16. Fill in the following table describing how this change affected people and their environment in both Ecuador and the United States and Canada. Identify the positive and negative effects (the winners and losers) in both regions.

	Positive Effects	Negative Effects
In Equador		
In the United States and Canada		

N. When you have finished, close all browser windows.

▶ DEFINITIONS OF KEY TERMS

Agribusiness An industrialized, corporate form of agriculture organized into integrated networks of agricultural inputs and outputs controlled by a small number of large corporations.

Agriculture The intentional cultivation of crops and raising of livestock.

Capital Goods such as equipment and buildings used to produce other goods.

Capital-Intensive Agriculture Agriculture in which a large amount of capital is applied per unit of output.

Commercial Agriculture Agriculture primarily for the purpose of selling the products for money.

Comparative Advantage When one region is relatively more efficient at producing a particular product compared with other regions.

Extensive Agriculture Large-area farms or ranches with low inputs of labor per acre and low output per acre.

First Agricultural Revolution The original invention of farming and domestication of livestock 8,000–14,000 years ago and the subsequent dispersal of these methods from the source regions.

Free Trade Imports and exports between countries that are unrestricted by tariffs, quotas, or excessive approvals and paperwork.

Friction of Distance A measure of how much distance discourages movement between places, based on the time, energy, or dollar cost that must be expended.

Globalization The increasing economic, cultural, demographic, political, and environmental interdependence of different places around the world.

Global-Local Continuum The interaction between global processes and local lifestyles. This continuum is a two-way process in which the local and the global shape each other.

Green Revolution The application of biological science to the development of better strains of plants and animals for increasing agricultural yields (the **Third Agricultural Revolution**).

Hunting and Gathering The collecting of roots, seeds, fruit, and fiber from wild plants and the hunting and fishing of wild animals.

Intensive Agriculture Small-area farms and ranches with high inputs of labor per acre and high output per acre.

Irrigation Artificial watering of farmland.

Labor-Intensive Agriculture Agriculture in which a large amount of human work is applied per unit of output.

Land Cover The general class of material or vegetation that dominates the surface of the land in a particular area.

Land Use The general class of activity for which land is used by humans in a particular area.

Livestock Domesticated animals such as cows, sheep, and poultry that are raised and managed to produce meat, milk, eggs, wool, leather, etc.

Mixed Farming An integrated agricultural system in which crops are grown and fed to livestock.

Monoculture Agriculture that uses a large area of land for production of a single crop year after year.

Nomadism Migratory movement of herders and their animals according to the availability of grazing land.

Plantation A large estate that produces a single cash crop. Mainly found now in the tropics.

Remote Sensing The use of satellite images of the earth's surface.

Second Agricultural Revolution A period of technological change from the 1600s to mid-1900s that started in western Europe, beginning with pre-industrial improvements such as crop rotation and better horse collars, and concluding with industrial innovations to replace human labor with machines and to supplement natural fertilizers and pesticides with chemical ones.

Sedentary Agriculture Agriculture that takes place in the immediate surroundings of a permanent settlement.

Shifting Cultivation A farming method in tropical areas in which wild vegetation is cleared and burned before crops are planted. When the soil fertility is diminished, farmers abandon the land to restore itself naturally, and they move to new areas where they repeat the process. Also known as *slash-and-burn agriculture*.

Subsistence Agriculture Self-sufficient agriculture, usually small scale and low tech, primarily for direct consumption by the local population.

Third Agricultural Revolution See **Green Revolution**.

Time-Space Convergence The rate at which the time separating two places decreases because of improvements in transportation or communication technology.

Yield Output per unit land per unit time (e.g., tons per acre per year).

▶ FURTHER READINGS

Anderson, Sarah. 2000. *Views from the South: The Effects of Globalization and the WTO on Third World Countries*. Chicago: Food First Books.

Bhagwati, Jagdish N. 2004. *In Defense of Globalization*. New York: Oxford University Press.

Borden, Tessie. 2003. Mexican Farmers Say NAFTA Ruins Lives, Forces Migration. *Arizona Republic* (Jan. 14):A1–A2.

Bowler, Ian R. (ed.). 1992. *The Geography of Agriculture in Developed Market Economies*. Harlow, Essex: Longman Scientific & Technical.

Collier, George A. 2000. *Basta! Land and the Zapatista Rebellion in Chiapas*. Chicago: Food First Books.

Duram, Leslie A., and Kelli L. Larson. 2001. Agricultural Research and Alternative Farmers' Information Needs. *Professional Geographer* 53(1):84–96.

Hall, Kevin. 2004. South American Soybeans Transforming Continent. *Arizona Republic* (Dec. 16):A26.

Kingsolver, Barbara. 2007. *Animal, Vegetable, Miracle: A Year of Food Life*. New York: HarperCollins.

Lanegran, David. 2000. Modern Agriculture in Advanced Placement Human Geography. *Journal of Geography* 99:120–131.

Lappé Moore, Francis, and Anna Lappé. 2002. *Hope's Edge: The Next Diet for a Small Planet*. New York: Tarcher/Putnam.

Lillesand, Thomas M., and Ralph W. Kiefer. 2000. *Remote Sensing and Image Interpretation*, 4th ed. New York; Chichester: Wiley.

Lopez, George, Jackie G. Smith, and Ron Pagnucco. 1995. The Global Tide. *Bulletin of the Atomic Scientists* (July/Aug.):33–39.

McAfee, Kathleen. 2004. Geographies of Risk and Difference in Crop Genetic Engineering. *Geographical Review* 94(1):80–106.

McAfee, Kathleen. 2003. Corn Culture and Dangerous DNA: Real and Imagined Consequences of Maize Transgene Flow in Oaxaca. *Journal of Latin American Geography* 2:18–42.

Meyer, William B., Derek Gregory, B. L. Turner II, and Patricia F. McDowell. 1992. The Local-Global Continuum, pp. 255–279 in *Geography's Inner Worlds*, Ronald F. Abler, Melvin G. Marcus, and Judy M. Olson (eds.). New Brunswick, NJ: Rutgers University Press.

Nabhan, Gary Paul. 2002. *Coming Home to Eat: The Pleasures and Politics of Local Foods*. New York and London: W.W. Norton & Co.

Pollan, Michael. 2006. *The Omnivore's Dilemma: A Natural History of Four Meals*. New York: Penguin.

Seitz, John L. 1995. *Global Issues: An Introduction*. Cambridge, MA: Blackwell.

Tarrant, John. (ed.). 1991. *Food and Farming*. New York: Oxford University Press.

Toffler, Alvin, and Heidi Toffler. 1993. The Twenty-First Century Global System. In *War and Anti-War*. Boston: Little, Brown and Co.

▶ WEB RESOURCES

Council for Biotechnology Information: www.whybiotech.com

Digital Globe. *Sample Imagery*: www.digitalglobe.com/sample_imagery.shtml

Fair Trade Federation: www.fairtradefederation.com

Food First: www.foodfirst.org

Global Exchange: www.globalexchange.org

Hsin, Honor. 2002. Bittersweet Harvest. *Harvard International Review* 24(1):38: www.harvardir.org/index.php?page=article&id=968&p=

Institute for Research on Public Policy. *Mapping the New North American Reality*: www.irpp.org/miscpubs/archive/NA_integ/papers.htm

Iowa State University, Leopold Center for Sustainable Agriculture: www.leopold.iastate.edu

National Aeronautics and Space Administration (NASA): www.nasa.gov

Native Seeds Search: www.nativeseeds.org

North American Center for Transborder Studies, Arizona State University: nacts.asu.edu

Office of the United States Trade Representative: www.ustr.gov

Scallion, Gordon-Michael. *Earthchange Maps and Map Database*: www.greatdreams.com/maps.htm

SECOFI. *NAFTAWORKS*: www.naftaworks.org

Shiva, Vandana. *The Threat of the Globalization of Agriculture*: www.hartford-hwp.com/archives/25a/007.html

Slow Food USA, Renewing America's Food Traditions Alliance: www.slowfoodusa.org/raft

Tremblay, Geneviève. *Agromedia*: collections.ic.gc.ca/highway/english/global/index.html

United Nations Food and Agricultural Organization (FAO): www.fao.org

University of Arizona Agricultural Extension: ag.arizona.edu/hydroponictomatoes/overview.htm

U.S. Department of Agriculture. *National Agricultural Statistics Service*: www.nass.usda.gov

Weiner, Tim. 2002 In Corn's Cradle, U.S. Imports Bury Family Farms. *New York Times*: www.globalexchange.org/ftaa/2002/nyt022602.html

▶ ITEMS TO HAND IN

Activity 1: • Questions 1.1–1.2, or answer all questions your instructor created in your WileyPlus assignments.

Activity 2: • Questions 2.1–2.4, including two product labels, or answer all questions your instructor created in your WileyPlus assignments.

Activity 3: • Questions 3.1–3.16, or answer all questions your instructor created in your WileyPlus assignments.

CHAPTER 9

Take Me Out to the Ball Game: Market Areas and the Urban Hierarchy

▶ INTRODUCTION

Although the uninitiated can look at a map of the United States or any other country and see a hodgepodge of cities—some big, some small, some close together, and others far apart—geographers see an interconnected, logically spaced system of cities (Figure 9.1). The key to understanding the nature of this system is to recognize that cities perform economic functions. Some of these functions are highly particular, for example, automobile production in Detroit, aerospace in Seattle, entertainment in Los Angeles, defense in San Diego, government in Washington, D.C., and tourism in Las Vegas. The growth and decline of cities is often keyed to the fates of their basic industries (see Chapter 6). Houston's celebrated boom and bust during the 1980s was strongly linked to the rapid rise and then spectacular fall of oil-related industries during the decade.

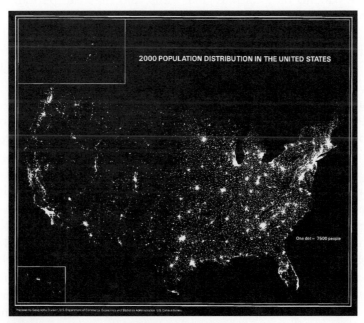

2000 POPULATION DISTRIBUTION IN THE UNITED STATES

One dot = 7500 people

Figure 9.1 Dot map of 2000 U.S. population.

Although these unique functions help us to understand growth and decline of cities in the urban system, the nature of the system itself is more strongly related to the more generic functions that all cities perform. Most cities offer a surprisingly similar array of goods and services for their residents and the people in surrounding areas. The same can be said of towns and villages, although the areas they serve are smaller and the goods they provide are fewer. Generally, we can talk about any city or town as a **central place** *to* which people travel in order to make purchases, and the areas that people travel *from* as their **market areas**. A market area is one example of the functional regions discussed in Chapter 2.

A **central place function** is a good or service that is provided by the central place for its trade area. These functions have an **order** or relative ranking based on how specialized they are, how large a market area is needed to keep them in business, and how far people are willing to travel to obtain them. The minimum market area size is known as the **threshold** of a good, whereas the maximum distance a customer is willing to travel is known as the **range** of the good. The threshold is a limit from the business's point of view, whereas the range is the limit from the consumer's point of view. A low-order central place function is obtained on a regular basis, it requires only a small market area to be profitable (i.e., it has a small threshold), and people are unwilling to travel far to obtain it (i.e., a small range). A grocery store is a classic example of a low-order central place function (Figure 9.2a). You probably purchase food regularly; you are reluctant to travel a great distance for these purchases, and the market areas for these products are small. A high-order central place function, such as a hospital, is required less frequently; you are willing to travel farther for it, and it requires a larger market area to remain profitable (Figure 9.2c). A shop selling oriental carpets, a toxicology lab, and an automobile repair shop specializing in Porsches are other high-order central place functions. Medium-order functions, such as lawyers, movie theaters, and shoe stores, require market areas of an in-between size (Figure 9.2b).

Medical doctors can be ordered by their functions, with family doctors, pediatricians, and obstetricians and gynecologists providing relatively low-order functions. We are not saying that their jobs are unimportant. We are saying that they see patients on a fairly regular basis, and they can be found in most small- and medium-sized towns. At the other end of the medical spectrum, a neurosurgeon and a cornea-transplant specialist provide higher-order central place functions and are found only in large cities.

Central place functions are provided in an **urban hierarchy**. We talked about hierarchical effects as they affect spatial diffusion in Chapter 3. The idea is the same here. Cities are organized into a hierarchy according to their size and importance. Importance in this context stems from whether they offer low- or high-order central place functions. Cities at the bottom of the urban hierarchy offer only low-order functions (Figure 9.3). Low-order cities are small, many in number, and relatively close together. Mid-sized cities offer low-order goods and services for their residents as well as medium-order functions for themselves and for those living in smaller cities within their sphere of influence (Figure 9.4). Mid-sized cities are fewer in number and farther apart than the lower-order centers. At the top of the hierarchy are the highest-order centers that offer all goods and services from gas stations and grocery stores (low order) to professional basketball and zoological gardens (high order) and everything in between (Figure 9.5). Geographers have confirmed the existence of urban hierarchies in many different countries and historical eras (Figure 9.6).

So far, we have dealt with the frequency, size, function, and spacing of central places and their market areas. **Central place theory** organizes these elements of

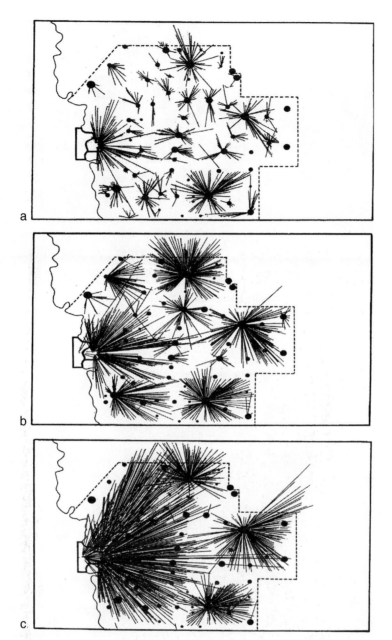

Figure 9.2 Farmers' shopping preferences in southwest Iowa in 1934 for (a) food, (b) lawyers, and (c) hospitals.

Source: Berry, Brian. 1967. *Geography of Market Centers and Retail Distribution*. Reprinted by permission of Pearson Education, Inc., Upper Saddle River, NJ, 07458.

the urban hierarchy into a unified spatial network of cities and towns. Developed initially by German economic geographer Walter Christaller in 1933, and refined by another German, August Lösch, in 1956, central place theory begins with some simplifying assumptions about the landscape. It assumes that the system of central places evolves on a flat, featureless, infinite plain of uniform population density and that customers prefer to shop at the nearest location that offers the product or service they need. To minimize travel distances for customers on a uniform landscape, the ideal shape for market areas would be a circle. Central place theory assumes that

Figure 9.3 This restaurant-garage-gas station in western Massachusetts illustrates the basic services that the lowest-order central places at the bottom of the urban hierarchy provide.

Figure 9.4 Main-street storefronts of Livingston, Montana, show a mix of low-order and medium-order central place functions.

businesses would spread out to cover an entire region with circular market areas, and that competition and entry of new firms would lead to market areas being packed together as tightly as possible, with each market area driven toward the minimum threshold size for that type of activity. Circles, however, cannot pack together perfectly without either leaving unserved spaces between the circles (Figure 9.7a) or overlapping each other (Figure 9.7b). Either assumption leads to a network of hexagonal market areas for each type of good or service (Figure 9.7c).

Central place theory takes these principles one step further, layering the networks of hexagonal market areas of different sizes on top of each other, like honeycombs

Figure 9.5 The glitz and glamour of Broadway theaters in New York City provide a good example of a very high-order central place function at the very top of the urban hierarchy. While other large cities have musical and dramatic theater venues, most major new shows premier in New York City, and only New York's theater district can be said to have a market area that truly encompasses the entire United States.

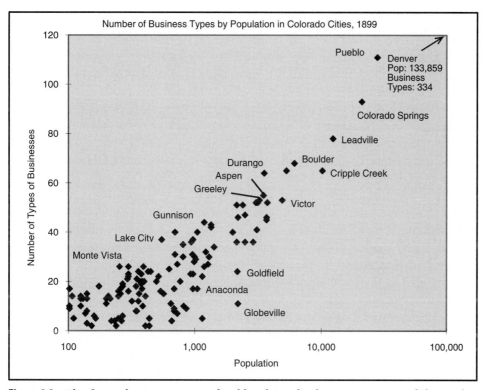

Figure 9.6 This figure shows a strong, predictable relationship between city size and the number of urban functions in Colorado in 1899. Small hamlets of less than 100 persons typically supported only five basic services, including a general merchandise store, blacksmith, hotel, and saloon. Centers between 100 and 500 offered a larger variety of services, including a bank, carpenter, druggist, hardware store, and newspaper. Larger cities such as Aspen and Durango (3,000 to 3,500) supported between 50 and 65 business types while Leadville, Colorado Springs, and Pueblo (10,000 to 30,000) provided between 80 and 120. At the top of the urban system, and off the scale of this graph, is Denver, which provided 334 different types of business services. Denver provided goods and services not found anywhere else in the state, including manicurists, detective agencies, and undertaker supplies.

Source: Reprinted from William Wyckoff (1989) "Central Place Theory and Location of Services in Colorado in 1899," *The Social Science Journal* 26(4), p. 388, with permission of Elsevier Science.

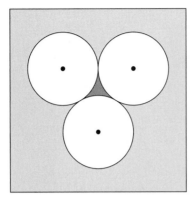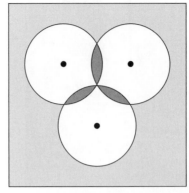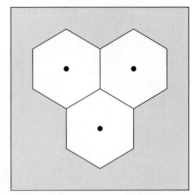

Figure 9.7 Theoretically, a circle is the ideal market area shape because it contains all space closest to a central place. However, with neighboring central places in the urban hierarchy, circles would either overlap (which indicates that some areas would have more than one central place to choose from) or leave gaps between adjacent circles (which indicates that some areas would not be served by any central place). Central place theory, however, assumes that all areas must be served and that people shop at their nearest central place offering a good or service. This can be accomplished by non-overlapping, space-filling hexagonal market areas, which can be derived from the network of circular market areas by assigning each point within the overlapping or unserved areas to its closest central place.

of small, medium, and large bees (Figure 9.8). But we aren't quite done yet because we still have to address how the different layers of hexagons relate to each other. Christaller offered a simple and sensible principle for this. His central place theory assumes that higher-order central places offer not only the goods and services of that level of the hierarchy but also all lower-order goods and services. For example, any place that has a concert hall and an airport will also have a movie theater and bus station, and any place with a movie theater and bus station will also have a video store and gas station. Thus, in Figure 9.8, the largest places have a large market area for their high-order goods and services, a medium market area for their medium-order functions, and a small market area for their low-order businesses. Likewise, the mid-sized towns have both medium market areas for their mid-level functions and a small market area for their low-order goods. The low-order places, however, have only small market areas. The market area layers therefore nest together in hierarchy across spatial scales that create the mature urban system.

As we said at the beginning, central place theory assumes that the system of central places evolves on a featureless, infinite landscape of uniform population density. The real world of course is not so neat and tidy, and therefore cities and towns are not so perfectly spaced. Many factors distort the ideal pattern, including rivers, mountains, coastlines, political boundaries, railroads, highways, and canals; and differences in population density, wealth, and cultural tastes. The idea is not to become obsessed with the exact size and shape of market areas but instead to focus on the spatial regularities of the size, frequency, and general spacing of places supplying low-order versus high-order central place functions.

Every time you go out shopping for something, you deal with the concepts of **central places, market areas**, and **urban hierarchies**. Although you may never have thought in these particular terms, you naturally think about where is the most convenient place to shop for a particular item no matter where you live. Ask any small-town resident, for instance, and that person will give you a detailed catalog of where to go to purchase a particular item, get something fixed, or see a certain

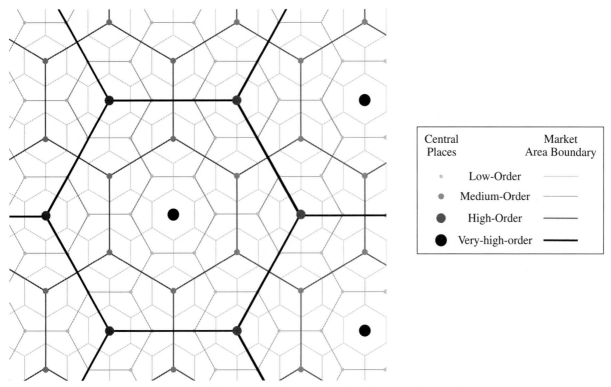

Central Places		Market Area Boundary
·	Low-Order	
●	Medium-Order	
●	High-Order	
●	Very-high-order	

Figure 9.8 Nested hexagon market areas predicted by central place theory.

kind of doctor. The rules of market areas and urban hierarchies also hold *within big cities*, but they are compressed into smaller spaces. Gas stations, video stores, and Quickie-Marts are at practically every major intersection; hospitals and furniture stores are spaced farther apart; megamalls are few and widely spaced; and one-of-a-kind functions, such as the baseball stadium, concert hall, and museums, are usually concentrated downtown, where they can serve the whole metropolitan area.

Activity 1 of this chapter shows you one way to measure the threshold of a specific central place function—pizza restaurants—by looking at their frequency throughout the urban hierarchy. Then, in Activity 2, you will experiment with the market areas for minor- and major-league baseball franchises. What does the geography of baseball franchises tell us about the U.S. urban system? What happens to the geography of market areas when franchises relocate? What happens when the American or National League adds teams?

Baseball and pizza make exemplary case studies of market area geography, but we could just as easily have chosen movie theaters and airports. Baseball in particular was chosen for two reasons. First, the relocation of sports teams has been in the news lately. Second, it is a central place function that has obvious low-order and high-order layers, namely minor leagues and major leagues. And pizza—well, almost everyone likes pizza!

▶ *CASE STUDY*

TAKE ME OUT TO THE BALL GAME

GOAL

To understand the geography of cities and towns as a system rather than as a haphazard distribution. You will analyze the relationship between the size of a city and the goods and services provided there, learn how to estimate thresholds, and use a geographic information system to study the market areas of major- and minor-league teams.

LEARNING OUTCOMES

After completing the chapter, you will be able to:

- Differentiate between low- and high-order goods and services.
- Construct and interpret a scatter diagram using a logarithmic scale.
- Estimate the minimum market size necessary to support a central place function.
- Relate high- and low-order goods and services to a city's position in the urban hierarchy.
- Use a geographic information system (GIS) to modify market areas.

SPECIAL MATERIALS NEEDED

- Calculator
- Computer with high-speed Internet access and a recent release of a Web browser. If using the Student Companion Site with the printed book, click on *Tech support* for system requirements and technical support. (If using the e-book in WileyPlus, click on *Help* for details about the system requirements.)
- Access to an Internet business telephone directory

BACKGROUND

The origins of baseball are in dispute. Conventional wisdom in the United States is that the modern game was invented by Abner Doubleday in 1839. Doubleday, a cadet at Otsego Academy in Cooperstown, New York, is often credited with drawing the first diagram of the field and writing the first set of basic rules. Historians, however, are skeptical of this scenario because the original diagram and rules cannot be found, and, with the exception of a close friend of Doubleday, no one in the area remembered anything about it.

A more plausible theory, and what most historians believe, is that the game dates back to the late eighteenth century when English boys played a game they called "rounders." Americans had played a version of this game since the early nineteenth century, although the names and rules of the game varied from place to place. Sources report the growing popularity of games called "town ball," "one old cat," "stick ball," "base," and "base ball."

Another myth about baseball is that it is a rural, small-town sport when, in fact, what we now know as baseball began in New York City, the birthplace of so many U.S. innovations. During the summer of 1842, a group of young gentlemen got together in Manhattan to play some version of the game, depending upon who showed up. At the behest of Alexander Cartwright, a 28-year-old shipping clerk, the group formally established themselves in 1845 as the New York Knickerbocker Base Ball Club. The Knickerbockers developed a standard set of rules, including the diamond-shaped playing field, foul lines, three missed swings make an out, and most important, runners were to be tagged or thrown out—not thrown at. Over the years, the Knickerbockers gradually refined the rules into the game we know today.

In the mid-eighteenth century, thousands of European immigrants flooded New York City—many of them young, male, and unmarried. Seeking leisure-time pursuits, they embraced baseball and began forming clubs. In 1857, a convention of amateur teams was called to discuss rules and other issues, and the following year they formed the National Association of Base Ball Players. Originally, the association contained 10 teams, all based in New York and neighboring areas; but not long after, Boston and Philadelphia franchises joined the league, giving wider coverage around the urban northeastern seaboard.

Baseball continued to gain popularity and to spread outward from its core in the Northeast. By 1861, there were 62 clubs in the National Association of Baseball Players, including clubs in Maine, Oregon, and California. The game was very popular with soldiers from both sides in the Civil War because it could be organized very easily without need for special equipment or facilities.

As the leagues grew, so did expenses. Teams began to charge admission and seek out donations or sponsors to make trips. Although the league was supposed to be composed of amateurs, players were secretly paid, and some were given jobs by sponsors. In 1869, the Cincinnati Red Stockings was the first team to pay players. The team attracted the best players and amassed a record of 65 wins and no losses. The idea of paid players quickly caught on.

The National Association of Professional Base Ball Players (forerunner to the National League) was founded in 1871 with nine teams—the Boston Red Stockings, Chicago White Stockings, Philadelphia Athletics, New York Mutuals, Washington Olympics, Troy (New York) Haymakers, Forest Way Kekiongas, Cleveland Forest Citys, and the Rockford Forest Citys—but quickly grew to 12 teams (Figure 9.9). National League owners maintained a tight grip on the game, crushing competition from other leagues and instituting a so-called reserve clause in players' contracts, restricting them to play for their current employer in perpetuity. When in 1899 the National League dropped its four least-profitable teams, an Ohioan named Ban Johnson, owner of a struggling circuit of minor-league teams, added new clubs in Boston, Philadelphia, Baltimore, and Washington, D.C., and declared his league the American League, competing head-to-head with the National League for players and fans. In 1903, the two leagues signed a national agreement promising to honor each other's contracts and retain the reserve clause.

© 2010 John Wiley & Sons, Inc.

Figure 9.9 Troy Haymakers.

At the turn of the century, major-league baseball was a big-city monopoly with teams in large industrial cities of the Northeast and Midwest (Figure 9.10). As high-order **central places**, these cities had large market **thresholds** to support a major-league baseball team—a very specialized entertainment activity and high-order central place function. The cities at the top of the **urban hierarchy** in 1900 dominated the sport. In fact, the five largest cities each had large enough populations to support multiple teams. New York, by far the biggest city, had three teams, followed in order by Chicago, Philadelphia, St. Louis, and Boston, all of which had two teams.

Between 1900 and 1950, baseball became one of the biggest entertainment industries in the country. Baseball became the national pastime. It drew huge audiences and fired population interest in charismatic players, such as Ty Cobb, Babe Ruth, Ted Williams, and Joe DiMaggio. Teams were concentrated in the urban Northeast and industrial Midwest, where the **market areas** were large enough to support team payrolls and operating expenses.

When President Roosevelt instituted the military draft at the start of World War II in 1940, every profession, including baseball, was affected. Starring players of both the major and minor leagues responded to their draft notices or enlisted. Despite the loss of many young players, President Roosevelt decreed that the game continue to be played to boost morale and provide entertainment. Baseball also was played overseas to ease the anguish and

boredom of war. Former professional stars played alongside sandlot players and high school athletes, and complicated league structures were established. The war years also introduced baseball to an international audience, particularly in Britain, where U.S. military teams played in local soccer, rugby, and cricket stadiums. To keep the troops occupied after hostilities ended in Europe, the military started a "Personal Athletic and Recreation Program" featuring baseball in May 1944. By midsummer, 200,000 troops were playing in competitive leagues, and military duties were scheduled around their games. More than 50,000 military personnel watched the Overseas Invasion Service Expedition play the 71st Infantry Division in the World Series of Europe that fall.

During the twentieth century, baseball reflected the changing ethnic relations of society in general. In 1947, the white-only segregated status of the game changed when Jackie Robinson of the Brooklyn Dodgers became the first African-American to play in a major-league game (Figure 9.11). Nearly three decades after the color barrier was broken, however, "Hammerin' Hank" Aaron was taunted and threatened as he eclipsed Babe Ruth's career home-run record. Earlier, two-time MVP Hank Greenberg had been an important symbolic figure for Jewish Americans during the rise of Hitler and the Nazis. More recently, Latin American, Japanese, and Korean stars have emerged as baseball has diffused around the world, especially to countries with strong U.S. ties.

▶ *CASE STUDY (continued)*

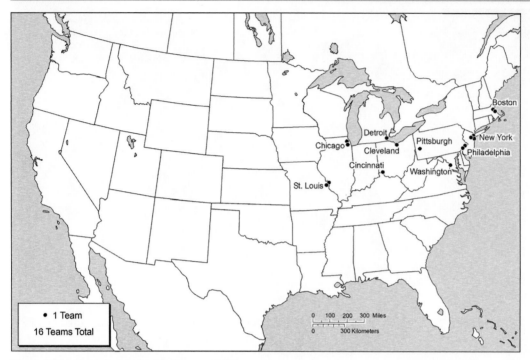

Figure 9.10 Major-league baseball teams, 1903.

Attendance began to fall in the early 1950s (from 21 million in 1948 to 17 million in 1952) because of increased television coverage, shifts in population, and obsolete, inner-city ballparks. Television provided baseball for free and broke people of the habit of going to the ballpark. With the advent of television, many fans shifted from in-park spectators to at-home television viewers, and the idea of a market area moved from a fan base large enough to support ticket sales to a television audience big enough to support television advertisements. The **range** for major-league baseball lengthened, as television allowed people to "consume" baseball farther from their homes. A second factor for reducing attendance at games was white exodus from the older eastern and midwestern cities to suburbs and to cities of the South and West. Third, all but three major-league ballparks had been built between 1915 and 1923 and did not provide the amenities that Americans had come to expect. Many owners tried to modernize their old-fashioned parks with electronic scoreboards. Yankee Stadium's scoreboard had several men behind it, operating more than five thousand keys!

After five decades of competition, Brooklyn finally won the World Series in 1955 only to be faced with the ultimate heartbreak two years later: the move of the beloved Dodgers to Los Angeles. Los Angeles had come from nowhere to become the fourth-largest city in America by 1950. Its market area was well above what was needed to support a major-league baseball team, but California was, at the time, geographically isolated from the baseball heartland of the Northeast. Demographics are destiny, however, and soon there was a move afoot to seed baseball on the West Coast. Walter O'Malley, the Dodgers

Figure 9.11 Jackie Robinson remains a symbol of desegregation in sports and an inspiration for baseball fans, especially minorities in the city.

owner, asked the City of New York to build the Dodgers a new stadium in Brooklyn. When the city turned him down, he began to look for greener pastures. Los Angeles offered good television potential, and there were promises to build a new stadium. A major impediment was that the Dodgers would be the only team in the West and thus geographically isolated from the rest of baseball. O'Malley approached fellow New Yorker Horace Stoneham, owner of the New York Giants, about the possibility of a two-club move: the Dodgers to Los Angeles and the Giants to San Francisco. With his outdated park, declining attendance, and limited television revenue, Stoneham agreed to the move, and the Giants–Dodgers rivalry was transplanted to the West Coast. New York, the cultural hearth of baseball, was left with only one major-league team.

The moves of the Dodgers and Giants to the West Coast were part of a flurry of moves in the late 1950s and early 1960s that reflected population growth of cities in the Midwest and California (Figure 9.12). The Boston Braves moved to Milwaukee in 1953; the St. Louis Browns became the Baltimore Orioles in 1954; the Philadelphia Athletics moved to Kansas City in 1955; and the Washington Senators became the Minnesota Twins in 1961. Nevertheless, many regions of the country were still not represented. With television offering a wider audience and demand in rapidly growing southern and western cities for teams of their own, the seeds of large-scale expansion and relocation were planted.

In 1960, a rival Continental League was established to serve the needs of Sunbelt cities. The Continental League planned head-to-head competition with the American and National Leagues. Faced with the prospect of losing their monopoly, major-league owners agreed on a compromise: to expand from 16 to 24 teams by the end of the decade. New teams were added in southern California (Angels), Washington (Senators), New York (Metropolitans, nicknamed the Mets), Houston (Colt 45s, who later became the Astros), San Diego (Padres), Montreal (Expos), Seattle (Pilots), and Kansas City (Royals), the last to replace the Kansas City Athletics, who had moved to Oakland, California.

It was inevitable that the absence of baseball in the South would be remedied with the region's post–World War II population growth and economic resurgence. As migrants from the North, with longstanding interest in baseball, relocated to the South, cities grew large enough to support a high-order **central place function** such as baseball. In 1966, the Milwaukee Braves sought to take advantage of a new, low-cost public stadium and the potential for good television ratings in Atlanta. The City of Milwaukee, owners of County Stadium where the Braves played, filed suit asserting that the move violated State of Wisconsin antitrust laws. As the Braves prepared to open their first season in Atlanta, the City of Milwaukee won the case in local court. Higher courts, however, overruled the decision, and the Braves said goodbye to Milwaukee for good. Soon thereafter, a group of local business leaders attracted the Seattle Pilots to Milwaukee and renamed the team the Brewers, after the city's long-standing heritage of beer making.

The 1960s were also a time for building new stadiums. Whereas ballparks had once been the creations of owners, now cities had to pay to attract and keep teams. Twelve new

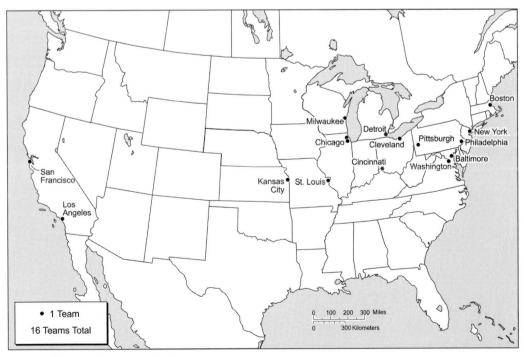

Figure 9.12   Major-league baseball teams, 1960.

© 2010 John Wiley & Sons, Inc.

▶ **CASE STUDY (continued)**

stadiums were built during the 1960s—all but Dodger Stadium with public funds. Many of these stadiums were located in the suburbs to reflect the suburban exodus of U.S. population, and most were cavernous, concrete multipurpose structures with Astroturf® fields designed to accommodate professional baseball and football.

Two economic issues defined baseball in the last decades of the twentieth century: continued expansion and the financial struggle between owners and players. Expansion in Seattle (Mariners) and Toronto (Blue Jays) in 1977, Colorado (Rockies) and Florida (Marlins) in 1993, and Tampa Bay (Devil Rays) and Arizona (Diamondbacks) in 1998 changed the game from two 8-team leagues in 1960 to six divisions with between 4 and 6 teams each (Figure 9.13). Through expansion and relocation, today's 30 teams cover a much broader geographic area than in 1900 but continue to be a big-city phenomenon. The huge expense of operating a major-league baseball team requires a large threshold population to support ticket sales and an even larger market area to support television advertisement. In naming themselves after states, the Florida Marlins, Colorado Rockies, and Arizona Diamondbacks are seeking to enlarge their fan base and television audience, while at the same time staying in the big cities that support season ticket sales, single-game ticket sales, and merchandising. Since 1960, players have strengthened their union and eventually won higher pay, independent arbitration, and free agency. By successfully challenging the long-standing "reserve clause," players won the

right to shop themselves to the highest bidder. Salaries skyrocketed as owners outbid one another for players. Eventually, owners balked, and adversarial player-owner relations led to several work stoppages. In 1994, when owners tried to limit free agency and impose a "salary cap" on total team salaries, players went on strike and the World Series was canceled for the first time in 89 years, leaving fans disheartened and disillusioned. Although play resumed in April 1995, it took until November 1996 to reach a labor deal.

Escalating player salaries have significant geographic implications. A more populous market area can translate into higher ticket sales and greater television revenues, which in turn allows the large-market teams to afford higher payrolls, field a more competitive team, win more games, and therefore sell more tickets, get more TV revenue, and afford even higher payrolls. This "positive feedback loop" (see Chapter 14) tends to make the rich teams richer and the poor teams poorer. Payrolls in 2005 ranged from a high of $208 million for the New York Yankees to a low of $30 million for the Tampa Bay Devil Rays, and the gap between the rich teams and the poor teams has been widening (Figure 9.14). From 1992 to 2000, the World Series winner had the highest payroll in five of the nine seasons. Every once in a while, however, a small-market underdog comes along and knocks off the big dog, as in 2003 when the Florida Marlins, with the twenty-fifth highest payroll ($50 million), upset the Yankees, with their league-leading $153 million payroll.

Figure 9.13 Major-league baseball teams, 2005.

© **2010 John Wiley & Sons, Inc.**

► **CASE STUDY** *(continued)*

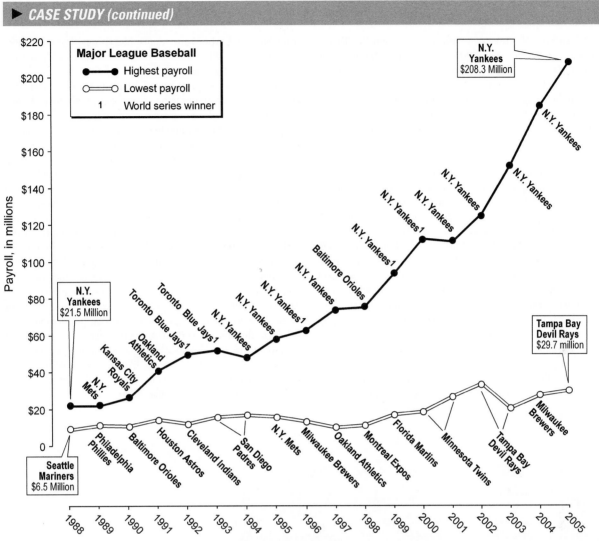

Figure 9.14 The widening payroll gap, shown here, is mirrored by a widening income gap. In 1999, the Yankees earned $176 million in local revenue compared to just $12 million for the Montreal Expos.

Source: ©2000, *USA Today.* Reprinted with permission. 2001–2005 statistics added.

The economic geography of baseball nearly torpedoed the national pastime once again in 2002, when a threatened August shutdown by baseball owners was averted by a last-minute compromise. The agreement tried to balance the needs of small-market teams, large-market teams, and players. The small-market teams benefit from increased sharing of the local revenues from the large-market teams. In addition, a luxury tax is assessed on teams exceeding defined payroll thresholds ($117 million in 2003 rising to $155 million in 2008) at a rate varying from 17 to 40 percent, which is redistributed to the poorer teams. The large-market teams got something they wanted by avoiding a hard salary cap like the one in the National Football League that strictly limits how much a team can spend on player salaries (and that led to recent Super Bowl appearances by small-market teams in Tampa Bay, St. Louis, Nashville and Pittsburgh). The rich teams can still spend what they want to sign the biggest stars. Finally, the players' union got two things they wanted. First, they received a 50 percent rise in the minimum salary from $200,000 to $300,000 (compared with an average of $2.3 million and a high of $26 million for New York Yankees third baseman Alex Rodriguez). Second, the owners agreed not to consider contraction—the outright elimination of teams. Contraction became an issue when the Minnesota Twins and Montreal Expos, two money-losing, small-market teams, offered to let the other owners buy them out and put them out of business, which would have saved the other owners from having to share revenues with them in the future. The players' union objected due to the loss of jobs. Thus each party in the talks got something it wanted, and the fans won the privilege of continuing to bankroll the entire circus. All this talk of contraction seemed to light a fire under the underpaid Minnesota Twins, who then confounded the experts *and their own owner* by not only making the 2002 playoffs but also winning their first-round series. Thank goodness money isn't everything!

Teams today look to supplement their revenue through merchandise sales, national TV (the Atlanta Braves are owned

© 2010 John Wiley & Sons, Inc.

▶ *CASE STUDY (continued)*

by Ted Turner, who televises them nationally on the Turner Broadcasting System, or TBS), and corporate boxes at the stadiums. It is not uncommon today for teams to threaten to move to another city unless their host cities build for them, using public funds, a new, baseball-only stadium with many corporate boxes. Cities are left with the distasteful choice of subsidizing a private business or losing a significant employer, a part of the city's history, and a substantial measure of status that comes with being a "major-league city."

As of the end of the 2005 season, only Boston's Fenway Park (1912) and Chicago's Wrigley Field (1914) remained of the ballparks built before 1920. Venerable Yankee Stadium, built in 1923, was replaced by a luxurious new venue in 2009, which will undoubtedly fuel substantial new revenue streams for the Yankees, who will be able to afford even higher payrolls than the $209 million they spent in 2008, almost ten times more than the Florida Marlins' $21.8 million. Any new locations of teams, through either expansion or relocation, must strike a balance between the financial needs of the team in question and the concerns of the other owners. New teams need to locate in large enough markets to be competitive, but they also cannot eat too much into nearby teams' markets. The Baltimore Orioles organization, which has been able to afford a high player payroll since moving into its new, retro-style stadium (Figure 9.15), surely is not thrilled by the move of the Expos

from Montreal, where attendance had dropped precipitously, to Washington, D.C.—only an hour's drive away—where they are now called the Nationals.

The location of professional baseball in North America always was and continues to be a story of **central place theory** in action. A major-league team requires a huge market area to support players' salaries and team operation expenses. It is the quintessential high-order central place function. Only big cities and large metropolitan regions have the population base and wealth to support such an economic activity. Baseball's farm system, which nurtures young talent, can afford to locate in smaller cities of the national urban hierarchy because these minor-league teams are lower-order central place functions. Baseball has responded to the changing demographics of the nation, relocating to and expanding in regions of rapid population growth and rapid urbanization. Many think of baseball in nostalgic terms as America's pastime and as a metaphor for life, and they bemoan the movement and renaming of teams. Economic and urban geographers, however, see baseball as an economic service that is provided to urban populations with adequate thresholds. As the nation's population is reorganized in response to global restructuring and demographic change, it is inevitable that urban services like baseball will follow suit. Where to locate a new franchise is one of the questions you will answer in the activities that follow.

Figure 9.15 The Baltimore Orioles moved into their new baseball-only stadium, built with state lottery money, in 1992. Its intimate retro style, brick facing, corporate boxes, and downtown location drew so many fans and generated so much revenue that it has inspired a wave of other retro, downtown stadiums in Seattle, Denver, Phoenix, Cleveland, Philadelphia, Detroit, and Pittsburgh. Named for the B&O railroad yards on which it sits, Camden Yards is located two blocks from Babe Ruth's birthplace.

Name: _____   Instructor: _____

Take Me Out to the Ball Game: Market Areas and the Urban Hierarchy

ACTIVITY 1: THRESHOLD OF A FUNCTION

Each central place function has a threshold, or minimum market size, needed to support the profitable sale of that particular good or service. Thresholds can be measured in numbers of people or, in areas of uniform population density, as a minimum area or radius. A good's threshold must be distinguished from its range, the maximum distance a consumer is willing to travel to purchase it. Threshold is from the seller's point of view; range is from the buyer's. For this reason, reliable estimates of a threshold would be very valuable information for a small-business owner or franchisee looking to open, say, a new pizza restaurant (Figure 9.16).

In Activity 1, you will estimate the threshold of a pizza restaurant based on its frequency in 10 central places spanning various levels of the urban hierarchy. You will relate the size of a city to the number of pizza restaurants found there and establish the minimum population size (threshold) needed to support a profitable pizza restaurant. You will find this information in a very familiar source—an online *Yellow Pages*-type of telephone directory.

Figure 9.16 Pizza restaurants are a fairly low-order central place function that can thrive even in small towns.

© 2010 John Wiley & Sons, Inc.

A. Pick one city in your state that represents each of these population ranges. You will need 10 in all. If your state has no cities in some of the population categories, simply leave that category out and report your results for fewer cities.

1. 500–2,000
2. 2,000–5,000
3. 5,000–10,000
4. 10,000–25,000
5. 25,000–50,000
6. 50,000–100,000
7. 100,000–250,000
8. 250,000–500,000
9. 500,000–1,000,000
10. more than 1,000,000

City populations can be found in U.S. Census Bureau and StatsCanada publications and in the index of most atlases. Alternatively, find city populations on the Internet: www.census.gov/popest/cities/ or factfinder.census.gov (select *population for a city or town* for your state) for the United States. For Canadian cities and towns, go to www.statcan.gc.ca and click on *Community Profiles*.

Write the city or town name in Table 9.1, or leave it blank if there is no city within that range. Also write the population of the city or town in Table 9.1. Use only city or municipal populations. Don't combine cities into metropolitan areas.

B. Go to any of the online Internet telephone directories, such as, www.switchboard.com, yp.yahoo.com, or yellowpages.msn.com and search for "pizza" for the same towns you selected in Question 1.1.

For your pizza data to be consistent with your population data, be sure you search for individual cities or towns, not metropolitan areas.

1.1. Count the number of different listings. Check the address of each pizza restaurant carefully to allocate it to the correct city and beware of repeat ads for one location. Be careful to include all outlets in a chain. Complete Table 9.1 with the number of pizza restaurants per city.

TABLE 9.1   City Populations and Pizza Restaurants

City	Population	Pizza Restaurants	City	Population	Pizza Restaurants
1.			6.		
2.			7.		
3.			8.		
4.			9.		
5.			10.		

C. Use the graph provided in Question 1.2 for making a scatter diagram. A scatter diagram depicts the relationship between two variables. One variable is measured on the x-axis (horizontal), and another is measured on the y-axis (vertical). You first locate the value of the x-axis variable and follow it straight up, then find the y-axis value for the second variable, follow that straight across, and place a dot where they intersect. The scatter diagram therefore is a "scatter" of these dots. It shows groupings or trends in the relationship between the two variables.

You will plot *population* on the x-*axis* (horizontal) and the *number of pizza restaurants on the* y-*axis* (vertical). A problem arises, however, if you plot the numbers using an ordinary graph. The difference in population for the smaller towns and the largest city is so great that you would need a very large graph to fit them both on a scale. It also would be difficult to accurately plot the dots for your smallest towns because they would tend to cluster in the lower left corner. We are therefore using a lognormal graph, which has the effect of "squeezing in" large numbers according to its logarithmic transformation.

A logarithm is a mathematical calculation in which the difference between 1 and 10 on a logarithmic scale is the same as the difference between 10 and 100, between 100 and 1,000, between 1,000 and 10,000, and so on. The log of a number is the exponent to which 10 must be raised in order to equal that number. For instance:

$$\log 10 = 1, \qquad \text{because } 10^1 = 10$$
$$\log 100 = 2, \qquad \text{because } 10^2 = 100$$
$$\log 1{,}000 = 3, \qquad \text{because } 10^3 = 1{,}000$$
$$\log 5 = 0.699, \qquad \text{because } 10^{0.699} = 5$$
$$\log 1 = 0, \qquad \text{because } 10^0 = 1$$

You can see this relationship on the lognormal graph provided (Figure 9.17). The y-*axis* starts at 1 and has tick marks at all integers up to 10. The distance between each tick mark gets progressively smaller until you reach 10. The next tick after 10 is 20, then 30, 40, and so on, up to 100. The patterning of tick marks between 10 and 100 looks the same as between 1 and 10, but each tick represents 10 rather than 1. After 100, each interval would be 100 rather than 10.

On the x-*axis*, the same pattern occurs, only the graph starts at 1,000. The second tick is 2,000, then 3,000, 4,000, and so on, up to 10,000. The first tick after 10,000 is 20,000, then 30,000, 40,000, and so on, up to 100,000. Make sure you understand how to read the graph and keep in mind that there is a "squeezing" effect for large numbers.

1.2. Make a scatter diagram depicting the relationship between the urban population and the number of pizza restaurants.

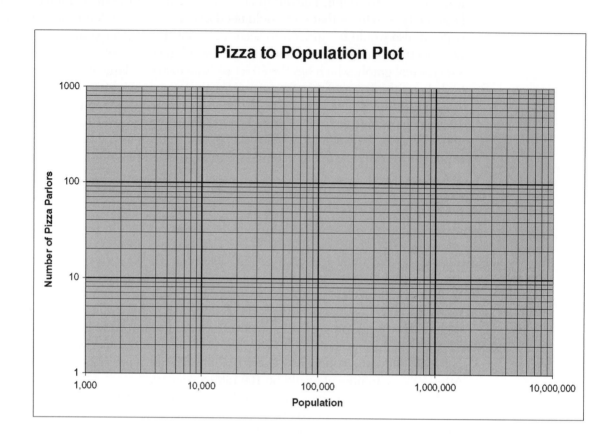

1.3. Draw the line that best fits the set of points in your scatter diagram. The line should be straight and need not (in fact, *cannot*) go through every dot. It is a line that best describes the trend in the relationship (caution: *do not simply connect the dots*). See Figure 9.17 for an example of a scatter diagram and the line of best fit.

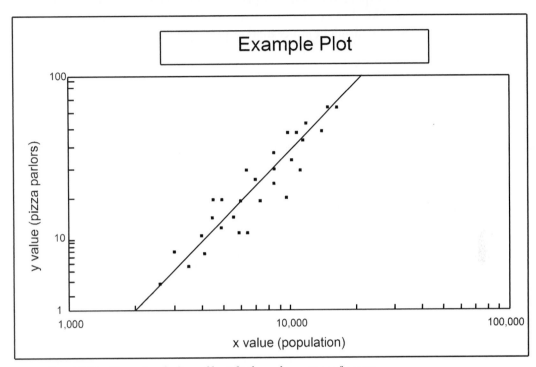

Figure 9.17   Example of a line of best fit through a scatter of points.

The line of best fit tells you, on average, how many pizza restaurants a given population size should be able to support. The x value at which your line hits the $y = 1$ level is the population at which exactly one pizza restaurant could remain in business. Any town with a population below this value could not support a pizza place. The value is the *threshold* necessary to support a pizza business.

1.4. At approximately what population value does your best-fitting line cross the $y = 1$ level? (That is, where does your line cross the *x-axis*?)_____.

1.5. What does it mean in terms of population per pizza restaurant when a city falls below (rather than above or exactly on) the best-fit line?

1.6. Suppose you were the site selection manager for a new chain of pizzerias in charge of expanding into your state. Write a short summary to the company president, interpreting the graph you made on page 272, to assess the potential to add profitable pizza restaurants in your study cities, given the level of competition in each city. For the *top 3 or 4 cities* with the most market potential, be sure to list the expected number of pizza restaurants, the actual number of pizza restaurants, and local place characteristics or any other insights you can glean from the graph data that might affect market potential.

Name: _____   Instructor: _____

Take Me Out to the Ball Game: Market Areas and the Urban Hierarchy

▶ ACTIVITY 2: MARKET AREA GEOGRAPHY

Like pizza restaurants, professional baseball teams are central place functions. Unlike pizza restaurants, they require a much larger market area to remain profitable. High-order central place functions have large thresholds (i.e., they require large market areas to maintain their competitiveness). Low-order central place functions have small thresholds; only a small market area is necessary for these activities to stay in business. Thus, low-order central place functions should be many in number and relatively close together, whereas high-order central place functions should be few in number and relatively far apart.

Notice that we are careful to use the word *should* in describing the pattern of urban goods and services. Central place theory assumes an even population distribution and a population with uniform buying power—assumptions that are rarely met. When population density is high or buying power is high, market areas will be geographically small. Conversely, when population density and/or buying power is low, market areas will be large in area. Other factors can influence the shape of market areas, including the transportation network, physical terrain, political or cultural barriers, the availability of information about the service, and people's behavioral whims and quirks. Market areas can and do take on highly irregular shapes.

In this chapter you will be asked to interpret maps of the market areas of major- and minor-league baseball teams as generated by a geographic information system (GIS). We have made a monumental assumption in instructing your computer how to draw the market areas for each team. We've told it that, all other things being equal, people root for the team closest to them. In the real world, all other things are not equal, and therefore many of our baseball market areas might not match the real fan boundaries. Many other factors, including historical and cultural connections, transportation, political boundaries, where you or your parents grew up, or just pure happenstance, can have you rooting for a more distant team.

There is also the question of whether such sharp boundaries exist at all. Boundaries are not cataclysmic divides where everyone on each side of the boundary roots for one team and not the other, but are transition zones where allegiances shift gradually from one team to another. For instance, baseball fans in Connecticut are often torn between the Boston Red Sox and the New York Yankees. Beginning with the fateful day the Red Sox's owner sold Babe Ruth to the Yankees, through the great Joe DiMaggio–Ted Williams rivalry, and on to the free-agent rent-a-hero of today, the most storied rivalry in baseball continues to be fought on the playgrounds and in the living rooms of Connecticut.

Before you go to the GIS activity, however, you should try drawing market areas by hand so you will have a better idea of what the computer is doing. Figure 9.18 shows you step-by-step instructions on how to draw market areas for the closest team. Use this example to answer Question 2.1.

© 2010 John Wiley & Sons, Inc.

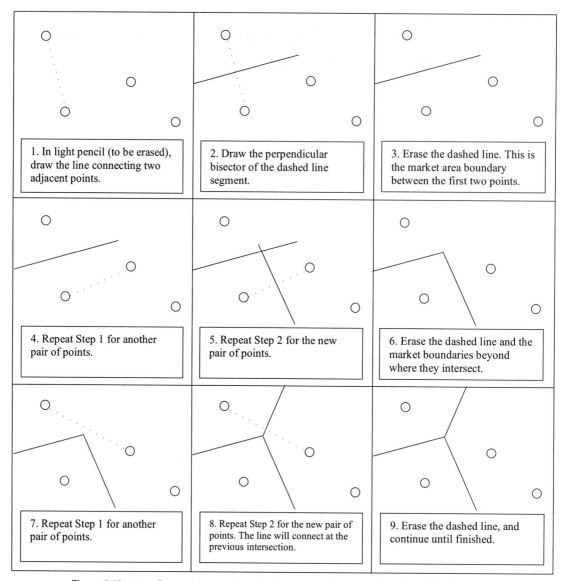

Figure 9.18 Step-by-step instructions for drawing market areas based on the closest team.

2.1. Figure 9.19 shows the distribution of minor-league baseball teams in Oregon, plus parts of neighboring states. Draw (*in pencil*) the market area for each city. In other words, for each central place providing these services, what area around it do you think it serves? Do as the computer would do: simply divide the distance evenly between each pair of central places and draw an irregularly shaped polygon around each central place. Follow the instructions in Figure 9.18 to help you draw your market areas. We have begun the exercise by completing one market area and partially completing adjacent areas. Use this guide to complete the remainder.

Now you are ready to examine the GIS-generated map of major- and minor-league baseball teams and their presumed market areas. Follow these instructions:

A. To start your activity, click on the *Student Companion Site* at www.wiley.com/college/kuby. (For students using WileyPlus, log on to your class Web site, select the *Assignment* tab, locate and click on this assignment, and follow all instructions.)

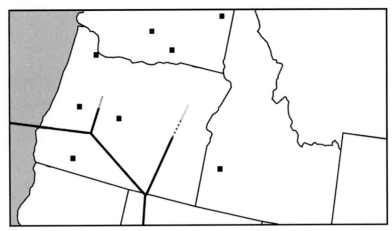

Figure 9.19 The distribution of minor-league baseball teams in Oregon and surrounding areas. Draw the rest of the boundaries to complete question 2.1.

B. Select the chapter from the drop-down list and then click on *Computerized Chapter Activities*.

C. Click on *Activity 2: Market Area Geography*.

The right margin is divided into upper, middle, and lower sections. The upper section lists four major themes you will be investigating: *All Teams 2005, Major Leagues 1997, Future U.S. Expansion and Future Latin America Expansion*. Depending on which theme is highlighted in the upper section, the choices in the middle section will change. The lower section lists population layers that can be turned on or off, including *Team Names*.

The starting screen shows a map of the United States and Canada with the current major-league baseball teams. A market area is drawn around each major-league central place. All points within each market area are closer to that central place than to any other city on the map.

The layer *Major League Teams* is highlighted in the middle section because that layer is on. Turn off this layer by clicking on its name; then turn on the layer *Major and Minor Leagues*. Now you see the distribution of all baseball central places (i.e., those that provide either minor-league or major-league teams). You can turn both layers on to show the distribution and market areas for both major- and minor-league teams superimposed on each other. Market areas for major-league teams have thick red lines; minor-league teams have thin blue lines. You can toggle one level on or off to see each layer better. A major-league team is a high-order urban service. It requires a large market area to be profitable, in contrast to a minor-league team, which requires a smaller market area.

You also can view a graduated circle map of metropolitan areas (2000 population over 30,000) as a background layer underneath each map of the baseball market areas. Click on the layer *Metropolitan Populations* to see the relationship between baseball team locations, market areas, and the cities they serve.

With the *Major League Teams* layer showing, click on *Market Area Population*, which will display the population within each major-league market area (excluding Mexico and the Caribbean). The metropolitan area populations and market area populations will assist you in answering questions about these maps, as will the *Team Names* layer.

© **2010 John Wiley & Sons, Inc.**

D. Turn on only the *Major League Teams* layer. Now, toggle the *Major and Minor Leagues* layer on and off to compare major and minor leagues on the following criteria:

2.2. The number of major-league teams vs. minor-league teams (it is not necessary to count each one):

2.3. The size of the market areas (major-league vs. minor-league teams):

2.4. The spacing of the teams (major-league vs. minor-league teams):

2.5. The size of the host cities (major-league vs. minor-league teams). You can turn the *Metropolitan Populations* layer back on for this question if you wish.

2.6. The GIS assumes that you will root for the team nearest you. Thus, it draws market areas based solely on the distance to the nearest baseball team. In real life, however, other factors can affect or distort the market area so that the distance is not equally divided between two central places. These factors can include transportation connections, physical terrain, communication links, state and national boundaries, and other cultural-historical ties. Using the *Major League Teams* layer, find at least two examples for which the "nearest center" rule does not apply, or ask some friends from different parts of the country if they know of team allegiances that do not match those drawn by the GIS. In other words, find at least two examples from these maps of baseball market areas that are not accurate. For each case, discuss what factors "override" distance and cause market areas to be distorted.

2.7. Why are there so few teams in the upper Great Plains?

E. Click on *Major Leagues 1997* in the upper section of the right margin. The screen will show the *Major League Teams 1997* layer. Phoenix, Arizona, and Tampa, Florida, are the two newest expansion teams in the major leagues (the Washington Nationals are a relocation from Montreal, not an expansion). You now see the map of major-league market areas prior to the 1998 addition of the Phoenix and Tampa teams, and the 2005 move from Montreal to Washington, D.C. Now click on the layer *Major League Teams* to see the 2005 teams. Turn on the *Metropolitan Population layer.*

2.8. Ignore for a minute the *relocation* of Montreal to Washington, D.C., and focus only on the *expansion* to Phoenix and Tampa. Were Phoenix and Tampa good choices for new expansion teams? Explain.

2.9. The addition of Phoenix and Tampa caused other cities in the system to lose market area. A smaller market area lowers stadium attendance and television revenue. Which cities were negatively affected when Phoenix and Tampa gained teams? List the decrease in each city's market area population caused by the new teams.

Cities Negatively Affected by
Phoenix Expansion:

Change in Market Area
Population:

Cities Negatively Affected by
Tampa Expansion:

Change in Market Area
Population:

2.10. Several teams moved to new cities over the last 50 years, in part to gain larger market areas; most recently, the Montreal Expos went to Washington, D.C., in 2005. Worse yet, as explained in the Background section, "contraction" (i.e., getting rid of some teams altogether) is not out of the question. Cities with small market areas can be vulnerable to losing their teams. Using the *Major League Teams* layer and *Market Area Populations*, find the three teams with the smallest market area in terms of population.

Team   *Market Area Population*

_____   _____

_____   _____

_____   _____

2.11. Can you understand why the owner of the Baltimore Orioles opposed the relocation of the Expos to Washington, D.C.? Major League Baseball offered the owner a stake in a new regional cable television network as compensation for the move because the Orioles' market area population went from _____ prior to the move to _____ after the move.

© 2010 John Wiley & Sons, Inc.

Now suppose you are on the Major League Baseball Expansion Committee, which is in charge of selecting new cities for teams. Suppose six cities have applied for new teams: Buffalo; Indianapolis; Memphis; New Orleans; Portland, Oregon; and San Antonio, Texas. (Make sure you know where these cities are.) Your job is to recommend to the committee the two best candidates.

F. Click on *Future U.S. Expansion* in the upper section of the right margin. Look at the existing major-league market areas and then select each city to see the new arrangement. Based on the market areas and the population served, choose the two you believe would be the best locations for new teams. You can again use the *Metropolitan Population* and *Market Area Population* layers to help.

2.12. Justify your choices.

a. Expansion Team 1:

b. Expansion Team 2:

G. One city that was negotiating for the relocation of Montreal was Monterrey, Mexico (in the state of Nuevo León). You saw on the *Major and Minor Leagues* layer that minor-league teams already play in Mexico, and a whole host of other Mexican baseball leagues are not shown on the map. The major leagues are also full of players from many Caribbean and Latin American countries, prompting Major League Baseball to introduce a World Baseball Classic starting in March 2006. Similar to soccer's World Cup, the 16-country tournament featured major-league players representing their home countries. With 6 of the 16 teams from Latin America, a bold future step might be for Major League Baseball to expand to Latin America, as it did to Canada in 1969. Click on *Future Latin America Expansion* in the upper section of the right margin. You see four possible new teams in Monterrey, Mexico; Havana, Cuba; Santo Domingo, Dominican Republic; and San Juan, Puerto Rico. Turn on the *Market Area Population* layer. Whereas the market area populations in all previous exercises showed only U.S. and Canadian populations, these numbers now include Mexico and the Caribbean countries shown on the map.

2.13. If indeed people root for the closest team, and all four of these cities in Mexico and the Caribbean are incorporated into the major leagues, how will current teams in the U.S. borderland states be affected?

Team	Pre-expansion, U.S.-only market population.	Post-expansion, U.S./Mexico market population
San Diego Padres		
Arizona Diamondbacks (Phoenix)		
Houston Astros		
Texas Rangers (Dallas)		

2.14. Write the name and market area population of the existing or new team that would conceivably have the largest fan base if the major leagues expanded simultaneously to all four Latin American cities.

2.15. The market area populations tell us about raw numbers of potential fans but nothing about the characteristics of those fans or of the place. If you were in the baseball business and were considering starting a new team in one of these four Latin American cities, you would need to know cultural and economic characteristics that might affect the success of a major-league baseball franchise there. Think of three population, economic, or cultural *place* characteristics that might make expansion there risky (i.e., what barriers are there to expansion into Latin America?).

H. When you have finished, close all browser windows.

▶ DEFINITIONS OF KEY TERMS

Central Place A city or town that provides goods and services to the surrounding population.

Central Place Function A good or service that a central place provides.

Central Place Theory A geographic model of the sizes and location patterns of settlements that serve as central locations for selling goods and services to hexagonal-shaped market areas.

Market Area The area in which residents favor a given central place over its competitors when shopping for a good or service.

Order The relative ranking of a central place function based on how specialized it is.

Range The maximum distance people are willing to travel to obtain a central place function.

Threshold The minimum market size needed to support a central place function.

Urban Hierarchy A system of cities consisting of various levels, with few cities at the top level and more and more settlements on each lower level. The position of a city within the hierarchy is determined by the types of central place functions it provides.

▶ FURTHER READINGS

Berry, Brian J. L. 1967. *Geography of Market Centers and Retail Distribution*. Englewood Cliffs, NJ: Prentice Hall.

Berry, Brian J. L., and William L. Garrison. 1958. The Functional Bases of the Central Place Hierarchy. *Economic Geography* 34:145–154.

Burns, E. K. 1997. Nested Hexagons: Central Place Theory, pp. 163–181 in *10 Geographic Ideas That Changed the World*, Susan Hanson (ed.). New Brunswick, NJ: Rutgers University Press.

Christaller, Walter. 1966. *Central Places in Southern Germany*. Englewood Cliffs, NJ: Prentice Hall.

Christaller, Walter. 1972. How I Discovered the Theory of Central Places: A Report about the Origin of Central Places, pp. 601–610 in *Man, Space, and Environment*, Paul W. English and R.C. Mayfield (eds.). New York: Oxford University Press.

Lewis, Michael. 2003. *Moneyball: The Art of Winning an Unfair Game*. New York: Norton.

Lösch, August. 1938. The Nature of Economic Regions. *Southern Economic Journal* 5(1):71–78.

Lösch, August. 1954. *The Economics of Location*. New Haven, CT: Yale University Press. Translated by W. H. Woglom and W. F. Stolper from *Die Raumliche Ordnung der Wirtschaft*, 2nd ed. Jena: Gustav Fischer, 1943.

Preston, R.E. 1983. The Dynamic Component of Christaller's Central Place Theory and the Theme of Change in His Research. *The Canadian Geographer* 27:4–16.

Rooney, John F. 1974. A *Geography of American Sport: From Cabin Creek to Anaheim*. Reading, MA: Addison-Wesley.

Shearmur, Richard, and David Doloreux. 2008. Urban Hierarchy or Local Buzz? High-Order Producer Service and (or) Knowledge-Intensive Business Service Location in Canada, 1991–2001. *Professional Geographer* 60(3):333–355.

Thrall, Grant Ian. 2002. *Business Geography and New Real Estate Market Analysis*. Oxford, UK: Oxford University Press.

Zimbalist, Andrew. 2003. *May the Best Team Win: Baseball Economics and Public Policy*. Washington, DC: Brookings Institution Press.

Zimbalist, Andrew, and Stefan Szymanski. 2005. *National Pastime: How Americans Play Baseball and the Rest of the World Plays Soccer*. Washington, DC: Brookings Institution Press.

▶ WEB RESOURCES

Baseball Almanac: www.baseball-almanac.com

Baseball Reference: www.baseballreference.com

BaseballParks.com: www.baseballparks.com

CBS Sportsline: cbs.sportsline.com/mlb

Center for Spatially Integrated Social Science. *Walter Christaller*: www.csiss.org/classics

dr1.com. *A Brief History of Baseball and the Dominican Republic*. dr1.com/articles/baseball.shtml

ESPN, Minor League Baseball: espn.go.com/minorlbb

Hargrove, William W., Richard F. Winterfield, and Daniel A. Levine. *Dynamic Segmentation and Thiessen Polygons: A Solution to the River Mile Problem*: gis.esri.com/library/userconf/proc95/to150/p114.html

Hedberg Maps. *Baseball Wall Map with League Insets*: www.mapsales.com/products/hedberg/baseball-wall-map.htm

Liga Mexicana de Beisbol: www.lmb.com.mx

Major League Baseball Collective Bargaining: www.mlb.com/NASApp/mlb/mlb/news/mlb_labor.jsp

National Baseball Hall of Fame and Museum: web.baseballhalloffame.org/index.jsp

National Treasury, Republic of South Africa. *Christaller's Central Place Theory*: www.treasury.gov.za/divisions/bo/ndp/TTRI/Day 2 - 30 Oct 2007/2c Reading Central Place Theory Christaller.pdf

Public Broadcasting System. *Baseball: A Film by Ken Burns*: www.pbs.org/kenburns/baseball
Sporting News: www.sportingnews.com/baseball
Sports Illustrated-CNN: sportsillustrated.cnn.com/baseball
The United Countries of Baseball: www.unitedcountriesofbaseball.com
USA Today. *Minor League Baseball Index*: www.usatoday.com/sports/baseball/minors/index.htm
USA Today. *Baseball Salaries*: asp.usatoday.com/sports/baseball/salaries
Yahoo! Yellow Pages: yp.yahoo.com

▶ ITEMS TO HAND IN

Activity 1: • Questions 1.1–1.6, including the completed Table 9.1 (Question 1.1) and the scatter diagram (Questions 1.2 and 1.3), or answer all questions your instructor created in your WileyPlus assignments.

Activity 2: • Questions 2.1–2.15, including your hand-drawn market areas for Oregon (Question 2.1), or answer all questions your instructor created in your WileyPlus assignments.

CHAPTER 10

Reading the Urban Landscape: Census Data and Field Observation

▶ INTRODUCTION

A city is a remarkable mosaic of sights, sounds, smells, and tastes. Think of the contrasts among an upscale downtown high-rise, an inner-city slum, a thriving ethnic neighborhood, and a brand-new tract housing development in the suburbs. Within a matter of minutes, urban dwellers can experience crushing poverty and deteriorating housing, on the one hand, and huge estates and luxury towers on the other. The small shops and exotic goods of immigrant neighborhoods such as "Little Italy," "Little Saigon," or "Koreatown" stand in stark contrast to the homogenized all-American mall nearby. Understanding the city involves coming to grips with these contrasts.

Three early models attempted to capture land-use patterns of the city (Figure 10.1). The **concentric ring model**, developed in the 1920s by the so-called Chicago

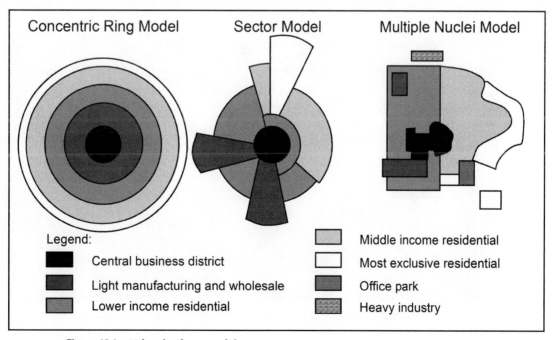

Figure 10.1 Urban land use models.

School of urban sociology, said that the city was organized in a series of concentric rings. The downtown or **central business district (CBD)**, packed with corporate offices, consumer services, shopping, and government buildings, was the focus of the city's commercial, social, and civic life (Figure 10.2). In the early twentieth century, urban employment was concentrated in and around the CBD. It was immediately surrounded by a fringe zone of land uses for which centrality is important for survival. The fringe included wholesaling, warehousing, light industry, and bus and train terminals, and is also marked by older, rundown housing and the encroachment of business from the CBD. Housing in this zone ran the gamut from crowded tenements to once-grand homes that wealthy occupants abandoned when they moved outward, and was home to the city's newest, poorest residents, often immigrants

Figure 10.2 Many U.S. cities still have a thriving CBD, particularly those that grew rapidly in the late nineteenth and early twentieth centuries. This image of San Francisco clearly shows the high-rise, high-rent CBD.

Figure 10.3 Row houses in densely populated North Philadelphia.

or ethnic minorities. The outer zones consisted of increasingly well-off residents, starting with the homes of blue-collar workers (Figure 10.3) who typically worked in the city's manufacturing plants adjacent to the downtown, then medium-income single-family houses, and finally the residences of high-income commuters.

The basic idea of this model was that the residential geography of the city was driven by a process of **invasion and succession** whereby new immigrants to the city moved into the oldest housing near the city center and pushed earlier groups outward (Figure 10.4). Each succeeding wave of immigration and the expansion of the downtown and its fringe produced a chain reaction, with each preceding group moving outward. This model of urban structure and growth was a good fit for the large cities of North America during the early twentieth century when immigration was high and nearly all factory, department store, and office jobs were either in the downtown or its fringe.

Proposed in 1939, the **sector model** of urban land use rejected the concentric zone theory, arguing instead that housing values in U.S. cities conformed to a pattern of sectors radiating out from the downtown rather than of concentric zones (see Figure 10.1). High-rent areas took the form of wedges leading outward along established lines of travel, fashionable boulevards, and environmentally desirable corridors such as high ground, ocean fronts, lakeshores, bays, and parks. Middle-income areas tended to locate on either side of the high-rent corridors, and low-rent areas were as far away as possible from high-income neighborhoods, usually in more central locations or adjacent to industrial zones along railroad tracks.

A third model of urban land use viewed the city as a grouping of specialized facilities such as retail districts, port districts, manufacturing districts, high-income housing, and so on. Known as the **multiple nuclei model** (see Figure 10.1), it was first proposed in 1945, when the growing popularity of the automobile was just beginning to create commercial, office, and industrial employment clusters outside the CBD for the growing suburban population. The multiple nuclei model was visionary in anticipating the postwar development of suburban shopping and office centers. It is a more flexible model than the other two models in the sense that the districts in the model are not always of the same shapes or the same spatial arrangement, as shown in Figure 10.1. What is general about this model is that not all employment is located in the CBD and that certain activities tend to be found in

Figure 10.4 Invasion and succession is illustrated by this Baptist church in North Philadelphia that earlier had been a synagogue. Once predominantly Jewish, the neighborhood is now mostly African-American.

adjacent districts of the city, such as middle-class neighborhoods bordering exclusive neighborhoods and lower-class neighborhoods bordering manufacturing and wholesaling. As the automobile became more prevalent and large suburban cities grew, the multiple nuclei model morphed into the concept of **urban realms**, or relatively independent suburban regions functionally tied to a mixed-use "suburban downtown." The concept of urban realms recognizes that the daily activities of many people occur within a fixed space in the metropolitan region, so that suburban dwellers interact on a regular basis with their nearby suburban downtown and its immediate vicinity (Figure 10.5).

As geographers and other social scientists worked to resolve the differences among the models, they found that certain characteristics tend to be organized more by rings, others more by sectors, and still others in clusters. Family life cycle characteristics (age, marital status, number of children, labor-force participation among women, and the presence of single-family housing) tend to be more organized around concentric zones with young families, large families, low rates of female labor-force participation, and single-family dwellings more prevalent in outlying areas. Nearer to the city center are people living alone or with roommates, few children, many working women, and a preponderance of multiple-family housing. "Empty nesters" whose children are grown and have moved away sometimes return to downtown areas for access to restaurants and cultural events. Characteristics

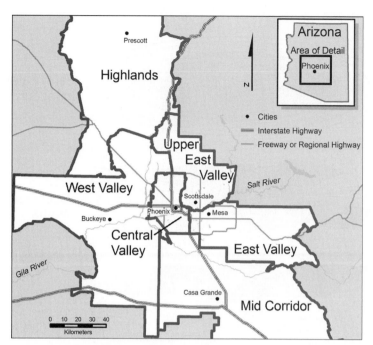

Figure 10.5 Metropolitan Phoenix stretches from the northwestern highlands around Prescott to the Tucson metro area in the southeast. Because of the great distances across this large urban area, most people do not negotiate the entire metropolis on a regular basis. Urban realms represent the functional spaces where residents regularly interact, and hence the part of the city they become most familiar with.

Source: modified from *Megapolitan: Arizona's Sun Corridor*, Morrison Institute for Public Policy, Arizona State University, May, 2008.

relating to socioeconomic status such as occupation, education, and income show more sector-like patterns, whereas clusters of racial and ethnic groups correspond more closely to the idea of specialized districts (Figure 10.6).

Although these early land-use models were helpful in describing the spatial organization of early twentieth-century industrial cities, they are less useful today in describing the structure of urban space. Urban geography today is greatly influenced by the concept of **postmodernism**, both as a theoretical viewpoint and as a style of architecture and urban design. To understand postmodernism, it helps to know a little about modernism. **Modernism** is based on a belief in the preeminence of scientific rationality and the inevitability of human progress. Modernism, which emphasizes function over form and universal models of how things are or should be, encompassed much of early- to mid-twentieth-century thinking (and doing) in many spheres of life. In architecture and urban design, modernism meant functional, boxy skyscrapers in the CBD, multistory apartment towers in the central city, and mile after mile of ranch houses in the suburbs. It meant a Detroit-made car in every garage. The stereotypical modern North American family, popularized and epitomized by 1950s and 1960s television programs such as *Father Knows Best* and *Leave It to Beaver*, was thought to contain a male breadwinner, his non-working wife, and minor children. In urban geography, the concentric ring and sector models represented modernistic thinking about urban form.

Postmodernism, on the other hand, flatly rejects the worldview that there are universal models for how the world does or should function. Postmodernism celebrates diversity and denies that any perspective, style, or subgroup has a monopoly on truth or beauty. Postmodern architecture emphasizes style, aesthetics, decoration,

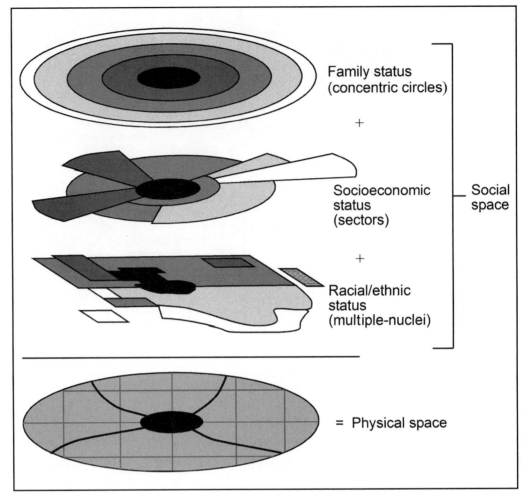

Figure 10.6 Patterns of family, socio-economic, and racial or ethnic status that make up the social space of the city tend to conform to each of the urban models discussed earlier in this chapter. When we overlay them, the residential structure forms a composite of the urban physical space.

context, and historic preservation—form as well as function. One economic parallel in today's postmodern world is Ford Motor Company, whose factory assembly lines once produced multitudes of vehicles in a few models, such as the Model T. Now an icon of postmodern activity, the company has dozens of different models, each customized to a highly segmented market of car buyers. Postmodernism is important for understanding the urban landscape because today's cities, while still bearing the imprint of modernity, have become more diverse collections of spaces and nodes designed for highly segmented markets of consumers.

Demographic trends have increased cultural diversity and led to social fragmentation along age, race, ethnic, income, class, and lifestyle lines in North American cities. Instead of just assimilating into the U.S. "melting pot," ethnic groups today celebrate their cultural heritage (Figure 10.7). Today, the stereotypical nuclear family represents a clear minority of all living arrangements as the population has aged, as divorce and remarriage have created more blended families with stepparents and stepchildren, as more adult children return home to live with their parents, and as more young and old choose to live alone. Persons living alone constitute one-quarter of all U.S. households, and single-parent units are the fastest-growing of all household types. The Chicago School's notion of suburban areas dominated by

Figure 10.7 Jackson Heights in New York City is a bustling immigrant neighborhood with many ethnic populations. The Mexican community demonstrates pride for their cultural heritage in this parade, which also serves to claim their space in the city and connect ethnic communities to place.

young families with children, large families, low female labor-force participation, and single-family housing is far too simplistic to capture the demographics of today's suburbs. Similarly, the idea of inner-city areas as dominated by childless couples and singles is often not matched by today's diverse inner-city populations.

With growing cultural and demographic diversity, many urban residents have sought to surround themselves with people similar to themselves and to shut out those who are different. The spectacular popularity of walled and gated communities and the rise of age-segregated retirement communities such as Sun City, Arizona, are the most obvious manifestations of this process. Ironically, in an age of globalization, the drive for local autonomy is at an all-time high. A record number of homeowner and neighborhood associations make decisions and represent the interests of an ever-narrower slice of the urban population. Many new suburban areas are like fortified honeycombs; each residential neighborhood is encased in its own space, with little regard for the metropolitan community as a whole. New master-planned communities dot the urban fringe and provide exclusivity and security; protection of property values; amenities such as tennis, golf, and swimming; and distinctive architectural features and physical layouts (Figure 10.8). In addition, they promote a sense of community and feelings of belonging for new residents—many of whom are recent migrants from other urban regions. This sense of community allows new residents to feel part of something larger than themselves, but these feelings of belonging are intensely focused on the self-contained master-planned community itself at the expense of the larger urban realm. Some social commentators worry that cities are losing their public consciousness and regional perspective as better-off citizens withdraw into master-planned communities where their tax dollars and community service no longer benefit the less fortunate who live elsewhere in the city.

Figure 10.8 A golf community/resort in California.

Figure 10.9 Abandoned slum buildings.

In nearly all North American cities, the relentless march of middle- and upper-class people and jobs to the suburbs, planned communities, and more recently to revitalized downtowns has left poor and disadvantaged populations in older, run-down inner-city neighborhoods called **slums**. The slums are home to many abandoned buildings (Figure 10.9) and an **urban underclass** with three defining characteristics. First, the underclass is persistently poor. Not all persons whose incomes fall below the poverty level are members of the underclass; only those who have been poor for an extended period of time are characterized as such. Second, the underclass is plagued by a variety of social ills, including out-of-wedlock births, high dropout rates, crime, gangs, and drugs. Third, the underclass lives in neighborhoods of concentrated poverty where most of their neighbors are also persistently poor. Underclass membership depends on geography, not just on income. We can meaningfully distinguish between poor who are mixed in with the population at large in other neighborhoods and underclass poor who are concentrated in inner-city slums. The spatial concentration of the underclass means they are physically distanced from the urban area's new job opportunities in the suburbs and socially isolated from middle-class lifestyles. As many urban critics point out, the spatial concentration of the underclass is partly a result of racial and ethnic discrimination, which has played a role in denying equal opportunity to bank loans, apartment rentals, jobs, and education that would enable aspiring individuals to improve, or move out of, their neighborhoods.

Depressed real estate values, in conjunction with larger sociodemographic forces such as rising immigration and the growth in nonfamily living arrangements, stimulated inner-city reinvestment and renewal, beginning in the 1960s. **Gentrification** involved the physical revitalization of some older, architecturally and historically significant neighborhoods (Figure 10.10). Initially, gentrifiers tended to be nontraditional households—gay partners, childless couples, and singles—seeking open neighborhoods where they would fit in and their lifestyles would be accepted. Later, gentrified neighborhoods attracted a diverse mix of the young and old, straight and gay, married and singles, and parents and the childless. Gentrified neighborhoods offer proximity to work, access to cultural and entertainment activities that have sprouted in many downtown districts, and the opportunity to live in an authentic, unique, and stimulating place that is connected with the city's history—a far cry from placeless suburban tract housing and strip malls that dominated new construction of the era (see Figure 10.8). Although gentrification has had a valuable and highly visible effect on some urban neighborhoods, it often drives out the neighborhood's previous population that can no longer afford high rents and real-estate taxes.

The postmodern hunger for neighborhoods that provide meaning, identity, diversity, and excitement in people's lives is linked to what public policy professor Richard Florida calls the rise of the **creative class**. As the economy changed from activities that emphasized raw materials and brute physical labor to activities based on human intelligence, knowledge, and creativity, economic growth became more closely tied to new ideas and new ways of doing things rather than to producing things. The creative class consists of scientists, engineers, artists, musicians, designers, and knowledge-based professionals who are engaged in the arts, knowledge production, innovation, and finding creative solutions to old and new problems.

Figure 10.10 Historic preservation in the colonial section of downtown Philadelphia.

© 2010 John Wiley & Sons, Inc.

Whereas fewer than 10 percent of American workers were doing creative work at the beginning of the twentieth century, the creative class now contains one-third of the workforce in the United States and in advanced European economies.

This pool of workers tends to be young, highly educated and paid, and creative by nature. They seek out cities and urban neighborhoods where they can settle in quickly, build support networks, put together a new life, and connect to place on a deep level. The line between work and home is not as finely drawn for these workers as for blue-collar workers and service-class workers. The creative class puts more emphasis on finding neighborhoods close to work that are compatible with their 24/7 lifestyles and craving for uniqueness, diversity, character, and authenticity. Talented, creative people value socially and ethnically diverse cities with a mix of influences and an openness to difference; a vibrant and varied nightlife; lively, engaging urban neighborhoods with sidewalk cafes, small galleries and bistros, street musicians, coffeehouses, and bookstores; and active outdoor recreational activities ranging from the more traditional bicycling and jogging to the new extreme sports such as trail running and snowboarding. Suburban tract housing and malls filled with chain stores are far less appealing to the creative class than are the hip downtown districts, historic neighborhoods, and certain types of suburban lifestyle communities with distinctive design elements, strong sense of identity, and unique outdoor recreational opportunities.

The urban regions and neighborhoods that offer these crucial place-based attributes have, according to Florida, a distinct advantage in the global competition for new ideas and new ways of doing things—the basis for twenty-first-century economic growth. Hot destinations for creative people are San Francisco, Austin, San Diego, Boston, and Seattle. San Francisco is blessed with a glorious natural setting, a host of charming and historic neighborhoods and hip districts, and lifestyle enclaves in Marin County and Silicon Valley. All five cities exude tolerance, diversity, and openness to creativity. The popularity of these ideas about the importance of the creative class in economic growth has spurred many small and large cities to reexamine their portfolios of downtown attractions and inner-city residential opportunities and market them as exciting places to live, work, and play in the twenty-first century.

In this urban environment of rapid economic and social change, downtown districts have had to reinvent themselves to survive. Downtowns of the twenty-first century are nerve centers for the new postindustrial, global information economy, and once again they are attracting new corporate headquarters. A new skyline of postmodern skyscrapers has appeared. The forces of decentralization have turned out to be selective: Activities that depend highly on electronic information and telecommunications such as credit-card–processing facilities and insurance companies are more likely to decentralize than are the activities of corporate decision making, financial trading, and investment banking that demand face-to-face interaction. Downtown businesses and government offices rely on the close proximity of business services (businesses that serve other businesses) such as marketing, accounting, advertising, personnel, repair, financial, and legal services.

New downtown entertainment and retail centers have helped revitalize central cities across North America. In addition to the museums and concert halls that never left, many downtowns are opening sports stadiums, convention centers, and new entertainment attractions including aquariums, IMAX theaters, and other attractions such as Cleveland's Rock and Roll Hall of Fame. Adding to the entertainment aspects of the downtown were more than 100 new downtown retail centers built

Figure 10.11 Built in 1929, Rockefeller Center in Manhattan includes 19 buildings on 11 acres with offices, shops, apartments, an ice-skating rink, NBC headquarters where *Saturday Night Live* and the *Today* show are taped, and, at Christmas, an 80-foot Christmas tree.

between 1970 and 1988. They were shopping centers with a downtown spin, such as Horton Plaza in San Diego and mixed-use developments such as Water Tower Place in Chicago and specialty markets including Pike Place Market in Seattle and Faneuil Hall Market in Boston. Downtown is once again "the place to be."

The postmodern urban landscape belies the modernist notion that it is beneficial to segregate residential, commercial, office, recreational, and industrial land uses from one another. Mixed-use developments such as Century City in Los Angeles, Rockefeller Center in New York City, and the Embarcadero Center in San Francisco combine opulent architecture with lavish interior design, upscale retail and office tenants, entertainment and recreation, and very high-income residential tenants (Figure 10.11). So-called festival centers such as Harbor Place in Baltimore, the Riverwalk in San Antonio (Figure 10.12), and Fisherman's Wharf in San Francisco are extensions of the mixed-use development concept that capitalizes on historical preservation to promote a city's unique identity. They are thriving entertainment centers, attracting special events such as concerts, art shows, street entertainment, and New Year's Eve celebrations.

Despite the immense success of downtown redevelopment events and gentrification efforts, the decentralization of the urban economy and population, or **suburbanization**, has continued apace. Urban decentralization has given rise to a new form of high-density, mixed-use development in the suburbs—so-called **edge cities**, a term coined by journalist Joel Garreau. Edge cities emerge from the "suburban downtowns" of the urban realm concept, but they are far more than just shopping malls. They are spread-out suburban downtowns with tall buildings, office space for white-collar jobs, shopping centers, entertainment complexes, hotels, corporate headquarters, and hospitals—pinnacles of a consumer/service-oriented society (Figure 10.13). Edge cities contain many of the urban functions typically found in the old downtown, but they are built to be served by automobile rather than pedestrian travel. Circumferential beltways further reduce the dependence of these suburban areas on the CBD. High-tech corridors with meticulously landscaped offices, research and development laboratories, clean industries, and hotels are a postmodern feature of the edge-city landscape.

Figure 10.12 Riverwalk in San Antonio, an urban festival center that first opened in 1941, is billed as America's Venice. Its cobblestone walkways, arched footbridges, and plentiful shops and romantic sidewalk cafés attract 7 million visitors a year.

Figure 10.13 This suburban office cluster (edge city) in Rockville, Maryland, is part of the sprawling Washington–Baltimore metro areas that have now merged into the nation's fourth-largest metropolitan area. Note the multistory buildings and the huge parking lots.

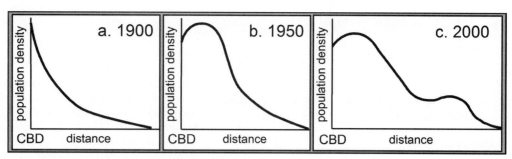

Figure 10.14 Generalized trends in population density with increasing distance form the CBD, 1900–2000.

When we consider the many changes that have occurred in North American cities since the nineteenth century, we can chart a general change in the population density from the central to the outer edges of the metropolitan area. In the early industrial days, the CBD was the most densely settled core, with a regular gradient of density decreasing outwards toward the low-density residential houses (Figure 10. 14a). By the middle of the twentieth century, suburbanization had been taking place for several decades, and importantly, both industries and people that were formerly located in the central cities were moving outward. Industries abandoned inner-city factories, and crowded inner-city slums were cleared. Office buildings replaced some of the downtown land use, but many of the white-collar workers for the industries that occupied these buildings commuted from the suburbs. The result was a lowered downtown population density as fewer people remained living in the CBD and an often empty and desolate appearance, yet a high-density ring remained immediately around the urban core where many people continued living in multi-family complexes, and many mixed uses of urban functions continued (Figure 10.14b). Finally, contemporary metropolitan areas sprawl ever outward in a gentle slope of decreasing density, with important spikes throughout the suburban regions where edge cities or other concentrations of housing, industry, or commerce might locate (Figure 10.14c).

Geographers who study the twenty-first-century city must have a bit of the archeologist in them because today's built environment includes elements from historic periods. The activities in this chapter ask you to do an in-depth study of one small piece of the urban mosaic to better understand the people who live there, the built environment, and other artifacts of local culture and the social geography. What kind of people do you see? What does the place look like? Does it look like any of the places described in the previous section? When were the structures built, what kinds of land uses are found, and what social, demographic, and economic forces are reflected in what you see?

▶ *CASE STUDY*

READING THE URBAN LANDSCAPE

GOAL

To develop a profile of a small area of the city using census data and field observation.

LEARNING OUTCOMES

After completing the chapter, you will be able to:

- Understand land-use patterns and trends in today's cities.
- Use electronic data from the U.S. Census Bureau or Statistics Canada.
- Relate a small geographic area to the larger urban context.
- Structure and sharpen field observation skills.

SPECIAL MATERIALS NEEDED

- Computer with high-speed Internet access and a recent release of a Web browser. If using the Student Companion Site with the printed book, click on *Tech Support* for system requirements and technical support. (If using the e-book in WileyPlus, click on *Help* for details about the system requirements.)

BACKGROUND

This chapter asks you to choose one tile from the urban residential mosaic and to become an expert on that tile. For the purposes of this chapter, a tile is a **census tract**. You will need to collect both primary and secondary data (see Chapter 1). Secondary data are available from the U.S. Census Bureau or Statistics Canada. What do the data tell you about the people who live in your tract? Describe the area in terms of its family orientation, socioeconomic status, and racial and ethnic composition (white-Anglo, African-American, Hispanic, Cuban, Vietnamese, etc.).

Although extremely useful, census data tell you just so much about your tract. The sights, sounds, and smells of the city are not captured in objective census information. The essence of a place also lies in the emotions and feelings people experience there. Fieldwork is fundamental to geography as a way to understand the world, and keen observation is a skill that provides deep insight into the place of study. The cultural landscape (see Chapter 2) is continually modified by humans, and clues about their lifestyles are everywhere to be seen. You will visit your particular area of the city and develop a profile based on what you see and experience. These impressions, based on primary observations, complement the information from secondary sources.

Students in small towns and rural areas can also do this activity. They will compare what they learn about their local area from the census information with what they learn from fieldwork. The only difference for rural students is that they may need to analyze data for a whole town instead of just one zone within it.

Name: _____   Instructor: _____

Reading the Urban Landscape: Census Data and Field Observation

► ACTIVITY 1: CENSUS TRACT DATA

In this activity, you will choose a census tract in your metropolitan area and collect statistics for that tract and for the entire metropolitan area that describe their demographic, economic, and social makeup. You may choose a tract with which you are familiar or one about which you wish to learn more. Maps of census tracts and census data are located on the U.S. and Canadian census Web sites and often can be found in the government documents section of university libraries. The next few paragraphs provide an overview for both U.S. and Canadian students, followed by detailed instructions for each country separately.

Consider what variables give a good profile of your census tract. *You* select which variables to use. Relevant variables can include these:

1. Percent Native American (United States) or Aboriginal (Canada)
2. Percent Hispanic (United States) or French ancestry (Canada) or other ethnic group
3. Percent of population under 18
4. Persons per household
5. Percent family/nonfamily households
6. Percent owner-occupied housing
7. Householders living alone
8. Median or average value of housing
9. Median or average rent
10. Vacancy or repair status of dwellings

This list is not inclusive, but a sample of variables that could describe your census tract. You will need to compare your tract with the average for your county or metropolitan area to assess its relative status for the entire metropolitan area. This means you must also record the values for the same variables for your metropolitan area. Try to avoid variables that depend on the size of the area of analysis, such as total population or total number of houses. It is not meaningful to compare the number of people in your tract to the number in the city. Instead gather percentages, median or mean values, or growth rates that can be directly compared with those of areas of differing sizes (such as a census tract and the Metropolitan Statistical Area).

► INSTRUCTIONS FOR STUDENTS IN THE UNITED STATES

Before we give you the instructions for downloading census data, you need some background on how the U.S. Census Bureau defines *metropolitan areas* and *census tracts*. The U.S. Office of Management and Budget (OMB) began using a new definition for metropolitan areas in 2003 called *core-based statistical areas* (CBSAs).

Based on census data, these are defined as any county containing at least one urban area of 10,000 or more population. The OMB recognizes three classes of CBSAs: *metropolitan statistical areas* (MSAs), *micropolitan statistical areas*, and *metropolitan divisions*. MSAs are defined as any county with one city of 50,000 or more inhabitants, plus any surrounding counties that are functionally connected to it as measured, for instance, by commuting patterns. *Micropolitan statistical areas* are counties that have at least one city of at least 10,000 but less than 50,000 people. Counties form the building blocks for metropolitan and micropolitan statistical areas. Finally, the largest MSAs with a population core of at least 2.5 million are often subdivided to form smaller groupings of counties, referred to as *metropolitan divisions*. A metropolitan division is a county or group of counties within a metropolitan statistical area that functions as a distinct social, economic, and cultural area within the larger region. For instance, Seattle and Tacoma are separate metropolitan divisions within the Seattle-Tacoma-Bellevue MSA. Of the top 15 newly defined MSAs in 2003, only 4 did not have metropolitan divisions: Houston, Texas; Atlanta, Georgia; Riverside, California; and Phoenix, Arizona.

Recognizing that many formerly separate metropolitan areas have coalesced (Dallas–Fort Worth and Baltimore–Washington, D.C., are examples), the OMB defines *combined statistical areas* (CSAs) as adjacent metropolitan and/or micropolitan statistical areas that have cross-commuting ties but at lower levels than are found among counties within individual metropolitan and micropolitan statistical areas. The largest of the nation's CSAs are New York–Newark–Bridgeport with 21.4 million people, Los Angeles–Long Beach–Riverside with 16.4 million, and Chicago–Naperville–Michigan City with 9.3 million. While the largest CSAs *may* have metropolitan divisions, *all* contain individual MSAs. For example, the Detroit–Warren–Flint CSA consists of four individual MSAs: Detroit–Warren–Livonia, Ann Arbor, Warren, and Flint. As of 2004, there were 578 micropolitan statistical areas and 369 MSAs in the United States and Puerto Rico, of which 11 were subdivided into 29 metropolitan divisions. There were also 123 CSAs that contained 334 MSAs and/or micropolitan statistical areas. A detailed map of these various metropolitan areas can be found at http://www.census.gov/geo/www/maps/msa_maps2003/msa2003_previews_htm/cbsa_csa_us_wall_0603_rev.htm.

The Census Bureau defines *census tracts* as "small, relatively permanent statistical subdivisions of a county delineated by a local committee of census data users for the purpose of presenting data. Census tract boundaries normally follow visible features, but may follow governmental unit boundaries and other non-visible features in some instances; they always nest within counties. Designed to be relatively homogeneous units with respect to population characteristics, economic status, and living conditions at the time of establishment, census tracts average about 4,000 inhabitants. They may be split by any sub-county geographic entity."

There is one drawback to the new definitions put in use by the OMB in 2003: the last U.S. decennial census of 2000 used different definitions that you will need to understand in order to gather data. The good news is that census tracts and MSAs remain the same, and that is what most students will use for this exercise. The only change you might see is that previously, CSAs were called *consolidated metropolitan statistical areas* (CMSAs), and the individual MSAs within a CMSA were called *primary metropolitan statistical areas* (PMSAs). Those of you searching for metro areas within a larger CMSA will need to recognize that PMSAs are listed within the larger CMSA, not as separate MSAs. Also recognize that prior to 2003, micropolitan statistical areas did not exist.

If you live in an urban area, you will get more detailed, localized information for a census tract than for your city as a whole. In rural areas, your instructor can have you get data for what the Census Bureau calls a "place" and compare that to your county as a whole.

► HOW TO DETERMINE CENSUS TRACT NUMBERS (OR LOCAL PLACE NAMES) FROM THE WEB

A. With any Web browser, go to www.census.gov.

B. Click on *American FactFinder*.

C. Click on *Maps*; then click on *Reference Maps*.

D. Click on *2000 Census Tracts and Blocks* and then select your state and zip code if you know it. Click *Go* and your map will appear. Because the *Zoom In* option is the default, every time you click on your area of interest, the map zooms in (you can also change the zoom scale at the top). With enough zooms, the 2000 census tract is outlined and numbers appear in brown. Write the number down.

E. For those of you in rural areas, "places" with census data are shown in pink. We recommend choosing whichever is smaller, census tract or place, for your local area. Write the number down.

► HOW TO ACCESS CENSUS DATA FROM THE WEB

F. Once you have found your census tract, go back to the Census's main Web page (www.census.gov) and choose *American FactFinder*.

G. Click on *Data Sets* and then click on *Decennial Census*. For demographic and racial information, click *Census 2000 Summary File 1*. For detailed social, economic, and housing information, click *Census 2000 Summary File 3*.

H. Read the description about the data available and then click on *Quick Tables*.

I. Your *Selection Method* will remain *List*. For the *Select Geographic Type*, choose *Census Tract* from the drop-down list. You will also need to select your state and county.

J. In the box labeled *Select One or More Geographic Areas*, scroll to your chosen census tract. Note that you can select the blue *Map It* button for a map of your selected area—very good for census tracts.

K. Click the blue *Add* button to list your selection in the lower box and then click on the *Next* button.

L. In the *Select One or More Tables* box, pick a data table that seems most suitable to you. Click the blue *Add* button so that the table appears in the box below.

M. Click the *Show Result* blue button.

N. After you have looked at the data table you selected for your geographic area, scroll to the top of the screen to select a different census variable (select *Tables*) or different census surveys (select *Data Set*).

O. Repeat these steps for as many variables as you require or select multiple tables at one time.

P. If you have finished collecting data for your census tract (or rural place), scroll to the top of the screen to select a larger area with which to compare it. Select *Geography* and choose your *Metropolitan Statistical Area* (or county, if you are in a rural area) to display the same variable for the larger region.

Q. To map census variables, on the *Data Sets* page, select *Thematic Maps* rather than *Quick Tables*. Follow the steps to make interactive census-variable maps for whatever geographic area you choose.

▶ INSTRUCTIONS FOR STUDENTS IN CANADA

Before we give you the instructions for downloading census data, you need some background on how Statistics Canada defines metropolitan areas and census tracts. Defined by Statistics Canada using census data, *census metropolitan areas* (CMAs) consist of a core urban area containing a large population nucleus and adjacent communities with which the core is socially and economically integrated. A CMA must have an urban core of at least 50,000 or a total population of at least 100,000. Areas whose urban cores contain between 10,000 and 49,999 are known as census agglomerations (CAs). All CMAs and CAs with more than 50,000 people are subdivided into census tracts. The largest CMA in Canada in 2001 was Toronto, with a population of 4.7 million. Montreal (3.4 million), Vancouver (2.0 million), and Ottawa-Hull (1.1 million) were the next largest CMAs. For the 2006 Census, Canada will have 33 CMAs and 111 CAs. Forty-eight of the CMAs and CAs participate in the census tract program.

When working with urban areas, do not confuse urban areas with politically defined cities. The City of Vancouver is a political unit that is distinct from the adjacent cities of Burnaby, Richmond, and North Vancouver. In contrast, the Vancouver CMA contains more than three dozen municipalities (census subdivisions), including the cities of Vancouver, Burnaby, Richmond, North Vancouver, and seven others, as well as adjacent villages, Indian reserves, and district municipalities.

Statistics Canada defines *census tracts* as "small geographic units representing urban or rural neighborhood-like communities" (Cat. No. 92-351-UIE, 1996 Census Dictionary). They are delineated by a local committee of census data users for the purpose of presenting data. Census tract boundaries normally "follow permanent and easily recognizable features" but can follow governmental unit boundaries and other nonvisible features in some instances. In any case, they always nest completely within CMAs and CAs as well as provincial boundaries. They can be split, however, by census subdivision boundaries. Designed to be relatively homogeneous units with respect to population characteristics, economic status, and living conditions at the time of establishment, census tracts range between 2,500 and 8,000 inhabitants. If you live in an urban area, you will get more detailed, localized information for a census tract than for your city as a whole.

Data are available only at the census-tract level for urban areas with a population of more than 50,000. For smaller communities and rural areas, your instructor can have you get data for what Statistics Canada calls a *census subdivision* instead of a census tract and compare that to the census division in which it is located. A census subdivision is a municipality or similar area whose boundaries are defined by law. Useful census subdivisions for rural areas include towns, villages, districts, and Indian reserves. Census subdivision data are available through *E-Stat*, although it may be easier to use Statistics Canada's *Community Profiles*. Ask your instructor for help.

▶ HOW TO DETERMINE CENSUS TRACTS (OR CENSUS SUBDIVISIONS) FROM THE WEB

A. With any Web browser, go to geodepot.statcan.ca/Diss/GeoSearch/index.cfm?lang=E.

B. Enter the name of a place or use the *Zoom In* (magnifying glass) tool to locate your place on the map.

C. After enough zooms, use the *Select Boundary* tool (icon of three yellow layers) to show the census unit outlines.

D. Use the *Information* tool ("i" with circle around it) to display the name of the census unit.

E. Scroll down to the very bottom of the *GeoSearch* page where you will find a hierarchical diagram of your census unit and the larger units within which it falls. Click on the name or number of the census unit, and the map will zoom in and recenter.

F. Write the name or number of your census unit.

▶ HOW TO ACCESS CENSUS DATA FROM THE WEB

G. Social and economic data from Census 2001 are readily available from Statistics Canada's E-Stat service. Go to the E-Stat main Web page (estat.statcan.ca/). *Note:* Access requires subscription to the service through your university. Data for census subdivisions and other large units, not census tracts or dissemination areas, can be freely obtained through Statistics Canada's (www.statcan.gc.ca/start-debut-eng.html) Community Profiles site.

H. For demographic and ethnic information, click the *Data* tab (it's under the *Table of Contents* heading).

I. Under the *People* subheading, you will have several choices. Click *Population and Demography* for age, religion, language, migration, birth, death, and other demographic data. Or, for detailed social, economic, and housing information, click the *Education, Labour, Health, Social Conditions*, or *Personal Finance and Household Finance* links under the same heading.

J. Choose a *Census* (not CANSIM) database on the subsequent page. Note the census dates and the general geographic units. If you are looking for a census subdivision, choose a table with *Provinces, Census Divisions*, and *Municipalities* in the title.

K. Select the appropriate census tract or subdivision from the *Geography* drop-down list and the variables you want from the scrolling *Characteristics* list.

L. Click the *Table: Areas as Rows* option at the bottom to display the data.

M. Scroll through the table to find your census tract or census subdivision.

© 2010 John Wiley & Sons, Inc.

N. You can use the options at the bottom of the page to add or sort variables and to calculate percentages.

O. After you have looked at the data table, use the *Back* button to navigate to the original table. Either select different census variables (from *Characteristics*) or go farther *Back* to select different census surveys (*Table of Contents* page). Repeat these steps for as many variables as you require.

P. If you have finished collecting data for your census tract or census subdivision, use the *Back* button to navigate to the original table and select a larger geographic region with which to compare it. Select *Geography* and choose your metropolitan area (or census division, if you are in a rural area) and repeat the steps for displaying the same variables.

Q. To map census variables, return to the page containing results of your *Table: Areas as Rows* command. At the bottom, you can choose the *Map* button to display the data for all tracts or census subdivisions in the table, which is very useful for comparing your area to others. Use the options to change the way that the data are displayed.

▶ FINAL INSTRUCTIONS FOR U.S. AND CANADIAN STUDENTS FOR ACTIVITY 1

1.1 Give the exact number of the census tract and where it is located in the metropolitan area. Does this neighborhood have a vernacular name (e.g., Maple-Ash, "Sin City," Dobson Ranch, South Philly, Uptown, Churchill Estates, etc.)?

1.2 Make a table that lists the specific variables you looked up that compares your tract and the metro area as a whole. For instance: Average Age tract=xx. x years Phoenix metro=yy.y years. Percent Hispanic tract=zz.z% Phoenix metro=ww.w%.

1.3 Describe the people who live there and their housing situation. How do they rate relative to the metro area (or county) as a whole in terms of wealth, social class, age, family orientation, race and ethnicity, and housing conditions?

Name: _____   Instructor: _____

Reading the Urban Landscape: Census Data and Field Observation

► ACTIVITY 2: FIELD SURVEY

Activity 2 requires you to visit your census tract (or rural place) and observe its people and landscape. Keep in mind what you learned about the tract from the census data you collected. The goals are to see whether your visual impression "matches" your mental image of the tract acquired from the census data and to find what you can see in the field that is not evident from census data alone.

Before you go into the field, it is helpful to know what to look for. This is a skill that develops over a lifetime, but we want to give you some help. Landscape interpretation requires paying attention to the everyday surroundings that you frequently take for granted (see Chapter 2 on the cultural landscape). The appearance of the world around us, from modifications to the natural terrain to the cities in which we live, provides clues to our culture and society. There is meaning in the built environment that reveals our values and that contributes to a "sense of place." There is much you can learn about your part of the city by looking closely at such things as the architecture (particularly house types), iconography and symbolism, and ethnic or religious landscapes. Subtle interpretations help unravel how landscapes reveal (and conceal) power relations.

Neighborhood demographics are evident by features such as the presence or absence of children's toys or sporting equipment, the types of stores located nearby and the products they sell, and the activities you see people undertaking. Do stores specialize in niche markets for ethnic minorities, for the elderly, or high-end consumer items? Are there many children running about? What types of cars are people driving (family-oriented minivans, sports cars for singles, or sturdy sedans for the elderly)? Are there clubs and cafés for the younger crowd, or perhaps assisted living, transportation services, and health care facilities for an older population?

Indicators of social status can be seen in the quality and condition of housing, cars, and other consumer items. Is there a predominance of single- or multi-family homes? Are yards well landscaped and litter free? Are there many luxury autos, or boats and other recreational vehicles? Is the neighborhood served by public transportation? Are people waiting at bus stops? Are people working on their cars in their front yard? Is there a predominance of security-related features, such as surveillance cameras, private security guards, gated communities, sturdy fencing, or warning signs?

Cultural tastes are everywhere displayed in the landscape. What types of food are sold locally, and what types of restaurants are there? Is public, shared space valued and used, or do the streets and parks seem vacant? Who uses the public space, if anybody? What types of churches and temples, or memorial monuments, are nearby? Do you hear or see any language other than English? Do you see any distinctive house decorations, garden types, or building modifications?

This exercise requires that you take time to stop, look, and think about the environment that surrounds you. Supplement your observations by any data you can gather. Does a local real-estate office list house values? What are the apartment rents in the area? Walk through the grocery stores and note unique food types. Talk to people and ask about the local place history and neighborhood characteristics. In sum, immerse yourself in the surroundings and reflect on the features that contribute to the quality of this place.

Before you begin, you will undertake a virtual field trip of Colorado Springs, where census data maps are linked to field observations with short explanatory text about what you see. This exercise is intended to help you think about field observations of your own.

A. To start your activity, click on the *Student Companion Site* at www.wiley .com/college/kuby. (For students using WileyPlus, log on to your class Web site, select the *Assignment* tab, locate and click on this assignment, and follow all instructions.)

B. Select this chapter from the drop-down list and then click on *Computerized Chapter Activities*.

C. Click on *Activity 2: Field Survey*.

D. Read and follow the instructions. Be sure to look at each map first to see patterns and then click on the highlighted census tracts to see visual representations of that variable from the field. The final page discusses variables not found in the census and has links to example photos.

E. When you have finished, close all browser windows.

When finished with the virtual field trip, you should have a good idea of the types of things you can examine in the field. Many geographers are surprised by what they did not expect to find once they get into the field. You can go to your area at different times of day and different days of the week to see how activity changes, but use caution and common sense about visiting certain parts of the city at night or alone. Don't put yourself in a dangerous or threatening situation. Now go out and do your study!

After you have conducted your field analysis, write approximately two pages (typed, double-spaced) to address the following issues:

2.1. Describe your impressions of the area. Did your field observations support the impressions formed by the census data? What differs from what you imagined the area to be based on the census data?

2.2. For each variable you select from the census, what did your field analysis reveal about that variable? This will involve "reading the landscape" on your part and asking questions about the people who live there. Think about the following questions a–d while conducting your field survey and answer these questions (and any other similar questions comparing your field observations to your census variables) in your write-up.

a. Does the tract (place) have an ethnic population that is significantly larger than the metropolitan (county) average? If so, what visible landscape clues reinforce this social geography? Pay attention to small details. How are the houses painted? What religious symbolism is apparent? Are there some characteristic land uses, such as gardens, plazas, or noticeable recreational sites? What vegetation do people plant and grow?

b. Does the tract (place) have a large population of children? If so, what can be observed about the uses of social space? Where do children play or hang out? What kinds of activities do they engage in?

c. Does the tract (place) contain high-income residents? What can you observe about vehicles parked in driveways, on the street, and in front of houses? Do many people ride the bus rather than drive?

© 2010 John Wiley & Sons, Inc.

d. How do your observations of housing compare to the statistical data from the census? What is the relationship between housing data and the physical condition and maintenance of houses or apartments? What *types* of housing prevail (i.e., apartments, row homes, duplexes, or single-family, detached houses)? Do people have large yards or common-use areas? Do people use backyards or front yards for socializing?

2.3. Do you think many changes have occurred since the 2000 census? Give examples.

2.4. What other information did you gather about your area that you could not get from census data alone? Do you believe that field observation can help you to better understand the cultural environment?

See Figures 10.15 through 10.17 for more examples of neighborhood landscape interpretation.

Figure 10.15 Union City, New Jersey.
Source: Courtesy Daniel D. Arreola

a. An older neighborhood, as evident by the Victorian three-story flats.

b. Likely not a neighborhood originally designed for the automobile, given the architectural style of the buildings and wide sidewalks.

c. A neighborhood built before zoning regulations because the lower floors were and still are commercial, and the upper floors are residential.

d. A foreign immigrant neighborhood, clearly Hispanic, but there could be clues that declare this a Cuban barrio rather than a Mexican-American or Puerto Rican one—use of the word *Hispania* rather than *Mexicana* or *Puertoriqueña*, or the kinds of fruit vended in stalls. What do auto types tell you about the income level of this immigrant community?

Figure 10.16 Paradise Valley, Arizona. Several landscape signatures broadcast that this is an elite neighborhood.
   a. Hillside location.
   b. Large houses on big lots.
   c. Houses set back from the street with curving driveways.
   d. Lush, well-manicured vegetation in a desert setting.
   e. No exposed utilities, no street lighting, and no sidewalks.
   f. No vehicles parked on street, and resident autos hidden from street.

Figure 10.17 Sacramento, California.
   a. A new subdivision, evident by small trees and contemporary house styles.
   b. Likely a middle-class population, evident by mixed house styles and garages facing street; also cul-de-sac street pattern and neighborhood watch sign.
   c. Retro fashion taste is evident in Craftsman house (an early-twentieth-century style) on corner and the purposely used old-style street lamp on corner.
   d. Sidewalks and vehicle parked on street.

▶ DEFINITIONS OF KEY TERMS

Census Tract An areal unit defined and used by the Census Bureau for presentation of data. Census tracts incorporate roughly 4,000 people, but considerable variation occurs.

Central Business District (CBD) The downtown or nucleus of the urban area. It has the peak value intersection, the densest land use, the tallest buildings, and traditionally was the urban area's major concentration of retail, office, and cultural activity.

Concentric Ring Model A model that explains urban land use in a pattern of concentric rings around the city center.

Creative Class The growing segment of the workforce engaged in arts, knowledge production, and innovation. The creative class includes scientists, engineers, artists, musicians, designers and architects, writers, editors, and cultural figures.

Edge Cities Suburban nodes of employment and economic activity featuring high-rise office space, corporate headquarters, shopping, entertainment, and hotels. Their physical layout is designed for automobile, not pedestrian, travel.

Gentrification The upgrading of inner-city neighborhoods and their resettlement by upwardly mobile professionals.

Invasion and Succession Settlement of new arrivals to a city in older housing near the city center (invasion) and outward push of earlier groups (succession).

Modernism As a worldview or philosophy, the belief in the preeminence of scientific rationality and the inevitability of human progress. As an architectural and urban planning movement, an emphasis on universal models and function over form.

Multiple Nuclei Model A model that explains urban land use as organized around several separate nuclei.

Postmodernism As a worldview or philosophy, rejects the notion that there are any universal models for how the world functions and what is best and denies that any perspective, style, or subgroup has a monopoly on truth or beauty. As an architectural and urban planning movement, emphasizes context, aesthetics, and mixing of land uses.

Sector Model A model that explains urban land use in pie-shaped sectors radiating outward from the city center.

Slums Older, run-down inner-city neighborhoods populated by poor and disadvantaged populations.

Suburbanization The process whereby growth in population and economic activity has been most intense at the fringes of urbanized areas.

Urban Realm Suburban regions functionally tied to a mixed-use "suburban downtown" with relative independence from the CBD.

Urban Underclass The disadvantaged population of inner-city slums who are persistently poor, plagued by a variety of social ills, and concentrated in neighborhoods where most of their neighbors are also persistently poor.

▶ FURTHER READINGS

Arreola, Daniel D. 1995. Urban Ethnic Landscape Identity. *Geographical Review* 85(4):527–543.

Cosgrove, Denis. 1989. Geography Is Everywhere: Culture and Symbolism in Human Landscapes, pp. 118–135 in *Horizons in Human Geography*, Derek Gregory and Rex Walford (eds.). Totawa, NJ: Barnes & Noble Books.

Dear, Michael J. 2000. *The Postmodern Urban Condition.* Malden, MA: Blackwell.

Duncan, James S. 1973. Landscape Taste as a Symbol of Group Identity: A Westchester County Village. *Geographical Review* 63:334–355.

The Economist. 2008. An Age of Transformation. (May 31).

Florida, Richard. 2002. *The Rise of the Creative Class.* New York: Basic Books.

Ford, Larry R. 1994. *Cities and Buildings.* Baltimore: Johns Hopkins University Press.

Ford, Larry R. 1994. Midtowns, Megastructures, and World Cities. *Geographical Review* 88:528–547.

Garreau, Joel. 1991. *Edge City: Life on the New Frontier.* New York: Doubleday.

Lewis, Peirce F. 1979. Axioms for Reading the Landscape, Some Guides to the American Scene, pp. 11–32 in *The Interpretation of Ordinary Landscapes: Geographical Essays*, Donald W. Meinig (ed.). New York: Oxford University Press.

Ley, David. 1983. *A Social Geography of the City.* New York: Harper & Row.

Lucy, William H. and David L. Phillips. 2006. *Tomorrow's Cities, Tomorrow's Suburbs.* Chicago: University of Chicago Press.

Knox, Paul L. and L. McCarthy. 2005. *Urbanization: An Introduction to Urban Geography* 2nd ed. Upper Saddle River, NJ: Pearson-Prentice Hall.

Knox, Paul L. 1995. *Urban Social Geography: An Introduction.* New York: Wiley.

Kunstler, J. 1993. *The Geography of Nowhere.* New York: Simon and Schuster.

McKenzie, Evan. 1994. *Privatopia: Homeowner Associations and the Rise of Residential Private Government.* New Haven: Yale University Press.

Powell, Jim. 1998. *Postmodernism for Beginners.* New York: Writers and Readers Publishing.

Rowntree, Lester B., and Margaret W. Conkey. 1980. Symbolism and the Cultural Landscape. *Annals of the Association of American Geographers* 70(4):459–474.

Schmandt, Michael J. 1996. Postmodern Phoenix. *Geographical Review* 85(3):349–364.

Short, John R. 1996. *The Urban Order.* Cambridge, MA: Blackwell.

Smith, Neil. 1996. *The New Urban Frontier: Gentrification and the Revanchist City.* New York: Routledge.

Smith, Neil, and Peter Williams (eds.). 1986. *Gentrification of the City.* Winchester, MA: Allen & Unwin.

Tierney, John. 2002. The Gentry, Misjudged as Neighbors. *The New York Times* (March 26): B1.

Walcott, Susan M. 1999. Fieldwork in an Urban Setting: Structuring a Human Geography Learning Exercise. *Journal of Geography* 98:221–228.

Walker, Richard, and Robert D. Lewis. 2001. Beyond the Crabgrass Frontier: Industry and the Spread of North American Cities, 1850–1950. *Journal of Historical Geography* 27(1):3-19.

Weiss, Michael. 1988. *The Clustering of America.* New York: Harper and Row.

Zelinsky, Wilbur. 2002. The Uniqueness of the American Religious Landscape. *Geographical Review* 82:282–294.

▶ WEB RESOURCES

Association of American Geographers. *Places Online*: www.placesonline.org

CreativeClass.org: www.creativeclass.org

Electronic Labyrinth. *Defining Postmodernism*: www.iath.virginia/edu/elab/hfl0242.html

FastCompany. *Where Are You on the Talent Map*: www.fastcompany.com/magazine/42/pp_florida.html

Lileks.com. *Historical and Contemporary Landscapes of Fargo, North Dakota*: www.lileks.com/fargo/index.html

Kotkin, Joel, and Fred Siegel. 2004. Too Much Froth. *Blueprint* (January 8): www.ndol.org/ndol_ci.cfm?contentid=252300&kaid=141&subid=301

Malanga, Steven. *The Curse of the Creative Class*: www.city-journal.org/html/14_1_the_curse.html

Philosophical Dictionary. *Postmodernism*: www.philosophypages.com/dy/p7.htm#pomo

Project for Public Spaces. *Great Public Spaces*: www.pps.org/gps

Rosin, Hanna. 2008. American Murder Mystery. *Atlantic Monthly* (July/August): www.theatlantic.com/doc/200807/memphis-crime

Statistics Canada. *New Criteria for Census Metropolitan Areas*: www.statcan.ca/Daily/English/030331/d030331f.htm

Terrain: A Journal of the Built and Natural Environment: www.terrain.org

University of California. *Downtown Los Angeles Walking Tour*: www.usc.edu/dept/geography/losangeles/lawalk

U.S. Census Bureau. *Metropolitan and Micropolitan Statistical Areas*: www.census.gov/popest/metro/index.html

U.S. Census Bureau. *American Factfinder*: factfinder.census.gov

▶ ITEMS TO HAND IN

Activity 1: • One- to two-page profile of your census tract (or place) answering Questions 1.1–1.3 based on statistics gathered from government documents, or answer all questions your instructor created in your WileyPlus assignments.

Activity 2: • Two additional pages answering Questions 2.1–2.4, or answer all questions your instructor created in your WileyPlus assignments.

CHAPTER 11

The Disappearing Front Range: Urban Sprawl in Colorado

▶ INTRODUCTION

Atlanta, Georgia, is expanding by more than 2 acres every hour. The New York metropolitan region now stretches almost 150 miles from New Haven, Connecticut, to Trenton, New Jersey, absorbing 15 other metropolitan areas in the process. When traffic is bad—which some would argue is *always*—it can take most of the day to drive the 110 miles from one end of the Los Angeles region to the other. **Urban sprawl** is the term we use for low-density development at, and sometimes beyond, the outer margins of our metropolitan areas. Sprawl is now the prevailing form of urban growth in North American cities. It gobbles up acre upon acre of valuable open space, exacerbates problems of traffic congestion, traps the population under a hood of smog, and adds to the expense of providing urban services. It is possible to plan urban growth that exhibits little of what we think of as "sprawl," but there are numerous influences that drive low-density growth on the **urban fringe** (Figure 11.1).

How did sprawl come to dominate growth in North American cities? Since the beginning of the Industrial Revolution, cities have been expanding due to rural-urban migration (Chapter 4). However, it has not always been possible to live far

Figure 11.1 New suburban growth encroaching on foothills in Laguna Michel, California.

away from the downtown central business district (CBD) where most jobs were located. In each era of urban expansion, the spatial extent of the **urbanized** (or built-up) **area** was constrained by the prevailing transportation networks. Each new transportation technology has made new areas on the urban fringe accessible to the city center and has been accompanied by new residential construction more spread out than those of the previous era (Figure 11.2).

Until about 1890, people got around in cities by walking or by horse, which limited cities to a dense, circular shape because of the slow speed of travel. Cities could not be any larger than the distance a person was willing and able to walk to work. By the 1880s, American cities were bursting at the seams. From 1890 to 1920, railroad-type technology, previously used for long-distance transport, was applied to short-distance urban travel with the building of commuter rail lines and electric streetcars. Once-rural areas became available for urban development with the arrival of a new streetcar stop or rail station. Cities of this age developed a star-shaped pattern with arms of growth along the rail lines. By the 1920s, mass-produced automobiles, typified by Henry Ford's Model T, became affordable to middle-class Americans. Cars provided accessibility to the areas between the streetcar lines, which began to fill in. Then, in the early 1950s, President Eisenhower initiated the interstate highway system, and urban freeways enabled people to commute to downtown from distant suburbs built far beyond the old urban fringe. Entire suburban towns served by freeways grew at the periphery of cities. Circular beltways, now common in most large metropolitan areas, further the development of outlying suburbs as cities in their own right, no longer subservient to the old downtown.

The inclusion of beltways in the freeway stage of Figure 11.2 recognizes that the CBD is no longer the sole destination to which people travel. Shopping, offices, and industry followed the middle class to the suburbs. The expression "bedroom suburbs," popular in the 1950s and 1960s, was first supplanted by the notion of **urban realms**, or relatively independent suburban regions, and then by **edge cities**, or "satellite towns" (see Chapter 10). Edge cities are huge retail and office clusters

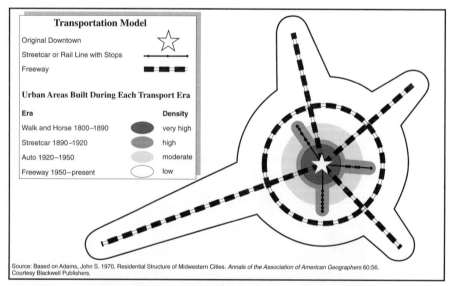

Source: Based on Adams, John S. 1970. Residential Structure of Midwestern Cities. *Annals of the Association of American Geographers* 60:56. Courtesy Blackwell Publishers.

Figure 11.2 The latest transportation technology has made new areas on the urban fringe accessible to the city center. Each transport era was accompanied by residential construction more spread out than the previous due to increasing ease of movement. The spatial structure of today's city reflects that different parts were built in different eras.

that have emerged around the intersections of major highways, around airports, and in older downtowns of what were once smaller surrounding cities now absorbed by the sprawling metropolis (Figure 11.3). High-tech companies frequently congregate in edge cities to be near their well-educated suburban workforce. Data transmission, electronic funds transfer, online information services, and e-shopping offer even greater locational flexibility for both companies and residents and hence promote further decentralization. Probably every metropolitan area with more than half a million people has at least one edge city. Some of the better-known national examples include the Galleria area west of downtown Houston, containing the 64-story Transco Tower; the area around the Massachusetts Turnpike and Route 128 in the Boston area; the Schaumburg area 30 miles west of downtown Chicago; the Perimeter Center near Atlanta; Tyson's Corner southwest of Washington, D.C.; and the Beverly Hills–Century City area in Greater Los Angeles.

Even though nonresidential land uses have moved to the suburbs, that does not mean people are traveling less. Quite often, the suburb in which they live is not the one in which they work (or go to college!). The average American in 2001 made

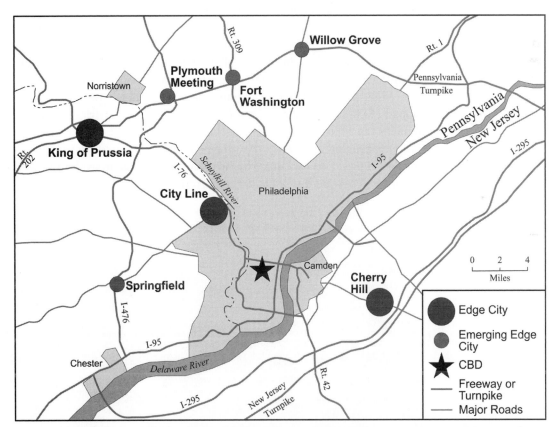

Figure 11.3 Founded in 1682, Philadelphia is the fifth-largest metropolitan area in the United States, with more than 5.8 million people. Suburban downtowns, or edge cities, have evolved in what used to be bedroom suburbs and outlying towns. The largest is in King of Prussia, where a huge complex of offices, high-tech companies, and warehouses has coalesced around one of the earliest and largest shopping malls at the intersection of the Schuylkill Expressway (I-76) and the Pennsylvania Turnpike. Total employment within a 5-mile radius is now more than 320,000 workers, many of whom commute to King of Prussia from other suburbs or even Philadelphia proper. Cherry Hill, New Jersey, and City Line Avenue are two other major suburban nuclei of jobs, shopping, and traffic. Others are emerging at strategic highway intersections, such as the Fort Washington and the Willow Grove areas.

4.1 trips per day totaling 40 miles, up from 2.9 trips and 26 miles per day in 1977. Automobile transportation is so pervasive today that our cities are built with the car in mind, and homes keep spreading outward in low-density development that typifies what we think of as sprawl. Since 1950, the federal government has built more than 4 million miles of highways. In 2007, the average U.S. household spent $8,220, or 17% of their budget, on expenditures related to private vehicles, including $2,384 on gasoline. Meanwhile, from 1990 to 2006, transport-related emissions of greenhouse gases grew by 25 percent over the same period, and U.S. oil imports rose 71 percent.

Today, with 2 to 3 times more people driving between suburbs than traveling from suburbs to the central city to work, flexibility in transportation becomes crucial. As demonstrated by the streetcar era in Figure 11.2, **mass transit** such as buses, subways, and light rail works best in bringing people along densely populated corridors to the CBD. New York and Chicago, two large, densely populated cities whose central areas were constructed in the streetcar era, account for one-third of all mass transit (or public transportation) trips in the entire United States. Private automobiles are better suited for anywhere-to-anywhere transportation. In the United States today, private automobiles account for 87 percent of commuting trips to work, followed by mass transit (4.8 percent), working at home (3.9 percent), and walking (2.9 percent). Transportation and land-use changes reinforce each other. Automobile use leads to increasingly decentralized, multinodal metropolitan areas. In turn, the multinodal urban geography makes the use of a car more important than ever because there is no longer a single focal downtown point on which public transportation routes converge.

While the prevalence of automobile transportation permits sprawl to occur, the primary factor driving sprawl is cost. Land is cheaper at the fringes of urban areas, where families can afford larger (and newer!) houses and more land than if they had purchased property near high-rent areas downtown. Simply put, you can get a better deal the farther out you move. This explains why, around some urban areas, **leapfrog development** occurs well beyond the limits of the current urbanized area (Figure 11.4).

Figure 11.4 Leapfrog housing developments isolated from the urbanized area. The contiguous "edge" of the suburbs is several miles behind the point from where the photo was taken.

Other factors that encourage low-density, sprawling cities result from ingrained cultural beliefs. Many Americans value individualism, which leads to a preference for stand-alone, single-family homes rather than row houses, communal living, or multi-family structures that are commonly found in other countries. The so-called American dream is a single-family home with a multicar garage and fenced-in yard on at least one-quarter of an acre of land. Combine this housing preference with the fact that as our society has become increasingly more affluent, our houses have gotten progressively larger (especially since the 1960s). The four-car garage, entertainment room, fourth bathroom, and pool have become standard features in new luxury homes (Figure 11.5).

Well-known policy analyst Anthony Downs identified 10 traits associated with sprawl:

1. Unlimited outward extension
2. Low-density development
3. Leapfrog development miles beyond the urban fringe
4. Fragmentation of political powers among many small municipalities
5. Dominance of transportation by private automobiles
6. Lack of centralized planning or control of land uses
7. Commercial strip development
8. Great fiscal disparities among towns and neighborhoods
9. Segregation of types of land uses in different zones
10. Reliance on a trickle-down process to provide low-income housing

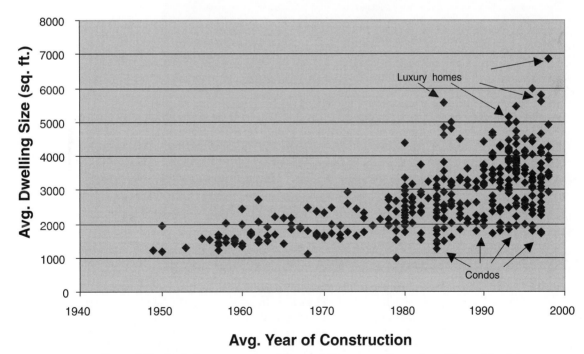

Avg. Year of Construction

Figure 11.5 Each dot represents a different 0.25-square-mile section of Scottsdale, Arizona, a wealthy suburb of Phoenix. The x-axis shows the average year in which the various dwellings in the quarter section were built. The y-axis is the average size of the dwellings in the quarter section. Today's luxury homes are two to four times larger than the average home of the 1950s, which are even smaller than today's average condos.

Several of these (such as traits #1, #2, #3, and #7) are measures or symptoms of sprawl, but others are causes. For instance, the fragmentation of governmental powers in a metropolitan area (trait #4) is a major issue that contributes to sprawl. Most cities rely heavily on sales taxes from retail and commercial activities. They therefore seek to attract stores that will generate revenue, many of which, such as malls and "big-box" retailers, require large amounts of land. The reliance on sales taxes for income leads cities to compete to attract these businesses rather than cooperating in a regional planning effort that could still serve market demand and use space more efficiently and with fewer negative environmental impacts (Figure 11.6). This competition, coupled with lack of **metropolitan government** (trait #6) and fiscal disparities between cities (trait #8), means there is frequently no coordinated effort to meet growth needs and avoid disjointed development that appears haphazard and sometimes dysfunctional.

Segregation of land uses (trait #9) also causes sprawl. City planners traditionally use **zoning** to separate incompatible land uses, such as housing and chemical factories (Figure 11.7). Each and every parcel in a city is zoned for one land use or another. Unfortunately, when residential, commercial, and industrial areas are required by zoning laws to be separated from one another, travel by private automobile (trait #5) is required in order for people to perform even the simplest errands or commutes. As Figure 11.8 shows, while the U.S. population increased

Figure 11.6 Tempe Marketplace (foreground) and Mesa Riverview (background) are two shopping malls on two of the four "corners" of the 101–202 freeway interchange in the Phoenix metropolitan area. They are located in such close proximity because the cities of Tempe and Mesa are both trying to capture the employment and sales-tax revenues within their boundaries. The two cities raced to construct the malls, knowing full well that the other city was proceeding with their own, and motivated by the idea that it would be better to get half of the business than none. While the strategy may benefit individual city finances, having two adjacent locations is not the optimal arrangement for the greater metropolitan region, which might be better served by regular spacing of malls, as suggested by Chapter 9's central place theory. Such competition for big retail complexes, with the surrounding surface parking lots that make them less accessible by walking, biking, and transit, leads to inefficient land use and dependence on private automobiles for shopping. This type of overbuilding of commercial space often leads to abandonment of commercial complexes across urban and suburban America.

31 percent from 1980 to 2006, the number of motor vehicles went up 57 percent, and the average miles driven per car went up 41 percent, leading to more than doubling of vehicle-miles traveled and more than tripling of **congestion** delays. Meanwhile, the percentages of people who carpool or take public transportation to work have fallen, as has the percentage of households without a car. These trends

Figure 11.7 This map illustrates zoning in an urban region, where each parcel has a designated land use and density that can be built upon it. Zoning is often beneficial towards maintaining property value because it keeps incompatible land uses separated, but the rigid spatial segregation of functional land uses greatly increases the probability that people must drive an automobile to move between their homes, shopping, work, school, or for most other functions. Advocates for more mixed-use zoning believe that an appropriate mixture of functions could facilitate less automobile dependency, if, for example, people could live, work, and shop all in the same immediate area.

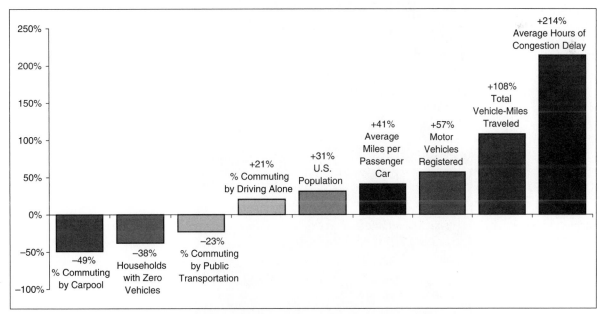

Figure 11.8 U.S. Automobile Dependency Trends, 1980–2006. Note: Some trends extrapolated from 1983–2007 or 1982–2005 on an annual percentage change basis.

Sources: Bureau of Transportation Statistics, Pocket Guide to Transportation, 2009; Pisarski, A.E. Commuting in America III, Transportation Research Board, 2006; Bureau of Transportation Statistics, Transportation Statistics Annual Reports, 1994, 2007; U.S. Census Bureau, Statistical Abstract of the United States, (1982, 1983, and 2009 editions).

are indicators of trait #5, the dominance of transportation by the private automobile, which is both cause and effect of urban sprawl. Transportation and land use are tied together inextricably, and geographers and urban planners have long known that freeway construction leads to the outward spread of cities, which increases traffic, which causes congestion (Figure 11.9), and leads back to needing more freeways in a vicious cycle. Likewise, any attempt to slow down or reverse sprawl and auto dependency must plan and develop the transportation and land-use components in tandem so they will reinforce, not counteract, each other.

Many people believe that sprawl, rather than being a problem, is simply a function of market forces that distribute resources in the most efficient manner. They argue that housing tracts could actually be a better land use than agriculture on what are often marginally productive lands. People buy the types of houses they prefer and shop at stores they like; therefore, one person's sprawl is another person's American dream. Others, however, counter that people buy not what they want but what is available; they have not been given a good choice of alternatives from which to choose. When shown photographs of urban scenery (called *visual preference surveys*), most people prefer images of neighborhoods and shopping centers that do not reflect the typical models being built today. More important, the "market forces" argument has been challenged by people who claim that market forces do not account for the social value of open space, the societal costs of traffic congestion and air pollution (Figure 11.10), or all public infrastructure and services costs associated with low-density development. A study of Custer County, Colorado,

Figure 11.9 Commuting in traffic jams is a daily routine for many Americans, as seen here in Los Angeles.

Figure 11.10 Smog continues to degrade the quality of life in many North American cities. Automobiles are the number-one contributor to air pollution.

found that for every dollar raised from taxes in low-density "ranchettes," the cost of providing services was $1.16. Market forces also have failed to adequately provide affordable housing (trait #10). Developers make their greatest profit by building expensive homes. There is little incentive to produce low-income housing from a strictly profit-making motive.

We have seen many reactions to urban sprawl in the news lately. A judge in Atlanta recently ordered all new highway construction halted until city planners could devise a better plan to deal with air pollution. Voters in Arizona and Colorado had ballot initiatives in 2000 that sought stronger limits on growth in urban areas (both were defeated after being labeled "too extreme," despite concern about sprawl in both states) (Figure 11.11). Voters in Ventura County, California, took the power to approve new subdivisions away from county officials; zoning changes now require voter approval.

While critics of sprawl abound, solutions are more difficult to come by. One popular alternative is called **New Urbanism**, a movement by architects and planners to build more traditional neighborhoods that foster a sense of community. New Urbanism emphasizes people, not cars. Garages are set back rather than facing the street, so that windows and porches out front act as buffers between private and public space. Front porches encourage greater socialization among neighbors. Grassy medians remain between sidewalks and streets, and the streets themselves are narrowed to slow traffic. **Mixed-use developments** (MUD), a new kind of zoning classification, stresses location of residential and commercial uses in close proximity and at a greater density so people can walk to work, stores, and schools (see Figure 11.12 and trait #9). House types are also mixed to promote diversity (see trait #10). All of these are seen as ways to promote neighborhood interaction instead of the sense of isolation that is characteristic of much of suburbia.

Austin, Texas, now measures any new commercial development proposals against a series of New Urbanist indicators (pedestrian access, mixed use, etc.) to

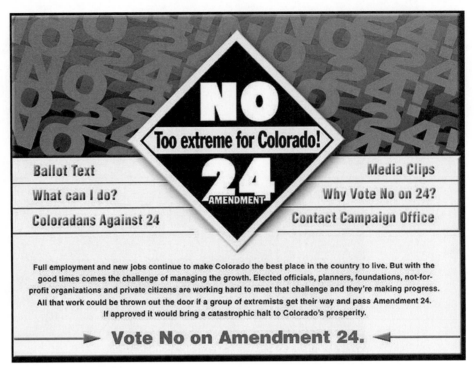

Figure 11.11 Web site advertisement encouraging a vote against a recent growth-management initiative in Colorado.

Figure 11.12 Mixed-use development in Arlington, Virginia, with commercial shops and services on the street level and a variety of residential options above.

© 2010 John Wiley & Sons, Inc.

Figure 11.13 These multifamily homes in an infill development of Tempe, Arizona, reduce outward sprawl and encourage alternate modes of transportation, as the built-in bike racks indicate. The front porches add a New Urbanist touch.

determine whether projects receive government subsidies. Cities around the country encourage people to move back downtown, convert old warehouses to lofts, and fix up historic districts. New Jersey and Maryland have both instituted new codes that encourage preservation of open space and **infill development**—construction of small-scale developments on vacant pockets of land remaining within the city (Figure 11.13).

Portland, Oregon, often is cited as a success story for "smart growth" policies that inhibit sprawl. The city emphasized human interaction over automobiles in its renewal projects in the 1970s. The focal point of the city is now the hugely popular Pioneer Courthouse Square, built in the early 1980s where a parking garage once stood. The also-popular Riverfront Park once was a 6-lane parkway that cut off the city from the Willamette River. City blocks are small in size, and all buildings have street-level shops (rather than blank walls) that encourage human interaction. In 1980, Portland instituted **growth boundaries** that put fixed limits on urban expansion (see trait #1). In addition, since 1986 Portland has invested $3 billion in a light-rail transit system that now consists of three lines and 64 stations, with two more lines under construction or planned. The result has been increasing density (but also increasing land values and house prices) in the urban downtown, and a very high rate of public transit ridership.

European and Japanese cities are far more compact and densely populated than are American cities, with much higher use of mass transit than even New York, Chicago, and Portland. Apartment living is the norm in central cities, and there is more travel by foot, bicycle, motorbike, and taxi. U.S. tourists often marvel at how lively and cosmopolitan foreign cities are. Of course, vacant land in these countries is far less plentiful and far more expensive than it is in North America, gasoline taxes raise the price to $3 to $6 per gallon, and people are used to a higher level of government intervention in their lives. Despite these differences, foreign cities also are experiencing a lesser version of sprawl on their urban fringes.

To be successful, antisprawl policies must satisfy many interest groups, or **stakeholders**. Developers need reassurance that investments they make will not be lost to policy or zoning changes prior to project completion. People need to be convinced that growth management policies will not overly restrict their housing type or render it unaffordable. People will always like the freedom of their automobiles, but other transit options should be available. Cities must simultaneously address transportation and housing needs while they encourage retail and commercial centers. Above all, planning must be flexible to adapt to many situations.

This chapter asks you to evaluate different **scenarios** for growth in the City of Colorado Springs, Colorado. You will be asked to look at each scenario from the perspective of different stakeholders. You will get a feel for the complexities of planning for growth and the difficulties of pleasing everyone.

► *CASE STUDY*

THE DISAPPEARING FRONT RANGE

GOAL

To understand the causes and effects of urban sprawl and proposed solutions to it, to recognize the perspectives of various stakeholder groups, and to see how those perspectives can be incorporated into realistic growth-management scenarios.

LEARNING OUTCOMES

After completing the chapter, you will be able to:

- Assess the relationship between urban growth and transportation technology.
- Articulate the causes of urban sprawl.
- Use GIS layering to visualize the uneven geographic effects of urban sprawl.
- Evaluate the alternative solutions to urban sprawl and recognize the inherent trade-offs among them.

- Advocate a position on urban sprawl.
- Negotiate an acceptable solution to urban sprawl with those who hold a different position.

SPECIAL MATERIALS NEEDED

- Computer with high-speed Internet access and a recent release of a Web browser. If using the Student Companion Site with the printed book, click on *Tech Support* for system requirements and technical support. (If using the e-book in WileyPlus, click on *Help* for details about the system requirements.)

BACKGROUND

The Front Range of Colorado is where the Great Plains meet the Rocky Mountains (Figure 11.14). The transition is abrupt, with 14,110-foot Pikes Peak rising from the plains just west of

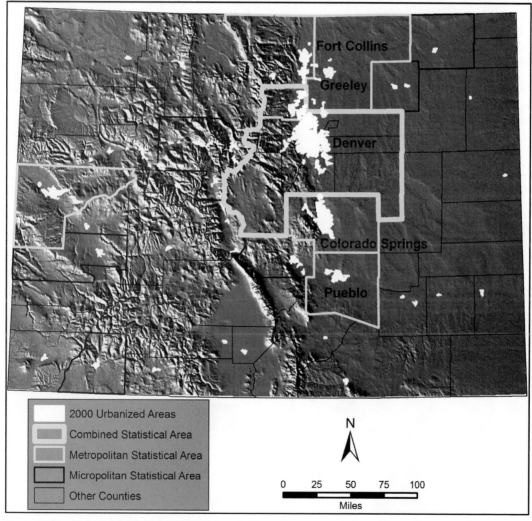

Figure 11.14 Urbanized areas along the Colorado Front Range stretch from Fort Collins to Pueblo.

© 2010 John Wiley & Sons, Inc.

Colorado Springs. This area has been a magnet for people since the gold rush days of the 1860s. Pueblo (on the Arkansas River) and Denver (on the South Platte) were early transportation and supply centers, and many other cities and towns have grown around them. Colorado's population picked up more than 1 million new residents in the 1990s, and its 30 percent growth over the decade was the third-fastest of any state. Denver, the focal point of the growth, was recently listed as one of the most sprawling cities in the United States, and the entire Front Range stretching from Fort Collins in the north to Pueblo in the south has grown rapidly. Colorado Springs, as the second-largest city in the region, is also undergoing rapid expansion.

Colorado Springs was founded in 1871 by General William Jackson Palmer to be a resortlike getaway for wealthy easterners. Palmer used his fortune from the Denver and Rio Grande Railroad to build a town according to his moral beliefs, characterized by many churches and parks and a lack of alcohol sales or taverns. Because of its clean air and abundant sunshine, the city soon became a popular destination for tuberculosis patients as well. While the Cripple Creek gold rush in the 1890s injected much wealth and industry into the community, the town remained quite small for many decades, relying on tourists who came to visit Pikes Peak, Garden of the Gods, and other nearby natural attractions. Beginning with World War II, military institutions formed a key part of the city's economic base. Fort Carson Army Post and what later became Peterson Air Force Base were founded during the war, and shortly after it, the United States Air Force Academy, the North American Air Defense Command (NORAD), and Schriever Air Force Base also located in the region. Today the economy has diversified greatly, with numerous high-tech companies (Intel,

Oracle, and MCI, among others) locating in this city known as a hub of silicon chip manufacturing plants.

Coloradans increasingly have become concerned with rapid growth. Numerous surveys identify urban sprawl as the number-one public concern, largely from fear of losing the quality of life that attracted people to the region to begin with: clean air, easy access to the mountains, and excellent outdoor opportunities.

The Colorado Springs Metropolitan Statistical Area (MSA) is expected to grow from about 507,000 people in the year 2000 to about 680,000 in 2020, an increase of around 33 percent. This translates into 70,000 to 75,000 new households. The bulk of these 173,000 new people will live within the city itself. Because growth is constrained to the west by the Rocky Mountains, to the south by Fort Carson Army Post and a new Cheyenne Mountain State Park, and to the north by the U.S. Air Force Academy, most growth will occur on the eastern plains (Figure 11.15). Currently, 40 percent of the Colorado Springs land is undeveloped, so planning for the future is essential. However, some of the remaining land has been highlighted by the city planners as **ecologically sensitive space**: fragile, rare, or valuable natural areas that are good candidates for preservation as parks, wilderness, or open space.

Colorado Springs' planners evaluate different **scenarios** or alternative ways in which the city could grow. Planners look at scenarios to decide which works best and then make suggestions to City Council, which in turn implements policies that encourage growth to follow the optimal pattern. Part of the problem is that what is "best" for one person or group is not "best" for another. For instance, a young family that wants room to grow could want the largest house it can afford in a new suburban

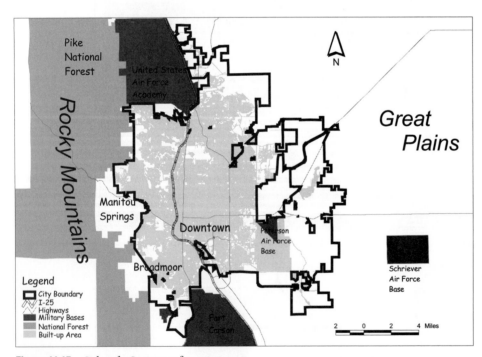

Figure 11.15   Colorado Springs reference map.

▶ **CASE STUDY** *(continued)*

tract at the farthest areas from the city. Environmentalists could decry this choice as contributing to increased traffic and air pollution and loss of precious open space and native prairie. A person with mobility restrictions (teenager, elderly, disabled) could favor tightly knit urban housing with nearby stores and entertainment that are easily accessible without the use of a car, whereas other people could lament the loss of privacy that accompanies living in a dense urban neighborhood.

One urban model will never fit all Americans. Geographers and planners refer to these types of situations as **trade-offs**, in which one objective must be sacrificed to achieve progress on another. Citizens must suffer more air pollution if they want cheaper housing, or suffer higher housing prices if they want cleaner air. Solutions that do not require trade-offs are known as **win-win solutions**. Zero-emission vehicles, for instance, could enable people to enjoy both cleaner air and cheap suburban housing. However, one needs to think clearly and comprehensively about these decisions: Even clean cars would not solve sprawl's effects on open space or traffic congestion on highways.

In the activities in this chapter, you will evaluate five different possible growth scenarios for Colorado Springs from the perspective of several different stakeholder groups. Your instructor will determine which stakeholder group you will represent. The five growth scenarios are guidelines to where the new developments of the city will be in 2020. They are all based on an increase of 72,000 housing units between 2000 and 2020.

Eastern Beltway

This growth scenario clusters development around what is anticipated to be a new interstate bypass to the east of the central city (shown on the GIS maps in Activity 2). On the eastern edge of the currently developed areas, the Powers Boulevard area is already experiencing rapid growth. When this becomes a major transportation corridor with connections to Interstate 25 on the north and south, commercial and industrial businesses are expected to favor locations nearby. Housing will also cluster along this corridor to take advantage of accessibility to transportation.

Urban Villages

The **urban village** concept is loosely based on the principles of New Urbanism so that mixed-use development of homes, shops, entertainment, and work are nearby. Although Colorado Springs' Urban Village growth scenario does not specify microscale urban design elements indicative of New Urbanist development, the idea is to concentrate new housing around several commercial and office nodes. Planners picked several retail and employment focal points, mostly in new-growth areas in the suburbs (shown by stars on the digital map) and proposed that medium- to high-density housing be clustered around these centers. The hope is that commuting to work by private automobiles can be minimized and "communities" will grow around these nodes.

Leapfrog

This scenario takes advantage of the most distant and least-developed land within the city limits to plan an entire new community. It is known as **leapfrog development** because

it jumps over available land on the urban fringe. Proponents cite the affordability of land, the vast tracts available, and the lack of constraints for planning new neighborhoods and transportation routes. It is usually cheaper *per mile* to build new residential streets and sewer lines in these empty areas than in areas that are already partially developed, but that includes only the costs within the development itself. Because of a leapfrog development's increased distance from existing public services such as emergency medical response, police and fire protection, and sewage treatment plants, either expensive connections must be built and maintained or new facilities must be built there. As a result, the *total* cost of public infrastructure is usually more expensive for leapfrog development. Leapfrog development would make possible larger homes in a new suburban setting, far from what many perceive as the social and environmental "problems" associated with inner cities, but it would encroach much farther into the rural areas, make open space less accessible to all, and add greatly to the city's total vehicle-miles traveled.

Northeast-Southeast Extensions

This scenario channels growth into two corridors that extend from the already developed areas. Compared with the leapfrog scenario, it focuses growth by keeping new areas contiguous with the already developed land. This scenario also has the benefit of serving two distinct markets: the northeast features more expensive housing serving a wealthier clientele, and the southeast has a larger contingent of smaller and more affordable housing for low- and middle-income citizens. Transportation needs can be better served with channeled growth such as this if major arteries are built into these sectors.

Infill

The final scenario is known as **infill** because it "fills in" most existing developable space in the city before new growth occurs on the periphery. The result would be a denser inner city that minimizes the spatial extent of developed land into the rural plains. Proponents cite increased energy efficiency with housing types such as multifamily homes and shorter commute distances. With amenities located closer, the need to use automobiles should decrease, and the population base for efficient public transportation should increase. Opponents decry the lack of private space (indoors and outdoors) associated with small lots or multifamily housing. They also cite the huge expense required to upgrade existing roads if the travel load is increased in older neighborhoods. The main policy instrument used to achieve the infill strategy is a **growth boundary**: literally, a line drawn on the map outside of which conversion of rural to urban land is prohibited. If such a line were drawn without including much available land, housing values would rapidly increase inside the boundary.

In Activity 1 of this chapter, you will first view an animated map showing the spread of the Colorado Springs urbanized area over time and assess the role of transportation networks and technology in shaping that growth, as idealized in Figure 11.2.

In Activity 2, you will prepare for the upcoming debate by using the map overlays to help you determine which scenario is most beneficial for various societal objectives. You won't

© 2010 John Wiley & Sons, Inc.

▶ *CASE STUDY (continued)*

yet be assigned to a stakeholder group, but you should begin thinking about whether criteria such as ecologically sensitive space, transit, or traffic congestion are important only to certain groups or to the overall city and community.

Finally, in Activity 3, you will be assigned to one of the stakeholder groups, and you will have to make a case for which growth scenario your group favors. After presenting your position statement to the class, your group will be divided among several citizens' working groups composed of members from each stakeholder group. The citizens' working groups will be charged with reaching a consensus on which scenario to recommend to the City Council.

Name: _____   Instructor: _____

The Disappearing Front Range: Urban Sprawl in Colorado

▶ ACTIVITY 1: TRANSPORTATION AND URBAN GROWTH

In this activity, you will watch Colorado Springs spread before your very eyes in the years from 1950 to 2000, and you will assess the relationship between transportation and the pattern of urban growth. Go back and review Figure 11.2. This idealized model of how urban growth is related to the spatial configuration of each new transportation technology was based on the historical experience of the midwestern cities of Chicago, Cleveland, Indianapolis, Cincinnati, and St. Louis.

Colorado Springs has some unique circumstances that have affected its growth patterns. Growth to the west of the city is limited by the massive wall of Pikes Peak, to the north by the Air Force Academy, and to the south by Fort Carson. The city has only one freeway, running north-south, with no major east-west corridor. Most important, the urban history of Colorado Springs (see Background) is quite different from that of the Midwest. Midwestern cities were founded earlier, and they experienced their most rapid growth during very different transportation eras. Midwestern cities grew rapidly during the late nineteenth and early twentieth centuries, but Colorado Springs did not mushroom until the late twentieth century. Colorado Springs is also much smaller. Many Midwestern cities were larger in 1900 than Colorado Springs was in 2000. Chicago surpassed the one million population level at the beginning of the streetcar era, when Colorado Springs was little more than a pleasant retreat near the mountains.

Despite the differences between Colorado Springs' situation and that of cities on which the idealized model was developed (or even because of them), it is instructive to compare Colorado Springs' growth pattern over time to the idealized model. Very often, one can learn just as much about a process by the way the model *doesn't* fit as by the way it does. As you look at the animation, think about the reasons that growth patterns in Colorado Springs do or do not fit the predicted model.

A. To start your activity, click on the *Student Companion Site* at www.wiley.com/college/kuby. (For Students using WileyPlus, log on to your class Web site, select the *Assignment* tab, locate and click on this assignment, and follow all instructions.)

B. Select this chapter from the drop-down list and then click on *Computerized Chapter Activities*.

C. Click on *Activity 1: Transportation and Urban Growth*.

D. You will see a map of Colorado Springs showing the built area in 1950. In the upper right is a graph with city and county population. At the bottom is a timeline from 1950 to 2000.

E. Move the slider manually to see the urbanized area change from 1950 to 2000. Click and drag the slider to move back and forth or freeze it at any year.

F. Move the slider to 1950. Turn on the *Streetcar* layer. Colorado Springs had an extensive streetcar system in the early twentieth century. One line ran westward from downtown to the suburb of Manitou Springs at the base of Pikes Peak (see Figure 11.15). The other ran southeast to The Broadmoor, a resort/country club/casino near Cheyenne Mountain. The city had no limited-access freeways at this time, but two major U.S. highways provided faster travel than the local street network.

1.1. Does the shape of the urbanized area in 1950 resemble any stage of the transportation/land-use model, and if so, which one? Explain.

1.2. Move the slider to the year 2000, by which time a north-south interstate highway had been built and a future beltway around the eastern circumference of the city had been announced. Describe the spatial pattern you see and explain its relationship to the transportation network.

1.3. How would you describe the growth pattern for Colorado Springs during the years between 1950 and 2000? Do you see any clear relationship with transportation?

1.4. Report the locations of any leapfrog developments that have been built beyond the urban fringe.

G. When you have finished, close all browser windows.

Name: _____ Instructor: _____

The Disappearing Front Range: Urban Sprawl in Colorado

▶ **ACTIVITY 2: URBAN SPRAWL SCENARIO ANALYSIS**

In this section, you will use the power of GIS to explore five real urban-growth scenarios developed by the Colorado Springs Planning Department. For each scenario, you will be able to overlay several different data layers to see what effect the scenario could have on transportation and sensitive ecological zones.

If you are doing Activity 2 in groups in a computer lab during class, please take turns as the *computer operator*. The other student(s) in the group can act as *timekeeper/taskmaster* or as *gatekeeper/consensus checker*. These roles are described in more detail in Activity 3.

A. To start your activity, click on the *Student Companion Site* at www.wiley.com/college/kuby. (For students using WileyPlus, log on to your class Web site, select the *Assignment* tab, locate and click on this assignment, and follow all instructions.)

B. Select this chapter from the drop-down list and then click on *Computerized Chapter Activities*.

C. If you have already taken the virtual field trip to Colorado Springs that is part of Chapter 10, go to Step G. If not, we encourage you to do so. Click on *Chapter 10 Virtual Field Trip to Colorado Springs* and follow the instructions on screen. When finished with the virtual field trip, close the virtual field trip browser window and proceed to Step D.

D. Click on *Activity 2: Urban Sprawl Scenario Analysis*.

E. You will see two side-by-side maps showing the already developed area of Colorado Springs in beige and the proposed growth areas for one scenario (refer to the legend to the right of the maps). In the left drop-down box above each map is a list of the five growth scenarios. View each scenario (refer to the descriptions in the background section for details). You can also click on the *Reference Map* to see Colorado Springs landmarks and roads.

F. In the right-hand box above each map, you have four additional layers for each scenario: *Ecologically Sensitive Space* (fragile, rare, or valuable areas that are potential candidates for preservation), *Mass Transit* (existing bus routes), *Traffic* (change in traffic volume that will likely occur for each scenario), and *Reference* (which lists landmarks and other reference features). Turn these on and off to see how they overlap with the proposed development area. Note that the *Growth* layer is the scenario without any of the additional four layers overlaid.

G. Click on any map to enlarge it in a new window. Scroll down to see a table of scenario attributes. Close the detailed map when finished.

H. You also have supplemental information to help you evaluate each scenario and make your choice as to which one is "best" for the different criteria (this information is also printed in Table 11.1). It is important to recognize that this information is our best "guesstimate" given today's situation. These values are not cast in stone; the changes brought about by the growth scenario will likely change the information in this table. For instance, if policies were set to constrain all development to infill sites, the price of housing and land would likely increase greatly. Similarly, as new residential areas develop, the public transportation network would likely change to better serve the market of potential riders (although the infill proponents use this as a motivation for their model, claiming that there would be no *need* to change if density increased). Be aware that housing types and values, traffic changes, utility costs, and housing densities are largely speculative and impossible to accurately predict.

TABLE 11.1   Scenario Planning Information

	Beltway	Urban Villages	Leapfrog	NE-SE	Infill
New housing units	72,000	72,000	72,000	72,000	72,000
Dwelling units per acre	8.4	8.4	3.58	3.58	16.8
Acres of land converted	10,865	10,743	20,035	20,097	7,548
Relative cost to provide electricity	medium	medium	high	medium	low
Relative cost to upgrade roads	medium	medium	low	medium	high
Approximate cost for sewer/ water lines	$262 million	$257 million	$627 million	$627 million	$147 million
Impact on central city traffic	slight increase	reduced	reduced	no change	increased
Potential for nonmotorized transit (walk, bike, skate)	low	high	low	low	high
Percent detached houses/ percent condos or townhouses	92/8	88/12	93/7	92/8	88/12
Average detached house value*	$180,000s	$200,000s	$120,000s	$200,000s	$160,000s
Average condo value*	$120,000s	$150,000s	$80,000s	$140,000s	$100,000s

*These real estate prices were estimated in 2000 and are not adjusted for housing inflation. Use them for *relative* comparisons only.

Source: Data courtesy of City of Colorado Springs, Colorado Springs Utilities, and El Paso County Assessor, © 2002.

Criteria	Best	Worst	Rationale
Preservation of rural land generally			
Preservation of *ecologically sensitive* space in particular			
Potential for nonmotorized trips			
Service by existing transit routes			
Inner-city congestion			
Suburban congestion			
Water, sewer, and electricity infrastructure expenses			
New road-building expenses (cost per mile)			
Detached housing prices (in terms of affordability)			
Condo and townhouse prices (in terms of affordability)			
Variety of types of residences within the new neighborhoods			
Revitalization of the CBD			
Proximity of housing to shopping, jobs, and services			
Air pollution			

2.1. In the table on the previous page, identify the scenario(s) that perform best and worst based on each criterion. In the event of an outright tie, write the names of both scenarios in the table. Some criteria have a clear-cut quantitative answer; you will need to make a value judgment for others. In the final column, write the rationale you used. By *rationale*, we mean not only the source (e.g., map, table) but also what you looked for on the map or table.

2.2. Compare and contrast the two given scenarios in terms of (1) the main geographic differences between them and (2) the main trade-offs between them. Base your responses on your answers to Question 2.1 and any other information at your disposal.

a. *The infill and leapfrog scenarios*
   (1) Describe how the two scenarios differ geographically.

   (2) Fill in the blanks to describe an important trade-off.
      The infill scenario performs well on _____ but poorly on _____, whereas the leapfrog scenario does the opposite.

b. *The urban villages and northeast-southeast extensions scenarios*
   (1) Describe how the two scenarios differ geographically.

   (2) Fill in the blanks to describe an important trade-off.
      The northeast-southeast extensions scenario performs well on _____ _____ but poorly on _____, whereas the urban villages scenario does the opposite.

I. When you have finished, close all browser windows.

Name: _____ Instructor: _____

The Disappearing Front Range: Urban Sprawl in Colorado

▶ **ACTIVITY 3: URBAN SPRAWL DEBATE AND CONSENSUS BUILDING**

Urban sprawl is a complex issue, in part because different stakeholder groups value different things and have different visions for the future. In Activity 3, you will play the role of one of the stakeholder groups. You will first participate in a debate about the issues. Then you will be appointed to a citizens' working group charged with reaching consensus and making a recommendation to the City Council.

Here are the major stakeholder groups and their driving interests:

Stakeholder	Driving Interests
Low-income single mother	Has two compelling interests: affordable housing and accessibility to work and day care. Time and financial constraints impose great mobility restrictions, which limit possible housing or work locations.
Real estate developer	Sole compelling interest is to maximize profits.
Middle-class family with school-age children, new migrant to Colorado Springs	Looking for best value, i.e., largest house for the money. Also needs good schools, not rundown or dangerous neighborhoods. Wants good views.
Middle-class family with school-age children, bought home on urban fringe 3 years earlier	Same as above, but also wants to preserve their own views of nearby open space and avoid continued sprawl that will make their area more congested and busy.
Environmentalist	Wants to preserve open space and farmland for wildlife habitats, cut pollution and water contamination, and conserve energy.
Elderly person	Needs easily accessible services such as grocery and drug stores and health care, but may not own a car or have a driver's license.
Single young urban professional (Yuppie)	Wants a truly urban, diverse, exciting environment with many entertainment activities, including a variety of arts, sports, restaurants, and clubs.
Farmer on urban fringe	Wants to either preserve farming lifestyle at a decent standard of living, or else sell off land for maximum profit.
Fast-growing high-tech employer	Needs easy commutes for workers, but also needs nearby access to urban and outdoor amenities to satisfy an educated and sophisticated workforce. Many employees have children, so good schools are necessary.

The debate will work best if each stakeholder group follows these traditional viewpoints. If you wish to play the role of a more enlightened mother, developer, family, or other stakeholder, please wait until step 3 to modify your position from the traditional driving interests listed above.

Your instructor will form your class into teams of three to five students each, and assign each team to one of the stakeholder groups. If there are more than 9 × 5 = 45 students in the class, the instructor will create multiple teams for some or all of the stakeholder groups (e.g., Developer 1, Developer 2).

Backstory: Tough Choices

Although it is not a large metropolitan area, the usual ills of urban sprawl have been accelerating in Colorado Springs: commercial strips; disappearing farmland; construction in foothills, ridgelines, and riparian areas; obstructed views; traffic congestion; longer commutes to work; increasing air pollution; lack of affordable housing in the newer suburbs; and flight of the middle class from the central city. Yet there is no shortage of people who want to buy the reasonably priced, low-density, new detached houses with amenities, fenced yards, and access to new schools that are springing up overnight on the prairies. Radio talk shows are filled with people complaining about urban sprawl. At the same time, proposals for a strict growth boundary have been met with vociferous opposition. As a result, the City Planning Department of Colorado Springs has prepared five alternative scenarios for accommodating 72,000 new dwelling units, the projected growth over the next 20 years. Maps and data have been made available to the general public in pamphlets and on the Internet. You have already studied the five scenarios and now are getting ready to speak at a public forum.

Step 1: Prepare a Written Position Statement (15 minutes for a 50-minute class; 20 minutes for a 75-minute class)

Prepare a written position statement for your stakeholder group based on your analysis of the five scenarios in Activity 2. Take the perspective of a typical member of your interest group. In your statement, first tell us a little about yourself and how you see the issue. Then advocate strongly for your interest group's first choice. You will have 1 to 2 minutes to read your statement aloud in the next step.

To enhance team functioning and facilitate completion of this step, students will be assigned to particular tasks. Count off and assign a number to each team member, beginning with 1. Your instructor will then randomly assign tasks to numbered students. Here are the tasks and some examples of what can be said to keep the group on track:

Timekeeper/Taskmaster, who keeps the group on schedule:

- "We have 3 minutes left to get the job done."
- "We're right on schedule."
- "We should have enough time to discuss this for another minute."
- "Let's get back to the main point."

Recorder, who drafts the statement in Step 2:

- "Shall we say it this way?"
- "Let me read this back to you to make sure it's right."

Consensus Checker/Gatekeeper

- "Do we all agree?"
- "Can anyone add any more before we move on?"

- "We haven't heard from you yet."
- "Thanks for your input. Can we get another opinion now?"

After Step 1, your instructor will randomly assign a number to the role of spokesperson, regardless of whether that individual was in one of the other roles. All students should be prepared to argue your team's position.

3.1. Write your position statement on this page.

Your stakeholder group _____

Step 2: Read Your Position Statement Aloud (1 to 2 minutes each; 10 minutes for a 50-minute class; 20 minutes for a 75-minute class)

Your instructor will randomly select the number of the student who will be the spokesperson. Be bold and forceful. Act the part!

3.2. Listen carefully to the other stakeholder groups' statements. Use the following table to take notes on their preferences.

Stakeholder Group	Preferred Scenario	Main Reasons
Low-income single mother		
Real estate developer		
Middle-class family with school-age children, new migrant to Colorado Springs		
Middle-class family with school-age children, bought home on urban fringe 3 years earlier		
Environmentalist		
Elderly person		
Childless young urban professional (Yuppie)		
Farmer on urban fringe		
Fast-growing high-tech employer		

Step 3: Citizen's Committee (12 minutes for a 50-minute class; 20 minutes for a 75-minute class)

The City Council has formed several Citizens' Working Groups to try to reach a consensus on the best overall scenario to recommend. Each Working Group is to be composed of one representative from each stakeholder group. You will advocate for your stakeholder group within the Working Group. All of the students numbered "1" in Step 1 will form Working Group 1, and likewise for Working Groups 2, 3, and so on.

Immediately upon convening, count off again; your instructor will randomly reassign the roles of recorder, taskmaster/timekeeper, and gatekeeper/consensus checker. We suggest you spend half your time trying to reach consensus and half your time drafting a position statement explaining the rationale for your recommendation. Keep in mind that any member of the group could be called upon as the spokesperson. You will have 1 to 2 minutes to present your recommendation.

Staying within your role, work with the other stakeholders to determine the best overall scenario. Consider short-term and long-term concerns and the needs and desires of all stakeholders.

3.3. Write your position statement here.

Step 4: Present Your New Position to the Class (1 to 2 minutes each; 8 minutes total for a 50-minute class; 15 minutes for a 75-minute class)

Your instructor will again randomly select the number of the student who will be the spokesperson. Don't be shy! Be persuasive.

3.4. Listen carefully to the other interest groups' statements. Use the following table to take notes on their recommendations.

Working Group	Recommendation	Main Reasons
Working Group 1		
Working Group 2		
Working Group 3		
Working Group 4		
Working Group 5		
Working Group 6		
Working Group 7		
Working Group 8		
Working Group 9		
Working Group 10		

▶ DEFINITIONS OF KEY TERMS

Congestion Heavy traffic volumes exceeding the capacity of roads, causing travel delays.

Ecologically Sensitive Space Fragile, rare, or valuable habitat that might merit preservation.

Edge Cities Suburban nodes of employment and economic activity featuring high-rise office space, corporate headquarters, shopping, entertainment, and hotels. Their physical layout is designed for automobile, not pedestrian, travel.

Growth Boundary A planning boundary beyond which conversion of rural land uses to urban land uses is strictly prohibited.

Infill Development Higher-density development in smaller patches of undeveloped or redevelopable land inside the urban boundaries.

Leapfrog Development Urban development well beyond the urban fringe, separated from the urban fringe by rural land.

Mass Transit Public transportation modes such as buses, subways, jitneys and vanpools, light rail (trolleys, streetcars), heavy rail (passenger trains), and monorails.

Metropolitan Government A regional governmental agency created to coordinate a variety of areawide functions such as water supply, transportation, open space, and waste management on behalf of the independent cities within the region. It is a response to the political fragmentation of the urban area.

Mixed-Use Development A single planned development designed to include multiple land uses, such as residential, retail, educational, recreational, industrial, or offices, in order to minimize the need for travel outside the development. MUDs range in size from office buildings that include some retail uses for lunchtime convenience of the employees to multiple building complexes and even huge planned communities covering several square miles.

New Urbanism A movement to make cities more livable and foster a greater sense of community by designing compact, pedestrian-friendly neighborhoods with sidewalks, front porches, and a larger variety of housing types and land uses.

Scenario A hypothetical planning alternative for accommodating future urban growth, which defines the assumptions for the analysis.

Stakeholder An individual or group with a strong interest or stake in how an issue is decided.

Trade-off A decision situation in which it is not possible to advance two conflicting goals simultaneously; that is, it is necessary to give up something in order to get something else. Compare with **win-win solution**.

Urban Fringe The edge of the urbanized or built-up area.

Urbanized Area The continuously built-up region of a metropolitan area.

Urban Realm Suburban region functionally tied to a mixed-use "suburban downtown" with relative independence from the CBD.

Urban Sprawl The spread of dispersed urban land uses outside compact urban centers into previously rural areas.

Urban Village A concentration of commercial land uses and higher-density housing outside the region's main central business district that is planned to be a focal point of shopping and employment for surrounding residential areas. Can be the anchor point of an urban realm.

Win-Win Solution A solution in which it is possible to advance two goals simultaneously. Compare with **trade-off**.

Zoning Planning regulations that define permissible land uses for parcels of the city.

▶ FURTHER READINGS

American Community Survey. 2007. *Most of Us Still Drive to Work – Alone: Public Transportation Commuters Concentrated in a Handful of Large Cities.* U.S. Census Bureau, U.S. Department of Commerce.

Barnett, Jonathan. 1995. *The Fractured Metropolis: Improving the New City, Restoring the Old City, Reshaping the Region.* New York: HarperCollins.

Beimborn, E., and R. Puentes. 2003. *Highways and Transit: Leveling the Playing Field in Federal Transportation Policy.* Washington, DC: Brookings Institution.

Brooks, David. 2009. I Dream of Denver. *New York Times* (Feb. 16):

Bruekner, Jan K. 2000. Urban Sprawl: Diagnosis and Remedies. *International Regional Science Review* 23(2):160–171.

Bullard, Robert D., Glenn S. Johnson, and Angel O. Torres. 2000. *Sprawl City: Race, Politics, and Planning in Atlanta.* Washington, DC: Island Press.

Calthorpe, Peter, and William Fulton. 2000. *The Regional City.* Washington, DC: Island Press.

Charles River Associates. 1997. *Building Transit Ridership: An Exploration of Transit's Market Share and the Public Policies that Influence It.* Transportation Research Board: Transit Cooperative Research Program, Report 27.

Chen, Donald T. 2000. The Science of Smart Growth. *Scientific American* (Dec.):84–91.

Cusack, Christopher. 2007. *Liquid City: Megalopolis and the Contemporary Northeast.* Washington, DC: RFF Press.

Downs, Anthony. 1994. *New Visions for Metropolitan America.* Washington, DC: Brookings Institution Press.

Jackson, Kenneth T. 1985. *Crabgrass Frontier: The Suburbanization of the United States.* New York: Oxford University Press.

Kay, Jane Holtz. 2000. *Asphalt Nation.* New York: Crown.

Marlin, John T. 1992. *Livable Cities Almanac: How Over 100 Metropolitan Areas Compare*. New York: HarperCollins.

Morrill, Richard. 2006. Classic Map Revisited: The Growth of Megalopolis. *Professional Geographer* 58(2):155–160.

Nijkamp, Peter, and Adriaan Perrels. 1994. *Sustainable Cities in Europe: A Comparative Analysis of Urban-Energy Environmental Policies*. London: Earthscan Publications.

Squires, Gregory D. (ed.). 2002. *Urban Sprawl: Causes, Consequences, and Policy Responses*. Washington, DC: Urban Institute.

Sucher, David. 2003. *City Comforts: How to Build an Urban Village*. Seattle: City Comforts, Inc.

Talen, Emily. 2005. *New Urbanism and American Planning: A Conflict of Cultures*. New York: Routledge.

Warner, Kee, and Harvey Molotch. 1999. *Building Rules*. Boulder, CO: Westview Press.

▶ WEB RESOURCES

American Planning Association: www.planning.org

Brookings Institution. *Improving Efficiency and Equity in Transportation Finance*: www.brookings.edu/es/urban/publications/wachstransportation.htm

Brookings Institution. *Metropolitan Policy Program*: www.brookings.edu/metro

Brookings Institution. *Mountain Megas*, 2008: www.brookings.edu/~/media/Files/rc/reports/2008/0720_intermountain_west_sarzynski/IMW_full_report.pdf

Center for Neighborhood Technology. *Housing and Transportation Affordability Index*: htaindex.cnt.org

Center for Urban Transportation Research, University of South Florida: www.cutr.usf.edu

City of Colorado Springs: www.springsgov.com

Congress for the New Urbanism: www.cnu.org

Downs, Anthony: www.plannersweb.com/sprawl/define.html

Federal Transit Administration. National Transit Database: www.ntdprogram.gov/ntdprogram/archives.htm

Google Maps (satellite images of any U.S. city): maps.google.com

Katz, Bruce, and Jennifer Bradley. *Divided We Sprawl*: www.theatlantic.com/issues/99dec/9912katz.htm

Langdon, Philip. *How Portland Does It*: www.theatlantic.com/issues/92nov/portland.htm

League of American Bicyclists. Bicycle Friendly Community Campaign: www.bikeleague.org/programs/bicyclefriendlyamerica/communities (scroll down to bottom)

Morrison Institute for Public Policy, Arizona State University. *Megapolitan: Arizona's Sun Corridor*: www.asu.edu/copp/morrison/megapolitan.htm

National Aeronautics and Space Administration. *Great Zooms*. Includes 17 U.S. cities: svs.gsfc.nasa.gov/stories/zooms/index.html

National Civic League: www.ncl.org

Pisarski, Alan A. *Commuting in America III: The Third National Report on Commuting Patterns and Trends*. Transportation Research Board, TCRP Report #110, 2006: www.trb.org/news/blurb_detail.asp?ID=6699

Prevention Magazine. *Best Walking Cities Finder*: www.prevention.com/bestcities

Puentes, R., and Tomer, A. *The Road . . . Less Traveled: An Analysis of Vehicle Miles Traveled Trends in the United States*. Brookings Institution, Washington, DC: www.brookings.edu/reports/2008/1216_transportation_tomer_puentes.aspx

Redefining Progress. *Community Indicators Project*: www.rprogress.org/projects/indicators

Schrank, D., and T. Lomax. *Urban Mobility Report*. Texas Transportation Institute: mobility.tamu.edu/ums

Sierra Club. *Stop Sprawl*: www.SierraClub.org/sprawl

Smart Growth America: *Measuring Sprawl and Its Impact*: www.smartgrowthamerica.org/sprawlindex/sprawlindex.html

Smart Growth Network: www.smartgrowth.org

Sustainable Measures: www.sustainablemeasures.com

UCLA Department of Urban Planning. *Critical Planning*: www.sppsr.ucla.edu/critplan

Urban Land Institute. *Reality Check: A Collaborative Regional Visioning Process of the Urban Land Institute*: commerce.uli.org/Content/NavigationMenu/MyCommunity/RegionalVisioningandCooperation/RealityCheck/Reality_Check.htm

U.S. Bureau of Transportation Statistics. *Transportation Statistics Annual Report*: www.bts.gov/publications/transportation_statistics_annual_report

U.S. Census Bureau. *Population Estimates: Maps*: www.census.gov/popest/gallery/maps

▶ ITEMS TO HAND IN

Activity 1: • Questions 1.1–1.4, or answer all questions your instructor created in your WileyPlus assignment.

Activity 2: • Questions 2.1 and 2.2, or answer all questions your instructor created in your WileyPlus assignment.

Activity 3: • Questions 3.1–3.4, or answer all questions your instructor created in your WileyPlus assignment.

CHAPTER 12

Do Orange and Green Clash? Residential Segregation in Northern Ireland

▶ INTRODUCTION

People of the same social class, occupation, race, ethnicity, and religion often cluster together in a process called **residential segregation**. Although North Americans tend to emphasize racial and ethnic segregation, people have long concentrated (or been forced to concentrate) along social class and religious lines. In early European and Middle Eastern cities, the most obvious feature of segregation was the Jewish ghetto. The term **ghetto** comes from the Italian word *getto*, meaning foundry, because the first ghetto in Venice, in 1516, was on the site of an iron foundry. Jewish residents were confined to certain districts by custom and by law, a process that magnified language and religious differences and contributed to the rampant anti-Semitism of the time. Segregated Jewish ghettos continued into the modern era in eastern Europe, and anti-semitism reached its height when Nazi forces targeted them in a campaign of genocide during World War II (Figure 12.1).

Figure 12.1 German occupation of Poland during World War II enforced extreme spatial segregation between Jewish ghettos and non-Jewish areas. This image shows a wooden bridge connecting the small and big ghettos in Warsaw, crossing over Chlodna Street where Jews were not allowed.

Figure 12.2 Specialized shops and signs make Asian shoppers feel at home on Union St., an Asian enclave in the borough of Queens in New York City.

Residential segregation can result from both voluntary and involuntary forces, although the two are sometimes difficult to separate. **Enclaves** are residential clusters that occur when people choose to live together, for example, to maintain their ethnic identity or to establish control over their territory. Immigrant enclaves such as the Hispanic barrios and Little Saigon of Los Angeles and Little Havana in Miami provide much-needed social support for new immigrants and are seedbeds for new immigrant businesses. They offer a wide array of restaurants, food markets, foreign-language newspapers, temples and churches, social clubs, and traditional medicine to those who live and work there (Figure 12.2). Enclaves also give social groups a measure of political influence that would not be possible if the group were spread out; witness the growing influence of Cuban Americans in South Florida. Currently, Los Angeles is one of the most ethnically and racially diverse cities in the nation due to high rates of immigration (Figure 12.3).

One of the best examples of voluntary segregation is the attraction of working-class and middle-class retirees to retirement communities in high-amenity regions. In these communities, retirees surround themselves with others usually of the same social class and race and pursue interests that befit their retired status: golf, crafts, potluck dinners, dancing, bowling, and so on. Formal age restrictions exclude children under 18 years and limit the community to people over the age of 50 or 55. Social critics argue that while fostering social interaction with like-minded people and an active lifestyle, retirement communities promote exclusivity and an attitude of being set apart from the rest of society. Critics also argue that retirement communities may not be as voluntary as they appear at first glance, because their very existence grows out of a societal attitude that favors youthfulness and shunts the elderly aside.

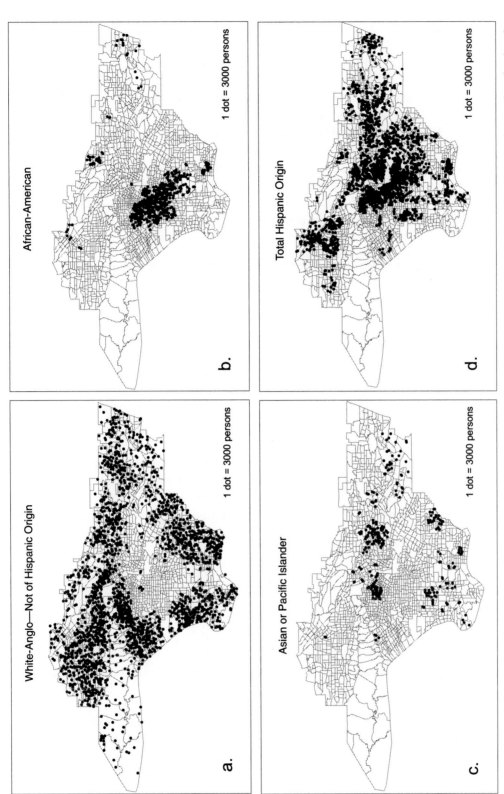

Figure 12.3 High levels of racial segregation characterize the racial and ethnic geography of metro Los Angeles County. White-Anglos are found in beach communities and in newly built suburbs. The black community is highly concentrated in a large area south of the downtown. Asians or Pacific Islanders are also concentrated but into smaller, more scattered nodes of settlement, reflecting their diverse ethnic makeup (Chinese, Japanese, Vietnamese, Cambodian, Filipino, Korean, etc.). The settlement pattern of Hispanics, the largest racial and ethnic minority group in Los Angeles County, represents the reverse of white-Anglos. For the most part, they are numerous in places where white-Anglos are absent.

347

Ghettos are products of involuntary segregation. The most blatant ghettos in North American cities were the early Chinatowns. The first wave of Chinese immigrants, most of them men, came to North America to build the railroads and to work in the mines. They eventually migrated to cities where they operated laundries, groceries, and bakeries and worked as household servants, cooks, gardeners, small farmers, and vegetable peddlers. They faced fierce discrimination from native-born North Americans. Ostensibly, prejudice against the early Chinese immigrants was based on the fact that their bachelor societies were alien to family life and on their culturally based customs of gambling and opium use, but hostility toward the Chinese extended far beyond the single men who frequented the gambling parlors and opium dens. Chinese were barred from owning property, and their communities were derided as morally aberrant, dirty, and disease ridden. Subjected to such hostility, the Chinese clustered into Chinatowns where they had relatively little contact with the general population.

Also subject to involuntary segregation were African-Americans who moved from the rural South to the urban North during the early to mid-twentieth century. (See Chapter 1 for a more complete discussion of African-American migration patterns.) Residential segregation stemmed from discriminatory practices in the housing and labor markets and by lending institutions. Now, even 40 years after these practices were ruled illegal, many African-Americans continue to be segregated in ghettos, particularly in the older cities of the industrial belt. The distinctions between voluntary and involuntary segregation are, however, more difficult to make. At other times in U.S. history, involuntary discrimination combined with the natural proclivities of immigrant groups to live together to form communities of Irish immigrants in Boston, Appalachian migrants in Chicago, and Puerto Ricans in New York.

The greater the degree of segregation of a particular group from the larger population, the greater the **social distance** between them. Social distance measures the likelihood that dissimilar groups will interact with one another or, in the case of racial and ethnic segregation, whether the minority group will be accepted and assimilated into the majority population.

Various dimensions of residential segregation, including evenness, concentration, and centralization, are measured by **segregation indices**. One such index, the *index of dissimilarity*, considers how the geographic distribution of a group compares to the distribution of a second reference group. This segregation index has values that range from 0 in cases of complete integration to 1.0 in cases of complete segregation. A value of 0.5 indicates that 50 percent of the particular group being studied would need to change their residences for the group to be distributed like the other group. Segregation indices calculated from census data tell us that African-Americans are the most segregated ethnic group, followed by Hispanics, Asians, and Native Americans (Table 12.1).

African-Americans are the most highly segregated, but their index declined dramatically due to the rise of their middle class, suburbanization of the nation's African-American population, and antidiscrimination legislation and programs (see Chapter 1). Levels of segregation among Asians and Hispanics, although lower than for African-Americans, remained constant due to large-scale immigration from Asia and Latin America. Meanwhile, those Native Americans living in large cities (not on reservations) congregate less than do the other ethnic groups.

Although residential segregation is often associated with city life, it also occurs at the larger regional scale. Spatial identity is a key feature in the rise of ethnic nationalism discussed in Chapter 13. Various groups (the Basques in Spain;

TABLE 12.1 **Segregation Indices in U.S. Metropolitan Areas at the Census Tract Level, by Ethnicity**

	1980	1990	2000
Native Americans	0.373	0.368	0.333
Asians	0.405	0.412	0.411
African-Americans	0.727	0.679	0.640
Hispanics	0.502	0.500	0.509

In these examples, the "other" group in each calculation are non-Asians, non-Hispanics, etc.

Source: U.S. Census Bureau, Housing and Household Economics Statistics Division. 2002. *Racial and Ethnic Residential Segregation in the United States: 1980–2000.* Washington, DC: www.census.gov/hhes/www/housing/resseg/pdftoc.html.

Chechens in Russia; Kurds in Iraq, Iran, and Turkey; and the Croats, Serbs, and Muslims in the former Yugoslavia) have attempted to enhance their ethnic identity through spatial isolation and residential segregation. Yugoslavia introduced the world to the term **ethnic cleansing**, a euphemism for genocide, house burnings, and forced migration for the purpose of achieving 100 percent residential segregation along ethnic lines. Sometimes groups do the opposite and use **integration** as a political weapon. In Israel, right-wing Jews have sought to build settlements in the Palestinian-dominated West Bank region to prevent Israeli leaders from giving the land to an independent Palestinian state. In this case, the segregation/integration varies by scale. At the local scale the settlements are nearly 100 percent Jewish, but at the regional scale the new Jewish settlements are purposely interspersed with the ancient Palestinian villages.

Until 1993, the white regime in South Africa practiced enforced segregation through a system of **apartheid**. In fact, the word *apartheid* means "separateness" in the Afrikaner language. Under apartheid, whites, "coloureds" (persons of mixed races), and Indians were restricted to certain urban neighborhoods. The white regime established ten homelands for different African peoples and argued that the homelands were, in effect, independent countries. As residents of separate countries, blacks were not seen as citizens of South Africa, and so-called pass laws regulated their movements.

This chapter asks you to evaluate residential segregation along religious lines at the regional scale in Northern Ireland. Religion is the distinguishing feature of the social, political, and economic life. Are Catholics and Protestants integrating into religiously mixed residential environments, or are they becoming more isolated over time? What does this change in residential segregation mean in regard to the search for a permanent solution to the violence and bloodshed that have dominated the country's recent history?

▶ *CASE STUDY*

DO ORANGE AND GREEN CLASH?

GOAL

To examine the changing residential segregation of Catholics and Protestants in Northern Ireland using a series of choropleth maps and **segregation indices** for 1971, 1991, and 2011.

LEARNING OUTCOMES

After completing the chapter, you will be able to:

- Compute an index of residential segregation.
- Use spreadsheet functions.
- Make choropleth maps using a GIS.
- Examine the geographical consequences of ethnic political turmoil.

SPECIAL MATERIALS NEEDED

- Computer with high-speed Internet access and a recent release of a Web browser. If using the Student Companion Site with the printed book, click on *Tech Support* for system requirements and technical support. (If using the e-book in WileyPlus, click on *Help* for details about the system requirements.)

BACKGROUND

Northern Ireland is a land with a long history of political turmoil. Although located on the same island as the independent country of Ireland, it is part of the United Kingdom of Great Britain and Northern Ireland (or United Kingdom [UK]), which also includes England, Scotland, and Wales. Today the population of 1.69 million, with a 2004 per capita gross domestic product of $23,690, is divided mainly between Catholics (about 44 percent of the population), who are mainly ethnic Irish, and Protestants (about 53 percent), who are predominantly ethnic Scots.

St. Patrick introduced Christianity to Ireland in the fifth century A.D. When the western Christian Church split during the Reformation in the early 1500s, the Irish remained overwhelmingly Catholic while the British became Protestants. Ireland at the time was divided into several local fiefdoms, each dominated by an aristocratic family. Although the British controlled only a small portion of Ireland around Dublin, many people had already given up the Irish language for English, which had been brought to Ireland by earlier English and Norman conquerors. The English monarchs, who had already consolidated British local fiefdoms under a single national government, saw several benefits to a final conquest of Ireland. It would add to their power, spread Protestantism, protect their "back door" from French and Spanish rivals on the continent (who also happened to be Catholic), and, not incidentally, provide a tidy profit to the British crown. In the northern part of Ireland known as Ulster, the O'Neill and O'Donnell ruling families had long resisted British efforts to control them and modify their traditional social system. The turning point came when the British defeated a combined Spanish-Ulster force in the battle of Kinsale in 1601 and shortly thereafter subdued the northern region (Figure 12.4).

As the British consolidated their control over the various parts of Ireland during the sixteenth and seventeenth centuries, they used a **plantation system** to alter the ethnic composition of entire regions. These are not plantations in the sense of a commercial farm like a coffee plantation, but deliberate, government-sponsored campaigns to "plant" pioneers loyal to the British Crown. Land was forcibly taken from the local Irish aristocracy, many of whom were forced into exile or killed, and given to British aristocrats, military officers, and others whom the king wished to reward. By 1700, less than 1 percent of Irish land was still in Irish Catholic hands.

The key to understanding why today's religious discord is concentrated in the northern part of the island is the difference between the Ulster Plantation and the other plantations (Figure 12.4). In three-quarters of the island, the plantations did not significantly alter the ethnic composition of the population, which remained predominantly Irish Catholic. The British colonizers mainly consisted of a few wealthy Protestant landowners whose land was farmed by local Irish Catholic **tenant farmers** and landless laborers.

Because Ulster had a history of rebelliousness, however, the British government imported large numbers of Scottish and English Protestants as the primary tenant farmers. Irish Catholics who remained in Ulster mainly worked as landless farm laborers or as tenant farmers on infertile farmland. The Ulster Plantation was an efficient and profitable way to control this rebellious territory because the Protestant "plantees," some of whom were former soldiers, would not only help defend their new land but also pay rent to the British Crown. Over the ensuing centuries, an entirely new Protestant social structure gradually took root in Northern Ireland, ranging from a landholding and industrial elite through a middle class of prosperous farmers to a working class of craftsmen, clerks, and laborers.

Fast forward to the twentieth century. After centuries of British control and Irish resistance to foreign domination, the southern three-quarters of Ireland gained its independence in 1921 as the Irish Free State (changed to the Republic of Ireland in 1949). Northern Ireland, however, remained part of the United Kingdom.

Political violence has plagued Northern Ireland since 1921. Catholics in Northern Ireland (descendants of the Irish tenants of the native aristocracy) resent their exclusion from independent Ireland, foreign domination by the United Kingdom, the loss of their ancestral lands, their lower economic status, and discrimination against them in jobs and local government housing. Protestants are a majority in Northern Ireland; they retain a strong British identity and resist the prospect of becoming a minority in a united Ireland dominated by Catholics. Since about 1969, Northern Ireland has been troubled by terrorist acts and political killings by both sides (Figure 12.5). The extreme Irish nationalist group calling itself the Irish Republican Army (IRA) rekindled a guerilla war against British institutions; paramilitary Protestant groups promoting the

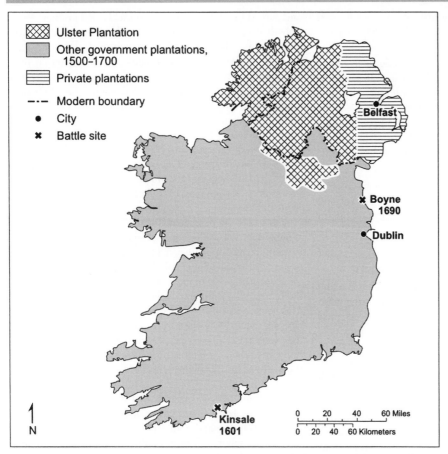

Figure 12.4 The current province of Northern Ireland includes most of the original Ulster Plantation sponsored by the British Crown plus some areas of private colonization, especially around the now capital city of Belfast.

Figure 12.5 The "car bomb" was a weapon of choice by the Irish Republican Army against British soldiers.

"unionist" cause (union with Britain) have responded in kind. An estimated 3,000 people have died in the conflict, including many innocent bystanders.

A 1994 cease-fire agreement led to a breaking of the impasse in 1998, with the help of some deft diplomacy by U.S. President Bill Clinton. To bring both sides to the negotiating table, Clinton convinced the British to admit that the Northern Ireland Troubles were not strictly an internal British matter and convinced the Irish nationalist political group, Sinn Féin ("We Ourselves"), that its hopes of reclaiming Northern Ireland were futile as long as it had a pro-British Protestant majority. Once in negotiations, Sinn Féin and the government of Ireland recognized British sovereignty over Northern Ireland in exchange for a dramatic increase in Irish Catholic political power. Details of the historic 1998 "Good Friday Agreement" reveal how difficult it was to forge a compromise:

1. Elections must be held at least once every seven years on whether the majority in Northern Ireland desires to stay part of the United Kingdom.

2. A 108-member elected Northern Ireland Assembly will control education and other local affairs. To ensure that the Protestant Unionist majority does not steamroll

© 2010 John Wiley & Sons, Inc.

▶ *CASE STUDY (continued)*

the Catholic Nationalist minority, votes will be decided on the basis of "minority veto" rather than "majority rule" (i.e., both sides must agree).

3. Assembly members must pledge to do their jobs in good faith but are not required to swear allegiance to the Queen of England, and the British Union flag will not fly over the Parliament Building.

4. Ireland changed its constitution to remove its claim of sovereignty over the entire island but will have some say in how things are run in the North through a North-South Ministerial Council.

5. The British government agreed in principle to give policing and judicial authority to local agencies and eliminate the traditional dominance of Protestants in the police force.

Unfortunately, the peace process has not gone smoothly in the wake of the Good Friday Agreement of 1998. Reforms moved slowly, with significant numbers of Protestants feeling that change was coming too quickly and Catholics frustrated at the government's unwillingness to seriously address their grievances. Moreover, Catholics came to believe that the idea of a shared state was not genuinely accepted by Protestants but a grudging concession offered in the face of mounting pressure by British, Irish, and U.S. public opinion. Protestants, in turn, came to question whether Catholics were sincere about giving up their weapons, a process called *decommissioning*.

Alas, the power-sharing government of Belfast collapsed in October 2002, and the British retook control. Violence continued with Protestants complaining they were "airbrushed" out of the negotiating process and the IRA unwilling to stand down in the face of Protestant paramilitarism. Recently, unclassified British documents from 1972 revealed a secret British proposal to deport all Catholics from Northern Ireland in a policy of "ethnic cleansing" (see Chapter 13). Although the plan was never implemented, the fact that it was even considered cast a shadow of distrust over the region.

More recently, the peace process may be back on track. In July 2005, the Irish Republican Army announced that it would resume disarmament and ordered its members to end the armed campaign to overthrow British rule. Calling for change through peaceful democratic means, the IRA move left "no possible excuse" for not implementing the Good Friday Agreement.

The St. Andrew's Agreement in October 2006 set out a time-table for power sharing, and elections for the Representative Assembly were held in 2007. The elections, while successful, saw the demise of more moderate parties and gains for the more hard-line republican (Catholic) and unionist (Protestant) parties. The new Assembly, and the executive body chosen to lead Northern Ireland, had approximately a 7:5 ratio of Protestants to Catholics, with strong Protestant support in the eastern counties and Catholic support in the western counties. In spite of the longstanding differences, the new leadership made many conciliatory gestures, and even some of the most ardent opponents in the long struggle met together in public

and agreed to work in a spirit of mutual collaboration. While nobody expects progress to be smooth, at least the open violence and hostility appears to have subsided.

Both Catholics and Protestants sponsor fraternal organizations to promote their group identities. Working-class Protestants join the Orange Order, named for William of Orange, the English king who consolidated Protestantism in Great Britain in the 1690s (Figure 12.6). Green, on the other hand, was the color the Catholic Irish adopted, in recognition of their ancestral homeland on the Emerald Isle. The Republic of Ireland flag—three vertical stripes of green, white, and orange—is a symbolic gesture of the hope that Protestants (orange) and Catholics (green) can live in neutral (white) harmony.

The exact percentage of Catholics in Northern Ireland is subject to intense debate because, in the 2001 census, 14 percent of the population said they had no religion or refused to answer the question. Catholics who revealed their religion made up 40 percent of the total population. Of the people who did indicate their religion, however, 47 percent were Catholic. The census also estimated the "community background" of citizens, which was their religion or the religion in which they were raised. Using this measure, the census indicated 44 percent Catholic, which is the figure we used at the start of this section. In short, 40, 44, and 47 percent are all correct in different ways.

One thing that is certain is that the number of Catholics in Northern Ireland has grown faster than the number of Protestants in recent decades. Historically, Catholic birth rates have been higher, and Protestants have emigrated at a faster rate in search of better economic opportunities (see Chapter 4). The Catholic percentage has risen from 33 percent in 1937 to 38 percent in 1981 to around 44 percent in 2001. It has long been assumed that the higher Catholic birth rate would eventually lead to Catholics surpassing Protestants in Northern Ireland, which could lead to a majority favoring reunification with Ireland. While the Catholic birth rate recently has been

Figure 12.6 Orangemen march in Portadown to commemorate the Battle of Boyne in 1690 when William of Orange, King of England, dealt the final crushing blow to the Irish resistors.

▶ CASE STUDY (continued)

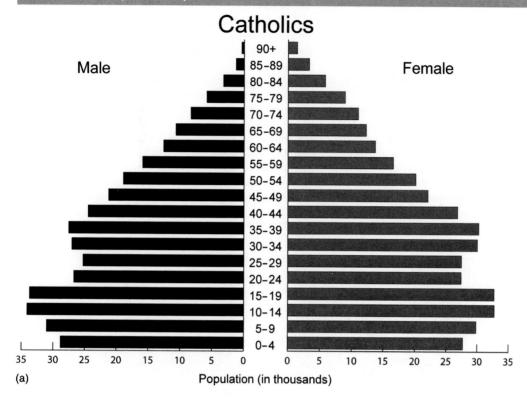

(a)

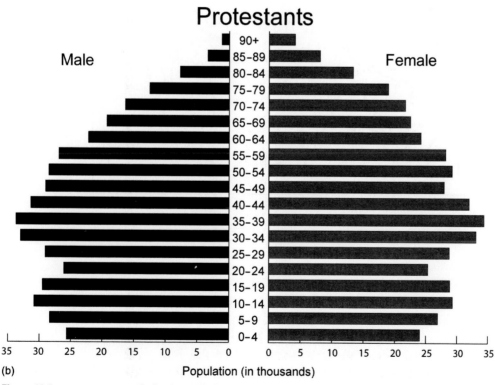

(b)

Figure 12.7 Age-sex pyramids for (a) Catholics and (b) Protestants in Northern Ireland. You can see that the upper half of the graph for the Catholics is the classic pyramid shape and the base is large, indicating a younger population overall, whereas the largest bars for the Protestant pyramid are between the ages of 30 and 45, and the higher number of elderly people give the top of the graph a rounded "beehive" shape rather than that of a steeply-sloping pyramid.

© 2010 John Wiley & Sons, Inc.

converging toward the Protestant rate, there is demographic momentum (see Chapter 5) on the Catholic side (Figure 12.7). The Protestant population is older, and Catholics outnumber Protestants from ages 0 to 25. Whether Catholics will eventually become the majority—and if so, when—remains an open question.

How has the political turmoil in Northern Ireland affected the settlement patterns of Catholics and Protestants? From the beginning of the plantation system, Protestants have outnumbered Catholics in the better farmlands of the eastern zone, while Catholics outnumber Protestants in the upland, rockier west. But even within the cities, the two groups tend to reside in separate neighborhoods, especially in working-class areas. Protestants have dominated the public school system,

while Catholic children largely attend state-supported church schools. Protestants typically dominate in manufacturing and government jobs, and Catholics dominate in port and construction work.

In Activity 2, you will measure residential separation of Protestants from Catholics with a numerical segregation index, which takes into account the ethnic percentages across the 26 governmental districts in Northern Ireland (Figure 12.8). You will examine how the residential geography has changed over time and predict how it will likely change in the future. **Spatial divergence** occurs if the two groups become spatially more segregated. **Spatial convergence** occurs if they become spatially more integrated. Which way do you think things are headed?

Figure 12.8 Northern Ireland local government districts.

Name: _____   Instructor: _____

Do Orange and Green Clash? Residential Segregation in Northern Ireland

▶ ACTIVITY 1: MAPPING RELIGIOUS AFFILIATION

A. To start your activity, click on the *Student Companion Site* at www.wiley .com/college/kuby. (For students using WileyPlus, log on to your class Web site, select the *Assignment* tab, locate and click on this assignment, and follow all instructions.)

B. Select this chapter from the drop-down list and then click on *Computerized Chapter Activities*.

C. Click on *Activity 1: Mapping Religious Affiliation*.

D. On the screen you see a choropleth map of the percentage of Catholics in Northern Ireland for local government districts in 1971. Try moving your mouse over the districts on the map: The percent Catholic will be displayed for the district at which you are pointing.

E. Like maps in Chapters 1 and 4, this one is an interactive choropleth map that allows you to change the number of classes and the break points between classes. For this exercise, you will assign the same class limits for each year—1971, 1991, and 2011—using the editable break-point boxes. The default map is set to six *Equal Interval* classes, with 16.7 percentage points per class. You must change the number of classes to five and interactively define the class limits. In the editable boxes, enter these class break points from top to bottom:

      Break point 1: 12

      Break point 2: 33

      Break point 3: 57

      Break point 4: 65

Select one of the six *Color Schemes* at the bottom of the screen so that a logical progression of colors or shades depicts the trend from high-percent Catholic to low-percent Catholic. Don't just pick a random selection of colors.

F. Look at the graphic array to the left of your map. This graph shows the distribution of data on the x-axis, in this case the percent Catholic for each district, from lowest value to highest value. The y-axis is the rank of local government districts from highest to lowest percent Catholic. The vertical bars show your class break points in this distribution. You can see that the class break points now match those you just typed, and the shading patterns between the bars match those of the map. You can scroll over the dots in the graphic array to see the name and exact percent Catholic of the district each dot represents.

G. Click the *Print* button so you can hand in the 1971 map. Check how well the color scheme you chose converts to black and white (those with color

© **2010 John Wiley & Sons, Inc.**

printers, of course, need not worry about this). Be sure all classes are easily distinguishable on your printed map. You can go back and change your color scheme after viewing the printed map.

H. Now repeat the process for 1991. Click on *Northern Ireland 1991* in the upper-right margin, set the identical class break points, and print. Repeat for *Northern Ireland 2011*. You will print a total of three maps. *You must use the same class break points for all three maps!*

1.1. In which part of Northern Ireland (e.g., near the capital of Belfast, along the Irish border, in the north) is the percent Catholic expected to grow most rapidly between 1971 and 2011?

1.2. In which part of Northern Ireland is the percent Catholic expected to decrease most rapidly between 1971 and 2011?

1.3. Add together the number of districts that are in the lowest class and the highest class for each year. Look for the number of districts in these categories on the activity map legend. How many districts fall into the combined top and bottom classes for each year?

	1971	1991	2011
Lowest category			
Highest category			
Total (add numbers from lowest and highest category)			

1.4. Does the presence of a larger number of districts in the extreme categories represent greater spatial convergence or divergence?

I. When you have finished the activity, proceed to *Activity 2* or close all browser windows.

Name: _____ Instructor: _____

Do Orange and Green Clash?
Residential Segregation in Northern Ireland

► ACTIVITY 2: INDEX OF SEGREGATION

Calculate an index of segregation for 1971, 1991, and 2011. The index of segregation is:

$$S = 0.5 * \sum_{i=1}^{n} \left| \frac{x_i}{X} - \frac{y_i}{Y} \right|$$

where:

S = segregation index

x_i = number of Catholics in district i

X = number of Catholics in all of Northern Ireland

y_i = number of non-Catholics in district i

Y = number of non-Catholics in all of Northern Ireland

n = number of districts

For those unfamiliar with the mathematical notation, the two vertical bars signify absolute value. The absolute value of a number is its magnitude regardless of sign (i.e., its distance from zero on the number line). The absolute value of any positive number is the number itself (e.g., |3.4| = 3.4). The absolute value of any negative number is the positive of that number (e.g., |−3.4| = 3.4).

The asterisk (*) means multiply.

The Σ is the *summation sign*. It should be read as "the summation from i equals 1 to n" of whatever is to the right of the symbol. In this case, it tells you to do the absolute value calculation for the first district ($i = 1$), add to that the absolute value calculation for the second district ($i = 2$), and so on until the nth district ($i = n$). Without the summation sign, we would have to write it this way:

$$S = 0.5 * \left[\left| \frac{x_1}{X} - \frac{y_1}{Y} \right| + \left| \frac{x_2}{X} - \frac{y_2}{Y} \right| + \cdots + \left| \frac{x_n}{X} - \frac{y_n}{Y} \right| \right]$$

The index of segregation has a minimum value of zero, meaning the ethnic group is distributed evenly throughout the region. Larger numbers (with a maximum value of 1.0) signify higher levels of segregation. The exact meaning of the segregation index is the proportion of the ethnic group's population that must relocate to achieve a perfectly integrated distribution of the group. Thus, a segregation index of 0.25 would mean that 25% of the group would have to relocate to be evenly distributed across all zones.

Now that we known *what* the formula is saying, let's try to understand *how* it works. Tables 12.2 through 12.4 show spreadsheets for calculating the segregation index just like those you will calculate in this activity, but with fewer rows. Each of the three spreadsheets is for a hypothetical region with 100,000 Catholics (ethnic group X) and 500,000 non-Catholics (group Y) spread over three districts.

TABLE 12.2 A Three-District Example

District$_i$	x_i	y_i	x_i/X	y_i/Y	$x_i/X - y_i/Y$	$|x_i/X - y_i/Y|$
1	50,000	350,000	0.5	0.7	−0.2	0.2
2	30,000	100,000	0.3	0.2	0.1	0.1
3	20,000	50,000	0.2	0.1	0.1	0.1

$X = 100,000 \qquad Y = 500,000$

0.4 Sum
0.2 Index

Let's begin with Table 12.2, a region with mild segregation. Look at the first row, which calculates $|x_1/X - y_1/Y|$. The first part of this term, x_1/X, is the fraction of the total Catholic population that lives in district 1. District 1 contains 50,000 Catholics out of 100,000 total Catholics in the whole country, so $x_1/X = 0.5$. The second term, y_1/Y, is the fraction of the non-Catholic population in district 1, which is 350,000/500,000, or 0.7. The difference between these two decimal fractions, $x_1/X - y_1/Y$, is equal to $0.5 - 0.7$, or -0.2. In other words, district 1 contains 50 percent of the country's Catholics but 70 percent of its non-Catholics, so you could say there's a "Catholic deficit" of 20 percent, signified by the -0.2 value. Likewise, districts 2 and 3 have Catholic "surpluses" of $+0.1$.

Why does the formula use absolute values? Notice that the three values in the $x_i/X - y_i/Y$ column add up to 0. This is no coincidence: it will always be the case. A surplus of an ethnic group in some districts is always canceled out by offsetting deficits of that group in other districts. By taking the absolute values of the differences, this canceling effect is avoided. You can think of the absolute value as measuring just the *size* of the difference; in other words, how far is the district from having equal percentages of both groups? In Table 12.2, adding all the $|x_i/X - y_i/Y|$s for all three rows yields a sum of 0.4. This is the sum of the sizes of the percentage differences for all three districts. The final segregation index is exactly half of that value, or 0.2.

Why is the final summation multiplied by 0.5 in the formula? The reason can be seen in Table 12.3. an example of complete segregation. All the Xs (Catholics) live in district 3, and none of the Ys (non-Catholics). Therefore,

$$\left| \frac{x_3}{X} - \frac{y_3}{Y} \right| \text{ equals } \left| \frac{100,000}{100,000} - \frac{0}{500,000} \right|,$$

or $|1 - 0| = 1$. Likewise, in districts 1 and 2, which contain 100 percent of the non-Catholics and 0 percent of the Catholics, the absolute differences of 0.4 and

0.6 also add up to 1. In a completely segregated country such as this, the sum of the absolute differences will always add up to 2. Therefore, to create an index with a scale from 0 to 1 instead of from 0 to 2, the sum is multiplied by 0.5.

TABLE 12.3   A Completely Segregated Example

$District_i$	x_i	y_i	x_i/X	y_i/Y	$x_i/X - y_i/Y$	$|x_i/X - y_i/Y|$
1	—	200,000	0	0.4	−0.4	0.4
2	—	300,000	0	0.6	−0.6	0.6
3	100,000	—	1	0	1	1
	$X = 100,000$	$Y = 500,000$				2 Sum
						1 Index

Finally, Table 12.4 shows the opposite extreme of complete integration of the two ethnic groups. In this case, equal percentages of Catholics and non-Catholics in each district yield a segregation index of 0.

TABLE 12.4   An Example in Which Both Groups have Identical Distributions

$District_i$	x_i	yi	x_i/X	y_i/Y	$x_i/X - y_i/Y$	$|x_i/X - y_i/Y|$
1	70,000	350,000	0.7	0.7	0	0
2	20,000	100,000	0.2	0.2	0	0
3	10,000	50,000	0.1	0.1	0	0
	$X = 100,000$	$Y = 500,000$				0 Sum
						0 Index

Use the spreadsheets for 1971, 1991, and 2011 to calculate the index of segregation for each year.

A. To start your activity, click on the *Student Companion Site* at www.wiley.com/college/kuby. (For students using WileyPlus, log on to your class Web site, select the *Assignment* tab, locate and click on this assignment, and follow all instructions.)

B. Select this chapter from the drop-down list and then click on *Computerized Chapter Activities*.

C. Click on *Activity 2: Index of Segregation*.

You will see a spreadsheet for 1971 with all the information you need. You will calculate the 1971 index first. The columns are as follows:

Column A: *District_i*   The name of the local government district.

Column B: x_i The number of Catholics in each local government district.

Column C: y_i The number of non-Catholics in each local government district.

Column D: x_i/X — The number of Catholics in District i divided by the total number of Catholics in Northern Ireland.

Column E: y_i/Y — The number of non-Catholics in District i divided by the total number of non-Catholics in Northern Ireland.

Column F: $x_i/X - y_i/Y$ — The difference between the Northern Ireland percentages of Catholics and non-Catholics in each local government district. This is a preliminary step in calculating the segregation index.

Column G: $|x_i/X - y_i/Y|$ — The absolute value of the previous column.

In a spreadsheet, each value is referenced according to the cell in which it is located. The letter of the column and the number of the row identify a cell. For instance, the number of Catholics in Antrim is in cell B2. The spreadsheet software will calculate values much like a calculator does if you tell it what formula to use and which cells to use in the formula.

D. Your first step is to divide the number of Catholics in the first district (x_{Antrim}) by the total number of Catholics in Northern Ireland (X). The total number of Catholics is in cell B28, at the bottom of Column B below the individual district values. You can scroll down the spreadsheet to find cell B28 by using the scroll bar on the right-hand side of the spreadsheet. For your convenience, the value of X for 1971 is also listed at the top of the screen as 558,800.

Click in cell D2, the first empty cell where you must calculate x_i/X. Type in the following formula:

$$= B2/558800$$

The $=$ is a code that tells the spreadsheet that you are entering a formula, not a number. This formula tells the software to divide cell B2 by 558800. An alternative to typing this formula using the keyboard is to use the formula buttons at the top right. Click the $=$ button, type B2, click the $\div$ button, and then type in 558800. Whichever way you enter the formula into the cell, if you did so correctly, the *Copy* button in the upper left will be highlighted. You have now calculated your first value. The answer will appear in the cell itself.

If you make a mistake, this message will appear: *The formula you have entered is incorrect. Try again.* Click *OK* and then return to the cell and edit or reenter the formula, following our instructions exactly. If you ever wish to restart the spreadsheet completely, go to the *View* menu and select *Refresh*.

E. Copy this formula to the entire Column D. First, click on *Copy* in the upper left. This copies the formula from cell D2 into a buffer that the computer remembers. Second, click on the *Column D* header to highlight the entire column. Third, click on the word *Paste* in the upper left. The computer has now copied the formula from cell D2 into each of the cells below it and has modified each formula to divide the B-column cells immediately to the left rather than always dividing cell B2.

F. Divide the number of non-Catholics per district by the total number of non-Catholics, much like you did in Step D for Catholics. For all of Northern Ireland, Y, the total of non-Catholics in 1971 was 960,300, which can be found in cell C28 or at the top of the screen. Click on cell E2 and type:

$$= C2/960300$$

Follow the *Copy* and *Paste* commands from Step E to copy this formula into Column E. All cell locations are updated when you paste the formula to the new cells.

G. Now you need to subtract the non-Catholic ratios from the Catholic ratios. Click on cell F2 and type:

$$= D2-E2$$

Copy this formula and *paste* it into all the cells for Column F.

H. Next, you must take the absolute value of each cell. The spreadsheet has a built-in function that converts a cell to absolute value. It is calculated by the operator *Abs*. Therefore, click on cell *G2*, and use the buttons and/or the keyboard to create the equation:

$$= Abs(F2)$$

Copy this formula and *paste* it into all the cells for Column G.

I. You now have the values you need to calculate S, the segregation index. Click on cell G28, just below the last column of values. You need to sum, or add up, all values in this column according to the formula. We will again use a spreadsheet function, this time the button Σ. Scroll down to row 28. Click on cell G28. You will now replace the formula you just inadvertently put there when you copied G2 and pasted it into the entire Column G. Press the = button, then the Σ button, and then type (G2: G27). Your formula should look like this:

$$= SUM(G2:G27)$$

This command sums all values from cell G2 through cell G27.

J. As the formula indicates, the one final step is to multiply this value by 0.5. Click on cell G29, and type the following exactly as it appears.

$$= G28 * 0.5$$

The value in G29 is the segregation index S for the year 1971. If done correctly, you will receive a congratulatory message on the screen that says you have completed this spreadsheet. Click *OK* and then click on *Print* in the right margin.

K. You must now repeat the preceding steps to calculate S for 1991 and 2011. Click on the year in the right margin and fill out each spreadsheet. Remember to substitute the 1991 and 2011 totals of Catholics and non-Catholics for the 558800 and 960300 figures, which applied only to 1971. The later values of X and Y can be found in cells B28 and C28 of each spreadsheet or at the top of the screen. Print out and hand in a completed spreadsheet for each year.

The index of segregation has a minimum value of zero, meaning Catholics would be distributed evenly throughout the Northern Ireland population. Larger numbers (with a maximum value of 1.0) would signify higher levels of segregation as Catholics and non-Catholics diverge spatially. The segregation index is the proportion of the Catholic population that must relocate to achieve a perfectly integrated distribution of Catholics and non-Catholics.

2.1. List your indices here:

1971	_____
1991	_____
2011	_____

2.2. Are Catholics becoming more or less segregated with respect to non-Catholics in Northern Ireland?

2.3. Describe how both the map patterns and the segregation indices show changes in segregation over time.

2.4. What are the long-term consequences of these changes in residential patterns? How do you think these changes could affect issues of religious tolerance, cultural pluralism (an acceptance of multiple cultures living together), and future negotiations for political change?

L. When you have finished, close all browser windows.

▶ DEFINITIONS OF KEY TERMS

Apartheid A system of forced segregation between races in South Africa in effect until 1993.

Enclave Residential clusters that result from voluntary segregation.

Ethnic Cleansing Forced residential segregation along ethnic lines.

Ghetto An urban area where, due to discrimination, ethnic segregation is largely involuntary.

Integration The residential mixing of subgroups within the larger population.

Plantation System An organized system of colonization used by the British government in the 1500s and 1600s to "plant" British colonists on Irish land.

Residential Segregation The residential separation of subgroups within the larger population.

Segregation Index A numerical measure of the degree of separation of two or more distinct groups.

Social Distance A measure of the likelihood that dissimilar groups will interact in society. Influences the degree of assimilation for minority groups.

Spatial Convergence Increased integration over time.

Spatial Divergence Increased segregation over time.

Tenant Farmer A farmer who rents land to farm. Although tenant farmers often live in debt to the landowner, they are considered more fortunate than landless laborers, who neither own nor rent their own land.

▶ FURTHER READINGS

Alba, Richard, and Victor Nee. 1997. Rethinking Assimilation Theory for a New Era of Immigration. *International Migration Review* 31:826–874.

Allen, James Paul, and Eugene James Turner. 1988. *We the People: An Atlas of America's Ethnic Diversity*. New York: Macmillan.

Anderson, K. J. 1987. The Idea of Chinatown: The Power of Place and Institutional Practice in the Making of a Racial Category. *Annals of the Association of American Geographers* 77(4):580–598.

Boal, F. W. 1976. Ethnic Residential Segregation. In *Social Areas in Cities, vol. 1*, D. Herbert and R. Johnston (eds.). New York: Wiley.

Cherny, R. W. 1994. Patterns of Tolerance and Discrimination in San Francisco: The Civil War to World War I. *California History* 73:130–141.

Clark, William A. V. 1998. *The California Cauldron: Immigration and the Fortunes of Local Communities*. New York: Guilford.

Doumitt, Donald P. 1985. *Conflict in Northern Ireland: The History, the Problem, and the Challenge*. New York: P. Lang.

Driedger, Leo (ed.). 1978. *The Canadian Ethnic Mosaic: A Quest for Identity, vol. 6*. Toronto: McClelland and Stewart.

Graham, D. T. 1994. Socio-Demographic Trends in Northern Ireland, 1971 to 1991. *Scottish Geographical Magazine* 110(3):168–176.

Lee, Trevor R. 1977. *Race and Residence: The Concentration and Dispersal of Immigrants in London*. Oxford: Clarendon Press.

Massey, Douglas S., and Nancy A. Denton. 1993. *American Apartheid: Segregation and the Making of the Underclass*. Cambridge: Harvard University Press.

Murtagh, B. 2002. *The Politics of Territory: Policy and Segregation in Northern Ireland*. London: Palgrave.

Roseman, Curtis C., Gunther Thieme, and Hans Dieter Laux (eds.). 1995. *Ethnicity: Geographic Perspectives on Ethnic Change in Modern Cities*. Lanham, MD: Rowman & Littlefield.

Ruble, Blair A. 2006. Mélange Cities. *The Wilson Quarterly* (summer): 43–68.

Shuttleworth I.G., and C.D Lloyd. 2009. Are Northern Ireland's communities dividing? Evidence from geographically consistent Census of Population data, 1971–2001. *Environment and Planning A* 41(1):213–229.

Van Kempen, Ronald, and A. Sule Ozuekren. 1998. Ethnic Segregation in Cities: New Forms and Explanations in a Dynamic World. *Urban Studies* 35:1631–1656.

Wong, D.W.S. 2003. Implementing spatial segregation measures in GIS. *Computers, Environment and Urban Systems* 27:53–70.

▶ WEB RESOURCES

Conflict Archive on the Internet: *Northern Ireland*: cain.ulst.ac.uk
Democratic Unionists Party: www.dup.org.uk
Fianna Fáil. *Fianna Fáil: The Republican Party*: www.fiannafail.ie
Irish Times. *Ireland.com*: www.ireland.com

Loyalist and Orange Information Services: www.lois.itgo.com/main.html
Northern Ireland Office: www.nio.gov.uk
Northern Ireland Statistics and Research Agency: www.nisra.gov.uk
Orangenet: www.orangenet.org
Sinn Féin: www.sinnfein.ie
UCLA Civil Rights Project. *State of Segregation Fact Sheet*: www.civilrightsproject.ucla.edu/policy/stateofsegregation.pdf
Ulster Unionists Party: www.uup.org
University of Ulster. www.ulst.ac.uk
U.S. Census Bureau. *Housing Patterns—Racial and Ethnic Segregation in the United States: 1980–2000*: www.census.gov/hhes/www/housing/housing_patterns/housing_patterns.html

► ITEMS TO HAND IN

Activity 1: • The three choropleth maps of percentage of Catholics
      • Questions 1.1–1.4, or answer all questions your instructor created in your WileyPlus assignments.
Activity 2: • The three completed spreadsheets
      • Questions 2.1–2.4, or answer all questions your instructor created in your WileyPlus assignments.

CHAPTER 13

Breaking Up Is Hard to Do: Nations, States, and Nation-States

▶ INTRODUCTION

The *political geography* of nations and states can explain most of the wars, civil wars, breakups, and mergers that dominated the international news at the end of the last millennium and start of the new one. Some 20 to 30 countries were engaged in active conflicts in 2008, yet they make headlines in the United States only when they boil over into horrific bloodshed—as in Sudan or the Congo—or when they involve familiar countries such as Iraq, Russia, Israel, and Ireland. Many new countries have emerged as the former Yugoslavia, Czechoslovakia, and the Soviet Union fragmented into pieces. Closer to home, French-speaking Québec narrowly defeated referendums on peacefully separating from English-speaking Canada, but the issue just won't go away. East and West Germany went in the opposite direction, dissolving the boundary between them and merging back into one country in 1990. Political realignments and so-called small wars (as opposed to wars between superpowers and their smaller allies) became more prevalent after the end of the Cold War. With communism's collapse, rivalry between superpowers no longer kept the lid on simmering ethnic feuds.

To understand political events such as these, you need the proper terms. Before you can learn these terms, however, you must first *un*learn them. Political geographers use the terms *nation, state,* and *nation-state* differently than most Americans do. For instance, Americans use *state* to describe each of the 50 federal subregions of the United States and use *nation* or *nation-state* to refer to the whole United States and to Canada. To a political geographer, however, a **state** refers to an independent, bounded, and internationally recognized territory with full sovereignty over the land and people within it—in other words, a country. In some cases, saying exactly when a political territory becomes fully independent and sovereign can be difficult. For instance, in 1949, the Chinese Communist Party, led by Mao Zedong, overthrew the ruling Nationalist Party, which fled to the island of Taiwan. They then declared Taiwan to be an independent state called Republic of China, but the mainland People's Republic of China still considers Taiwan to be a breakaway part of its own country. Equally ambiguous is determining when the United States went from being a **colony** of Britain to a state: on July 4, 1776, when the Declaration of Independence was signed, or in 1789 after defeating the British, ratifying the Constitution, and electing the first president?

While a state is a political unit, a **nation** is a cultural unit, a group of people with a common ancestry—regardless of whether the group controls its own country.

The root of the word *nation* comes from the Latin *natio*, meaning "birth, nation, race, species, or breed." It connotes blood ties between people. A nation is the largest such grouping of people, which distinguishes it from a family, clan, or tribe. Nations see themselves as a cohesive group and as distinct from other groups. Most nations share a common religion, a common language, and accepted social ways of behavior that give it a common culture. These common cultural traits act as a glue to unite people within a nation and as a barrier to divide them from other nations. Not all people in the nation need to have the same language, religion, and biological ancestry as long as they come to believe in the myth of their common ancestry. The Greeks, for instance, hold to the view that they are the direct descendants of peoples of the ancient Greek city-states even though a massive influx of Slavs beginning in the sixth century so overwhelmed the native Greek population that Greece in the Middle Ages was referred to as *Slavinia (Slavland)*.

Now we know *what* a nation is, but we also need to consider *when* a cultural group becomes a nation. To become a nation, a cultural group needs to develop a consciousness of being a nation and of foreigners as being different. The group members need to start seeing themselves as Brazilians, Tibetans, or Scots, not just as residents of a particular village and worshippers of a particular religion. Political geographers often trace the origins of national identity to the political philosophies of the U.S. and French revolutions in the late 1700s. Before then, most states were considered personal property of their rulers, but the new thinkers introduced the idea that states should express the will of their people. When ancestral cultural groups develop a *political* consciousness that they should be united and should rule their own lands, they become a nation. Most political geographers hold that even the Chinese, who have had cultural continuity over two millennia, did not evolve a national identity until European political ideals diffused to East Asia during the nineteenth century.

A nation is usually territorially based. We call that territory its **homeland**. It is the motherland or fatherland, the sacred soil. Some nations are lucky enough to rule their own homelands, as the French rule France. Other nations lie within a sovereign state but are officially recognized by that state and are granted varying degrees of **regional autonomy**, such as Québec (in Canada), Scotland (in the United Kingdom), Chechnya (in Russia), and the Navajo Indian Reservation (in the United States). Still others, with names like Zululand or Baluchistan, or Galicia, have no official status but are every bit as real to their sons and daughters. The vast majority of the estimated 5,000 nations in the world fall into this category.

There is thus a mismatch between the political geography of states and the cultural geography of nations. Several prototypical cases can be defined. If a nation's homeland corresponds exactly to a state's territory, that nation is said to be a **nation-state** (see Figure 13.1a), which is the political-geographic ideal because it does not give cause to anyone from within or from outside of the country to try to peaceably or forcefully alter the state's boundaries. Nation-states, however, are the exception rather than the rule. A survey of territories generally considered to be full-fledged states in 1971 found that only 9 percent of them could be considered nation-states. Some examples include Japan, Sweden, Portugal, and Costa Rica, although even these are rarely perfectly "pure."

If the state and national boundaries do not match, the potential for conflict exists. A basic distinction can be drawn between a multination state and a multistate nation. A *multination* state occurs when several distinct nations are found together in the same political state as, for example, in Canada or South Africa. While this is

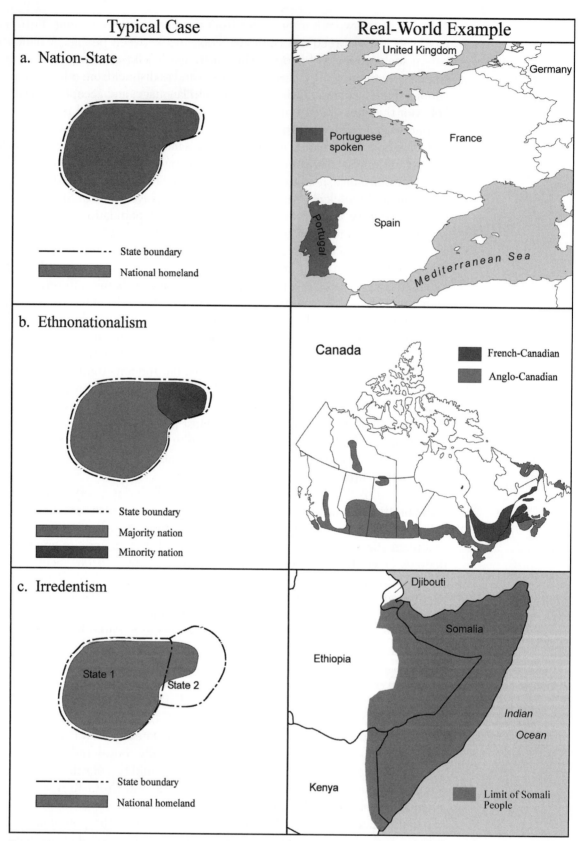

Figure 13.1 Examples of the political geography of nations and states.

not always a recipe for unrest (e.g., multi-national Switzerland), more often than not it leads to **ethnonationalism**, which is a strong feeling of belonging to a minority nation that is contained within a state dominated by a more powerful nation (see Figure 13.1b). In its weak form, ethnonationalism can lead to a desire for regional autonomy to maintain one's native language and traditions (e.g., Wales); in its strong form, it can lead to **separatism**, the desire to break away and form one's own nation-state (e.g., Québec in Canada or Tibet in China) or outright **secession** (e.g., Lithuania, which left the Soviet Union in 1991, or the Slovaks, who divorced the Czechs in 1993). Many separatist groups will resort to violent means to achieve their desired ends, and most states feel justified in using force to suppress these revolts and keep their territory intact. In fact, of the estimated 122 wars in 1993, 97 could be categorized as a state versus a minority nation within its borders.[1]

A *multistate* nation, on the other hand, exists when a national homeland overlaps into more than one state. In this case, one state encompasses the majority of the nation, and "outliers" exist in neighboring states (see Figure 13.1c). A multistate nation can give rise to **irredentism**, which occurs if a nation's homeland spills over into another state and the people on the "wrong side" of the boundary wish to join their territory with the rest of their homeland. Often, a sign of irredentism at work is when one of the nations refers to its homeland as "Greater _____," as in Greater Somalia or Greater Germany, which implies that the nation believes it has been constrained into only a portion of its true homeland. This situation existed for Germany prior to World War II, when many ethnic Germans lived in Czechoslovakia and Poland, giving Hitler an excuse to expand. The term *irredentism* originates from the Italian expression *Italia irredenta*, or "unredeemed Italy." Until the 1860s, the Italian peninsula was divided among a handful of kingdoms, duchies, republics, and papal states. In 1871, when the state of Italy was finally unified, Italian nationalists began referring to South Tirol, a key Italian-speaking region still in Austro-Hungarian hands, as *Italia irredenta*.

The French Canadian nation is a classic example of ethnonationalism that has led to a separatist movement. As with many such cases, one needs to venture across centuries and oceans to trace the roots of the current situation. In 1608, the French established a colony on the banks of the St. Lawrence River where the City of Québec now lies, two years before the first British colony in Newfoundland. Both the French and the British were after land, glory, aboriginal converts to their brand of Christianity, a shipping route to the Orient, and the furs of animals found in the cold northern forests. After 150 years of struggle between the two empires, France ceded virtually all of its North American claims to the British in 1763. Eleven years later, the British, in the face of unrest among the French population of 70,000 and not wanting to be diverted from the task of holding on to its more lucrative colonies to the south, proclaimed the Québec Act, guaranteeing French rights to speak the French language, practice Catholicism, and abide by the French legal system. Canadian provinces united in 1867 into the British-ruled Dominion of Canada, and its young people, including French speakers, fought alongside other soldiers from the British Empire in various colonial wars from South Africa to India. Canada was granted full legislative authority over domestic and external affairs in 1931 and acquired its own constitution and charter of rights (with full independence from the United Kingdom)

---

[1] Nietschmann, Bernard. 1994. The Fourth World: Nations Versus States, pp. 225–242 in *Reordering the World: Geopolitical Perspectives on the 21st Century*, George J. Demko and William B. Wood (eds.). Boulder, CO: Westview Press.

in 1982. As of 2006, the French-speaking population, living disproportionately in the province of Québec, had grown to 6.8 million of Canada's 31.6 million.

The French Canadian nation makes up the majority in Québec, and a substantial minority in the provinces of New Brunswick and Newfoundland (see Figure 13.1b). Because French speakers are such a large minority, the Canadian government conducts all public business in both French and English. The Québec provincial government, on the other hand, passed laws requiring that children of immigrants attend French-language schools and that Québec provincial affairs be conducted in French only. As a result, many Canadian corporations and English speakers moved to other provinces. French nationalism reached new heights in the 1960s and 1970s with the rise of an extremist group, the *Front Libération de Québec*, and a strongly nationalist political party in 1976. However, separatist referendums for Québec sovereignty failed in 1977 and 1995 because only a slight majority of French speakers supported it (Figure 13.2) while the vast majority of English speakers opposed it (Figure 13.3). In contrast to many other ethnonational situations around the world, English- and French-speaking Canadians have eschewed violence and pursued territorial goals through dialogue.

Not all international conflicts lend themselves to a clear explanation using the concepts of nations and states and homelands. The ongoing crisis in Israel between the Hebrew-speaking Jews and the Arabic-speaking Islamic Palestinians is a case in point. In this complex situation, both nations claim the same territory as their homeland. The Jewish historical claim is based on ancient occupation before the Jews were forcibly expelled from Palestine in two **diasporas** (dispersals of a population), first by the Babylonians in the seventh century B.C. and then by the Romans in the first century A.D. For the next two millennia, the region was home to Arab people who converted to Islam in the seventh century A.D.

Figure 13.2 Québec pro-secession march in the last days before the referendum in October 1995. Supporters of a *"Oui"* ("Yes") vote to secede from Canada carried Québec flags and brandished nonviolent symbols such as flowers and peace signs.

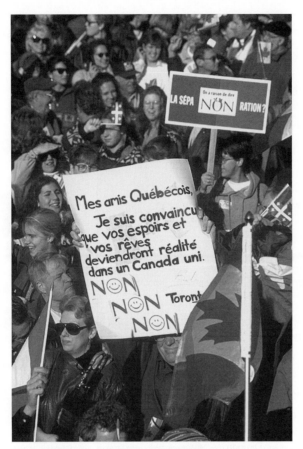

Figure 13.3 At a rally against Québec separatism in Montreal, the largest city in Québec, supporters of a *"Non"* vote pleaded to the *"Oui"* voters in French: "My Québecois friends—I am convinced that your hopes and dreams can become reality in a united Canada. No, no, no. Toronto."

Jews began returning to Palestine and buying up land in the 1920s when the region came under British control. From the 1920s to 1940s, the British, the League of Nations, and the United Nations tried unsuccessfully to broker partition plans for dividing the territory. After the first of many wars, Israel became a state in 1948. The Palestinian people—who may or may not have seen themselves as a distinct nation at that time, but who most certainly do today—found themselves divided between those within the new state's boundaries and almost a million **refugees** who had fled Israel proper to neighboring states on the eve of war. Today the Palestinians have won a limited form of regional autonomy in the West Bank and Gaza Strip territories (Figure 13.4), two of the areas where the refugees settled but that were not the Palestinians' original homelands. Any lasting peace agreement must overcome the resistance of hard-liners on both sides, the need of both states for a sustainable water supply, and the particularly thorny issue of Jerusalem, which both religions regard as holy ground (Figure 13.5).

Political geographers recognize two primary forms of territorial organization and government: unitary and federal. A **unitary state** is largely governed as a single unit by the central government. Although it may be subdivided into provinces or counties for administrative purposes, the central government dictates the degree of regional political control. A **federal state**, on the other hand, employs a two-tiered system of government with a clear and formal distinction between the powers of

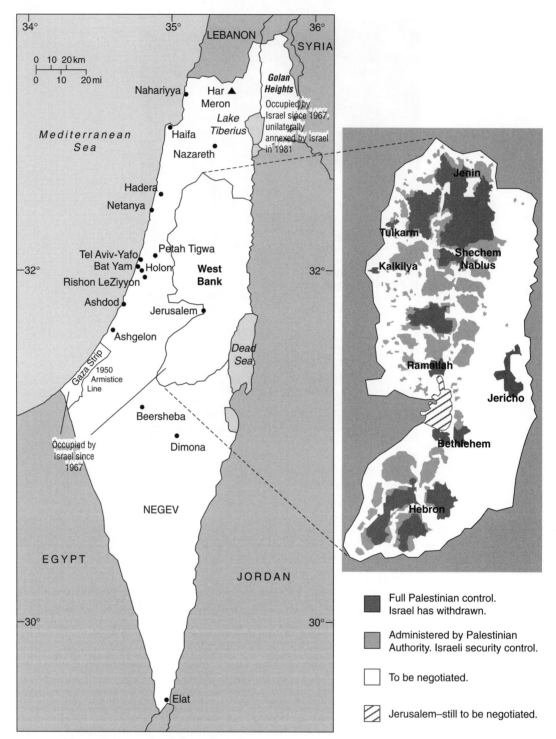

Figure 13.4 Israel and the Occupied Territories.

the central (federal) government and those of the lower-level administrative units within the country, often spelled out in a written constitution. Each region has its own capital, government, courts, and budget. Depending on the country, the regions can be called provinces as in Canada, republics as in the former Yugoslavia or former Soviet Union, or states as in the United States, although this usage is incorrect and

Figure 13.5   In Jerusalem, Jews pray at the Western (or "Wailing") Wall that is the last surviving remnant of the Temple of Solomon. Just above it can be seen the Dome of the Rock mosque, the oldest existing Islamic structure in the world, built in the seventh century on the spot from which Muhammad is believed to have ascended to heaven.

confusing from a political-geographic perspective. Most countries in the world are organized as unitary states, including France, Saudi Arabia, and Japan. Only 10 to 20 are federations, including the United States, Canada, Mexico, Brazil, Australia, and India. China is organized into 32 provinces, autonomous regions, and special municipalities, but it is not considered a good example of a federal state because the central government can override provincial decisions whenever it pleases.

A unitary form of organization tends to work best in smaller states that are more compact in shape, have a single core region, and are dominated by a single nation. In such cases, the different regions often share the same agenda. Many European states and most former colonies have adopted a unitary system. Dictatorships are usually unitary as well. Federalism, on the other hand, allows diverse regions to coexist under a common umbrella that allows each province to maintain some of its distinct regional character. Large multinational, multilingual states with diverse environments, cultures, economies, or histories can function well as federations. States with multiple core regions, perhaps consisting of fragmented topography or islands, or facing communication difficulties, may function better as federations. The degree of integration can vary on a spectrum from a loose federation sharing only a few things like a common currency, passport. and army, to a tight federation with little regional differentiation of policy. Both federal and unitary states sometimes allow certain minority nations to have a higher degree of regional autonomy. Spain is a unitary state that gives some autonomy to the Basque region and Catalonia, while Canada is a federal state that gives some autonomy to Québec. In both cases, regional autonomy has helped blunt, but not eliminate, separatist movements.

Federalism often sounds great in theory, but history is littered with failed federations. When Latin American colonies won their independence from Spain, a Central American Federation was formed but lasted only from 1825 to 1838 before breaking up into Costa Rica, Nicaragua, El Salvador, Honduras, and Guatemala. Other federations were proposed but never really got off the ground. In the 1950s and 1960s, the Arab/Islamic countries of North Africa almost united in a Maghreb federation as part of a pan-Arab, anticolonial union. The United States was almost added to the list of failed federations, when the South seceded from the North in 1861, precipitating the Civil War. In this chapter, you will either read about the former Yugoslavia, where a federation was not enough to hold together a group of nations with long histories of bloodshed and betrayal, or Iraq, which is hoping that a federal structure will encourage its nations to stay together without the threat of force from Saddam Hussein.

Many factors can tear at the cohesion of a federation—or of a unitary state, for that matter. Ethnonationalism and irredentism, of course, can divide a state, but other factors can exacerbate or mitigate their effects. If one region is much wealthier than another, the wealthier one may object to subsidizing the poorer region, while the poorer region may feel that the richer region exploits its natural resources or labor. Persecution of minority nations, underrepresentation in government and army positions, environmental degradation, and culturally insensitive policies can also fan the flames of ethnonationalism. On the other hand, many differences can be overcome if a state has a powerful **raison d'être**, or literally "reason for being." Switzerland is a multinational state that is 65 percent German, 18 percent French, 10 percent Italian, and 1 percent Romansch, but its national ideals of nonaggression and international neutrality have proven to be a powerful glue to its diverse nationalities.

American students typically have little trouble understanding this concept of raison d'être because the ideas upon which the United States was founded—that all people are created equal and entitled to inalienable rights to life, liberty, and the pursuit of happiness—are so well known. When it comes to the concepts of nation and state, however, vernacular usage of these words here and abroad creates a terminological chaos that clouds our understanding of current events. The United States of America is actually not a union of independent states but perhaps would be described better as the United **Provinces** of America. If the United Nations were really an organization of nations, it would have more than 5,000 members instead of the approximately 200 states that currently have seats in it. The term *international* in fact refers to *interstate*, while Americans' use of *interstate* (as in interstate highways) really means *intrastate*. **Nationalism** has come to mean loyalty to the state, when it is often quite the opposite—loyalty to one's nation. Of course, it is understandable that the dominant nations would confuse nationalism and **patriotism** (loyalty to the state) because for them, the nation and state are the same.

An example of proper usage of *nation* is in the *Pledge of Allegiance* to the U.S. flag. The expression "One nation under God" refers properly, if wishfully, to *a group of people with a common culture and ideals* (nation). Despite their lack of blood ties, most (but not all) Americans do share a common historical experience in that they or their ancestors came to the United States in search of opportunity or freedom. The lack of blood ties to other Americans, however, makes it difficult for us to fathom why neither the Serbs, Croats, Bosnian Muslims, and Kosovo Albanians of the former Yugoslavia (Activity 1), nor the Shiites, Sunnis, and Kurds of Iraq (Activity 2), seem to be able to peacefully coexist in a "melting pot" or "cultural stew," as Americans and Canadians do, without slaughtering each other. This same lack of understanding undoubtedly has led U.S. political and military leaders to underestimate the difficulty of stabilizing Bosnia, Kosovo, and Iraq to the point where foreign troops can be withdrawn.

► *CASE STUDY*

BREAKING UP IS HARD TO DO

GOAL

To explain what can happen when **nations** and **states** don't coincide geographically. Using news articles, you will analyze the nations and states involved in either the breakup of Yugoslavia or the reconstruction of Iraq.

LEARNING OUTCOMES

After completing the chapter, you will be able to:

- Distinguish between the concepts of a nation and a state, ethnonationalism and irredentism, and nationalism and patriotism.
- Recognize whether a country is a nation-state, and if not, why not.
- Explain the advantages of regional autonomy and of unitary and federal systems of government.
- Critically analyze news stories on ethnic conflicts around the world.
- Interpret current events in the former Yugoslavia or Iraq in the context of their history and geography.

SPECIAL MATERIALS NEEDED

- Computer with high-speed Internet access and a recent release of a Web browser. If using the Student Companion Site with the printed book, click on *Tech Support* for system requirements and technical support. (If using the e-book in WileyPlus, click on *Help* for details about the system requirements.)

BACKGROUND

The crisis in the former Yugoslavia dominated international news during the 1990s. Iraq has done the same for the beginning of the new millennium. This chapter will help you understand these distant conflicts.

War in Yugoslavia killed about one-quarter of a million people, forced several million more to leave their homes and become refugees, and devastated a once beautiful country. The discovery of modern-day genocide just a few hundred kilometers from the borders of the European Union was truly shocking to many Europeans. Organized rape was used not only as an act of hatred and a means to demoralize the enemy but also as a way to dilute the bloodlines that form the very core of a nation's existence. A peace plan forged in 1995 by the Clinton administration was grudgingly accepted by the three major combatants in Bosnia—the Serbs, Croats, and Muslims—only to see the entire bloody scenario repeat itself in 1999 in Kosovo. An international coalition led by the United States intervened militarily to stop the Serbs from further ethnic cleansing of Kosovo. As of 2009, international peacekeepers, headed by the European Union but including U.S. and Canadian troops, still were based in Kosovo to keep the lid on the conflict and

enforce the peace accord, but had moved back from an executive role to one of monitoring and support of local institutions. The peacekeeping operation is—hopefully—in its final chapter before Kosovo's status is formally resolved.

Yugoslavia lies in southeastern Europe in an area that political geographers describe as a **shatterbelt**—a region in which state boundaries have been drawn and redrawn many different times over the years, largely as a result of being caught between powerful forces. The nations in the shatterbelt of southeastern Europe have been ruled by one empire after another, with occasional periods of independence. Shatterbelts tend to form in areas with two geographical characteristics. First, the areas tend to be topographically fractured (very mountainous), which prevents the emergence of a major power that might have integrated the many small independent nations and expelled outside invaders. Second, shatterbelts tend to be at a crossroads of trade and migration, which opens them up to outside powers and deposits new groups of people in their midst. Shatterbelts can have very complex geographies of nations and states. In the words of Vuk Draskovic, a leading Yugoslavian dissident, "The ethnic map of prewar Bosnia, and indeed prewar Yugoslavia, was like a jaguar's skin. The people were inseparably mixed. No magician could make ethnic borders on such a jaguar's skin."[2] Other shatterbelts are in the Caucasus and Southeast Asia.

Unlike Yugoslavia, Iraq is not in a shatterbelt. In fact, Iraq's Tigris and Euphrates river plains were the heartland of several ancient empires. Like Yugoslavia, however, some of its past, present, and future troubles stem from the way its political boundaries cut across nations. Similar to Yugoslavia, the state of Iraq and its boundaries were created by an outside power—in this case, the British—in the first half of the twentieth century. Unlike in Yugoslavia, however, the war in Iraq erupted not over ethnic divisions but over global geopolitics, religion, terrorism, dictatorship, and oil. The ethnic makeup of Iraq, however, with Sunni Muslims, Shia Muslims, and Kurds, hinders resolution of the conflict.

Activities 1 and 2 of this chapter deal with the situations in Yugoslavia and Iraq, respectively. You will read a variety of news stories, analyses, and government reports about the ancient and modern histories of Yugoslavia and Iraq. Ethnic maps will help you analyze the current situations. Both case studies provide different types of print or online news media or official sources, each of which has only part of the story, instead of a single comprehensive summary. You will use these sources to answer fill-in-the-blank questions about the background to the crises, the conflagrations of violence, and the reasons it is so difficult to disentangle the nations within a state from each other cleanly. You will learn the reasons that, once a state is in place, breaking it up is indeed hard to do.

The U.S. Department of State and the CIA both recruit geographers (among others) to write intelligence reports, analyze foreign situations, study boundary disputes, make

---

[2]Quoted in Roger Cohen, "The Tearing Apart of Yugoslavia: Place by place, Family by Family," *New York Times* (May 9, 1993), p. 4.

▶ **CASE STUDY** *(continued)*

maps, and interpret satellite images and aerial photographs. In addition to several regional bureaus, the State Department has an Undersecretary for Democracy and Global Affairs, who deals with population, refugees, migration, human rights, oceans, and environmental issues. Some of the skills you will use in these activities are those that the agencies value highly in geographers, namely the abilities to read maps, apply terms and definitions to messy situations, and synthesize the historical, cultural, economic, demographic, and physical forces that act on a region.

A recent survey by the National Geographic Society found that only one in seven Americans age 18 to 24, the prime age for military service, could locate Iraq on a world map. Since the September 11, 2001, terrorist attacks on the World Trade Centers and the Pentagon and with the recent war with Iraq, the importance of Activity 2 on Iraq is painfully obvious. But why should you, a college student far from the conflict, personally care about Yugoslavia? First, the United States still maintained about 1,450 troops in Kosovo in 2008. Second, the United States has a population of minorities: Native American, Polish American, Hispanic American, African-American, Jewish American, Asian American, and so on. Although you may not be of Slavic or Muslim ancestry, the concepts you learn here will help you understand what is going on in other areas of the world to which you could have personal attachments. Nation-state conflicts continue to flare up between Protestants and Catholics in Northern Ireland (see Chapter 12); in Punjab, Kashmir, and Sri Lanka on the Indian subcontinent; in East Timor in Indonesia; in Tibet (controlled by China); in Israel and Palestine; in Armenia, Azerbaijan, and Chechnya in the former Soviet Caucasus; and between Hutus and Tutsis in Rwanda, Burundi, and Congo. Third, ethnonational issues exist in North America. As recently as the 1970s, Native Americans clashed with the U.S. government, and the two still

have conflicts over water rights, fishing, dumping of waste, gambling, and burial sites. Canada is officially a bilingual state because of French-speaking descendants in Québec, many of whom still want to secede from Canada. In southern Mexico, a rebellion by indigenous (Indian) peoples in Chiapas is ongoing; they believe the government does not represent their interests in struggles for land and improvements to their living conditions. Therefore, as a voter, as a taxpayer, as a friend or relative of a U.S. or Canadian soldier or peacekeeper, as a descendant of immigrants, or as a Native American or Québecois, you need to be informed about these issues.

Note: We realize that, by the time you do this exercise, the situations in Iraq and the former Yugoslavia could have changed drastically or faded from view. *In political geography, change is unavoidable.* We have tried to make this chapter as relevant and up-to-date as possible at the time of publication. Students interested in keeping up with the current situation should consult our sources: *The Christian Science Monitor, The New York Times*, PBS, *The New York Review of Books*, the United Nations, and the U.S. Department of State, or others including *Time, Newsweek, The Economist*, and *U.S. News and World Report*, or in-depth journals such as *Foreign Affairs, The Atlantic Monthly, Current History, International Affairs, Journal of Peace Research, Ethnic Racial Studies*, and the *American Journal of International Law*. In addition, you can find current updates on the Internet (see Web References at the end of the chapter).

Name: _____ Instructor: _____

Breaking Up Is Hard to Do: Nations, States, and Nation-States

▶ ## ACTIVITY 1: THE RISE OF NATIONALISM AND THE FALL OF YUGOSLAVIA

Activity 1 requires you to read six selections about the former Yugoslavia and then answer questions about them. The first article (Goodrich, 1993) is from *The Christian Science Monitor*. It is one of several articles we have selected from the *Monitor* because of its world-famous coverage of international affairs—not because of its religious affiliation. The Goodrich article provides a 1,500-year historical overview that is not usually available in newspapers. We have added a few key points to this article [in square brackets], and some useful maps (Figures 13.6–13.12, Table 13.1).

The second reading consists of excerpts from a United Nations research article by Ali Karaosmanoğlu (1993) that offers a concise summary of how and why the former Yugoslavia fell apart. It highlights the most important fact about the political geography of the area: that the former Yugoslavia was a multination state, but breaking it into its individual republics (i.e., provinces) did not solve the problem because both Bosnia and Croatia were also each a mix of nations.

In the third article, photojournalist Lee Malis of *The Christian Science Monitor* tells the harrowing tale of one young Muslim woman's nightmare at the hands of the Bosnian Serbs. We warn you of the graphic nature of this short feature article; you could find it disturbing. It should be emphasized that the Serbs were not the only nation to engage in such war crimes.

Why not carve Bosnia up into three states, and let the Serbian part of Bosnia join with Serbia and the Croatian part of Bosnia join with Croatia? Why does the rest of the world care about keeping Bosnia in one piece? This is the subject of the fourth reading, a short analysis by Laura Kay Rozen from *The Christian Science Monitor* in September 1996, at the time of the first-ever Bosnian elections. Five key points summarize why keeping Bosnia whole was important to the foreign policies of other countries. Note that neither we (the textbook authors) nor the article author herself necessarily espouse all of these arguments. In fact, one of the points regarding a fear of Islamic terrorism from a Muslim-dominated Bosnian state is an example of prejudicial thinking. However, all five arguments frequently were heard on talk shows and seen on op-ed pages of the time.

The final reading consists of excerpts from two U.S. Department of State reports on the Kosovo (pronounced Koh-SOH-vah) crisis. The stated purpose of these reports was to document the extent of ethnic cleansing by the Serbs against the Albanians in Kosovo. Aerial photography and other forms of evidence accompanied these reports, which were delivered to the Executive Branch of the U.S. government and Congress, U.S. allies, and the international community. They were important documents in the decisions to use U.S. military power to stop the ethnic cleansing in Kosovo and to justify the deployment of U.S. troops as peacekeepers. The reports were also made available to the media and the public over the Internet. In reading these excerpts, you should think about some of the geopolitical issues that could explain why the United States chose to intervene in this particular crisis but not in others. The Serbs have historically been allies with the Russians, who are also Slavs who follow an Eastern Orthodox form of Christianity. Other issues to consider are the U.S.'s historic alliance with Western Europeans, the importance of not appearing to be anti-Islamic, and the power of media images of mass graves, burning houses, and refugees.

It would take many newspaper articles to fill you in on all that happened in the aftermaths of the Bosnia and Kosovo crises. We wrap it up for you with a short summary and map that updates you to early 2009.

▶ ACTIVITY 1 READINGS

Goodrich, Lawrence J. 1993. Old Animosities, Exploited Today, Underlie Complex Balkans Puzzle. *The Christian Science Monitor* (Oct. 13, 1993):1–2.

Karaosmanoğlu, Ali L. 1993. *Crisis in the Balkans*. United Nations Institute for Disarmament Research, Research Paper no. 22, UNIDIR/93/37. New York: United Nations.

Malis, Lee. 1993. Bosnia: The Flight from Ethnic Cleansing. *The Christian Science Monitor* (Feb. 17, 1993):9–11.

Rozen, Laura Kay. 1996. Keeping Bosnia Whole: Why the World Cares. *The Christian Science Monitor* (Sept. 19, 1996):5.

U.S. Department of State. 1999. *Erasing History: Ethnic Cleansing in Kosovo*: www.state.gov/www/regions/eur/rpt_9905_ethnic_ksvo_toc.html (May 1999).

U.S. Department of State. 1999. *Ethnic Cleansing in Kosovo: An Accounting*: www.state.gov/www/global/human_rights/kosovoii/homepage.html (Dec. 1999).

▶ QUESTIONS

(Note: Answers to questions marked by * cannot be obtained directly in the readings. You'll need to think critically about the readings and apply concepts properly to figure them out.)

A. History of Hatred

Refer to articles by Goodrich and Karaosmanoğlu and Figures 13.6 and 13.9.

1.1. What cultural trait, language, or religion, divides the Serbs and Croats?

_____

1.2. Name the religion of the Serbs _____ and of the Croats. _____

1.3. What historical development is responsible for this religious divide between Serbs and Croats? _____

1.4. How did Islam come to this region of Europe?

_____

1.5. In what century did the Muslims defeat Serbia in the battle of Kosovo?

_____

1.6. What other outside empire next dominated the northern parts of the region in the several centuries prior to World War I? _____

1.7. A country called Yugoslavia (Land of the Southern Slavs) first came into being after World War I. Which of its member nations dominated Yugoslavia at that time?

_____

1.8. What happened during World War II that further increased Serb-Croat hatred and added to the Serb sense of victimhood?

_____

_____

B. The Pre-Breakup Situation

Refer to articles by Goodrich and Karaosmanoglu, Figures 13.7 and 13.8, and Table 13.1.

After World War II, Yugoslavia adopted a federal system of government. The country was divided into six "republics," similar to the 50 U.S. states and 13 Canadian provinces, but with one important difference. In Yugoslavia, the government tried to define the republics along ethnonational lines.

1.9. Which republic was most ethnically uniform?* _____

1.10. Which republic was least ethnically uniform?* _____

1.11. Prior to its breakup, was Yugoslavia a nation-state, a multistate nation, or a multination state?* _____

1.12. The pre-war state of Yugoslavia referred to its component regions as "republics." Would a political geographer have called them states, nations, or provinces?*
_____

1.13. From World War II until its breakup, Yugoslavia had what kind of government—communist, capitalist, or monarchy? _____

C. The Breakup

Refer to article by Karaosmanoglu, Figures 13.7 and 13.8, and Table 13.1.

From 1991 to 1993, Slovenia, Croatia, Bosnia, and Macedonia all claimed independent status. In fact, the breakup of Yugoslavia consisted of three wars, not one.

1.14. Did Yugoslavia break up because of ethnonationalism or irredentism?*

_____

1.15. The first war, which lasted only 10 days, was between Slovenia and the Yugoslavian government after Slovenia declared its independence in the spring of 1991. Would the declaration of independence by Slovenia be described as an act of irredentism or secession?* _____

1.16. Why didn't the Serb-dominated government of Yugoslavia put up more of a fight to keep Slovenia from breaking away?*

_____

_____

1.17. After Slovenia became independent, could it have been characterized as a nation-state (see Figure 13.8)?* _____

1.18. The second war also started in the spring of 1991, but in Croatia. The two warring nations were _____ and _____.

D. Bosnia
Use article by Rozen, Table 13.1, and Figures 13.7, 13.8, and 13.12.

To answer the next set of questions, you need to adjust your mental map. What used to be the single state called Yugoslavia broke up into five separate independent states. In addition to Bosnia, Croatia, Macedonia, and Slovenia, the remaining two republics, Serbia and Montenegro, stayed together under the name of Yugoslavia. They were sometimes referred to as the "rump Yugoslavia" to distinguish it from the former, larger Yugoslavia. The third war within the former Yugoslavia began in Bosnia in the spring of 1992.

1.19. Which was the dominant nation within Bosnia in terms of population?

_____

1.20. Name the second and third most populous nations within Bosnia's borders.

_____ _____

1.21. Which, if any, of these two minority nations in Bosnia were irredenta of other states?* _____ _____

1.22. After Bosnia established its independence, would it have been best described as a state, a nation, or a nation-state?* _____

1.23. Why would the breakup of Bosnia worsen the refugee problem?

_____

_____

_____

1.24. What message would the permanent breakup of Bosnia into two or three separate states send to other ethnic groups in the Balkans and around the world?

_____

_____

_____

1.25. Why wouldn't the Serb-dominated part of Bosnia, which the Bosnian Serbs call *Republika Srpska*, be a viable independent state?

_____

_____

_____

E. Kosovo and Ethnic Cleansing (1999)

Refer to articles by U.S. State Department, Karaosmanoğlu, and Goodrich, Figures 13.7 and 13.8, Table 13.1, and the author's update.

1.26. In 1999, in what state was Kosovo? _____

1.27. What two nations cohabit Kosovo? _____ and _____

1.28. What nation is the majority in Kosovo? _____

1.29. What state's citizens would likely have irredentist feelings toward Kosovo?*

_____

1.30. What is the aim of "ethnic cleansing?"

_____

_____

_____

1.31. Name five methods of ethnic cleansing. _____

_____   _____

_____   _____

F. All's Not Quiet on the Balkan Front

Refer to Update by authors and Figures 13.7–13.13.

1.32. Is there still a state called Yugoslavia? _____

How many states are there now in what used to be Yugoslavia before 1991?
_____

1.33. Aside from the smoldering conflicts in Bosnia and Kosovo, what other political geographic issues remain that might break up an existing state and create a new state in the region?

_____

_____

_____

_____

_____

_____

▶ ACTIVITY 1 READINGS

▶ *THE CHRISTIAN SCIENCE MONITOR*

Old Animosities, Exploited Today, Underlie Complex Balkans Puzzle[3]
by Lawrence J. Goodrich, staff writer of *The Christian Science Monitor*.
October 13, 1993. Reprinted by permission.

Boston—As the likelihood grows that American forces will be directly involved in trying to restore the peace in the former Yugoslavia, many Americans are asking how the slaughter there began.

Unfortunately, what is happening today in the Balkans is nothing new. It is the continuation of the ethnic and religious hatreds that have swept the region for centuries, made worse by radical nationalists' cynical exploitation of these animosities.

The ethnic mixture of the Balkans began to form about the fifth century A.D. Vast tribal migrations swept across Europe: Germanic tribes came west, followed by Slavs to their east. In succeeding centuries Magyars (Hungarians), Mongols, Tatars, and Bulgars ranged over the Balkans. Between Western and Eastern Europe, a great gulf developed. Rome had fallen, but the Roman Empire in the East, with its capital at Constantinople (Byzantium), lasted another 1,000 years. The Roman church without a state and the Byzantine church subservient to the emperor split over long-standing political and theological disputes. This chasm went right through the

[3]Adapted by the authors.

Balkans: Hungarians, Slovenes, and Croats were Roman Catholic, while Romanians, Bulgarians, Greeks, and Serbs were Eastern Orthodox [see Figure 13.6a].

All across Europe nation-states began to form around the most powerful tribes. But in the 14th and 15th centuries, a series of catastrophes struck the Balkans. First the Ottoman Turks defeated Serbia at the battle of Kosovo in 1389. Constantinople (now Istanbul) fell in 1453. [The Ottoman Turks introduced the Muslim (i.e., Islamic) religion into the region.] By 1529 the Turks had fought their way to the gates of Vienna, which they besieged again in 1683 [see Figure 13.6b]. All political, cultural, and economic evolution in those parts of the Balkans under Turkish rule stopped under the oppression of the Turkish sultan.

For the next 400 years, the history of the Balkans was a history of rivalry among the Ottoman, Austro-Hungarian, and Russian empires. Croats, Slovenes, and Transylvanian Romanians lived under the influence of Vienna and Budapest [see Figure 13.6c]. Romanians, Bulgarians, Macedonians, Serbs, and some Albanians clung tenaciously to their Eastern Orthodox faith, which became entwined with their national aspirations. Most Albanians and some Slavs, however, converted to Islam.

The Balkan peasantry was kept impoverished as agricultural riches were shipped off to feed the Ottoman Empire. The Turks played off tribes, clans, and families against each other, poisoning the political culture.

Christianity was barely tolerated.

None of the subsequent development of Western and Central Europe—the growth of guilds and the middle class, the decline of feudalism, the Reformation and the Counterreformation, the Renaissance and the Enlightenment—touched the Balkans.

By the nineteenth century, the Ottoman Empire was in serious decline. Most of the Balkan ethnic groups began to agitate for independence and their own states. But their villages were often scattered among each other.

Little by little each group threw off Turkish rule. Russia felt a special calling to help its Orthodox Slav brethren, the Serbs and Bulgarians, and provided political or military support.

But the rule of the Balkans is: Everything for my ethnic group and nothing for yours. The group on top now governs at the expense of the others; the groups out of power wreak vengeance when the power balance shifts. People see themselves as Serbs, Croatians, or Albanians first and as individuals second.

This attitude is preserved by the region's economic backwardness and low educational levels. It is especially true in rural areas. While cities may be ethnically mixed, villages usually are ethnically pure, or nearly so.

[In 1908, Austria-Hungary directly annexed Bosnia, inciting the Serbs to seek the aid of Montenegro, Bulgaria, and Greece in seizing the last Ottoman-ruled lands in Europe. In the ensuing Balkan Wars of 1912–1913, Serbia obtained northern and central Macedonia, but Austria compelled it to yield Albanian lands that would have given Austria access to the sea. Serb animosity against Austria-Hungary reached a climax on June 28, 1914, when the Austrian Archduke Franz Ferdinand was assassinated in Sarajevo by a Bosnian Serb, Gavrilo Princip—the spark that lit the powder keg of World War I.[4]]

---

[4]U.S. Department of State, Bureau of European Affairs. 1999. *Background Notes: Serbia and Montenegro:* www. state. gov/www/background_notes/serbia_9908_bgn. html (August 1999).

© 2010 John Wiley & Sons, Inc.

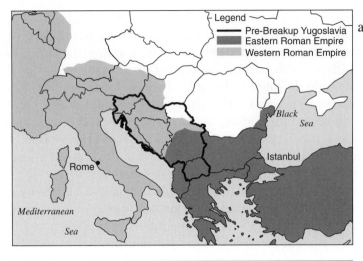

a. The Roman Empire adopted, Christianity in the fourth century and split administration between a western half centered on Rome, and an eastern half whose capital was Constantinople (now Istanbul, Turkey). The western half became predominantly Catholic, the eastern half predominantly Orthodox. This divide still runs through the former Yugoslavia: Slovenes and Croats are mostly Catholic, while Serbs, Macedonians, and Montenegrins are mostly Orthodox.

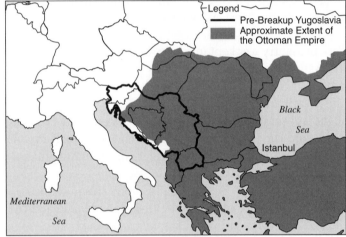

b. Islam originated in Mecca in current-day Saudi Arabia, but soon spread to include what is now Turkey. Centuries later, the Ottoman Empire arose in Turkey and spread Islam well into the Balkans and Europe. Current-day Bosnian Muslims are mostly Slavs who converted to Islam during the long reign of the Ottomans.

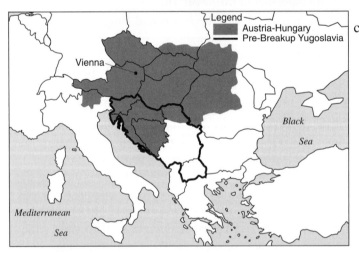

c. The outside power that controlled most of the Balkans on the eve of World War I was the Austro-Hungarian Empire. In fact, World War I was triggered when a Bosnian Serb, irate over the latest chapter of outside domination, assassinated the Austro-Hungarian Archduke Ferdinand in Sarajevo on June 28, 1914.

Figure 13.6 Three major empires that divided the Slavic-speaking peoples in the Balkans.

© 2010 John Wiley & Sons, Inc.

After the Turkish and Austrian Empires collapsed at the end of World War I, the victorious Allies carved up the remains into a series of new, artificial Balkan states. The southern Slav groups were lumped together in what officially was christened Yugoslavia [literally "land of the southern Slavs"] in 1918. Serbia was the dominant partner, which led to constant friction with the Croats. The new country never had a chance. Nazi Germany invaded in 1941 and set up a fascist Croatian puppet state. [The Croatian] Ustashe troops committed terrible atrocities against Bosnian and Croatian Serbs [murdering approximately 350,000 Serbs]. Serbian nationalist guerrillas, the Chetniks, retaliated in kind.

Communist partisans under Josip Broz Tito, armed by the Allies, fought the Germans to a standstill, broke with the Chetniks, and took power at the end of the war. [Post–World War II Yugoslavia had the same external boundaries as before, but internally it was divided into six republics: Serbia, Croatia, Slovenia, Bosnia-Herzegovina, Macedonia, and Montenegro (Figure 13.7a). There was some attempt to define these republics along ethnonational lines, but of the six, only Slovenia was even close to being ethnically pure; see Table 13.1 and Figure 13.8.] Communist rule under Marshal Tito kept a tight lid on ethnic feuding, but it continued to

Figure 13.7 (a) Pre-breakup Yugoslavia; (b) Post-breakup Yugoslavia; (c) the former Yugoslaviva in 2009.

© 2010 John Wiley & Sons, Inc.

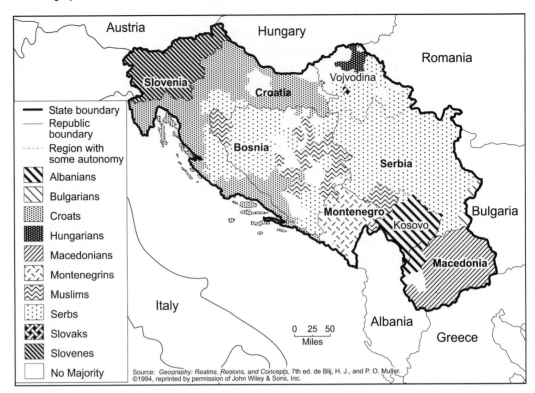

Figure 13.8 Pre-war ethnic distribution in the former Yugoslavia.

TABLE 13.1 Percentages of Pre-war Ethnic Populations, by Republic or Autonomous Region

	Albanians	Croats	Muslims	Serbs	Slovenes	Others
Bosnia		18	40	33		9
Croatia		75	12			13
Kosovo	90			10		
Macedonia	23			2		67 Macedonians 8 others
Montenegro	7	1	15	9		68 Montenegrins
Serbia	20	2		65		13
Slovenia		3		2	90	5
Vojvodina				56		21 Hungarians 23 Others
Former Yugoslavia (all republics)	14	20	9	36	8	13

Sources: James Gow, "Deconstructing Yugoslavia," *Survival* 33:293 (1991): *Encyclopedia Britannica*: *CIA Factbook;* and PC-Globe software (1989).

smolder. [Under communist rule, Serbia was transformed from an agrarian to an industrial society.] When Tito died in 1980, he left in place a collective presidency of Yugoslavia that rotated among the six republics.

But without Tito's personal magnetism and willingness to use force, the system soon began to break down. After communism collapsed in the former Soviet Union and Eastern Europe, the Yugoslav federation began to dissolve as Croats and Slovenes demanded independence, partly in pursuit of historic aspirations but also in fear of Serbian President Slobodan Milosevic's repression of the Albanian minority in Kosovo. Mr. Milosevic and Croatian President Franjo Tudjman made things worse by their inflammatory rhetoric and their policies of grabbing land from neighboring republics, to create a greater Serbia and a greater Croatia, and to expel other groups. [By the time the fighting died down, Yugoslavia had broken into five new states.] (Figure 13.7b.)

The region remains a tinder box: Greeks are nervous about the former Yugoslav republic of Macedonia; Montenegrins, still united with Serbia in rump Yugoslavia, are growing restless; and serious tensions persist between Hungarians and Romanians.

The most dangerous area is Kosovo province in Serbia. An historical Serbian heartland, it is now inhabited mostly by ethnic Albanians, who have seen their rights suppressed by the Milosevic government. Almost half the Albanians in the world live in Serbia; should the Serbs start an ethnic-cleansing campaign, it is doubtful Albania could stand by. Such a conflict could ignite tensions between Greece, which likely would side with the Orthodox Serbs, and Turkey, which would support the Muslim Slavs and mostly Muslim Albanians.

The question now is whether the United States can provide the leadership that will take the Balkans in the direction of peace or whether the region will sink deeper into disaster.

► THE UNITED NATIONS INSTITUTE FOR DISARMAMENT RESEARCH

UNIDIR/93/37, Research Paper No. 22, 1993. Reprinted by permission.

Excerpted from "Crisis in the Balkans"
by Ali L. Karaosmanoğlu

The 19th and 20th centuries have undoubtedly left scars that are difficult to cure. But the immediate cause of the present Yugoslav crisis is neither external power intervention nor traditional ethnic animosities. The latter could well be prevented from escalating to a bloody conflict situation if moderate policies were adopted by the conflicting regional entities. First of all, Serbia's, and its extreme nationalist leader Milosevic's, ambition to create a "Greater Serbia" constitutes the major cause of the crisis.[5] To some extent, the crisis is also the product of the Croatian and Bosnian policies of independence which failed to show sufficient consideration for the large Serbian communities in both countries.

Yugoslavia's nations had "very different and often mutually exclusive needs and aspirations." For the Serbs [who were the dominant power], Yugoslavia's future depended on further and tighter centralization. The non-Serb majorities, on the contrary, were in favor of creating their own sovereign states, or at least a confederation of sovereign states. . . .

A series of events in 1990–91 contributed to the deterioration of the crisis. In April 1990, the Croatian Democratic Union (HDZ) and the Democratic United

[5As Roskin and Berry (1997) point out: "It's easy to blame the Serbs, but understand where they are coming from psychologically. The Serbs argue: 'All right, you bastards who murdered us during World War II, if you want an independent Croatia and Bosnia, we have the right to pull the Serb areas out of your republics and gather them into a Greater Serbia, where they will be safe.' The attitude of Serbs closely parallels that of Israelis: 'We have historically been the victim of massacres, and we aren't going to take it anymore.'" In fact, there's plenty of blame to go around in Yugoslavia.]

Opposition of Slovenia (DEMOS) came to power as a result of multi-party elections. Both political parties were centre-right and pro-independence. During the election campaign, the HDZ advocated a "Greater Croatia" that would annex Croat-populated regions of Bosnia while condemning "greater Serbian hegemony" [i.e., dominance]. This created considerable concern among the Serbian population living in the border areas of Croatia. The Serbian perception of this threat was reinforced, on the one hand, by the increasingly secessionist stance of Croatia, and on the other, by the expulsion of Serbs from government positions. Moreover, the Croatian authorities threatened the Serbs by saying they would take measures to weaken the Serbian economic position in the republic. These moves of the Croatian government led to growing Serbian fears, and, eventually, to insurrections and armed clashes. . . .

In February, [Serbian President] Milosevic and [Croatian President] Tudjman agreed on Serbian and Croatian annexations in Bosnia. . . . [A Bosnian referendum on independence] was held in March 1992 without Serbian participation. The Muslims and Croats voted in favor of a "sovereign and independent Bosnia and Herzegovina" while the Serbs were erecting barricades around Sarajevo.

So far there have been three wars in the Yugoslav succession. The first took place in Slovenia in the Spring of 1991 and lasted for 10 days. The Serbian minority in Slovenia is only 2.4% of the population and is not implicated in the Serbian design of creating a "Greater Serbia." The conflict remained local without regional or international implications. The second war [between Croats and Serbs from Croatia and Serbia] started in Croatia in the spring of 1991. The hostilities were resumed again in February 1993 while the UN and EC representatives were working on a peace plan. The third began in Bosnia and Herzegovina in the spring of 1992 and is still being waged.

The last two conflicts had a significant similarity. One of their common features was the application by the Serbs of policies of "ethnic cleansing." This involved changing the demographic composition of villages, towns, and regions and clearing land corridors to link up ethnic Serbian enclaves in Croatia and in Bosnia-Herzegovina with Serbia. These policies were (and still are) extensively applied to Bosnian Muslims and Croats. The victims were either directly driven out or intimidated to flee their homes. The methods of intimidation included murder, rape, and imprisonment in concentration camps. The Yugoslav conflict brought more than two million refugees and displaced persons. Countries such as Croatia, Austria, Italy, Germany, Hungary, Slovenia, and Turkey were put under migratory pressure. Serbia resettled ethnic Serbs in areas that were ethnically cleansed, thereby using refugees to change the demographic composition of regions and thus contributing to the creation of a Greater Serbia. . . .

The Kosovo problem constitutes one of the most dangerous crisis areas in Yugoslavia's ongoing process of disintegration. The origins of this problem can be traced back to the creation of an independent Albanian state after the defeat of Turkey in the Balkan Wars of 1912–1913. The independent Albania included only 50 percent of the Albanian population in the area. A great number of Albanians remained in Kosovo, an Ottoman province, most of which was given to Serbia. Today there are more than 2 million Albanians in Kosovo (an overwhelming majority of them are Muslims; the figure includes 15,000 Turks) and they account for over 90 percent of the population, the remaining 10 percent being Serbian and Montenegrin. However, the Serbs regard Kosovo as their historic heartland. Kosovo was the cradle of the medieval Serbian state. [See Figure 13.9.] It is the historic

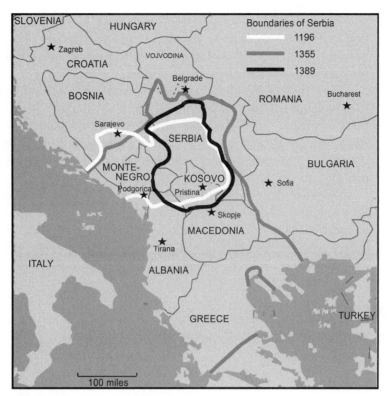

Figure 13.9 Former borders of Serbia.

battlefield where the Serbs fought against the Ottomans in 1389. It is also a region containing many Orthodox churches and monasteries. These factors make the province a cultural and spiritual centre for the Serbs. Kosovo has greatly contributed to the formation of a Serbian collective memory and consciousness, and this has become particularly significant in the process of building a Serbian state based on ethnic nationalism.

While the Serbs view Kosovo as a part of the Serbian historical patrimony that cannot be negotiable, the Albanians base their claims on self-determination. Kosovo was in fact a self-governing province of Serbia in terms of the 1974 Yugoslav Constitution. Kosovo had its semi-autonomous status gradually eroded by the central government in Belgrade in 1990–1991. The basic cultural and educational rights of the Albanian population were abrogated. The Serbian authorities shut down the Albanian language schools. They dismissed Albanians from the police force, which has been totally serbianized. Belgrade also reinforced the local security force by sending in Serbian and Montenegrin military units. Moreover, the economy was almost entirely serbianized. Most of the Albanian workers and managers were replaced with the Serbs.

The Albanians, for their part, took measures to set up their own state organization in a gradual and clandestine manner. In September 1991 they held a referendum in which they voted for a "sovereign and independent" Kosovo. In May 1992 they held elections [and elected the moderate intellectual Ibrahim Rugova]. They also set up an underground school system financed by parents. Despite these efforts, the Kosovars have not been able to develop an effective means to defend themselves should the fighting spread to Kosovo. The lack of adequate defensive means, on the one hand, and the offensive Serbian strategy on the other, have brought about a very deep sense of insecurity, not only in Kosovo but also in Albania. It should be noted that this feeling of insecurity, combined with the measures of democratization in Albania and Kosovo, increased the assertiveness of Albanians. As a matter of fact, the democratic elections in both countries have further increased popular pressure for an Albanian-Kosovar reunion.

Nevertheless, in spite of popular pressure, Albanian authorities in both countries prevented numerous incidents from escalating to all-out conflict. [Remember that this was published in 1993.] Moreover, many Albanians seem willing to accept some form of autonomy within a new Yugoslavia. But this type of settlement is abhorred by the Milosevic administration which still views Kosovo as an integral part of a unitary Serbia.

The Albanians are careful not to provide the Serbian authorities with an excuse for a violent crackdown and the Albanian government has been urging the Kosovars to contribute to a peaceful solution of the Kosovo problem. But Albanian leaders have repeatedly declared that ethnic cleansing in Kosovo would not be tolerated by Tirana [Albania's capital] and would lead to Albania's military intervention.

▶ THE CHRISTIAN SCIENCE MONITOR

February 17, 1993; Copyright © 1993 Lee Malis/Spectrum Pictures. Reprinted by permission.

Bosnia: The Flight from Ethnic Cleansing
by Lee Malis
(photos by Lee Malis)

Travnik, Bosnia-Herzegovina—The war in Bosnia continues. Diplomats still talk about what needs to be done, and how to make it stand once it is agreed upon. But the television news broadcasts say the bombings continue in Sarajevo. Another Bosnian village with a strange name falls to Serbian militias, and another massacre occurs in an unfamiliar place. Muslims try to retake eastern towns, and Serbs block UN attempts to break through with aid.

I have worked in the former Yugoslavia three times over the past two years as a freelance photographer for US magazines. During my first trip to Sarajevo, my guide was killed, a young Spanish photographer I had become friends with died, and my friend who is an Associated Press photographer was wounded.

Hundreds of other men, women, and children also died in those two or three weeks in Sarajevo.

On my last trip, in late November, I tried to make a portrait of the refugees in Travnik, a small city in the mountains of Bosnia 60 miles northwest of Sarajevo. I spent nine days living in a refugee camp there.

These were average Muslim Bosnians. They were not diplomats or generals or politicians. They were moms and dads, electricians and farmers, and children. Their names cannot be used because they have left families behind in villages under Serbian control.

There are hundreds of thousands of refugees in Bosnia, primarily because of "ethnic cleansing" by the Serbs. In Travnik and surrounding communities 20,000 to 30,000 refugees are scattered in homes, schools, and sports halls.

When the Serbs take an area, they "cleanse" cities and towns of non-Serbs, who make up about two-thirds of the Bosnian population. Just over half are Muslims, and the rest are Croatians. Those "cleansed" are either killed, sent to refugee camps or prison camps, or more often just told to leave or they will be killed. The Muslim population is taking the worst of the atrocities.

Since the war began last year [1992], Serbian militias have taken control of close to 70 percent of the country. The refugees lose their homes and belongings. When the Muslims reach a refugee camp, they can go no farther. Many European countries have closed their borders, because they say they have no more room for Bosnian refugees.

Four People Managed to Escape Through the Window

High in the mountains, in a quiet village nine miles from Travnik, are a few remnants of a family from the town of Visegrad, in eastern Bosnia. They are staying in the home of a family they have never met before, just one of thousands of families living in strangers' homes.

I was led there by a 10-year-old boy from a nearby town who spoke little English. The boy told me that I should talk with this family of refugees, because there is a survivor of a massacre there.

The family invites me into their one room. The atmosphere is brittle, as if the world is made of eggshells. The first thing they do is make coffee for everyone. It seems that if Bosnian Muslims have absolutely nothing, they will always manage to make coffee for guests.

The family consists of a woman, her child, and her parents.

In the spring of last year, the woman says, Visegrad had been taken over by Serbs. On the morning of June 13, she talked with a good friend of hers who is Serbian. The friend told her that she should get out of town as fast as possible, and try to go to another village that was safer.

When she returned home from visiting her friend, it was already too late. The Serbs were rounding up the men and taking them away. Young women were being taken to "rape hotels" for the soldiers.

The people who remained were told to leave at gunpoint. From her neighborhood, there was a group of 64 old men, women, and children. One baby girl was only two days old. They got as far as the Drina River, still in the city of Visegrad. They were stopped on the bridge that leads out of town.

There they were searched for money, jewelry, and anything else of value, and it was stolen from them. They stood on the bridge for two hours. During that time, the woman saw about 10 bodies either floating in the river or lying along its banks.

The five soldiers holding them on the bridge were all familiar to her. She had grown up with some of them and knew some of their families.

The 64 Muslims were led into a house and forced into one room. The soldiers made them take off their clothes, and their clothes were taken away.

The people waited in the room for a short time, and then the door was opened and someone threw in a bomb. It was not a regular bomb, but something that burned. In the madness, people tried to escape through the window. Then the commander came in with a machine gun and opened fire. Four people managed to escape through the window; the other 60 were killed, including her mother-in-law, with whom she lived. She herself was shot twice, once in the arm and once in the leg.

Of the people who died, she knew the names and families of 26 women, nine elderly men, and 19 children. The oldest was a 93-year-old man, and the youngest was the two-day-old baby girl.

She could not keep up with the other three who had escaped. There was a woman, the woman's son, and an elderly man. But she could only get a short distance away, where she found a sewer and crawled inside. She lay there for three days.

A Muslim woman who was still in Visegrad found her, after the other survivors said where they had last seen her. The woman administered some minor first aid, gave her food, and contacted her mother and father, who had also heard that their daughter was still alive.

They managed to come to her. In the evening, they had to crawl and walk, carrying her for more than a mile along sewage ditches to avoid being seen. Then they walked and hitchhiked 30 miles to the Muslim-held town of Gorazde, where she stayed in the hospital 22 days.

As soon as she was well enough, she was let out of the hospital to make room for others. Gorazde was under siege at the time, and the city was being bombed.

She, her son, and her parents again walked and hitchhiked through dangerous territory for five days until they reached Zenica.

During the whole interview, the mother had not said a word. She sat quietly, listening to the story, distractedly serving coffee now and then, but mostly looking down or out the window. The tears were in her eyes as the interview ended, and she was embarrassed for crying. She told the ten-year-old guide that four of her sons also have disappeared. There has been no word from them in six months.

They Have to Leave the Men Behind

A young woman says goodbye to her brother and father as she gets into a car. Her mother, sister, and a younger brother are going with her. They have to leave the men behind at the refugee center in Travnik. If the men were caught traveling, they would be put into the Bosnian Army or imprisoned by the Serbs. The family's visa is forged, but they are going to try to get out of Bosnia anyway. The women say they are afraid they will never see the older brother and father again.

▶ *THE CHRISTIAN SCIENCE MONITOR*

September 19, 1996; Copyright © 1996 by Laura Kay Rozen. Reprinted by permission.

Keeping Bosnia Whole: Why the World Cares—Five Reasons International Officials Aim for United State

by Laura Kay Rozen, special to *The Christian Science Monitor*

Sarajevo, Bosnia-Herzegovina—The international officials charged with keeping Bosnia together as a multi-ethnic state liken their task to building a house of cards—one they can only hope will get stronger with time. In the meantime, they say, only one thing will continue to be the cement holding the country together: international will.

Although last weekend's elections bolstered the power of nationalists who would split the country apart, the mediators charged with implementing the Dayton peace accords—the blueprint for peace—are now gearing up to overcome the obstacles to a united Bosnia.

But why all the effort? The cost of ethnic partition and secession, they say, would be too high for the West, as well as for the Balkans.

Specifically, there are five reasons driving the international community's efforts:

Bosnian Serb Independence Won't Work

Contrary to the nationalist aims of the Bosnian Serbs, independence of their entity, so-called Republika Srpska, is not viable, analysts say. "There is simply no real future for that little jagged piece of territory if it is not integrated into [Bosnia]," said U.S.

Balkans envoy, Assistant Secretary of State John Kornblum. "It is not a place that can secede and survive."

The dividing line between the Bosnian Serb area and Muslim-Croat Federation agreed to at the Wright-Patterson Air Force Base in Dayton, Ohio, last November was never meant to be an international border. It is a zig-zagging and impractical line that would impede economic and political development for both sides, as well as be militarily indefensible.

"The boundaries between the Serb and Muslim-Croat parts of Bosnia are meant to be fluid," explains Ambassador Michael Steiner, deputy to UN mediator Carl Bildt.

"Besides, the Republika Srpska has nowhere to secede into. [Serbian President Slobodan] Milosevic is not going to risk international ostracization and sanctions to support a secessionist Bosnian Serb state."

A Muslim State in Europe

U.S. and European officials are particularly concerned that a Muslim ministate—what would remain if Bosnia's Croats and Serbs secede—would be manipulated by radical Islamic countries. "Europe would have a very serious problem. Radical forces are just waiting for this to happen. You would have a Gaza Strip situation here," said Steiner, referring to the area the Israelis charge is a terrorist hotbed.

"At the [Muslim-led Party for Democratic Action] SDA rally at Kosovo stadium last week, there were 70,000 people. At the left and right of the crowd, there were the radicals, shouting in Farsi," explains Steiner. "The radical fringe of SDA is still a minority. But if things go the wrong way, they will be hardened. These radical forces will become dominant." It's not what the SDA wants, he says, "but they will be used." [*Authors' note*: This argument represents a prejudiced point of view that automatically associates countries with Islamic majorities with radical Islamic terrorism. Nevertheless, the reporter is correctly reporting it as a concern that was voiced.]

Regional Example. Diplomats say that international sanction of Serb secession would send a message to other ethnic groups in the region that aggression and genocide are acceptable ways to achieve their territorial and national goals.

"Look, 200,000 people were killed in this war, 3 million people were forced from their homes, many by ethnic cleansing, men and women were raped, tortured, starved, and slaughtered in Europe's first death camps since World War II. For them to let the Bosnian Serbs who sanctioned this behavior get their own state is morally despicable," says a UN official.

U.S. Envoy Richard Holbrooke also makes a moral case for why Serb secession cannot be tolerated. "No one objected to the 'Velvet Divorce' of Czechoslovakia. It was done in a democratic way. . . . But what happened here is aggression. Because of the nature of the process that unfolded here, it would not have been appropriate to sanction secession or partition."

Analysts say that many areas in the Balkans share conditions that led to ethnic conflict in Bosnia. The Albanians in Kosovo and Macedonia, the Hungarians in Romania and Slovakia, the Muslims in Sandzak share the problems of ethnic minorities in undemocratic states that offer minorities few rights and security, and have equally devastated economies. These minorities and their governments are watching Bosnia closely.

Refugees. Secession would mean refugees would never be able to return to their homes which are now held by other ethnic groups, and would therefore remain a source of political and economic tension. Steiner points out that over half of Bosnia's pre-war population—3 million people—has been displaced by the war, and are now living as refugees abroad or in refugee housing in other parts of Bosnia. The majority of refugees in Europe are Muslims who were ethnically cleansed from areas now controlled by Serbs.

Bosnian refugees are creating economic and social burdens in Croatia and Europe. Germany in particular—which has taken in more refugees than any other Western European country—has an interest in sending its 300,000 Bosnian refugees home.

"I don't think we will ever get stabilization without allowing those refugees who want to go back," says Steiner.

NATO Credibility

Analysts here are concerned that the failure to follow the multiethnic vision of the Dayton accord would devastate the organizations that have been sent here to implement the peace. NATO and U.S. leadership in the Bosnia peace effort would have failed to bring a permanent solution to Europe's worst conflict since World War II.

A breakdown of the multiethnic government would likely require a long-term engagement of NATO forces in Bosnia and would place these forces in a more dangerous situation.

Officials say that international will to end a new Bosnian war after the huge effort to implement Dayton would be exhausted. They also say that renewed fighting would seriously damage the credibility of the NATO alliance, whose first active engagement was to send 60,000 forces to enforce the Bosnia peace.

▶ U.S. DEPARTMENT OF STATE

From "Erasing History: Ethnic Cleansing in Kosovo"
Report released by the U.S. Department of State, Washington, D.C., May 1999

What began in late February 1998 as a Serb government campaign against the separatist Kosovo Liberation Army (KLA) has evolved into a comprehensive, premeditated, and systematic program to ethnically cleanse the Serbian province of Kosovo of its roughly 1.7 million ethnic Albanian residents (also referred to as Kosovar Albanians). Because Serbian authorities have denied access to international monitors, documentation efforts have been too fragmented to estimate definitively the number of missing and dead. . . .

The term "ethnic cleansing" first came into use during the mass expulsions of ethnic Muslims from towns in eastern Bosnia-Herzegovina in 1992; since then, media outlets, human rights groups and governments have used it on enough occasions to require careful definition. As used in this report, ethnic cleansing is defined as the systematic and forced removal of the members of an ethnic group from a community or communities in order to change the ethnic composition of a given region. In Bosnia, many ethnically cleansed towns and regions were eventually reoccupied by members of another ethnic group (who themselves often had been cleansed).

From the beginning, the [Serbian] regime in Belgrade has deliberately misled the international community and its own people about its ethnic cleansing campaign. Counterinsurgency operations against the KLA began in late February and early March 1998, when Serbian Ministry of Internal Affairs Police (MUP) attacked the villages of Likosane and Cirez. These attacks resulted in the death of 25 Kosovar Albanians, of which as many as 14 may have been summarily executed. . . .

In late March 1999, Serbian forces dramatically increased the scope and pace of their efforts, moving away from selective targeting of towns and regions suspected of KLA sympathies toward a sustained and systematic effort to ethnically cleanse the entire province of Kosovo. To date, Serb forces conducting ethnic cleansing operations have not yet tried to repopulate the over 500 towns and villages from which residents have been evicted. Some villages are now used as cover for Serb military emplacements. Many, however, remain depopulated. NATO is committed to ensuring the return of all Kosovars to their homes.

Since March 19, 1999, the Office of the United Nations High Commissioner for Refugees (UNHCR) estimates that over 700,000 Kosovars have fled to the Former Yugoslav Republic of Macedonia (211,000), Albania (404,000), Bosnia-Herzegovina (17,000), the Republic of Montenegro (62,000), and elsewhere (as of May 5, 1999). [See Figure 13.10.] The Governments of Macedonia, Albania, Bosnia, and Montenegro have provided land for camps, logistical support, and protection. NATO forces in Macedonia and Albania have helped establish transit camps. Other governments have begun to accept varying numbers of refugees to ease the pressure on the so-called "front-line" states. Even with such support, however, the front-line states will continue to bear the brunt of these mass expulsions, which has badly burdened the economies and upset the political balances of these states.

Although the media has focused almost exclusively on the story of the hundreds of thousands of exhausted refugees arriving at camps in Macedonia and Albania, another story has escaped their attention, in large part because Serbian authorities have not permitted entry into Kosovo. Those left behind in Kosovo—known as internally displaced persons, or IDPs—suffer under much worse conditions than even those faced by refugees. While independent sources have not been able to confirm reports of starvation among IDPs in Kosovo, many in all likelihood are experiencing food shortages, malnutrition, health problems, and other types of deprivation as a result of having to hide from Serbian forces for weeks in neighboring mountains and forests. Needless to say, they also likely face attack by Serbian forces. According to some reports, VJ [Yugoslav Army] units have thrown grenades from helicopters at fleeing IDPs. Shelling of civilians reportedly has been used to herd groups of refugees for later deportation.

Figure 13.10 Serb attacks in Kosovo and refugee flows from Kosovo.
Source: U.S. State Department, www.state.gov/www/regions/eur/map1.html.

From "Ethnic Cleansing in Kosovo: An Accounting (Executive Summary)"
Report released by the U.S. Department of State, Washington, D.C., December 1999

"Ethnic Cleansing in Kosovo: An Accounting" is a new chapter in our effort to document the extent of human rights and humanitarian law violations in Kosovo, and to convey the size and scope of the Kosovo conflict. The information in this report is drawn from refugee accounts, NGO [nongovernmental organizations] documentation, press accounts, and declassified information from government and international organization sources.

The atrocities against Kosovar Albanians documented in this report occurred primarily between March and late June, 1999.

A central question is the number of Kosovar Albanian victims of Serbian forces in Kosovo. Many bodies were found when KFOR [U.N. Kosovo Peacekeeping Force] and the ICTY [International Criminal Tribunal for the Former Yugoslavia] entered Kosovo in June 1999. The evidence is also now clear that Serbian forces conducted a systematic campaign to burn or destroy bodies, or to bury the bodies, then rebury them to conceal evidence of Serbian crimes. On June 4, at the end of the conflict, the Department of State issued the last of a series of weekly ethnic cleansing reports, available at www.state.gov/www/regions/eur/rpt_990604_ksvo_ethnic.html, concluding that at least 6,000 Kosovar Albanians were victims of mass murder, with an unknown number of victims of individual killings, and an unknown number of bodies burned or destroyed by Serbian forces throughout the conflict.

The Prosecutor said her office had exhumed 2,108 bodies from 195 of the 529 known mass graves. . . . Enough evidence has emerged to conclude that probably around 10,000 Kosovar Albanians were killed by Serbian forces [see Figure 13.11].

Death represents only one facet of Serbian actions in Kosovo. Over 1.5 million Kosovar Albanians—at least 90 percent of the estimated 1998 Kosovar Albanian

Figure 13.11 Before and after aerial photography evidence of mass graves.
Source: www.state.gov/www/regions/eur/rpt_9905_ethnic_ksvo_7a.html.

© 2010 John Wiley & Sons, Inc.

population of Kosovo—were forcibly expelled from their homes. Tens of thousands of homes in at least 1,200 cities, towns, and villages have been damaged or destroyed. During the conflict, Serbian forces and paramilitaries implemented a systematic campaign to ethnically cleanse Kosovo—aspects of this campaign include the following:

- *Forcible Displacement of Kosovar Albanian Civilians:* Serbian authorities conducted a campaign of forced population movement. In contrast to actions taken during 1998, Yugoslav Army units and armed civilians joined the police in systematically expelling Kosovar Albanians at gunpoint from both villages and larger towns in Kosovo.

- *Looting of Homes and Businesses:* There are numerous reports of Serbian forces robbing residents before burning their homes. Another round of robbery occurred as Serbian forces stole from fleeing Kosovars as they crossed the border to Montenegro, Albania, or Macedonia.

- *Widespread Burning of Homes:* Over 1,200 residential areas were at least partially burned after late March, 1999. Kosovar Albanians have reported that over 500 villages were burned after March, 1999.

- *Use of Human Shields:* Refugees claim that Serbian forces used Kosovar Albanians to escort military convoys and shield facilities throughout the province. Other reporting indicates that Serbian forces intentionally positioned ethnic Albanians at sites they believed were targets for NATO airstrikes.

- *Detentions:* Serbian forces systematically separated military-aged men from the general population as Kosovars were expelled. These men were detained in facilities ranging from cement factories to prisons. Many of these detainees were forced to dig trenches and were physically abused. At least 2,000 Kosovar Albanians remain in detention in around a dozen Serbian prisons today.

- *Summary Executions:* There are accounts of summary executions at about 500 sites across Kosovo.

- *Exhumation of Mass Graves:* Serbian forces burned, destroyed, or exhumed bodies from mass graves in an attempt to destroy evidence. Some were reinterred in individual graves.

- *Rape:* There are numerous accounts indicating that the organized and individual rape of Kosovar Albanian women by Serbian forces was widespread. For example, Serbian forces systematically raped women in Djakovica and Pec, and in some cases rounded up women and took them to hotels where they were raped by troops under encouragement of their commanders. Rape is most likely an underreported atrocity because of the stigma attached to the victims in traditional Kosovar Albanian society.

- *Violations of Medical Neutrality:* Kosovar Albanian physicians, patients and medical facilities were systematically attacked. Many health care facilities were used as protective cover for military activities; NGOs report the destruction by Serbian forces of at least 100 clinics, pharmacies, and hospitals.

- *Identity Cleansing:* Kosovar Albanians were systematically stripped of identity and property documents including passports, land titles, automobile license plates, identity cards, and other forms of documentation. As much as 50 percent of the population may be without documentation.

By systematically destroying schools, places of worship, and hospitals, Serbian forces sought to destroy social identity and the fabric of Kosovar Albanian society.

- *Aftermath:* Following the withdrawal of Serbian forces in June, Kosovo saw manifestations of a new set of human rights problems. These include acts of retribution against the Serb minority, including the killing of 200–400 Serb residents. In addition, as many as 23,000 conscientious objectors, draft evaders, and deserters in Serbia are threatened with legal action.

► BY THE AUTHORS

Update on the Former Yugoslavia to March, 2009

Bosnia

The fighting in Bosnia described in these readings was not easily brought to a halt. As definitive evidence of genocide mounted, the United Nations and North Atlantic Treaty Organization (NATO) finally moved to stop the bloodshed. A "no flight" zone was declared over Bosnia, and international economic sanctions were imposed on Yugoslavia. Eventually, the ban on weapons imports into Bosnia—originally designed to douse the fire—was lifted to enable the Muslims to defend themselves. The Bosnian Muslims then joined forces with the Croats to mount a counteroffensive against Serbian strongholds. The Croats successfully regained control of the Serb-populated regions of Croatia, and the Muslims succeeded in reestablishing some territorial corridors between their safe havens.

Finally, an on-again, off-again cease-fire was reached, and U.N. peacekeeping forces from a variety of countries, including the United States and Canada, moved in. Bosnian Serbs at that time controlled about 70 percent of Bosnia, with the Muslim-Croat alliance controlling the rest. As the economic embargo began causing real hardship, Yugoslavia's President Milosevic pressured the Bosnian Serbs to the peace table. In 1995, U.S. Secretary of State Warren Christopher brokered a peace deal known as the *Dayton Accords* that all parties reluctantly accepted. Bosnia was to remain a multination state but was divided into two autonomous parts. The Bosnian Serbs received 49 percent of the territory, which they renamed *Republica Srpska*, with 51 percent for the still-combined Muslim-Croat Federation (see Figure 13.12). Notice how the boundaries were designed to make each group's territory a contiguous whole, even if it means having a narrow corridor as a connector. This way, there is free unrestricted movement within each ethnic republic and one less excuse to restart the war.

In the Muslim-Croat Federation, the predominantly Croatian area of Bosnia known as *Herceg-Bosna* had evolved into a ministate of sorts, with stronger ties to Zagreb than to Sarajevo. While all three nations have some "multiculturalists" who favor a unified Bosnia and nationalists who favor separatism or irredentism, a July 1996 poll found that 95 percent of Bosnian Serbs and two-thirds of Bosnian Croats opposed a unified country. Only Muslims favored keeping Bosnia whole. The U.S. Department of State's policy was that, unless indicted war criminals are brought to justice, per the Dayton Accords, the festering rivalries that produced the war in the first place would prevent a lasting peace. Some European governments, however, argued that punishing the Serbs would be counterproductive because it is more important to rebuild Bosnia economically. Then, when the peacekeeping troops

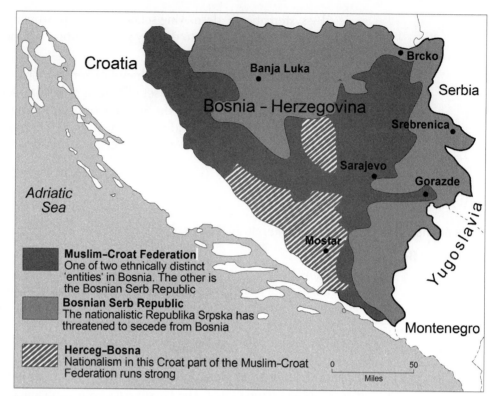

Figure 13.12 Bosnia-Herzegovina after the 1995 Dayton peace accords.

do pull out, there will be a functioning economy so that all three ethnic groups will have a stake in preserving the peace. The United States has poured billions of dollars into Bosnia to help with reconstruction, humanitarian assistance, economic development, and military reconstruction. European Union Forces (EUFOR) took over peacekeeping duties from NATO in December 2004. In October 2007, EUFOR's mission changed from peacekeeping to civil policing, and the number of European troops was reduced from 7,000 to 2,500.

Kosovo

The United States and its European allies bear some responsibility for the Kosovo crisis. The Kosovo Liberation Army (KLA) was a small fringe organization with little popular support for armed insurrection in Kosovo until after the Dayton peace conference. The conference excluded any Kosovar Albanian delegates, and many Albanians concluded that "the reward for nonviolence was international neglect" (Hooper, 1999).[6] When increased Albanian unrest led to a Serbian crackdown in 1998, the U.S. unwillingness to follow through on its threats of air strikes against Yugoslavian military targets emboldened the Serbs and helped convince the Albanians to take matters into their own hands. International attempts to broker a peace settlement in February 1999 failed dismally, as Yugoslavian military, police, and paramilitary units amassed within and around Kosovo.

Having learned its lesson in Bosnia, NATO responded to Serbian attacks much faster in Kosovo, although not fast enough to stop the Serbs from ethnically cleansing most Albanians from Kosovo (see U.S. Department of State reports). On March

[6]Hooper, James. Kosovo: America's Balkan Problem. *Current History* (April 1999):159–164.

© 2010 John Wiley & Sons, Inc.

24, 1999, two weeks after the start of the Serbian offensive, NATO began launching air strikes against Yugoslavian military, police, television, transportation, electricity, and water supply targets. The air war eventually crippled Yugoslavia, and two to three months after the fighting began, Yugoslavia accepted a cease-fire and began to withdraw. Peacekeeping troops have been contributed by 19 NATO members (including the United States, Canada, and almost all of their European allies) as well as 18 non-NATO countries (including Russia, other Slavic former Soviet states such as Ukraine, other Muslim former Soviet states such as Azerbaijan, and Islamic Middle Eastern states such as Jordan). Peacekeeping forces are involved in rebuilding infrastructure and institutions and removing land mines but have been unable to completely prevent Albanians from revenge attacks and ethnic cleansing against the remaining Serbs. An estimated 500 to 1,000 Serbs have been murdered since the Yugoslavian Army pulled out. Many Kosovar Serbs have abandoned their homes and fled to Serbia proper, fueling another chapter in the long annals of Serbian victimhood. As in Bosnia, a de facto partition has taken place, with Serbs concentrating in North Mitrovica, an area adjacent to Serbia and home to a vast gold and zinc mining complex.

In June 1999, following the 78-day NATO campaign to quell the violence, the U.N. Security Council Resolution 1244(1999) placed Kosovo under a transitional administration, the U.N. Interim Administration Mission in Kosovo (UNMIK), to establish and oversee "the development of provisional democratic self-governing institutions to ensure conditions for a peaceful and normal life for all inhabitants in Kosovo."[7] In interim elections in October 2000, all three major parties advocated eventual independence. From 2000 to 2008, as Kosovo's Provisional Institutions of Self Government (PISG) were established and began to assume more responsibilities, UNMIK has gradually scaled back from running the region to monitoring and supporting local institutions. A U.N.-led process to determine Kosovo's final status began in late 2005 but failed to reach agreement between Serbia and Kosovo. On February 17, 2008, the Kosovo Assembly declared Kosovo independent. Since then, over 50 countries have recognized Kosovo. Serbia continues to reject Kosovo's independence and has asked the International Court of Justice for a ruling on the legality of Kosovo's independence declaration under international law.

Macedonia

In March 2001, ethnic violence erupted in Macedonia, one of the six former republics of Yugoslavia. Bordered by Albania, Kosovo, Serbia, Bulgaria, and Greece, Macedonia's population is 23 percent Albanian (see Figure 13.8, Table 13.1). Macedonia had been lauded as the only former Yugoslavian republic that had seceded without bloodshed. Its multinational population was thought to coexist peacefully. Less than two years after the war in Kosovo ended, however, Albanian nationalist fighters and their weapons began crossing the border from Kosovo to attack Slavic Macedonian targets in the mountainous Albanian majority zone. The rebels called for a change in the Macedonian constitution to upgrade the status of the Albanian minority—a change that would essentially partition the country along ethnic lines. Although the situation sounds hauntingly familiar, Macedonia's situation contains some unique elements. When Macedonia seceded from Yugoslavia in 1991, the neighboring state of Greece refused to recognize its independence

---

[7]United Nations Interim Administration Mission in Kosovo (UNMIK). 2008. *Kosovo in June, 2008:* www.unmikonline.org/docs/2008/Fact_Sheet_July_2008.pdf.

until it agreed to change its official name to the Former Yugoslavian Republic of Macedonia (FYROM) to distinguish it from the Macedonian region of Greece. Greece imposed a trade blockade on Macedonia, which it finally lifted in 1995. Meanwhile, the neighboring state of Bulgaria has questioned whether Macedonians are a nation at all or really an offshoot of the Slavic Bulgarian nation. There is also a small Serbian minority (2 percent) in Macedonia.

Serbia and Montenegro

In one of the most unexpected and dramatic events of the entire saga, the Serbian people succeeded in overthrowing President Slobodan Milosevic, the architect of a decade of ethnic cleansing. The Serbian people, although still strongly nationalistic, had grown tired of war, air raids, poverty, and ostracism from the international community. Average income had dropped to $40 per month, and the streets of Belgrade had become one large flea market. Elections were held in September 2000, and by all reports the opposition party triumphed, although the government denied it. In early October 2000, after a general strike, massive crowds began gathering in the streets of Belgrade for speeches and protests. On October 5 the crowd stormed the Parliament building, and with Serbian troops unwilling to fire on their own people, the Milosevic era came to a quick, bloodless end. Milosevic was charged with crimes against humanity by the U.N. International Criminal Tribunal at The Hague, Netherlands, but was found dead in his cell in 2006 before the trial was completed.

In new elections on December 24, 2000, moderate reformer Vojislav Kostunica was elected President of Yugoslavia with the promise to complete democratic reforms. Many thorny issues faced the new regime, including international war crime indictments against former Serbian leaders, economic reconstruction, trade relations with other former Yugoslavian republics, and pressure for unification with, and protection of, Serbs in Bosnia and Kosovo. Yugoslavia was readmitted to the United Nations in 2001.

On March 12, 2003, a sniper killed the prime minister of Serbia, Zoran Djindjic, the charismatic philosopher-politician who rallied the people to oust Slobodan Milosevic in 2000. Former members of the Milosevic regime now involved in organized crime were believed to be behind the assassination. The reform-minded and pro-Western Djindjic had threatened to arrest Gen. Ratko Mladic, who, in 2009 is still wanted by the tribunal for war crimes in Bosnia.

Meanwhile, the party in Montenegro favoring independence from Yugoslavia and its Serb majority narrowly won national elections in April 2001. Montenegrins, who comprise about two-thirds of the population, share a similar religion and language with the Serbs but historically have developed separately from them (see Figure 13.8, Table 13.1). Prior to the downfall of Milosevic, the United States was encouraging Montenegrins to seek independence as a way of weakening the Milosevic regime in Yugoslavia. After Milosevic fell, however, the United States did an about-face and began discouraging them because independence for any new Balkan nation could send a "green light" to the others and precipitate new wars.

In 2002, the Serbian and Montenegran regions of Yugoslavia began negotiations to forge a looser relationship. These talks became a reality on February 4, 2003, when their parliament restructured the country into a loose federation of two republics; The new state was officially called *Serbia and Montenegro* for three years.

Under the Constitutional Charter of Serbia and Montenegro, each region within the state retained the right to hold a referendum on independence from the state union. In May 2006, Montenegro invoked that right. The support for seceding from Serbia was 55.5 percentage, just barely exceeding the 55 percentage threshold required. Montenegro formally declared its independence on June 3, 2006. There are now two separate democratic states, one called Serbia and the other called Montenegro (Figure 13.7c).

As of March 2009, the status of the autonomous region of Vojvodina, which contains 27 percent of Serbia's population and a sizable Hungarian minority, is unclear. Vojvodina currently enjoys a degree of autonomy, and in October 2008 its Assembly passed a new draft Statute of Autonomy that has yet to be approved by the Serbian Parliament. Serbian nationalist groups have accused the Vojvodina Assembly of attempting to divide the country. The Assembly spokesman has reiterated that "Vojvodina does not want secession" and emphasized that the Vojvodina situation should not be confused with Kosovo.

Name: _____   Instructor: _____

Breaking Up Is Hard to Do: Nations, States, and Nation-States

▶ ACTIVITY 2: IRAQAPHOBIA

Activity 2 requires you to read articles and reports about Iraq (pronounced i-RAK) and then answer questions about them (see Figure 13.13). The first reading is excerpted from the U.S. Library of Congress's online country study of Iraq, edited by Helen Chapin Metz. The *Country Study* Web site contains online versions of books previously published in hard copy by the Federal Research Division of the Library of Congress under the Country Studies/Area Handbook Program sponsored by the U.S. Department of the Army. The Army originally sponsored this series to provide background on regions in which U.S. forces might be deployed. "The books represent the analysis of the authors and should not be construed as an expression of an official United States Government position, policy, or decision." Over 100 countries are covered; some, like Afghanistan, have just recently been added. We, the authors of *Human Geography in Action*, have selected (and occasionally added to) various sections of *Iraq: A Country Study* to weave into a narrative of Iraq prior to the Gulf War in 1991. The Iraq Country Study has not been updated since 1988, but your next reading picks up the story from there.

The second source is a detailed chronology of *The Long Road to War* from the Web site of the television newsmagazine *Frontline*, produced by the Public Broadcasting System (PBS). PBS is the TV network partially funded by the federal government to bring quality TV to the population. PBS is independently

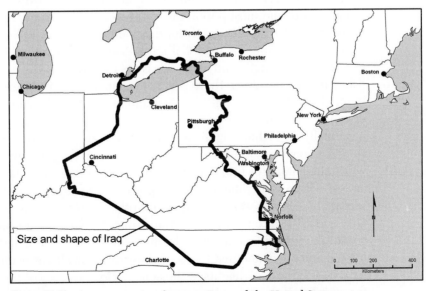

Figure 13.13 Area comparison between Iraq and the United States.

© 2010 John Wiley & Sons, Inc.

run, however, and is not a propaganda mouthpiece for U.S. government policies. Chronologies are becoming an ever more popular information resource on Web sites and are a good way to familiarize yourself with the background of a long-running crisis. Chronologies by themselves may not give you enough deep background information to make sense of the sequence of events, but paired with a political-historic-geographic background like the Library of Congress Country Study, they can provide most of what you need to make sense of international crises. This chronology actually begins with Saddam Hussein's childhood, but we pick it up in 1979 when he becomes president of Iraq. The chronology ends a few months before the war began, and so we, your textbook authors, have filled in some key events up until the time this book went to press.

The third source is an article from the *New York Review of Books* called "How to Get Out of Iraq." According to its Web site, the *New York Review of Books* is a biweekly magazine "in which the most interesting and qualified minds of our time . . . discuss current books and issues in depth." Armed with the deep background and the chronology leading to war, you are now ready for this kind of in-depth analysis. The author is Peter Galbraith, a senior diplomatic fellow at the Center for Arms Control and Non-Proliferation, and formerly a professor at the National War College in Washington, D.C. and U.S. Ambassador to Croatia from 1993 to 1998 during the Yugoslav crisis. He brings that experience to bear on the possibility of breaking Iraq into three semi-independent regions. He is known as one of America's leading experts on the Kurdish people, having investigated Saddam's use of chemical weapons against the Kurds for Congress and helped establish the "No-Fly Zone" protecting the Kurds after the first Gulf War. He has extensive experience working with the United Nations in various capacities. Ambassador Galbraith holds an A.B from Harvard College, an M.A. from Oxford University, and a J.D. from Georgetown University Law Center. Galbraith published this article in May 2004, and while the new Iraqi constitution had not been drafted, let alone approved, at that time, his analysis was extremely relevant. We chose this article over more recent ones for several reasons. First, it strives for a certain degree of balance by telling you what has gone right and what has gone wrong with the war. Second, it describes the first year of the U.S. occupation and reconstruction of Iraq, which is so crucial to the current situation yet was not covered by other articles we found. Third, and most important, it delves *deeply* into the nation and state issues so important to this chapter, from the point of view of the Sunni Arabs, the Shiite Arabs, and the Sunni Kurds. Galbraith discusses a three-region federal system of government at length, and while this is not exactly what the new constitution established in October 2005, there are many similarities. As you read this article, keep in mind that (a) it was written a year and half before the constitution, and (b) it is, of course, just one expert's opinion.

Finally, we include highlights of the new Iraqi constitution, using selected quotes from the document itself. The constitution sets up the governmental structure under which the nations of Iraq will try to coexist. Whether the nations of Iraq peacefully coexist within something called Iraq, break into separate states, plunge into civil war, ignite a wider war, or merge with other states or regions—and how long the U.S. and U.K. troops remain in Iraq—may largely depend on the success of this constitution. Keep in mind that the draft constitution contained provisions allowing it to be amended, and that the U.S. constitution itself has been amended 27 times. Attached to these highlights of the constitution is a map of the referendum results for each Iraqi province, along with a brief commentary on it, made by us.

▶ ACTIVITY 2 READINGS

Frontline (WGBH, Public Broadcasting System). 2003. *The Long Road to War—Chronology:* www.pbs.org/wgbh/pages/frontline/shows/longroad/etc/cron.html

Galbraith, Peter W. 2004. How to Get Out of Iraq. *The New York Review of Books* 51(8), May 13, 2004: www.nybooks.com/articles/17103

Metz, Helen Chapin (ed.). 1990. *Iraq: A Country Study* (4th ed.). Library of Congress, Federal Research Division. Area Handbook Series: http://lcweb2.loc.gov/frd/cs/iqtoc.html

Text of the Draft Iraqi Constitution: www.un.int/iraq/TAL_Constitution/Draft_Iraqi_Constitution_english.pdf (highlights quoted by the authors)

▶ QUESTIONS

These questions are arranged in the order in which the answers are found or implied in the four sources. Occasionally, however, you will have to combine the new information with previous information to come up with the correct answer. Answers to questions marked by an asterisk (*) cannot be obtained directly in the readings. You'll need to think critically about the readings and apply concepts properly to figure them out.

Section A: From Ancient Times to the Creation of Iraq

Refer to Iraq: A Country Study, *the sections on "Historical Background" and "Enter Britain."*

2.1. What is the ancient name of the area presently called Iraq? _____

Name one of the ancient civilizations that flourished there. _____

2.2. What are the two main rivers running through the region?

_____ and _____

2.3. Throughout Iraqi history Iraq's many autonomous social units, its lack of stone for road building, its location at the eastern flank of the Arab world, and the periods when the irrigation systems fell into disrepair—all these were forces of political _____. (centralization or fragmentation)

2.4. What outside empire dominated this region in the several centuries prior to World War I?

_____.

2.5. After World War I, control of Iraq was given to what country? _____. What international organization gave away control of Iraq? _____.

2.6. The boundaries of Iraq were drawn by _____ with virtually no consideration of _____

_____

© 2010 John Wiley & Sons, Inc.

2.7. Iraq became independent in what year? _____

2.8. Iraq's first type of government was _____
(communism, democracy, military dictatorship, or monarchy).

Section B: Nation and State Geography

Refer to Iraq: A Country Study, *sections on "Religious Background," "Language Background," "Kurdish Background," and "Religion/Language Summary" and Figures 13.15, 13.17, and 3.6 in Chapter 3.*

2.9. In which half-century did Islam arrive in the area that is now Iraq (see Figure 3.6)? _____ half of the _____ 00s.

2.10. What historical event is responsible for the divide between Sunni Muslims and Shia Muslims?

_____

_____

_____

2.11. What are the *five* pillars of Islam? Give the Arabic words and explain each one.

_____

_____

_____

_____

2.12. What was the official language of Iraq from its inception to the U.S. overthrow of Saddam Hussein? _____

2.13. Iraq is a _____ (nation, state, nation-state).*

2.14. The Kurds are a _____ (nation, state, nation-state)*, and their homeland overlaps which five countries?

_____ _____ _____ _____ _____

2.15.   Fill in the following table based on your readings and maps:

	Language	Sect of Islam	Percentage of Iraqi Population*	Region of Iraq (e. g., north, west, central, etc.)
Iraqi Shia				
Iraqi Sunni Arabs				
Iraqi Kurds				
Kuwaiti majority			n.a	n.a
Iranian majority			n.a	n.a

*Note that there are also several small minority groups in Iraq in addition to the three largest groups.

2.16. According to the "Religion/Language Summary" of the *Iraq Country Study*, Saddam Hussein, like most past rulers of Iraq, belonged to which ethnic group?

_____

Section C: The Iran-Iraq War

Refer to Iraq: A Country Study, *the section on "Enter Saddam," including text box on "U.S. Support of Saddam Hussein," and* The Long Road to War, *section on 1980–1988: "Geopolitics and the Iran-Iraq War," and Figures 13.15, 13.17, and 13.18.*

2.17. In 1980, Iraq invaded Iran. What was the importance of the territory over which Iran and Iraq were fighting? _____

_____

_____

2.18. This territory, however important, was not the only reason for Iraq's attack on Iran. According to the *Iraq Country Study*, Saddam Hussein was "threatened by the 1979 Islamic Revolution in Iran and by its potential influence on Iraq's majority population." Why? (Refer to the table in Question 2.15.*)

_____

_____

_____

2.19. Which country did the United States support in the Iran-Iraq war from 1980 to 1988? _____

Why?

_____

_____

_____

2.20. Name *three* specific kinds of military and technical support the United States offered to Saddam Hussein's regime during the Iran-Iraq war.

_____

_____

_____

Section D: The Gulf War

Refer to Iraq: A Country Study, *section on "Enter Saddam" and* The Long Road to War, *sections on "1990–1991: The Buildup to War," "1991: The Gulf War and Its Aftermath," and "1991–1998: Trying to Disarm Saddam," and Figures 13.15 and 13.17.*

2.21. In 1990, Iraq invaded _____.

2.22. What were Iraq's reasons for the invasion? (*Note: Be sure to check both the* Iraq Country Study *and* The Long Road to War *for reasons, because different reasons are given.*)

_____

_____

_____

2.23. The people of the invaded country *differ* from Saddam's Sunni/Arab nation on the basis of: (check one—see table in Question 2.15*).

language _____
religious group _____
both _____
neither _____

2.24. After the Gulf War in 1991, the United Nations Security Council adopted Resolution 687 that required Saddam to

_____

_____

2.25. One year after the September 11, 2001, terrorist attack on the World Trade Center towers in New York, the Bush Administration released its National Security Strategy, which came to be known as the Bush Doctrine. What were the *three* key elements of the Bush Doctrine?

_____

_____

_____

Section E: The Invasion of Iraq and Overthrow of Saddam Hussein

Refer to The Long Road to War, *sections on "2001–2003: Iraq—Test Case of a New Foreign Policy," "Saddam Overthrown," and "Occupation and Reconstruction of Iraq," and to* How to Get Out of Iraq, *sections 1–4.*

2.26. What were the two reasons publicly stated by the United States at that time for their invasion of Iraq in March 2003?

_____

_____

2.27. Which major countries supported the U.S.-led invasion?

_____

Which major countries opposed it?

_____

2.28. According to Peter Galbraith, the main thing that went right in the U.S. invasion/occupation of Iraq was the overthrow of Saddam Hussein and the Baath Party. Give *two* of Galbraith's specific examples of why it was "one of the two most cruel and inhumane regimes in the second half of the twentieth century."

_____

_____

2.29. According to Peter Galbraith, what are some important things that went wrong in the U.S. invasion/occupation of Iraq? Fill in the blanks to complete each one.

Discontent with the U.S.-led occupation boiled over into an _____ in the Shiite areas of Iraq and a persistent _____ in the Sunni Triangle.

U.S. credibility abroad has been undermined by the failure to find _____.

Unchecked looting effectively gutted every important public institution in the city with the notable exception of the _____ Ministry.

The U.S. official in charge of prisons decided to work with the warden of _____ prison, apparently unaware of its fearsome reputation as the place where tens of thousands perished under Saddam Hussein.

Section F: Will Iraq Stay Together?: The Geography of Nations and States

Refer to How to Get Out of Iraq, *sections 5–7, What the New Constitution Says (including election map), Figures 13.15, 13.17, and 13.23.*

2.30. Since 1991, the Iraqi Kurds have effectively governed themselves through the semi-independent Kurdistan Regional Government. This is best described as a form of _____ (federal state, nation, nation-state, regional autonomy, or unitary state).*

2.31. The people of Kurdistan almost unanimously prefer independence to being part of Iraq. This is best described as an example of _____. (ethnonationalism, irredentism, nationalism, separatism, or secession)*

2.32. Iranian Shiites, such as the Ayotollah al-Sistani and, from the grave, Ayotollah Khomeini, have enormous political and spiritual influence in southern Iraq. Hypothetically, if the Shiites in Iraq wanted to join their territory with that of their fellow Shiites in Iran, or if the government in Iran tried to claim the Shia region of southern Iraq on the basis of a common national religion, the political geography term that would describe this desire best is _____. (ethnonationalism, irredentism, or nationalism)*

2.33. In contrast to Shiite Arabs and Sunni Kurds, Sunni Arabs have always felt a strong sense of _____ toward Iraq as a whole. (nationalism, ethnonationalism, or irredentism)

2.34. According to Galbraith, "The breakup of Iraq is not a realistic possibility for the present." Which outside countries have the most to lose if the Iraqi Kurds become independent?

_____ _____ _____

Why?

_____

_____

2.35. Why wouldn't the Sunni Arabs want to divorce themselves from the Kurds and Shiites and create a separate Sunni-majority state of their own in the central and western regions where they are a majority?

_____

_____

2.36. If the three main nations of Iraq were to try to divide Iraq into three separate ethnically based independent states, which "unresolved territorial issue" would be most "explosive" and possibly plunge Iraq into violent conflict? _____ (name a city)

What makes this issue so explosive and contentious?

_____

_____

_____

_____

On October 15, 2005, the Iraqi people voted to approve a new constitution for Iraq. Answer the following questions about it.

2.37. Which form of government did they adopt?

___ Unitary state

___ Unitary state with regional autonomy

___ Federal state

___ Federal state with regional autonomy

2.38. Which nation would likely be most in favor of each of the following parts of the constitution? (*While you may be able to find answers to some parts of questions 2.38 and 2.39 by going back through the Galbraith article and the *Iraq Country Study*, what we have in mind here is for you to use the general knowledge you have learned about the three nations of Iraq.)

"Its Arab people are part of the Arab nation."

___ Sunni Arabs ___ Shiite Arabs ___ Kurds ___ All groups

"Islam is the official religion of the state and is a basic source of legislation. No law can be passed that contradicts the undisputed rules of Islam."

___ Sunni Arabs ___ Shiite Arabs ___ Kurds ___ All groups

"No law can be passed that contradicts the principles of democracy."

___ Sunni Arabs ___ Shiite Arabs ___ Kurds ___ All groups

"Arabic and Kurdish are the two official languages for Iraq. Iraqis are guaranteed the right to educate their children in their mother tongues."

___ Sunni Arabs ___ Shiite Arabs ___ Kurds ___ All groups

"The federal authority will maintain the unity of Iraq, its integrity, independence, sovereignty and its democratic federal system."

___ Sunni Arabs ___ Shiite Arabs ___ Kurds ___ All groups

"The governments of regions have the right to practice legislative, executive and judicial powers according to this constitution, except in what is listed as exclusive powers of the federal authorities. The regional authority has the right to amend the implementation of the federal law in the region in the case of a contradiction between the federal and regional laws in matters that do not pertain to the exclusive powers of the federal authorities."

___ Sunni Arabs ___ Shiite Arabs ___ Kurds ___ All groups

"The region's government is responsible for all that is required to manage the region, in particular establishing and organizing internal security forces for the region such as police, security and regional guards."

___ Sunni Arabs ___ Shiite Arabs ___ Kurds ___ All groups

2.39 Which nation would likely be least in favor of each of the following parts of the constitution?

"Entities or trends that advocate, instigate, justify or propagate racism, terrorism, 'takfir' (declaring someone an infidel), or sectarian cleansing are banned, especially the Saddamist Baath Party in Iraq and its symbols, under any name."

___ Sunni Arabs ___ Shiite Arabs ___ Kurds ___ All groups

The federal authorities will have "exclusive powers" over foreign policy and national defense.

___ Sunni Arabs ___ Shiite Arabs ___ Kurds ___ All groups

"A quota [on revenues from oil and gas] should be defined for a specified time for affected regions that were deprived in an unfair way by the former regime or later on, in a way to ensure balanced development in different parts of the country."

___ Sunni Arabs ___ Shiite Arabs ___ Kurds ___ All groups

► ACTIVITY 2 READINGS

► THE LIBRARY OF CONGRESS

Adapted by the authors from: **Iraq: A Country Study**

Helen Chapin Metz, editor.

Historical Background

Iraq became a sovereign, independent state in 1932. Although the modern state, the Republic of Iraq, is quite young, the history of the land and its people dates back more than 5,000 years. Indeed, Iraq contains the world's richest known archaeological sites. Here, in ancient Mesopotamia ("the land between the rivers"), the first civilization—that of Sumer—appeared in the Near East, followed later by Babylon and Assyria. Despite the millennium separating the two epochs, Iraqi history displays a continuity shaped by adaptation to the ebbings and flowings of the Tigris and Euphrates Rivers [Figure 13.14]. Allowed to flow unchecked, the rivers wrought destruction in terrible floods that inundated whole towns. When the rivers were controlled by irrigation dikes and other waterworks, the land became extremely fertile.

Mesopotamia could also be an extremely threatening environment, however, driving its peoples to seek security from the vicissitudes of nature. Throughout Iraqi history, various groups have formed autonomous, self-contained social units that exerted a powerful fragmenting force on Iraqi culture. Two other factors that have inhibited political centralization are the absence of stone and Iraq's geographic location as the eastern flank of the Arab world [see Chapter 2, Activity 1: Mapping Culture Regions]. For much of Iraqi history, the lack of stone has severely hindered the building of roads. As a result, many parts of the country have remained beyond government control. Also, because it borders non-Arab Turkey and Iran and because of the great agricultural potential of its river valley, Iraq has attracted waves of ethnically diverse migrations. Although this influx of people has enriched Iraqi culture, it also has disrupted the country's internal balance and has led to deep-seated schisms.

Throughout Iraqi history, the conflict between political fragmentation and centralization has been reflected in the struggles among tribes and cities for the food-producing flatlands of the river valleys. When a central power neglected to keep

Figure 13.14 The Tigris and Euphrates rivers have been the water source for agriculture and the lifeblood for civilization for millennia.

© **2010 John Wiley & Sons, Inc.**

the waterworks in repair, land fell into disuse, and tribes attacked settled peoples for precious and scarce agricultural commodities. For nearly 600 years, between the collapse of the Abbasid Empire in the thirteenth century and the waning years of the Ottoman Empire in the late nineteenth century, government authority was tenuous and tribal Iraq was, in effect, autonomous. At the beginning of the twentieth century, Iraq's disconnected—and often antagonistic—ethnic, religious, and tribal social groups professed little or no allegiance to the central government. As a result, the all-consuming concern of contemporary Iraqi history has been the forging of a nation-state out of this diverse and conflict-ridden social structure and the concomitant transformation of parochial loyalties, both tribal and ethnic, into a national identity.

Enter Britain

By the beginning of the twentieth century, enfeebled Ottoman rule had invited intense competition among European powers for commercial benefits and for spheres of influence. The British feared that a hostile German presence in the Fertile Crescent would threaten British oil interests in Iran and perhaps even India itself. In 1914 when the British discovered that Turkey, home of the Ottomans, was entering the war on the side of the Germans, British forces from India landed, and by March 1917 the British had captured Baghdad. At the 1919 Paris Peace Conference, under the League of Nations Covenant, Iraq was formally made a Class-A mandate entrusted to Britain. [A *mandate* was a mechanism for the winning powers of World War I to temporarily take over the former colonies of the losing powers and prepare them for independence.]

The League of Nations actually granted a broad swath of formerly Ottoman territory to Britain, from Egypt to Iraq, as mandated territory. As the controlling power, Britain was able to define the boundaries of the countries to be created out of the mandated territory. Britain defined the territorial limits of Iraq with little correspondence to natural frontiers or traditional tribal and ethnic settlements. Britain also paid little heed to Iraq's need for a port at the Tigris' and Euphrates' outlet to the Persian Gulf, a delta area known as the Shatt al Arab. Britain made Kuwait a separate territory and eventually a separate state, pinching Iraq's access to the Gulf.

Between 1918 and 1958, British policy in Iraq had far-reaching effects. At the Cairo Conference of 1921, the British chose Emir Faisal ibn Hussain as Iraq's first King. The British saw in Faisal a leader who possessed sufficient nationalist and Islamic credentials to have broad appeal, but as a Saudi Arabian he was also vulnerable enough to remain dependent on their support. Faisal traced his descent from the family of the Prophet Muhammad, and his ancestors had held political authority in the holy cities of Mecca and Medina since the tenth century. From 1921 to 1932, Iraq remained a British mandate territory that Faisal ruled with the permission and guidance of the British. After independence from Britain in 1932, the monarchy lasted until a coup d'etat ended the reign of Faisal's grandson, King Faisal II, in 1958.

Ultimately, the British-created monarchy suffered from a chronic legitimacy crisis: The concept of a monarchy was alien to Iraq. Despite his Islamic and pan-Arab credentials, Faisal was not an Iraqi, and, no matter how effectively he ruled, Iraqis saw the monarchy as a British creation. The majority of Iraqis were divorced from the political process, and the process itself failed to develop procedures for resolving internal conflicts other than rule by decree and the frequent use of repressive measures. Also, because the formative experiences of Iraq's post-1958 political leadership centered around clandestine opposition activity, decision-making and government activity in general have been veiled in secrecy. Furthermore, because the country lacks deeply rooted national political institutions, political power frequently has been monopolized by a small elite, the members of which are often bound by close family or tribal ties.

Religious Background

Islam came to Iraq by way of the Arabian Peninsula, where in A.D. 610, Muhammad—a merchant in the Arabian town of Mecca—began to preach the first of a series of revelations granted him by God through the angel Gabriel. A fervent monotheist, Muhammad denounced the polytheism of his fellow Meccans, which because the town's economy was based in part on a thriving pilgrimage business to the Kaaba shrine and other pagan religious sites in the area, earned him the enmity of the town's leaders. In A.D. 622 he and a group of followers accepted an invitation to settle in the town of Yathrib, later known as Medina. The move, or *hegira*, marks the beginning of the Islamic era and of Islam as a force in history; the Muslim calendar begins in A.D. 622. In Medina, Muhammad continued to preach and eventually defeated his detractors in battle. He consolidated the temporal and the spiritual leadership in his person before his death in A.D. 632. After Muhammad's death, his followers compiled those of his words regarded as coming directly from God into the *Quran* (or *Koran*), the holy scriptures of Islam.

After Muhammad's death, the leaders of the Muslim community consensually chose Abu Bakr, the Prophet's father-in-law and one of his earliest followers, to succeed him. At that time, some persons favored Ali, Muhammad's cousin and the husband of his daughter Fatima, but Ali and his supporters (the *Shiat Ali*, or Party of Ali) eventually recognized the community's choice. The next two caliphs (successors) were recognized by the entire community. When Ali finally became caliph in A.D. 656, Muawiyah, governor of Syria, rebelled. After the ensuing civil war, Ali moved his capital to Iraq, where he was murdered shortly thereafter.

Ali's death ended the last of the so-called four orthodox caliphates and the period in which all of Islam recognized a single caliph. Muawiyah proclaimed himself caliph from Damascus. The Shiat Ali refused to recognize him or his line and withdrew to establish the dissident sect, known as the *Shias*, supporting the claims of Ali's line to the caliphate based on descent from the Prophet. The larger faction, the *Sunnis*, adhered to the position that the caliph must be elected. This ancient schism accounts for contemporary Islam's separate Sunni and Shia sects [Figure 13.15].

Originally political, the differences between Sunni and Shia interpretations rapidly took on theological and metaphysical overtones. In principle, a Sunni approaches God directly; there is no clerical hierarchy. Some duly appointed religious figures, however, exert considerable social and political power. *Imams* usually are men of importance in their communities, but they need not have any formal training; among the Bedouins, for example, any tribal member may lead communal prayers. Shia Muslims, also known as *Shiites*, hold the fundamental beliefs of other Muslims. But, in addition to these tenets, the distinctive institution of Shia Islam is the Imamate—a much more exalted position than the Sunni imam, who is primarily a prayer leader. In contrast to Sunni Muslims, who view the caliph as only a temporal leader who lacks a hereditary view of Muslim leadership, Shia Muslims believe the Prophet Muhammad designated Ali to be his successor as Imam, exercising both spiritual and temporal leadership. Each Imam in turn designated his successor—through 12 Imams—each holding the same powers [Figure 13.16].

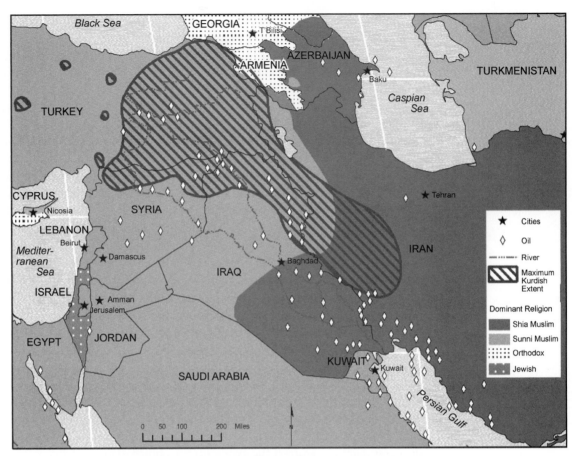

Figure 13.15   Major religions in and around Iraq.

Figure 13.16   The ayatollah of an Iraqi Shiite Muslim group prays with his followers. Photos on the wall are portraits of the ayatollah's eight brothers and other martyrs killed by the Iraqi regime.

The duties of Muslims form the five pillars of Islam, which set forth the acts necessary to demonstrate and reinforce the faith. These are the recitation of the *shahada* ("There is no God but God, and Muhammad is his prophet"), daily prayer (*salat*), almsgiving (*zakat*), fasting (*sawm*), and pilgrimage (*hajj*). The believer is to pray in a prescribed manner after purification through ritual ablutions each day at dawn, midday, midafternoon, sunset, and nightfall. Prescribed genuflections and prostrations accompany the prayers, which the worshiper recites facing toward Mecca. Whenever possible, men pray in congregation at the mosque with an imam, and on Fridays make a special effort to do so. The Friday noon prayers provide the occasion for weekly sermons by religious leaders. Women may also attend public worship at the mosque, where they are segregated from the men, although most frequently women pray at home. A special functionary, the *muezzin*, intones a call to prayer to the entire community at the appropriate hour. Those out of earshot determine the time by the sun.

The ninth month of the Muslim calendar is Ramadan, a period of obligatory fasting in commemoration of Muhammad's receipt of God's revelation. Throughout the month all but the sick and weak, pregnant or lactating women, soldiers on duty, travelers on necessary journeys, and young children are enjoined from eating, drinking, smoking, and sexual intercourse during the daylight hours.

All Muslims, at least once in their lifetime, should make the *hajj* to Mecca to participate in special rites held there during the twelfth month of the lunar calendar. Muhammad instituted this requirement, modifying pre-Islamic custom, to emphasize sites associated with God and Abraham (Ibrahim), founder of monotheism and father of the Arabs through his son Ismail.

The lesser pillars of the faith, which all Muslims share, are *jihad*, or the crusade to protect Islamic lands, beliefs, and institutions, and the requirement to do good works and to avoid all evil thoughts, words, and deeds. In addition, Muslims agree on certain basic principles of faith based on the teachings of the Prophet Muhammad: there is one God, who is a unitary divine being in contrast to the trinitarian belief of Christians; Muhammad, the last of a line of prophets beginning with Abraham and including Moses and Jesus, was chosen by God to present His message to humanity; and there is a general resurrection on the last or judgment day.

Islam is a system of religious beliefs and an all-encompassing way of life. Muslims believe that God (Allah) revealed to the Prophet Muhammad the rules governing society and the proper conduct of society's members. It is incumbent on the individual therefore to live in a manner prescribed by the revealed law (*sharia*) and on the community to build the perfect human society on earth according to holy injunctions. Islam recognizes no distinctions between church and state. The distinction between religious and secular law is a recent development that reflects the more pronounced role of the state in society, and Western economic and cultural penetration. The impact of religion on daily life in Muslim countries is far greater than that found in the West since the Middle Ages.

Language Background

Arabic is the official language and mother tongue of about 76 percent of the population and is understood by a majority of others. The term *Arab* therefore refers to people from Morocco to Iraq who speak Arabic as their primary language [see Chapter 2, Activity 1: Mapping Culture Regions]. One of the Semitic languages, Arabic is related to Aramaic, Phoenician, Syriac, Hebrew, various Ethiopic

© 2010 John Wiley & Sons, Inc.

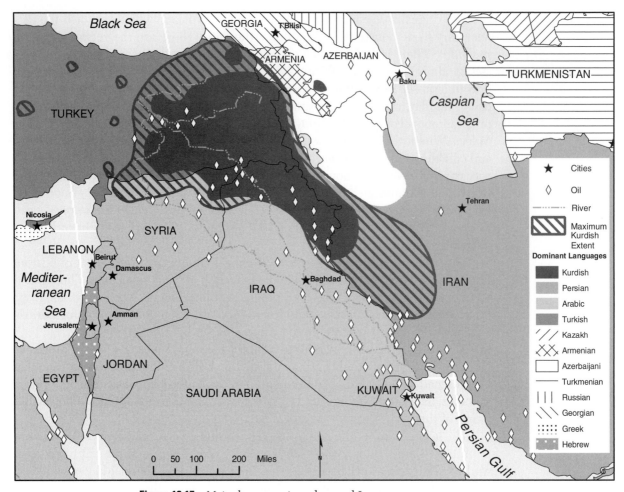

Figure 13.17 Major languages in and around Iraq.

languages, and the Akkadian of ancient Babylonia and Assyria. Minorities speak Turkic, Armenian, and Persian [Figure 13.17].

The other main language spoken in Iraq is Kurdish, spoken by Iraq's Kurdish minority. Kurdish is not a mere dialect of Farsi or Persian, as many Iranian nationalists maintain, and it is certainly not a variant of the Semitic or Turkic tongues. It is a separate language, part of the Indo-European family.

Kurdish Background

Kurds represent by far the largest non-Arab ethnic minority, accounting in 1987 for about 19 percent of the population, or around 3.1 million. Ranging across northern Iraq, the Kurds are part of the larger Kurdish population (probably numbering close to 16 million) that inhabits the wide arc from eastern Turkey and the northwestern part of Syria through Soviet Azerbaijan and Iraq to the northwest of the Zagros Mountains in Iran. Although the largest numbers live in Turkey (variously estimated at between 3 and 10 million), it is in Iraq that they are most active politically. Although the government hotly denies it, the Kurds are almost certainly a majority in the region around Kirkuk, Iraq's richest oil-producing area.

The Kurds inhabit the highlands and mountain valleys and have traditionally been organized on a tribal basis. Historians have traced the Kurds' existence in these mountains back at least 3,000 years, and throughout their history they have been feared as fierce warriors. Once mainly nomadic or semi-nomadic, Kurdish society was characterized by a combination of urban centers, villages, and pastoral tribes since at least the Ottoman period. The migration to the cities, particularly of the young intelligentsia, helped develop Kurdish nationalism in the twentieth century.

The historic enmity between the Kurds and Iraq's Arabic-speaking central government has contributed to the tenacious survival of Kurdish culture. The Kurds' most distinguishing characteristic and the one that binds them to one another is their language. The Kurds have been locked in an unremittingly violent struggle with the central government in Baghdad almost since the founding of the Iraqi republic in 1958. It appeared in the early 1970s that the dissident Kurds—under the generalship of the legendary leader Mulla Mustafa Barzani—might actually carve out an independent Kurdish area in northern Iraq. The war between Iraq and Iran that broke out in 1980 afforded Iraqi Kurdish groups the opportunity to intensify their opposition to the government.

Religion/Language Summary

At least 95 percent of the population adheres to some form of Islam. The government gives the number of Shias as 55 percent but probably 60 to 65 percent is a reasonable figure. Most Iraqi Shias are Arabs. Almost all Kurds, approximately 19 percent of the population, are Sunnis. About 13 percent are Sunni Arabs, including Saddam Hussein and most past rulers of Iraq. The remainder of the population includes small numbers of Turkomans, mostly Sunni Muslims; Assyrians and Armenians, predominantly Christians; Yazidis, of Kurdish stock with a syncretistic faith; and a few Jews.

Enter Saddam

Between the overthrow of the monarchy in 1958 and the emergence of Saddam Hussein in the mid-1970s, Iraqi history was a chronicle of conspiracies, coups, countercoups, and fierce Kurdish uprisings. Saddam finally became president of Iraq in 1979 after gradually becoming the moving force behind his party. Beginning in 1975, however, with the signing of the Algiers Agreement—an agreement between Saddam Hussein and the Shah of Iran that effectively ended Iranian military support for the Kurds in Iraq—Saddam Hussein was able to bring Iraq an unprecedented period of stability. He effectively used rising oil revenues to fund large-scale development projects, to increase public sector employment, and significantly to improve education and health care. This tied increasing numbers of Iraqis to the ruling Baath (Arab Socialist Resurrection) Party. As a result, for the first time in contemporary Iraqi history, an Iraqi leader successfully forged a national identity out of Iraq's diverse social structure. Saddam Hussein's achievements and Iraq's general prosperity, however, did not survive long. Threatened by the 1979 Islamic Revolution in Iran and by its potential influence on Iraq's majority population, Iraq attacked Iran on September 22, 1980.

The border with Iran had been a continuing source of conflict and was partially responsible for the outbreak in 1980 of the Iran-Iraq war. The terms of a treaty negotiated in 1937 under British auspices provided that in one area of the Shatt al Arab, the boundary would be at the low-water mark on the Iranian side [Figure 13.18].

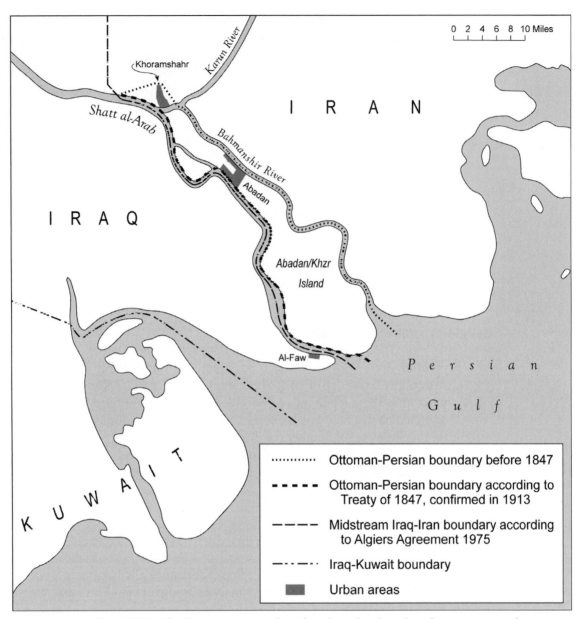

Figure 13.18 The changing Iraq-Iran boundary along the Shatt al–Arab waterway over the years.

The narrow Shatt is Iraq's only access to ocean transportation. Iran subsequently insisted that the 1937 treaty was imposed on it by "British imperialist pressures." Through Algerian mediation, Iran and Iraq agreed in March 1975 to define the common border all along the Shatt estuary as the middle of the main channel. To compensate Iraq for the loss of what formerly had been regarded as its territory, pockets of territory along the mountain border in the central sector of its common boundary with Iran were assigned to it. Nonetheless, in September 1980 Iraq went to war with Iran, citing among other complaints the fact that Iran had not turned over to it the land specified in the Algiers Accord. [See the box, "U.S. Support of Saddam Hussein in the 1980s."]

U.S. Support of Saddam Hussein in the1980s

According to *Newsweek* "American officials have known that Saddam was a psychopath" since the early 1970s. Yet after radical Islamic fundamentalists overthrew the pro-American, westernized Shah of Iran in 1979 and took U.S. embassy employees hostage, the Reagan administration was eager to use Saddam as a "surrogate" against Iran. When Iran's "human wave attacks" began to tilt the balance in the Iran-Iraq war, the United States began providing Iraq with assistance that would give it an edge against its common enemy, Iran (Figure 13.19). The United States provided Saddam with satellite photos, tanks, "dual-use" (commercial-military) equipment such as database software, helicopters, and video surveillance equipment. Most troubling, the United States also shipped chemical analysis equipment and "bacteria/fungi/protozoa," which could be used to make anthrax, to the Iraqi Atomic Energy Commission. It is not known for certain whether any of the materials provided by the Americans were used by Iraq against its own people. After the Iran-Iraq War, *Newsweek* writes that "the State Department was equivocating with Saddam right up to the moment he invaded Kuwait in August 1990."

Source: Dickey, Christopher, and Evan Thomas. 2002. How Saddam Happened. *Newsweek* (Sept. 23, 2002): 34–41.

In 1988 the boundary with Kuwait was another outstanding problem. It was fixed in a 1913 treaty between the Ottoman Empire and British officials acting on behalf of Kuwait's ruling family, which in 1899 had ceded control over foreign affairs to Britain. The boundary was accepted by Iraq when it became independent in 1932, but in the 1960s and again in the mid-1970s, the Iraqi government seized parts of Kuwait, basing its claim on the fact that Kuwait was part of the Basra Province of the Ottoman Empire, the rest of which went to Iraq, and therefore was unfairly separated from Iraq by Britain. Kuwait made several representations to the Iraqis during the war to fix the border once and for all, but Baghdad repeatedly demurred, claiming that the issue was a potentially divisive one that could enflame nationalist sentiment inside Iraq. On August 2, 1990, Iraq attacked and then annexed Kuwait. Iraqi president Saddam Hussein accused Kuwait of illegally pumping oil from Iraq's Rumaila oil field, which spans the border; of not paying off its debt to Iraq for defending the Arab nation against the Persians (Iran); and of refusing to negotiate Iraq's needs for a deepwater port at the Shatt al Arab.

Sources: Iraq: A Country Study (sections on "Boundaries"; "Historical Setting"; "National Security"; "World War I and the British Mandate"; "Islam"; "Kurds"; "Religious Life"; "Shias"; "Society"; "Sunnis"; and "The People").

Figure 13.19 Iranian soldiers, some only children, shout "Allahu Akhbar" or God is Great, during the Iran-Iraq war of 1980–1988.

▶ *FRONTLINE*

The Long Road to War
Excerpted from: **Frontline (Public Broadcasting System).** *The Long Road to War— Chronology*: **www.pbs.org/wgbh/pages/frontline/shows/longroad/etc/cron.html**
Copyright © 1995–2002. From Frontline and WBGH Educational Foundation © 2005 WBGH Boston.

July 1979
Saddam Hussein seizes presidency
    Saddam stages a palace coup and President Bakr resigns for health reasons. Among Saddam's first actions after assuming the presidency is purging the Ba'ath Party of any potential enemies.
    Several weeks into his presidency, Saddam calls a meeting of the Ba'ath Party leadership and insists it be videotaped. He announces there are traitors in their midst and reads out their names. One by one, the individuals are led out, never to be seen again. Tapes of the meeting are sent throughout the country, allowing Saddam to send a message to the Iraqi elite.

1980–1988: Geopolitics and the Iran-Iraq War

Sept. 22, 1980

Iraq attacks Iran

In one of the largest ground assaults since World War II, Saddam sends 200,000 troops across the Iranian border, initiating what would become a bloody eight-year conflict.

When Ronald Reagan becomes president in 1981, he endorses a policy aiming for a stalemate in the war so that neither side emerges from the war with any additional power. But in 1982, fearing Iraq might lose the war, the U.S. begins to help. Over the next six years, a string of CIA agents go to Baghdad. Hand-carrying the latest satellite intelligence about the Iranian front line, they pass the information to their Iraqi counterparts. The U.S. gives Iraq enough help to avoid defeat, but not enough to secure victory.

1981

Israel attacks Iraqi nuclear reactor

In a surprise raid, Israeli forces destroy the nuclear reactor at Osirak that the Iraqis had built with French assistance. Most countries, including the U.S., condemn Israel for violating Iraqi sovereignty.

1986

Iran-Contra scandal breaks

The Iran-Contra scheme is conceived by Reagan administration officials. Iran had been running out of military supplies in its war with Iraq, and Reagan is advised that the U.S. could strike a deal in which secret arms sales to Iran could lead to the release of U.S. hostages held by pro-Iranian terrorists in Lebanon.

Public exposure of the plan—which also involved illegally diverting the proceeds from the arms sales to the U.S.-backed Contras in Nicaragua—leads to the end of the U.S. policy. However, when Saddam learns of America's actions, he vows never to trust the U.S. again.

1987

U.S. Navy aids Iraq

In the name of freedom of navigation, the U.S. throws the weight of its navy behind Iraq's position in the Persian Gulf. A large American armada protects tanker traffic and cripples the Iranian navy. A war, which at that point had been going against Iraq, is again transformed into a stalemate.

March 1988

Saddam gasses Iraqi Kurds

U.S. hopes for a civilized Iraq are shattered when Iraqi forces unleash a devastating gas attack in the town of Halabja, killing an estimated 5,000 Kurds.

Richard Murphy, the State Department's top Middle East diplomat for most of the 1980s, told FRONTLINE in 1990 that after the attack at Halabja the U.S. expressed its dismay at Iraq's use of chemical weapons. He recalled that Secretary of State George Schultz persuaded the Iraqis to "articulate a position that they would forswear future use of chemical weapons."

1988

Ceasefire in Iran-Iraq war; U.S. declares its policy successful

The end of the war comes with a cease-fire under conditions that reflect the U.S. government's best hopes. A classified State Department document states: "We can

Figure 13.20 Kurdish victims of an Iraqi poison-gas attack lie where they were killed on March 22, 1988, in northern Iraq.

legitimately assert that our post-Irangate policy has worked. The outward thrust of the Iranian revolution has been stopped. Iraq's interests in development, modernity and regional influence should compel it in our direction. We should welcome and encourage the interest, and respond accordingly."

1990–1991: The Buildup to War

July 17, 1990

Saddam threatens Arab neighbors

By 1990, Saddam Hussein has the fourth-largest army in the world and his program to build weapons of mass destruction is well under way. However, after its eight-year war with Iran, Iraq is billions of dollars in debt and angry with its Arab neighbors about the low price of oil, its chief source of cash.

In a speech celebrating the 22nd anniversary of his party's rise to power, Hussein threatens Kuwait and the United Arab Emirates. "Iraqis," he says, "will not forget the maxim that cutting necks is better than cutting the means of living. Oh, God almighty, be witness that we have warned them."

Within two weeks of the speech, Iraq masses 100,000 troops at the Kuwaiti border.

July 25, 1990

Saddam meets with U.S. ambassador

April Glaspie, U.S. ambassador to Iraq, is summoned to meet with Saddam. According to an Iraqi transcript, Saddam harangues her about his dispute with Kuwait over oil prices. Ambassador Glaspie tells Saddam, "The president personally wants to deepen the relationship with Iraq." She expresses concerns about the Iraqi troops on the Kuwaiti border, but reflecting the official State Department position, she says, "We don't have much to say about Arab-Arab differences, like your border differences with Kuwait. . . . All we hope is you solve these matters quickly."

In the final week of July, Saddam reinforces his troops. But several Arab leaders privately assure the U.S. that Iraq will not invade Kuwait. The State Department continues to make it clear the U.S. will not intervene in the dispute.

Aug. 2, 1990
Kuwait invaded; world condemns Iraq
   On the day of Iraq's invasion, President George H. W. Bush flies to Aspen, Colorado, for a previously scheduled meeting with British Prime Minister Margaret Thatcher. She encourages Bush to "draw a line in the sand" not only to protect Saudi Arabia, but to warn Saddam that an attack on Saudi Arabia will be considered an attack on the U.S.
   Less than 48 hours after the invasion, the U.S. and the Soviet Union issue an unprecedented joint statement condemning Iraq. On Aug. 5, Bush declares, "This will not stand, this aggression against Kuwait."

Aug. 8, 1990
U.S. troops sent to Persian Gulf
   In one of the president's rare speeches from the Oval Office, Bush announces his decision to send U.S. troops to the Gulf. He emphasizes that the action is defensive and that he is banking on sanctions to force the Iraqis from Kuwait. "The United States will do its part to see that these sanctions are effective and to induce Iraq to withdraw without delay from Kuwait," he says. "America does not seek conflict, but America will stand by her friends."

August–September 1990
U.S. builds worldwide coalition; Saddam resists
   On Sept. 11, six weeks into the crisis, President Bush visits Capital Hill, where he gives a glowing report of his diplomatic success in building a worldwide coalition. The president had just returned from a quickly called summit with Soviet leader Mikhail Gorbachev, who had firmly endorsed the U.S. policy toward Iraq.
   Because of Soviet support, the U.S.—for the first time since the Korean War—is willing and able to use the United Nations to organize world support against the aggression. In the first five weeks of the crisis, the Security Council adopts five tough resolutions against Iraq.
   However, by the end of September, Saddam Hussein has 360,000 troops in place, and they are digging in deep along the Saudi border. Despite his isolation, it appears Saddam is not planning to leave Kuwait.

Nov. 29, 1990
UN authorizes use of "all means necessary" to eject Iraq from Kuwait
   Secretary of State James Baker personally conducts the last-minute lobbying at the UN to convince the Security Council to authorize the use of force if Iraq does not leave Kuwait by Jan. 15, 1991. "Simply put," he tells the Security Council, "it is a choice between right and wrong."

Jan. 12. 1991
Congress authorizes use of force
   After three days of debate, the U.S. House and Senate both adopt a resolution giving President Bush the authority to make war on Iraq.

Jan. 15, 1991
UN deadline for Iraqi withdrawal from Kuwait
   The deadline passes without any Iraqi action.

1991: The Gulf War and Its Aftermath

Jan. 17, 1991

Gulf War begins

The air war lasts for six weeks, during which coalition forces drop more bombs than had been dropped during all of World War II. On Feb. 24, the ground attack begins, and within days, the U.S. military realizes that the Iraqis are not going to stand and fight (Figure 13.21). After Chairman of the Joint Chiefs of Staff Colin Powell expresses concern that the allied rout of Iraqi forces would be seen as a massacre, Bush decides to end the war. On Feb. 28, a cease-fire takes effect at 8 A.M.

March 1991

Saddam brutally suppresses rebellions in north and south of Iraq; U.S. does not intervene

During the war, President Bush repeatedly calls for Iraqis to rise up against Saddam. Within days of the cease-fire, Shia Muslims in the south of Iraq, close to the allied front lines, take up arms against Saddam. In the first heady days of the uprising, the rebels control the streets.

Saddam quickly moves loyal forces and uses armed helicopters to suppress the uprising in the south. U.S. troops can see the fighting from their positions, but are ordered not to intervene. There are estimates that tens of thousands of Shia Muslims were killed.

A few days after the Shia uprising begins, the Kurds start a rebellion in northern Iraq. While the southern uprising had been somewhat incoherent, the Kurds have political leaders who can shape the revolt. As the rebellion gathers momentum,

Figure 13.21 Burning oil fields were one of the worst forms of environmental destruction left after Iraq deliberately set oil wells ablaze as it withdrew from Kuwait.

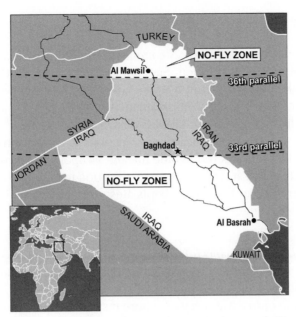

Figure 13.22 No-fly zones over Iraq since the First Gulf War in 1991.

Kurdish leaders who had been living abroad return. They hope to trigger a coup against Saddam that will result in a new Iraqi leader who will let the Kurds run their own affairs.

Saddam's forces soon attack the rebels, who are not supported by Washington, which had decided against backing an uprising that might lead to Iraq's breakup. The rebel forces are hopelessly outgunned. As Kurdish cities are shelled, there is panic among the population. The cities of Kurdistan empty, and a million people head toward the mountains in an attempt to reach the safety of Turkey and Iran. Again, U.S. forces, who see the exodus, are ordered not to intervene.

With Saddam clinging to power, Bush decides on a containment strategy toward Iraq: tough U.N. inspections, economic sanctions, and no-fly zones to protect the Kurds and Shia Muslims in the north and south of the country (Figure 13.22).

1991–1992
U.S. inaction catalyzes foreign policy hawks

Saddam's brutality and America's failure to support the Shia and Kurdish uprisings deeply affects a group of neo-conservative thinkers in Washington, including Richard Perle, William Kristol, and Under Secretary of Defense for Policy Paul Wolfowitz, who complains that the U.S. inaction is comparable to "idly watching a mugging."

In 1992 Paul Wolfowitz takes the lead in drafting an internal set of military guidelines—"Defense Planning Guidelines"—which is prepared every few years by the Defense Department. Wolfowitz's draft argues for a new military and political strategy in a post–Cold War world. Containment, it says, is an old idea, a relic of the Cold War. America should talk loudly and carry a big stick—and use it—to preempt the use of weapons of mass destruction. And if America had to act alone, so be it.

Controversy erupts after the draft is leaked to the press. The Bush White House orders Defense Secretary Cheney to rewrite it. In the new draft there is no mention of preemption and U.S. willingness to act alone.

© 2010 John Wiley & Sons, Inc.

1991–1998: Trying to Disarm Saddam

April 3, 1991

UN passes Resolution 687, creates commission to inspect Iraqi weapons facilities

As a result of the resolution, Saddam stays in power, but economic sanctions remain. Saddam must destroy his weapons and allow inspection of all weapons facilities by a UN Special Commission, known as UNSCOM. Iraq is given 15 days to provide a list of its weapons of mass destruction.

The next day, Iraqi deception over weapons of mass destruction begins. Iraqi nuclear scientists are ordered to hide nuclear weapons from inspectors, collect and move computer data, and formulate a justification for the existence of Iraqi nuclear labs. On April 6, Iraq formally accepts Resolution 687 and UNSCOM makes its first inspection in June.

June 1991

Iraqis defy UNSCOM inspectors

On one of UNSCOM's first assignments, inspectors demand access to an Iraqi military facility. The base commander will not allow inspectors into the building, but lets them climb onto a water tower, where inspectors spot Iraqi trucks slipping out the back gate. Although UN vehicles catch up with the trucks and try to pull them over, the Iraqis refuse to stop and fire warning shots at the inspectors. However, the inspectors obtain photographs showing the trucks are carrying calutrons—giant iron magnets that can be used to enrich uranium.

September 1991

UNSCOM raid discovers Saddam's nuclear plans

In a surprise raid on an Iraqi government building, UNSCOM inspectors, led by David Kay, discover a hidden archive of documents that reveals Saddam's plans to develop a nuclear weapon.

Incensed by the inspectors' discovery, the Iraqis haul off the original documents, and demand the inspectors turn over their photographs of the documents. The standoff lasts for four days and the weapons inspectors are held hostage in the parking lot outside of the building. They are finally allowed to leave with their evidence when the U.S. announces it will intervene militarily on behalf of UNSCOM.

June 26, 1993

Clinton orders bombing of Iraqi intelligence headquarters

The U.S. fires 23 Tomahawk cruise missiles in response to a plot to assassinate former President Bush with a car bomb when he traveled to Kuwait the previous April. The plot is linked to Iraqi intelligence.

Aug. 7, 1995

Saddam's son-in-law reveals biological weapons program

Hussein Kamel, a high-ranking Iraqi general—and one of Saddam's sons-in-law—announces in Jordan that he has defected with his brother and their wives. Kamel had been in charge of hiding Iraq's weapons of mass destruction and he tells the chief UN arms inspector of a vast arsenal of weapons UNSCOM had failed to find and where the cache is hidden.

The inspectors raid Al Hakam, which Kamel had described as Iraq's top-secret germ warfare production facility. The Iraqis had denied having any biological weapons programs, but there UNSCOM discovers Russian-built fermenters used to produce anthrax and growth medium used to grow biological toxins. The inspectors bury 17 tons of it and blow up the entire facility.

Nine months later, Kamel accepts Saddam's guarantee that he can safely return to Iraq. The moment they cross the border, Saddam's two daughters are separated from their husbands; Kamel and his brother are killed several days later.

Fall 1997–Winter 1998
Inspections reach crisis point

In September 1997, UNSCOM inspector Dr. Diane Seaman leads a surprise inspection of an Iraqi food laboratory suspected of housing biological weapons work. Entering through a back door, Dr. Seaman catches men running out with briefcases that contain records of biological weapons activity on the stationery of the Iraqi Special Security Organization (SSO)—the organization that guards Saddam Hussein. That night, UNSCOM attempts to inspect the SSO offices but is blocked.

The Iraqis are furious, and in October they accuse the American UNSCOM inspectors of spying. They threaten to expel all American inspectors and shoot down U-2 surveillance planes.

In response, UNSCOM Chairman Richard Butler withdraws all weapons inspectors on Nov. 13, and an exasperated President Bill Clinton orders a bombing campaign. At the last minute, the Russians convince the Iraqis to back down and the planes are turned around.

The inspectors return to Iraq in late November (Figure 13.23). Confrontations resume almost immediately and continue throughout the winter, with the U.S. continuing to threaten military action to force Iraqi compliance.

Figure 13.23 UN weapons inspectors search a presidential palace in Iraq.

© 2010 John Wiley & Sons, Inc.

UN Secretary General Kofi Annan travels to Baghdad and negotiates a compromise in which Saddam allows the inspectors to return to Iraq but restricts their access to sensitive sites. Saddam agrees to allow inspectors to visit eight disputed "presidential sites" with diplomatic escorts.

Dec. 16–19, 1998

Weapons inspectors leave Iraq; U.S. and Britain embark on Operation Desert Fox

In December, Saddam ends Iraqi cooperation with UNSCOM and accuses the UN of espionage. On Dec. 15, UNSCOM Chairman Richard Butler reports that the Iraqis are refusing to cooperate with inspectors and the next day, President Clinton—on the eve of the House impeachment vote—orders Operation Desert Fox, a four-day bombardment of key Iraqi military installations. It is conducted without UN Security Council approval.

On Dec. 16, the day the bombing begins, the UN withdraws all weapons inspectors. Inspectors will not return to Iraq until November 2002, following the passage of UN Security Council Resolution 1441.

March 1999[7]

George W. Bush considers presidential run

Bush sets up an exploratory committee for a presidential campaign, and foreign policy experts descend on Austin, Texas, to help prepare him for a White House run.

His tutors include both neo-conservative hawks, such as Wolfowitz and Rumsfeld, and pragmatic realists, including Colin Powell and Condoleezza Rice. During the campaign, neither side will really know where it stands with the candidate.

Jan. 20, 2001

The second Bush presidency begins

Both hawks and realists present Bush with candidates for foreign policy posts in the new administration. The hawks end up with three important jobs: Lewis "Scooter" Libby becomes Cheney's chief of staff, Donald Rumsfeld becomes secretary of defense, and Paul Wolfowitz becomes deputy secretary of defense. But Colin Powell's nomination as secretary of state is viewed as a formidable counterweight to the Pentagon hawks.

The two groups express varying views on how to deal with Saddam Hussein. The hawks develop a military option and push for increased aid to the Iraqi opposition. Colin Powell advocates "smart sanctions" that would allow more humanitarian goods into Iraq, while tightening controls on items that could have military applications.

2001–2003: Iraq—Test Case of a New Foreign Policy

Sept. 11, 2001

Attacks on World Trade Center and Pentagon

In his address to the nation on the evening of Sept. 11, President George W. Bush announces that the U.S. will "make no distinction between the terrorists who committed these acts and those who harbor them."

Sept. 15, 2001

Administration debates Iraq at Camp David

Four days after the Sept. 11 attacks, Bush gathers his national security team at a Camp David war council. Deputy Secretary of Defense Paul Wolfowitz argues that

---

[7]Frontline's *Long Road to War* Chronology has a break from 1998 to 2001. This entry and the next are excerpted from: Frontline (WGBH, Public Broadcasting System). 2003. *Chronology: The Evolution of the Bush Doctrine*: http://www.pbs.org/wgbh/pages/frontline/shows/iraq/etc/cron.html.

it is the perfect opportunity to move against state sponsors of terrorism, including Iraq. But Secretary of State Colin Powell tells the president that an international coalition would come together only for an attack on Al Qaeda and the Taliban in Afghanistan, not an invasion of Iraq.

The war council votes with Powell; Secretary of Defense Donald Rumsfeld abstains. The president ultimately decides that the war's first phase will be Afghanistan. The question of Iraq will be reconsidered later.

Sept. 20, 2001
Bush addresses joint session of Congress
Bush's speech to Congress builds on his address from the night of Sept. 11. "We will pursue nations that provide aid or safe haven to terrorism," he declares. "Every nation, in every region, now has a decision to make. Either you are with us, or you are with the terrorists. From this day forward, any nation that continues to harbor or support terrorism will be regarded by the United States as a hostile regime."

Jan. 29, 2002
State of the Union signals possible action in Iraq
Bush's State of the Union address introduces the idea of an "axis of evil" that includes Iraq, Iran, and North Korea, and signals the U.S. will act preemptively to deal with such nations.

He continues to build the case against Iraq, saying,

"Iraq continues to flaunt its hostility toward America and to support terror. The Iraqi regime has plotted to develop anthrax, and nerve gas, and nuclear weapons for over a decade. This is a regime that has already used poison gas to murder thousands of its own citizens—leaving the bodies of mothers huddled over their dead children. This is a regime that agreed to international inspections—then kicked out the inspectors. This is a regime that has something to hide from the civilized world."

The president warns, "We'll be deliberate, yet time is not on our side. I will not wait on events, while dangers gather. I will not stand by, as peril draws closer and closer. The United States of America will not permit the world's most dangerous regimes to threaten us with the world's most destructive weapons."

August 2002
Within administration, an open debate on Iraq
Powell reports trouble getting U.S. allies on board for a war with Iraq and wants to consult the UN. At a private dinner with the president on Aug. 5, Powell warns that the United States should not act unilaterally and must fully consider the economic and political consequences of war—particularly in the Middle East.

Powell's view is championed by Brent Scowcroft, former national security adviser in the Bush I administration, who publishes an op-ed in *The Wall Street Journal* on Aug. 15. Scowcroft argues that Bush is moving too quickly on Iraq and advocates pressing for the return of UN inspectors.

Soon after, Vice President Cheney emerges as the administration voice advocating action. In a Nashville speech to the Veterans of Foreign Wars, Cheney warns that "a return of inspectors would provide no assurance whatsoever of [Saddam's] compliance with UN resolutions."

In the same speech, Cheney also outlines a larger, long-term strategy whereby regime change in Iraq could transform the Middle East:

"Regime change in Iraq would bring about a number of benefits to the region. When the gravest of threats are eliminated, the freedom-loving peoples of the region will have a chance to promote the values that can bring lasting peace. As for the reaction of the Arab 'street,' the Middle East expert Professor Fouad Ajami predicts that after liberation, the streets in Basra and Baghdad are 'sure to erupt in joy in the same way the throngs in Kabul greeted the Americans.' Extremists in the region would have to rethink their strategy of Jihad. Moderates throughout the region would take heart. And our ability to advance the Israeli-Palestinian peace process would be enhanced, just as it was following the liberation of Kuwait in 1991."

As Bush leaves for an August vacation in Crawford, Texas, he agrees to take his case to the UN and asks his advisers to start preparing the speech.

Sept. 12, 2002
Bush addresses UN on Iraq

In the United Nations speech, Bush calls for a new UN resolution on Iraq. But the president also warns: "The purposes of the United States should not be doubted. The Security Council resolutions will be enforced—the just demands of peace and security will be met—or action will be unavoidable. And a regime that has lost its legitimacy will also lose its power."

Sept. 17, 2002
Bush National Security Strategy released

Twenty months into his presidency, George W. Bush releases his administration's National Security Strategy (NSS) (see Figure 13.24). It is the first time the various elements of the Bush Doctrine have been formally articulated in one place. The 33-page document presents a bold and comprehensive reformulation of U.S. foreign policy and outlines a new, muscular American posture in the world—a posture that will rely on preemption to deal with rogue states and terrorists harboring weapons of mass destruction. [First,] the document says that America will exploit its military and economic power to encourage "free and open societies." [Second,] it states for the first time that the U.S. will never allow its military supremacy to be challenged as it was during the Cold War. And [third], the NSS insists that when America's vital interests are at stake, it will act alone, if necessary.

Figure 13.24 President George W. Bush introduced a new, preemptive National Security Strategy in September 2002, which came to be known as the Bush Doctrine.

Policy analysts note that there are many elements in the 2002 NSS document that bear a strong resemblance to recommendations presented in the controversial Defense Department document authored by Paul Wolfowitz back in 1992, under the first Bush administration.

Nov. 8, 2002
UN Security Council passes Resolution 1441
The resolution is adopted by a unanimous vote of the Security Council. It warns of "serious consequences" if Iraq does not offer unrestricted access to UN weapons inspectors.

Authors' Note: The Frontline Chronology stops here. We have added key events. Consider these first two events a continuation of the chronology section "2001–2003: Iraq—Test Case of a New Foreign Policy."

February 5, 2003
Powell Addresses UN about Weapons of Mass Destruction
U.S. Secretary of State outlined the evidence that Iraq was purposely concealing its biological, chemical, and nuclear weapons of mass destruction program (Figure 13.25). He pointed out that Iraq was in violation of UN Resolution 1441, which entailed "serious consequences" for noncompliance with UNSCOM, and that everyone knew that "serious consequences" meant the use of force when the resolution was crafted. He also tried to make a case for growing Iraqi involvement with the al-Qaeda terrorist organization.

Figure 13.25 U.S. Secretary of State Colin Powell presented satellite images such as this to the United Nations as "evidence" of Iraqi weapons of mass destruction. No such weapons were ever found.

© 2010 John Wiley & Sons, Inc.

March 2003
Breakdown of diplomacy

Many countries remained unconvinced that war was the best course of action at this time. Germany and France led the opposition, arguing that peaceful diplomatic options had not yet been exhausted, and that war could further the rift between the Islamic world and the West. In addition, they felt that international action had effectively contained Iraq's threat, albeit not eliminated it.

France, Russia, and China—all permanent members of the UN Security Council—threatened to veto any UN resolution authorizing an invasion of Iraq. UN Secretary-General Kofi Annan warned that war on Iraq without a new resolution endorsing it "will not be in conformity with the (UN) Charter," a cornerstone of international law.

The international focus began to turn away from the danger of a tyrant with weapons of mass destruction and toward the danger of a world with a single superpower—the United States—that is willing and able to project that power around the world unilaterally (i.e., on their own).

In addition, many people in the United States and worldwide doubted that Iraq had any substantial contribution to the September 11 attacks.

Among the more prominent supporters of the U.S. position were the United Kingdom, Australia, Spain, Islamic countries like Qatar and Kuwait, and former Soviet-bloc countries like Bulgaria and Poland. Several Arab and Islamic countries in the Persian Gulf called on Saddam Hussein to step down voluntarily to save the region from war. Turkey, however, refused to let U.S./Coalition forces launch a ground assault on Northern Iraq from Turkey, and reasserted its right to send troops into Iraq to stem Kurdish refugee flows and suppress any movement toward an independent Kurdish state.

On the eve of war, chief weapons inspector Hans Blix reports that Iraq is once again cooperating and the inspectors need more time.

Saddam Overthrown

March 20, 2003
War begins

American missiles strike Baghdad. Several days later, U.S. and British ground troops invade Iraq from the south.

April 9, 2003
Fall of Baghdad

Iraqis celebrate in the streets, topple the statue of Saddam Hussein, and loot many important government, education, and cultural sites (Figure 13.26).

May 2003
UN Security Council backs U.S.-led administration in Iraq

With the overthrow of Saddam now a historical fact, the UN tries to help legitimize the U.S.-led transitional administration so as to maintain peace and order in Iraq.

Occupation and Reconstruction of Iraq

July 6, 2003
Doubts raised about rationale for war

Former U.S. Ambassador to Niger Joseph Wilson writes a now-famous op-ed piece in the *New York Times* entitled "What I Didn't Find in Africa." The article suggested that the Bush Administration knew that some of the evidence presented

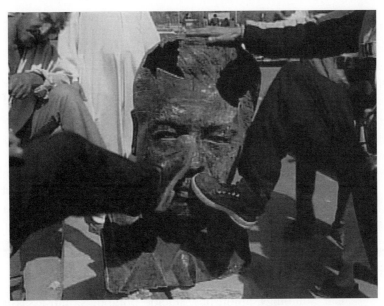

Figure 13.26 After U.S. troops took Baghdad in April 2003, Iraqi citizens toppled a statue of Saddam Hussein and showed their contempt for the ousted dictator by touching the bottoms of their shoes to the statue's broken head.

to the UN by Secretary of State Colin Powell on February 5, 2003, was unsubstantiated. Wilson had been sent to Niger by the CIA to investigate rumors that Iraq had tried to buy yellowcake uranium, but upon arriving he had discovered that the rumors were based on forged documents.

One week later, columnist Robert Novak, citing senior administration officials, published a column entitled "Mission to Niger" revealing Wilson's wife, Valerie Plame, as an undercover CIA agent. An entire CIA operation and front company had to be shut down.

Two and a half years later, Special Prosecutor Patrick Fitzgerald would indict Vice President Richard Cheney's Chief of Staff "Scooter" Libby for obstructing the investigation into the leak of this classified information.

December 14, 2003
Saddam Hussein captured in a "spider hole" in Tikrit

April–November 2004
Coalition forces battle Shia militia in Fallujah
Month-long U.S. military siege of the militia of radical cleric Moqtada Sadr in the Sunni Muslim city of Fallujah, followed by more fighting in Najaf.

May 2004
Abu Ghraib torture scandal
Photos of abuse of Iraqi prisoners by U.S. forces are published.

June–July 2004
Reports Question Validity of War
The 9/11 Commission concludes there is "no credible evidence that Iraq and al-Qaeda cooperated on attacks against the United States." The bipartisan Senate Intelligence Committee unanimously concludes that reports on Iraq's weapons of mass destruction were "either overstated, or were not supported by, the underlying

intelligence report." Senate findings were echoed by British and Australian reports on pre-war intelligence.

June 28, 2004
Iraqi sovereignty

The United States officially hands over sovereignty to an Iraqi interim government.

January 30, 2005
Election of Iraqi Transitional National Assembly

Eight million people vote for a Transitional National Assembly. The Shia United Iraqi Alliance wins a majority of assembly seats. Kurdish parties come in second, and most Sunnis boycott the election. The main task of this assembly is to draft a constitution for Iraq and, having largely boycotted the elections, the Sunnis have relatively little say in it—a potentially significant strategic mistake.

2005
Shia uprising lapses, Sunni insurgency rages

Car bombings, ambushes, suicide bombings, and assassinations of collaborators with foreign authorities escalate. The number of Iraqi civilians killed since the invasion is estimated at between 25,000 and 100,000. The number of U.S. soldiers killed passes 2,000.

August 2005
Constitution drafted

Shia and Kurdish negotiators draft a constitution for Iraq with the help of U.S. negotiators. Sunni representatives do not get involved until the last minute.

October 15, 2005
Referendum on constitution passes

Voters in all but three Sunni-dominated provinces approved a draft constitution. The constitution can be vetoed if three provinces oppose it by at least a two-thirds majority. Two heavily Sunni provinces vote it down, but opposition is not strong enough in the third province, Niniveh, to reach the two-thirds level necessary (see Figure 13.31, page 456, for constitutional election results).

The constitution creates a federal democratic republic consistent with Islamic principles, with rights for women, and regional autonomy for the Kurds and other groups of provinces that so desire it (see page 454, Text of the Draft Iraqi Constitution, for details).

December 2005
Elections held

Pursuant to the new constitution, a 275-member Council of Representatives was elected. Shia alliance wins plurality but lacks two-thirds majority to rule without coalition partners. Interim Prime Minister Ibrahim al-Jaafari, the Shia spokesman of the Islamic Dawa Party, continues in role without official confirmation.

April 22, 2006
Iraqi Prime Minister replaced

After four months of uncertainty, the Council of Representatives replaced Ibrahim al-Jaafari with fellow Shia and Dawa Party member Nuri al-Maliki. al-Jaafari was blamed for continuing violence, lack of effective government services, and bias against Sunnis and Kurds. The new Prime Minister, al-Maliki, was a Shia dissident under Saddam Hussein who fled Iraq in 1979 and returned after the U.S. overthrow of Saddam in 2003.

May 15, 2006
Saddam Hussein charged with crimes against humanity.

May 20, 2006
Government formed
The Council of Representatives approves most of Maliki's cabinet minister appointments, marking Iraq's first constitutional government in nearly a half century.

July–December 2006
Allegations about subcontracting
Questions raised about wasteful subcontracts to private companies such as Parsons, Halliburton, and Blackwater hired by U.S. government to rebuild infrastructure and provide security and services to U.S. military. National Intelligence Estimate concludes that "the Iraq war has made the overall terrorism problem worse." Bipartisan report by Iraq Study Group concludes that "the situation in Iraq is grave and deteriorating" and "U.S. forces seem to be caught in a mission that has no foreseeable end."

December 30, 2006
Saddam executed
Iraqi government hangs Saddam Hussein for crimes against humanity. U.S. cumulative death toll in Iraq reaches 3,000. Iraqi death toll for 2006 is 34,000, according to the United Nations.

February–August 2007
The "Surge"
The United States increases troop levels by 20,000 to quell sectarian violence in Baghdad and Anbar Province and give the Iraqi government a chance to stabilize. Half a year later, there is little doubt that violence has declined, but questions persist over what caused the decline and whether it was sustainable. The National Intelligence Estimate warned that a withdrawal of troops would "erode security gains achieved thus far." An independent U.S. military commission headed by General James Jones attributed improvements to mixed neighborhoods being ethnically cleansed into purely Shia or purely Sunni. The U.S. also recruited and paid over 50,000 Sunni militia, known as "Awakening Councils," to turn against al-Qaeda in Iraq.

August, 2007
The leading Sunni political group in Iraq—the Iraqi Accordance Front—withdraws from the government in a disagreement over power-sharing.

December, 2007
Turkey strikes Iraqi Kurdistan
After ongoing raids into southwestern Turkey by Iraqi Kurdish rebels, Turkey launches air strikes against Kurdish rebels in Iraqi Kurd territory

December, 2007
U.K. withdraws from Basra Province
British troops withdraw from Basra Province in southern Iraq, handing over the security duties to the Iraqi government.

January 12, 2008

Justice and Accountability Law

In an important benchmark of political healing, the Iraqi government created a commission with the power to allow former low-level Baath Party members under Sadaam Hussein back into Iraqi government positions.

July, 2008

The leading Sunni political group in Iraq—the Iraqi Accordance Front—rejoins the Iraqi government after almost a year.

September–October, 2008

Progress on security in Sunni areas

U.S. hands over security of Anbar Province to the Shia-led Iraqi government. It is the first Sunni province to reach this benchmark. The Baghdad Awakening Council, a Sunni militia of about 54,000 men, is transferred from the U.S. payroll to the Iraqi government payroll.

December 31, 2008

End of UN Mandate

Expiration of UN Security Council Mandate authorizing U.S. forces to be in Iraq. Thereafter, U.S. forces remained in Iraq under a bilateral Status of Forces Agreement to provide security and to support the freely elected government. The agreement calls for withdrawal of U.S. combat troops by Dec. 31, 2011. After rebuffing the U.S. request for immunity for all U.S. personnel, the final agreement allows Iraq to prosecute Americans for major crimes committed off duty and off base. Iraq takes control of the Green Zone where most American and Iraqi government officials live.

January 31, 2009

Provincial elections

Elections held for provincial councils in all provinces except for the three provinces under the Kurdistan Regional Government and at-Ta'mim province, home to the contested city of Kirkuk.

February 27, 2009

Obama announces intention for withdrawal

President Obama announced plans to withdraw most American troops from Iraq by August 31, 2010, although leaving up to 50,000 personnel for smaller missions and training of Iraqi troops.

▶ *THE NEW YORK REVIEW OF BOOKS*

How to Get Out of Iraq

By Peter W. Galbraith

Volume 51, Number 8 (May 13, 2004). Reprinted with permission from *The New York Review of Books*. Copyright © 2004 NYREV, Inc.

1. In the year since the United States Marines pulled down Saddam Hussein's statue in Baghdad's Firdos Square, things have gone very badly for the United States in Iraq and for its ambition of creating a model democracy that might transform the Middle East. As of today the United States military appears committed to an open-ended

stay in a country where, with the exception of the Kurdish north, patience with the foreign occupation is running out, and violent opposition is spreading. Civil war and the breakup of Iraq are more likely outcomes than a successful transition to a pluralistic Western-style democracy.

Much of what went wrong was avoidable. Focused on winning the political battle to start a war, the Bush administration failed to anticipate the postwar chaos in Iraq. Administration strategy seems to have been based on a hope that Iraq's bureaucrats and police would simply transfer their loyalty to the new authorities, and the country's administration would continue to function. All experience in Iraq suggested that the collapse of civil authority was the most likely outcome, but there was no credible planning for this contingency. In fact, the U.S. effort to remake Iraq never recovered from its confused start when it failed to prevent the looting of Baghdad in the early days of the occupation.

Americans like to think that every problem has a solution, but that may no longer be true in Iraq. Before dealing at considerable length with what has gone wrong, I should also say what has gone right.

Iraq is free from Saddam Hussein and the Baath Party. Along with Cambodia's Pol Pot, Saddam Hussein's regime was one of the two most cruel and inhumane regimes in the second half of the twentieth century. Using the definition of genocide specified in the 1948 Genocide Convention, Iraq's Baath regime can be charged with planning and executing two genocides—one against the Kurdish population in the late 1980s and another against the Marsh Arabs in the 1990s. In the 1980s, the Iraqi armed forces and security services systematically destroyed more than four thousand Kurdish villages and several small cities, attacked over two hundred Kurdish villages and towns with chemical weapons in 1987 and 1988, and organized the deportation and execution of up to 182,000 Kurdish civilians.

In the 1990s the Saddam Hussein regime drained the marshes of southern Iraq, displacing 500,000 people, half of whom fled to Iran, and killing some 40,000. In addition to destroying the five-thousand-year-old Marsh Arab civilization, draining the marshes did vast ecological damage to one of the most important wetlands systems on the planet. Genocide is only part of Saddam Hussein's murderous legacy. Tens of thousands perished in purges from 1979 on, and as many as 300,000 Shiites were killed in the six months following the collapse of the March 1991 Shiite uprising. One mass grave near Hilla may contain as many as 30,000 bodies.

In a more lawful world, the United Nations, or a coalition of willing states, would have removed this regime from power long before 2003. However, at precisely the time that some of the most horrendous crimes were being committed, in the late 1980s, the [United States] strongly opposed any action to punish Iraq for its genocidal campaign against the Kurds or to deter Iraq from using chemical weapons against the Kurdish civilians.

On August 20, 1988, the Iran-Iraq War ended. Five days later, the Iraqi military initiated a series of chemical weapons attacks on at least forty-nine Kurdish villages . . . near the Syrian and Turkish borders. As a staff member of the Senate Foreign Relations Committee, I (along with Chris Van Hollen, now a Maryland congressman) interviewed hundreds of survivors in the high mountains on the Turkish border. Our report . . . established conclusively that Iraq had used nerve and mustard agents on tens of thousands of civilians. . . .

Except for a relatively small number of Saddam Hussein's fellow Sunni Arabs who worked for his regime, the peoples of Iraq are much better off today than they were under Saddam Hussein. The problems that threaten to tear Iraq apart—Kurdish aspirations for independence, Shiite dreams of dominance, Sunni Arab nostalgia for lost power—are not of America's making (although the failure to act sooner against Saddam made them less solvable). Rather, they are inherent in an artificial state held together for eighty years primarily by brute force.

2. American liberation—and liberation it was—ended the brute force. Iraqis celebrated the dictatorship's overthrow, and in Baghdad last April ordinary citizens thrust flowers into my hands (Figure 13.27). Since then, however:

- Hostile action has killed twice as many American troops as died in the war itself, while thousands of Iraqis have also died.

- Terrorists have killed the head of the United Nations Mission, Sergio Vieira de Mello; Iraq's most prominent Shiite politician, the Ayatollah Baqir al-Hakim; and the deputy prime minister of the Kurdistan Regional Government, Sami Abdul Rahman, along with hundreds of others.

- Looting has caused billions of dollars of damage, most of which will have to be repaired at the expense of the US taxpayer.

- $150 billion has already been spent on Iraq, an amount equal to 25 percent of the non-defense discretionary federal budget. (By contrast, the first Gulf War earned a small profit for the US government, owing to the contributions of other nations.)

- Discontent with the US-led occupation boiled over into an uprising in the Shiite areas of Iraq on the first anniversary of liberation and a persistent insurgency in the Sunni Triangle degenerated into a full-scale battle in Fallujah. Many on the US-installed Iraqi Governing Council strongly opposed the US military response, and the US-created security institutions—the new Iraqi police and the paramilitary Iraqi Civil Defense Corps—refused to fight, or in some cases, joined the rebels.

- US credibility abroad has been undermined by the failure to find weapons of mass destruction. Spain's elections, Tony Blair's sinking poll results,

Figure 13.27 American troops welcomed into Baghdad in April 2003.

and the prospective defeat of Australia's Howard government underscore the political risk of too close an association with the United States.

- Relations with France and Germany have been badly hurt, in some cases by the gratuitous comments made by senior US officials.

- The United States does not now have the military or diplomatic resources to deal with far more serious threats to our national security. President Bush rightly identified the peril posed by the nexus between weapons of mass destruction and rogue states. The greatest danger comes from rogue states that acquire and disseminate nuclear weapons technology. At the beginning of 2003 Iraq posed no such danger. As a result of the Iraq war the United States has neither the resources nor the international support to cope effectively with the very serious nuclear threats that come from North Korea, Iran, and, most dangerous of all, our newly designated "major non-NATO ally," Pakistan.

With fewer than one hundred days to the handover of power to a sovereign Iraq on June 30, there is no clear plan—and no decision—about how Iraq will be run on July 1, 2004. . . .

As is true of so much of the US administration of postwar Iraq, the damage here is self-inflicted. While telling Iraqis it wanted to defer constitutional issues to an elected Iraqi body, the US-led Coalition Provisional Authority could not resist trying to settle fundamental constitutional issues in the interim constitution. [*Authors' note:* The constitution to which Galbraith refers in this and the following paragraph is not the one approved by Iraqi voters in October 2005, which is described in the next reading. Galbraith refers here to interim laws, not the basis for the long-term future of Iraq, which was decided the year after this article was written.] The US government lawyers who wrote the interim constitution, known formally as the Transitional Administrative Law, made no effort to disguise their authorship. All deliberations on the law were done in secret and probably fewer than one hundred Iraqis saw a copy of the constitution before it was promulgated. To write a major law in any democracy—much less a constitution—without public discussion should be unthinkable. Now that Iraqis are discovering for the first time the contents of the constitution, it should come as no surprise that many object to provisions they never knew were being considered.

Iraq's Shiite leaders say that the National Assembly due to be elected in January 2005 should not be constrained by a document prepared by US government lawyers, deliberated in secret, and signed by twenty-five Iraqis selected by Ambassador Bremer. In particular, the Shiites object to a provision in the interim constitution that allows three of Iraq's eighteen governorates (or provinces) to veto ratification of a permanent constitution. This, in effect, allows either the Kurds or the Sunni Arabs, each of whom make up between one fifth and one sixth of Iraq's population, to block a constitution they don't like. (It is a wise provision. Imposing a constitution on reluctant Kurds or Sunni Arabs will provoke a new cycle of resistance and conflict.) The Shiite position makes the Kurds, who are well armed, reluctant to surrender powers to a central government that may be Shiite-dominated.

At the moment the Sunni Arabs have few identifiable leaders. The Kurds, however, are well organized. They have an elected parliament and two regional governments, their own court system, and a 100,000 strong military force, known as the Peshmerga. The Peshmerga, whose members were principal American allies in the 2003 war, are better armed, better trained, and more disciplined than the minuscule Iraqi army the United States is now trying to reconstitute.

Early in 2005, Iraq will likely see a clash between an elected Shiite-dominated central government trying to override the interim constitution in order to impose its will on the entire country, and a Kurdistan government insistent on preserving the de facto independent status Kurdistan has enjoyed for thirteen years. Complicating the political struggle is a bitter territorial dispute over the oil-rich province of Kirkuk involving Kurds, Sunni Arabs, Shiite Arabs, Sunni Turkmen, and Shiite Turkmen.

It is a formula for civil war.

3. How did we arrive at this state of affairs?

I arrived in Baghdad on April 13, 2003, as part of an ABC news team. It was apparent to me that things were already going catastrophically wrong. When the United States entered Baghdad on April 9 last year, it found a city largely undamaged by a carefully executed military campaign. However, in the two months following the US takeover, unchecked looting effectively gutted every important public institution in the city with the notable exception of the Oil Ministry. The physical losses include:

- The National Library, which was looted and burned. Equivalent to our Library of Congress, it held every book published in Iraq, all newspapers from the last century, as well as rare manuscripts. The destruction of the library meant the loss of a historical record going back to Ottoman times.

- The Iraqi National Museum, which was also looted (Figure 13.28). More than 10,000 objects were stolen or destroyed. The Pentagon has deliberately, and repeatedly, tried to minimize the damage by excluding from its estimates objects stolen from storage as well as displayed treasures that were smashed but not stolen.

- Baghdad and Mosul Universities, which were stripped of computers, office furniture, and books. Academic research that took decades to carry out went up in smoke or was scattered. . . .

Figure 13.28 The Deputy Director of the Iraqi National Museum, Mushin Hasan, holds his head in his hands as he sits on destroyed artifacts on April 13, 2003 in Baghdad. U.S. troops did little to protect thousands of priceless artifacts being taken or destroyed.

Even more surprising, the United States made no apparent effort to secure sites that had been connected with Iraqi WMD programs or buildings alleged to hold important intelligence. As a result, the United States may well have lost valuable information that related to Iraqi WMD procurement, paramilitary resistance, foreign intelligence activities, and possible links to al-Qaeda.

- On April 16, looters attacked the Iraqi equivalent of the US Centers for Disease Control, stealing live HIV and live black fever bacteria. UNMOVIC [United Nations Monitoring, Verification, and Inspection Commission] and UNSCOM had long considered the building suspicious and had repeatedly conducted inspections there. The looting complicates efforts to understand and account for any Iraqi bioweapons research in the past. A Marine lieutenant watched the looting from next door. He told us, "I hope I am not responsible for Armageddon, but no one told me what was in that building."

- Although US troops moved onto the grounds of Iraq's sprawling Tuwaitha nuclear complex, they did not secure the warehouse that contained yellowcake and other radiological materials. Looters took materials that terrorists could use for a radiological weapon, although much of that material was eventually recovered. The looted nuclear materials were in a known location and already had been placed under seal by the International Atomic Energy Commission.

- Ten days after the US took over Baghdad, I went through the unguarded Iraqi Foreign Ministry, going from the cooling unit on the roof to the archives in the basement, and rummaging through the office of the foreign minister. The only other people in the building were looters, who were busy opening safes and carrying out furniture. They were unarmed and helped me look for documents. Foreign Ministry files could have shed light on Iraqis' overseas intelligence activities, on attempts to procure WMD, and on any connections that may have existed with al-Qaeda. However, we may never know about these things, since looters scattered and burned files during the ten days, or longer, that this building was left unguarded.

  The looting demoralized Iraqi professionals, the very people the US looks to in rebuilding the country. University professors, government technocrats, doctors, and researchers all had connections with the looted institutions. Some saw the work of a lifetime quite literally go up in smoke. The looting also exacerbated other problems: the lack of electricity and potable water, the lack of telephones, and the absence of police or other security.

  Most importantly, the looting served to undermine Iraqi confidence in, and respect for, the US occupation authorities.

4. In the parts of Iraq taken over by rebels during the March 1991 uprising, there had been the same kind of looting of public institutions. In 2003, the United States could not have prevented all the looting but it could have prevented much of it. In particular, it could have secured the most important Iraqi government ministries, hospitals, laboratories, and intelligence sites. It could have protected the Iraq National Museum and several other of Iraq's most important cultural and historical sites.

In the spring of 2003, Thomas Warrick of the State Department's Future of Iraq Working Group prepared a list of places in Baghdad to be secured. The Iraq

National Museum was number two on the list. At the top of the list were the paper records of the previous regime—the very documents I found scattered throughout the Foreign Ministry and in other locations. What happened next is a mystery. My State Department informants tell me the list was sent to Douglas Feith, an undersecretary in the Department of Defense, and never came out of his office. Feith's partisans insist that uniformed American military failed to take action. In either case, the lack of oversight was culpable.

During the war in Kosovo, the Clinton White House was criticized for insisting on presidential review of proposed targets. President Bush, notorious for his lack of curiosity, seems never to have asked even the most basic question: "What happens when we actually get to Baghdad?"

The failure to answer this question at the start set back US efforts in Iraq in such a way that the US has not recovered and may never do so.

The Bush administration decided that Iraq would be run by a US civilian administrator—initially, Retired General Jay Garner—and American advisers who would serve as the de facto ministers for each of the Iraqi government ministries. All this was based on the expectation that the war would decapitate the top leadership of the Saddam Hussein regime, and the next day everyone else would show up for work.

Predictably, this did not happen. In 1991, all authority disappeared in the areas that fell into rebel hands. But even had things gone as the Bush administration hoped, it was not prepared to run Iraq. As the war began, the Bush administration was still recruiting the American officials who would serve as the de facto Iraqi ministers. The people so recruited had no time to prepare for the assignment, either in learning about Iraq or in mastering the substantive skills needed to run the ministry assigned to them. Many mistakes were made. For example, the US official in charge of prisons decided to work with Ali al-Jabouri, the warden of Abu Ghraib prison, apparently unaware of the prison's fearsome reputation as the place where tens of thousands perished under Saddam Hussein. The coalition rehabilitated Abu Ghraib and today uses it as a prison. The symbolism may be lost on the US administrators but it is not lost on Iraqis. [*Authors' note*: Galbraith's article was written shortly before the photos of U.S. troops torturing and ridiculing Iraqi prisoners were discovered and published.]

In late 2002 and early 2003, I attended meetings with senior US government officials on Kirkuk, the multi-ethnic city that is just west of the line marking the border of the self-governing Kurdish region. When Kirkuk, which is claimed by the Kurds, was held by Saddam Hussein, horrific human rights abuses had taken place there. I had been to Kirkuk in the 1980s, and I was concerned that Kurds brutally expelled in the 1980s and 1990s would return to settle scores with Arabs who had been settled in their homes. The week the war began, I asked the US official responsible for Kirkuk how he planned to deal with this problem. We will rely on the local police, he explained. I asked whether the local police were Kurds or Arabs. He did not know. It remains astonishing to me that US plans for dealing with ethnic conflict in the most volatile city in all of Iraq rested on hopes about the behavior of a police force about which they did not have the most basic information.

The Kirkuk police were, in fact, Arabs, and had assisted in the ethnic cleansing of the city's Kurds. [*Author's note*: The US State Department defines ethnic cleansing as "the systematic and forced removal of the members of an ethnic group from a community or communities in order to change the ethnic composition of a given region."] They were not around when Kurdish forces entered the city on

April 10, 2003. Many other Arabs also fled, although this was largely ignored by the international press.

The United States' political strategies in Iraq have been no less incoherent. . . . The United States, it was decided, would turn power over on June 30, 2004, to a sovereign Iraqi government that would be chosen in a complicated system of caucuses held in each of Iraq's "governorates (or provinces)." By January this plan was put aside (it was widely described as "election by people selected by people selected by Bremer"). . . .

The Bush administration's strategies in Iraq are failing for many reasons. First, they are being made up as the administration goes along, without benefit of planning, adequate knowledge of the country, or the experience of comparable situations. Second, the administration has been unwilling to sustain a commitment to a particular strategy. But third, the strategies are all based on an idea of an Iraq that does not exist.

5. The fundamental problem of Iraq is an absence of Iraqis.

In the north the Kurds prefer almost unanimously not to be part of Iraq, for reasons that are very understandable. Kurdistan's eighty-year association with Iraq has been one of repression and conflict, of which the Saddam Hussein regime was the most brutal phase. Since 1991, Kurdistan has been de facto independent and most Iraqi Kurds see this period as a golden era of democratic self-government and economic progress. In 1992 Kurdistan had the only democratic elections in the history of Iraq, when voters chose members of a newly created Kurdistan National Assembly. During the last twelve years the Kurdistan Regional Government built three thousand schools (as compared to thousand in the region in 1991), opened two universities, and permitted a free press; there are now scores of Kurdish-language publications, radio stations, and television stations (Figure 13.29). For the older generation, Iraq is a bad memory, while a younger generation, which largely does not speak Arabic, has no sense of being Iraqi.

Figure 13.29 Kurds are taking advantage of their new-found autonomy to build institutions and develop an infrastructure to serve their people.

The people of Kurdistan almost unanimously prefer independence to being part of Iraq. In just one month, starting on January 25 of this year, Kurdish nongovernmental organizations collected 1,700,000 signatures on petitions demanding a vote on whether Kurdistan should remain part of Iraq. This is a staggering figure, representing as it does roughly two-thirds of Kurdistan's adults.

In the south, Iraq's long-repressed Shiites express themselves primarily through their religious identity. In early March I traveled throughout southern Iraq. I saw no evidence of any support for secular parties. If free elections are held in Iraq, I think it likely that the Shiite religious parties—principally the Supreme Council for Islamic Revolution in Iraq (SCIRI) and the Dawa (the Call)—will have among them an absolute majority in the National Assembly.

The wild card is Moqtada al-Sadr, the leader of the Shiite uprising. If he is allowed to compete in elections, he will certainly take a share of the Shiite vote. If he is excluded (or imprisoned or killed), his supporters will likely influence the policies of the mainstream Shiite parties, or conceivably disrupt the elections. None of this is good for hopes of creating a stable, democratic Iraq.

The Shiites are not separatists but many of them believe their majority status entitles them to run all of Iraq, and to impose their version of an Islamic state. They also consider connections with Shiites elsewhere as important as their nationalist feelings about Iraq. Iranian Shiites, such as the Ayatollah al-Sistani and, from the grave, Ayatollah Khomeini, have enormous political and spiritual influence in southern Iraq. Their portraits are ubiquitous. Mainstream Iraqi Arab Shiites, such as SCIRI's leader Abdel Azziz al-Hakim, often advocate a very pro-Iranian line.

Sunni Arabs have always been the principal Iraqi nationalists, and a part of the anti-US uprising in the Sunni Triangle is a nationalist one. The Sunni Arabs have long been accustomed to seeing the Iraqi state as a part of a larger Arab nation, and this was a central tenet of the Baath Party. As Sunni Arabs face the end of their historic domination of Iraq, they may seek to compensate for their minority status inside Iraq by further identifying themselves with the greater Arab nation. Connections with other Sunni populations may eventually become even more important among the Sunni Arabs than pan-Arabism. As elsewhere in Arab Iraq, the Sunni religious parties appear to be gaining ground in the country's Sunni center at the expense of the secular parties.

Radical Sunni Islamic groups, including those with recent links to al-Qaeda, appear to have an ever more important part in the uprising in the Sunni Triangle (which explains the increasing use of suicide bombers, not a tactic that appeals to the more worldly Baathists). By attacking Shiite religious leaders and celebrations (for example the deadly bombings this March during the as-Shoura religious holiday in Baghdad and Karbala, and the car bomb assassination of SCIRI leader Baqir al-Hakim), Sunni extremists seek to provoke civil war between Iraq's two main religious groups.

6. [Initially], the United States strategy [was] to hold Iraq together by establishing a strong central government. . . .

Little of this will come to pass. The Kurdistan National Assembly has put forward a comprehensive proposal to define Kurdistan's relations with the rest of Iraq. . . . [*Authors' note*: Galbraith was mostly right. See your next reading—Text of the Draft Iraqi Constitution—to see the regional autonomy provisions that were approved in October 2005.]

This places the Kurds on a collision course with the Shiites and the Sunni Arabs. The Shiite religious parties insist that Islam must be the principal source of law throughout Iraq. Both Shiites and Sunni Arabs object to downgrading Arabic to one of two official languages. Sunni Arab nationalists and Shiite religious leaders object to Kurdistan retaining even a fraction of the autonomy it has today. [*Authors' note:* Here Galbraith was wrong about the Shiites, who overwhelmingly approved the new constitution recognizing Kurdish as an official language and granting substantial regional autonomy to any group of provinces that wants it.]

There are also acute conflicts between Shiite Arabs and Sunni Arabs. These have to do with the differing interpretations of Islam held by the two groups' religious parties and conflicts between pro-Iranian Shiites and Arab nationalist Sunnis. . . .

In my view, Iraq is not salvageable as a unitary state. From my experience in the Balkans, I feel strongly that it is impossible to preserve the unity of a democratic state where people in a geographically defined region almost unanimously do not want to be part of that state. I have never met an Iraqi Kurd who preferred membership in Iraq if independence were a realistic possibility.

But the problem of Iraq is that a breakup of the country is not a realistic possibility for the present. Turkey, Iran, and Syria, all of which have substantial Kurdish populations, fear the precedent that would be set if Iraqi Kurdistan became independent. Both Sunni and Shiite Arabs oppose the separation of Kurdistan. The Sunni Arabs do not have the resources to support an independent state of their own. (Iraq's largest oil fields are in the Shiite south or in the disputed territory of Kirkuk.)

Further, as was true in the Balkans, the unresolved territorial issues in Iraq would likely mean violent conflict. Kirkuk is perhaps the most explosive place. The Kurds claim it as part of historic Kurdistan. They demand that the process of Arabization of the region—which some say goes back to the 1950s—should be reversed. The Kurds who were driven out of Kirkuk by policies of successive Iraqi regimes should, they say, return home, while Arab settlers in the region are repatriated to other parts of Iraq. While many Iraqi Arabs concede that the Kurds suffered an injustice, they also say that the human cost of correcting it is too high. Moreover, backed by Turkey, ethnic Turkmen assert that Kirkuk is a Turkmen city and that they should enjoy the same status as the Kurds.

It will be difficult to resolve the status of Kirkuk within a single Iraq; it will be impossible if the country breaks up into two or three units. And while Kirkuk is the most contentious of the territories in dispute, it is only one of many.

The best hope for holding Iraq together—and thereby avoiding civil war—is to let each of its major constituent communities have, to the extent possible, the system each wants. This, too, suggests the only policy that can get American forces out of Iraq.

In the north this means accepting that Kurdistan will continue to govern its own affairs and retain responsibility for its own security. US officials have portrayed a separate Kurdistan defense force as the first step leading to the breakup of Iraq. The Kurds, however, see such a force not as an attribute of a sovereign state but as insurance in case democracy fails in the rest of Iraq. No one in Kurdistan would trust an Iraqi national army (even one in which the Kurds were well represented) since the Iraqi army has always been an agent of repression, and in the 1980s, of genocide. The Kurds also see clearly how ineffective are the new security institutions created by the Americans. In the face of uprisings in the Sunni Triangle and the south, the new Iraqi police and civil defense corps simply vanished.

Efforts to push the Kurds into a more unitary Iraq will fail because there is no force, aside from the US military, that can coerce them. Trying to do so will certainly inflame popular demands for separation of the Kurdish region in advance of January's elections.

© 2010 John Wiley & Sons, Inc.

If Kurdistan feels secure, it is in fact more likely to see advantages to cooperation with other parts of Iraq. Iraq's vast resources and the benefits that would accrue to Kurdistan from revenue sharing provide significant incentives for Kurdistan to remain part of Iraq, provided doing so does not open the way to new repression. (Until now, most Iraqi Kurds have seen Iraq's oil wealth as a curse that gave Saddam the financial resources to destroy Kurdistan.)

In the south, Iraq's Shiites want an Islamic state. They are sufficiently confident of public support that they are pushing for early elections. The United States should let them have their elections, and be prepared to accept an Islamic [republic]—but only in the south. In most of the south, Shiite religious leaders already exercise actual power, having established a degree of security, taken over education, and helped to provide municipal services. In the preparation of Iraq's interim constitution, Shiite leaders asked for (and obtained) the right to form one or two Shiite regions with powers comparable to those of Kurdistan. They also strongly support the idea that petroleum should be owned by the respective regions, which is hardly surprising since Iraq's largest oil reserves are in the south.

There is, of course, a logical inconsistency between Shiite demands to control a southern region and the desire to impose Islamic rule on all of Iraq. Meeting the first demand affects only the south; accepting the second is an invitation to civil war and must be resisted.

Federalism—or even confederation—would make Kurdistan and the south governable because there are responsible parties there who can take over government functions. It is much more difficult to devise a strategy for the Sunni Triangle—until recently the location of most violent resistance to the American occupation—because there is no Sunni Arab leadership with discernible political support. While it is difficult to assess popular support for the insurrection within the Sunni Triangle, it is crystal clear that few Sunni Arabs in places like Fallujah are willing to risk their lives in opposing the insurgents.

We can hope that if the Sunni Arabs feel more secure about their place in Iraq with respect to the Shiites and the Kurds, they will be relatively more moderate. Autonomy for the Sunni Arab parts of Iraq is a way to provide such security. There is, however, no way to know if it will work.

Since 1992, the Iraqi opposition has supported federalism as the system of government for a post-Saddam Iraq. Iraq's interim constitution reflects this consensus by defining Iraq as a federal state. There is, however, no agreement among the Iraqi parties on what federalism actually means. . . .

Last November, Les Gelb, the president emeritus of the Council on Foreign Relations, created a stir by proposing, in a *New York Times* Op-Ed piece, a three-state solution for Iraq, modeled on the constitution of post-Tito Yugoslavia. The Yugoslav model would give each of Iraq's constituent peoples their own republic. These republics would be self-governing, financially self-sustaining, and with their own territorial military and police forces. The central government would have a weak presidency rotating among the republics, with responsibilities limited to foreign affairs, monetary policy, and some coordination of defense policy. While resources would be owned by the republics, some sharing of oil revenues would be essential, since an impoverished Sunni region is in no one's interest.

This model would solve many of the contradictions of modern Iraq. The Shiites could have their Islamic republic, while the Kurds could continue their secular traditions. Alcohol would continue to be a staple of Kurdish picnics while it would be strictly banned in Basra.

The three-[republic] solution would permit the United States to disengage from security duties in most of Iraq. There are today fewer than three hundred coalition troops in Kurdistan, which would, under the proposal being made here, continue to be responsible for its own security. By contrast, introducing an Iraqi army and security institutions into Kurdistan, as the Bush administration says it still wants to do, would require many more coalition troops—because the Iraqi forces are not up to the job and because coalition troops will be needed to reassure a nervous Kurdish population. If the United States wanted to stay militarily in Iraq, Kurdistan is the place; Kurdish leaders have said they would like to see permanent US bases in Kurdistan.

A self-governing Shiite republic could also run its own affairs and provide for its own security. It is not likely to endorse Western values, but if the coalition quickly disengages from the south, this may mean the south would be less overtly anti-American. Staying in the south will play directly into the hands of Moqtada al-Sadr or his successors. Moderate Shiite leaders, including the Ayatollah al-Sistani, counseled patience in response to al-Sadr's uprising, and helped negotiate the withdrawal of al-Sadr's supporters from some police stations and government buildings. The scope of the uprising, however, underscores the coalition's perilous position in the south. The failure of the Iraqi police and the Iraqi Civil Defense Corps to respond highlights the impotence of these American-created security institutions. The sooner power in the south is handed over to people who can exercise it, the better. Delay will only benefit anti-American radicals like al-Sadr.

As for the Sunni Triangle, one hope is for elections to produce a set of leaders who can restore order and end the insurrection. Presumably this is an outcome the Sunni rebels do not want to see happen; they will use violence to prevent a meaningful election in large parts of the Sunni Triangle. In these circumstances, the United States may face the choice of turning power over to weak leaders and living with the resulting chaos, or continuing to try to pacify the Sunni Triangle, which may generate ever more support for the insurrection. There may be no good options for the United States in the Sunni Triangle. Nevertheless the three-state approach could limit US military engagement to a finite area.

Baghdad is a city of five million and home to large numbers of all three of Iraq's major constituent peoples. With skilled diplomacy, the United States or the United Nations might be able to arrange for a more liberal regime in Baghdad than would exist in the south. Kurdish and Shiite armed forces and police could provide security in their own sections of the capital, as well as work together in Sunni areas (with whatever local cooperation is possible) and in mixed areas. Such an arrangement in Iraq's capital is far from ideal, but it is better than an open-ended US commitment to being the police force of last resort in Iraq's capital.

Because of what happened to Yugoslavia in the 1990s, many react with horror to the idea of applying its model to Iraq. Yet Yugoslavia's breakup was not inevitable. In the 1980s, Slovenia asked for greater control over its own affairs and Milosevic refused. Had Milosevic accepted a looser federation, there is every reason to think that Yugoslavia—and not just Slovenia—would be joining the European Union this May.

Still, a loose federation will have many drawbacks, especially for those who dreamed of a democratic Iraq that would transform the Middle East. The country would remain whole more in name than in reality. Western-style human rights are likely to take hold only in the Kurdish north (and even there not completely). Women's rights could be set back in the south, and perhaps also in Baghdad.

In administering elections and allowing a federation to emerge, the US would badly need the help of the UN and other international organizations and, if it can get it, of the principal European nations as well. The alternative is an indefinite US occupation of Iraq in which we have fewer and fewer allies. It is an occupation that the US cannot afford. It also prevents the US from addressing more serious threats to its national security.

7. The American involvement in Iraq will be a defining event for the US role in the world for the coming decades. Will it be seen as validating the Bush administration's doctrines of preventive war and largely unilateral action?

In my view, Iraq demonstrates all too clearly the folly of the preventive war doctrine and of unilateralism. Of course the United States must reserve the right to act alone when the country is under attack or in imminent danger of attack. But these are also precisely the circumstances when the United States does not need to act alone. After September 11, both NATO and the UN Security Council gave unqualified support for US action, including military action, to deal with the threat of international terrorists based in Afghanistan. After the Taliban was defeated, other countries contributed troops—and accepted casualties—in order to help stabilize the country; and they have also contributed billions to Afghanistan's reconstruction. . . .

In Iraq the United States chose to act without the authorization of the Security Council, without the support of NATO, and with only a handful of allies. Aside from the British and the Kurdish Peshmerga, no other ally made any significant contribution to the war effort. The United States is paying practically all the expenses of the Iraq occupation. Even those who supported the unilateral intervention in Iraq seem by now to realize that it cannot be sustained. The Bush administration, having scorned the United Nations, is now desperate to have it back.

It turns out that there are some things that only the United Nations can do—such as run an election that Iraqis will see as credible or give a stamp of legitimacy to a political transition. But the most urgent reason to want United Nations participation is to share the burden. . . . The reason is cost. Taking all expenses into account, one year of involvement in Iraq costs between $50 billion and $100 billion. Under the mandatory assessment scale for the United Nations this would cost France and . . . Germany some $5 billion to $10 billion each, and they would face pressure to put their own troops in harm's way. NATO assessments are similarly costly. [O]ur allies may not be willing to commit resources on this scale to help the United States get out of Iraq. As a European diplomat told me before last year's war, "It will be china shop rules in Iraq: you break it, you pay for it."

I believe United States policy is most successful when it follows international law and works within the United Nations, according to the provisions of the Charter. This is not just a matter of upholding the ideals of the UN; it is also practical. As our war in Iraq demonstrates, we cannot afford any other course.

—April 15, 2004

▶ TEXT OF THE DRAFT IRAQI CONSTITUTION

(Highlights quoted by the authors)
www.un.int/iraq/TAL_Constitution/Draft_Iraqi_Constitution_english.pdf

Preamble

We the sons of Mesopotamia, land of the prophets, resting place of the holy imams, the leaders of civilization and the creators of the alphabet, the cradle of arithmetic: on our land, the first law put in place by mankind was written; in our

Figure 13.30 Voters in Baghdad try to deposit their votes on the referendum for the new constitution, October 15, 2005.

nation, the most noble era of justice in the politics of nations was laid down; on our soil, the followers of the prophet and the saints prayed, the philosophers and the scientists theorised and the writers and poets created. . . .

We the people of Iraq, newly arisen from our disasters and looking with confidence to the future through a democratic, federal, republican system, are determined—men and women, old and young—to respect the rule of law, reject the policy of aggression, pay attention to women and their rights, the elderly and their cares, the children and their affairs, spread the culture of diversity and defuse terrorism.

We are the people of Iraq, who in all our forms and groupings undertake to establish our union freely and by choice, to learn yesterday's lessons for tomorrow, and to write down this permanent constitution from the high values and ideals of the heavenly messages and the developments of science and human civilization, and to adhere to this constitution, which shall preserve for Iraq its free union of people, land and sovereignty [Figures 13.30 and 13.31].

Government

The Republic of Iraq is an independent, sovereign nation, and the system of rule in it is a democratic, federal, representative (parliamentary) republic.

National Identity

Iraq is a multiethnic, multi-religious and multi-sect country. It is part of the Islamic world and its Arab people are part of the Arab nation.

Capital

Baghdad with its administrative boundaries is the capital of the Republic of Iraq.

Baath Party

Entities or trends that advocate, instigate, justify or propagate racism, terrorism, "takfir" (declaring someone an infidel), or sectarian cleansing, are banned, especially

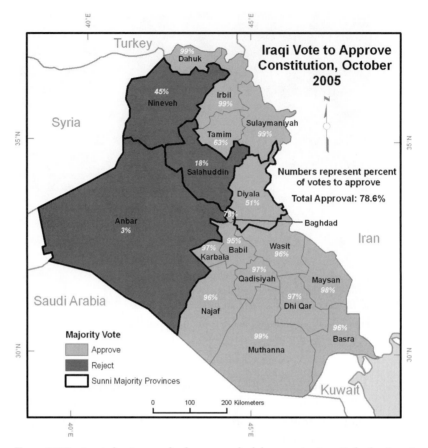

Figure 13.31 Iraqi election results for approval of the constitution. Only the Sunni-majority provinces voted against the constitution.

the Saddamist Baath Party in Iraq and its symbols, under any name. It will not be allowed to be part of the multilateral political system in Iraq.

Individual Rights

Iraqis are equal before the law without discrimination because of sex, ethnicity, nationality, origin, color, religion, sect, belief, opinion or social or economic status. The state guarantees social and health insurance, the basics for a free and honorable life for the individual and the family—especially children and women—and works to protect them from illiteracy, fear and poverty and provides them with housing and the means to rehabilitate and take care of them.

Islam

Islam is the official religion of the state and is a basic source of legislation:

(a) No law can be passed that contradicts the undisputed rules of Islam.

(b) No law can be passed that contradicts the principles of democracy.

(c) No law can be passed that contradicts the rights and basic freedoms outlined in this constitution.

This constitution guarantees the Islamic identity of the majority of the Iraqi people and the full religious rights for all individuals and the freedom of creed and religious practices.

© 2010 John Wiley & Sons, Inc.

Language
> Arabic and Kurdish are the two official languages for Iraq. Iraqis are guaranteed the right to educate their children in their mother tongues, such as Turkomen or Assyrian, in government educational institutions, or any other language in private educational institutions, according to educational regulations.

Women's Rights
> Citizens, male and female, have the right to participate in public matters and enjoy political rights, including the right to vote and run as candidates. A proportion of no less than 25 percent of the seats in the Council of Representatives is specified for the participation of women.

Powers of the Federal and Regional Governments
> The federal authority will maintain the unity of Iraq, its integrity, independence, sovereignty and its democratic federal system. The federal authorities will have the following exclusive powers: foreign policy; national defense; customs, currency, and trade; weights and measures; passports and residency; mail and broadcasting; general budgets; guaranteeing levels of water flow into Iraq; census, and certain aspects of oil (see below). All that is not written in the exclusive powers of the federal authorities is in the authority of the regions.

Regional Autonomy
> The regions comprise one province or more, and two regions or more have the right to join into one region. One province or more have the right to form a region, based on a request for a referendum. The governments of regions have the right to practice legislative, executive and judicial powers according to this constitution, except in what is listed as exclusive powers of the federal authorities. The regional authority has the right to amend the implementation of the federal law in the region in the case of a contradiction between the federal and regional laws in matters that do not pertain to the exclusive powers of the federal authorities. A fair share of the revenues collected federally is designated to regions, in a way that suffices their duties and obligations, taking into consideration the (region's) resources and needs. The region's government is responsible for all that is required to manage the region, in particular establishing and organizing internal security forces for the region such as police, security and regional guards. . . . Laws legislated in Kurdistan since 1992 remain in effect, and decisions made by the government of the Kurdistan region—including contracts and court decisions—are effective unless they are voided or amended according to the laws of the Kurdistan region by the concerned body, as long as they are not against the constitution.

Provinces
> Provinces that were not included into a region are given extensive administrative and financial authorities to enable them to self-manage according to the principle of administrative decentralization.

Oil Wealth
> The federal government will administer oil and gas extracted from *current* fields in cooperation with the governments of the producing regions and provinces on condition that the revenues will be distributed fairly in a manner compatible with the demographical distribution all over the country. A quota should be defined for a

specified time for affected regions that were deprived in an unfair way by the former regime or later on, in a way to ensure balanced development in different parts of the country. The federal government and the governments of the producing regions and provinces together will draw up the necessary strategic policies to develop oil and gas wealth to bring the greatest benefit for the Iraqi people, relying on the most modern techniques of market principles and encouraging investment.

Amendments

[Amendments require approval by] two-thirds of the members of the Council of Representatives, the consent of the people in a general referendum, and the endorsement of the president within seven days. No amendment is allowed that lessens the powers of the regions that are not among the exclusive powers of the federal authority, except with the agreement of the legislative council of the concerned region and the consent of a majority of its population in a general referendum.

▶ DEFINITIONS OF KEY TERMS

Colony An area conquered and administered by a foreign power.

Diaspora Scattered settlements of a particular national group living abroad.

Ethnonationalism A strong feeling of belonging to a nation that is a minority within a state, has its own distinctive homeland within the state's territory, and has deeply rooted feelings that they are different from the rest of the state's population.

Federal State A state with a two-tiered system of government with a clear and formal distinction between the powers of the central (federal) government and those of the lower-level administrative units within the country. This system of government is called *federalism*, and the country can be called a *federation* or *confederation*. Contrast federal state with *unitary state*.

Homeland Perceived ancestral territory of a nation.

Irredentism A movement to reunite a nation's homeland when part of it is contained within another state. The piece of homeland that is ruled by the other state is known as an *irredenta*.

Nation The largest human grouping characterized by a common origin or ancestry. A territorially based community of people who usually have similar language or religion, a common history (real or imagined), and accepted social ways of behavior that give it a common culture.

Nationalism Loyalty to the nation to which you belong. Often misused today to refer to *patriotism*.

Nation-State A state that has the same boundaries as a nation.

Patriotism Loyalty to the governing state in which you live.

Province A first-level administrative subregion of a state.

Raison d'être Literally translates as "reason for being." A state idea that helps rally diverse peoples together.

Refugee A person who is outside his or her country due to a well-founded fear of persecution and who is unable or unwilling to return.

Regional Autonomy Limited self-rule for a region within the larger state.

Secession Complete break-off of a region into an autonomous, independent state. This occurs when a separatist movement achieves its goals.

Separatism The desire to break a region away from its state and form a new independent state.

Shatterbelt A region caught between powerful forces whose boundaries are continually redefined.

State An independent, bounded, and internationally recognized territory with full sovereignty over the land and people within it—in other words, a "country."

Unitary State A state largely governed as a single unit by the central government. It may be subdivided into provinces or regions for administrative purposes, but the central government dictates the degree of regional political control. Contrast unitary state with *federal state*.

▶ FURTHER READINGS

Agnew, John. 2007. No Borders, No Nations: Making Greece in Macedonia. *Arnals of the Association of American Geographers* 97(2):398–422.

Bergen, Peter. 2008. Al Qaeda at 20 Dead or Alive? *Washington Post* (Aug. 17): B01.

Boyd, Andrew. 1998. *An Atlas of World Affairs*, 10th ed. London: Routledge.

Burg, Steven L. 1993. Why Yugoslavia Fell Apart. *Current History* (Nov.):357–363.

Cohen, Roger. 1993. The Tearing Apart of Yugoslavia: Place by Place, Family by Family. *New York Times* (May 9):4.

Connor, Walker. 1994. *Ethnonationalism: The Quest for Understanding*. Princeton, NJ: Princeton University Press.

Cornell, Svante E. 2008. War in Georgia, Jitters All Around. *Current History* (Oct.):307–314.

Dahlman, Carl, and Gearóid Ó Tuathail 2005. Broken Bosnia: The Localized Geopolitics of Displacement and Return in Two Bosnian Places. *Annals of the Association of American Geographers* 95(3):644–662.

Dickey, Christopher, and Evan Thomas. 2002. How Saddam Happened. *Newsweek* (Sept. 23, 2002):34–41.

Drummond, Dorothy. 2003. *Holy Land, Whose Land? Modern Dilemma, Ancient Roots*. Seattle: Educare Press.

Fallows, James. 2005. Why Iraq Has No Army. *Atlantic Monthly* (Dec.):60–77.

Flint, Colin (ed.). 2005. *The Geography of War and Peace: From Death Camps to Diplomats*. New York: Oxford University Press.

Fournier, P. 1991. *A Meech Lake Post-Mortem: Is Québec Sovereignty Inevitable?* Montreal: McGill-Queens University Press.

Gow, James. 1991. Deconstructing Yugoslavia. *Survival* 33:293.

Gregory, Derek. 2004. *The Colonial Present: Afghanistan, Palestine, Iraq*. Malden, MA: Blackwell Publishing.

Kifner, John. 1999. Crisis in the Balkans: Horror by Design—The Ravaging of Kosovo: A Special Report; How Serb Forces Purged One Million Albanians. *New York Times* (May 29):A1, A4–A5.

Klare, Michael. 2004. *Blood and Oil: The Dangers and Consequences of America's Growing Dependency on Imported Petroleum*. New York: Metropolitan Books.

Munson, Henry. 2004. Lifting the Veil: Understanding the Roots of Islamic Militancy. *Harvard International Review* 25(4): 20–23.

Post, Jerrold, Ehud Sprinzak, and Laurita M. Denney. 2003. The Terrorists in Their Own Words: Interviews with 35 Incarcerated Middle Eastern Terrorists. *Terrorism and Political Violence* 15(1):171–184.

Poulsen, Thomas M. 1995. *Nations and States: A Geographic Background to World Affairs*. Englewood Cliffs, NJ: Prentice Hall.

Ricks, Thomas E. 2006. *Fiasco: The American Military Adventure in Iraq*. New York: Penguin Press.

Robinson, Glenn E. 2007. The Fragmentation of Palestine. *Current History* (Dec.):421–426

Yergin, Daniel. 2008. *The Prize: The Epic Quest for Oil, Money, and Power*. New York: Simon and Schuster.

▶ WEB REFERENCES

Albanian.com. *Kosovo*: www.albanian.com/information

Amnesty International: www.amnesty.org

Bennis, Phyllis. 2005. *The Iraqi Constitution* ZNet (October 13): www.zmag.org/znet/viewArticle/5213

British Broadcasting Corporation News. *Text of the Draft Iraqi Constitution*. news.bbc.co.uk/l/shared/bsp/hi/pdfs/ 24_08_05_ constit.pdf

British Broadcasting Corporation News. *Timeline Iraq*: news.bbc.co.uk/1/hi/world/middle_east/737483.stm

Brown, Nathan J. 2005. *The Final Draft of the Iraqi Constitution: Analysis and Commentary*. Carnegie Endowment for International Peace: www.carnegieendowment.org/files/FinalDraftSept16.pdf

Cable News Network (CNN.com). *War in Iraq*: www.cnn.com/SPECIALS/2003/iraq

Central Intelligence Agency. *The World Factbook*: www.cia.gov/library/publications/the-world-factbook

Christian Science Monitor: www.christiansciencemonitor.com

Common Dreams News Center. *News in Depth: The Kosovo War*: www.commondreams.org/kosovo/kosovo.htm

Council on Foreign Relations. *Iraq*: www.cfr.org/region/405/iraq.html

CountryReports.org: www.countryreports.org

Fallows, James. 2002. The Fifty-First State? *Atlantic Monthly* 290(4):53–64: www.theatlantic.com/issues/2002/11/fallows.htm

Frontline (WGBH, Public Broadcasting System). 2003. *The Long Road to War—Chronology*: www.pbs.org/wgbh/pages/frontline/shows/longroad/etc/cron.html

Galbraith, Peter. 2004. How to Get Out of Iraq: www.nybooks.com/articles/17103

Global Policy Forum. *Iraq*: www.globalpolicy.org/security/issues/irqindx.htm

Goldberg, Jeffrey. 2008. After Iraq. *The Atlantic* (Jan./Feb.): www.theatlantic.com/doc/200801/goldberg-mideast

Guardian Unlimited. *Special Report: Oil and Petrol*: www.guardian.co.uk/oil

History News Network. *About the History of Iraq*: hnn.us/articles/1032.html

Infoplease. *Iraq Timeline*: www.infoplease.com/spot/iraq-timeline-2008.html

IslamiCity: www.islamicity.com

Kurdistan Democratic Party—Iraq: www.kdp.pp.se

Library of Congress, Federal Research Division. *Country Studies*: 1cweb2.loc.gov/frd/cs/cshome.html

Noah, Timothy. 2004. *Kurd Sellout Watch, Day 421: Should We Partition Iraq?* (April 27): www.slate.com/id/2099574

North Atlantic Treaty Organization (NATO), *NATO's Role in Kosovo*: www.nato.int/issues/kosovo/index.html

Novak, Robert. 2003. *Mission to Niger* (July 14): http:// www.townhall.com/opinion/columns/robertnovak/2003/07/14/160881. html

Permanent Mission of Iraq to the United Nations: iraqunmission.org

Rubin, Barnett R., and Ahmed Rashid. 2008. Frorn Great Game to Grand Bargain: Ending Chaos in Afghanistan and Pakistan. *Foreign Affairs* (Nov./Dec.): www.foreignaffairs.com/articles/64604/barnett-r-rubin-and-ahmed-rashid/from-great-game-to-grand-bargain

Serbian Orthodox Diocese of Raska and Prizren, Media Publishing Center. *Kosovo: Land of the Living Past*: www.kosovo.net

Srpska Mreza. *The Saga of Kosovo*: www.srpska-mreza.com/mlad

United Nations Development Program. *The Republic of Iraq*: www.iq.undp.org

United Nations High Commissioner for Refugees (UNHCR): www.unhcr.org/home.html

United Nations, Interim Administration Mission in Kosovo: www.unmikonline.org

United Nations Special Commission (UNSCOM): www.un.org/Depts/unscom

U.S. Department of State, *Building Peace in Kosovo*: www.state.gov/www/regions/eur/kosovo_hp.html

U.S. Department of State, Department Organization: www.state.gov/r/pa/ei/rls/dos/436.htm

U.S. Department of State, *Iraq:* www.state.gov/p/nea/ci/iz

U.S. Department of State. *Kosovo Chronology:* www.state.gov/www/regions/eur/fs_kosovo_timeline.html

University of Texas, Perry-Castañeda Library Map Collection. *Iraq Maps:* www.lib.utexas.edu/Libs/PCL/Map_collection/iraq .html

United Nations Assistance Mission for Iraq. *Map Center:* www.uniraq.org/docsmaps/maps. asp

United Nations International Criminal Tribunal for the Former Yugoslavia: www.icty.org

United Nations Peacekeeping: www.un.org/Depts/dpko/dpko/index.asp

The White House. *The Agenda: Iraq:* www.whitehouse.gov/agenda/iraq

Wilson IV, Joseph C. 2003. *What I Didn't Find in Africa* (July 6): http://www.commondreams.org/views03/0706-02.htm

World News Network. *Iraq Daily:* www.iraqdaily.com

▶ ITEMS TO HAND IN

Activity 1: • Questions 1.1–1.33, or answer all questions your instructor created in your WileyPlus assignments.

Activity 2: • Questions 2.1–2.39, or answer all questions your instructor created in your WileyPlus assignments.

Ask your instructor which activity to complete.

CHAPTER 14

Preserving the Planet: Human Impact on Environmental Systems

▶ INTRODUCTION

The study of **human-environmental interactions** is a long-standing theme in geography. The interaction is a two-way street in that the natural environment affects humans' ways of life, and these ways of life, in turn, affect the natural environment. From prehistoric times, humans left an imprint on the landscape by diverting water from rivers into rice-paddy fields, cutting forests for crops and pasture, terracing hillsides to create more agricultural land (Figure 14.1), and burning wood and coal to keep warm, cook food, and produce tools. In some cases, prehistoric populations degraded their natural environments greatly. Among the Hohokam of the American Southwest, overirrigation rendered the natural environment incapable of supporting the existing population. Ultimately, the entire civilization collapsed. Depleted soil fertility also is thought to have contributed to the downfall of some Mayan civilizations in Mesoamerica.

Figure 14.1 Terracing hillslopes for rice paddies has been practiced for centuries in China.

Concern with human-environmental interactions is at the forefront of public debate today. There is growing awareness that humans are affecting their environment at increasing rates, in fundamentally new ways, and at larger scales. Human actions now cause global-scale environmental impacts such as planetary warming due to higher levels of greenhouse gases, extinction of species, and degradation of the stratospheric ozone layer that protects life on the surface from harmful ultraviolet rays. Geographers were among the first scientists to sound the alarm that human-induced changes to the environment are affecting the balance of life itself on our fragile planet. Humans cannot ignore these changes in Earth's natural systems.

Although each environmental problem is different, one common theme underlying human-environmental interactions is the idea of a **system**, a group of elements in which a change in one element or process causes direct or indirect changes in others. The basic building blocks of any system are **stocks** (amounts of energy, materials, and organisms) and **flows** (movements of energy, materials, and organisms). Stocks and flows are connected in **cycles**, circular series of flows that replenish the stocks of the system and allow it to continue functioning. Examples include (a) the hydrologic cycle, where water continually evaporates from water bodies only to precipitate elsewhere; (b) the nutrient cycle, where food energy is transferred up the food chain and eventually returns to the earth where plants and animals decompose; and (c) the carbon cycle, where carbon is released into the atmosphere by fossil fuel and wood combustion and through animal respiration, only to be reabsorbed by plants through photosynthesis (Figure 14.2). Energy provided by the sun is the ultimate mechanism driving these three systems.

Sustainable environmental cycles remain in a balanced or **equilibrium** state in which stocks are replaced by returning flows. The cause-and-effect loops that affect balance in a system are known as *feedback loops*. When a stock rises or falls out of its normal range, feedback loops determine what happens. **Negative feedback loops** offset the original change and restore the balance. For instance, when the stock of predators in a food chain falls, their prey will multiply, providing a substantial food supply to help the predators rebound. These relationships are "negative" in the sense that the original change is reversed or negated through system dynamics. **Positive feedback loops** do the opposite. They multiply the original change and send the system snowballing further out of balance. For instance, denudation of the rain forest leads to soil erosion, which causes further denudation, which causes further erosion, and so on. Positive feedback loops are sometimes known as *vicious cycles*. Negative feedback loops lead to sustainability; positive feedback loops detract from it.

Various ecological systems are intertwined. Changes to the carbon cycles can modify the composition of the atmosphere, which can influence atmospheric circulation, which alters precipitation patterns in the hydrologic system, which in turn affects plants and animals in the food chain. Small ecosystems (such as a coral reef) exist within larger ones (the continental shelf), which exist within global systems (the circulation of ocean currents). At the intersection of many of these systems, life exists in the **biosphere**, the thin layer of air (atmosphere), water (hydrosphere), and earth (lithosphere) that supports life.

Next we must insert humans into the environmental system. We do this by first acknowledging that humans are part of the natural world, not independent of or dominant over it. Second, we must recognize that the human society itself functions as a system. A simplified general model of human-caused environmental change is shown in the systems diagram in Figure 14.3. If this were a physical geography course, the focus would be mainly on the third box in the model: environmental

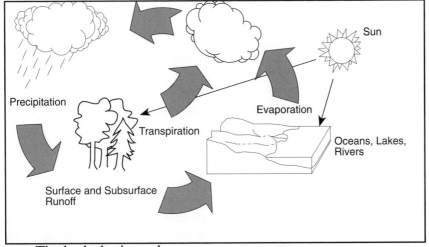

Water continually evaporates through energy from the sun. The water then precipitates elsewhere, creating surface runoff in the form of streams and rivers, subsurface runoff, and aquifers underground. Much water is stored in lakes and oceans, which are important evaporation sources. The water is also used by plants, which transpire some of it back into the atmosphere.

a. The hydrologic cycle

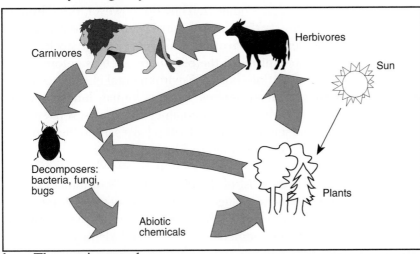

The sun provides energy for plants to grow. Energy is transferred up the food chain as complex organisms eat simpler ones. All life forms eventually die and return to the earth to decompose. Small insects, bacteria, and fungi aid in the decomposition process. Final organic decomposition results in abiotic chemicals, which are nutrients for plants.

b. The nutrient cycle

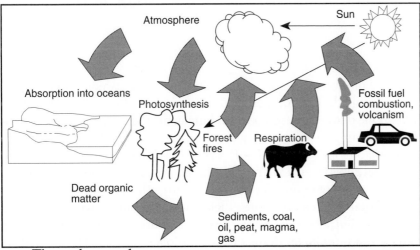

Carbon is released into the atmosphere by fossil fuel and wood burning, from animal respiration (we eat carbohydrates and breathe out CO_2), and through volcanic activity. Plants, using energy from the sun, convert much of this CO_2 into carbohydrates through photosynthesis. Some of it is also absorbed into the oceans. Dead organic matter contains carbon, which is stored in the earth's sediments and in coal, oil, gas, and peat—four fossil fuels that release carbon into the atmosphere when burned.

c. The carbon cycle

Figure 14.2 Energy-material cycling through three environmental systems.

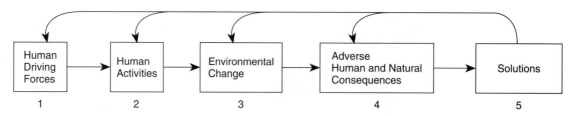

Figure 14.3 Generalized systems model of human-caused environmental damage.

change. However, for a human geography course, we are more interested in the human-environment interface, where human activities cause environmental change and where change in natural systems affects the way humans live and work.

Human driving forces are the underlying trends or processes in society that are indirectly responsible for environmental degradation but do not directly hurt the environment (box 1). For instance, population growth, greater affluence, more sophisticated technology, public policy, and materialistic culture do not necessarily, in and of themselves, damage the environment. They do, however, drive **human activities** such as forestry or industry that directly damage environmental systems (box 2). These human activities lead to **environmental change** to the stocks and/or flows of energy, materials, and organisms in the biosphere, such as deforestation, soil erosion, and air and water pollution (box 3). Environmental changes can have **adverse human and natural consequences**, such as human lung disease or species extinction (box 4). Finally, when the consequences become severe enough, and when humans come to understand how our activities have caused them, people begin to seek **solutions** to treat the problem (box 5).

In the rest of this introductory section, we go into greater detail about each of these five boxes. We provide you a list of the different kinds of human driving forces, human activities, environmental changes, adverse human and natural consequences, and solutions. Then, in Activity 2 of the exercise, your task will be to read magazine articles about regional environmental problems and identify the specific driving forces, human activities, environmental changes, adverse consequences, and solutions that are involved. In short, you will be asked to fill in the boxes in the human-environmental systems flowchart.

Human Driving Forces

The systems model of environmental change distinguishes between human activities that directly change the environment and the underlying forces that drive those human activities. One of the earliest models of human driving forces is the **IPAT** formula. Environmental impacts I were seen as a multiplicative result of population P, affluence A, and technology T; that is, $I = P \times A \times T$. The idea was simple: 10 families in 500-square-feet apartments use roughly the same amount of heating oil as one family in a 5,000-square-feet house. Technology creates a third multiplicative effect. Insulation, solar design and heating, more efficient furnaces, and a switch from oil to natural gas lessen the impacts. Conversely, heating by burning raw coal in a simple stove, as is often done in China, dramatically multiplies the impacts. In Activity 1 of this chapter, you will use the IPAT formula to look at how more-developed and less-developed countries contribute to the global warming problem.

For Activity 2, however, we expand the list of human driving forces from three to five, in recognition of criticisms that IPAT ignores cultural and governmental influences.

1. *Population*. All else being equal, more people will use more land and more resources and produce more waste. Less-developed countries (LDCs) have three-quarters of the world's population. Their populations also are growing faster than in more-developed countries (MDCs), and this increase creates **population pressure** on the land and resource base. Population pressure often leads to shortsighted overuse of sensitive land and water resources. Also, rapidly growing populations, because of their young age structures (see Chapter 5), consume more of their economic production in food, health care, and education, and thus have less left over to invest in environmental stewardship.

2. *Affluence*. Individuals in MDCs consume more resources *per capita*: more gasoline used to drive more cars more miles; more electricity generated for industry, offices, and homes; more forests cleared for more beef consumed; more land converted to urban uses; and so on. Not surprisingly, individuals also generate more waste of every kind per person: wastewater, toxic waste, CO_2 emissions, and solid waste (Figure 14.4c). High rates of consumption, however, are counterbalanced partly because wealthier societies can afford to spend money on mitigating environmental consequences—a fact that the IPAT model ignores. Measures that affluent countries take include setting aside lands for parks and wilderness; installing expensive pollution control devices; protecting endangered species; regulating pesticides; locating noxious facilities far from population centers; and providing safe drinking water for all (Figure 14.4a). With their focus on alleviating hunger and poverty, LDCs cannot afford to go quite so far to protect the environment. So where do these conflicting trends leave us—does affluence have a positive or negative impact on the environment? Some environment scientists think that all

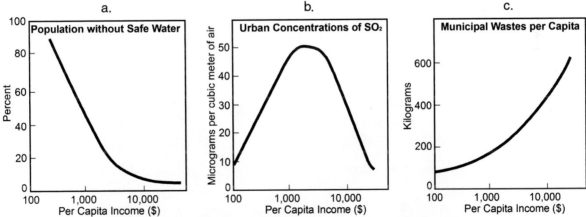

Figure 14.4 As a country becomes wealthier, environmental conditions can (a) improve, (b) get worse and then get better, or (c) deteriorate. Scientists surmise that the reverse-U curve in (b) is the general case, and the examples in (a) and (c) would in fact resemble (b) over a very long time span. For instance, if we could go back far enough in history to measure water quality in (a), we might find that the preagricultural human societies had very clean water to drink, which gradually grew worse during the agricultural and industrial revolutions before getting better. Likewise, if we could go far enough into the future in (c), we might find that society has eliminated most forms of municipal waste through recycling, composting, less packaging, digital newspapers, and other technologies not yet invented, and this upward slope would turn downward eventually.

Source: The World Bank. 1992. *World Development Report 1992: Development and the Environment.* Reprinted by permission of Oxford University Press.

© 2010 John Wiley & Sons, Inc.

environmental impact functions resemble the reverse-U curve in Figure 14.4b, which could be confirmed if one could only obtain data far enough into the past or future to capture the entire life cycle. In Figure 14.4b, very poor countries emit little sulfur dioxide (SO_2) pollution because they have little mechanization. As these countries develop and industrialize, SO_2 emissions rise. Eventually, as the societies become rich through substitution of capital and fossil fuels for human labor, two things happen. High SO_2 concentrations begin to cause acid rain and other problems, and societies become rich enough and technologically sophisticated enough to spend billions of dollars to reduce SO_2 emissions. The IPAT model, however, assumes a linearly increasing impact function, such as a straight-line version of Figure 14.4c or the upward-sloping first part of Figure 14.4b. The IPAT model would attribute Figure 14.4a and the downward-sloping part of Figure 14.4b to technology (T), not affluence (A), which is only half correct.

3. *Technology*. Better technology wastes fewer natural resources, develops more ways of tapping **renewable resources**, and provides more effective methods of treating and cleaning waste products. However, technology also creates new types of environmental damage, for example, industrial waste from the computer chip industry, CFC emissions, and high-level radiation.

4. *Political Economic Systems*. Government encourages wasteful use of resources when it leases mineral extraction or when it supplies fresh water at prices below the long-term costs, when it refuses to force polluters to control or pay for the damage caused by their emissions, or when it builds free roads into virgin forest (Figure 14.5). Development policy often favors short-term job creation over long-term environmental management. For instance, a coal-burning power plant generates the electricity needed for jobs, yet many of the citizens pay in the form of respiratory problems from air pollution or reduced outdoor recreational opportunities resulting from forests and fish dying from acid rain. Communist countries are notorious for their

Figure 14.5 South American governments encourage development and migration to the Amazon frontier by building roads and offering incentives. Deforestation follows in the wake of the roads.

© 2010 John Wiley & Sons, Inc.

Figure 14.6 Dead rhino with horn cut off by poachers in Southern Africa. Only the horns are of value to the poachers, who export them to the Far East where they are believed to provide great medicinal and sexual benefits.

environmental degradation, largely because state-owned industries and the government itself are not accountable to the people.

5. *Cultural Values*. Cultural values can directly affect the environment, even in countries with similar government systems, levels of affluence, and use of technology. The U.S. preference for detached, large houses with private yards contributes directly to our high consumption of lumber for furniture and building materials and of fossil fuels for heating, cooling, and driving. High mobility rates and sprawling cities add to our heavy use of fossil fuels. In contrast, smaller houses and less reliance on the automobile in Japan lead to lower levels of resource consumption. Cultural driving forces also include beliefs, practices, and dietary preferences (Figure 14.6).

These five factors are, of course, interrelated. For instance, as you learned in Chapter 5, birth rates usually diminish with increasing affluence. Also, cultural values affect which technologies are developed, and political systems become more sophisticated with sustained affluence.

Human Activities

Human activities that directly cause environmental changes can be grouped into five general categories. The categories used here are loosely based on the primary, secondary, and tertiary sectors of the economy we encountered in Chapter 6, plus a fourth category for residential consumption and a fifth category combining all aspects of transportation. Note that all five types of human activities use energy and water.

1. *Extractive Activities*. This is the primary sector of the economy, which harvests and extracts raw materials from the earth. Extractive activities are subdivided as follows:

   a. Hunting and gathering of wild plants and animals, including forestry.

   b. Raising livestock (domesticated animals), which covers everything from ranching on wild lands to grazing on planted areas to raising animals in pens and feeding them with harvested feed crops.

   c. Farming, or planting of crops.

   d. Mining.

2. *Industry*. This includes the secondary sector of the economy that processes raw materials into finished products.

3. *Services*. This includes the tertiary and quaternary sectors of the economy that either sell the finished products or use products to perform services (excluding transportation).

4. *Household Consumption*. This includes activities inside a person's home or yard.

5. *Transportation*. This includes both construction and use of transportation infrastructure by private individuals as well as corporate and government entities.

Environmental Change

All forms of life depend on systems of energy and material flows that provide them with the light, food, water, heat, nutrients, and space they need to survive. Humans cause environmental change by altering flows of energy and materials in the environmental system in three basic ways:

1. *Energy/Material Redistribution*. This category includes all ways that humans redistribute, sequester, or otherwise change nonliving materials and energy in the natural world. Materials and energy include water, nutrients, soil, mineral deposits, heat, and sunshine. In **energy and material redistribution**, humans do not introduce new substances into the environment (see Pollution)—they disrupt natural flows of energy and materials. Redistributing means moving things around that otherwise would not change, such as draining a wetland and eroding soil from a field or mountain.

   Sequester means to impound or stop natural movement, as in the way dams stop water and fertile sediments from flowing downstream (Figure 14.7). Redistribution of natural materials includes transformation of the earth's surface, which can involve strip mining, paving lots and roads, field leveling, hillside terracing, and so on. Earth, air, and water redistribution are all grouped in this category.

2. *Pollution*. Humans put waste materials, such as harmful substances from agriculture (DDT) and industry (carbon monoxide, PCBs) into the environment. If natural processes cannot readily dispose of these waste materials, or if they harm any form of life because of their quantity, chemical nature, or temperature, we have a special word for them: **pollution**. Pollution can be emitted into the atmosphere (Figure 14.8), hydrosphere, or lithosphere. Carbon dioxide is a special case: As a natural product of animal respiration, forest fires, and volcanoes, it is not an unnatural substance. In fact, its presence in the atmosphere keeps the surface of the earth from freezing. The very large quantities that humans emit through the burning of fossil fuels, however, are disrupting the planet's carbon and heat cycles. CO_2 can therefore be considered a form of pollution.

3. *Direct Biological Interference*. Humans directly remove, redistribute, and modify living creatures by harvesting them (e.g., fishing, grazing, or logging, as in Figure 14.9), transplanting them (both plants *and* animals),

Figure 14.7 Uribante Caparo hydroelectric dam in Venezuela shows both the upstream and downstream impacts of impounding and releasing massive amounts of water.

Figure 14.8 Smoke spews out of smokestacks at this factory in Cananea, Mexico. Tall smokestacks are often used to lessen the impacts on the local area, but if they are too tall, they can create a plume that goes for hundreds of miles.

and breeding or genetically engineering new hybrids (again, plants *and* animals). Overgrazing of livestock on grasslands is one of the oldest environmental impacts known to humans (Figure 14.10). We call this **direct biological interference** to distinguish it from one of the categories in Figure 14.3—box 4, adverse natural consequences—that result *indirectly* from redistribution of natural resources or pollution.

Figure 14.9 Humans modify the ecosystem on a massive scale, as seen by this enormous clear-cut area in Washington.

Figure 14.10 Overgrazed grasslands with cattle carcass, Carrizo Plain, California.

Adverse Consequences

The fourth component of our simplified model of environmental change is adverse consequences. This is the "so what?" of environmental change (i.e., why we should be concerned about it):

1. *Adverse Human Consequences.* Environmental change affects human health in a variety of ways. These range from short-term incidents such as high air-pollution days; to lifelong problems such as malnutrition, birth defects, and respiratory problems; to fatalities due to cancer-causing toxic and nuclear waste, deadly natural disasters such as floods and landslides, infant mortality, unsafe drinking water, and the like. Economic consequences range from lost days of work and increased health care costs to reduced agricultural productivity, damage to bridges and buildings, loss of recreational opportunities and tourism income, and loss of species that could have medicinal or agricultural value. Human consequences also include the loss of habitat for indigenous peoples in remote areas whose subsistence culture can depend on the existence of unspoiled habitat.

2. *Adverse Natural Consequences.* The adverse consequences to other life-forms include extinction, loss of biodiversity (the variety of species), disruption of the food chain or other nutrient cycles, and climate change that modifies or moves habitats (Table 14.1). Soil erosion that happens *after* logging is a good example of an adverse natural consequence of the initial environmental change (Figure 14.11).

Figure 14.11   Human removal of the natural forest cover in the Amazon rain forest leads to soil erosion. The tree roots hold the soil in place; without them, heavy rains wash it away.

© 2010 John Wiley & Sons, Inc.

TABLE 14.1 **World's Most Endangered Species**

Animal Species	Geographic Range	Estimated Wild Population
AMPHIBIANS		
Puerto Rican Crested Toad	Puerto Rico, British Virgin Islands	< 300
REPTILES		
Chinese Alligator	China	800–1,000
Western Swamp Turtle	Australia	55
BIRDS		
St. Vincent Amazon	St. Vincent	700–800
California Condor	United States [re-int.]	27
Regent Honeyeater	Australia	< 1,000
Blue-throated Macaw	Argentina (?), Bolivia, Paraguay (?)	< 1,000
Red-fronted Macaw	Bolivia	1,000
Blackiston's Fish Owl	China, Japan, Russia	680–900
Orange-bellied Parrot	Australia	150
Edwards Pheasant	Vietnam	Extinct (?)
Bali Starling (Bali Mynah)	Indonesia	30–35
MAMMALS		
Addax	North Africa and the Sahel	< 250
Somali Wild Ass	Ethiopia, Somalia	100–250
Black-footed Ferret	United States	60
Rodrigues Flying Fox	Mauritius (Rodrigues)	350
Silvery Gibbon	Indonesia	1,000
Amur Leopard	China, North & South Korea, Russia	28–31
Asiatic Lion	India	300
Pygmy Loris	Cambodia (?), China, Laos, Vietnam	300–500
Sumatran Rhinoceros	Southeast Asia	250–400
Golden Lion Tamarin	Brazil	< 650
Amur Tiger	China [ex?], N. Korea [ex?], Russia	330–371
Sumatran Tiger	Indonesia	400–500
Red Wolf	United States	92

Source: World Resources Institute, Table 14.4, "Endangered Species Management Programs, 1996" (www.wri.org/facts/data-tables-biodiversity.html).

Solutions

The last component of our simplified model involves solutions to environmental problems. Solutions can be thought of as negative feedback loops because, as a result of adverse consequences, changes are made to other parts of the system that eventually reduce those same adverse consequences. The range of responses that humans can take to environmental problems falls into six categories:

1. *Prevention.* Prevention refers generally to actions that address the initial driving forces of a problem. We use this term in the same way as in medicine, where prevention refers to living a healthy lifestyle that prevents illness from occurring in the first place. For example, given that population growth in China will lead to greater energy and food needs, which will lead to more coal emissions and more soil erosion, the Chinese one-child policy is a powerful solution for preventing these problems from growing out of hand. Another preventive solution is to change governmental

policies that have inadvertently encouraged activities that damage the environment, such as low livestock grazing fees, cheap gasoline, or road-building into the Amazon rain forest. The least popular form of prevention is the suggestion that people accept a lower economic standard of living.

2. *Technological Change.* In Activity 2, the arrow from the technological change solution box is directed toward human activities and the technology component of human driving forces. In the former case, technological change is directed specifically at making a particular activity less damaging:

- Fishing techniques that do not capture dolphins and other nontargeted species
- Ranching that does not overgraze grasslands
- Farming that uses organic pesticides
- Forestry that avoids clear-cutting entire hillsides and leaves some old growth standing
- Mining methods that do not leach heavy metals into nearby streams
- Industries that install pollution-capturing filters
- Services that recycle their wastes
- Households that purchase more fuel-efficient vehicles and water-saving showerheads

   The second arrow leads back to the human driving force of technology and refers to more far-reaching technological changes, such as genetic engineering and computerization that affect many or even all human activities.

3. *Natural Feedbacks.* Natural negative feedbacks can reduce the adverse consequences of an environmental change, and humans can allow these processes to do their work. This arrow is directed at the environmental change box. Oil spills in warm water can be broken down by certain naturally occurring bacteria. In some lakes with a limestone base, acid rain can be naturally returned to a normal pH. CFCs are eventually broken down by sunlight, but not until the average CFC molecule destroys 100,000 ozone molecules in the ozone layer. Some introduced species will have natural predators that keep them in check. When you are reading about an environmental problem, it is important to determine whether the natural feedbacks can be relied upon rather than more aggressive human solutions.

4. *Land-Use Change.* Land-use change refers to either changing the location of an activity or changing the land uses around the activity that the activity can harm. A billion-dollar nuclear power plant built in Shoreham, Long Island (New York), but never approved for use, stands as testament to the fact that it could be impossible to evacuate the population around a nuclear power plant if it is located in a congested urban area. Some people want to ban housing on barrier islands because the house lights discourage sea turtles from laying eggs on the beaches. The not-in-my-backyard (NIMBY) response makes it increasingly difficult to locate any undesirable facility, such as incinerators, landfills, and airports.

5. *Mitigation.* Mitigation refers to after-the-fact solutions that try to undo the damage or reduce the adverse consequences of an event that has

already occurred. The arrow in Activity 2 is thus directed at both the environmental change and adverse consequences boxes in Figure 14.3. Mitigation examples include cleaning up chemical spills, deacidifying lakes, rehabilitating strip mines, reintroducing peregrine falcons and wolves that were hunted to near extinction, and adding fish ladders to dams (Figure 14.12).

6. *Compensation*. Sometimes, if the political will, economic means, or technological know-how are inadequate for preventing, relocating, or mitigating a problem, policy makers will settle for compensating the victims. This is most common in environmental problems where the costs and complications are high and the effects are not life threatening. Compensation is a common solution to the environmental problem of airport noise. It is also the term that applies to relief granted by lawsuits to the victims, as in the movie *Erin Brockovich*, about victims of chemical dumping who sued an electric utility company.

A recent ecological study illustrates how environment systems are interconnected in surprising ways; and it also gives us a chance to show how the terminology in this chapter can help you understand a real environmental problem. In the late 1700s, Russian trappers introduced arctic foxes to some of Alaska's Aleutian Islands (Figure 14.13). By the early 1800s, seabirds began disappearing from these

Figure 14.12 Adult salmon migrate from the ocean up rivers and creeks to spawn, but dams disrupt this natural process. Fish ladders added onto a dam to try to restore salmon migration after it was cut off would be considered a form of *mitigation*. However, a fish ladder designed into the original dam so that migration is never disrupted would be considered a *technological change* to the human activity that would otherwise have caused environmental change.

© 2010 John Wiley & Sons, Inc.

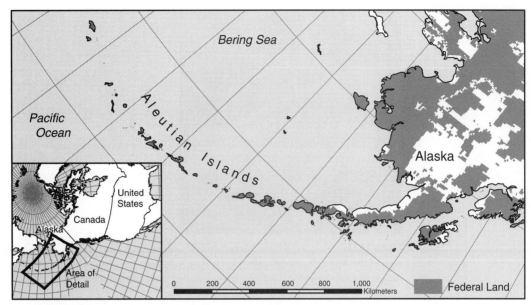

Figure 14.13 Alaska's Aleutian Islands, where Russian trappers introduced foxes in the late 1700s, setting off a domino effect throughout the ecological system from which the islands have never recovered.

islands as the foxes ate the birds and eggs. In 1949, the U.S. Fish and Wildlife Service began hunting, trapping, and poisoning foxes on 17 islands so that endangered birds could return. Recently, scientists began surveying places to reintroduce the Aleutian Canadian goose on these islands, but found little suitable habitat. The vast grasslands of beach rye had been replaced by scruffy tundra of shrubby and leafy plants. Scientists discovered that the foxes had set off a surprising cascade of effects. It turns out that seabird guano (feces) was an essential source of nitrogen for the island soils. Islands that never had foxes produced 63 times more guano and had much higher nitrogen levels in the soils, much healthier grasslands, and a hundred times more birds than the fox-infested islands had. Unfortunately, eradicating foxes from the 17 islands did not reverse the degradation of the grasslands, and the endangered seabirds did not return due to lack of suitable habitat.

We can translate this ecological disaster into system terms, starting with box 3 in Figure 14.3: environmental change. The environmental change that started it all was direct biological interference in the form of introduction of foxes. Working backward from the environmental change, we see it was caused by the human activity of hunting and trapping, which in turn was driven by increasing affluence and a cultural taste for fox-fur coats. Working forward from the environmental change, we see the domino effect of adverse natural consequences in box 4: As the stock of foxes increased, the stock of geese decreased, the flow of nitrogen from the sea to the land via guano decreased, the stock of nitrogen in the soils decreased, the stock of beach rye decreased, and the stock of shrubby plants increased. This created a positive feedback loop in that, as the grassy habitat degraded, fewer geese nested, leading to less guano, less nitrogen, less beach rye, and still fewer geese. These adverse consequences set off a search for solutions. Mitigation (killing foxes) turned out not to be enough to enable natural negative feedback loops to restore balance;

Figure 14.14 We get only one planet: No refunds or returns allowed. Earth observation taken aboard the Space Shuttle Discovery, Orbiter Vehicle (OV) 103, during late afternoon shows the Andes Mountains and a sunglint on the Pacific Ocean (Image courtesy of STS-31).

despite the lack of predators on the fox-free islands, geese could not return because the habitat had changed and the food chain had unraveled.

In a book of this nature, emphasizing hands-on activities, there is no way that we can introduce you to all of the important environmental problems that face Earth at the start of the twenty-first century (Figure 14.14). Even an incomplete list—including soil erosion, acid rain, desertification, species extinction, wetlands destruction, the ozone hole, global warming, algal blooms, coral reefs, tropical deforestation, overgrazing, solid waste, toxic waste, radioactive waste, air pollution, water pollution, noise pollution, indoor pollution, overfishing—is long and growing. The five categories and subcategories in Figure 14.3, however, and systems thinking in general, are applicable to any environmental problem you read about.

▶ **CASE STUDY**

PRESERVING THE PLANET

GOAL

To give students the tools to understand environmental problems. These tools include basic math, systems thinking, and seeing a problem from different perspectives.

LEARNING OUTCOMES

After completing the chapter, you will be able to:

- Calculate total carbon dioxide emissions from population, affluence, and technology data for different country groups.
- Work with data in different units of measurement.
- Relate levels of development and geographic location of countries to environmental impacts.
- Break down environmental problems into five system components: human driving forces, human activities, environmental change, adverse consequences, and solutions.
- Describe the causes and effects of the disappearing Aral Sea, cattle grazing in tropical Latin America, and wildlife corridors in North America.
- Understand different stakeholder groups' perspectives on environmental problems.
- Advocate a position on an environmental problem, and search for solutions that are amenable to several groups.

SPECIAL MATERIALS NEEDED

- Calculator
- Computer with high-speed Internet access and a recent release of a Web browser. If using the Student Companion site with the printed book, click on *Tech Support* for system requirements and technical support. (If using the e-book in WileyPlus, click on *Help* for details about the system requirements.)

BACKGROUND

This chapter contains four environmental case studies and several approaches for making sense of them. Three of the case studies (on the disappearing Aral Sea, cattle in tropical Latin America, and wildlife corridors in North America) are introduced through newspaper and magazine articles. You will apply the systems framework from the Introduction to one or more of these articles in Activity 2, and you will engage in role-playing about these case studies in Activity 3.

In the first case study, you will use IPAT to understand global warming. This requires that you know the basics about the planet's energy balance (Figure 14.15a). Incoming energy in the form of sunlight enters Earth's atmosphere, where about one-quarter of it is reflected back into space. Most of the remainder is absorbed by Earth, which then radiates that energy back toward space in the form of heat. Earth is surrounded by a blanket of atmosphere, consisting of many gases such as oxygen, nitrogen, water vapor, and CO_2. Different atmospheric gases intercept radiation of different wavelengths, and some, such as CO_2, act as a kind of natural greenhouse that insulates the planet. CO_2 absorbs some of the radiant heat energy and reradiates it in all directions, which means that some heat is sent back to Earth.

The greenhouse effect is not new. CO_2 is an essential stock in the natural atmosphere that is absorbed by plants during photosynthesis, converted into carbohydrates, eaten by animals, and breathed back out by animals as CO_2 again. What is new since the Industrial Revolution is the enormous amount of CO_2 being emitted into the atmosphere by humanity through the burning of fossil fuels and forests (Figure 14.15b). Humans are burning stocks of carbon in the form of oil and coal that accumulated underground for billions of years. This carbon has been released into the atmosphere in the form of CO_2 over the course of but a few centuries (Figure 14.16). The CO_2 concentration in the atmosphere is building up to levels not surpassed since the Cretaceous Period—when there were dinosaurs in polar regions—more than 60 million years ago. The CO_2 concentration in the atmosphere has risen from 280 parts per million (ppm) in 1750 to 386 ppm in 2008 (Figure 14.16). Other industrial and agricultural waste gases, such as methane, CFCs, and nitrous oxide, are also effective insulators, and have also been increasing in the atmosphere. In conjunction with these atmospheric changes, we have seen the mean global temperature rise about 0.8°C (1.4°F) since 1900 (Figure 14.16). The 10 warmest years on record have all occurred between 1997 and 2008, and analysis of "proxy" climate data such as tree rings, ice cores, and coral indicate the past 10 years were the warmest in the past millennium.

While there is no disputing the fact that CO_2 is accumulating in the atmosphere, there was much scientific debate in the 1980s and 1990s over whether the observed warming was within the normal range of natural climate fluctuation. To assess and update the current state of knowledge on climate change, the United Nations Environment Programme and the World Meteorological Organization established the Intergovernmental Panel on Climate Change (IPCC), composed of the leading scientific experts from around the world. In 2007, the IPCC's Fourth Assessment Report concluded: "Most of the observed increase in global average temperatures since the mid-20th century is *very likely* due to the observed increase in anthropogenic GHG [greenhouse gas] concentrations." In addition: "Observational evidence from all continents and most oceans shows that many natural systems are being affected by regional climate changes, particularly the observed impacts of temperature increases." In other words, global warming is no longer a vague future threat—it is here and now.

The IPCC summarized some of the main consequences of global warming so far. Sea-level rise, which averaged 1.8 mm per year since 1961, has accelerated to 3.1 mm per year since 1993, as warmer sea and air temperatures melt polar ice caps and thermal expansion increases the volume of existing

▶ **CASE STUDY (Continued)**

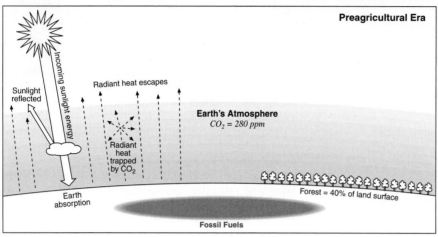

a.

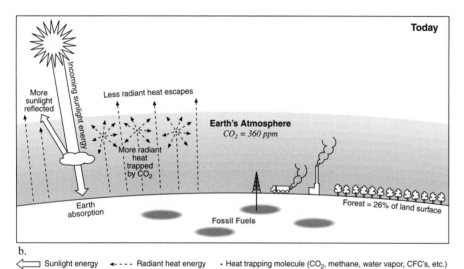

b.

⟨══ Sunlight energy ◀---- Radiant heat energy • Heat trapping molecule (CO₂, methane, water vapor, CFC's, etc.)

Figure 14.15 CO_2 and Earth's energy balance.

oceans. Arctic summer sea ice has thinned 40 percent in recent decades. Nonpolar glaciers have retreated in the Rockies, Andes, Alps, Himalayas, and other mountain ranges. Coral reefs are suffering from increased bleaching. Plant and animal ranges have shifted poleward and up in elevation. Plants are flowering earlier, birds are migrating and nesting earlier, and insects are emerging earlier in the year. The frequency and severity of summer droughts have increased, as have, ironically, heavy precipitation events in northern latitudes. Not all consequences have been adverse, however. The growing season has lengthened by 1 to 4 days per decade since 1960, making farming possible where it once was not and allowing multiple crops per year in some new regions. Again, it is important to emphasize that these are scientific observations, not predictions.

And yet, despite the preponderance of evidence, uncertainty does exist over future changes and the extent to which natural feedbacks will offset the warming trend. Four negative feedbacks in particular have been the subject of recent scrutiny. First, the oceans absorb a substantial amount of CO_2. Second,

other man-made pollutants such as sulfates are increasing the reflectivity of clouds, meaning that less sunlight reaches Earth's surface (Figure 14.15b). Third, more CO_2 in the atmosphere means more nutrients for plants that can reabsorb some of the CO_2. Fourth, the cold water released into the oceans by melting glaciers could trigger a reversal.

The latest IPCC report predicts that, without any major changes in climate policy, greenhouse gas concentrations in the atmosphere will increase 30 to 240 percent by 2100, which will force average temperatures up by 1.8°–4.0°C (3.2°–7.2°F). This temperature increase is 2 to 5 times higher than the increase experienced in the twentieth century. Sea level is expected to rise up to 2 feet in the twenty-first century, flooding low-lying coastal areas and heavily populated islands. Global circulation patterns would change in ways climatologists don't fully understand, but there is consensus that the hydrologic cycle is becoming more intense, bringing more intense drought, heat waves, storms, and flooding. Agricultural and biotic regions will continue to shift, and some species will

© **2010 John Wiley & Sons, Inc.**

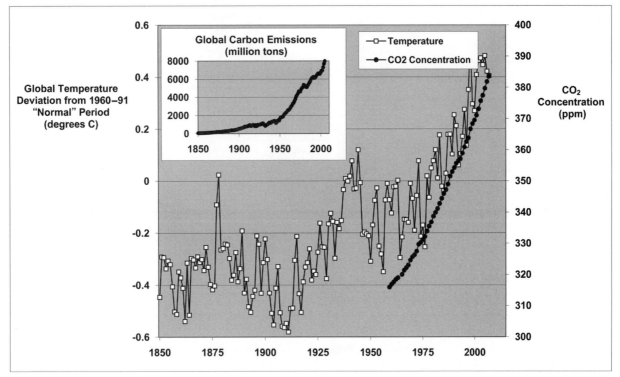

Figure 14.16 Trends in global average temperature (since 1850) and atmospheric CO_2 concentration (since 1959). Inset graph shows estimated global carbon emissions (since 1850) from fossil fuel burning, cement manufacturing, and gas flaring. Sources: www.cru.uea.ac.uk/ and cdiac.esd.ornl.gov/.

be irreparably harmed. While some areas may benefit from a warmer climate, like Russia, Scandinavia, Tibet, and Canada, many rainy areas could get rainier, and semiarid regions like the U.S. Great Plains could become drier.

The IPCC concludes that the larger the changes become, the more the adverse consequences will predominate over beneficial changes. Furthermore, the adverse consequences will fall mainly on the LDCs, and within each country, will fall hardest on the poorest citizens. The IPCC further warns that any delay in dealing with the crisis will be costly. Greenhouse gases have long lifetimes in the atmosphere. Sea levels could continue rising for thousands of years after CO_2 concentrations stabilize.

As the riddle of global warming unfolded at the end of the twentieth century, the MDCs and LDCs of the world increasingly found themselves on opposite sides of the debate about policy solutions. Many of these disagreements came to the fore at the UN's Kyoto Conference in 1997, when the international community gathered together to address the problem of global warming. LDCs looked to MDCs to curb their enormous emissions of CO_2, while MDCs asked LDCs to conserve their rain forests because of the many unique and valuable species they harbor, not to mention the CO_2 they absorb. Poor countries asked for financial aid in protecting their environments and for a share of profits from medicines made from rain-forest ingredients, at the same time that rich countries urged poor countries to slow their population growth. Poor countries

retorted that "development is the best contraceptive," and hoped there would be some oil left by the time most of their population becomes rich enough to own a car.

There were also disagreements among the MDCs that have kept the United States from ratifying the Kyoto Protocol. In the Kyoto Protocol, the industrialized countries of the world agreed to reduce their emissions of greenhouse gases. Under President Clinton, the United States signed the treaty in 1998, pledging to cut CO_2 and other gases by 2012. Congress, however, refused to ratify the treaty, and President Bush formally pulled the United States out of the Kyoto Protocol in March 2001. In addition to what they felt was unequal treatment of MDCs and LDCs (see above), the United States argued for more flexibility in satisfying the targets. In particular, the agreement faltered over U.S. demands to get emissions-reduction credits for establishing carbon sinks by planting carbon-absorbing forests and other land-use changes, and for helping LDCs lower their emissions by improving their technology. Despite the U.S. pullout, 183 countries have ratified or accepted the Kyoto Protocol as of January 2009, including the Russian Federation, Canada, the European Community, Australia, Japan, and China. The European countries agreed to lower emissions cuts and give credits for reforestation. As of March 2009, the United States remains the only MDC not to accept the Kyoto Protocol, although the Obama administration has made addressing climate change one of its top priorities.

▶ *CASE STUDY (Continued)*

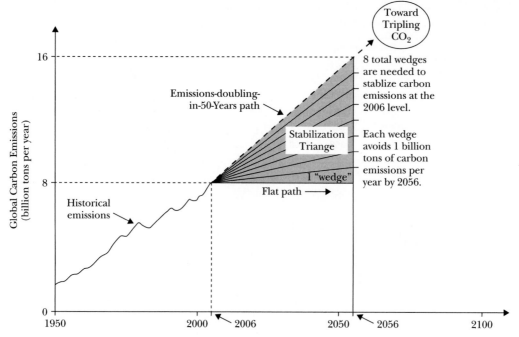

Figure 14.17 To stabilize emissions at the 2006 level, Princeton scientists suggested a divide and conquer strategy. Each carbon "wedge" in the "stabilization triangle" is capable of reducing one billion tons of annual carbon emissions by 2056, and 25 billion tons over the entire 50 years. It is important to recognize, however, that even investment of this scale would only stabilize CO_2 *emissions*, not the CO_2 *content* of the atmosphere. With global emissions of 8 billion tons per year in 2006, humanity was emitting CO_2 faster than the natural environment could absorb it, and as a result the CO_2 content of the atmosphere was rising. Stabilizing emissions at the 2006 level would only prevent the rate of increase of the atmospheric content of CO_2 from rising even faster. Based on Socolow, Robert H. and Stephen W. Pacala. 2006. A Plan to Keep Carbon in Check. *Scientific American* (September): 50–57.

Stabilizing carbon emissions will not be easy. Princeton University scientists Stephen Pacala and Robert Socolow illustrated the monumental scale of this task in their influential stabilization-wedge diagram (Figure 14.17). The graph shows the historic trend of world carbon emissions and extrapolates the rate of increase from eight billion tons of carbon per year in 2006 to roughly 16 billion tons by 2056. They coined the term "stabilization triangle" to describe the total cumulative amount of carbon emissions between the projected growth curve to 16 billion tons in 2056 and the "flat path" that keeps global emissions at eight billion tons. Preventing this amount of emissions is too massive an undertaking, they argue, for any one solution to accomplish single-handedly. Instead, they divide the stabilization triangle into eight separate "wedges." Each wedge consists of a gradual ramping up of one technology, reducing .02 billion tons in the first year, .04 in the second, and so on until it reduces 1 billion tons of carbon per year by 2056. Cumulatively, each wedge avoids 25 billion tons of carbon over the 50-year period. Pacala and Socolow identified fifteen possible carbon-reduction technologies and estimated the scale of the infrastructure needed for each one to reduce one wedge's worth of emissions (Table 14.2). These solutions are presented here to give you an idea of the size of the task

at hand. The list is not all-inclusive and does not include measures that reduce other greenhouse gases. It does not address the driving forces of the problem, such as population and income growth, and it doesn't include mitigation measures to reduce solar radiation or remove carbon from the atmosphere after it has been emitted.

And yet, despite the enormity of completing eight wedges worth of solutions, all this would do is stabilize carbon emissions at 8 billion tons per year. Stabilizing emissions would not stabilize global warming. To understand why, it helps to think of the atmosphere as a bathtub. As we pour more water into a bathtub than the drain can empty, the water level will rise. The level of CO_2 in the bathtub/atmosphere has been growing for decades because we have been putting more CO_2 in than natural processes are removing. When emissions levels were below today's 8 billion tons per year, they were already causing the CO_2 level in the bathtub to rise to its current level and causing the climate to change. Thus, stabilizing emissions at 8 billion tons per year will only keep the level rising at roughly the current rate rather than an accelerating rate. Of course, the feedback loops in the carbon cycle and climate system are more complicated than the bathtub analogy, but it is clear that the world needs to reduce emissions well below

▶ *CASE STUDY (Continued)*

Table 14.2 Types and Scale of Potential Solutions for Reducing One Wedge Worth of Carbon Over 50 Years

End-User Efficiency and Conservation

1. Efficient cars	Increase the fuel economy of 2 billion cars from 30 to 60 miles per gallon
2. Less driving	Reduce vehicle-miles traveled from 10,000 per year to 5,000 for 2 billion 30-mpg cars
3. Electricity conservation	Lower residential and commercial electricity use by 25%

Electricity Generation

4. Power plant efficiency	Increase the efficiency of converting coal energy to electricity from 40% to 60% at 1,600 large power plants
5. Natural gas substitution	Replace 1,400 large coal-fired power plants with natural-gas plants

Carbon Capture and Storage

6. Carbon Capture and Storage (CCS)	Build facilities to capture the CO_2 from 800 large coal-fired power plants and pump it through pipelines to geologic formations (including depleted oil fields) where it can be injected underground for long-term storage
7. Hydrogen from coal, and CCS	Introduce CCS at coal power plants to produce hydrogen for 1.5 billion fuel-cell vehicles
8. Syngas from coal, and CCS	Build synfuels plants to produce 30 million barrels a day from coal and capture and store the carbon, replacing more than one-third of the world's daily oil supply

Alternative Energy Sources

9. Nuclear power	Increase nuclear power capacity 3× above 2006 levels to replace coal power
10. Wind power	Increase wind power capacity 40× above 2006 levels to replace coal power
11. Solar power	Increase solar power capacity 700× above 2006 levels to replace coal power
12. Wind to hydrogen	Increase wind power capacity 80× above 2006 levels to fuel hydrogen fuel-cell vehicles
13. Ethanol	Use one-sixth of the world's cropland to grow crops for ethanol for 2 billion cars (and do so using a negligible amount of fossil fuels for fuel and fertilizer in growing the crops)

Agriculture and Forestry

14. Stop deforestation	Stop all deforestation globally
15. Conservation tillage	Grow crops in the residue of the previous crops on all cropland worldwide

Source: Socolow, Robert H., and Stephen W. Pacala. 2006. A Plan to Keep Carbon in Check. *Scientific American* (September): 50–57.

the 8 billion-ton flat path in Figure 14.17 if we are to stabilize or eventually lower the atmospheric level of CO_2.

Another important theme in environmental geography is that different **stakeholder** groups have conflicting interests in the global warming debate. The divide between the MDCs and LDCs on this issue masks the fact that there will be winners and losers within both kinds of country. The Canadian farmer's gain will be the Mexican farmer's loss. If high taxes are placed on carbon-based fuels, some oil-drilling and coal-mining communities will lose their entire economic base. Other industries and communities, such as areas with above-average solar and wind

power, will benefit from the new technologies designed to replace carbon-based fuels. Coastal communities will suffer while inland residents could soon be sitting on oceanfront property.

The increasingly popular idea of **sustainable development** calls for economic development without compromising the resource base and the environment for future generations. Around the world, many promising initiatives are under way, ranging from reforestation, energy and water conservation, commercialization of renewable energy sources, organic farming, self-regulation by fishermen, pollution control technologies, hydrogen cars, and reintroduction of endangered species

© 2010 John Wiley & Sons, Inc.

▶ *CASE STUDY (Continued)*

into the wild. Sustainable development promotes policies appropriate for each particular region, given its natural, political, economic, and social systems.

Environmental problems are intimately related to the other aspects of human geography we studied in Chapters 1 through 13. This chapter draws your attention to the demographic, economic, technological, political, and cultural factors that contribute to environmental change. Environmental problems reach across scales, spread diseases, cause migrations, and exacerbate ethnonational tensions. In fact, one would be hard pressed to find an earlier chapter in this book that does not come into play somewhere in this final chapter.

Name: _____   Instructor: _____

Preserving the Planet: Human Impact on Environmental Systems

▶ ACTIVITY 1: ENVIRONMENTAL IMPACTS (IPAT) BY DEVELOPMENT CATEGORY: A GLOBAL WARMING CASE STUDY

The IPAT formula is a highly simplified model designed to capture the multiplicative aspects of population, affluence, and technology on resource use and environmental impacts. The idea is that a few wealthy individuals can consume enough to create the same environmental impact as many poor people—unless one group or the other uses less-damaging technologies. In Activity 1, we will apply this formula to carbon dioxide emissions.

Table 14.3 lists population, gross domestic product (GDP) per capita, and carbon dioxide emissions per dollar of GDP for the World Bank's three categories of development: low-income, middle-income, and high-income countries (Figure 14.18). In addition, the United States and Canada are separated from the other high-income countries to see how the North American model of development differs from that of Europe, Japan, Australia, and the other high-income countries.

Table 14.3   IPAT Table for Carbon Dioxide Emissions, 2002

Region	I Carbon Dioxide (CO_2) Emissions (million kg)	$=$	P Population (millions of persons)	$\times$	A Affluence (Gross Domestic Product in US$ per capita*)	$\times$	T Technology (kg of CO_2 emissions per US$ of GDP†)
Low-Income Countries		$=$	2,257	$\times$	$2,181	$\times$	0.38
Middle-Income Countries		$=$	2,986	$\times$	$5,597	$\times$	0.59
High-Income Countries Excluding the United States and Canada		$=$	646	$\times$	$24,997	$\times$	0. 37
United States and Canada		$=$	322	$\times$	$35,138	$\times$	0.56
World		$=$	6,211	$\times$	$7,906	$\times$	0.49

Source: CO_2 emissions from UN Statistics Division, Millennium Indicators Database (CDIAC data): unstats.un.org/unsd/mi/mi_series_1ist.asp. Population and GDP data from World Resources Institute, Earth Trends Environmental Information Portal: earthtrends.wri.org. Missing data estimated from Population Reference Bureau. World Population Data Sheet: www.prb.org and from U.S. Central Intelligence Agency, *World Factbook*: www.cia.gov. Country rankings from the World Bank: www.worldbank.org. Based on 191 countries.

*Gross domestic product converted to international dollars using purchasing power parity (PPP) rates.
†Based on carbon dioxide emissions from burning fossil fuels and manufacturing cement.

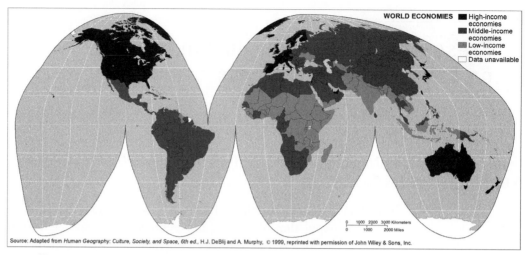

Source: Adapted from *Human Geography: Culture, Society, and Space, 6th ed.*, H.J. DeBlij and A. Murphy, © 1999, reprinted with permission of John Wiley & Sons, Inc.

Figure 14.18   Income-level categorization of countries.

In selecting variables to plug into the IPAT formula, it is important to make sure that the units of measurement will multiply to a result that is measured in the correct units. If you "cancel" similar terms in the numerators and denominators of the following formula, you will see that the units of measurement of $P \times A \times T$ work out to equal the units in which I is measured.

$$I = P \times A \times T$$

$$\text{million kg CO}_2 = \text{million persons} \times \frac{\$GDP}{\text{person}} \times \frac{\text{kg CO}_2}{\$GDP}$$

1.1. Multiply $P \times A \times T$ for each row in Table 14.3, and write the answer in the I column. Which group of countries emits the most CO_2: low income, middle income, or high income? (In answering, remember to add United States and Canada to the high-income countries.)

1.2. The affluence and technology columns are repeated in Table 14.4. Multiply $A \times T$ for each row to get the average kg of CO_2 emissions *per person*. Write the answers in the AT column.

Table 14.4 IPAT Table for Carbon Dioxide Emissions, 2002

Region	A Affluence (Gross Domestic Product in US\$ per capita)	$\times$	T Technology (kg of CO_2 emissions per US\$ of GDP)	$=$	AT Per Capita Emissions Factor (kg of CO_2 emissions per person)
Low-Income countries	2,181	$\times$	0.38	$=$	
Middle-Income countries	5,597	$\times$	0.59	$=$	
High-Income countries, excluding United States and Canada	24,997	$\times$	0.37	$=$	
United States and Canada	35,138	$\times$	0.56	$=$	
World	7,906	$\times$	0.49	$=$	

1.3. How many times higher than the average for low-income countries is the average per capita CO_2 emissions factor for the United States and Canada? (Use Table 14.4.)

Than the average for other high-income countries?

We have previously studied world population patterns (Chapter 5) and world affluence patterns (Chapter 7). Let's now take a look at the third factor: technology. In this analysis, everything that is not population or affluence gets lumped into a catchall "technology" category. Technology therefore incorporates a whole slew of factors besides the efficiency of energy-using equipment:

- *A country's mix of commercial and traditional energy types.* The World Bank data in Table 14.3 do not include CO_2 from traditional, nonmarket sources of energy such as firewood and animal and plant wastes.
- *A country's mix of renewable and nonrenewable energy sources.* Most renewable resources (wind, solar, hydropower, tidal) do not directly emit CO_2, whereas most nonrenewable resources (coal, oil, natural gas) do.

- *A country's mix of types of fossil fuels.* Coal, oil, and natural gas produce different amounts of CO_2 for the same amount of thermal energy, with coal producing the most CO_2 and natural gas the least.

- *A country's mix of economic sectors.* Think back to Chapter 6, which distinguished among the primary, secondary, and tertiary sectors of the economy. Low-income countries tend to get most of their GDP from the primary sector. Middle-income countries tend to have a more even mix of all three sectors, while the tertiary sector dominates in high-income countries. Now combine that with the fact that these three sectors do not use the same amount of energy to create a dollar's worth of GDP. The secondary sector (manufacturing) uses the most energy, and the tertiary sector (services) the least. The primary sector (agriculture, mining, forestry, fishing) may use a lot of energy or a little, depending on whether it employs capital-intensive or labor-intensive methods.

- *The value of a country's products.* The denominator of the technology factor is GDP. If a country produces low-value or low-quality goods, the pollution in the numerator will be spread over a smaller value base in the denominator.

- *A country's climate.* Countries with extreme temperatures require more energy use for space heating and cooling.

- *A country's size and import/export patterns.* All else being equal, large countries may pollute more because of the long transportation distances that must be covered. For small countries that import many of their goods and raw materials, the energy use for manufacturing and transporting some of what they consume may be charged to the exporting country.

- *A country's cultural values.* Some cultural values that may contribute to greater energy use include larger houses, more divorces (i.e., more separate households), more private automobiles, less mass transit, more meat consumption, and so on. Many of these factors are more related to affluence, but they can also differ between two equally rich countries.

- *A country's government policy.* Government regulation of pollution, taxes on gasoline and energy use, government subsidies for roads and automobiles versus rail and transit, land-use and parking policies, and zoning laws are just some of the governmental influences on energy use and pollution. *Note that in Activity 2 of this chapter, these last two factors (cultural values and governmental policy) are separated from technology and treated as independent factors. But in Activity 1, their influence is bundled together with technology in the CO_2-per-$GDP factor.*

- *Energy efficiency.* Yes, finally, technology also includes the efficiency of energy-using and pollution-controlling devices, which directly lower the T factor.

1.4. Now, given the long list of factors just related, use your prior knowledge about how the United States and Canada differ from Western Europe and Japan to give some specific reasons that explain why the United States and Canada emit so much more CO_2 per dollar of GDP than other high-income countries do.

1.5. If the entire world's population had the GDP per capita of the United States and Canada and emitted CO_2 at the same per \$GDP rate as the United States and Canada, how much CO_2 would the entire world emit? How does this compare to the current world total? (Use Table 14.3.)

1.6. If the entire world's population had the GDP per capita of the middle-income countries and emitted CO_2 at the same per \$GDP rate as the high-income countries excluding the United States and Canada, how much CO_2 would the entire world emit? How does this compare to the current world total? (Use Table 14.3.)

Name: _____ Instructor: _____

Preserving the Planet: Human Impact on Environmental Systems

▶ ACTIVITY 2: HUMAN-ENVIRONMENT SYSTEMS ANALYSIS

Activity 2 asks you to apply the systems model of environmental change to one of the following three case studies:

Royte, Elizabeth. 2002. Wilding America. *Discover* 23 (Sept. 2002):43–47.

Frederick, Kenneth D. 1991. The Disappearing Aral Sea. *Resources* 102:11–14.

Parsons, James J. 1988. The Scourge of Cows. *Whole Earth Review* 58:40–47.

You will read an article on your computer screen and identify (1) the human driving forces ultimately generating the environmental change; (2) the human activities directly causing it; (3) the mechanism of environmental change; (4) its adverse consequences; and (5) the proposed solutions. Learning to think about every environmental problem in this framework will give you a basis for understanding and comparing the many threats that we hear about daily.

This activity is self-correcting. If you give a wrong answer, the software will give you some helpful comments to point you in the right direction, and you can try again.

A. To start your activity, click on the *Student Companion Site* at www.wiley.com/college/kuby. (For students using WileyPlus, log on to your class Web site, select the *Assignment* tab, locate and click on this assignment, and follow all instructions.)

B. Select this chapter from the drop-down list and then click on *Computerized Chapter Activities.*

C. Click on *Activity 2: Human-Environment Systems Analysis.*

D. Read the activity description and then click *Continue.*

E. Click on one of the three case studies, depending on which article your instructor has assigned.

F. Begin reading the article.

G. When you reach a highlighted passage of text, first consider which of the five main boxes it represents. Then identify which of the subcategories the passage describes. When you are ready, click anywhere within the highlighted passage to select it.

H. Click on *Flowchart* in the right margin.

I. The software will automatically switch to the flowchart diagram, in which the five components of Figure 14.3 are represented by five distinct columns of boxes. Click anywhere within the box you think is correct.

J. If your answer is correct, the key points of the highlighted text are pasted into the correct box of the flowchart. As adjoining boxes are filled in,

© 2010 John Wiley & Sons, Inc.

arrows will be drawn connecting them. If your answer is wrong, a message box appears, giving you some advice. Try clicking in another box.

K. Click on *Article* in the right margin to return to the article and continue reading.

L. When you have successfully pasted all of the highlighted passages into the flowchart, a message will appear to say that you have finished. Go to the *File* menu, choose *Page Setup*, set the orientation to *Landscape*, and click *OK*. Then go to the *File* menu and *Print* the finished flowchart.

Think about the following issues in applying the systems terms to the articles:

- There may be more than one driving force for each activity and more than one activity that is causing a particular kind of environmental change.

- To determine which category of human activity is causing an environmental change, you must focus on the direct agent, not the underlying cause. Is sulfur dioxide emitted by the industrial plant that converts coal to electricity or by the homes and offices cooled by electricity—or both? In this case, the SO_2 is emitted from the power plant smokestack, not the air conditioning unit. Are tropical forests cut by the settlers that raise the cattle, the industry that processes cattle into hamburgers, or by the fast-food restaurant that sells the burgers?

- Some problems are due to only one kind of environmental change; others consist of multiple kinds of human-caused change. For instance, the destruction of the ozone layer is exclusively a pollution problem; redistribution of natural resources or direct biological interference play no role in it. In contrast, the damage caused by gold mining near Yellowstone National Park consists of three distinct changes: (1) changes to the land surface by digging and moving soil and rock, (2) pollution from the chemicals used, and (3) cutting the forest.

- It is important, and sometimes difficult, to distinguish between natural adverse consequences in box 4 of Figure 14.3 and the human-caused environmental changes in box 3. If the environmental change is caused directly by human activities, it should be placed in box 3, but if one ¨environmental change is caused by another environmental change, it should go into box 4, adverse consequences. For instance, if agriculture (a human activity) leads to deforestation (direct biological interference), which in turn leads to soil erosion (redistribution of materials), the latter should be listed as an adverse consequence of deforestation. However, if road building (human activity) leads to the soil erosion directly, it should be listed as a human-caused environmental change. Another complex example would be depletion of the stratospheric ozone layer. CFC pollution would be listed as the human-caused environmental change, and ozone depletion, plant damage, and skin cancer all would be adverse consequences of the CFC pollution.

M. When you have finished, close all browser windows.

Name: _____ Instructor: _____

Name: _____

Name: _____

Name: _____

Name: _____ Stakeholder Group: _____

Preserving the Planet: Human Impact on Environmental Systems

▶ ACTIVITY 3: CONFLICTING VIEWPOINTS ON ENVIRONMENTAL PROBLEMS

Activity 3 is a role-playing activity designed to enhance your ability to see an environmental problem from various points of view. All people working in the environmental arena must recognize that many different stakeholder groups are involved in any environmental problem, and any solutions must take into account their perspectives. You will engage in a role-playing activity that will sensitize you to the perspectives of the different stakeholder groups.

You will work in a team to represent the stakeholder group to which you have been assigned in a debate. The role-playing activity is divided into several steps.

Step 1: Assign an article, form teams, and exchange e-mail addresses (during the class prior to the role-playing activity).

Step 2: Individual homework: read the article and answer Question 3.1, exploring your stakeholder group's perspective on the problem. You can download a document of Question 3.1 from the Activity 3 Web page (or from the CD) and then do this step at home and e-mail your completed answers to your teammates.

Step 3: Back in class, discuss and resolve any differences in your team's answers to Question 3.1.

Step 4: Prepare a written position statement for your stakeholder group.

Step 5: Advocate your position statement to the class.

Step 6: Without completely repudiating your past position, modify your statement to satisfy some of the concerns of the other stakeholder groups.

Step 7: Present your modified position to the class.

For each article, these are the stakeholder groups:

Stakeholder	Driving Interests
Big business proponent	Primary interest is to maximize profits. Locations are therefore sought where products can be produced most cheaply by minimizing costs. Businesses can minimize costs by using cheap labor or operating in locations where the costs of negative externalities (i.e., pollution, habitat destruction, or other hazardous side effects of production) are not paid for by the business itself.
Local workers	Seek employment. In developing countries with few jobs, often a hazardous and/or low-paying job is the only choice (other than no job at all or subsistence farming [see Chapter 8]). Workers therefore are frequently forced to overlook issues such as environmental degradation or poor work conditions in the name of mere survival.
Government	In countries where governments are held accountable (i.e., through fair elections), policies seek to provide the most benefit for all citizens. There are widely varying strategies to accomplish this (see Chapter 7), but generally providing jobs is a very high priority. In any case, alleviating extreme poverty is usually a goal, and often environmental protection comes second to the basic needs of the people. Unfortunately, many governments are also self-serving and use power merely for personal gain or to benefit a select group of elites. In these cases, even the basic needs of the people may be neglected.
Environmentalists	Want to strengthen natural ecosystems by preserving habitats. Seek protected lands that will not be developed and regulations on pollution and on other destructive human behavior. Tropical rain forests, with very rich biodiversity, are of particular concern, given their importance as both species habitats and in regulating global warming gases.
Consumers	Most consumers want the best products for the cheapest price. Particularly in poorer places, affordability is most important. However, in more educated and affluent societies, some are willing to pay higher prices for products that are less harmful to the environment and provide more social justice to those who produce them.

The debate will work best if each stakeholder group follows these traditional viewpoints. If you wish to play the role of a more enlightened business, worker, government, environmentalist, or consumer, please wait until step 6 to modify your position from the traditional driving interests listed in the table.

The recommended group size is three to five students. If the class has more than 25 students, we recommend having several teams representing each stakeholder group. You can think of them as different corporations, different families, different political parties, and different environmental groups. Your instructor will randomly select which team will get the opportunity to present its statement.

Step 1: Form Teams and Exchange E-mail Addresses

Prior to the role-playing activity, your instructor will assign one of the three articles in the book or another of his or her choice. The instructor will also form the teams. Write your teammates' names and e-mail addresses here:

_____

_____

_____

_____

Step 2: Read the Article and Answer Questions Exploring Your Stakeholder Group's Perspective and E-mail Your Answers to Your Team

Outside of class, answer the following sets of questions from the perspective of your particular stakeholder group, based on the article. You can download a Microsoft Word file from the Activity 3 Web page (or from the CD) and type in the blanks. Don't interject your personal opinion but answer them as you would if you really were a member of this stakeholder group.

E-mail your answers to your team. Print your answers and those of your teammates. Read them before class and identify any discrepancies. Bring these materials to class.

To access Question 3.1 from the Web site or CD:

A. To start your activity, click on the *Student Companion Site* at www.wiley.com/college/kuby. (For students using WileyPlus, log on to your class Web site, select the *Assignment* tab, locate and click on this assignment, and follow all instructions.)

B. Select this chapter from the drop-down list and then click on *Computerized Chapter Activities*.

C. Click on *Activity 3: Conflicting Viewpoints on Environmental Problems*.

D. Read the activity description and then click *Continue*.

E. Click on one of the three case studies, depending on which article your instructor has assigned.

F. Click on *Printable Article* to open a copy of the article in Acrobat Reader (.pdf) format.

G. Once in Acrobat Reader, print the article to read and bring to class and then close Acrobat Reader.

H. Click on *Answer Question 3.1*.

I. Copy and paste these questions into a word processing file or an e-mail file. Answer the questions and e-mail them to your group.

J. When you have finished, close all browser windows.

3.1. What is your stakeholder group's perspective on this environmental problem?

a. Questions about your group
 (1) Who exactly are you? Tell us some details about yourself.

 (2) Where are you located?

 (3) What is your role in this issue?

 (4) What motivates your interest in this issue?

b. Questions about the environmental problem
 (1) What exactly is the environmental change that your stakeholder group sees happening in this region?

 (2) What human activities would your group think are causing the change, and who is engaged in those activities?

c. Question about the causes of the problem
   (1) What are the primary macro-level trends that your stakeholder group sees as driving this change? (You could start with the human driving forces given in the chapter introduction: population, affluence, technology, government, and cultural values. However, be specific; expand on these general terms as much as possible. Also, you can add your own terms.)

d. Questions about the consequences of the problem
   (1) Is this environmental change affecting your group, and if so, how?

   (2) How does this environmental change affect other stakeholder groups?

Step 3: Resolve Any Discrepancies with Your Team (5 minutes)

Review your answers with your teammates and come to agreement on the best answers.

Step 4: Prepare a Written Position Statement (15 minutes)
Count off and assign each student a number. To enhance team functioning and facilitate completion of this step, your instructor will randomly assign roles to student numbers. Here are the roles and some examples of how they can keep the group on track:

Timekeeper/Taskmaster, who keeps the group on schedule:

- "We have three minutes left to get the job done."
- "We're right on schedule."
- "We should have enough time to discuss this for another minute."
- "Let's move on to the next question."
- "Let's get back to the main point."

Recorder, who drafts the statement in Step 2:

- "Shall we say it this way?"
- "Let me read this back to you to make sure it's right."

Consensus Checker/Gatekeeper:

- "Do we all agree?"
- "Can anyone add any more before we move on?"
- "We haven't heard from you yet."
- "Thanks for your input. Can we get another opinion now?"

Prepare a written position statement for your stakeholder group that incorporates your answers to the preceding questions. Tell us about yourself and how you see the issue. Take the perspective of a typical member of your stakeholder group. Advocate your stakeholder group's position strongly. You will have 2 minutes to read your statement aloud in the next step.

After Step 4, your instructor will randomly assign a number to the role of spokesperson, regardless of whether that individual was in one of these roles. **All students should be prepared to argue their team's position.**

Write your team's position statement here:

Step 5: Read Your Position Statement Aloud (2 minutes each, 10 minutes total)

Your instructor will randomly select the number of the student who will be the spokesperson. Be bold and persuasive. Act the part!

Also, listen carefully to the other stakeholder groups' statements and, in the following table, take notes on exactly who they are (i.e., what company, what level of government), and what their position is.

Stakeholder Group	Who Exactly Are They?	Position Statement
Big Business Proponents		
Local Workers		
Government		
Environmentalists		
Consumers		
Other		

Step 6: Modify Your Position (10 minutes)

In recognizing what you have heard from the other stakeholder groups, take your same position but try to modify it to satisfy at least some of the concerns of the other groups. You can also change your rhetoric. Write a revised statement offering your team's new position, detailing what, if anything, you are willing to change.

Step 7: Present Your New Position to the Class (2 minutes each; 10 minutes total)

Your instructor will again randomly select the number of the student who will be the spokesperson.

Also, listen carefully to the other stakeholder groups' statements, and in the table below, take notes on how they have modified their stance.

Stakeholder Group	Modifications to Their Positions, If Any
Big Business Proponents	
Local Workers	
Government	
Environmentalists	
Consumers	
Other	

▶ DEFINITIONS OF KEY TERMS

Adverse Consequences Negative impacts of environmental change on humans and/or nature (plants and animals).

Biosphere The regions of the earth's crust and atmosphere occupied by living matter. The biosphere includes the atmosphere (air), the hydrosphere (surface and subsurface waters), and the lithosphere (upper reaches of the earth's crust).

Cycle A circular flow of energy, materials, or organisms that replenishes the elements of a system, enabling the system to continue to function.

Direct Biological Interference Human-caused alteration of species through removal, redistribution, or modification of living creatures.

Energy and Material Redistribution Human-caused alteration of energy or material flows through impoundment, redistribution, or transformation.

Environmental Change Changes in an environmental system caused by an alteration or disruption of the natural cycles.

Equilibrium A balanced state of a system in which stocks and flows are fairly stable or fluctuate within their normal range.

Flow Movement or transformation of energy, materials, or organisms from one stock to another.

Human Activities Things people do—in this case, things they do that affect the environment.

Human Driving Forces Social and cultural conditions that influence human use and perception of the natural environment

Human-Environmental Interactions The ways in which human society and the natural environment affect each other.

IPAT Shorthand for a multiplicative model of human impacts on the environment; holds that Impacts (I) are proportional to Population (P) × Affluence (A) × Technology (T).

Negative Feedback Loop A cause-and-effect chain that begins with a change to a stock and ends up reversing the original change and bringing the system back toward equilibrium.

Pollution Human introduction of materials into the biosphere that have a negative environmental impact.

Population Pressure Strain on the natural and economic resources that occurs when the needs of a large or rapidly growing population cannot be met by the resources available.

Positive Feedback Loop A cause-and-effect chain that begins with a change to a stock and ends up amplifying the original change and pushing the system further from equilibrium.

Renewable Resources Resources that can be used and restored after use or that have an unlimited supply.

Solutions Efforts to solve environmental problems.

Stakeholder An individual or group with a strong interest or stake in how an issue is decided.

Stock Amounts of energy, materials, or organisms that exist in a system.

Sustainable Development Providing for the needs of the present without diminishing the options of future generations.

System A set of elements along with the connections between them that form a whole unit and work together.

▶ FURTHER READINGS

Brown, Lestor, R. 2008. *Plan B 3.0: Mobilizing to Save Civilization*, 3rd ed. New York: Norton.

Buttel, F. H., A. P. Hawkins, and A. G. Power. 1990. From Limits to Growth to Global Change. *Global Environmental Change* (Dec.):57–66.

Cameron, Silver Donald. 1990. Net Losses: The Sorry State of Our Atlantic Fishery. *Canadian Geographic* 110:28–37.

Carson, Rachel. 1962. *Silent Spring*. Greenwich, CT: Fawcett.

Croll, D. A., J. L. Maron, J. A. Estes, E. M. Danner, and G. V. Byrd. 2005. Introduced Predators Transform Subarctic Islands from Grassland to Tundra. *Science* 307:1959–1961.

Dotto, Lydia. 2000. Proof or Consequences. *Alternatives Journal* 26:8.

Goldfarb, Theodore D. (ed.). 2000. *Taking Sides: Clashing Views on Controversial Environmental Issues*, 9th ed. Guilford, CT: Dushkin Publishing Group.

Hayes, R. Dennis. 1993. Ravaged Republics. *Discover* 14:67–75.

Hawken, Paul, Amory Lovins, and L. Hunter Lovins. 1999. *Natural Capitalism: Creating the Next Industrial Revolution*. New York: Little Brown.

Lean, Geoffrey, and Don Hinrichsen (eds.). 1992. *Atlas of the Environment*. Oxford: Helicon.

Meadows, Donella H., Jorgen Randers, and Dennis L. Meadows. 2004. *Limits to Growth: The 30-Year Update*. White River Junction, VT: Chelsea Green.

Park, Chris C. 1992. *Tropical Rainforests*. London: Routledge.

Pryde, Phillip R. (ed.). 1995. *Environmental Resources and Constraints in the Former Soviet Republics*. Boulder, CO: Westview Press.

Revkin, Andrew C. 2009. The Greenhouse Effect and the Bathtub Effect. *New York Times* (January 28, 2009).

Ryan, John C. 2001. Indonesia's Coral Reefs on the Line. *World Watch* 14:12–19.

Sheppard, Robert. 2002. Beyond Kyoto: How Your Life Will Change. *Macleans* (Nov. 11, 2002):18.

Sharp, Zachary. (ed.). 2008. *Annual Editions: Environment 08/09*, 27th ed. New York: McGraw-Hill.

Socolow, Robert H. and Stephen W. Pacala. 2006. A Plan to Keep Carbon in Check. *Scientific American* (September): 50–57.

Stevens, William K. 2000. Global Warming: The Contrarian View. *New York Times* (Feb. 29, 2000):F1, F6.

Turner, Billie L. II, et al. 1990. *The Earth as Transformed by Human Action: Global and Regional Changes in the Biosphere over the Past 300 Years*. Cambridge: Cambridge University Press.

Vitousek, Peter M., Harold A. Mooney, Jane Lubchenco, and Jerry M. Melillo. 1997. Human Domination of Earth's Ecosystems. *Science* 277:494–499.

Webster, Donovan. 1999. Walking a Wildlife Highway from Yellowstone to Yukon. *Smithsonian* 30:58–72.

Wines, Michael. 2002. Grand Soviet Scheme for Sharing Water in Central Asia Is Foundering. *New York Times* (Dec. 9, 2002):A14.

Worldwatch Institute (ed.). 2009. *State of the World 2009: Into A Warming World*. New York: Norton.

▶ WEB RESOURCES

Alternatives Journal: www.alternativesjournal.ca/

Arctic Council and the International Arctic Science Committee: *Arctic Climate Impact Assessment*: www.acia.uaf.edu

Bleja, David. *Breathing Earth*: www.breathingearth.net/

Carbon Dioxide Information Analysis Center: cdiac.esd.ornl.gov/home.html

E/The Environmental Magazine: www.emagazine.com/

Greenhouse Network: www.greenhousenet.org/

Intergovernmental Panel on Climate Change: www.ipcc.ch/

National Council for Science and the Environment. *Improving the Scientific Basis for Environmental Decision Making*: www.cnie.org/

National Climatic Data Center: www.ncdc.noaa.gov/oa/ncdc.html

Natural Resources Defense Council: www.nrdc.org/

National Geographic Society. Wild World: www.nationalgeographic.com/wildworld/

Nature Conservancy: www.nature.org

New York Times. The Changing Environment: A Look at the Aral Sea Over Time, Using Google Earth: video.nytimes.com/video/playlist/science/119481622277/indexhtml#1231546884681

Resources for the Future: www.rff.org/

SEED: Schlumberger Excellence in Educational Development. Global Climate Change and Energy, Stock and Flow (Bathtub Simulation): www.seed.slb.com/subcontent.aspx?id=4014

The Atlantic Monthly. Articles from *The Atlantic Monthly's Archive and Related Links*: www.theatlantic.com/politics/environ/environ.htm

United Nations Environment Programme. One Planet Many People: Atlas of our Changing Environment: www.unep.org/onePlanetManyPeople/index.php

United Nations Framework Convention on Climate Change: unfccc.int/2860.php

U.S. Energy Information Administration: www.eia.doe.gov/

U.S. Environmental Protection Agency: www.epa.gov/

World Bank: www.worldbank.org/environment/

World Resources Institute: www.wri.org/

World Wildlife Fund: www.worldwildlife.org/

Worldwatch Institute: www.worldwatch.org/

▶ ITEMS TO HAND IN

Activity 1: • Questions 1.1–1.6, or answer all questions your instructor created in your WileyPlus assignments.

Activity 2: • A printed systems flowchart for each environmental problem assigned by your instructor, or answer all questions your instructor created in your WileyPlus assignments.

Activity 3: • One copy of the worksheet for Steps 1–7 (check with your instructor whether one worksheet is required per individual or per group), or answer all questions your instructor created in your WileyPlus assignments.

Appendix

Reference Maps

North America Cities

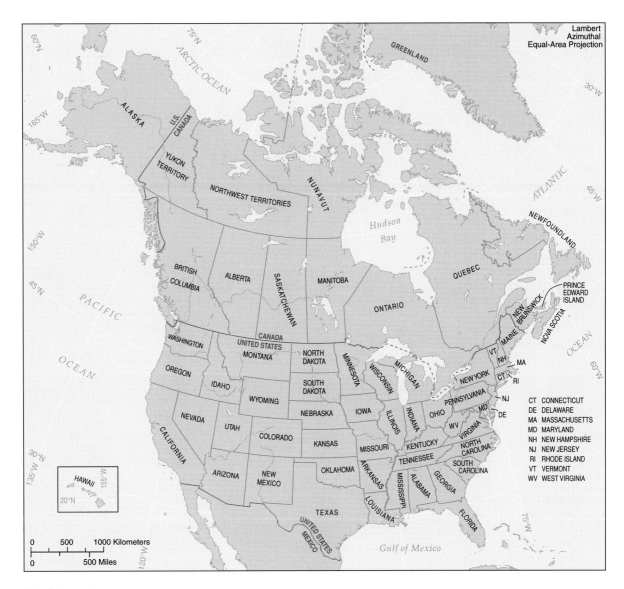

North America

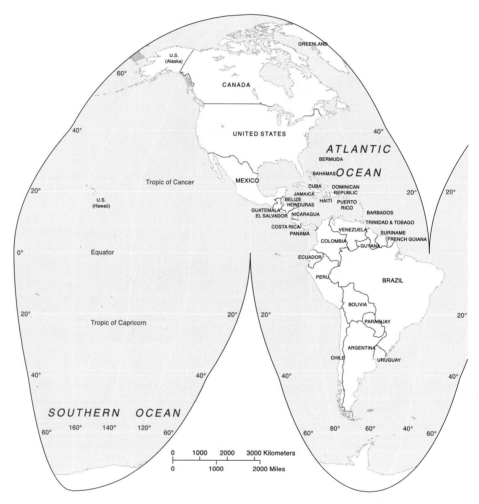

World Map

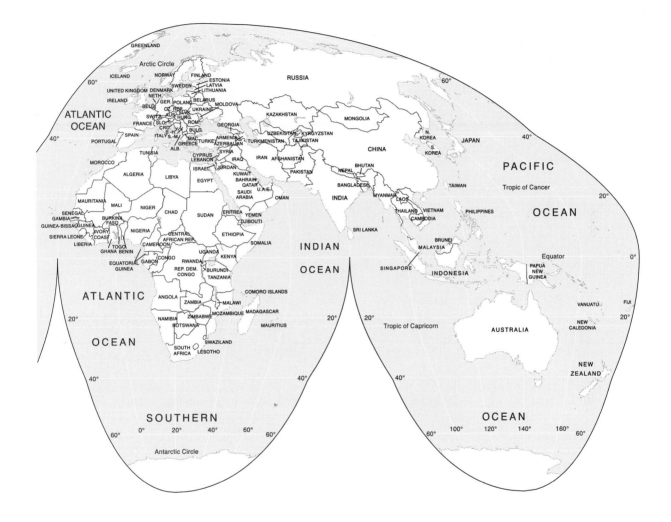

Index

Photo Credits

Chapter 1

Fig. 1.3: Mark Leibowitz/Masterfile. Fig. 1.7: Jim Erickson/Corbis Stock Market. Fig. 1.8: Najlah Feanny/Corbis Images. Fig. 1.9: Bettmann/Corbis Images. Fig. 1.10: Willie L. Hill, Jr./The Image Works. Fig. 1.11: Photo from Wikipedia: http://en.wikipedia.org/wiki/File:US_President_Barack_Obama_taking_his_Oath_of_Office_-_2009Jan20.jpg.

Chapter 2

Fig. 2.3: Fraser Hall/Getty Images, Inc. Fig. 2.5: Behrouz Mehri/AFP/Getty Images. Fig. 2.6: Getty Images, Inc. Fig. 2.8: Michael Kuby. Fig. 2.9: Hubertus Kanus/Photo Researchers. Fig. 2.10: Will Yurman/The Image Works. Fig. 2.11: Patrick Ward/Corbis Images. Fig. 2.12: Courtesy John Harner. Fig. 2.14: Courtesy John Harner. Fig. 2.15: Courtesy John Duncan Shaeffer. Fig. 2.16: Courtesy John Harner.

Chapter 3

Fig. 3.1: ©AP/Wide World Photos. Fig. 3.7: Allan Tannenbaum/The Image Works. Fig. 3.9: Dorigny/REA/SABA. Fig. 3.12: John Giordano/SABA.

Chapter 4

Fig. 4.1: Courtesy Michael Kuby. Fig. 4.3: John Harner. Fig. 4.9: Howard Dratch/The Image Works. Fig. 4.6: Dorothea Lange/Corbis Images.

Chapter 5

Fig. 5.5: Ingram Publishing/Photolibrary Group Limited. Fig. 5.11: Sheldan Collins/Corbis Images. Fig. 5.12: James P. Blair/National Geographic Society. Fig. 5.13: NAMAS BHOJANI/©AP/Wide World Photos. Fig. 5.14: Courtesy Michael Kuby.

Chapter 6

Fig. 6.1: Joel Sartore/National Geographic Society. Fig. 6.5: Dr. Jurgen Scriba/Photo Researchers. Fig. 6.8: Bob Krist/Corbis Images. Fig. 6.11: Courtesy Martin J. Pasqualetti. Fig. 6.12: Spencer Platt/Getty Images, Inc.

Chapter 7

Fig. 7.5: Courtesy Michael Kuby. Fig. 7.6: Chris Kapolka/Stone/Getty Images. Fig. 7.9: Courtesy Michael Kuby. Fig. 7.10: Courtesy Michael Kuby. Fig. 7.11: Lauren Goodsmith/The Image Works. Fig. 7.13: Getty Images News and Sport Services.

Chapter 8

Fig. 8.1: Leslie Hugh Stone/The Image Works. Fig. 8.2: Michael Melford/The Image Bank/Getty Images. Fig. 8.5: Michael Melford/Getty Images, Inc. Fig. 8.6: David McNew/Getty Images News and Sport Services. Fig. 8.7: Courtesy John Harner. Fig. 8.8: Stephen Ferry/Getty Images News and Sport Services. Fig. 8.9: Fridman Pauo/Corbis Sygma. Fig. 8.10: Visions LLC/Photolibrary Group Limited.

Chapter 9

Fig. 9.1: U.S. Census Bureau. Fig. Fig. 9.3: Kevin R. Morris/Corbis Images. Fig. 9.4: JTB Photo/Photolibrary Group Limited. 9.5: Visions LLC/Photolibrary Group Limited. Fig. 9.9: Rensselaer County Historical Society. Fig. 9.11: Courtesy Michael Kuby. Fig. 9.15: Ted Mathias/©AP/Wide World Photos. Fig. 9.16: Courtesy John Harner.

Chapter 10

Fig. 10.2: Satellite image courtesy of ©GeoEye www.geoeye.com. All rights reserved. Fig. 10.3: Courtesy Michael Kuby. Fig. 10.4: Courtesy Michael Kuby. Fig. 10.7: KIKE CALVO/©AP/Wide World Photos. Fig. 10.8: Mike Powell/Stone/Getty Images. Fig. 10.9: Michael Kuby. Fig. 10.10: Courtesy Michael Kuby. Fig. 10.11: Richard Berenholtz/Corbis Stock Market. Fig. 10.12: Greg Probst/Stone/Getty Images. Fig. 10.13: J. Pickerell/The Image Works. Fig. 10.15: Courtesy Michael Kuby. Fig. 10.16: Courtesy Daniel D. Arreola. Fig. 10.17: Courtesy Daniel D. Arreola.

Chapter 11

Fig. 11.1: J. Nordell/The Image Works. Fig. 11.4: Courtesy John Harner. Fig. 11.7: Photo by Todd Photographic Services. Fig. 11.9: David Butow/SABA. Fig. 11.10: Steve Starr/SABA. Fig. 11.11: Michael Kuby. Fig. 11.12: © Telegraph UK/Zuma Press. Fig. 11.13: Courtesy Michael Kuby.

Chapter 12

Fig. 12.1: Image from Wikipedia: http://commons.wikimedia.org/wiki/File:Bundesarchiv_Bild_101I-270-0298-14,_Polen,_Ghetto_Warschau,_Br%C3%BCcke.jpg. Fig. 12.2: Rafael Macia/Photo Researchers. Fig. 12.5: Nascimento/REA/SABA. Fig. 12.6: Getty Images News.

Chapter 13

UN 13.1-p. 395 (top) Lee Malis/Spectrum Pictures. UN 13.2-p. 395 (bottom) Lee Malis/Spectrum Pictures. UN 13.3-p. 397 Lee Malis/Spectrum Pictures. Fig. 13.2: © Brooks Kraft/Sygma/©Corbis.

Fig. 13.3: Christopher Morris/SABA. Fig. 13.5: D. Wells/The Image Works. Fig. 13.11: U.S. Department of State. Fig. 13.14: Georg Gerster/Photo Researchers. Fig. 13.16: Scott Peterson/Getty Images News and Sport Services. Fig. 13.19: ©AP/Wide World Photos. Fig. 13.20: CNN/Getty Images News and Sport Services. Fig. 13.21: Allen Tannenbaum/The Image Works. Fig. 13.23: Ahmed al Rubayyh/Getty Images News and Sport Services. Fig. 13.24: Paul J. Richards/AFP/Getty Images. Fig. 13.25: ©AP/Dept. of State. Fig. 13.26: ©AP/Wide World Photos. Fig. 13.27: ©AP/Wide World Photos. Fig. 13.28: Mario Tama/Getty Images. Fig. 13.29: ©AP/Wide World Photos. Fig. 13.30: ©AP/Wide World Photos.

Chapter 14

Fig. 14.1: Keren Su/Stone/Getty Images. Fig. 14.5: Wesley Bocxe/The Image Works. Fig. 14.6: James Hancock/Photo Researchers. Fig. 14.7: Simon Jauncey/Stone/Getty Images. Fig. 14.8: Courtesy John Harner. Fig. 14.9: Still Pictures/Peter Arnold, Inc. Fig. 14.10: Stephen J. Krasemann/Photo Researchers. Fig. 14.11: Martin Wendler/Peter Arnold, Inc. Fig. 14.12: Jeri Gleiter/Taxi/Getty Images. Fig. 14.14: Courtesy NASA.